A History of Psychology

GLOBALIZATION, IDEAS, AND APPLICATIONS

Robert B. Lawson • Jean E. Graham • Kristin M. Baker

John Dewey Hall
University of Vermont
Burlington VT USA

PEARSON

Prentice Hall

Upper Saddle River, New Jersey

Library of Congress Cataloging-in-Publication Data

Lawson, Robert B.
  A history of psychology : globalization, ideas, and applications / Robert B. Lawson,
Jean E. Graham, Kristin M. Baker.
    p. cm.
  Includes indexes.
  ISBN 0-13-014123-2
  1. Psychology–History–Textbooks. I. Graham, Jean E. II. Baker, Kristin M. III. Title.

  BF81.L39 2006
  150.9–dc22

2006043756

*This book is dedicated to those who have made history
and to those who have been inspired by it.*

Editorial Director: Leah Jewell
Executive Editor: Jessica Mosher
Editorial Assistant: William Grieco
Senior Marketing Manager: Jeanette Moyer
Marketing Assistant: Laura Kennedy
Assistant Managing Editor: Maureen Richardson
Production Liaison: Randy Pettit
Manufacturing Buyer: Sherry Lewis
Manufacturing Manager: Nick Sklitsis
Interior Design: GGS Book Services, Inc.

Cover Design: Jayne Conte
Director, Image Resource Center: Melinda Reo
Manager, Rights and Permissions: Zina Arabia
Manager: Visual Research: Beth Brenzel
Manager, Cover Visual Research & Permissions:
  Karen Sanatar
Composition/Full-Service Project Management:
  GGS Book Services, Inc.
Printer/Binder: R.R. Donnelley & Sons, Inc.
Cover Printer: Lehigh Press, Inc.

Credits and acknowledgments borrowed from other sources and reproduced, with permission, in this textbook
appear on appropriate page within text.

Pearson Education LTD.
Pearson Education Singapore, Pte. Ltd
Pearson Education, Canada, Ltd
Pearson Education–Japan

Pearson Education Australia PTY, Limited
Pearson Education North Asia Ltd
Pearson Educación de Mexico, S.A. de C.V.
Pearson Education Malaysia, Pte. Ltd

10 9 8 7 6 5 4 3 2 1
ISBN 0-13-014123-2

Contents

SECTION II ■ EARLY PHILOSOPHICAL AND BIOLOGICAL FOUNDATIONS OF SCIENTIFIC PSYCHOLOGY

SECTION III ■ SCHOOLS OF PSYCHOLOGY

Preface

History is frequently dismissed as simply a record of past events, dry, stale, and inorganic, yet this is far from the truth as history is a living, reactive, and organic entity. Illuminating the past helps us to understand who we are now, while at the same time, our current understanding of reality in turn changes our view of past events. History also shapes the future. This is true of history in general as well as the more specific history of a scientific discipline such as psychology.

When you are trying to chart a course forward, it is essential to have points of reference that include where you are now as well as where you have been. Experiment and investigation without direction is not science, it is simply aimless curiosity. To engage fully as a scientist and/or practitioner in any scientific discipline, you need to understand the history of that discipline.

In this book, *A History of Psychology: Globalization, Ideas, and Applications,* we seek to provide the necessary points of reference that allow the reader to engage fully in the discipline of psychology. By understanding where psychology has been and the factors that have contributed to what psychology is today, the next generation of psychologists can more effectively plot the course for the future of the discipline.

Psychology has not developed in a vacuum, but rather has evolved within a larger cultural context. As a result, a history of psychology that is purely an internal history considering only developments within psychology, independent of cultural influence, is inadequate. Accordingly, although this book presents primarily an internal history, we take into account the broader intellectual and social context within which psychology has developed. This is particularly critical since this is one of the first textbooks on the history of psychology to go beyond American and Western European psychology.

The general framework of this book is designed to promote the view of psychology as a global enterprise, the development of which is moderated by the dynamic tension between the move toward globalization promoting homogeneity and concomitant local forces promoting diversity and indigenization.

In **Section I—The Present: Globalization, Psychology, and History**, we provide an overview of the concept of globalization and its impact on psychology, a treatment of psychology in America, and close with a discussion of the nature, methods, and purpose of history.

In **Section II—Early Philosophical and Biological Foundations of Scientific Psychology**, we present a general history of scientific psychology that focuses primarily on the Western intellectual traditions of the discipline.

In **Section III—Schools of Psychology**, we examine the major schools of psychology, namely, voluntarism and structuralism, functionalism, behaviorism, Gestalt psychology, and psychoanalysis; we conclude this section with continuing developments in psychotherapy—object relations and humanistic psychology. In each of the six chapters of Section III, we focus upon global issues addressed by each school of psychology, the leaders of each school, the defining ideas of each school, and the applications of those ideas in contemporary psychology.

Section IV—Diversity in Psychology expands the scope of our discussion of the history of psychology beyond the Western and white male traditions of exclusion to include a systematic examination of the contributions of previously marginalized women and minority practitioners as well as the development of psychology outside of the Western cultural context.

Each chapter begins with an overview and a list of learning objectives to aid the reader in determining focal points in the material, and we conclude each chapter with a brief summary discussion of the presented material. This book is intended primarily for an audience of undergraduate students in psychology who have already completed some introductory courses in the subject. The text is intended to be a challenging one that provokes discussion and deeper consideration of the forces influencing the development of psychology, and could also be appropriately used for a graduate-level course on the history of psychology. The book is intended for use as a stand-alone text for a one-semester course in the history of psychology that can be supplemented by focused readings selected by the instructor. Different configurations are possible for the use of the various sections of the text, depending on the individual goals of the instructor; for example, a one-semester course using Sections I, II, and IV would emphasize the impact of globalization on psychology, the development of indigenous Western psychology, and the critical role of diversity in psychology around the globe. No matter how you use this text, we are confident that you will appreciate fully that history has a future, and that for all of humanity to craft an enhanced future around the globe requires that we all think logically and act compassionately.

To aid them in appreciating the dynamic interaction between the development of psychology and the sociocultural context which surrounds it, we strongly recommend that students take the opportunity to engage in a "Personal Timeline Exercise"; preferably near the beginning of the course. To develop this timeline, we suggest that students examine their own "history" to determine what experiences, events, or people have shaped who they are as individuals and also as psychologists. This timeline should look beyond the personal sphere to include the individual's social and cultural context and is not necessarily limited to events following the student's birth, since our lives are often significantly impacted by the lives and experiences of those who came before us. For example, a personal timeline could include items similar to the following:

- World War II—My father's experience serving as an American soldier in World War II led him to instill in his children a deep commitment to the ideals of service and duty.
- The invention of the computer—Computers and the Internet play a significant role in my life to the extent that it would have conceivably taken a very different path had computers not been invented.
- Battling cancer at the age of 19.
- Witnessing a sibling's battle with alcohol and drug addiction.
- September 11, 2001.
- Having Mr. Miller as my third grade teacher.
- Taking up running as a regular exercise activity.

Since this timeline reflects the individual student's perspective, there are no rights or wrongs to its construction. The final product is less important than the act of engaging in reflective and mindful analysis of one's own life. In doing so, the student will hopefully gain a deeper understanding and appreciation for history.

Acknowledgments

Writing a textbook of this scope is an undertaking that could not be accomplished without the assistance and support of many individuals. We are grateful for the encouragement and support of the textbook division of Pearson Prentice Hall and psychology editor Jessica Mosher. We express our gratitude to Doug Bell at GGS Book Services for coordinating the final production phase of the project. We are also indebted to chapter contributors Barnaby Riedel (chapter 1) and Matthew Mishkind (chapter 9); Ingrid Lunt, Olga Mitina, Stanislas Golubenko, and Zhenhua Ma for providing material, perspective, and translation assistance for chapters 16 and 17, respectively; and Jenny Marcotte, Diana St. Louis, and Irene Knight for their able administrative support.

Robert B. Lawson
Burlington, Vermont

Jean E. Graham
Burlington, Vermont

Kristin M. Baker
Burlington, Vermont

TIMELINE OF PHILOSOPHY AND PSYCHOLOGY IN THE CONTEXT OF GENERAL HISTORY

Key: ▨ Century Interval ▨ Decade Interval ▨ Millenium Interval

General History		Famous People	Events in Philosophy and Psychology
	600 B.C.		
-580 B.C.–Anaximander organizes a world map -550 B.C.–Pythagoras of Samos proposes the Pythagorean Theorem -550 B.C.–Siddhartha Gautama Buddha establishes Buddhism -526 B.C.–First codes of law are issued in China	500 B.C.	(-563 to -483)–Siddhartha Gautama Buddha (-551 to -479)–Confucius	
-431 to -404–The Peloponnesian Wars	400 B.C.	(-472 to -370)–Democritus (-470 to -399)–Socrates (-460 to -377)–Hippocrates (-427 to -347)–Plato	
-367–Plato founds the Academy -335–Aristotle founds the Lyceum	300 B.C.	(-384 to -322)–Aristotle (-369 to -286)–Chuang Tzu (-341 to -270)–Epicurus (-336 to -264)–Zeno	-350–Aristotle writes *De Anima* and *On Memory and Reminiscence*
-204–The Chinese construct the Great Wall of China -200–The Chinese manufacture paper	200 B.C.	(-298 to -238)–Xun Zi, or Xuncius (-298 to -212)–Lao Tzu	
-44–Julius Caesar is assassinated	100 B.C.		
The Books of the New Testament are compiled The Silk Road opens trade between China and Europe	100	(120–201)–Galen	170–Claudius Galen describes the anatomy of the brain and ventricles
	200		
380–Christianity becomes the official religion of the Roman Empire 393–The last Olympic Games are held before the games are forbidden in 394 395–The Roman Empire is divided into eastern and western halves	300		
476–The Fall of Rome	400		406–Augustine writes *Confessions*
	500		
621–Buddhism becomes the state religion of Japan 622–Muhammed is expelled from Mecca and flees to Yathrib; his flight, the hegira, marks the beginning of the Islamic Calendar 630–The Muslim Empire is formed	600		
740–First printed newspaper appears in China 750–The Arabs learn the art of papermaking from China	700		
835–First reference to a printed book in China	800		

850—First European medical school is founded in Salerno, Italy

900
1000
1010
1020 — 1020—Ibn Sina, or Avicenna, suggests 5 distinct cognitive functions for the 3 ventricles of the brain
1030
1040
1050
1060 — 1060—The Norman Conquest; William the Conqueror claims the throne of England in 1066
1070 — (1079–1142)—Peter Abelard
1080 — (1098–1179)—Hildegard von Bingen
1090 — (1096–1099)—The first Crusade
1100
1110
1120
1130
1140 — (1147–1149)—The second Crusade
1150
1160 — 1163—In Europe, dissection of the human body is discouraged by the Church; 1168—Oxford University is founded
1170
1180 — (1189–1191)—The third Crusade
1190 — 1190—Islam spreads through India
1200 — (1202–1204)—The fourth Crusade
1210 — 1213—Genghis Khan invades China; 1215—The Magna Carta is signed; (1218–1221)—The fifth Crusade
1220 — (1225–1274)—Thomas Aquinas; (1228–1229)—The sixth Crusade
1230
1240 — 1247—World's first mental hospital, Bethlehem Royal Hospital, opens in London; (1248–1250)—The seventh Crusade
1250 — 1252—The beginning of the Inquisition
1260 — 1264—Thomas Aquinas publishes *Summa Theologica*
1270 — 1275—Marco Polo reaches China

(Continued)

General History	Year	Famous People	Events in Philosophy and Psychology
	1280		
	1290	(1290–1350)—William of Occum	
	1300	(1304–1374)—Francesco Petrarch	
	1310		
	1320		
1333—The Black Death begins in China	1330		
1337—The Hundred Years' War begins	1340		
1348—The Black Death reaches Europe	1350		
	1360		
	1370		
	1380		
	1390		
	1400		
	1410		
	1420		
1431—Joan of Arc is burned at the stake	1430		
1438—Johann Gutenberg develops the printing press	1440		
1453—The Hundred Years' War ends	1450	(1452–1519)—Leonardo da Vinci	
	1460	(1469–1527)—Niccolò Machiavelli	
1474—William Caxton prints the first book in English; 1478—The Spanish Inquisition begins	1470	(1473–1543)—Nicolas Copernicus	
1480—Ivan III unites the Russian nation and strengthens the authority of the monarchy	1480	(1483–1546)—Martin Luther	
1492—Christopher Columbus sails to the Americas	1490		
	1500		1506—The term psichiologia is first used by Marco Marulik
1513—Niccolo Machiavelli publishes *The Prince*; 1517—The beginning of the Protestant Reformation	1510		
1519—Spain invades Mexico	1520		1524—Marco Marulik publishes *The Psychology of Human Thought, Volume 1*
1533—Ivan the Terrible becomes the first Russian Czar; 1534—The Church of England is founded by Henry VIII	1530		
	1540		
1558—Elizabeth I becomes Queen of England	1550	(1552–1610)—Matteo Ricci	
	1560	(1561–1626)—Francis Bacon	
1564—The birth of William Shakespeare	1570	(1564–1642)—Galileo Galilei	

Year	Events	Births/Deaths	Publications
	1587—Virginia Dare is born; the first child of English parents born in America		
1580		(1582–1649)—Julius Alenis (1582–1649)—Franciscus Sambiasi (1588–1679)—Thomas Hobbes (1596–1650)—René Descartes	
1590			
1600			1605—Francis Bacon publishes *The Proficiency and Advancement of Learning*
1610	1616—William Harvey develops model of the human circulatory system The King James Bible is published		
1620			
1630	1632—Galileo publishes *Dialogue on the Two Great Systems of the World* 1636—Harvard University is founded	(1632–1677)—Baruch Spinoza (1632–1690)—John Locke	1637—René Descartes publishes *Discourse on Method*
1640		(1642–1727)—Isaac Newton	1649—René Descartes theorizes total separation of body and soul in *Passions of the Soul*
1650			1651—Thomas Hobbes publishes *Leviathan*
1660	1660—The beginning of the Restoration period in England 1664—The Royal Society founds the journal *Philosophical Transactions*, the oldest existing scientific journal The Greenwich Observatory is founded		
1670			
1680		(1685–1753)—George Berkeley	
1690			1690—John Locke publishes *An Essay Concerning Human Understanding*
1700		(1705–1757)—David Hartley	1709—George Berkeley publishes *An Essay Toward a New Theory of Vision*
1710		(1711–1776)—David Hume	
1720		(1724–1804)—Immanuel Kant	
1730		(1734–1815)—Franz Anton Mesmer	
1740			1745—Julien Offray de La Mettrie publishes *The Natural History of the Soul* 1748—David Hume publishes *An Inquiry Concerning Human Understanding* 1748—Julien Offray de La Mettrie publishes *L'Homme Machine*
1750	1755—Moscow State University is founded 1756—Wolfgang Amadeus Mozart is born	(1751–1825)—Marquis de Puysegur (1758–1832)—Franz Joseph Gall	
1760			1765—Gottfried Wilhelm von Leibniz publishes *New Essays on the Human Understanding*
1770	1776—The Declaration of Independence is signed	(1774–1842)—Robert Whytt (1774–1842)—Charles Bell	1774—Franz Mesmer performs his first cure using "animal magnetism"
1780		(1783–1855)—Francois Magendie	1782—Immanuel Kant publishes *The Critique of the Pure Reason* 1786—Luigi Galvani reports results of experiments on stimulation of muscles of the frog through application of electrical pulse 1789—Thomas Malthus publishes *An Essay on the Principle of Population*

(Continued)

General History	Year	Famous People	Events in Philosophy and Psychology
(1792–1795)—The French Revolution	1790	(1794–1867)—Marie-Jean Pierre Flourens	1790—Erasmus Darwin produces theory of human behavior and experience
The Rosetta Stone is discovered	1800		
	1801		
	1802	(1802–1887)—Dorothea Lynde Dix	
	1803		
	1804		
	1805		
	1806		
	1807		
	1808	(1808–1858)—Johannes Müller	Franz Thomas Gall and Johann Kaspar Spurzheim publish *Recherches sur le System Nerveux*
	1809		
	1810		
	1811		Sir Charles Bell describes at a dinner party the anatomical separation of sensory and motor function of the spinal cord
The War of 1812	1812		
	1813		
	1814		
Napoleon is defeated at Waterloo	1815		
	1816		
Establishment of the New York Stock and Exchange Board	1817		
	1818	(1881–1903)—Alexander Bain	
	1819		
	1820		
	1821		
	1822		Francois Magendie publishes article postulating separation of sensory and motor function of the spinal cord
	1823	(1823–1860)—Phineas Gage	
	1824	(1824–1880)—Pierre-Paul Broca	
	1825		
	1826		
	1827		
	1828		
	1829	(1829–1905)—Ivan Michailovich Sechenov	
The U.S. Congress makes abortion a statutory crime	1830		

1831			
1832		(1832–1920)—Wilhelm Wundt	
1833			
1834			
1835			
1836	Queen Victoria of England begins her 64-year reign		
1837			
1838		(1838–1917)—Franz Brentano	
1839			
1840			
1841			
1842			
1843			John Stuart Mill publishes *A System of Logic*
1844			
1845			
1846			
1847		(1847–1930)—Christine Ladd-Franklin	
1848	Karl Marx and Friedrich Engels publish *The Communist Manifesto* / A Women's Rights Convention is held in Seneca Falls, NY		
1849		(1849–1936)—Ivan Pavlov	
1850		(1850–1909)—Hermann Ebbinghaus	
1851		(1851–1943)—Lillien Jane Martin	
1852			
1853			
1854			
1855			
1856		(1856–1939)—Sigmund Freud	
1857		(1857–1927)—Vladimir Bekhterev	
1858			Wilhelm Wundt becomes assistant to Hermann von Helmhotz
1859			Charles Darwin publishes *On the Origin of the Species*
1860	The American Civil War begins / New York State passes a law allowing women to collect their own wages, mount lawsuits, and inherit property from their husbands		
1861			Paul Broca demonstrates localization of speech functions in the left frontal lobe of the brain
1862		(1862–1915)—Oswald Kulpe / (1862–1936)—Georgy Chelpanov	

(Continued)

Year	General History	Famous People	Events in Philosophy and Psychology
1863	Abraham Lincoln delivers the Emancipation Proclamation	(1863–1930)—Mary Whiton Calkins	
1864			
1865	The American Civil War ends The 13th Amendment prohibiting slavery is ratified in the United States		
1866			
1867		(1867–1927)—Edward Bradford Titchener	
1868		(1868–1940)—Cai Yuanpei	
1869	Wyoming Territory becomes the first American political body that allows women to vote		Francis Galton publishes *Hereditary Genius* and first employs the concept of normal distribution for purposes of classification
1870		(1870–1937)—Alfred Adler (1870–1952)—Maria Montessori	Jean Marie Charcot begins to teach in La Salpêtrière
1871		(1871–1939)—Margaret Floy Washburn	
1872			
1873			
1874		(1874–1949)—Edward Lee Thorndike	
1875		(1875–1961)—Carl Jung	
1876	The telephone is patented by Alexander Graham Bell		
1877			
1878		(1878–1972)—Lillian Moller Gilbreth	
1879		(1879–1957)—Konstantin Kornilov (1879–1985)—Ernest Jones	Wilhelm Wundt establishes first psychological laboratory at the University of Leipzig in Germany Francis Galton utilizes the method of word association Lightner Witmer is first to use the term "clinical psychology"
1880		(1880–1943)—Max Wertheimer	
1881			Max Friedrich is the first recipient of a doctoral degree in experimental psychology
1882		(1882–1960)—Melanie Klein	
1883			Johns Hopkins University establishes first American psychology laboratory Wilhelm Wundt establishes the journal *Philosophische Studien*
1884			
1885		(1885–1952)—Karen Horney	
1886	The Vermont Legislature passes a bill granting women suffrage	(1886–1939)—Leta Stetter Hollingworth (1886–1941)—Kurt Koffka	Vladimir Bekterev founds the first Russian psychology laboratory
1887		(1887–1967)—Wolfgang Köhler	
1888	Chromosomes are visualized for the first time.		James McKeen Cattell becomes the first American professor of psychology
1889		(1889–1960)—Sergie Rubinstein (1889–1964)—W. R. D. Fairbairn	

Year	Psychologists (birth–death)	Psychology events	World events
1890	(1890–1947)—Kurt Lewin (1890–1970)—Ai Wei	The American Psychological Association is founded	
1891			
1892		Christine Ladd Franklin completes the doctoral program in psychology	
1893	(1893–1988)—Henry Murray		
1894	(1894–1970)—Heinz Hartmann (1894–1970)—Lu Zhiwei	J. M. Cattell and J.M. Baldwin found the journal *Psychological Review* Margaret Floy Washburn becomes the first woman to receive a PhD in psychology	
1895	(1895–1954)—Francis Cecil Sumner (1895–1982)—Anna Freud		
1896	(1896–1934)—Lev Vygotsky (1896–1966)—Nikolai Bernstein (1896–1971)—D. W. Winnicott (1896–1987)—Mary Cover Jones	Lightner Witmer establishes the first psychological clinic in America at the University of Pennsylvania	The first modern Olympics are held in Athens, Greece
1897	(1897–1967)—Gordon Allport (1897–1985)—Margaret Mahler		Guglielmo Marconi achieves long distance radio transmission
1898	(1898–1970)—Kuo Zing Yang		
1899			
1900	(1900–1980)—Erich Fromm		
1901		Pierre Janet and George Dumas found the French Psychological Society	
1902	(1902–?)—Chen Li (1902–1977)—Alexander Luria (1902–1987)—Carl Rogers (1902–1994)—Erik Erikson		
1903	(1903–1979)—Alexei Leontiev	First Japanese psychology laboratory established at Tokyo University	The Wright Brothers make the first successful flight in an airplane
1904		James Ward and W.H. Rivers launch the *British Journal of Psychology*	
1905		Mary Whiton Calkins becomes the first woman president of the American Psychological Association	Albert Einstein proposes a special theory of relativity
1906		James McKeen Cattell publishes first edition of *American Men of Science* Ivan Pavlov publishes his research on classical conditioning	
1907	(1907–1996)—Evelyn Hooker		
1908	(1908–1970)—Abraham Maslow (1908–2001)—Anne Anastasi		
1909	(1909–1994)—Rollo May	Sigmund Freud and C.C. Jung travel to Clark University in the United States *The Journal of Education Psychology* is founded	The National Association for the Advancement of Colored People (NAACP) is founded
1910			China abolishes slavery

(Continued)

General History		Famous People	Events in Philosophy and Psychology
The Kansas attorney general rules women may wear trousers	1911		Sigmund Freud publishes *The Origin and Development of Psychoanalysis* A.A. Brill founds the Psychoanalytical Association of New York The *Journal of Animal Behavior* is established
Hsuan-t'ung, the last emperor of China, abdicates	1912		Max Wertheimer publishes the article *Experimental Studies of the Perception of Movement*
The first refrigerator for domestic use is produced in Chicago	1913	(1913–1981)—Heinz Kohut (1913–1999)—Mary Salter Ainsworth	John Watson publishes *Psychology as a Behaviorist Views It* Wolfgang Köhler begins conducting studies with chimpanzees in Tenerife
(1914–1918) World War I	1914	(1914–2005)—Kenneth B. Clark	
	1915		India establishes its first psychology department at Calcutta University
The first birth control clinic in the U.S. opens in Brooklyn, NY Jeanette Rankin becomes the first woman elected to the U.S. House of Representatives	1916		The *Journal of Experimental Psychology* is established Enrique Aragón establishes the first Mexican psychology laboratory
(1917–1922)—The Russian Revolution Frozen food processing is invented in the U.S.	1917	(1917–1983)—Mamie Phipps Clark	The *Journal of Applied Psychology* is established The American Association of Clinical Psychology separates from APA Cai Yuanpie establishes the first Chinese psychology laboratory at Beijing University
The Pulitzer Prize is established The Russian Communist Party is founded	1918		Robert S. Woodworth publishes *Dynamic Psychology*, in which he introduces the concept of drive Mary Whiton Calkins becomes the first woman president of the American Philosophical Association
Benito Mussolini founds the Italian Fascist Party	1919		
The 19th Amendment gives women in the U.S. the right to vote	1920	(1920–1992)—Carolyn Attneave	John B. Watson and Rosalie Rayner publish *Conditioned Emotional Reactions* First Chinese independent department of psychology established at Nanjing University
	1921		Köhler, Koffka, and Wertheimer establish the journal *Psychologische Forschung* The first Australian psychology department is established at the University of Sydney
	1922		
	1923	(1923–present)—Janet Spence	
Joseph Stalin becomes leader of the Communist Party in the Soviet Union	1924		The Indian Psychological Association is established
	1925		
The Jazz Singer, the first talking film, debuts	1926		
The Stock Market Crash of October 24 sparks the Great Depression	1927		

World Events	Year		Psychology
Charles Lindbergh makes first nonstop solo transatlantic flight	1928		
	1929		Edward Boring publishes *A History of Experimental Psychology*
	1930		
	1931	(1931–2001)—Martha Bernal	
	1932	(1932–present)—Florence Denmark	
	1933	(1933–1998)—Dalmas A. Taylor	
	1934		The first psychological clinic in Egypt is founded at the Higher Institute of Education
	1935		
	1936		
New York State law allows women to serve as jurors	1937		
	1938		
(1939–1945) World War II	1939		The Canadian Psychological Association is established
	1940		
The U.S. enters WWII following the bombing of Pearl Harbor on December 7th	1941		
	1942		
	1943		
	1944	(1944–present)—Sandra Bem (1944–present)—Elizabeth Loftus (1944–present)—Stanley Sue	
The United Nations is established The Arab League is founded Tupperware is first marketed	1945		The first U.S. state law for certification or licensure of psychologists is signed by the governor of Connecticut
India gains independence from Great Britain	1946		
	1947		The first issue of *American Psychologist* is published The Korean Psychological Association is established The Egyptian Association for Psychological Societies is established
Israel is created as the Jewish homeland The Universal Declaration of Human Rights passes the UN General Assembly	1948		
The Soviet Union explodes an atomic bomb ushering in the nuclear arms race between the U.S. and U.S.S.R. NATO is formed	1949		The Boulder Conference outlines a scientist-practitioner model for clinical psychology
Apartheid is established in South Africa The Korean War begins	1950		
	1951		The Israel Psychological Association is established
	1952		The International Union of Psychological Science (IUPS) is founded DSM-I is published by The American Psychiatric Association

(Continued)

Year	General History	Famous People	Events in Philosophy and Psychology
1953	The execution of Julius and Ethel Rosenberg		The American Association of Psychology publishes the first *Code of Ethics of Psychologists*
1954	The first TV dinners are sold in the U.S.		
1955	Rosa Parks is arrested for refusing to take a seat at the back of a public bus; her action sparks the Civil Rights Movement		
1956	The first transistorized computer is completed at MIT		The Czechoslovak Psychological Society and the Slovak Psychological Society are founded
1957			
1958			
1959	Fidel Castro takes power in Cuba		Mexico establishes its first school of professional psychology
1960			
1961	Soviets construct the Berlin Wall in Germany; The U.S. military buildup in Vietnam begins with combat advisors. President John F. Kennedy declares that they will respond if fired upon.		*The Journal of Humanistic Psychology* is established
1962			The Psychological Association of the Philippines is established
1963	John F. Kennedy is assassinated		
1964	The U.S. Civil Rights Act is passed prohibiting discrimination on the basis of race, sex, religion, or national origin		Humanistic psychology emerges as the 'Third Force' in psychology
1965	The Beatles appear on the Ed Sullivan Show; First American combat troops arrive in Vietnam		The military regime dissolves the Department of Psychology at the Universidade de Brasília in Brazil
1966	China's Cultural Revolution begins		The first master's program in humanistic psychology is established at Sonoma State College; The study of psychology is banned in China: The Chinese Institute of Psychology is closed, all publication of psychology journals and books in China is stopped
1967	Microwave ovens become available for home use		The Department of Psychology is established at the University of Hong Kong; The Hong Kong Psychological Society is established; The Psychological Association of Iran is established; *The Korean Journal of Psychology* is established; The Pakistan Psychological Association is established; The first Doctor of Psychology (PsyD) degree program in Clinical Psychology is established at the University of Illinois
1968			
1969	Americans land on the moon; The largest antiwar demonstration ever held in Washington, D.C. protests the Vietnam War		

World Events	Year	Psychology Events
Honeywell releases the H316 "Kitchen Computer," the first home computer, priced at US$10,600 in the Neiman Marcus catalog. Four students are killed by National Guardsmen at Kent State University in Ohio. The killings sparked hundreds of protest activities across college campuses in the United States.	1970	
	1971	
U.S. Congress passes the Equal Employment Opportunity Act	1972	
U.S. Supreme Court decision in Roe v. Wade legalizes abortion for women up to 6 months pregnant. The last U.S. combat troops leave Vietnam	1973	The PsyD degree is endorsed for professional practice at the APA Conference in Vail, Colorado
	1974	The *Journal of Black Psychology* is established
	1975	
The trade name "Microsoft" is registered	1976	
	1977	
The Muslim fundamentalist revolution in Iran ousts the shah and establishes the rule of Ayatollah Khomeini	1978	The Columbian Society of Psychology is established. The Chinese Society of Psychology is re-established
The first test-tube-fertilized infant is born in England	1979	
(1980–1989) Iran–Iraq War	1980	It is estimated that 1 in 10 doctorates granted in the U. S. is in psychology
	1981	M. Rosenzweig estimates the total number of psychologists in the world to be around 260,000. APA has approximately 50,500 members
	1982	
	1983	
	1984	
Mikhail Gorbachev assumes power in the Soviet Union	1985	
The Space Shuttle Challenger explodes during liftoff	1986	
	1987	
	1988	
The Berlin Wall is torn down	1989	
Iraq invades Kuwait triggering U.S. involvement in what becomes known as "The Gulf War"	1990	
	1991	
	1992	
	1993	

(Continued)

xxix

General History		Famous People	Events in Philosophy and Psychology
	1994		
	1995		The European Federation of Professional Psychologists Association accepts the *Meta-Code of Ethics*
	1996		
	1997		
	1998		Martin E. P. Seligman coins the term "Positive Psychology" to describe an alternative vision for psychology less focused on treatment of pathology which explores instead the more positive end of the continuum of human behavior and experience
	1999		Martin E. P. Seligman teaches the first undergraduate seminar on "Positive Psychology"
	2000		

Contemporary Psychology: Global Forces

CHAPTER OVERVIEW

Globalization affects all aspects of our lives as well as the field of psychology. Although globalization has evolved over many centuries, it is often considered a relatively new phenomenon. We focus upon globalization starting with the European Renaissance, then moving to the period of colonialism dominated by the West, through the world wars, and today as manifested in many international economic structures and alliances that increasingly connect nations, organizations, and individuals.

Psychological globalization embraces every country throughout the world, and is crystalized as the *The Three Worlds of Psychology*. In this theory, the United States is considered the first world because to date it is the major producer of psychological knowledge that is exported to both the second world of psychology (e.g., England, Canada, and Australia) and the third world of psychology (i.e., developing countries such as Nigeria, Cuba, and India). This theory presumes that each of the three worlds has an unequal capacity to produce and disseminate psychological knowledge that shapes the field of psychology. As all countries on the globe continue to be interconnected by economics, media, and travel, the field of psychology continues to grow globally, with the number of psychologists in the world, in both the traditional academic/research field and health service provider specializations, nearly doubling between 1980 and 1991. Interestingly, there also has been a recent strong move toward the formation of regional organizations, as reflected in the formation of the European Federation of Professional Psychologists' Association (EFPPA) and the Interamerican Society of Psychology (Sociedad Interamericana de Psicologia; SIP), which reflect the dynamics between global and regional local forces seen throughout the world.

Four core functions of internationality in psychology are identified, the first of which is the promotion of cross-national understanding and goodwill among people. Second, since concepts are often imported through culture-specific language traditions, internationality serves to safeguard against locking the discipline into culture-dependence. The third function is capacity building through international research and practice programs and projects, and lastly the development of cross-national training curricula.

The current expression of globalization has been influenced by the evolution of postmodernism which is thought of by some as an attack on scientific inquiry promoting relativism. Postmodernism calls for a reevaluation of psychology due to the limitations of hypothesis testing, and the tendency to universalize the findings of Western psychology to cultures around the globe, that is, one psychology fits all.

The developing regions of the world (Africa, Asia, and Latin America) are in a hurry to grow economically and to eradicate poverty. To accomplish their goals these regions must develop their own indigenous psychologies because such psychologies embrace the cultural views and values, theories, and assumptions about human nature that shape psychological functions in each respective culture. It is crucial that emerging regions of the world develop their own indigenous psychologies, as Western psychology alone is unable to assist in their current economic, cultural, and psychological challenges.

In large measure, Western psychology has proven inadequate in dealing with the social issues of non-Western cultures because it carries the culture-specific vision of individualism and objectivity while many other cultures around the world embrace collectivism and the primacy of the subjective. To move toward a global paradigm is to encourage the development of distinctly indigenous psychologies while at the same time seeking their integration. At a time when the secular, scientific, religious, technological, and spiritual cultural traditions of different regions of the world seem to conflict more and more, global psychology welcomes all of them as important perspectives within a diverse global whole.

LEARNING OBJECTIVES

When you finish studying this chapter, you will be prepared to:

- Identify the key economic and political events in the evolution of globalization to the present
- Discuss the impact of some of the forces of globalization upon theories as well as the practice of psychology
- Explain **The Three Worlds of Psychology** including their countries, historical development, and characteristics
- Identify and discuss the distinctive characteristics of global organizations bringing together the field of psychology
- Address the four functions of internationality in psychology
- Define postmodernism and speak to its influence on our self-identity and contribution to expanding psychological research
- Identify the purposes of cross-cultural psychology, theoretical orientations, and methodologies
- Define culture and discuss how it is employed in the study of cross-cultural psychology as well as have a clear view of how culture can assist in dealing with the challenges presented by globalization
- Identify and further address the fundamental reasons why Western psychology has been unable to come together with other indigenous psychologies to assist in economic and social development
- Identify the social and economic deterrents to the development of psychology in the developing world

INTRODUCTION

The emergence of a global psychology paradigm is the result of a radically changing world marked by rapid information exchange, unprecedented mobility, and the vanishing of ideological coherence. Advances in telecommunications, transportation, and economics have linked all of us to global forces. The fabled "global village" (McLuhan & Fiore, 1968) has arrived, yet unforeseen social, cultural, political, and environmental problems increasingly challenge its viability. As Vaclav Havel wrote, "without a global revolution in our sphere of consciousness, nothing will change for the better in the sphere of our being as humans, and the catastrophe toward which we are headed . . . will be unavoidable" (Lasley, 1994, p. 3). In short, the challenge before all of us is to learn how to be part of rather than apart from each other.

The present forces of globalization are pitting secular, scientific, religious, technological, and spiritual cultural traditions against one another in what seems to be an irreconcilable conflict over ways of knowing (Marsella, 1998). These fundamental differences are being represented by a growing sense of confusion and bewilderment over how to live meaningfully within the emerging global context of human life. The scale and complexity of global events and forces constitute an extraordinary challenge for psychology as a science and profession because they impose complex and intense demands on individual and collective psyches around the world and challenge our sense of identity, control, and well-being. While psychology has a critical role to play in addressing and resolving these problems, its efficacy will only be realized if we are prepared to make a major disciplinary response. Such a response requires a reorientation toward the individual in a global context as well as a reconsideration of the premises, methods, and practices of Western psychology in particular, and an increased appreciation, support, and use of other diverse indigenous psychologies. In the minds of some, psychological science tells more about the history, culture, and values of the West than about any universal psychology.

Globalization has led to the rapid and worldwide spread of Western cultural lifestyles, values, and priorities. The cause of this global culture-change process is a result of the economic, political, and military dominance of the West and the inequities imposed by power asymmetries. Although there is much that is admirable about Western culture, especially its stated commitment to human rights, democratic values, and intellectual and social progress, serious questions can be raised about the wisdom of establishing it as a universal standard without including other cultural perspectives in the discussion. Driven by the necessity of capitalist expansion and an ethnocentric justification of its values, the West's notion of "progress" is leading to the creation of a Westernized Global Village in which peoples from all over the world have little political or economic power to defend their unique cultural identities and lifestyles. Accordingly, it is no surprise that tensions between democratic and hegemonic forms of globalization are a central feature of our era (Tehranian & Reed, 1997).

A resurgent determination has risen among marginalized groups and indigenous peoples to resist the loss of their social, cultural, and religious identities. These forces of resistance have made indigenization a defining characteristic of the past two decades (Huntington, 1996). Opposition is expressing itself in a variety of complex ways including localist, ethno-nationalist, pan-nationalist, regionalist, environmentalist, feminist, and religious movements (Tehranian & Reed, 1997). At the same time as hegemonic globalization strives to integrate humanity into a single Western vision, the world's people increasingly resist by asserting the basic right to determine their own cultural identity and way of life. Thus, a paradox exists between globalization and indigenization that threatens our capacities to counteract devastating economic, political, cultural, and environmental events and forces. In order for diverse peoples to collaborate constructively in the midst of global challenges, we must strive to answer whether there are certain values we can and should share even as we promote cultural diversity. This question, and the ongoing challenge of answering it, requires a new paradigm of psychology that places both psychologists and psychologies in their appropriate local and global contexts.

Any examination of the history of psychology as an academic discipline exposes its deeply rooted Western origins and its dependence on largely Western cultural assumptions regarding human behavior and the nature of truth (Sexton & Hogan, 1992). Although the growth of Western psychology continues worldwide, non-Western and ethnic minority psychologists are increasingly claiming that their culturally distinct experiences cannot be explained by Western concepts and methods (Gergen et al., 1996). The coupling of Western ethnocentric psychology with the aim of becoming increasingly international is leading to the creation of a Westernized global psychology that negates global ethnocultural diversity, jeopardizes the validity of varied forms of psychological research, and allows psychology to function as a sociopolitical stabilizing mechanism of Western hegemonic globalization (Moghaddam, 1987).

Inasmuch as global challenges threaten the survival of humanity as a whole, a superordinate psychology must arise that is concerned with understanding, evaluating, and addressing the consequences of global events and forces upon differing cultures and their members (Marsella, 1998). This need to identify and value the similarities and differences between people within and across different cultures of the world is the reason for a global psychology which must employ multicultural, multisectoral, multidisciplinary, and multinational knowledge, methods, and interventions. A global psychology makes plain that dominant mainstream Western psychology is itself a culture-specific indigenous psychology with limited applicability to people outside the Western cultural tradition. Global psychology requires all of us to realize the global context of the individual and the importance of local culture in shaping affective or emotional, behavioral, and cognitive systems. In order to do so, global psychology supports the aim of cross-cultural research to (a) construct if appropriate universal laws governing affective, behavioral, and emotional systems through cross-cultural collaboration among psychologists around the world; (b) identify different cultural expressions of these three systems; and (c) identify those affects or emotions, behaviors, and cognitions (memories, beliefs, and thoughts) that are unique to different cultures around the world. Global psychology asserts that to a certain degree all psychologies are cultural manifestations, and to meet the above cross-cultural goals indigenous psychologies must be supported and given equal expression in the formation of a global psychology.

The expansion of technology, population growth, crowding, environmental devastation, and multiethnic living as a result of migration are all forces that mandate a need for the development of coordinated local and global ethics, conflict management, behavioral health education, and disease prevention strategies. International psychological organizations are increasing, indigenous psychologies are developing, and the psychological bases of global challenges are being recognized. This chapter focuses upon the present and the future of psychology in a global world which increasingly calls for the emergence of a new paradigm of psychology, one that is capable of meeting the demands of globalization so that we may appreciate and embrace more deeply that we are a part of rather than apart from each other.

GLOBALIZATION AND THE FIELD OF PSYCHOLOGY

Globalization refers to a transformation in time and space. The present world, as a result of rapid global communication systems and mass transportation, is changing ever so rapidly into a type of global village where goods are exchanged, cultures intersect, and national boundaries disappear (Giddens, 1994). For example, consider the impact that Internet computer technology has had on our lives. With the push of a button, people from all over the world can transcend national and natural borders creating cyber-subcultures that have powerful socializing influences (Marsella, 1998). Accordingly, these local and global transformations have been the central reason for a critical reevaluation of psychology and its role in a global context.

Coming Together: The Evolution of Globalization

Although globalization is a novel phenomenon in relation to the history of humankind, it is not unique, as many think, to the latter half of the twentieth century. For our purposes, we begin with globalization as manifested in the fifteenth century, when the Renaissance of European culture (1450–1600) was well under way and social pluralism, expanding commerce, and technological achievements provided the basis for a new era in global politics (Huntington, 1996). The history of globalization is inseparable from the rise of the West (i.e., European cultures and countries such as Italy, France, Germany, and England). For some 400 years after the advent of the European Renaissance, intercivilizational relations consisted of the subordination of other societies to Western civilization. However, as Westerners often forget, this was not by the superiority of Western ideas, values, or religion, but by its superiority in reaching distant peoples (ocean navigation) and conquering them through military prowess.

The stage of globalization that is of particular importance to this chapter is the era of colonialism or the kind of social, political, and economical arrangements made and fought over by the West during the 19th and early 20th centuries. This stage saw, for the first time, a single civilization establish itself as a leader around the globe. Europeans controlled 35% of the earth's land surface in 1800, 67% in 1878, and 84% in 1914 (Huntington, 1996). Capitalism, as an economic force, was the primary catalyst behind this rapid expansion of the West. New colonies were not created to advance primarily a religious or political cause, but rather, to establish and control world markets as a means of fighting against the tendency for profits to fall. On the other hand, the progressive values of the Enlightenment (individualism, reason, and human rights) led, with some obvious irony, to the West's perception of other civilizations as "backward." So while colonization was primarily the result of economic motives, the West's belief in its own cultural superiority also played a crucial role in rationalizing colonization as not only legitimate but God's will. The idea of "the white man's burden," taken from a poem by Rudyard Kipling (1899), and the spirit of "manifest destiny" in the United States expressed the ethnocentric justification for Western expansion anywhere and everywhere there were opportunities for economic profit.

In the early 1900s, Europe, the United States, Canada, Australia, New Zealand, South Africa, and the countries of South America constituted the so-called Western world. All were formally Christian, all regulated their affairs by European systems of law, and all had access to the cultures of Europe with which they shared their languages. Accordingly, the Western world was a world of shared standards. Philanthropists and progressives, oblivious to any disruptive effects, believed that the values of European civilization were better than indigenous values and envisioned a world united under Reason. Science was beginning to overtake religion as the standard for accumulating knowledge of the natural world, including human affective, behavioral, and cognitive systems. Psychology, as a science, emerged out of the West at the height of the colonial period with the establishment of the first psychological laboratory under Wilhelm Wundt at the University of Leipzig in 1879.

By 1910 the world was more unified politically and economically than it had ever been, with the West dominating other cultures and regions. All this changed in 1917 as a result of the Russian Revolution, which marked the dawn of an ideological conflict between liberal democracy and communism or between the West and the non-West, ultimately culminating in the cold war. The rise of Marxism, first in Russia then in China and Vietnam, represented a transition phase from the European international system to a post-European multiciviliza-tional system (Huntington, 1996). At this stage, identified by Robertson (1990) as "the struggle-for-hegemony phase," the unilateral international system gave way to a more bipolar model in which relations were increasingly dominated by reactions of the West to developments in those societies not characterized by liberal democracy.

With the passing of the two world wars on European soil, America established itself as a global superpower and arbitrator of international affairs. Beginning in the late 1960s, and con-tinuing into the present, a new stage of globalization arrived, identified as "the uncertainty phase" (Robertson, 1990). The end of the cold war, the heightening of global consciousness, the spread of nuclear weapons, the increase in global institutions, and new problems of multi-culturality within societies all characterize this new phase and mark it as a time of uncertainty. While globalization has facilitated connection and coordination among people, the negative consequences of globalization are many, including the diminished or lost sovereignty of states, constraints on democracy, loss of community, increased centralization of corporate and governmental elites, concentration of the global power structure, and increased dependency among less-developed nations on globalizing powers (Farazmand, 1999).

There is a growing awareness that globalization is driven by the hegemony of Western capitalism and its need to expand continually to promote profit. New markets, cheap labor, and unrestricted production sites have made "going global" a profitable move for businesses. Since profit is the lifeblood of capitalism, businesses have expanded internationally with little concern for local ecology or indigenous cultures. As these businesses have expanded to become multinational and transnational corporations they have accrued such substantial economic and political power that they have become a threat to state sovereignty, democ-racy, community, and psychological wellness. The International Monetary Fund (IMF), the World Bank (WB), and the World Trade Organization (WTO) are organizations that give inter-national loans, mostly to the developing world, to promote the growth of the international private sector. However, such loans are only given if the country is willing to meet certain conditions that deepen financial, military, and economic dependency on Western powers (Farazmand, 1999). The very fact that global organizations can dictate fiscal, monetary, and other structural adjustment policies of poor and less-developed countries is a negation of local democracy, community, and human rights. For much of the developing world, globalization has resulted in deepening poverty, social disintegration, and environmental devastation. Globalization of corporations has meant for many less-developed countries a destruction of domestic production economies in favor of export-oriented, cash-crop activities, and global interests (Farazmand, 1999).

As a result, worldwide anti-globalization movements have arisen, which speak against such developments as the displacement of indigenous people, human rights violations, envi-ronmental destruction, the suppression of ethnocultural diversity, the decline of democracy, the breaking of the social contract, and the illegitimacy of the State as an instrument of cor-porate power and interest rather than the collective good. The popular press has also called our attention to the consequences of hegemonic versus democratic forms of globalization. Samuel Huntington (1996), in his book *The Clash of Civilizations*, argued that Western, Arabic, and Eastern civilizations are moving toward a potentially catastrophic conflict because of competing worldviews and values. George Soros (1997), in his article "The Capitalist Threat," asserted that free-market global capitalism might undermine the required values for an open society. Noreena Hertz (2001), in her book *The Silent Takeover: Global Capitalism and the Death of Democracy*, contends that global capitalism in its present form destroys democracy by making the State powerless relative to the interests of big business.

Global psychology prizes diverse psychologies, the call for universal human rights, and democratic/participatory forms of globalization. Inasmuch as global psychology opposes the privileging of any national or cultural psychology and aims to alleviate social and psychological misery worldwide, global psychology is as much about the appropriate research and application of psychological knowledge as it is about mandating an emancipatory political role for psychology.

While we have been focusing on the evolution of globalization and its inherent power asymmetries, globalization in the late twentieth century was especially different from earlier stages in the shift from primarily economic to increasing cultural exchanges between countries within a multicultural, multinational, and multiethnic context (Appadurai, 1990; Featherstone, 1990). This shift in globalization concerns psychology because in addition to material exchanges between countries, people are increasingly coming into daily contact with the varied behaviors, beliefs, and feelings of the members of many varied cultures around the world.

The influences of globalization on psychological functioning are only now being explored, with the primary psychological consequence impacting the formation of identity (Arnett, 2002). Many scholars of globalization have argued that now more than ever adolescents are growing up with a consciousness of the world as a whole. This global consciousness among the young is resulting in diminished ties to the specific place of their upbringing, raising new problems and possibilities for identity formation. Arnett (2002) argues that we may be seeing the development of bicultural identities among adolescents who attain both a local identity and an identity tied to the global culture. Although a healthy integration of these two cultural identities can be seen in a variety of cultural contexts, as evidenced by the Inuit in Canada (Condon, 1988) or young Indians in the global high-tech economy (Verma & Saraswathi, 2002), signals of alienation and identity confusion have also arisen (Arnett, 2002). Indeed, having a global consciousness involves wrestling with a lack of cultural certainty. An important job for psychologists around the world is to begin researching the effects of having both a local and global consciousness. What are the costs and benefits? What are the conditions that foster a healthy integration of both cultural identities? How do indigenous psychologies differ in their understanding of the consequences of globalization?

The Three Worlds of Psychology

The worldly domain of psychology can be categorized according to the power structure of psychological communities at the global level. Moghaddam (1987) argues that there are three worlds in psychology, each having an unequal capacity to produce and disseminate psychological knowledge and to shape the field of psychology. While the three worlds are differentiated solely on the development of productive forces in psychology, the strength of these forces has been influenced by political and economic differences, most notably the availability of material resources. In effect, the differential wealth in the three worlds has translated into the unequal development of psychological resources such as laboratories, psychological journals, universities, and trained psychologists.

The **first world** is represented by the United States where the discipline of psychology has flourished to such a degree that even seemingly esoteric psychological constructs and associated studies have social and economic support (e.g., creativity and self-enhancement). Although U.S. psychology is the offspring of European psychology, it has developed of its own accord, and since the end of World War II has expanded so that its productive capacity stands unparalleled. The first world is the major producer of psychological knowledge and is able to export this knowledge to both the second and third worlds without being much influenced by their psychological developments.

The **second world** consists of countries like England, Canada, Australia, and the former Soviet Republics. The second world rivals the first world in some areas, but its influence is far greater in the second and third worlds than it is in the first world (Moghaddam, 1987). The influence of the second world upon the third world stems largely from the legacy of colonialism and the traditional ties established during those times. The relative lack of resources does not allow the second world to study the range of research topics comparable to the first world, thus limiting the second world's scope of influence.

The **third world** mainly imports psychological knowledge from both the first and second worlds due to the limited economic and sociopolitical capacities to produce psychological knowledge (Moghaddam, 1987). Countries in the third world include developing countries such as Nigeria, Cuba, and India. Aside from blatant economic differences, another important reason for the third world's lack of capacity to produce psychological knowledge is a direct result of inherent social-structural characteristics. An example of these characteristics is the duality of the traditional and modern sectors. While the population of the modern sector tends to be more affluent, literate, and influenced by Western culture, the traditional sector tends to be poor, illiterate, and indigenous in lifestyle. The impact of psychology remains limited to the minority modern sector, and third world psychologists have had little success in applying their skills to the traditional sector (Moghaddam & Taylor, 1985).

Moghaddam (1987) has noted that these three worlds are not defined by absolute boundaries, so as with the case of India, some countries seem to fall between the second and third worlds. However, the importance of the categorization lies not in differentiating clearly between worlds, but to make clear the power inequalities involved in the production and dissemination of psychological knowledge and the shaping of mainstream psychology. Through an awareness of how culture guides research and influences findings, these power imbalances become of great concern for the discipline of psychology and its aim to lend relevant expertise to issues of global and local importance. The formation of an international community of psychological organizations is coming to play an important role in the reevaluation of psychological science and the cultivation of a commons where genuine global dialogue can occur among psychologists from a wide and diverse array of cultures.

The Growth of Psychology Around the Globe

According to data from the International Union of Psychological Science (IUPsyS), the total number of psychologists and psychological researchers in the world doubled between 1980 and 1991, from 260,000 to 500,000 (Rosenzweig, 1992, 1999). Growth in psychology was predicted in almost all of the countries surveyed, so it is likely that at present the total number of psychologists in the world is nearing the one million mark!

Since the amount of training required in each country to be considered a psychologist differs, local definitions were used in these surveys. For instance, in the United States and Canada most psychologists have a PhD or master's degree while in other countries four or five years of postsecondary education is required to become a psychologist and in some countries just three years of training is necessary (Rosenzweig, 1992). Obviously, an international issue for the discipline has been to gain legal protection for the title of psychologist that would include the development of training standards. Campaigns to achieve this goal are being pursued in many parts of the world so that the public will be protected from people without proper qualifications.

The wealth of the United States both intellectually and economically has contributed to it becoming the most active country in the field of psychology. In the early 1990s, the United States had the greatest concentration of psychologists in general (250,000) and research psychologists in particular (36,000 out of 72,000) around the world (Rosenzweig, 1992). Moghaddam (1987) found that most of the psychologists who ever lived or are now living can be found in the United States. As a result, there has been an Americanization of psychology in the twentieth century that many believe is compromising the applicability of the discipline around the globe.

Rosenzweig (1992) notes that the differences between the developing and industrialized nations can be examined in terms of two major areas of psychology: the traditional ademic/research fields (e.g., developmental, cognitive, and social psychology) and the health service provider fields (e.g., clinical psychology and counseling). In general, psychological research in developing countries tends to be more focused on the health service provider fields while research in the industrialized world gravitates more toward the academic/research fields. This difference in concentration is highly related to the availability of material resources. While developed countries can afford to do research for the sake of general knowledge and the development of theory, developing countries must focus their limited resources on research that has direct relevance for their economic and social development.

One trend of considerable importance is the overall decline in the basic research fields of psychology such as cognitive, behavioral, and experimental psychology. Since the 1950s there has been substantial growth in the practice of psychology worldwide but only minimal increases in psychological research. Without a strong academic/research base the practice of psychology will suffer. If psychological research does not continue to draw interest and replenish its research base, there will be fewer people qualified to train psychologist-practitioners. The result, many fear, would be a psychology without a science (Sexton & Hogan, 1992).

For both the developed and developing countries the most active fields of research are social, educational, cognitive, and clinical psychology. Although most psychologists are working on these areas of psychology around the world, some psychologists in certain countries are investigating topics of special local or regional interest. Rosenzweig (1992) lists a variety of countries whose psychology programs emphasize a special interest related to national concerns: Japan, the psychology of Zen and other Eastern systems; Hong Kong, Chinese psychology; Turkey, immigration studies in social psychology; Colombia, experimental analysis of behavior; the United Kingdom, cognitive neuropsychology; Yugoslavia, self-management; and in India, Indonesia, Israel, and South Africa, cross-cultural psychology.

Global Psychological Associations

International cooperation and exchange is a necessary component so psychology can become more global in scope and applicability. Cross-national understanding and goodwill among psychologists may be seen as the prevailing impetus for the growth of international psychological organizations around the world. The importance of international collaboration was recognized as early as 1889 with the founding of the National Congress of (Physiological) Psychology in Paris. Today international organizations, conferences, congresses, workshops, and cross-national research teams play a central role in the life of professional psychologists around the world. Internationalization serves psychology in both the contexts of basic and applied research, theoretical and conceptual development, and in the improvement of infrastructural resources for the continued internationalization of psychology.

Founded in 1951 as the organizational successor to the International Congresses of Psychology, the **International Union of Psychological Science (IUPsyS)** is the most encompassing international organization of psychology (Rosenzweig, 1999). As is the rule for international scientific unions, IUPsyS has no individual members, but instead is an organization composed of national member organizations with no more than one national member per country. Every four years it schedules International Congresses with the 28th International Congress held in Beijing, China in 2004. As stated in its aims, IUPsyS has worked to promote "the development of psychological science, whether biological or social, normal or abnormal, pure or applied" (Pawlik, 1985). The IUPsyS currently has sixty-nine national members on the five continents and through them has access to hundreds of thousands of psychologists around the world, making it the international voice of psychological science. This voice is served by a number of important publications put out by the IUPsyS, including *The International Journal of Psychology*, the *International Directory of Psychologists,* and the *Proceedings of the International Congresses*, as well as other occasional publications (Pawlik, 1985).

Many smaller international organizations exist alongside and as a rule are affiliated with IUPsyS. For example, the International Council of Psychologists (ICP) holds conventions annually and aims to increase communication among psychologists around the world. There are also a number of international organizations that are either topically or regionally organized. The **International Association of Applied Psychology (IAAP)**, also affiliated with IUPsyS, was founded in 1920 and is made up of individual members. IAAP has gradually expanded its membership to include psychologists from all over the world and has incorporated a wide variety of applied fields, as reflected through the work of its thirteen divisions: organizational psychology, community psychology, health psychology, economic psychology, and political psychology to name a few (Pawlik & d'Ydewalle, 1996, p. 489).

Many other topically focused international organizations have developed over the years and are affiliated with IUPsyS. Some examples include the International Association for Cross-Cultural Psychology (IACCP), the International Society of Comparative Psychology (ISCP), and the International Society for the Study of Behavioral Development (ISSBD). In recent years, however, there has been a strong tendency for the formation of regional organizations. This trend has been facilitated, if not necessitated, by economic and political developments toward integrated regionalization (Rosenzweig, 1999).

The **European Federation of Professional Psychologists' Association (EFPPA)** includes twenty-five European countries, represents about 100,000 psychologists, and was founded in 1981. The two major objectives of the EFPPA are to (1) reduce differences between European countries in the standards of training and professional practice and (2) ensure that expert advice is available to relevant intergovernmental and nongovernmental bodies on matters relating to psychology. The role of the EFPPA has become even more important with the advent of the European Union and the creation of a standard European currency (i.e., the euro).

One of the oldest regional organizations is the **Interamerican Society of Psychology** (Sociedad Interamericana de Psicologia; **SIP**). Founded in 1951, the SIP advances psychology as both a science and a profession within the Americas and has held over twenty-three congresses in various parts of North, Central, and South America. Other regional groups exist around the world, for example, the Afro-Asian Psychological Association, the Asia-Oceania Psychological Association, and the Southeast-Asian Psychological Association. The establishment of a Pan-Arab Psychology Association is under discussion at present.

Functions of Internationality

The four core functions of internationality in psychology include first the promises of cross-national understanding and goodwill among people (Pawlik, 1992). Cooperation across nations is essential to the advancement of the psychological discipline with societal well-being a precondition for the existence of the discipline itself. As is well known, psychology is especially vulnerable when social conditions become oppressive and intellectual freedom is restricted, as we have witnessed in Germany under Hitler, Cambodia under Pol Pot, and China under Mao Zedong (Pawlik & Rosenzweig, 1994). Psychology contributes to and is essentially dependent upon societal freedom and cross-national benevolence.

Second, since psychological concepts are often imported through culture-specific language traditions, internationality in psychology serves to safeguard against conceptual cultural-dependence. Translating terms from one language to another without diluting or distorting their core meanings is a difficult task. However, if we are to learn from the concepts derived in other cultural contexts as well as cooperate in their development, then effective translation is of the utmost importance. To help overcome translation problems, the IUPsyS produced a trilingual glossary of psychological terms (Duijker & van Rijswijk, 1975), but the challenge continues as more cultures participate in the formation of concepts. More recently, Jing (1991) edited a concise encyclopedia of psychology with cross-references from Chinese to Japanese and vice versa (Pawlik & d'Ydewalle, 1996). Despite the importance of translation, the effort to internationalize psychology requires sensitivity to cultural specifics and generalities that may not lend themselves to direct translation. Thus, an important international task and emerging challenge for psychology is to become multilingual instead of English-dependent (Pawlik & d'Ydewalle, 1996).

The third function of internationality is capacity building through international research programs and projects of professional practice. Program activities may be devised to bring specialized research training and research facilities to third world countries. Capacity building may also take the form of research cooperation through network projects. Such projects promote communication and facilitate research through the exchange of literature, newsletters, workshops, and other means suitable to the topic of study.

The fourth function of internationality in psychology is the development of cross-national training curricula. Academic training of future psychologists in an increasingly global world will require international cooperation at the level of curriculum planning. Standards must be set so that academic and/or professional degrees in psychology equate to similar levels of experience. A master's degree from Austria, for example, must have some basic similarities to one from Ecuador. To protect the public, persons without adequate training and experience must be prevented from representing themselves as psychologists. Currently, almost all psychology programs around the world include courses in research methodology and statistics, a positive sign that standards are increasingly shared (Rosenzweig, 1992). On the other hand, curricular formation must be sensitive to different cultural perspectives of proper psychological training and aim to support curricula that enhance the flowering of indigenous psychologies and their methods of inquiry. In other words, equality of curricular standards need not suggest they have exactly the same components but rather include a standard variety of methodologies, intentions, and content areas.

Globalization has brought psychology to peoples from all over the world but it has also led to the questioning of its fundamental premises and a growing sense of uncertainty within the discipline. The "uncertainty phase" of globalization in which we now live has been a result of this uncoupling of culture from place and an unprecedented exposure to otherness. One of the key developments during and as a result of this exposure has been the philosophical transition from modernity to postmodernity, a transition that has affected both the way we conceive of the world and the way we view the discipline of psychology.

POSTMODERNISM AND THE MULTICULTURAL MOVEMENTS

The present era is commonly referred to as "postmodern" and the term itself highlights the uncertain age that has called it forth; an age, as Stephen Toulmin (1985, p. 268) states, "that has not yet discovered how to define itself in terms of what it is, but only in terms of what it has **just-now ceased to be**." Postmodernism is an elusive construct with many meanings (Featherstone, 1990). Some equate it with an attack on scientific inquiry especially in the social sciences and psychology, the rejection of standards to judge one theoretical model against another, and the acceptance of relativism. Others see it as an extension of established knowledge by new methods of inquiry, such as deconstructionism, that place knowledge into cultural or other more focused contexts (Anderson, 1996; Fish, 1996; Rosenau, 1992). Postmodernism fully arrived into global attention in the early 1980s, but it developed out of the earlier works of scholars such as Baudrillard (1983), Derrida (1976), and Foucault (1979, 1980) as well as advances in physics (Bohr's Principle of Complementarity) and mathematics (Godel's Proof). Although elusive, we can say that postmodernism is a movement that aims to extend and transcend modernism through a reevaluation of what defined it; namely, reason, linear progress, and a belief that truth can be (and must be) objectively harvested through science and incorporated into a universal system.

Postmodernism

Three features, as outlined by Burbles and Rice (1991), distinguish postmodern thought. **First**, postmodernists reject absolutes and insist that no single rationality, morality, or theoretical framework has the ability to explain all of the universe. As the philosopher Richard Rorty (1989) puts it, **truth is made rather than found**. This, however, is not a new idea, since it came into the Eastern world with Buddhism and the Western world in the works of Heraclitus some 2,500 years ago. The search for an ultimate system that explains the universe is considered to impinge upon the infinity of human creative potential. Postmodernism means understanding that all our stories about what's out there—all our scientific facts, all our religious teachings, our society's beliefs, even our personal perceptions—are the products of a highly creative interaction between human minds and the cosmos (Anderson, 1996). Postmodernism doesn't ask us to change **what** we believe, but rather to examine **how we came to** believe it. For example, rather than considering science the only way to arrive at truth we might consider it one important way out of many so as to give credibility to other ways of knowing such as truths revealed by the arts.

The **second** feature of postmodernism is the belief that all social and political discourses are saturated with cultural and ideological biases that seek legitimacy. Each of us wants to believe in the rightness of our perspective and the correctness of our judgments, but post-modernists believe that truth is largely a social construction rather than an absolutely accurate representation of reality. People need to learn to recognize and appreciate that what they do and think is to a great degree a product of social constructions (most importantly, language and culture), rather than a product of some ultimately verifiable and defendable reality. When people let go of the need to defend their perspective of reality as absolute, and recognize all perspectives as a product of the dynamic interaction between culture and the cosmos, they then can validate the perspectives of others and find a deeper meaning in their own construals of reality.

The **third** idea that recurs in postmodern thought is the celebration of difference. Since human ideas about the world are constructions, both socially and personally derived, there is no reason to grant one view exclusive explanatory power while dismissing other explanatory possibilities as less valuable or obsolete. Instead, postmodernism is an acceptance of the unavoidable plurality of the world and an abandonment of the modern urge to promote universalism at the cost of diversity. Diversity, and its encouragement, is at the core of post-modern thought.

While postmodernism has raised consciousness by sensitizing people to the subjective nature of truth, it can also promote a perspective of meaninglessness. The basic argument is that since previous claims to morality were ethnocentric and led to the oppression of power-less groups, commitment to any moral or ethical framework means stepping in the direction of dogmatism, fanaticism, and authoritarianism. Ironically, an unwillingness to pursue the moral act or partake in ethical discourse secures the existence of oppression and injustice. Although we are all limited by our social and subjective constructions, we all have within us the potential for open-mindedness, humility, and collaboration, and we all have similar needs. Likewise, while there may not be a single moral or ethical framework, we are all bound to pursue the moral act and discuss visions of the good society.

Postmodernism emphasizes eclecticism and paradox and asks all people to be flexible and attuned to the many different strands of locally generated knowledge. For the field of psychology, this means recognizing that traditional psychological concepts and theories have developed in a predominantly Euro-American context that limits their applicability to cultur-ally diverse populations (Sue, Bingham, Burke, & Vasquez, 1999).

A Reevaluation of Psychology

According to some scholars psychological science tells more about the history, culture, and values of the West than it does about any universal psychology. In embodying these cultural values, the expansion of psychology around the globe is seen by many as serving the function of ideological hegemony. One of the core constructs of Western psychology that produce this ideological effect both in theory and practice is the absolute faith in science

(Gergen et al., 1996; Marsella, 1998; Sloan, 1996). Many aspects of Western psychological science have come under scrutiny, namely, the uncritical acceptance of science as the source of absolute truth and universal knowledge and the neglect of culture as a moderator of both human psychology and science itself.

Psychological science is based on certain assumptions regarding human nature that shape and define it. For example, the empiricism of science assumes that the scientist possesses an observing mind that is capable of reflecting and recording the nature of a world external to it. Many years ago, Thomas Kuhn, a historian of science, challenged this assumption with the concept of "paradigm shift," as presented in his book *The Structure of Scientific Revolutions* (1970). Kuhn argues that scientists periodically recreate the world to make room for new ideas and discoveries. Paradigms shape the way we interpret the world so rather than scientists having minds that are capable of objectively reflecting the external world, we are increasingly seeing scientists and scientific discoveries as products of worldviews. However, while the history of science reflects the individual and cultural history of scientists, truths can still be ascertained through science. Individual interests may frame research but this does not mean there are no scientific standards to which evidence must conform with more or less accuracy. After all, science has had a tremendous impact on our ability to control and predict forces external to us.

Paradigms or systems of knowledge, though oversimplified, are indispensable to human thought and action. It is impossible for the human mind to grasp reality in its entirety. As in the example of reversible figures studied extensively by Gestalt psychologists where either two profiles or a candlestick can be seen but not at the same time, the minute we focus on one quality of the world we fail to see other important qualities. Paradigms order our perceptions and lend coherence to experience, but problems occur when we stick to one paradigm at the expense of a more holistic understanding. In the words of Abraham Maslow (1908–1970), "If the only tool you have is a hammer, you tend to see every problem as a nail." Postmodernism and globalization demand that psychology have a multi-paradigmatic vision of the universe, one that recognizes the benefits of having a diversity of worldviews and perspectives. A global psychology recognizes that ethnocultural diversity is as important as biological diversity in that it provides social and psychological options in the face of formidable environmental challenges (Marsella, 1998).

Another assumption of Western psychological science has been that the psychologist must remain as detached, objective, and value free as possible through the safeguards of the scientific method. Criticism shows, however, that this has tended to isolate Western psychology and divorce it from other modes of investigation (Gergen et al., 1996). Historical, mythological, and philosophical data are often viewed as incompatible with science because they invariably entail subjective as well as objective elements. David Bakan (1969) pointed out that the use of rigorous scientific methodology might actually divorce psychology from the empirical rather than illuminate it. In a well-developed experiment, events are carefully chosen and controlled to prevent the haphazard events of the world from interfering with results. Thus, the more carefully designed the experiment the more separate it becomes from the world of experience it seeks to clarify.

If science were to have a publicly stated value it would be the quest for certainty and the goal of establishing absolutes (Krippner & Winkler, 1996). The modern era was the age of what is sometimes called scientism or the naïve acceptance of science as the source of absolute truth, yet with the arrival of postmodernism the perception is increasingly taking hold that much of our knowledge is both locally generated and locally applicable rather than universal. This development recognizes the existence of multiple truths and multiple means of arriving at truth. As a consequence, this increasingly puts pressure upon the field of psychology to accept the premises, methods, and findings of indigenous psychologies and to scrutinize its own tendency toward monocultural universalism (as exemplified by behaviorism), a tendency that undermines its aim of being both a science of human behavior and a promoter of human welfare.

From the perspective of cross-cultural psychology, Berry, Poortinga, Segall, and Dasen (1992) distinguish four levels of ethnocentrism in psychology: the use of culturally inappropriate stimuli or items; the use of inappropriate instruments and methods; culture-specific conceptualizations; and the choice of topics for research and application focused on the perceived needs of one's own society. As globalization has proceeded, culture has come to be seen as playing a definitive role in the construction of science and its methods.

Cross-Cultural Psychology

The process of globalization has brought an increase in diversity within nations and an interdependence among nations that makes it difficult for psychologists to assume a unicultural stance. Cross-cultural psychology is the systematic study of behavior and experience as it occurs in different cultures, is influenced by culture, or results in changes in existing cultures (Triandis, 1980, 1996; Triandis & Vassiliou, 1972; Triandis, Malpass, & Davidson, 1972). A major purpose of cross-cultural psychology is to test the generality of psychological laws through a comparison of cultures. These comparisons include an investigation of both similarities and differences across ethnic-cultural boundaries and focus not so much on cultures per se but on the individual-in-a-cultural-context (Ho, 1994).

Berry, Poortinga, Segall, and Dasen (1992) identify three theoretical orientations in cross-cultural psychology that explain the relationship between human psychology and culture in different ways: **absolutism, relativism**, and **universalism**. The absolutist position assumes that human nature is qualitatively the same across all cultures and that culture has little effect upon the meaning or display of human characteristics: depression is depression, hatred is hatred, and love is love. The relativist position represents the opposite pole, asserting that culture is a primary determinant of human nature and dispositions. Depression, from this perspective, is expressed and experienced so differently across cultures that it cannot be understood outside of the particular cultural context. For the relativist, it is impossible to construct and measure context-free concepts.

Cross-cultural psychologists typically expect both biological and cultural factors to influence human behaviors and experiences. Like the relativists, they assume the influence of culture to be substantial but, like the absolutists, they believe comparisons can be made across cultures. The resulting theoretical stance is universalism, a kind of common ground. Universalism assumes that basic human characteristics are common to all members of the species and that culture influences the display of them. An example of a universal law is that all instrumental behaviors are shaped by their consequences. Culture modifies this basic law in specific ways. For instance, consequences that advance or enrich the group, as opposed to the individual, are more valuable and frequent in collectivistic rather than individualistic societies. Thus, from the perspective of universalism, assessment assumes the existence of basic psychological givens while measures are developed in culturally meaningful ways.

Cross-cultural psychology is not so much defined by unique theories but rather by unique methodologies (Triandis, 1980). For the past thirty years or so, the hallmark of cross-cultural psychology has been the recognition that one cannot take a psychological method and use it in another culture without drastic modification. Three terms, as discussed by Ho (1994), serve as analytical concepts and methodological safeguards for cross-cultural psychologists. An **emic** refers to a culture-specific dimension of human psychology. Emic constructs apply to only one culture and make no claim of applicability to other cultures. For example, **philotimo**, meaning the extent to which an individual conforms to the expectations of his ingroup, is an emic construct applicable only to Greece (Triandis & Vassiliou, 1972). It is especially salient in Greece and characterizes Greek culture. No purpose would be served in studying how philotimo dictates behavior patterns among the French.

An **etic**, on the other hand, aims to make a cross-cultural comparison and is characterized as a true universal. Measuring across cultures with items appropriate for each culture is etic while measuring in one culture only is emic. What is not appropriate is taking an emic scale, for instance, the one used to measure philotimo among Greeks, and using it as if it were an etic scale say, among the French. In the early years of cross-cultural psychology, unsophisticated Euro-American emics were ethnocentrically and indiscriminately imposed upon the interpretation of behaviors across cultures. The results yielded pseudoetics or assumed etics (Triandis, Malpass, & Davidson, 1972). It is now an integral part of cross-cultural psychology to begin with careful internal exploration of psychological phenomena in local cultural terms so as to avoid uninterpretable results. An important assumption of cross-cultural psychology is that extensive use of emic approaches in a number of cultures will produce instruments that satisfy the requirements of etic research. Over time, it is assumed that a universal psychology might emerge.

Culture and Boundaries

In the early days of cross-cultural psychology, culture was conceptualized as something "out there" to be studied, observed, and described (Segall, Lonner, & Berry, 1998). Definitions and methodologies have tended to neglect the active role people play in constructing culture daily through their interaction with others and the surrounding environment. More recently, individuals have come to be viewed not as mere consequences or victims of culture, as a computer is to its programmer, but as active contributors to a dynamic interactive process. Culture is no longer seen as being outside the individual, where it influences behavior, but "as an intersubjective reality through which worlds are known, created, and experienced" (Miller, 1997, p. 103). Cross-cultural psychology views culture and the self as interdependent, mutually reinforcing processes.

Interestingly, agreement over the definition of culture in the social sciences has not yet emerged. Cultural anthropologists have defined it in more than 100 ways, and psychologists have not reached much more consensus either (Kroeber & Kluckhohn, 1952). Such a diversity of perspectives highlights both the subjective element in defining reality as well as the multidimensional complexity of culture. On the other hand, a large proportion of definitions suggest that culture consists of **shared elements** (Shweder & LeVine, 1984). For our purposes, **culture** is defined as standards for perceiving, believing, evaluating, communicating, and acting among those who share a language, a historic period, and a geographic location (Triandis, 1996).

The most meaningful way to grasp the concept of culture, as it exists today in the field of cross-cultural psychology, is to consider how it is used. Segall, Lonner, and Berry (1998, p. 1101) have noted, "it is meant to serve as an over-arching label for a set of contextual variables (political, social, historical, ecological, etc.) that are thought by the researcher to be theoretically linked to the development and display of a particular behavior." The primary objective of cross-cultural psychology is to discover how culture relates to psychological differences.

For example, the **individualism-collectivism** dimension has served many researchers in recent years as a cultural characteristic capable of predicting behavioral differences across cultures. The structure of goals is one attribute that defines collectivism and individualism. Collectivists set their goals to be compatible with the goals of their ingroups. If there is a discrepancy between the two sets of goals, collectivists give priority to the ingroup goals. Individualists use goals that may or may not be compatible with the goals of their ingroups, but if they are discrepant, the individualist will give priority to personal goals (Triandis, 1996). In this sense, culture is the overarching label under which the contextual dimension of individualism-collectivism operates and defines uniquely each culture.

In a world of increasing mobility, cultural regions are becoming less distinct and the identification of one cultural group from other cultural groups is becoming increasingly difficult. What exactly is common among a culture's members? What criteria identify the boundaries of membership? Social scientists have been tempted to define a cultural group by its social structure, language, national identity, or contact group, but in a world of international migration and mobility the psychological dimension of culture is coming to be seen as the most useful way to define and understand a culture.

Triandis (1996, p. 409) devised a test that examines what he calls **cultural syndromes** or "a pattern of shared attitudes, beliefs, categorizations, self-definitions, norms, role definitions, and values that is organized around a theme that can be identified among those who speak a particular language, during a specific historic period, and in a definable region." One identifiable cultural syndrome is the individualist-collectivist dimension described above (Hui & Triandis, 1986). Other cultural syndromes include tightness-looseness (i.e., number of norms across situations), active-passive (i.e., competition vs. cooperation) and complexity-simplicity (i.e., high-low number of role definitions; Triandis, 1996). Two methods of measuring cultural syndromes include (a) identifying questionnaire items to which 90% of a sample responds on the same side of a neutral point and (b) identifying items to which 90% of triads agree among themselves in less than sixty seconds (Triandis, 1996). These measures of cultural identification emphasize that cultural group membership is internalized within an individual or a group and can represent attitudes and beliefs specific to differing groups even within similar regional boundaries. In line with this reasoning, contemporary cross-cultural psychology demonstrates clearly that culture is represented less by place or time and more by internalized beliefs that subsequently influence the thoughts and behaviors of individuals in each distinct culture. Most studies in the field of cross-cultural research involve data collection from at least two cultural groups while some studies are monocultural with comparisons made to other cultures through previous research. It is generally agreed that a minimum of three cultures must be involved to yield meaningful comparisons.

Cross-cultural psychologists have tended to focus on a limited range of topics. Three of the more popular topics are deviance, perception, and personality (Hogan & Tartaglini, 1994). Other topics of interest are child development (Gardiner, 1994), language (Beatty, 1994), organizational psychology (Wang, 1993), and the self (Baumeister, 1987; Sampson, 1988). Interest in these areas gives rise to the question of how much culture really exists in cross-cultural psychology? Cross-cultural research emphasizes the importance of attitudes, beliefs, needs, personality, and the self because Western culture is individualistic and Western psychology focuses on individuals and internal processes. If more research were led by non-Western cultures the focus would likely change from the individual to norms, collective needs, collective self-definitions, and values (Triandis, 1996). External processes, such as membership of the individual in a collective (i.e., family, work group, religious community, etc.) and the context of behavior are culturally more important for non-Western cultures.

DEVELOPMENT INITIATIVES AND THE CALL FOR INDIGENIZATION

Developing countries are in a hurry to grow economically and eradicate poverty so as to catch up with the level of socioeconomic status that has taken hundreds of years to achieve in the West. This "temporal compression of change" obviously contrasts with the gradual evolution of such systems in the West, raising distinct and unanticipated issues for the developing world (Sinha, 1994a; Sinha & Holtzman, 1984). Rapid socioeconomic development and modernization are not without their dangers. Apart from causing various environmental hazards, such rapid changes also have psychological fallouts. Not only will it require the building of certain economic infrastructures but also the general modernization of social structure, institutions, families, attitudes, and value systems, that is, a large-scale transformation of society (Sinha, 1994b; Sinha & Holtzman, 1984).

Psychology's interest in social change and development did not begin to emerge until the mid-1960s because the area of national development and social change unfortunately constituted only a peripheral interest at best for psychology in the latter half of the 20th century (Sinha & Holtzman, 1984). Many of the challenges posed by rapid socioeconomic development and social change in the developing countries of Africa, Asia, and Latin America include risks to the psychological stability of their inhabitants. Increases in the ambiguity of values, suicide, riots, social violence, crime, delinquency, HIV-AIDS, alcoholism, the stresses of urban overcrowding, and alienation have all been consequences of concern to psychologists (Arnett, 2002; Sinha & Holtzman, 1984; Triandis, 1971, 1996; Verma & Saraswathi, 2002). These forms of social and psychological disorganization have resulted from both the impersonality of modern life as well as the rapidity of change. In spite of the important role that psychology can play in developing countries, the impact and growth of psychology has been limited by the discipline's Euro-American origins.

Western Psychology in the Developing World

Sinha and Holtzman (1984) outlined four reasons for the inability of Western psychology to make an impact in the developing world. First, the importation of Western psychology by the developing world carried with it a set of research questions that arose specifically from Western society and its cultural traditions. As a consequence of emulating the Western paradigm, psychological research conducted in the developing world has often been a mere replication of studies done in the West with little relevance to indigenous needs (Sinha, 1994a).

As a result, the focus of developing-world scholars has shifted away from the problems of their own countries to culturally irrelevant problems within Western psychology.

Second, mainstream psychological knowledge has been the product of an advanced industrial society characterized by literacy, impersonality, universality, and a wide range of beliefs, ideas, and attitudes derived from that social milieu (Jahoda, 1980; Sinha, 1994a). While this knowledge base has been very effective in contributing toward the more efficient functioning of relatively stable institutions in the West, the unstable climate of the developing world limits their appropriateness and relevance. Inasmuch as particular social systems require the study of particular psychological processes, an effective psychology in one social system is likely to be ineffective, if not disastrous, when applied to other diverse social systems.

Western psychology has focused primarily upon the personal or dispositional characteristics of individual actors at the expense of recognizing the influence of sociocultural factors upon psychological processes (Sinha, 1994a). In contrast, problems of social development invariably have contextual, structural, and institutional components.

Lastly, Sinha and Holtzman (1984) note that a major constraint of psychology in approaching the complexities of development has been its reliance on a Western methodology modeled after mathematics and pure science. While this has led to a vast output of neatly designed research into social processes, one wonders how much relevance it has to real-life psychological phenomena. Some truths unique to a particular culture may be inaccessible to science employing hypothesis testing. In Africa, for example, much wisdom is embedded in folklore, idioms, spatial use of cues, and touch, yet the ability of rigorous scientific methods to extract this knowledge is doubtful. Pressing social problems are highly complex and do not lend themselves well to controlled experimental study. The narrow conception of acceptable methods has limited the ability of contemporary Western psychology to account for and react to the urgent social problems that face countries in the process of development.

After decades of uncritical reliance on Western psychological knowledge, psychologists of the developing world now view the application of Western psychological knowledge to developing countries as a form of Western hegemony (Marsella, 1998). While these countries are anxious to modernize, they do not wish to sacrifice their cultural heritage in the process. Psychology has an important role in facing issues of national development and social change brought on by the forces of globalization, but not until the discipline adapts itself to the unique demands of each culture and becomes a force against the hegemonic imposition of any national or cultural psychology. The call for indigenization by developing-world psychologists is very likely to promote assistance in national development and the amelioration of social problems as well as fresh perspectives for the discipline as a whole (Sahoo, 1993).

The Call for Indigenization

Long before the development of psychology as a formal academic discipline, people throughout the world had their own religious and metaphysical systems that contained rich theories about human nature, behavior, personality, and interrelationships with the world. Indigenous cultures have provided their own unique solutions to human problems since the dawn of humankind from coping with frustration through fatalism, to the treatment of mental illness through suggestion, herbal medicine, prayer, song and dance, or other culturally meaningful practices. Indigenization can be seen as a project to restore the true identity of people (Sinha, 1994a). At the same time, the indigenization of psychology will enable mainstream psychology to become more global by expanding its vision of what forms psychological functioning may take in diverse cultures (Sinha & Holtzman, 1984).

According to Heelas (1981), **indigenous psychologies** consist of the cultural views, theories, classifications, and assumptions together with overarching social institutions that influence psychological functions in each respective culture. Indigenous psychologies are concerned with issues that are often applied in nature and have immediate relevance to the culture from which they emerge. These psychologies are very pragmatic and hope to foster a sense of unity and prestige among local people and the psychological enterprise (Bernal, 1985). They are not the same as "specialist" psychologies, such as industrial/organizational psychology, which are created by academic psychologists to develop esoteric understanding of a specific phenomenon or topic (Heelas, 1981). Indigenous psychologies represent culturally pervasive psychological opinions and can include the fields of anthropology, religion, sociology, and nonpsychological traditions (Heelas, 1981). A move toward indigenous psychologies implies a move toward culturally relevant applied psychologies.

India has been cited as a successful case of indigenization (Moghaddam, 1987). As reflected in the establishment of the section of Applied Psychology at Calcutta University in 1938, Indian psychology assumed an applied stance from the outset. Today, seventy universities in India have well-established psychology departments and institutes for both applied research and the provision of psychological services to the public (Sinha, 1994b). Indian psychology is called to contribute its share to the resolution of national problems such as population growth, poverty, family planning, community development, education, and health (Sinha, 1994b).

The culturally appropriate application of psychology in India is leading to the formulation of a truly Indian psychology that integrates Hindu constructions of psychological functioning and personhood. Indian psychology emphasizes a holistic-organic worldview, coherence and order across all forms of life, nonlinear growth and continuity in life, the socially constituted nature of the person, behavior as transaction, the temporal and atemporal existence of human beings, the search for eternity in life, the desirability of self-discipline, the transitory nature of human experience, control that is distributed rather than personalized, and a belief in multiple worlds including both material and spiritual realities (Sinha, 1994b). As can be seen, the fruition of an Indian psychology would differ greatly from the Western emphasis on individualism, mechanism, and objectivity.

The major purpose of indigenization is not to generate a set of mutually exclusive alternative psychologies, but rather to develop more culturally grounded and locally useful forms of knowledge to respond appropriately to urgent social issues, and to encourage multiworld dialogue between psychologies that may eventually lead to a universal psychology. While there exists a great local and global urgency for indigenization, many factors currently exist that are impeding the growth of psychology in developing countries.

Systematic Deterrents to the Development of Psychology in the Developing World

A lack of economic resources, impoverished living conditions, political instability, and a minimum of perceived applied value are shared systematic deterrents to growth in the developing world. For example, psychologists in the developing world must face the personal difficulties and daily hassles that arise from impoverished life conditions. The personal problems that result from having to meet social and familial obligations in conditions of poverty can excessively tax one's capacity to conduct research. One study done among Bangladeshi psychologists showed that 60% considered personal challenges posed by poverty to be a very serious deterrent to research (Adair et al., 1995). Psychologists must face the myriad of challenges of poverty before energy can be devoted to discipline development. Likewise, many developing countries face problems of political instability. The uncertainty that a volatile political system creates leads to unstable leadership, short-term planning, and an inability to sustain enduring lines of research. Worker strikes, military coups, tribal warfare, terrorism, and vast systems of corruption are all political forces that can paralyze an entire nation and detract from both the funding and advancement of psychology in such contexts.

Sociopolitical factors of the developing world can also be a great hindrance to the psychological enterprise. Although psychology is a science that seeks to increase the knowledge base and general well-being of all people, it might be seen as a threat to the ideology and values of elite decision makers in a particular society. Often this sentiment is tied to the identification of psychology with Euro-American traditions, and may link a leader's development agenda with a call for Westernization. As a consequence of the restricted growth of psychology in the developing world, people may have little knowledge of psychology as a full-fledged international discipline. In China and Hong Kong, for example, many people are ignorant of the discipline's scientific basis and some still regard psychologists as "fortune tellers" or "palm-readers" (Leung & Zhang, 1995). Thus, psychologists have a difficult time promoting the importance of the discipline and garnering public support for its development due, in part, to the public's perception of psychology in the developing world as negative, foreign, or restricted.

The most pervasive problems confronting psychology in the developing world are tied to wealth. Lack of funding makes it extraordinarily difficult for psychologists to have access to current books and journals, technical instruments, money for research projects, and transportation to international conferences. The net result of limited funding is isolation from the psychological community at large, which in turn leads to a narrow scope of training, research, and overall development.

Linking the Social and the Economic

Knowledge of people's motivations and habits, and their participation in implementing development schemes, are some of the critical areas where psychology can make contributions to economic development (Sinha, 1994b). Since the cognitive and motivational characteristics of individuals in the developing world determines their ability to exploit opportunities provided under new socioeconomic circumstances, psychological services are essential to the success of development strategies. In India, facilities for easy bank loans have been made available in rural areas but most poor small farmers have been unable to derive full benefits from them due to a lack of experience with modern economic practices (Sinha, 1994b). What if some indigenous people consider borrowing money from outside the family inappropriate? What if money isn't the most important motivating factor for a farmer to develop his farm? As these questions suggest, economic inputs need to be grounded in knowledge of the interaction between local culture and the psychological processes of motivation and decision making.

While development must be seen as a complex interaction of variables (economic, political, sociocultural, and psychological), current development strategies place almost exclusive importance upon economic inputs. International agencies such as the World Bank, the International Monetary Fund, and the World Trade Organization give enormous loans that are contingent upon developing countries reorienting their economies to export-oriented, cash-crop activities and global interests. The aim is to cultivate an economic infrastructure capable of returning a profit that could then be used for further development and the growth of social services. While there are numerous problems with the capitalist approach to development (e.g., destruction of domestic production economies, deepening dependency on Western powers and globalizing elites, restrictions on democracy, and favoring of the wealthy), the exclusive emphasis on capital as the solution to development is the major misconception inhibiting the development initiative. To think that economic infrastructure can be developed without a concern for indigenous values or worldviews is to assume blindly that it is possible to separate the economic sphere from its sociocultural context.

TOWARD A GLOBAL PSYCHOLOGY PARADIGM

This chapter has been a means of pointing toward the future of psychology in a global world, one that increasingly calls for the emergence of a new psychology paradigm that is capable of responding to the demands of globalization as well as maintaining local cultures. Environmental devastation, urbanization, national development, crowding, interethnic conflict, terrorism, human rights abuses, health management, disease prevention, population control, and family planning are just a few global social challenges where psychological expertise is essential and desperately needed.

Global challenges require locally applicable and relevant intervention strategies that can only be developed in collaboration with indigenous worldviews. If a better world is to be promoted by the psychological enterprise, then Western psychology can no longer assume an independent stance at the cost of ignoring other substantive possibilities from disparate cultural traditions. The time has come to further the development of indigenous psychologies globally, and to place Western psychology in its appropriate global context as one indigenous psychology within a diverse global landscape. Facilitating indigenous psychologies, however, goes beyond a mere expansion of psychology's horizons; it mandates political action and calls for recognition of the moral implications inherent in the multicultural movement. Postmodernity has forced psychologists to become very forthright in questioning the value base of their work yet skeptical about replacing criticisms with a moral vision for the future. Global psychology does not assume the existence of an impervious version of right and wrong, but it does argue for the aspiration to be ethical (Prilleltensky, 1997).

The human rights struggle, for instance, is central to the aim of promoting indigenous psychologies and the rights of minority voices. Some postmodernists, however, have suggested that the call for human rights is an imposition of Western values, especially individualism and autonomy. While these criticisms have their basis, they ignore the fact that non-Western people from all over the globe have participated in the struggle for human rights, particularly as a resistance to Western hegemony. Although we should be skeptical of universals, we should **not** avoid discussing and searching for them. Global psychology considers the struggle for human rights morally universal because it stresses that humans need specific freedoms **from** political oppression, environmental degradation, impoverished living conditions, and ignorance but does not go on to define what their freedom **to** should comprise (Ignatieff, 2001).

Global psychology aspires to be as integrative as possible; that is, to include all cultural and paradigmatic perspectives in the discussion of human behavior and experience so as to eventually form a truly representative and dynamic psychology. Accordingly, we present a history of psychology that is broader and more inclusive than standard treatments to date, we examine the relationship(s) between religions of the world and psychology, we devote almost one-fourth of the entire book to diversity issues, we present Western psychology in the context of globalization, and we present detailed histories of psychology in Russia, China, Africa, Asia-India, Latin America, and other parts of the world as well. We believe, finally, that many global components of psychology need to be acknowledged, developed, and supported in order for the big picture of global psychology to emerge. Although the challenges are formidable, psychology is finding a global identity in leaps and bounds. International psychological organizations are increasing, indigenous psychologies are developing, and the psychological bases of global challenges are being recognized and addressed. Indeed, the global embrace **is** the "brighter future" which has been with us all this time and within each of us to cultivate.

HISTORY OF PSYCHOLOGY: A FRAMEWORK

The framework for our treatment of the history of psychology consists of four sections mirroring the epochs of psychology, namely, **the present, the early foundations of scientific psychology, schools of psychology**, and **diversity in psychology** which embraces eastern and western psychologies (see Table 1-1).

The first section of the book, **The Present: Globalization, Psychology, and History** consists of three chapters which includes this one on psychology and global forces while Chapter Two focuses upon the ideas of appreciating and valuing the growing diversity of the

TABLE 1-1	Framework for the History of Psychology		
The Present	**Early Foundations of Scientific Psychology**	**Schools of Psychology**	**Diversity in Psychology**
■ Contemporary Psychology: Global Forces	■ Philosophical Foundations	■ Voluntarism and Structuralism	■ Women in Psychology
■ Psychology: The American Approach	■ Biological Foundations	■ Functionalism	■ Racial Diversity in Psychology
■ Nature of History and Methods of Study	■ Phrenology, Mesmerism, and Hypnosis	■ Behaviorism	■ Psychology in Russia
			■ Psychology in China
	■ Associationism	■ Gestalt Psychology	■ Indigenous Psychologies
		■ Psychoanalysis	
		■ Beyond Psychoanalysis	

content and applied strategies of American psychology. The third chapter examines the nature of history, methods for studying history, the paradigms and revolutions in psychology, and the effectiveness of psychology.

The second section, **Early Foundations of Scientific Psychology**, consists of four chapters and examines first some of the early ideas of psychology shaped by religions of the world, philosophy, and biological science, then we turn to the systematic modification of consciousness by "talking methods" including phrenology, mesmerism, and hypnosis, and conclude this section with associationism focusing upon how mind acquires content. The many ideas about mind leads us to examine the issue of whether other living creatures (infrahumans) besides humans are also mindful or whether they have no access to their mind thus making humans unique creatures amongst all other creatures.

The third major section of this book, **Schools of Psychology**, consists of six chapters and on the surface resembles the standard approach of most textbooks on the history of psychology, which focus primarily upon the 19th and the first half of the twentieth century as the golden era in the history of Western psychology. In fact, significantly much more has been learned and published in psychology during the twentieth century, and thus the need for extension of the foundational ideas presented in each chapter to contemporary research and applications in psychology.

The final section of this book is **Diversity in Psychology** and serves as the gateway to the future of psychology in the 21st century. This is a very exciting and challenging time for humanity as well as for the field of psychology. We believe many of the topics covered in this final section represent the infrastructure for the further development and strengthening of psychology over the next twenty-five years and beyond.

We hope this book is of value to you, and we welcome your suggestions and comments about what did and did not work for you. Please feel free to e-mail, fax, phone, write, or best of all, stop by and visit us. Whatever works for you works for us!

Summary

There is a brighter future on the horizon embodying the potential power of the world as a truly global community. The Three Worlds of Psychology creates a framework which allows us to reference countries in different stages of development and the effects this may have on their indigenous psychologies and contribution to global psychology. The Three Worlds of Psychology theory presumes that each of these worlds has an unequal capacity to produce and disseminate psychological knowledge which shapes the field of psychology.

As illustrated by the growing numbers of psychologists throughout the world, cross-national cooperation is clearly essential to the global advancement of psychology. The fundamental functions of internationality have been identified and include the promotion of cross-national understanding and goodwill among people. Second, since concepts are often imported through culture-specific language traditions, internationality serves to safeguard against locking the discipline into complete culture-dependence. The third function is capacity building through international research programs and projects of professional practice, and the fourth function of internationality in psychology is the development of cross-national educational curricula.

Postmodernism is often thought of as an attack on scientific inquiry while at the same time accepting relativism. The deconstructionist methods of inquiry introduced by postmodernism require a reevaluation of psychology that focuses upon both methodological issues and the expansion of Western psychology around the globe and its dominance of other cultures. As psychologists we must be careful before establishing universals, especially given the possibility of dismissing other worldviews. Accordingly, we must recognize the process of globalization, which includes increasing diversity within nations as well as interdependence among nations that makes it difficult for psychologists to embrace only a unicultural model of psychology.

As we have seen, the developing world is presented with challenges of economic growth and the eradication of poverty as well as developing an indigenous psychology. Western psychology has proven in large measure to be inadequate in dealing with the social issues of non-Western cultures because of the dominant voices of individualism, mechanism, and objectivity. In order to move toward a more global paradigm of psychology, it is essential to address this dominance through the development and integration of indigenous psychologies into a global paradigm for psychology. At a time when secular, scientific, religious, technological, and spiritual cultural traditions of different regions seem at conflict, global psychology welcomes all of them as important perspectives within a diverse global whole.

■ Chapter 1—Contemporary Psychology: Global Forces

Discussion Questions

- ■ What are the three worlds of psychology? Explain.
- ■ Where is modern psychology rooted and what are some of the associated advantages and disadvantages?
- ■ How do the core functions of internationality influence psychology?
- ■ Does postmodernism believe in universal truths? Explain.
- ■ What were the major landmarks in the evolution of globalization?
- ■ How can a global psychology overcome the challenges introduced by the strong Western influence?
- ■ What are the major schools of psychology?

Psychology: The American Approach

CHAPTER OVERVIEW

In these times, people around the world are becoming more connected and interdependent, exchanging goods and cultural practices, and seeking the knowledge to live wholesome and rewarding lives free from fear and the threats of terrorism around the globe. Psychology can assist all of us in these pursuits, and help us construct a meaningful and sustainable peace.

Psychology as a science seeks knowledge to understand primarily human **affective, behavioral**, and **cognitive** systems while as a profession, psychology seeks to apply this knowledge to enhance further the lives of individuals and groups around the world. Psychology, like the marketplace, is becoming more and more global and there is likewise tension between the identification of invariant laws that describe and shape affective, behavioral, and cognitive phenomena and the unique local expressions of affect, behaviors, and cognitions found in particular cultures. To understand the global and local challenges and opportunities of today and tomorrow it is essential to be informed about the history of psychology in different countries and cultures. Psychology without a sound historical and systematic research base of ideas and principles yields fads. On the other hand, psychology without application to everyday challenges yields pedantry and irrelevance that is limited and nonadaptive to a changing world in which the sustained interplay between global and local forces is shaping the present and future of the discipline.

The major focus of this chapter is upon psychology in the United States as an example of an indigenous psychology that has in many respects dominated the history and development of psychology around the globe. Accordingly, we examine some of the fundamental ideas of American psychology and their applications. We also examine the dynamics of global and local forces as they impact psychology in the United States, and identify three critical challenges facing psychology here as well as in other countries and cultures. We conclude the chapter by emphasizing the importance of applied knowledge grounded in solid data sets and theory.

LEARNING OBJECTIVES

When you finish studying this chapter, you will be prepared to:

- Describe psychology as a science and a profession
- Appreciate the breadth of psychology and its relationship to other disciplines
- Appreciate local and global dynamics influencing psychology in the United States, the American Psychological Association, and the Association for Psychological Science
- Describe the three issues in psychology in the United States focusing upon credentials, diversity, and prescription privileges
- Define psychology and identify a new vision for the field

INTRODUCTION

Psychology, the science and profession, focuses upon the *"ABCs"* of life, that is, the systematic study of the affective (**A**), behavioral (**B**), and cognitive (**C**) systems and their interaction in living creatures, especially but not exclusively human beings, in a variety of contexts.

Although psychology focuses upon affects or feelings, behaviors, and cognitions (i.e., thoughts, memories, and expectations) of individuals and groups, it shares this interest with many other disciplines ranging from the arts and humanities, the social sciences, the biological sciences, and medicine. Accordingly, psychology is a rich mix of scientific and artistic methods of inquiry and applied strategies.

Scientific psychology seeks to discover invariant laws that govern the affective, behavioral, and cognitive systems of all humans and infrahumans (e.g., hominids such as chimpanzees and apes as well as other mammals such as dogs and cats). Scientific psychology is most often conducted in university laboratories with an emphasis upon understanding and explaining affective, behavioral, and cognitive systems while professional psychology focuses upon the application of psychological knowledge. Most psychologists around the world practice psychology by providing psychotherapy to individuals or groups. For our purpose, applied psychology refers to the broader delivery of psychological services in a variety of settings to a wide variety of persons in our communities, schools, workplaces, and governments.

To be an effective psychologist anywhere around the globe today, it is essential to envision the world with an informed view of the historical development of key psychological ideas and findings. It is also important to be informed about applied strategies derived from systematic research which may have involved many different methods of inquiry, ranging from controlled laboratory experiments and field-based studies to postmodern methods of inquiry and analysis such as deconstructionism. Psychology without application can lead directly to pedantry or irrelevance while psychology without a grounding in systematic research findings can lead to fads and inconsequential or even harmful interventions.

No matter where we live or work, each of us yearns to know about ourselves and our world. This need to know has expressed itself over the millennia through personal reflection, religions, spiritual and rational philosophies, and the sciences, all of which still play a fundamental part in a fuller understanding of the contemporary human experience. Accordingly, perhaps this long-standing and universal need to know led Herman Ebbinghaus (1850–1909), a psychologist who did some of the first systematic studies of human memory, to comment that "Psychology has a long past but a short history." People have always been interested in understanding people long before psychology began as a formal science and profession.

Unlike the **history** of psychology as an independent science which many acknowledge began in 1879 at the University of Leipzig with Professor Wilhelm Wundt (1832–1920), the **past** of psychological inquiry is relatively richer and more varied. Perhaps the past of psychology began about 50,000 years ago when some cultural hominid, a human or human-like creature living in a group, took some time out from the pressing demands of daily survival and reflected on fundamental questions about the meaning of existence and community. As the evolving inquiry became more shared, public, and systematic over the millennia, persons from religion, philosophy, the arts, and the sciences stepped in to answer enduring existential questions, leading eventually to the formal establishment (in 1879) of the science and later the profession of psychology.

Unfortunately, for a variety of reasons, the knowledge of most psychologists about the history of predominantly Western psychology is limited to the 19th century, coupled with, perhaps, some more recent historical developments in psychology (Mays, Rubin, Sabourin, & Walker, 1996; Pawlik & d'Ydewalle, 1996). Psychology in most places around the globe is comparatively ethnocentric or culturally bound in contrast with the current Zeitgeist or Spirit of the Times of globalization (Triandis, 1996). Worldwide webs of communication, trade, and travel along with the international transfer of technology contribute to the need for a global psychology (Gergin, Gulerce, Lock, & Misra, 1996; Lunt & Poortinga, 1996). Psychology must move in the inevitable direction of globalization or risk being left behind.

LOCAL-GLOBAL DYNAMICS IN PSYCHOLOGY IN AMERICA

The development of psychology is influenced by local economic, philosophical, and governmental systems as well as the cultural traditions and the resources devoted to psychology. These internal forces interact with global economic, governmental, and external cultural forces resulting in either the absorption, adaptation, or rejection of these global forces. Psychology in all countries around the world has been increasingly influenced by this local and global dynamic, which will continue to shape all of our indigenous psychologies in the years ahead. We now turn to examine briefly the dynamic between global and local forces by looking at the American Psychological Association and the American Psychological Society, three pressing issues in psychology in the United States, and examples of other indigenous psychologies.

American Psychological Association (APA)

The American Psychological Association (APA) was founded in most part as a result of the organizing efforts of Granville Stanley Hall (1844–1924), held its first organizational or preliminary meeting on July 8, 1892, and today is the largest psychological association in the world (Evans, Sexton, & Cadwallader, 1992). Presently, there are approximately 147,527 APA members compared to approximately, for example, 4,200 in the Chinese Psychological Society. Although there are in most cases large absolute differences in membership between APA and other national psychological associations, the rate of growth of psychologists is decreasing in the United States while increasing rapidly in many other countries such as Israel, China, and South Africa (Mays, Rubin, Sabourin, & Walker, 1996; Sexton & Hogan, 1992).

A profile of the 2004 APA membership is presented in Table 2-1. Notice the marked gender asymmetry for the "fellows" which is the highest membership category requiring nomination by colleagues, and noteworthy achievements in research, practice, or applied psychology (American Psychological Association, 2004). **This gender asymmetry is reversed** when we examine enrollment patterns for the late 1980s through the early 1990s which most likely have persisted up to the present and we see then that 72% of graduating seniors majoring in psychology were women, and 67% of graduate students and 62% of those completing their doctoral degrees were women (Dey, Astin, & Korn, 1991; National Science Foundation, 1994). Likewise, as Table 2-1 makes plain, there are three times more women than men student affiliates, which suggests that in the next five to ten years women will most likely serve in many more APA leadership roles than at present. The increasing representation of women in psychology and the related diversity is a positive phenomenon, and reflects a growing demand for diverse knowledge and skills from psychology (Pion, 1991; Pion et al., 1996).

Just as there are tensions between local and global forces shaping psychology around the world, there have been tensions within the APA that have shaped psychology in the United States over the past 100 years, and they are still operating today, particularly between the

TABLE 2-1	American Psychological Association Membership Statistics: 2004				
	Total	**Men**	**Women**	**% Men**	**% Women**
Fellows	4,742	3,506	1,236	74	26
Members	77,448	37,049	40,399	48	52
Associates	7,150	2,829	4,321	40	60
High School Teacher Affiliates	2,111	811	1,300	38	62
Community College Teacher Affiliates	811	104	199	34	66
International Affiliates	3,878	1,875	2,004	48	52
High School Student Affiliates	475	97	378	20	80
Community College Student Affiliates	336	96	240	29	71
Student Affiliates	51,085	12,220	38,866	24	76
Total	**147,527**	**58,587**	**88,943**	**40**	**60**

Adapted from American Psychological Association, *APA membership statistics: 2004*. Retrieved June 7, 2004 from http//www5. apa.org/membership/memstat.cfm. Copyright © 2004 by the American Psychological Association. Adapted with permission.

science and practitioner wings (Rice, 1997). For example, at the beginning of the twentieth century there was division between two types of science in psychology. One was the older, laboratory-based experimental psychology imported from Germany and advocated by Edward Bradford Titchener (1867–1927) known as structuralism. Titchner was an Englishman who earned his PhD from Wilhelm Wundt at Leipzig University and believed that psychology was a laboratory science. He founded "The Experimentalists" separate from the APA to focus the attention of psychologists primarily upon psychology as a laboratory science rather than a profession (Goodwin, 1983). The alternative to structuralism was called functional psychology or functionalism, which was the original indigenous psychology in America. Functionalism stressed individual differences, the application of psychological knowledge to address individual and social needs, and mental measurement of intelligence, personality, and job skills. American psychology is still searching for the optimal balance between psychology as a science and as a profession (i.e., the applied and practice sides of psychology).

At the end of World War II (1945), the Veterans Administration sponsored an extensive program to train clinical psychologists to augment the efforts of psychiatrists dealing with the massive psychological needs of returning veterans (Albee, 1959). The Boulder Conference, a signal event in the history of American psychology, attempted to codify and standardize clinical training and yielded a clinical training model of scientist-practitioner to achieve a working relationship between psychology as a science and a practice, which worked, although somewhat awkwardly, for about twenty-five years (Peterson, 2000; Raimy, 1950).

In the 1980s a new division within the APA emerged between many academic psychologists engaged primarily in research as contrasted with the much larger number of those providing clinical and counseling services (Rice, 1997). Despite this division between science and practice, the general membership of APA voted to maintain what was then the organizational structure of the APA Council of Representatives and the divisional structure focused upon specific areas within psychology such as clinical, developmental, gay and lesbian issues, and sports psychology, rather than a federation of semiautonomous societies reflecting major constituent identities (Dewsbury, 1997; Rice, 1997). Today the APA consists of fifty-six divisions, with each division maintaining its own mission, structure, and literature. Further information pertaining to each division housed within APA can be linked to from the APA main Web site, **www.apa.org**. The science-oriented group known as the Assembly of Scientific and Applied Psychologists (ASAP) broke away from the APA in 1988, and formed a rival organization known as the Association for Psychological Science (APS).

Association for Psychological Science (APS)

The Association for Psychological Science (APS) was founded in 1988 to advance scientific psychology and its representation as a science on the national level. In 2006, APS membership exceeded 15,000 and includes the leading psychological scientists and academics, clinicians, researchers, teachers, and administrators.

The society rapidly became involved in advocacy for psychological science. In January 1989, APS organized the first Summit of Scientific Psychological Societies, a collection of representatives from over forty psychological organizations, to discuss the role of scientific advocacy, the enhancement of psychology as a coherent scientific discipline, the protection of scientific values in education and training, the use of science in the public interest, and the scientific values of psychological practice.

In response to some of the issues above, and convinced of the need for a new cadre of young behavioral science investigators, APS prompted the creation of the Behavioral Science Track Award for Rapid Transition (B/START) program at the National Institute of Mental Health, which was launched in 1994. The B/START program was expanded to the National Institute on Drug Abuse (NIDA) in 1996, and later to the National Institute on Alcohol Abuse and Alcoholism (NIAAA) in 1999.

THREE ISSUES IN AMERICAN PSYCHOLOGY

The relationship between psychology as a science and a profession is still evolving and there are three areas that psychology in the United States in particular and many other indigenous psychologies need to address. First is the designation of the doctoral degree as either PhD (**Doctor of Philosophy**—the research degree) or the PsyD (**Doctor of Psychology**—the professional degree); second is the appropriate educational and service response to the changing demographics of the clientele served by psychologists, and third is the issue of drug prescription privileges for psychologists.

Credentials

Although psychology began in most places around the world in the academic setting of universities, it has clearly progressed beyond that heritage to become a science-based health services profession (Shapiro & Wiggins, 1994). In the United States there are about

140 accredited PhD programs that prepare health service provider professional psychologists (APA, 1995). Interestingly, the number of APA members earning the PsyD has increased steadily over the past ten years with 630 awarded in 1993, representing about 15% of all psychology doctorates earned in psychology (APA, 1995; Rice, 1997). Shapiro and Wiggins (1994) proposed that students in clinical training for the practice of psychology earn a PsyD degree from an accredited program, preferably within a university setting. The degree designation issue needs to be resolved so as to make plain to the public the appropriate professional credentials for the legitimate provision of psychological services.

Diversity

Recently, Hall (1997) has argued that American psychology must make substantive modification to its curriculum, training, research, and practice components to respond appropriately to the changing demographics of the U.S. population. For example, one third of the U.S. population is now people of color which will climb to 50% by 2050. Similarly, the rising acceptance of bisexuality among the youth of America (Leland, 1995), and a gay and lesbian population of about 10 to 12% in the United States makes plain the need for the further diversification of psychology (Crooks & Baur, 1990). Although the APA has been supportive of diversity, there is still the need to make substantive curricular and policy changes within psychology (Hall, 1997). For example, Bernal and Castro (1994) reported that whereas approximately 25% of the U.S. population are people of color, forty-eight or 46% of clinical programs had no minority faculty, thirty-seven had one faculty member of color, and nineteen of the programs had two or more minority faculty members! At the policy-setting level, there have been only eight female presidents in the over 100-year-old history of APA, two people of color; and only three ethnic minorities have been members of the board of directors (Hall, 1997). Table 2-2 presents some specific steps that must be taken to diversify more fully American psychology and the APA.

TABLE 2-2 Some Suggested Strategies for Diversification in American Psychology

Education and Training

- The psychology curriculum must be culturally inclusive
- Recruit and retain diverse faculty and students

Research

- Acknowledge the credibility and utilize research of diverse publications such as, for example, *Journal of Black Psychology, Women & Therapy,* and *Cultural Diversity and Mental Health*
- Increase number of journal editors and reviewers from diverse backgrounds

Practice and Leadership

- Be knowledgeable about current research with diverse populations
- Enhance further diversity in APA governance, membership, and staff

Adapted from Hall, C. C. I. *Cultural malpractice: The growing obsolescence of psychology with the changing U.S. population,* pp. 642–651. Reprinted by permission of the author.

A failure to vigorously pursue these steps will lead to the further isolation of psychology from a growing segment of the U.S. and world populations. As William James (1956) once said, "There is very little difference between one person and another, but what little difference there is, is very important" (pp. 256–257).

Prescription Privileges

The third force that is a source of tension within psychology is the issue of prescription privileges for psychologists. DeLeon, Sammons, and Sexton (1995) have argued that prescription privileges would enhance the scope of health care services provided by psychologists, can be implemented based upon a two-year psychopharmacology curriculum including a clinical internship similar to that employed by the U.S. Department of Defense Psychopharmacology Demonstration Project (PDP) initiated in 1991, and would allow psychologists to join the growing ranks of other prescribing nonphysician health care providers, as found, for example, in optometry, podiatry, and advanced practice nursing. In a subsequent paper, DeLeon and Wiggins (1996) addressed concerns expressed by some outside of psychology (e.g., psychiatrists) that the quality of mental health care will deteriorate if psychologists gain prescription privileges by citing the fact that 82% of prescriptions for psychotherapeutic medications written in 1991 were by internists and family practitioners who did not possess significant training in the mental health field. DeLeon and Wiggins (1996) conclude that doctoral psychologists can be educated readily to use psychotropic medications in a safe, cost-effective, and competent manner, and that prescription privileges are the next frontier for psychology in the 21st century. In 2002, New Mexico was the first state to give specially trained psychologists the authority to prescribe certain drugs related to the diagnosis and treatment of mental health disorders (Holloway, 2004). Presently, there is prescription privilege legislation pending in eighteen states. In 2004, the state of Louisiana granted prescription privileges to trained psychologists.

DeNelsky (1991, 1996) has argued that prescription privileges for psychologists would "medicalize" psychology as is the case for psychiatry, and move psychology away from being the premier provider in assisting people in acquiring **more effective thinking and behavior patterns**, which have been shown to be highly effective strategies. In fact, psychotherapy is at least as effective as medication in the treatment of depression, even severe depression, and lower relapse rates are associated with psychotherapy compared to psychoactive medications (Antonuccio, Danton, & DeNelsky, 1995). A *Consumer Reports'* survey of approximately 4,000 persons who received only psychotherapy for a broad range of disorders indicated that they improved as much as those who received therapy plus drugs without the side effects frequently associated with medications ("Mental Health," 1995; Seligman, 1995). Furthermore, even though the American Psychological Association's legislative body, the Council of Representatives, voted in August 1995 to support efforts to obtain prescription privileges for psychologists, there was no legislative requirement or mandate from the council that individual state psychological associations (e.g., California, Illinois, and New York associations) actively seek to modify the laws in their states so that psychologists can prescribe medications (Martin, 1995). Inasmuch as the "scope of practice" laws indicating what psychologists can do legally is determined by each state, some psychologists believe that costly and single-focus legislative battles will arise in every state legislature depleting each associations' financial resources and ignoring other important issues before psychology (DeNelsky, 1996; Hayes & Heiby, 1996).

We believe the future of psychology is extremely promising, the challenges are many yet not insurmountable, and those most fit for the future will be those who cultivate a sound grounding in the history of psychology from a global perspective that includes indigenous psychologies. We now turn to the new vision for psychology in both the science and profession of psychology.

DEFINITION AND A NEW VISION FOR PSYCHOLOGY

Although there are hundreds of definitions of psychology, common to almost all of them is that psychology is the science and profession that focuses primarily upon the **A**ffective, **B**ehavioral, and **C**ognitive systems of living creatures, especially, but not exclusively, human beings. Accordingly, we define psychology as:

> The systematic investigation of affective, behavioral, and cognitive systems and their interaction in a variety of creatures and contexts.

Psychology as a science focuses upon knowledge that promotes understanding while psychology as a profession focuses upon using knowledge to solve problems and enhancing the capacities of an individual or group. The future of psychology requires the continuing interaction between the scientific and applied sides of psychology, which was noted as early as the first annual meeting of the American Psychological association in 1892 in Philadelphia, Pennsylvania.

> We accumulate figures, but we forget too often what those figures imply. People rightly say of it (psychology) that it is rich in decimals but poor in ideas. (Münsterberg, 1892, p. 11)

According to Martin Seligman (1998), the 1998 president of the American Psychological Association, there is emerging a new vision for psychology in the United States which has evolved from events over the past 100 years. From 1900 to 1945, psychology in the United States focused upon finding solutions and developing appropriate strategies to treat mental illness, making the lives of all people fulfilling, and identifying and nurturing talented persons. However, from the end of World War II (1945) up to the present, American psychology has focused primarily upon understanding and providing psychotherapy for individuals with behavioral, cognitive, and/or emotional problems or dysfunctions (Seligman, 1998). In short, the bulk of psychology in the United States for the second half of the twentieth century has focused an inordinate amount of attention and resources on individual illness, dysfunction, and morbidity rather than wellness, prevention, and further strengthening of effective and resilient individuals as well as understanding and providing services to groups and families.

The new vision for psychology as reflected in Seligman's work and that of many others (Fredrickson, 2001; Sheldon & King, 2001) focuses upon positive psychology as "the scientific study of ordinary human strengths and virtues" (Sheldon & King, 2001) and is a reaction to the primary focus of psychology upon pathology over the past fifty-plus years. Likewise, although there are some links to religious movements and related positive-thinking campaigns, positive psychology is more grounded in empirical observations and experimentation.

As a consequence of working in a medical model focusing upon personal weakness and on the damaged brain for the past fifty years, psychology in the United States is not well-equipped to deal with a broad range of applied problems and is like other indigenous psychologies around the world, which also face massive applied social problems. As

Seligman (1998) makes plain, we need to focus our resources upon studying and enhancing human strengths and virtues. Psychologists need to appreciate that much of the best work they do is amplifying the strengths rather than repairing patients' frailties and dysfunctions. The new vision for psychology requires that psychologists around the world continue to develop psychological models or theories to support a psychology of strength and resilience and continue to repair individuals damaged by corrosive habits, drives, childhood experiences, or brains. As we move deeper into the new millennium of the 21st century, psychology in the United States is shifting attention to prevention and addressing a wider array of applied social challenges by understanding and applying the forces of courage, optimism, interpersonal skills, value of work, hope, integrity, mutual respect, and endurance. Psychologists are now seeing more clearly individuals as decision makers with choices, preferences, and competencies who can manage their own lives, families, and communities, and who periodically need support to avoid or escape from helplessness and hopelessness.

This vision for psychology requires sustained and systematic communication between scientists and practitioners so as to make certain that applications of psychology are firmly grounded in a systematic body of knowledge. Beutler, Williams, Wakefield, and Entwistle (1995), based upon a national survey of 325 psychologists, found that clinical practitioners value and listen to science more than scientists value and listen to clinicians with the possible consequence that scientists may be missing important avenues for identifying critical areas of research. Beutler et al. (1995) present five specific steps to enhance richer communications between practitioners and scientists including the presentation of scientific knowledge beyond the usual outlet of refereed scientific journals and meetings to include workshops, newsletters, practice journals, and an increasing need for scientifically grounded trade books written in an engaging and informative fashion for the practitioner community. In short, practitioners and scientists must implement new patterns of communication, otherwise psychological practice runs the risk of becoming based solely upon anecdote, practical experience, and seductive yet ineffective and misleading information.

▧ Summary

As people around the world become increasingly interdependent and connected, psychologists must move with flexibility toward a global psychology or be left behind.

Psychology is a science-seeking knowledge for understanding the affective, behavioral, and cognitive systems of primarily but not exclusively human beings. Likewise, psychology is also a profession which consists of practice strands focused upon the delivery of individual and group psychotherapy as well as applied interventions grounded in systematic psychological knowledge to address the wide variety of challenges and opportunities for preventing problems and strengthening further thoughtful, resilient, and courageous individuals and communities. To be an effective psychologist today and in the future, it is essential to be grounded in the historical development of key empirical psychological ideas and findings and their application in a variety of contexts around the world.

Psychology around the world, whether in the United States, China, India, Latin America, or anywhere, is influenced by global and local forces and issues. What counts in contemporary psychology is a sound grounding in the historical development of empirical foundational ideas and systematic findings and the application of these to the many challenges facing humanity around the world.

■ Chapter 2—Psychology: The American Approach

Discussion Questions

- ■ Define psychology and explain the ABCs of psychology.
- ■ What are the distinguishing characteristics separating the science and profession of psychology?
- ■ How does psychology influence other disciplines?
- ■ What is the role of the two largest psychological organizations in the United States?
- ■ What are the three pressing issues of psychology in the United States?
- ■ Where is the future of psychology headed?

Nature of History and Methods of Study

CHAPTER OVERVIEW

History is an event or set of events that has happened while the present is a point on a continuum of change. History has a future because the **interpretation** of the relics or evidence of historical persons and events can change as a result of the discovery of new relics while the events and persons themselves remain unchanged. So even though historical events and persons do not change, the interpretation of their significance can change, thus making the study of history known as historiography a dynamic enterprise. Inasmuch as history is elusive, different approaches for understanding the nature of history are examined, including the cyclical (history repeats itself), progressive (we learn and benefit from the past), and dynamic systems or chaotic (patternless events happen) models of history. We indicate some of the consequences of these models for the history of psychology.

Two major forces that make history include the **Naturalistic** and the **Personalistic** forces with the former emphasizing the importance of the time and place of the cultural context while the Personalistic explanation stresses that there are great individuals who make history.

We consider the chronological approach to the study of the history of psychology in which the historian selects a time period such as from the present back to 200 years B.C. and then organizes the historical analysis of events and persons within this temporal framework. The schools of thought is another approach in which a group of psychologists align themselves around a particular pattern of ideas promoted by a leader of a school of psychology such as, for example, structuralism, behaviorism, or psychoanalysis.

According to some scholars, it is our methods of study rather than our subject matter that make psychology scientific, and thus we review briefly methods of study employed by research and applied psychologists. We provide historical examples of the authority and boundaries of scientific laboratory studies within psychology by examining the apparent supernatural powers of an early 20th-century psychic and by an examination of the Salem witchcraft trials. Thereafter, we turn to the new history of psychology, which is critical rather than ceremonial and focuses upon the political and social contexts in which ideas developed.

Paradigms or frameworks guide and influence the collection and interpretation of observations and findings so that findings are not created equally. We examine the process of paradigm formation and revolutionary change in science as reflected in the mythical revolutions in psychology in the United States. Inasmuch as there is no overarching paradigm that embraces all of psychology we examine the advantages and limitations of specialization, which began at the outset of psychology in the late 19th century and which is extremely pervasive in contemporary psychology. We review the findings of meta-analytic, efficacy, and effectiveness studies of psychological interventions that demonstrate unequivocally that psychology yields positive affective, behavioral, and cognitive benefits for individuals as well as groups.

LEARNING OBJECTIVES

When you finish studying this chapter, you will be prepared to:

• Define history, historiography or the study of history, and discuss the nature of history

- Identify the criteria for determining historical importance as well as discuss how history has a future as a result of the changing interpretations of events and persons based upon expanding and updated historical data sets
- Make plain the differences between the deterministic forces of the Naturalistic (cultural connections) and the Personalistic (great person) models of cardinal historical developments
- Identify and discuss the major approaches to the study of the history of psychology
- Identify methods of study in psychology which are employed in almost all psychological studies around the world
- Discuss the importance of methodology in the history of psychology, including the study of spiritualism and science and the Salem witchcraft trials
- Identify the unique features of the new history of psychology as well as discuss paradigms and the so-called revolutions in the history of psychology in the United States
- Discuss areas of specialization in psychology and the forces of unification, including methodology and theories of psychological phenomena
- Make plain that psychology makes a difference based upon the findings of extensive meta-analytical studies that demonstrate the positive beneficial outcomes from a diverse array of psychological interventions

INTRODUCTION

History is an event or set of events that has happened while the present is a point in time on a continuum of change. At first glance, history is about what happened, and, therefore, may be considered by some as a stable and fixed discipline. However, history is the continuing discovery of new historical relics and data sets that may give rise to changing interpretations of prior events and persons indicating clearly that history is a dynamic field of study that has a future.

The study of history is known as **historiography**, which encompasses issues about the historical data set, the nature of history, the forces that shape history, and the writing of history. History is an empirical and interpretative discipline. The empirical part of history is the collection and cataloguing of historical relics or artifacts that serve as the record(s) of the events and persons involved in these events. Relics or data sets might include, for example, stones, tools, letters, books, videotapes, e-mail, Web pages, satellite and spacecraft images, bones, and DNA specimens. In historical research, there is always the possibility that the data set may be incomplete and the discovery of new data could change dramatically our interpretation of the historical events or persons. Accordingly, the interpretative side of history focuses upon attributing meaning to the data set, which usually involves the historian looking at the larger social and temporal contexts in which the data are embedded.

Another important issue of historiography is the nature of history itself; for example, is history repetitive, progressive, or chaotic in nature (Henle, Jaynes, & Sullivan, 1973)? Perhaps you have heard the comment about current events that the news doesn't change, it just happens to different people. In other words, history repeats itself. According to the **cyclical hypothesis of history**, the inherent nature of history is that events repeat themselves over time, there is a pattern to these repetitions, knowledge of the past provides insight into the future, and the historian's job is to identify and explain these patterns or rhythms. Although the particulars of events may change over time the patterns of these events do not, such as the repetitiveness of ethnic and national conflicts, good and bad economic times, the seasons of the year, and the stages of our individual lives. Cycles in the history of psychology are evident when we realize, for example, that the analysis of consciousness was considered the primary subject matter in the early years of psychology, but it was then replaced with a focus upon behavior during the first half of the twentieth century. Now consciousness (awareness and experiences of affect and cognitions) is back again as an important part of the subject matter of psychology along with behavior.

According to some historians, history is progressive with the current generation building upon the accomplishments of prior generations (Gawronski, 1975). According to the **linear progressive model of history**, new discoveries and knowledge emerge over time arising from earlier experimentation and inquiry so that life today is better than life 100 years ago. Just pause for a moment and think about all the many conveniences of your daily life, none of which probably existed fifty to one hundred years ago. Likewise, in the history of psychology we have seen over the years advances in our understanding in areas such as color vision, learning, and the development of different therapies to treat different psychological disorders.

Another model of the nature of history is the **chaos hypothesis**, according to which "stuff happens." There are no inherent patterns nor is history a quasi-orderly progressive phenomenon. Rather, events arise as a result of the apparently random interactions of events or systems, although some patterns may be observable depending upon the level of analysis such as the length of the time span or breadth of the context of the observations of the historian. For example, Koch (1993) has argued extensively that psychology is misconceived when seen as a coherent science or discipline focused upon the empirical study of humans and infra humans. According to Koch (1969, 1993), psychology is still searching for a unique methodology to study its subject matter and has been misguided in its attempts to emulate the natural sciences, especially physics.

What's Important

Each year in the United States and many other countries around the world, every adult taxpayer has to file an annual income tax return indicating total income; deductions, some of which may be related to professional expenses incurred (e.g., expenses for studying the history of psychology); and how much tax may still be owed to the government.

One of us was audited or called in to talk with an official auditor or examiner of the Internal Revenue Service (IRS) about some deductions for research expenses associated with the history of psychology that were listed on a recent tax return. The IRS auditor was a very courteous, no-nonsense kind of person interested only in the facts and figures, so she inquired about the basic nuts and bolts of studying the history of psychology. Accordingly, the first point to keep in mind about the study of history is that historical truth is more elusive than scientific truth because all that remains of historical events are relics. These relics need to be inspected and studied carefully, and may be maintained in some archive, museum, or laboratory requiring the historian to travel, and thus the reason for the travel expenses listed on the tax return. On the other hand, it is sometimes possible to purchase relics, books, videotapes, and newspapers, which accounts for some of the other expenses shown on the tax return. The important point to remember here is that once you have access to or possess historical relics you then have to calculate their significance by determining what the relic signifies about the historical event(s) of interest.

Another important point about the study of the history of psychology is that there are a variety of criteria for historical importance as a result of the discovery of new relics about a particular person, event, or both. For example, it may be recorded that an important person met with a particular group of people, which was considered historically to be a very important meeting, while later in time it is discovered that another group was excluded from the meeting, and thus it is the exclusion rather than inclusion of a certain group that is important in the analysis and possible present-day impact of the historical event. Another historian may argue that an event may not be significant in and of itself while another may argue to the contrary, or the event may not be important in the short run but rather in the long run. For example, the tearing down of the Berlin wall in 1989 was momentous then and even more so today because it may well have been an international event of such magnitude that it contributed significantly to the elimination of other barriers or walls such as the dissolution of the Soviet Union or USSR in 1991. The Berlin wall (1989) and the dissolution of the Soviet Union (1991) are excellent examples of the issues for determining the criteria of importance of political history. In the history of psychology, John Dewey's paper on the reflex arc (1896) is considered by some as very important because it was the beginning of the school of psychology known as functionalism.

Another factor in determining what is important out of all the things that have happened is the historian herself or himself. For example, as more women enter psychology, move into leadership positions, and become historians of psychology, the role of women becomes more central and will reshape the history of psychology.

Making History

We have identified above some of the forces that shape the study of history and which make plain that history is a dynamic and changing discipline, even though historical events only happen once involving a particular set of persons or events. We now turn to the identification of some of the **forces that make history itself**, and these include the spirit of the times and the place (Naturalistic) and the Personalistic theory of history making.

According to the Naturalistic or Zeitgeist approach, history is in large part made by the spirit of the time and place so that, for example, Sigmund Freud came onto the global psychological scene as a result of having lived and worked during a time when science was prized, especially in the intellectual and cosmopolitan atmosphere in Vienna, Austria. Likewise, Mahatma Gandhi, Mao Zedong, John Fitzgerald Kennedy, Elvis Presley, Mother Theresa, Marie Montessori and all other world-renowned global figures rose to prominence because they happened to be in the right place at the right time. The Naturalistic approach de-emphasizes the individual in shaping history, is deterministic in that contextual or situational forces are paramount, and supports heartily the perspective that "culture informs mind."

The Personalistic theory of history argues that there are great persons endowed with an abundance of intelligence, insight, skills, personality, or some other dispositional feature or trait so that it is the person that shapes the culture and the times. Here, "mind informs culture" and the Personalistic theory stresses the centrality of the uniquely gifted, talented, and motivated person who makes history. This is a nondeterministic model which stresses the importance of the unique individual in making history. Thus, the civil rights movement in the United States or in South Africa would not have been launched nor its accomplishments and struggles to the present moment been possible without the unique persons of the Reverend Martin Luther King Jr., and Nelson Mandela, respectively. According to the Personalistic model, it was these unique persons that had the intellectual, moral, and personal courage to lead and shape the civil rights movement in the United States and South Africa. As most would agree, both the Naturalistic and Personalistic models of historical causation have merit and at one point in time one force may be a more robust predictor of historical events than the other, yet over time they both interact so that both models are valuable (Simonton, 1994).

Approaches to the History of Psychology

One of the most widely used methods for studying and writing about the history of psychology is the chronological approach. The historian picks some point in time and moves to some other point in time, usually, but not always, from the present to the past. Obviously, the historian establishes some criteria for her or his time line, and examines important persons and events during the selected period. An example of the chronological approach to the history of psychology is Edwin G. Boring's classic work, *A History of Experimental Psychology* (first published in 1929 and revised for the 1950 edition), which focuses primarily upon philosophical, physiological, and psychological developments during the 19th century and the early part of the 20th century.

Another approach to the study of the history of psychology is the focus upon the schools of psychology. A school of psychology is a group of psychologists who have aligned themselves around a particular pattern of ideas promoted by a leader(s) of a movement, such as Wilhelm Wundt and Edward Titchener (**psychology of consciousness**); William James, James Rowland Angell, and John Dewey (**functionalism**); John B. Watson (**behaviorism**), Max Wertheimer, Wolfgang Köhler, and Kurt Koffha (**Gestalt psychology**); and Sigmund Freud (**psychoanalysis**). Note that all these leaders of the schools of psychology were men reflecting the exclusionary nature of 19th- and early 20th-century psychology and the larger European and American cultures of those times. The school or systems approach to the history of psychology is represented by Robert S. Woodworth's *Contemporary Schools of Psychology* (1931), Edna Heidbreder's *Seven Psychologies* (1933), or Melvin H. Marx and William Cronan-Hillix's *Systems and Theories in Psychology* (1987). The schools of psychology dissipated around the early 1940s as the persons entering psychology were more diversified, there was increasing specialization as psychological knowledge accumulated in the literature, and the range of psychological topics grew broader. The schools or systems of psychology no longer exist, although orientations to psychological problems endure today such as behavioristic (behaviorism), applied (functionalism), cognitive (Gestalt), or dynamic (psychoanalysis) perspectives on a variety of psychological topics.

In the autobiographical approach well-known psychologists write personal or professional content autobiographies as reflected by Carl Murchinson's *History of Psychology in Autobiography* (1952). Lastly, a topical approach focuses upon particular areas of psychology such as, for example, perception, learning, and personality as reflected in J. P. Chaplin and T. Krawiec's *Systems and Theories of Psychology* (1960) or E. Hilgard and G. Bower's *Theories of Learning* (1966). Recent treatments of the history of psychology have become more focused upon highly specialized topics such as Donald K. Freedheim's *History of Psychotherapy* (1992).

METHODS OF STUDY IN PSYCHOLOGY

Just as there are a number of fundamental methods for studying the history of psychology, there are also some fundamental methods of study employed in almost every area of specialization in psychology. The search for the appropriate methods of study dates back to the beginnings of psychology as a formal, separate discipline in 1879 and continues right up to the present moment. This emphasis upon the importance of methodology in psychology has led some to observe that psychology is more a set of methods in search of subject matter than a discipline with a fixed subject matter.

Although there are many methods of study in psychology, most are related to four primary methods employed by many research and applied psychologists around the world. The psychological literature is located in textbooks, journals, electronic list servers, World Wide Web sites, personal correspondence, and archives. The value and applicability of any of these data sets are determined by the method of inquiry used to obtain the data.

Table 3-1 presents the four primary methods of study that are used most often in psychology. In general, as you move from case study to laboratory experiment you gain increasing control over the independent and dependent variables at the expense of losing realism, ecological validity, or touch with indigenous individuals or groups.

TABLE 3-1	Methods of Study and their Advantages and Disadvantages	
Method of Study	**Advantages**	**Disadvantages**
	■ Generates new topic areas	■ Affords little control of variables
Case study	■ Provides insights	■ Makes determinants of actions and experiences difficult to discern
	■ Suggests hypotheses	
	■ Permits causal inferences	■ Affords a limited degree of control of variables
Field experiment	■ Makes it easier to generalize results	■ Does not allow for subjects to be randomly selected
	■ Enhances realism	
	■ Allows for a high degree of control and precision	■ Results are often artificial and unrealistic
Laboratory experiment	■ Permits strong causal inferences	■ Results have limited generalizability
	■ Involves the random assignment of subjects to treatment conditions	■ Arouses suspicion in subjects
	■ Is unobtrusive	■ Is limited to using available data
Archival research	■ Is relevant to the topic of interest	■ Yields correlational data

From Lawson, R. B., & Shen, Z. *Organizational psychology: Foundations and applications.* Copyright © 1998. Reprinted by permission of The Oxford University Press.

A working knowledge of all four methods is definitely of value when examining foundational studies and experiments in the history of psychology.

We now examine a significant challenge in the beginning of the 20th century that faced American psychologists as they attempted to construct and maintain boundaries between the new science of psychology and its "pseudoscientific" counterparts of psychic research and spiritualism. It is interesting that the psychologists involved in these events relied almost exclusively upon issues of method of study of psychological phenomena to make plain that the new science of psychology could study both natural and so-called supernatural events. In demonstrating the power of the methods of study, psychology was further legitimized as a separate and scientific discipline. Interestingly, this earlier focus upon the centrality of methods in psychology is extremely timely today as Eastern and Western psychologies merge into a global psychology requiring the alignment of vitalistic, spiritual, and scientific explanations of events and experiences. Also, contemporary public interest in spirituality, especially in the Western world, has given rise to a creative tension between the public's demand for alternative psychological services, while psychologists seek to maintain the credibility of psychology by using scientific methods while being open to methods that focus upon individual phenomenological or experiential narrative reports.

Spiritualism and Science

At the beginning of the 20th century, psychology was deemed by some as incapable of becoming a science because the subject matter, consciousness, was unquantifiable and its methodology was unclear and adrift in a metaphysical morass (Coon, 1992). Interestingly, Coon (1992) has argued that early 20th-century psychologists used their battles with spiritualists to legitimize further psychology as a science and thus established a new role for themselves as the guardians of the science of psychology. For example, Hugo Münsterberg (1913), director of the Harvard Psychological Laboratory, studied the alleged psychic or mind reader Beulah Miller, a young girl from Rhode Island, and concluded that she was not a fraud nor was she a clairvoyant (capacity to sense the thoughts of others as a result of supernatural communication). Münsterberg (1913) claimed that Miller had "supernormal sensitiveness" to the minute muscular movements made by a person when concentrating, and if she was prevented from seeing the person while concentrating then she lost her psychic powers. Münsterberg (1913) asserted that all persons made minute muscular movements when concentrating, a fact that "we can easily show with delicate instruments in the psychological laboratory" (p. 17).

Psychologists demonstrated the authority of science, the laboratory, and its instruments to the public, which reinforced the idea that psychology is a science and that this natural science can explain natural and apparently supernatural phenomena as well! Explaining a phenomenon doesn't necessarily minimize interest in it as many people today still seek psychics in Boston, Rhode Island, and almost any place around the world. People seeking psychics may be looking for comfort, knowledge to inform important life choices, and a sense of predictability to life, all of which are psychological needs. Psychics provide services which are very natural such as presence, attentiveness, emotional support, and an aura of deep insight and package these services as supernatural. Unfortunately, psychics are not regulated by law nor are their practices regularly open to systematic study, so it is difficult to learn further about how their services work and don't work in assisting people in learning about themselves and how they manage their lives.

Sorcery in Salem

As indicated earlier in this chapter, the interpretation of a historical event may change even though the event(s) itself happens only once, and the relics or evidence of that event may not change as dramatically as the interpretation. We turn now to an event that many considered to be the result of mass hysteria, while some thought the event was the result of witchcraft or other supernatural forces that influenced significantly the affective, behavioral, and cognitive systems of hard-working and pious people. The event took place in Salem, Massachusetts, in 1692, and is widely known as the Salem witchcraft trials. The relics of this event include legal documents, letters, and personal diaries, which have been studied and reviewed.

A third and extremely ingenious interpretation of the so-called sorcery in Salem was proposed by a psychologist Linnda Caporael in 1976. According to Caporael (1976), many of the young girls who exhibited symptoms of what some in Salem then considered "bewitchment" may well have been suffering from a disease known as convulsive ergotism, which is due to **ergot**. This is the sclerotia of the fungus **Claviceps purpurea**, which usually grows on rye. Ergot grows densely on rye harvested from low, moist, shaded land, especially if the land is newly cultivated. Interestingly, all twenty-two of the Salem households affected in 1692 were located on or at the edge of soils ideally suited to rye cultivation, namely, moist, acid, and sandy loams.

The supposed witchcraft at Salem village was not initially identified as such. In late December 1691, about eight girls, including the niece and daughter of the minister, Samuel Parris, were afflicted with unknown "distempers." Their behavior was characterized by disorderly speech, odd postures and gestures, and convulsive fits. There was no apparent medical explanation and in February 1692, a doctor suggested the girls might be bewitched. Reluctant to accept this explanation, Minister Parris resorted to prayer and fasting, while a neighbor instructed Parris' Barbados slave "Tituba" to prepare a "witch cake" made in part from rye. Shortly thereafter, the girls accused Tituba and two other women in Salem Village, Sarah Good and Sarah Osborn, of witchcraft. The three women were taken into custody in February 1692. The affliction of the girls continued and in March they also accused Martha Corey and Rebecca Nurse. Further accusations by the children followed. The first case of witchcraft was tried on June 2, and the first condemned "witch" was hanged on June 10, 1692. By the time the witchcraft episode ended in the late fall of 1692, twenty persons had been executed and at least two had died in prison of the total 150 accused that were waiting to be hung.

The original eight girls and others accused or afflicted experienced the following symptoms: (a) crawling sensations in the skin; (b) tingling in the fingers, vertigo, tinnitus aurium, headaches; and (c) disturbances in sensation, hallucination, convulsions, vomiting, and diarrhea. These are exactly the same symptoms of convulsive ergotism that result from eating contaminated rye bread and other foods prepared with rye which was the basic grain of Salem, Massachusetts in 1691–1692. Ergot, a parasitic fungus, contains a large number of potent pharmacologic agents, including "isoergine" (lysergic acid amide), which has similar behavioral effects to those produced by LSD. It is very possible that the Salem witchcraft crisis was the result of ergot poisoning carried by the rye grain harvested in the fall of 1691. One Satan in Salem may well have been convulsive ergotism. Although the surviving records make certainty impossible, what is available indicates that the witchcraft accusations of 1692 were most likely a public health problem due to ergot poisoning rather than the work of Satan.

Other outbreaks of ergotism have been reported, such as the epidemic during the Middle Ages known then as Ignis Sacer or the holy fire but which has not been widely interpreted as the work or result of Satan or witchcraft (Matossian, 1982; Spanos & Gottlieb, 1976).

The New History of Psychology

In a series of presentations, papers, and books, Professor Laurel Furumoto and her colleagues have introduced and refined the historiographical methods of "the new history of psychology" (Furumoto, 1979, 1981, 1985, 1988; Furumoto & Scarborough, 1986). Within the discipline of history itself, Professor James H. Robinson argued, in his *The New History*, that we need to turn from the study of history "as a chronicle of heroic persons and romantic occurrences" (p. 10) to the study of institutions as the path to a more accurate historical understanding. Institutions, according to Robinson (1912), represented national habits or "the ways in which people have thought and acted in the past, their tastes and their achievements in many fields besides the political" (p. 15). The "new history" is now well established in the discipline of history as well as the specialty area of the history of science (Himmelfarb, 1987; Kuhn, 1970). Interestingly, Stephen J. Brush (1974), a historian of science focusing upon physics and early astronomy, published a paper in *Science* in 1974, titled "Should the history of science be rated X?" In essence, Brush was advocating for the "new history" over the traditional history which portrayed the scientist as an objective fact finder and neutral observer compared to the approach of the new history which presents scientists often operating in a subjective fashion under the influence of a variety of extra-scientific factors such as funding opportunities, public opinion, and worldviews or metaphysical commitments within the given scientific discipline.

The appearance of the *Journal of the History of the Behavioral Sciences*; the establishment of Division 26—the History of Psychology of the American Psychological Association; the founding of the Archives of the History of American Psychology at the University of Akron, Ohio, all in 1965, along with the first graduate program (1967) in the history of psychology (through the leadership of Robert I. Watson); and lastly, the founding of Cheiron, the International Society for the History of the Behavioral and Social Sciences in 1969, established the study of the history of psychology as a legitimate area of specialization within psychology.

The initial model for the study of the history of psychology was the traditional approach, and it wasn't until the mid-1970s that the new or critical history began to emerge in the history of psychology (Blumenthal, 1975; Furumoto, 1988). According to Furumoto (1988), the new history of psychology tends to be critical rather than ceremonial, contextual rather than simply the history of ideas, and inclusive going beyond just the study of great white men. Furumoto also believes that it utilizes primary sources (those authored by the historical person of interest) and archival documents (correspondence and diary materials), and aspires to see issues as they appeared at the time rather than just as antecedents of contemporary ideas. The new history of psychology rejects the model of scientific activity as a continuous progression from error to truth, and considers scientific change as a shift from one paradigm or worldview linked to another. The new history of psychology seeks to ground psychology in a history that is more diversified, chromatic, and positioned to deal with the challenges of globablization coupled with the tensions to preserve, respect, and foster indigenous psychologies and local cultures.

According to Furumoto (1988), the new or critical history of psychology has evolved through the following stages:

Compensatory history—examination of the past to identify lost or overlooked persons such as women, to fill up the empty niches in the traditional history of psychology.

Contribution history—focus upon the contributions of neglected or marginalized persons in the history of psychology.

Unique histories—focus upon the experiences of particular groups of persons and how their collective experience influenced their contributions to psychology.

Scarborough and Furumoto (1987) have stressed five gender-specific themes and barriers to participation that are essential for understanding the contributions of women to the history of psychology:

Barriers to graduate education—women not allowed to matriculate for officially recognized study in graduate psychology programs at prestigious institutions such as Harvard and Columbia.

The family claim—socially mandated that women should stay at home to raise children or care for aged parents rather than pursue a career.

The marriage versus career dilemma—women had to choose one or the other while men had both.

Uncollegiality of white males—the old boy networks that excluded women from key academic and professional positions.

The myth of meritocracy—connections, networking, and mentoring essential for prestigious academic appointments and promotions rather than decisions based solely upon performance.

Unfortunately, some of these barriers to participation still exist. However, as a consequence of the leadership of Furumoto (1988) and others the history of psychology is now more critical, inclusive, and contextual.

Paradigms and Revolutions

Science doesn't just happen; rather, it arises from the labors of scientists, the communities in which they work and live (e.g., different laboratory groups which may embrace a particular school or system of thought), and serendipitous or chance observations or findings. In his book *The Structure of Scientific Revolutions* (1962/1970), Thomas Kuhn suggests that in the stage of prescientific development, the preparadigmatic phase, the focus is upon fact finding, which is a fairly random process since no single framework, system or school of thought, or in Kuhnian terms, paradigm, is dominant to guide and direct the fact-finding process. Thus, in the beginning all facts are created equally. However, eventually one of the paradigms becomes dominant as the accepted or correct way to interpret findings, and to guide the search for new findings to support the predominant paradigm. A particular paradigm becomes dominant for a variety of reasons such as the validity of the findings, as well as the relative economic and political strength of one of the communities of scientists compared to others. Once a paradigm is established, we enter, according to Kuhn (1962/1970), the period of normal science when there are no more arguments about basic definitions of the subject matter, methods, and assumptions about what to look for and what it means when you find it, because a paradigm is now dominant.

According to Kuhn, revolutions in science as contrasted with economic, political, or social revolutions are smaller dramas, involve a clash of ideas, and usually one worldview gives way to another (Kuhn, 1970; Leahy, 1992). Kuhn (1970) suggested that scientific revolutions pass through four stages: (a) **normal science**, characterized as a period with a dominant paradigm that sets the research agenda, sanctifies the methods of study, and provides the calculus for interpreting the reported findings; (b) **appearance of anomaly**, in which some difficult puzzles can't be solved, and if they persist are then seen as fundamental and generate a period of crisis; (c) **crisis**, in which the predominant paradigm begins to crack and then crumble; and (d) **revolution**, in which the adherents of the emerging paradigm gain control of the levers of power in science such as journal editorships, textbooks, listservers, and even granting agencies (Leahy, 1992). In effect, the new replaces the old paradigm and the cycle or revolution begins again with the normal science, appearance of anomaly, crisis, and then revolution.

Cohen (1985) has also proposed a model of scientific revolutions in which the four stages of revolution are more clearly defined than in Kuhn's model, and he also proposed clear criteria to evaluate whether or not a scientific episode was revolutionary. The primary criterion to determine if a scientific revolution was taking place according to Cohen (1985) was the opinion of scientists involved in the event itself, what he called contemporary testimony. To this major criterion for scientific revolution, Cohen added later documentary history, historians' judgment, and the opinion of working scientists. Porter (1986) has also put forth a model of scientific revolutions that combines the central features of Kuhn's and Cohen's models. In essence, scientists must be aware that the entrenched orthodoxy is being overthrown, and scientific revolutions must be at least international or global in extent.

Leahy (1992), in an insightful and important journal article titled "The Mythical Revolutions of American Psychology," has argued that the so-called three major revolutions in American psychology (i.e., mentalism, behaviorism, and cognitive psychology) were in fact periods of rapid and continuous rather than revolutionary change. According to Leahy (1992), the widespread yet mythical story of the development of American psychology consists of three chapters. In chapter 1, mentalism, psychology was born in 1879 as the study of consciousness, using the method of introspection or systematic and skilled self-reports of conscious experiences relative to controlled stimuli presented in the psychological laboratory. The second chapter, behaviorism, began in 1913 when mentalism was challenged and taken to task by the behaviorists, who made behavior or "bodies in motion" the subject matter of psychology, stressed the centrality of behavioral learning methods such as classical or Pavlovian conditioning, and asserted unequivocally that mind didn't matter in psychology as it was private and subjective. Lastly, chapter 3, cognitive psychology, began in 1956 with the so-called cognitive revolution which was facilitated by the outside forces of linguistics and artificial intelligence. After twenty years of struggle, information-processing cognitive psychology became the dominant paradigm in American psychology (Leahy, 1992). Thus, the psychology evolved along a continuum of change marked by mentalism, behaviorism, are finally cognitive psychology focused upon information processing.

Leahy (1992) believes that the story of the above three revolutions in psychology is more appropriately portrayed as a narrative of research traditions that have changed over time, moving from the early efforts of Wundt to represent mental life by means of introspective reports, then to the realism of John B. Watson's behaviorism, and finally to the research tradition of reductionism in cognitive psychology. This analysis of changing research traditions in psychology is a more accurate reflection of the development of psychology in the United States because within each of these three systems of psychology there had been a difficult time identifying unifying methods of study; extensive debate raged regarding the subject matter of focus within each school; and none of the so-called revolutionary changes had been international in scope save for Wundt's establishment of psychology as a separate discipline of study in 1879.

Specialization in Psychology

There is no doubt that psychology today appears fractured, made up of many areas of specialization, and is populated by the proliferation of subspecialties and specific proficiencies such as the different psychotherapeutic techniques or different forms of psychometric assessment for personality, intelligence, or abilities (Benjamin, 1997). As we noted earlier, the schools or systems of psychology gave way in the 1940s to areas of specialization such as clinical, developmental, industrial/organizational, and school psychologies reflecting the conceptual diversity of psychology. These areas of specialization gave rise to the many divisions of the American Psychological Association (Benjamin, 1997; Bower, 1993; Dewsbury, 1997; Wolfe, 1997). Interestingly, however, organized psychology began to specialize almost from the outset when the American Psychological Association (APA) began with its first informal meeting in Granville Stanley Hall's study at Clark University in Worcester, Massachusetts, on July 8, 1892, and the first annual meeting held on December 27, 1892, at the University of Pennsylvania. The thirty-one charter members consisted primarily of experimental or laboratory-based psychologists, philosophers, psychiatrists, and educators (Sokal, 1992). The then fastest-growing part of the APA was made up of philosophers, whom the psychologists attempted to balkanize into a separate section (Benjamin, 1997). The philosophers objected and started to bolt from APA, and they formed the American Philosophical Association in 1902. For those psychologists remaining in the APA, controversy then developed around psychologists who might destroy the scientific purity of psychology through application of laboratory-based findings to practical problems. Lightner Witmer, who was considered the founder of clinical psychology, established the first psychological clinic rather than laboratory in 1896, encouraged his colleagues to appreciate applied or practical psychology, and charged them to use their laboratory findings to "throw light upon problems that confront humanity" (Witmer, 1897, p. 116). Thus, from the outset, American psychology consisted of different emerging areas of specialization, especially laboratory and applied psychologies.

Another force promoting specialization in psychology is the maturing of the discipline giving rise to the view that psychology really has three distinct subject matters, namely, behavior, neurobiological processes of behavior, and phenomenological experience (Bower, 1993). As a consequence, there is no longer any systematic attention focused upon identifying an overarching paradigm for all of psychology but rather the identification and analyses of paradigms in specific areas of specialization. As psychology becomes more specialized, areas will grow apart so that graduate educational programs may be quite different fifty or so years from now, with biopsychology being taught in medical schools. Cognitive psychology may well be a part of information sciences, and social psychology will be found in the professional schools (e.g., business).

One of the ways, in "the current sea of specialization," to identify some influential areas of specialization in psychology is to examine the eminence or importance of psychologists as judged by historians of psychology and influential contemporary psychologists. Korn, Davis, and Davis (1991) in combination with Estes, Coston, and Fournet (1990) reported the eminence rankings of contemporary psychologists based upon ninety-three chairpersons of graduate psychology departments and twenty-three members of Division 26—History of Psychology of the American Psychological Association, who disclosed their eminence rankings on a blank sheet with columns for All-Time and Contemporary. Table 3-2 presents the rankings for the historians, which include prominent psychologists in learning, cognition, clinical, developmental, and psychobiological areas of psychology with even greater emphasis upon the area of learning represented in the rankings by department chairpersons. As you might have surmised, all of the psychologists ranked in Table 3-2 are white males with a similar demography found for the rankings of all-time importance psychologists as well! There is need for further diversification of psychologists in the United States regardless of what area of specialization they may represent. Although given the growing preponderance of areas of specialization in psychology that moderates the possibility of an overarching paradigm for psychology as a science and profession, it is clear that a person-participation paradigm shift is needed to fix the mix and bring psychology more in line with the increasing diversity around the world.

McGovern, Furumoto, Halpern, Kimble, and McKeachie (1991) examined undergraduate psychology curricula, developed four alternative psychology curricula, and inquired if there is a canon in psychology. They suggested that the canon is probably focused upon evolving methodologies for studying affective, behavioral, and cognitive systems. This focusing upon methodology is very important because it cuts across areas of specialization in psychology, thus bringing some unity to psychology and also allowing psychologists to study a wide

TABLE 3-2	**Historians' and Chairpersons' Rankings of the Importance of Contemporary Psychologists**	
Rankings	**Historians**	**Chairpersons**
1	Skinner, B. F.	Skinner, B. F.
2	Miller, G. A.	Bandura, A.
3	Simon, H. A.	Miller, N.
4	Miller, N.	Miller, G. A.
5	Hilgard, E. R.	Neisser, U.
6	Sperry, R.	Bower, G.
7	Bandura, A.	Estes, W.
8	Eysenck, H. J.	Seligman, M.
9	Piaget, J.	Eysenck, H. J.
10	Neisser, U.	Hilgard, E. R., Rescorla, R.

Adapted from Korn, J. H., Davis, R., & Davis, S. F. Historians' and chairpersons' judgments of eminence among psychologists, pp. 789–792. Reprinted by permission of the author.

range of applied problems such as racism, conflict resolution, and educational strategies for an increasingly diversified global cultural environment. The centrality of methodology is an important historical and contemporary unifying force in psychology.

Lastly, Slife and Williams (1997) have argued that another unifying force, like methodological issues, that existed in the formative years of psychology that can also play an important role in contemporary psychology is the area of theoretical psychology. In the 1930s, schools of psychology such as behaviorism, functionalism, and psychoanalysis still existed and attempted to embrace all or most of the subject matter of psychology under one unifying theoretical model. By the 1940s, these schools had given way to more focused but still "grand" theories that aspired to explain psychological processes such as learning, perception, and social action. These smaller theories have been replaced by even more focused theories that are restricted, for example, to specific types of learning, motivation, and psychotherapy.

Slife and Williams (1997) have argued that subject matter fragmentation in the discipline, biologizing of psychology, and postmodern challenges to mainstream methods of inquiry within psychology (see Table 3-1) make plain the need for a specialization in theoretical psychology. Theoretical psychologists would serve as disciplinary consultants much like statisticians and methodologists do on thesis, dissertation, and research projects and programs. Some have suggested that we don't need a theoretical psychology because we already have too many theories. However, a major purpose of theoretical psychology would be the clarification and critical evaluation of psychology's ideas and practices. Theoretical psychology can embrace the study of method, globalization of psychology, and an appreciation of indigenous psychologies. Lastly, all data sets always need interpretation, thus requiring a theoretical framework to bring meaning to the data. Slife and Williams (1997) argue that theoretical psychology needs to be transdisciplinary, including philosophical contributions from epistemology (nature of knowledge) and ontology (nature of existence) as well as ethics.

PSYCHOLOGY MAKES A DIFFERENCE

Although psychology consists of many areas of specialization constructed around focused theories or models, it is important to determine if there is any global or transspecialization assessment of the outcomes of psychological interventions derived from a variety of settings using a variety of psychological interventions.

Prior to the advent of meta-analysis in the mid-1970s (Glass, 1976), assessments of psychological interventions were limited to single-study experimental or quasi-experimental approaches and research reviews of such studies with mixed outcomes supporting clear positive outcomes, or studies that presented a "parade of close-to-zero effects" (Rossi & Wright, 1984). The advent of meta-analysis affords a very powerful technique to gather systematic knowledge about the efficacy of psychological, educational, and behavioral interventions for individual and social problems (Lipsey & Wilson, 1993). Meta-analysis treats eligible research studies as a population to be systematically sampled and surveyed. Accordingly, the features and findings of individual studies are abstracted, quantified, coded, and assembled into a database that is statistically analyzed, similar to other quantitative survey studies. Lipsey and Wilson (1993) examined the effect sizes (i.e., the difference between the means of the treatment and control groups divided by usually the pooled standard deviation or that of the control group) for 302 meta-analytic studies directed at practical individual- or group-level problems and included interventions such as general and cognitive behavioral psychotherapy, treatment programs for offenders, meditation, biofeedback, tobacco smoking cessation programs, computer-based education, science and math instruction, test anxiety, job enrichment programs, organizational development programs, and many other areas of specialization.

The fundamental finding of the Lipsey and Wilson study is that psychological interventions have a robust positive impact upon individuals and groups—psychology works! Lipsey and Wilson (1993) performed a more refined meta-analysis controlling for some possible biases that might have inflated the initial positive outcomes, such as nonrandomized assignment of participants to treatment conditions or the use of one group for the pre- and post-intervention research designs or protocols, which tend to yield higher positive outcomes. Lipsey and Wilson (1993) found robust positive effects of psychological interventions (83% of mean effect sizes with the refined distribution were 0.20 or greater) based upon 156 out of the original 302 meta-analyses, which encompassed approximately 9,400 individual treatment effectiveness studies and **more than one million individual subjects!** These findings are comparable to the range of outcomes for a variety of medical treatments such as drug treatment for arthritis. Obviously, not every psychological intervention works, but clearly the overall outcomes are very positive and the challenge now is to determine which interventions are most effective, the mediating causal processes through which they work, and the characteristics of recipients, providers, and settings that most influence outcomes.

In summary, many types of psychological interventions yield positive outcomes for individuals and groups. We must continue to develop transcultural interventions and assessment strategies to deal with the many challenges and opportunities that arise from around the world.

■ Summary

History has a future because it shapes the future through **the changing interpretations** of the relics or evidence of fixed historical events and persons that may change as new historical evidence is discovered, even though the original events and persons themselves do not change.

We examined the cyclical (history repeats itself), linear progressive (present is an improvement over the past), and the chaotic (stuff happens) models of the nature of history. Historical importance is determined by a variety of criteria including the method of study of history, the availability of historical relics, and the interests of the historian. History happens as a result of a variety of forces, including the Naturalistic model, which proposes that the context shapes history or culture informs mind. This deterministic perspective is in contrast to the Personalistic model, according to which history is shaped by great, unique, and gifted persons so that mind informs culture.

We examined different approaches to the history of psychology, including the most frequently used chronological approach in which events and persons during a particular period of time are focused upon giving the appearance of an orderly unfolding of history. Thereafter, we identified methods of study employed in various combinations and degrees by almost all psychologists around the world to develop empirically foundational ideas and applications. Spiritualism and science have always coexisted uneasily as alternative explanatory mechanisms for understanding physical and psychological phenomena. We reviewed alleged historical instances of the supernatural, as espoused by some psychics, and the so-called Salem witchcraft trials to indicate the authority as well as the limitations of laboratory-based scientific methods for explaining natural as well as supernatural phenomena.

We then turned to the method of the new history of psychology that focuses upon the contributions of previously marginalized persons (e.g., African Americans and women) to psychology. We reviewed the constructs of paradigm and revolution which have been employed to understand the history of science in general and the so-called mythical revolutions in American psychology. We examined the historical and contemporary expression of areas of specialization in psychology, and concluded that psychology works by reviewing the unequivocal findings from meta-analytical studies demonstrating that a wide variety of psychological interventions yield positive outcomes within and across the affective, behavioral, and cognitive systems of individuals and groups.

■ Chapter 3—Nature of History and Methods of Study

Discussion Questions

■ What are the models and the nature of history?

■ What are the differences between the Naturalistic (cultural connections) and the Personalistic (great person) models of cardinal historical developments?

■ What are some advantages and disadvantages of the four predominant methods of study in psychology?

■ According to Furumoto, how did the new or critical history of psychology evolve?

■ How can specialization benefit and hinder the field of psychology?

Philosophical Foundations of Psychology

CHAPTER OVERVIEW

Humans have always sought knowledge about themselves, other living creatures, the earth, and the universe beyond so as to adapt effectively and efficiently to a wide variety of environments. Accordingly, to bring some meaning, stability, and purpose to our individual and collective lives we have created over the millenia different ways of knowing and learning. We begin our journey with a brief examination of the four river valley civilizations, the first of which arose around 5000 B.C. It is noteworthy that important religious and philosophical components of these four early civilizations still inform many different cultures around the world today.

Three important ways of knowing include **faith** derived from divine revelation and dogma, which forms the basis of religion; **rationality** (thinking and reflecting), which forms the infrastructure of philosophy; and **systematic observation**, which forms the basis of science. These three fundamental ways of knowing are not mutually exclusive, and indicate that living is about facts and faith. We examine the concept of animism as an early explanatory system which in turn gave rise to questions about the nature of soul or spirit.

We then examine the four philosophical-religious systems that arose directly from the four river valley civilizations and which represented revolutionary breakthroughs in faith- and rational-based systems. Specifically, we review briefly the major principles of Chinese philosophy, the Indian religions of Hinduism and Buddhism, Judaism, and Greek philosophy. Thereafter, we present some of the foundational features of Roman philosophy and examine the ascendance of Christianity across Europe and Islam throughout the Middle East and northern Africa.

We then review briefly Islamic science and philosophy, both of which produced new knowledge as well as preserved the works of the Greek philosophers during the repressive reign of Christianity in Western Europe. We see the leading edge of the Renaissance in the work of the Judaic philosopher Maimonides, who attempted to reconcile the forces of faith and reason in his *The Guide for the Perplexed*, published in 1190, a challenge that was also embraced by Scholasticism as reflected in the works of Peter Abelard (1079–1142), Thomas Aquinas (1225–1274), and William of Occam (1290–1350).

The Renaissance covers the period from about 1450 to 1600, and was centered in Europe, especially in Italy and the city of Florence. The Renaissance was about personal agency as the individual was seen as powerful and capable of adding value to the world. We examine briefly the work of Francesco Petrarch (1304–1374), who focused upon personal spirituality rather than the then-confining coda of religion and rationality. We next review briefly the contributions of Martin Luther (1483–1546), and of Niccolò Machiavelli (1469–1527), who provided an important handbook, *The Prince*, for getting things done in the world in response to the demands of efficiency, practicality, and the common good, rather than in response to rigid moral concerns. Machiavelli was clearly of this world and captured in his political and social writings the Renaissance theme of the centrality of humanity and the inherent potential powers of every individual. Renaissance science also reflected the centrality of humanity as a powerful force for understanding as, for example, in the works of Nicolas Copernicus (1473–1543), Galileo Galilei (1564–1642), Isaac Newton (1642–1727), and Francis Bacon (1561–1626). All of these persons made plain the Renaissance theme that "humanity is a part of rather than apart from the world," although in some cases at great cost of personal persecution and humiliation. It is essential to note that many during the

Renaissance came to believe that human experiences could be explained and understood in natural rather than supernatural terms.

We conclude this chapter with the life and works of René Descartes (1596–1650), who is considered by many to have ushered in the modern period (1600 to about 1960) in which science and rationality were championed as the most valid and accurate ways of knowing. For Descartes, only that which could not be doubted, namely, the act of doubting itself or **Dubito, ergo sum** (I doubt, therefore I am) served as the gateway to certainty arising primarily from systematic scientific studies and rationality. In his *Discourse de la Mèthode* (*Discourse on Method*) published in 1637, Descartes presented his four rules for determining certainty in any area of inquiry. Descartes also wrestled with the nature of the relationship between mind and body as well as between humans and infrahumans (all other animals). Lastly, he gave us the concept of **undulatia reflexa** or automatic bodily movement not supervised or determined by conscious awareness, which informed many 17th-, 18th-, and 19th-century experiments that form the physiological foundation of psychology and also served as the basis of 20th-century stimulus–response psychology.

LEARNING OBJECTIVES

When you finish studying this chapter, you will be prepared to:

- Describe the four river valley civilizations, the first of which arose around 5000 B.C.

- Identify and discuss the foundational ideas of the four philosophical-religious systems, Chinese philosophy, Indian religion (Hinduism and Buddhism), Judaism, and Greek philosophy that arose directly from the four river valley civilizations

- Present the foundational ideas of the religious systems of Christianity and Islam

- Discuss the significant features of Islamic science and philosophy which produced new knowledge as well as preserved the important works of the Greek philosophers

- Summarize Maimonides' *The Guide for the Perplexed* and the foundational ideas of Scholasticism, both of which attempted to reconcile the forces of faith and reason and set the stage for the Renaissance

- Identify the major developments in religion, philosophy, science, and politics that formed the central core of the Renaissance (1450–1500), all of which emphasized that "humanity is a part of rather than apart from the world."

- Discuss the contributions of René Descartes (1596–1650) and his maxim of **Dubito, ergo sum** (I doubt, therefore I am) as well as his foundational idea of **undulatio reflexa** (or automatic bodily movement), both of which served as points of departure for the modern period (from about 1600 to 1960) and the physiological foundations of psychology

INTRODUCTION

Our planet Earth, third from the sun and one of nine planets that orbits around the sun, is about five billion years old. Homo sapiens, modern humans, first appeared on Earth about 200,000 B.C., while civilization began about 5000 B.C. when Homo sapiens had clearly switched from being hunter-gatherers following the food supply to growing food in a fixed place, giving rise to agriculture. Since the beginnings of civilization human control over the environment has accelerated constantly, and the changes of our many diverse cultures (i.e., the learned and shared beliefs, values, and behaviors of an identifiable group of people) have outpaced tremendously evolutionary changes in our biology. Modern humans have been living in increasingly organized cultures since the dawn of civilization around 5000 B.C., while we still retain the foundational emotional patterns and motor reflexes of primitive humans (Craig, Graham, Kagan, Ozment, & Turner, 1994).

We now examine briefly the major changes in the history of humanity focused upon ways of acquiring and using knowledge that takes us from the beginning of civilization to the modern period that began around A.D. 1600. From the beginning up to the present moment, humans have been seeking answers to evolving fundamental questions including, for example, who am I and what are my origins, how am I like and different from others, will what I do matter and to whom, what is the meaning or purpose of life, and what is the origin of the earth and the universe? Humans constructed organized knowledge systems to address these questions including supernaturalism, religion, philosophy, and science.

THE DAWN OF CIVILIZATION—FOUR RIVER VALLEY CIVILIZATIONS

At the dawn of civilization, preliterate and prehistoric human beings lived closer to nature than their more civilized descendants who started to live about 5000 B.C. in more highly organized cities surrounded by rich and fertile land in river valleys. The beginning of river valley civilization is marked by three major historical events, namely, the establishment of **agriculture** for a stable food supply; the development of **writing** so as to keep records of the behaviors of the rivers and weather, both critical to a stable food supply; and the **organization** of complex systems to regulate and control the exchange of goods, services, and properties (Roberts, 1995).

River valley civilizations arose in four distinct places around the world so from the outset diversity has been a central and key feature of human civilization (Craig et al., 1994). The first **Sumarian civilization** arose in Mesopotamia (the land between the rivers) in the valley of the Tigris and Euphrates rivers (modern Iraq) founded by a people called Sumarians who lived in the city of Sumer near the head of the Persian Gulf. Thereafter, early **Egyptian civilization** that spanned almost three thousand years (3100 to 100 B.C.), began in the Nile valley along the northernmost portion of the 4,000-mile-long Nile River, and featured a religion that focused upon the afterlife. On the Indian subcontinent of Asia an **Indus** or **Harappan civilization** began near the Indus and Ganges Rivers that lasted some 500 years, spanned a much larger area than its contemporaries of Mesopotamia and Egypt, and was a fairly uniform culture suggesting a highly organized government, an integrated economic system, and sound internal communications. Although a relatively short-lived civilization, a noteworthy feature of the organization of the cities of the Indus civilization was an intricate system of covered drains and sewers with private houses serviced by wells, bathrooms, latrines, and great baths. Lastly, the **Chinese civilization** emerged along the southern bend of the Yellow River in central China. The early Chinese civilization was divided into the Hsia, Shang, and Chou dynasties that spanned the period from 2200 to 256 B.C.,

Four River Valley Civilizations

- Sumarian Mesopotamian: Arose between the Tigris and Euphrates Rivers.
- Egyptian Civilization: Arose in 3100 B.C. along the northernmost segment of the Nile River.
- Indus or Harappan Civilization: Arose near the Indus and Ganges Rivers and lasted about 500 years.
- Chinese Civilization: Arose along the southern bend of the Yellow or Yantze River around 2200 B.C.

FIGURE 4-1 The Dawn of Civilization

with the Hsia considered a legendary civilization. Like other river valley civilizations, as the Chinese gained freedom from nature through agriculture they created a highly stratified society so that instead of wrestling with the forces of nature they wrestled with the forces of expanding and increasingly complicated organized cultures. For example, commerce required a good road system to transport goods across large areas and a strong and organized army as well as a literate bureaucracy to administer the functions of government, including keeping the roads open and safe.

In summary, the Mesopotamian and Egyptian civilizations of the Near East (modern day Iraq and Egypt, respectively) arose first, followed by those of India and China (Figure 4-1). Each of the four river valley civilizations exhibited a similar pattern of development, namely, agriculture, writing, and increasingly organized cities and economic and social systems. Although it is not clear if these river valley civilizations around the globe arose independently or were the result of diffusion due to increasing contacts between them (Craig et al., 1994).

From the beginning, we see many diverse civilizations and religions, all of which were concerned with knowledge about the nature of the natural and supernatural worlds. Religions represent ways of knowing based primarily upon faith in truths given through revelation or poignant and mystical experiences of the founder. Interestingly, religions from the outset and up to the present moment shape markedly how many different people around the world feel, behave, and think in their daily lives, and, accordingly, contemporary psychologists must know about them to be effective around the globe.

EARLY EXPLANATORY SYSTEMS—ANIMISM AND SPIRITS

Humans, in order to survive in pre-civilized (prehistoric) and civilized (historic) times, have always needed to understand, explain, and even predict our own affect (emotions), behaviors, and cognitions (thoughts) as well as those of infrahumans. In addition, to strengthen their cultures and societies, humans have also needed knowledge of plants (e.g., for herbal medicines), animals, the weather, the earth, and the universe.

In general, three important ways of knowing include **faith** derived from divine revelation and dogma, which forms the basis of religion; **rationality** (thinking and reflecting), which forms the infrastructure of philosophy; and **systematic observation**, which forms the basis of science. In our everyday lives, most of us behave like scientists by observing events and others, forming hypotheses or guesses about what is going to happen, and keeping track of outcomes. We also behave as believers in that we have faith in ourselves (confidence), others, and explanatory systems such as, for example, religion. Thus, living is about knowing facts and faith!

One of the earliest explanatory systems of life events is **animism** or the belief that all of nature is alive with no distinction between animate (living) and inanimate (nonliving) objects (Cornford, 1957). In its original form, animism did not differentiate between the animate and the inanimate but, rather, saw all of nature as alive.

Another early explanatory principle of life events was the concept of **breath, spirit**, or **soul** which led to the distinction between animate and inanimate objects. Animate objects were said to have the property of self-induced motion while inanimate objects do not because the former have a soul or spirit and the latter do not. The soul housed in the human body was the **sine qua non** (i.e., an indispensable condition) for human life, and when the breath, spirit, or soul left permanently from the body then death resulted (Hulin, 1934). Dreams were explained as the temporary release of the spirit from the body so that it could wander across great distances, achieve heroic deeds, deal with the dead, fly, survive near misses with death, and return to the body with knowledge and insight which might then inform critical decision when the person awoke from sleep.

The spirit explanation of life was refined into "good and evil spirits," an explanatory model that is still alive today as expressed in some contemporary religions, cults, and even in psychology when we speak of persons with positive and negative moods, spirits, or dispositions. Thus, an "evil spirit" was associated with sickness and deviant or unexplainable behaviors while a "positive spirit" was responsible for sound health and adaptive behaviors. Elaborate practices were devised to influence the spirits, giving rise first to magic, symbol worship, and eventually to systematic religions and philosophies.

EARLY PHILOSOPHIES AND RELIGIONS

The four river valley civilizations, namely, the Mesopotamian (Tigris-Euphrates rivers), the Egyptian (Nile River), the Indus-Vedic (Indus and Ganges rivers), and the Chinese (Yellow River), evolved over a 5,000-year period beginning around 5000 B.C. This then gave rise, between 800 and 300 B.C., to the first stage of a two-stage revolution of major philosophies and religions followed by the second stage between 300 B.C. and A.D. 700 (Craig et al., 1994). Figure 4-2 presents an outline of the two stages of these intellectual and spiritual breakthroughs that still inform contemporary thought and guide the actions of millions of people around the world today. It is interesting to note that the philosophies and religions of the original or first stage share common features, which include (Craig et al., 1994):

- All of the philosophical and religious systems developed in the river valley civilizations, which at that time had highly structured agricultural, urban, writing, and organizational systems that provided a fairly stable platform for revolutionary breakthroughs in faith and rational systems.

- Each philosophical and religious system arose in response to the need to develop more universal ethical systems and codes of behavior to align more harmoniously with the ever-increasing rate of technological and social changes in each of the river valley civilizations.

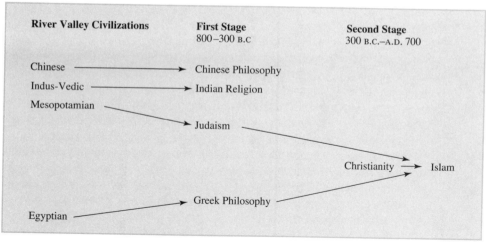

FIGURE 4-2 The Two-Stage Philosophical and Religious Revolutions of the Four River Valley Civilizations

Adapted from Craig, A. M. et al. (1994). *The heritage of world civilizations*. (3rd ed.). Copyright © 1994. Electronically reproduced by permission of Pearson Education, Inc., Upper Saddle River, New Jersey.

■ Once these early philosophical and religious systems developed global (Judaism, Christianity, and Islam) or regional (Buddhism and Confucianism) momentum they took on a life of their own, became increasingly insulated from and resistant to each other, and ignored, resisted, or eventually coexisted with the later development of modern science right up until the present. Given the robustness and resiliency of these traditional philosophical and religious systems, it is important for contemporary psychologists to be aware of the richness and defining features of each of these traditions and those that followed. Accordingly, Figure 4-3 presents a coarse calendar of significant periods and events in the history of humanity to guide our brief review of each of the philosophical and religious systems arising from the four river valley civilizations. We begin with a brief examination of the Chinese philosophies known as Confucianism and Taoism.

Confucianism and Taoism

Confucius (551–479 B.C.) is the Latinized form of K'ung Fu-tzu or Master K'ung, as he is known in China (Chan, 1967; Roberts, 1955). Confucianism is not a religion although it is very spiritual and is an updated version of the aristocratic codes of behaviors and moral qualities of the fading period of the Chou dynasty (1050–256 B.C.). We know mostly about Confucius through the **Analects**, a series of four books which are a collection of his sayings compiled after his death by his first- and second-generation disciples. The sayings appear in the following format:

> The Master (Confucius) said: Yu, shall
> I tell you what it is to know. To say
> you know when you know, and to
> say you do not when you do not,
> That is knowledge (Lau, 1979, p. 65).

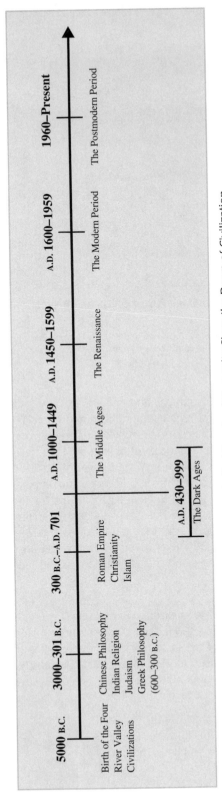

FIGURE 4-3 A Coarse Calendar of Significant Periodical Events of Humanity Since the Dawn of Civilization

In the Confucian system, **any** person can become noble by embracing **chun-tzu** which is a set of behaviors and an attitude or demeanor that reflect the virtues of integrity (truth telling), righteousness, altruism, and loyalty. Table 4-1 presents the fundamental moral qualities that Confucius insisted his followers embrace and use in their daily actions and thinking.

Confucius taught that genuine happiness and harmony arise from the practice of specific guidelines for managing relationships. According to his Five Forms of Human Relationship (ruler–subject, father–son, husband–wife, older–younger brothers, and friend–friend; note that all save friendships are male-dominant relationships), if everyone fulfilled the duties of her or his status and practiced courtesy, reverence, and the correct form of social interaction at all levels of the Five Forms, then individual and social harmony would prevail (Chan, 1967). In short, Confucianism teaches that the well-being of any society depends on the morality of its members. Confucianism was developed further by his philosopher disciples Mencius (370–290 B.C.) and Hsun-tzu (300–237 B.C.). These and all other Confucian philosophers believe that through education individuals overcome human weakness.

Confucianism was not adopted as the official Chinese philosophy until 200 B.C., and since then over the last 2,000 years has influenced approximately 25% of the world's population. Although Confucianism was eventually replaced by the philosophy and social-economic system of communism in A.D. 1949, an effort has recently been made in China and around the world to preserve the great intellectual and cultural heritage of Confucianism. Today, Confucians number around 300 million, mostly in China.

Lao-tzu (591–479 B.C.) was an older contemporary of Confucius and was generally considered to have authored the *Tao Te Ching* (*Book of the Tao and Its Powers*), which is a poetic treatise stressing that in the material world everything is relative (Garraty & Gay, 1981). Everything exists in contrasts yet behind the duality and illusions is the primary unifying principle called the **Tao** or **Way**. The Tao can only be apprehended intuitively rather than intellectually as through a mystical state achieved by meditation. The Taoist symbol for the forces of **yin** (light, masculine, forceful) and **yang** (dark, feminine, submissive) represents the condition of absolute balance in the universe, ☯.

Taoism offered a refuge from the burden of social responsibilities demanded by Confucianism and was more focused upon cosmic rather than daily issues. The verses of the *Tao Te Ching* are engaging and mystifying, using few words to invite reflection rather than convey specific instructions. Such verses include reference to the **Tao** as:

> both knowledge and experience are real, but reality has many forms, which seem to cause complexity. By using the means appropriate, we extend ourselves beyond the barriers of such

---

TABLE 4-1 **Confucian Moral Qualities**

- **Personal Authenticity**—loyalty to one's inner self
- **Thoughtfulness**—consideration toward others
- **Prudence**—moderation in all things
- **Relationships**—meticulous observation of the rites and ceremonies that pertain to human actions
- **Civility**—a cultured manner

complexity, and so experience the Tao.
(www.clas.ufl.edu/users/gthursby/taoism/ttcstan3.html#1)

The **Way** or **Tao** is constantly changing yet never changes! The Way has no limits and cannot be defined or bounded. Once the weak conquers the strong, weakness now becomes strength and in turn is conquered as new weak forces arise. The *Tao Te Ching* also reflects on the cyclical nature in reference to overcoming:

> It is the way of the Tao, that things which expand might also shrink; that he who is strong, will at some time be weak, that he who is raised will then be cast down, and that all men have a need to give, and also have a need to receive.
> (www.clas.ufl.edu/users/gthursby/taoism/ttcstan3.html#1)

This perpetual behavior of individuals and organized groups such as government reflects an important Taoist dynamic, namely, the cyclical nature of all natural and human phenomena. Change is the Way through the unbounded universe!

Indian Religions: Hinduism and Buddhism

Initially, Indian religion known as Hinduism focused upon the **Upanishads** texts written around 1200 B.C. in Sanskrit (an ancient language) by Brahmans or scholars and philosophers who acquired their power through knowledge rather than ritual acts (Craig et al., 1994). The Upanishads are in turn based upon the **Vedas** which is an extensive book of knowledge (six times the length of the Bible) revealed to "seers" (sage or prophet) during states of deep contemplation. The Vedas were written around 1500 B.C. by the Vedic Indians who settled on the banks of the Indus River in northern India. A distinguishing feature of Hinduism is its diverse and at times contradictory beliefs. For example, when a Hindu dies the body is cremated and the ashes are usually thrown over a sacred river such as the Ganges. Interestingly, a human can be reborn after death into a higher or lower form of life depending upon one's karma or the effect of one's actions during one's prior life, which exert a positive or negative influence upon one's next life. Thus, good or positive karma causes one to be born into a higher life and the reverse if one has negative karma from one's former life. Lastly, Hindus have a generally pessimistic view of life, believing that as a result of **samsara** or reincarnation life moves in an endlessly repetitive pattern of circular motion, life, death, life, death, and so on endlessly, that is, **The Wheel of Life**. The way out of samsara is through either vast knowledge or intense devotion to a personal god leading to **moshka** or ultimate liberation from the life–death cycle.

Buddhism was founded in the fifth century B.C. by Siddhartha Gautama (ca. 566–486 B.C.), who gave up Hinduism to seek the "Truth." A "seer" (sage or prophet) predicted that Gautama, who was born into a powerful ruling family in northeastern India, would become either a world ruler or a homeless wanderer (Roberts, 1995). At the age of 29, Gautama gave up all of his possessions, social position, and family, turning first to an intense study of Hinduism. One day, while meditating under an "Enlightment Tree," he learned how to stop the karmic outflows that fuel suffering. At that point, he became the Buddha—he achieved full enlightment. Thereafter, he spent the remaining forty-five years of his life travelling extensively and spreading his message of salvation.

TABLE 4-2	The Four Noble Truths of Buddha

- **All life is suffering**.
- **Suffering arises from desire**.
- **Overcome suffering by eliminating desire**.
- **Meditation and the attainment of wisdom can eliminate desire**.

The Buddha translated his "experience of enlightment" into the Four Noble Truths presented in Table 4-2 (Rahula, 1974). The first Noble Truth is that life is difficult yet by following the Eightfold Path of right understanding, thought, speech, action, livelihood, effort, mindfulness, and concentration one can overcome desire or **dukkha**. Buddha called his teachings the **dharma** or spiritual law (Craig et al., 1994). According to the dharma or Buddhist teachings, once the desire for earthly possessions, including life itself, is eliminated the believer can reach Nirvana, that is, the state of extinguishment or serene detachment. Nirvana represents an escape from The Wheel of Life or the endless cycle of life and death which is a doctrine carried over from Hinduism. The Buddha rejected the Hindu belief that the soul is reunited with Brahman (The Creator) after escaping The Wheel of Life because the Buddha did not believe in Brahman or the human soul.

There are hundreds of variations of the basic teachings and practices of Buddhism. Thus, for example, Zen Buddhism teaches that meditation is the only path to salvation. From Zen arises the famous "Unanswerable Questions" such as "what is the sound of one hand clapping?" Tantric Buddhism preaches that repeating a mantra, a series of meaningless symbols, fitted to an individual after studying with a Buddhist teacher, can yield magical results. Of the approximately 250 million Buddhists around the world, only a half million live outside of Asia and only small minorities in India.

Judaism

Judaism was the first universal or global monotheistic (one God) religion like that of the later religions of the Christian and Muslim faiths. Judaism arose most likely during the period of 2000 to 500 B.C., in the region of Mesopotamia and Egypt which was characterized by polytheistic (multiple gods and goddesses) religions (Craig et al., 1994; Roberts, 1995). Judaic monotheism rests upon two foundational ideas, namely, God through his prophets had a direct involvement in the history of humanity rather than the aloofness or indifference of the polytheistic religions, and, second, the nature of Yahweh or the God of all was seen by the prophets as the ideal or the epitome of justice and goodness. Yahweh, because of his righteousness, was a God for all and he demanded righteousness from his followers. Judaism changed the score card of life so that what counted were just and good deeds and thoughts rather than only specific rituals.

The history of the Hebrew people, later called the Israelites, is carried by the **Torah** or Hebrew Bible (the first five books of the Old Testament) which is divisible into four major sections and considered by Jews as the foundation of their religious worship. The earliest written

TABLE 4-3	The Essential Components of Judaism

- **Love of Learning**—Jews consider education a privilege and a responsibility.
- **The Worship of God**—An observant Jew tries to embrace as her or his own the merciful, just, compassionate, and tolerant qualities of God.
- **Good Works**—Good deeds in support of the less fortunate are obligatory and must come from the heart.

sections go back to about 900 B.C., and the first section is the story of Abraham and the patriarchs in Canaan (The Books of Genesis and Job). The second section includes the period from Israel's bondage in Egypt, and the Exodus in pursuit of the Promised Land. The history of Israel as a united and then divided Kingdom in the land of Canaan is in the third section of the Torah, and the fourth section covers the fall of the two major kingdoms, Israel and Judah, the Babylonian Captivity, and the release of the Jews to rebuild their shattered country.

The **Talmud**, a supplement to the Torah or Old Testament, is a collection of religious and civil Jewish laws and their scholarly interpretations, and is considered the textbook for training rabbis or teachers. The Talmud is a veritable storehouse of wisdom that includes thousands of engaging parables, anecdotes, and historical notes. Many of the Talmudic maxims are well known, such as "why are we born into the world with clenched fists and leave it with outstretched fingers? . . . to remind us that we take nothing with us." The Talmud makes plain that knowledge and an awareness of God is obtainable through reason and rational discourse rather than revelation confined to unique and transcendent experiences. The three fundamental components of the Jewish faith are presented in Table 4-3. In Judaism, the essence of God is knowledge, especially of the truth, law, and traditions.

There are three branches of Judaism: Orthodox, Conservative, and Reform, with their differences based more upon traditions than doctrines. There are approximately fourteen million Jews around the world, six million in North America, and only four million living in Israel.

GREEK PHILOSOPHY

The last development of the first stage of the major philosophical and religious systems arising from the original four river valley civilizations was Greek philosophy, which spanned the period from about 600 to 300 B.C. (MacLeod, 1975). The Greek philosophical system focused upon an explanatory system of the universe that promoted materialism, rationalism, and empiricism for understanding the universe, the world, and the human experience (Craig et al., 1994). Supernaturalism took a backseat in Greek philosophy, although Grecians still embraced homage and deference to the many gods and goddesses that swirled around the universe. Greek philosophers advocated that people put their faith in the processes of **rationalism** (explanation of phenomena based upon systematic observation of things and events) and **naturalism** (the idea that the physical and experienced worlds can be understood without recourse to the forces under the control of the gods and goddesses but rather, can be based upon physical principles and laws [Garraty & Gay, 1981]).

Thales

The Greek philosophers produced an intellectual revolution by speculating about the nature of the universe and its origin, relying exclusively upon naturalistic hypotheses without any reference to supernatural powers. For example, Thales, around 600 B.C., addressed the question of the basic substance of the world, and answered that the primal substance of the world is water from which all else is derived (Urmson, 1960). The foundational idea is that Thales and those who followed boldly dethroned the gods and goddesses and replaced them with impersonal elements. Gone was an explanation of the origin of the world based on the erotic adventures of Kronos and Uranus, replaced by permanent substances and general causes derived from observation and reason (Garraty & Gay, 1981). The work of Thales is probably the point of departure for the rational investigation of the universe, thus launching the era of science that stood as an alternative to earlier mystical and religious explanations of the world. There followed Thales a sterling chain of about a dozen pre-Socratic philosophers who extended naturalistic explanations into every nook and cranny of the external world. Interestingly, these pre-Socratics or Sophists were paid for their knowledge, especially regarding such practical problems as determining the distance of a ship at sea, the transport of an army over a river, or the accurate calculation of the four seasons of the year.

Anaximander and Pythagoras

Anaximander (610–547 B.C.) gave us the idea that humans arose from other species (evolution) rather than from the action of a god, goddess, or both, and the first map of the world as well as the sun dial for telling time based upon a rational system of light and shadow (Urmson, 1960). Pythagoras (570–508 B.C.) founded a combined scientific and religious community in Croton in southern Italy around 530 B.C. He gave us the term *philosophy* combined from *philo* (love) and *sophia* (knowledge or wisdom). Pythagoras and his followers began the movement away from explanations of the world grounded in primordial substances such as water, air, earth, and/or fire to explanations based upon the underlying mathematical relationships between elements in the world as, for example, the musical scale, which is essentially a numerical scale. In addition, we see a shift from cosmological explanations (explaining the universe) to an interest in human issues such as using music as therapy. Women such as Theana, spouse of Pythagoras, and their daughter Myia played a vital role in the development of the breadth of Pythagorean philosophy stressing the centrality of harmony in daily life to maintain sound mental and physical health as well as providing guidelines for nurturing child care.

The Eleatics

The Eleatics, based in Elea in southern Italy, consisted of the pre-Socratic philosophers including Xenophanes (570–525 B.C.), Parmenides (515–451 B.C.), and Zeno (450–443 B.C.). The Eleatics turned away from cosmology or explanations focused upon finding the foundational elements of the universe. They instead focused upon epistemology, which is the branch of philosophy concerned with knowledge or ways of knowing, the nature of human knowledge, and the identification of the universal essence of ideas such as beauty, justice, and truth (Kirk & Raven, 1957; Urmson, 1960). Xenophanes argued that humans have only opinions or speculations derived primarily from their personal experiences about things and events rather than knowledge that transcends the particulars of personal experiences. Parmenides wrote a philosophical poem, *On Nature*, which consists of a dialogue between him and a goddess. The poem focused upon the dualistic tension between knowing the world through our senses, which gives us particulars and change, while reason gives us awareness of universal realities, which is unified and permanent.

It is also noteworthy that during this pre-Socrates period, the Greeks invented the scientific study of history or *istoric*, a Greek word meaning inquiry (Roberts, 1995). Herodotus (484–425 B.C.) is considered the founder of scientific history as he attempted to document in writing the economic, political, and social events and interactions between Greece and Persia that led up to the Persian war. Thucydides picked up where Herodotus left off and wrote the history of the Peloponnesian War (431–404 B.C.) which was a lengthy, demoralizing, and destructive internal war between the city-states of Athens and Sparta.

Heraclitus, Empedocles, and Democritus

We conclude our treatment of the pre-Socratic philosophers with Heraclitus (540–475 B.C.), Empedocles (554–495 B.C.), and Democritus (460–370 B.C.). Heraclitus was born into an aristocratic family, withdrew from society, and believed most people are stupid because they fail to appreciate that the physical world is governed by **Logos** (i.e., reason) and can be understood by reason (Kirk & Raven, 1957; Urmson, 1960). He believed the world is constantly changing so that any sense of constancy is illusory, and change is represented symbolically by fire which is in constant flux, as seen in the continuous change of the shape, color, intensity, and size of the flames of a fire. For Heraclitus, we are constantly in a state of becoming which raises the problem of how we can know anything with certainty if everything is changing. To answer, in part, Empedocles distinguished between sensation, which is the detection of physical energy such as movement on your skin and perception or interpretation of the awareness of movement. What varies is the interpretation of the energy while the detection of the energy is constant. Empedocles believed there are four basic elements in the world, namely, fire, earth, air, and water, and the forces of love and strife give rise to attraction and repulsion amongst the four elements yielding all possible things and experiences. Empedocles believed that objects (i.e., distal stimuli) give off faint copies of themselves—**eidola**—which enter the blood (which contains the above four basic elements) through pores of the body. The eidola of the external elements combine with like internal elements, and the fusion of like elements gives rise to the perception of the target object.

Democritus (460–370 B.C.) was a **materialist** and thought the universe was composed of an infinite number of small, indivisible, indestructible atoms (Urmson, 1960). Democritus developed the idea of the atom as the underlying substance of all of the natural world, which could vary in size, shape, and motion. Physical atoms accounted for the natural world while soul atoms (smaller, smoother, and livelier than physical atoms but still atoms) were responsible for psychological actions so that, for example, when a person thinks, the soul atoms are agitated. The apparent difference between the physical and mental is resolved as mind is composed of atoms which are more subtle than physical atoms. Humans are a part of the physical world and can be explained in terms of physical laws, mind is matter and matter is mind.

Socrates

The Golden Age of Greece includes the work of Greek Idealists, namely, Socrates, Plato (a pupil of Socrates), and Aristotle (a pupil of Plato) that spanned the period from about 470 to 320 B.C. The historical record of Socrates is based not upon his writing, as he apparently did none, but rather upon the writings about him by Aristophanes, Xenophan, Aristotle, and most notably Plato. Socrates was first and foremost an Athenian, a courageous soldier in the Peloponnesian War pitting the city-states of Athens and Sparta against each other, and a very principled and practical person, although he himself was not preoccupied with the practicalities of daily life such as holding a secure job or maintaining a household (Craig et al., 1994; Urmson, 1960).

Socrates believed firmly in the power of human reason, and that by clear reasoning we can discover the enduring and universal reality behind sensory-based experiences. Reasoning rather than observation alone is the true instrument of science. Socrates encouraged the pursuit of not just knowledge of external objects and the world, but also knowledge of the self. Socrates challenges us to seek self-knowledge, which he believed would lead to virtue and in turn to a more harmonious world by making our actions consonant with our thoughts. Socrates championed authenticity based upon reason and introspection; he urged each of us to "Know Thyself," and believed an unexamined life was worthless.

Socrates believed that evil arises from ignorance, and knowledge of one's inner mental life would lead to a host of socially desirable behaviors. Thus, the social contract between society and the individual member is grounded in self-knowledge, which advances both the individual member and society (Smith, 1974). Knowledge of the self is the means by which the individual and society advance. The Socratic Method is a form of logical argumentation to reveal the truth regarding a particular issue. Socrates would ask for a definition of a term such as beauty or justice, then point out the limitations of the answer, ask for further clarification, and repeat this process until a clear and consistent answer which could not be questioned further was identified. He also gave us the reasoning tool of induction, which involves systematic and specific observations based upon serial questioning of assumptions and assertions.

Socrates challenged popular assumptions and ideas to seek clarity rather than to overthrow them. However, this strategy proved irritating to many conservative Athenians yet appealing to young Athenians who generally were attracted to ideals, integrity, intellectual potency, and inspiration. Ultimately, Socrates was tried on fabricated charges of corrupting the youth, denying the Greek gods, and attempting to establish new gods. He was found guilty and sentenced to death, mostly because of his unwillingness to compromise his views and appease his prosecutors. By this he showed his courage in the courtroom as he had done earlier on the battlefield.

Plato, in his magnificent *Phaedo*, describes the last few hours of the life of Socrates, who at age 70 announced to his faithful students and supporters that his time of departure had come, he then calmly drank the hemlock poison, walked briefly around the room reporting the effects of the poison, and then died.

Plato

Plato was born in Athens in 427 B.C., lived there most of his eighty years, was a student of Socrates, and he witnessed the devastating effects of the drawn out Peloponnesian War that reduced Athens from a population of 80,000 to 21,000 persons. When Plato was

27 years of age, Socrates was condemned to death by an Athenian court, and Plato, like many other students of Socrates, left Athens for a time for solace and the pursuit of new knowledge so as to restore a decent and just Athenian government (Craig et al., 1994; Roberts, 1995; Urmson, 1960).

Plato wrote in the literary style of **dialogue**, expressing his ideas in the form of conversations. Plato was an Idealist, according to which humans can think and by thinking alone one can discern the permanently real World of Ideas or Forms that exist behind the World of Appearances conveyed by our senses. In one of his finest dialogues, *The Republic*, Plato gives us the allegory or the myth of the cave to make plain the differences between the World of Appearances and the World of Ideas or Forms. In the dialogue, we encounter people who have been chained to a cave since childhood so that all they have ever seen is a continuously changing pattern of shadows dancing on a wall cast by a fire at the opening of the cave. Now when one of the cave dwellers is liberated and moves toward the light, he or she no longer sees shadows but experiences directly the permanent forms that give rise to the changing shadows. Thus, Plato gives us the foundational idea that access to the World of Ideas or Forms is by thinking rather than observation based solely upon sensory knowledge. For example, in a lifetime we may experience via our senses many different examples of a triangle all of which are imperfect compared to our grasping through thinking the Idea or Form of triangularity. Plato believed the psyche (*psuche*, Greek) or soul has mental properties and can also be thought of as mind. The soul or mind perceives, thinks, feels, and guides behaviors or actions. Plato thought the soul was influenced by rational as well as nonrational, animalistic, or asocial forces, and that the higher rational functions had to be constantly vigilant to keep the irrational forces in check. Plato structuralized the soul into three parts; the rational soul, the affective or feeling soul, and the appetitive soul. As is well known, this type of structural modeling of the psyche or mind was developed further by many subsequent scholars including most notably Sigmund Freud (1856–1939).

Plato founded an academy in Athens to educate potential ruler-philosophers about the way to access by rational means the World of Forms or Ideas. Plato died in 347 B.C.

Aristotle

Aristotle (384–322 B.C.) was born in Stagira in Macedonia; his father, Nichomachus, a physician, died when Aristotle was a young boy; and eventually, Aristotle, at the age of 17, was sent to Athens to study with Plato in the Academy, where he remained for twenty years. After the death of Plato in 347 B.C., Aristotle traveled in Asia Minor collecting information derived from the observations of beekeepers, fishermen, and hunters about the structures of many different mammals, fish, insects, birds, and the anatomy of humans. These activities, which were quite a departure from the rational approach of Plato's Academy, reflected Aristotle's faith in the importance of observation, classification, and then deduction of implications from specific observations. In 342 B.C., the young scholar returned to Macedonia to become the private tutor for King Philip's 13-year-old son who seven years later ascended to the throne of Macedonia and is known to us as Alexander the Great. Thereafter, Aristotle returned to Athens in 336 B.C., and established his own school known as the Lyceum. Here empirical observations were classified into categories with the intent of constructing an encyclopedia of human knowledge (Craig et al., 1994; Guthrie, 1960; Roberts, 1995; Urmson, 1960).

Aristotle is credited with writing about 170 books of which 47 still survive today. The range of topics is exceedingly broad, including biology, physics, ethics, psychology, rhetoric, and politics. In all fields, the method of inquiry was the same, namely, beginning with observations of empirical evidence followed by reasoned analysis for inconsistencies which were then explained by metaphysical principles. Unlike Plato, who believed that first or universal principles are identified by pure thought, Aristotle believed they were discovered by examining nature directly. Thus, for Plato, all knowledge existed independently of nature while for Aristotle nature and knowledge were inseparable. Aristotle's view on all matters, like that of Plato's, was teleological in that he believed that there is an inherent purposiveness within the processes of nature. Nature has a purpose—it is directed toward a goal. For Plato, purposes were found in the Ideas or Forms or transcendental concepts outside the experience of most people while for Aristotle the purposes of most things, *entelechy* (inherent purpose), are readily inferred by observation of their behaviors in the world.

Aristotle spent twelve years teaching at the Lyceum; married Pythias who became the mother of their two children, Pythias and Nicomachus; and ultimately became a sought-after public figure for whom knowledge and teaching were inseparable. When Alexander died in 323 B.C., funding of the Lyceum by the Macedonian king vanished, and Aristotle, because of his association with Alexander, was scorned by the Athenian "anti-Macedonians" who came into power. Aristotle remembered what happened to Socrates, saw the handwriting on the wall of public sentiment, and fled Athens, dying a few months later in 322 B.C. This marked the beginning of the end of the "Golden Era of Greece."

The most important of Aristotle's work for psychology is treated primarily in his book *De Anima* (*About the Soul*). Like other Greek philosophers, Aristotle believed the soul has a purpose (entelechy) which is to give life, and there were three different kinds of souls (Ross, 1931). The purpose of the vegetative soul is growth, namely, the pursuit of food and reproduction. The purposes of the sensitive soul, possessed by animals but not plants, include growth, responsiveness to the external environment, experiences of pleasure and pain, and memory. Lastly, the rational soul is possessed only by humans, includes the functions of the other two souls, and, most importantly, provides reasoning and thinking. Throughout history humans are separated from infrahumans or animals because it had been suggested and argued by Aristotle and many other philosophers that only humans were capable of rational thought such as problem solving. Today, we now know, based upon systematic observations and experimentation, that this distinction is more a matter of degree (continuous) than kind (discontinuous) between humans and infrahumans.

Aristotle believed there were five senses that provide the gateway to the mind: vision, audition, taste, smell, and touch, from which all experience is constructed. In addition, he believed there was a second-order common sense, *sensus communis*, that synthesized the sensory data into meaningful perceptions. Our memory and imagination allowed us to recombine the sensory data and preserve them as ideas.

Aristotle also wrote about imagination and dreaming. Images arise from sensations, they long outlast the physical or sensory stimuli, and the retention of the images constitutes memory. The images are the linkage between sensation and rational thought with the images acted upon by reason. Active reason abstracts principles or true knowledge from the synthesized experience of *sensus communis* while passive reason uses the synthesized experiences for adapting to situations in everyday life. Dreaming arises from the images of past experience, which are activated by events inside or outside of the body such as digesting a meal while sleeping or a loud noise or sound, respectively. Most of our dreams are about prior experiences while some vivid dreams might suggest a future course of action. Aristotle suggested that we pay attention to our dreams.

The Golden Age of Greece ended with the death of Aristotle in 322 B.C., and was followed by the philosophies of the Roman Period with Rome as a powerful global force from about 300 B.C. to A.D. 476. Around A.D. 200, Rome had a population of about one million while the expanding Roman Empire, which spanned from England to Africa, had a population of 50 to 100 million people.

ROMAN PHILOSOPHIES

The Roman philosophies of stoicism, epicureanism, skepticism, and Neoplatonism focused primarily upon identifying guidelines on how to live a good life, unlike Greek philosophy that focused upon cosmological issues of the origin and nature of the universe or epistemological issues of the nature and validity of human knowledge (Craig et al., 1994; Russell, 1945).

The Stoics stressed living a simple life, accepting one's fate with indifference, and the emptiness of material possessions; they considered courage in the face of suffering or danger as most admirable. Epicureanism stressed that our earthly life is all we have and is not followed by life after death. For the Epicurean, we must attain the good life now by seeking moderation in all things and avoiding extremes such as intense pleasures which are usually followed by intense pain. Skepticism rejected the notion of true knowledge or universal truths suggesting instead that all we can know with some certainty are our individual experiences and opinions. Thus, for the Skeptic, it is best to live a simple life by adapting to the social customs or practices wherever we live—be practical and pragmatic, or "when in Rome do as the Romans do." The Neoplatonists, led by Plotinus (A.D. 204–270), revised the work of Plato emphasizing the mysticism and the World of Ideas or Forms central to Platoism.

For the Neoplatonists, the physical or sensory world, although beautiful at times as reflected in art, music, and attractive people, was constantly changing. Conversely, it was only when we accessed the Other World of Ideas and Forms by meditation and withdrawal from the physical world that we would experience changeless principles or truths and lasting bliss. Neoplatonism is important because it pointed to the similarities between Judaism, Christianity, and early Greek philosophy that stressed the inherent corruption of the pursuit of only material goods and pleasures, the problem of evil, and the presence of a higher other World known to the soul that could be accessed by faith or reason. Neoplatonism combined religion and philosophy, which served as a model throughout the balance of the Roman Period and for centuries beyond into the Middle Ages, covering the period from the fall of Rome to the start of the Renaissance (400–1400).

The fall of Rome around A.D. 400 was a consequence of a variety of forces including a geographically expanding empire that required enormous resources for the Roman army which in turn strained the economic, ethical, and political systems of the entire Roman enterprise, especially the city of Rome. Another important contributor to the fall of Rome was the tensions between Rome and the Christian Church, which leads us directly from primarily rational philosophies to the second stage of the philosophical and religious revolutions of the four river valley civilizations, namely, the establishment of Christianity and Islam.

CHRISTIANITY

Christianity arose from a remote province of the Roman Empire, stirred the hearts and provided hope to poor people, and was opposed by the established religious institutions and the sophisticated philosophies of the educated classes of the Roman Empire. In addition, Christianity was also opposed by the imperial government of Rome and followers were persecuted so as to suppress the challenges to established religious and political practices. Eventually, Christianity, once despised and feared, became the official religion of the then mightiest empire of the world (Craig et al., 1994). The Catholic religion is the largest of the different denominations of Christianity with approximately 650 million Catholics worldwide and almost two thirds of all of contemporary Christianity made up of Catholics.

The Christian Church or the fellowship of the faithful arose from the teachings of Jesus of Nazareth, and then those of Saul (A.D. 5–67), later known as the apostle Paul following his conversion from Judaism to Christianity on the road outside of Damascus. In large measure, Paul, based upon his faith in Jesus Christ, was a pivotal person who solidified the establishment of the Christian Church in Rome known then and today as the Roman Catholic Church. The Roman Catholic Church continued to grow, eventually dominated the European region of the Roman Empire, and later separated into the Western and Eastern factions with headquarters in Rome and Constantinople, respectively. One of the major differences between these factions was that the Western Church recognized the pope as the only and infallible leader of the Church while the Eastern Church recognized four patriarchs as the leaders of the Church. Eventually, the Great Schism or divide arose and the two movements separated and became the Roman Catholic Church and the Eastern or Greek Orthodox Church.

The historical Jesus of Nazareth was born around 4 B.C. and died by crucifixion probably in A.D. 30. Jesus was born into a modest Jewish family and developed into an extremely effective teacher. Jesus was not a philosopher but rather a simple man who encouraged people to follow the wisdom of their experiences, informed primarily by their heart rather than exclusively by books and sophisticated philosophies (Brett, 1965).

Jesus had increasing success, especially among the poor, with his teachings framed mostly as parables or stories and sayings, and as his reputation grew so did suspicion of him among the upper classes. In violation of then existing attitudes and gender-biased practices which forbade talking or even looking at women in public, Jesus spoke to women in public and included them in his teaching sessions and also as travel companions in his moving entourage. Likewise, his criticism of then current religious practices annoyed the religious establishment. Eventually, the Roman governor, Pontius Pilate, was inclined to think of Jesus and his followers as dangerous revolutionaries, and consequently Jesus was put to death by crucifixion in Jerusalem in an attempt to promote a more stable social order in accord with the then prevailing political, religious, and social codes (Roberts, 1995).

Christianity grew swiftly during the period of A.D. 300 to 600, especially after the conversion to Christianity of the Roman Emperor Constantine who in 324 appointed himself the sole emperor of the reunited Roman Empire. Constantine built the new city of Constantinople on the site of the city of Byzantium making it the new capital of the Roman Empire rather than Rome, and in so doing fortified the eastern boundaries of the Empire. Historically, Constantinople served as the shield for the old Graeco-Roman world of the Mediterranean and Western Christendom to protect it against invasion by the Persians and the spread of Islam into Western Europe.

An extremely important spokesman for the Church was St. Augustine (354–430) or Aurelius Augustinus. Augustine was educated in the law, rhetoric, and philosophy; he taught in Milan, returned to his birthplace of Hippo in northern Africa (modern Tunisia), and became a bishop of the Christian Church in 396 (Urmson, 1960). Initially, Augustine wanted to separate the fates of the Roman Empire and Christianity. According to Augustine, in his book *City of God*, the Roman Empire represented the terrestrial or earthly City of Man which was evil and doomed to destruction while the latter, the heavenly City of God (Christianity) was good, immortal, and was populated by all the saints on earth and in heaven. Augustine stressed that Christian faith is essential for salvation but not a substitute for reason, which is the foundation of classical Greek philosophy. His writings focused upon the tension between the forces of faith and reason, and marked the beginning as well as the dominant philosophical force of the medieval period of history or the Middle Ages (400–1450).

In his classic autobiography *Confessions*, written about 400, Augustine describes his worldly youth and intense bodily appetites which, while consistently fulfilled, still yielded a lack of personal peace and deeper meaning to life until his conversion to Christianity in 387 (Outler, 1955). Augustine believed that humans have free will, and, therefore, responsibility for their affect or feelings, behaviors, or cognitions or thoughts so we can choose between evil or good, which are direct outcomes of our decision-making process. Thus, the locus of control for behavior is shifted from external forces such as the emperors and other authority figures to internal forces shaped by knowledge derived from both reason and faith for, although reason without faith is possible, it is incomplete. According to Augustine, contemplating God can give rise to a sense of unsurpassed joy and peace and this emotional experience can serve as the referent for evaluating all other experiences. Thus, anything that promotes experiences of comparable joy and peace is good while, if not, then such actions and experiences are evil. Faith and emotions were then considered the guides to true knowledge and leading a good life. Augustinian philosophy requires that facts fit faith and any that do not are suspect, totally ignored, or suppressed. We now turn to another global religion that also struggled with the reconciliation of the forces of faith and reason.

ISLAM

The Middle Ages spanned from about 400 to 1450. The period from about 430, marked by the death of Augustine, to about 1000 is known as the Dark Ages because Greek and Roman books were lost or destroyed and there were no substantial advances in Europe in science, philosophy, or the arts. With the final fall of Rome around 500, there arose many small villages which were ruled by local customs rather than uniform Roman law. As a consequence, the Roman Catholic Church quickly became the voice of authority rather than Roman law for unifying the villages of Western Europe. Dogma dominated, and until the end of the first millenium the Western world was unable to see and acknowledge the realities of the earthly world. Western Europe was on hold while some parts of the world were active and alive with a new religion and framework for understanding the human experience.

Islam, which means submission or surrender to the will of God, is the last of the religious revolutions to arise out of the early river valley civilizations (Figure 4-2), and originated in the city of Mecca in now Saudi Arabia. Arabs considered this the center of pilgrimage for the veneration of the **Ka'aba** or a black meteoric stone from the heavens, and continue today to make pilgrimages to Mecca (Craig et al., 1994; Roberts, 1995). Muhammad ibn Abd Allah (570–632), the founder of Islam, considered himself only the messenger of God rather than a deity. Muhammad was orphaned at age 6, raised most likely by his grandfather, and eventually married a wealthy widow which allowed him to become a tradesman and to experience the growing moral and social unrest of Mecca. Muhammad, an introspective man, reflected on the increasingly worldly ways of his hometown by retreating for a month during the summer to a cave outside Mecca. One day, in the cave, when Muhammad was about 40 years of age he heard the word of Allah spoken to him by the angel Gabriel. As he continued to receive spiritual messages or short passages of inspiration from Allah, Muhammad was instructed to carry the messages first to the people of Mecca and then everywhere throughout the world. Muhammad was faithful to the command of Allah and he indeed carried the messages for the remaining twenty-two years of his life. Muhammad collected the sacred messages from Allah into chapters with the rest written after his death, and they formed the book of Islam known as the **Koran** which means recitation (Lester, 1999). The Koran is believed to be the actual word of God revealed to the Prophet Muhammad with parts of it comparable to the Bible and Talmud containing stories about the prior prophets of God such as Abraham, Moses, and Jesus. The Koran is divided into seven chapters with sixty-six sections known as *suras*.

Persons who believe in Allah and accept Muhammad as his Prophet are Muslims or Moslems, meaning ones who submit to God. As Islam grew throughout the Middle East, Africa, Spain, and southeastern Europe, it was necessary to discern the will of God from the perspective of the community which often faced local or situational problems different from those addressed by the Koran alone. Accordingly, local Muslim leaders studied best how to apply Koranic instructions to local situations, and as a consequence Islam divided into two major sections, the Sunnite (regard the first four caliphs or spiritual leaders as legitimate successors to Muhammad), consisting of about 90% of all Muslims, and the Shiite, who regard Ali the son-in-law of Muhammad and one of the four caliphs as the legitimate successor. Today, Islam is the most widespread religion on Earth, claiming a billion members in fifty countries with ten to fifteen million Muslims in the United States and Europe.

The Koran contains the Five Pillars of Faith that include belief in one God (Allah), angels, many prophets but only one message, judgment, and dignity arising from knowledge of God. The Five Pillars of Observance are presented in Table 4-4. Islam is not just a religion but a total way of life so that the sacred is not separated from the secular. Learning is promoted and encouraged, especially learning about oneself. Likewise, hard work and determination are important for psychological, spiritual, and physical health, "Nobody is better spoken than a good doer." The Koran teaches that Allah is just and merciful and that by doing good works, repenting, and purifying oneself by following the Five Pillars of Faith and Observance one can lead a good life and achieve eternal salvation in heaven. According to tradition, the Prophet Muhammad said it is better that women should pray at home rather than in Muslim mosques. In general, Jewish and Christian women have throughout history enjoyed relatively more freedom than Muslim women, although all three religions are basically patriarchical or male dominated. A mosque in Jerusalem, the Dome of the Rock, is considered to be the

TABLE 4-4	The Five Pillars of Observance of Islam

- **Shahada** or the creed—"There is no God but Allah and Muhammad is His prophet."
- **Salat** or prayer—While facing Mecca, the five compulsory daily prayers are said at dawn, noon, afternoon, sunset, and nightfall.
- **Zakat** or charity—An obligation and an act of worship amounting to giving to the poor approximately 2.5% of one's income or valuables.
- **Siyam** or fasting—An opportunity to practice restraint.
- **Hajj** or pilgrimage—All Muslims, unless ill or impoverished, are required to journey to Mecca at least once in their life.

place from which Muhammad ascended into heaven at the end of his earthly life. Within 100 years of the death of Muhammad, the Muslim Empire included a larger area than the Roman Empire and as a consequence Arab philosophers came in contact with the great works of classical Greece and Rome with a special focus on the works of Aristotle. By utilizing this knowledge, the Arabs made great progress in applied knowledge in medicine, science, and mathematics as well as philosophy, including the work of Avicenna (980–1037) and Averröes (1126–1198).

Islamic Science and Philosophy

Avicenna was a great Islamic scientist and scholar, author of up to 100 books on topics in science and philosophy, and most famous for his book on medicine, *The Canon*, which was used in European universities for 500 years up until about 1650 (Gordon, 1959). Avicenna attempted to reconcile the forces of faith and reason, particularly the theology of Islam with the science of Aristotle, similar to what Maimonides (1135–1204) would do for Jewish and St. Thomas Aquinas (1225–1274) for Christian intellectual histories, respectively. In his medical practice, Avicenna believed both physical and mental illness were due to imbalances of humors or bile similar to Galen (129–199), the great Greek physician. Unlike Aristotle, who believed humans had three internal senses, common sense, imagination, and memory, Avicenna believed we had seven internal senses starting with common sense which in accord with Aristotle's views synthesized information provided by the five external senses. However, unlike Aristotle, Avicenna believed that the active intellect, the highest of the seven internal senses, allowed us to enter into a relationship with God rather than understand universal principles based upon observing empirical events. Reason and faith are compatible rather than mutually exclusive. Avicenna, in accord with Islamic teachings, believed the soul lives on after the body dies. Avicenna died in 1037.

Averröes (1126–1198) was an active Islamic scholar like Avicenna who, although a physician, focused upon philosophy especially the integration of faith and reason (Tsanoff, 1964). Unlike Avicenna, Averröes taught that all human experiences provide knowledge of God rather than such knowledge arising only from the process of reason of the active intellect. Averröes commented extensively upon Aristotle's philosophy, and like him believed the soul dies with the body. However, like Aristotle, he believed that only the active intellect survives death, and because the active intellect is like a collective intellect no personal experiences and memories survive death. Averröes is most important for advocating that reason and faith can be independent as well as complementary of each other, a belief that was incompatible with orthodox Islamic as well as Christian teachings of his time.

JUDAIC PHILOSOPHERS

Lastly, before we enter the final phase of the Middle Ages, which set the stage for the Renaissance around 1450, we treat briefly the work of Maimonides and some Christian philosophers who were inspired by their Arabian colleagues to reconcile faith and reason so as to bring back Aristotlean philosophy to the Western world and most importantly set the stage for the reemergence of science in Europe.

Maimonides (1135–1204) was an influential Jewish philosopher and physician educated by Arabian teachers (Craig et al., 1994; Urmson, 1960). Maimonides wrote *The Guide for the Perplexed* (1190), which attempted to reconcile the forces of reason or science and faith or religion, which were aimed initially at educated Jews caught in the enduring intellectual dilemma between rationalism based on critical thinking and religious tradition based on authority and revelation. *The Guide* enjoyed broad appeal, was used in European universities, and basically argued that ancient scriptual texts such as the Talmud, Bible, and Koran presented truths about life and were intended primarily for the uneducated and simple-minded. Maimonides argued that God, reason, and truth are inseparable, so that truth revealed through reason is from God and such truth is as sacred as the truths revealed by the great texts. Thus, conflict between reason and faith arise when the reader takes scriptural stories too literally rather than seeing them as illustrative teaching texts. Maimonides legitimized the value of reason. Eventually, Maimonides was considered suspect by hard-line Jewish, Christian, and Islamic clerics, although fortunately his work contributed substantially to the impending scientific revolution of the Renaissance less than 250 years after Maimonides' death in 1204.

The Crusades, which started around the beginning of the 11th century, were initiated by the Christians in Europe with the intent of reclaiming the Holy Land from the Muslims and culminated in the fall of Constantinople on May 29, 1453 to the Osmanli Turks (later known as Ottomans) led by the Ottoman Sultan, Mehmet II, who defeated Constantine XI (Craig et al., 1994; Garraty & Gay, 1981; Roberts, 1995). The Crescent of Islam then flew over Byzantium which replaced the Cross which had flown over Christian Constantinople, and most importantly this urban conflict divided Europe into western and eastern factions, a division based in large part upon the dictates of religious beliefs, which continues right up to the present moment. Thus, we see today that Christianity, Judaism, and Islam all make claims upon the City of Jerusalem as their city based upon their sacred histories. Despite all the hideous horrors and travesties against humanity in the name of religion rather than reason, the Crusades brought the West back in contact with Greek and Roman classics, especially Aristotle and the forces of reason, as the basis for understanding the human experience. The return of reason made it necessary for some scholars of the Roman Catholic Church to reconcile and harmonize the forces of faith and reason. The destructive potential of unchecked religious systems is clearly visible in the many lives that have been lost over the centuries as well as in the many people around the world today who are involved in conflict around a mix of religious, economic, and cultural issues and claims.

SCHOLASTICISM: THOMAS AQUINAS AND WILLIAM OF OCCAM

Scholasticism is the synthesis of Aristotelian philosophy with Christian dogma which began with the book *Faith Seeking Understanding,* written by St. Anselm (1033–1109), which attempted to employ reason to support religious belief. Peter Abelard (1079–1142), a brilliant philosopher and widely acclaimed teacher in Paris, challenged the Catholic Church as well as social convention because of his passionate love of philosophy and Héloïse the young niece of the church official Fulbert, respectively (Grane, 1970). In his book *Sic et Non* (*Yes and No*), Abelard posed well over 100 theological questions addressed by his dialectic method which highlighted the inconsistencies of the answers to these questions provided by Scripture and theologians. Thus, he believed it was possible to get to the truth of a matter or at least see both sides of an issue by examining arguments and counterarguments. Abelard's intent was not to overthrow Church dogma, but rather to point out by reason that one would conclude inevitably that God existed thus aligning faith and reason as ways of knowing God and the natural world as well. As Abelard's reputation as a teacher grew, he secured an appointment at Notre Dame Cathedral in Paris where, when he was 42 years old, he met and fell in love with 17-year-old Héloïse, the niece of Fulbert. They had a child, were secretly married, and eventually Abelard was castrated by Fulbert, who felt betrayed by Abelard, to whom he had entrusted Héloïse for tutoring. Fulbert and others had considered Abelard to be the greatest teacher in all of Paris. Ultimately, Abelard became a monk and Héloïse a nun, separated from each other and living out their lives in loneliness. This was quite the counterpoint or dialectic of how they began their lives together in the early part of their relationship.

St. Thomas Aquinas (1225–1274) was educated first at the University of Naples and then by Albertus Magnus (1193–1280) in Cologne, Germany. Albertus Magnus was a major Aristotelian scholar, was among the first since the Greeks (well over a 1,000 years earlier!) to make detailed observations of nature, and he made noteworthy contributions to the field of botany. However, it was primarily St. Thomas Aquinas who brought back Aristotelian philosophy and science to the West by arguing that reason and faith are compatible (Coplestone, 1962; Gerard, 1966). All ways of knowing, whether from reason, revelation, scripture, introspection, or observation of nature, led to knowledge of God. Aquinas' view was also known as the **doctrine of double truths**. This doctrine states that something can be true in rational philosophy but false in religious belief because faith and reason are separate ways of knowing and, for some, philosophy is the highest form of knowing. This fusion between the rationalism of philosophy and the dogma of theology created a double truth that could be grasped by the general public; thus, Aquinas was responsible for the coherent synthesis of the doctrine in which the strength of a faith was indicated by its relativity to empirical science (Hourani, 1961). In effect, St. Thomas' work eventually led to the separate study of faith or theology and reason or philosophy and indicated that it was possible to argue and debate Church dogma without the ultimate loss of one's faith. The foundational idea that the study of natural phenomena on Earth could go forward without eroding faith and a focus on the world beyond set the stage for the Renaissance.

The work of William of Occam or Ockham (1290–1350), a Franciscan monk, was the final leap to reason that takes us to the Renaissance. Occam asserted that universal ideas (e.g., dog) do not exist independent of the empirical awareness of a specific object (a dog) but that such universal ideas exist in name only (nominalism), unlike realism that holds that there are universal ideas that, like Plato's Forms or Ideas, lie behind specific perceptions. Occam said we can trust our senses to inform us of the real nature of the world without recourse to believing there is some supernatural world that is manifested in our perceptions. Therefore, explanations of our experiences need be based on the fewest assumptions possible without reference to the supernatural; thus, **Occam's razor or the principle of parsimony**, that is, the fewer the assumptions when explaining a phenomenon or object the better.

THE RENAISSANCE: THE PLACE AND THE PEOPLE

Very little, in history or in life in general, happens neatly, and, accordingly, our treatment of the Renaissance, like the historical developments to date and to follow, is based upon finding threads that connect together places, people, and events probably more so than they were in the reality of their time. Renaissance means "rebirth," and the Renaissance stands as the transition from the medieval to the modern period of history. The Renaissance was about a rebirth or a liberation from old ways of feeling, behaving, and thinking and a search for new codes of conduct and thought. There was an increasing growth of an "attitude of curiosity" based upon human reason focused upon articulating humanity's place in the world of the living, the here and now, rather than focusing upon the possibility and nature of life after death.

The Renaissance covers the period from about 1450 to 1600, and was centered especially in Italy and the city of Florence (Craig et al., 1994; Garraty & Gay, 1981; Roberts, 1995). It was primarily about a vigorous questioning of the acceptance of Church as well as Aristotelian received dogmas with the latter fully incorporated into Christian teachings as a result of Scholasticism. The Renaissance was a period of individual agency in which there was an enhanced belief in the power of the individual to add value to the world. Belief in the power of the individual gave rise to a spirit of optimism which, in general, encouraged people to take chances, explore, and discover their humanity and the world in which they lived; this spirit had been previously suppressed by the sole reliance upon the dogma of the Church and Scholasticism as the sources of all knowledge.

Although it is difficult to identify one single place, person, or event that marks clearly the actual beginning of the Renaissance, most would agree that the establishment of European universities provided the intellectual infrastructure for the Renaissance. The first European university was the University of Bologna established in 1119, followed by the universities of Paris, Oxford, Cambridge, and others in France and Portugal. The initial curricula included theology, law, and medicine, which were soon complemented by the liberal arts. The universities provided the fertile grounds for learning about the world, humanity, and ideas that eventually challenged the dogma of the Church and Scholarticism.

Francesco Petrarch

Many consider the writings of Francesco Petrarch (1304–1374) as the beginning of the Renaissance or the transition from the medieval to the modern period of history (Kristeller, 1967). Petrarch focused upon freeing the human spirit from Scholasticism, which fused together religion and Aristotelian rationalism thus making religion too much of a rational rather than a rich spiritual experience. Petrarch promoted the rebirth of a personal Christianity like that advocated by St. Augustine, which was based upon the Bible, personal faith, and personal feelings. Petrarch also argued that life on earth is as important as life after death, and thus must be lived fully and freed from the chains of dogma.

Martin Luther

Martin Luther (1483–1546), a German monk, member of the Augustinian order of the Roman Catholic Church, and biblical scholar, started the Reformation in 1517 when he nailed his ninety-five theses to the castle church in Wittenberg while a professor at the local university (Craig et al., 1994; Roberts, 1995). Luther tapped into German resentment toward the Roman Catholic Church for the practices of tithing or the requirement that a Church member give one tenth or twelfth of her or his resources to the Church with the threat of excommunication or eternal damnation used as leverage for failure to pay up. In addition to raising money by tithing for the construction and maintenance of St. Peter's Cathedral in Rome, the Church also instituted the practice of indulgences by which, for contributions of money, the pope assured such faithful that they would get time off in Purgatory, then considered a temporary way station of the after-world for cleansing of the soul before final passage to heaven. Luther was also upset with the uneven education of the clergy of the Roman Catholic Church while his most robust challenge to the Church focused upon the blind and unquestionable acceptance and buttressing of dogma. Luther did not want to start a new church; rather, he wanted to reform Catholic dogma and practices. Eventually, as a consequence of his continuing protests, he was excommunicated from the Roman Catholic Church in 1520 and became the leader of **Protestantism**. Protestants denied the authority of the pope, and believed each individual had the capacities and the right to interpret the Bible for herself or himself. This belief was advanced significantly when the Bible was translated from Latin into the German vernacular. The elevation of individual conscience and judgment for determining appropriate conduct and thought rather than relying upon the interpretations of the intermediaries or clergy of the Roman Catholic Church was indeed revolutionary and added further fuel to the Renaissance.

Niccolò Machiavelli

Italy, during the Renaissance, was a land of autonomous city-states that cooperated with each other to gain strength in numbers as reflected, for example, in the Treaty of Ledi (1454–1455), which brought Milan, Naples, and Florence into a military alliance. Later, in 1494, Naples, with the support of Florence, prepared to attack Milan which in turn sought a new political alignment with France. This began the invasion of Italy by first the French and then Spanish and German armies. Like Francesco Petrarch, Niccolò Machiavelli (1469–1527) was interested in human nature and the forces that govern human actions and thoughts, especially group behaviors based upon the exercise of power (Craig et al., 1994; Gilbert, 1967; Wood, 1968). Machiavelli, the founder of the discipline of political science, was born of a poor family in Florence, was educated in the humanities, secured an appointment as a bureaucrat in the Florentine government, and became an effective administrator. In short, he learned how to get things done in an organization by observing and studying the use of power, leadership, and authority. He sought, like the humanists, to explain social behavior using objective methods of observation rather than moralistic and theological principles.

Machiavelli wrote *The Prince* and *The Discourses* in 1513. In *The Prince*, he argued that in almost all cases when efficiency, practicality, and the common good are the goals these goals then supercede moral principles as ends in themselves. Getting things done is more important than rigid moral concerns about how they get done. In *The Discourses*, Machiavelli praised democracy and believed that socialization and suggestibility are forces that can be harnessed by the effective leader to shape individual and group behaviors. He identified both positive and negative features of human nature, observed that religion can be used as a powerful tool to promote unity, and that the effective leader uses religion to assuage fear of the unknown.

RENAISSANCE SCIENCE

The Spanish Inquisition began in 1478, and was essentially the brutal and myopic attempt to impose Catholicism as the only true religion upon all the people of Spain and other parts of Europe. The Inquisition was basically about the Roman Catholic Church's efforts to suppress alternative views of humanity and the world, which were based not upon Church dogma but rather upon observation and reason championed during the Renaissance. The rationale for the Inquisition was grounded in the belief held by the then all-powerful clergy that the Roman Catholic Church was founded by the Son of God, Jesus Christ, and the institution of Church was the earthly reflection of God despite the human foibles and failings of some of the clergy. Therefore, the Roman Catholic Church had to be defended at all costs including severe persecution and death to those who challenged the foundational doctrines and teachings of the Church.

Nicolas Copernicus

Renaissance science opened new perspectives on human nature and the world such that humans were considered more and more as a part of, rather than apart from, the natural world. The Renaissance scientists established the foundation of modern science, although many times at a high personal price because of the Church's resistance to change and reluctance to give up power and influence over the minds of the people.

The scientific enterprise of the Renaissance began with the work of Nicolas Copernicus (1473–1543), a devout Roman Catholic priest (Craig et al., 1994). Copernicus, in his book *On the Revolution of the Celestial Spheres*, published within a week of his death, argued that the earth revolved around the sun (Heliocentric theory) rather than the sun revolving around the earth (Geocentric theory). The Geocentric theory, also known as Ptolemy's theory, dominated Western thought for about 1,300 years because it was compatible with Church doctrine, which considered humanity and the earth as the center of the universe around which all other things revolved.

Galileo Galilei

Next came Galileo Galilei (1564–1642), who first studied medicine at the University of Pisa, then changed to the study of mathematics and physics, and was awarded a chair in mathematics at the University of Padua, Italy, in 1592 (Craig et al., 1994). Galileo improved upon the optical power of the telescope invented earlier in Holland, which allowed him and others who dared to look into the telescope to observe directly the movement of celestial bodies around the sun rather than the earth. Galileo also observed that the planet Jupiter had four moons, indicating that there were at least eleven (11) bodies in the solar system instead of seven (7) as believed by the Church. Galileo also observed that all earthly objects fall at the same rate of speed, challenging Aristotle's belief that heavy objects fall faster than lighter objects. In fact, Galileo made plain that movement of any body in the heavens or on the earth obeyed physical laws which could be derived through observation and experimentation. For Galileo, once a law was discovered no further experimental observations were necessary because mathematical deductions could describe all specific examples of the law.

Galileo distinguished sharply between the physical world and the subjective world of experiences with the former governed by laws and existing independent of anyone's experience of physical reality. Features of the physical world were later called primary qualities and included quantity, shape, size, position, and motion. According to Galileo, the subjective world consisted of perceived or secondary qualities and included color, temperature, smell, and sound, none of which were stable or behaved lawfully. Thus, only the physical world could be studied scientifically, which forced thinkers of his time to consider human conscious experience as secondary to the physical world and beyond the reach of scientific inquiry.

In 1611, Galileo was invited to the Pontifical Court in Rome to demonstrate his telescope and to present his observations using the telescope. Within five years, in 1616, Galileo was invited back to Rome to face charges of heresy, and although not found guilty he was ordered by the Church to stop promoting the Copernican theory of the universe (White, 1896/1910). Galileo published his *Dialogue Concerning the Two Chief World Systems—Ptolemaic and Copernican* in 1632, which advocated Copernican rather than Church doctrine. As a consequence he was recalled to Rome, forced to kneel before a panel of cardinals, and mandated to deny all he believed in based upon his careful observations and experiments over the years. Thereafter, he was confined, away from family and friends, and died in 1642. Both Galileo's *Dialogue* and Copernicus' *Revolutions* were placed on the Church's Index of Forbidden Books. Science in service of religion or politics comes at a very high price, including extreme pressures to deny one's personal views of the physical and social worlds. In the end, as you know, Copernican theory won out and set the stage for the beginning of the modern period in which science predominated and in many ways started to take the place of religion as the cardinal way of knowing about the world and humanity.

Isaac Newton

Isaac Newton (1642–1727) believed that the universe is a lawful machine created by God which, when studied objectively, affords further knowledge of God, thus aligning faith and reason as comparable ways of knowing (Craig et al., 1994). Newton is perhaps best known for his law of gravitation, which grew out of the earlier work of Galileo, according to which *all* objects in the universe attract each other. This single law explained the motion of all bodies everywhere in the universe; it made plain that science can unlock the secrets of the natural world and is a cumulative enterprise in that scientific findings, when added up over time, can yield a more complete understanding of the world and the place of humanity in the world.

Francis Bacon

Francis Bacon (1561–1626) was born in London, educated at Cambridge University, admitted to the bar in 1575, elected in 1584 to the British Parliament or House of Commons, and advanced rapidly in the legal and political professions until 1621 when he was accused of taking bribes from some of his clients (Boorstin, 1998; Craig et al., 1994). He was then deprived of further political office, and, accordingly, intensified his activities as a commentator upon the state of human knowledge, published his major work *Novum Organum* (*New Instrument of the Mind*) in 1621, and died in 1626 while collecting data on the preservative effects of freezing chickens by packing them with snow. Bacon's primary contribution to the philosophical foundations of psychology was in the area of scientific methodology.

Unlike Galileo, who sought general principles or laws based upon a science of deduction (the general to the specific), Bacon advocated a science built upon induction or a series of specific observations of nature without any preconceived views or theories of nature or the intended observations. Bacon believed that science would be most accurate going from specific observations to generalizations (induction) rather than from generalizations or universals that didn't necessarily always involve observations of specific empirical events (deduction). For Bacon, the way of knowing truth is observation without any preconceived expectations or theories.

Bacon believed that scientific knowledge provided understanding of phenomena and could also improve the world and humanity. Accordingly, by first understanding from **experimenta lucifera** (experiments of light) and then by **experimenta fructifera** (experiments of fruit), science can indicate how understanding of causal relationships can be applied, providing both types of experiments involved direct observation. Thus, Baconian inductive methodology can explain events in our natural world and improve the well-being of humanity in this world rather than the anticipated after life, which had never been directly observed but only constructed upon the many assumptions and arguments without empirically based experimentation or observation.

We are indebted to Francis Bacon, who gave us the foundational idea of the importance of systematic observation as the way of knowing about the world and humanity. The universe and humanity are what we discover through our observations and "humanity is a part of rather than apart from the world." Accordingly, if there is to be a science of humanity then it must be grounded in systematic and specific observation of our affective, behavioral, and cognitive systems.

THE MODERN PERIOD: RENÉ DESCARTES

The last person we encounter on this long historical odyssey focused upon the history of ways of knowing is René Descartes (1596–1650). Descartes was born in La Haye (now called La Haye–Descartes), a small town near Tours, France (Boorstein, 1998; Urmson, 1960). His mother died of tuberculosis within a year of his birth, and his father, a wealthy lawyer, provided a lifelong stipend for Descartes so he could be freed from the necessity to work for a living and instead love to work. Descartes was a child of frail health, and as a consequence his formal education began when he was 8 years old when he was enrolled in a Jesuit School at La Flèche, graduating eight years later at the age of 16.

In 1616, Descartes earned a law degree from the University of Poitiers, fulfilling his family's hope that he would follow in his father's footsteps and become a lawyer, although he was not interested in practicing the law. As a consequence, Descartes traveled to Holland to serve as a soldier and then to other parts of Western Europe and eventually returned to France to live in St. Germain, a suburb of Paris. There he enjoyed for a time the attractions of the city including dancing, socializing, gambling, and walking through the Palace Gardens of St. Germain while observing the new and captivating statues that seemingly moved automatically as an observer approached them, much like the electronically guided statues we see today in some of the theme parks around the world.

In November 1619, at the age of 23, Descartes was earnestly seeking a direction in life, and when he arose from a dream-filled sleep he was led to it. He dedicated his life to determining what knowledge was beyond doubt through the formulation of an analytical geometry and the establishment of a philosophical system grounded in mathematics and rationalism. Although always a person inclined to worldly pleasures, Descartes now concentrated more and more on the life of the mind.

In his *Discours de la Méthode* (*Discourse on Method*), published in 1637, Descartes began by rejecting all dogma, authority, and everything else except that of which he was absolutely certain, including those ideas that he claimed were indubitable or intrinsically incapable of being doubtful. He identified four rules for determining certainty in any area of inquiry, which included (a) trust your doubt so as to accept as true only those clear and distinct ideas about which you have absolutely no doubt, (b) divide big problems into smaller parts to promote a series of small wins, (c) begin by first fully understanding simple ideas and then move to more complex ideas in an orderly step-like fashion, and, lastly, (d) enumerate all elements of the problem and review them again to be without doubt that nothing was left out. As is well known, Descartes' use of the above four rules or guidelines to find truth found his starting point for certainty in himself, which is reflected in one of the great one-liners of philosophy: "**Cogito, ergo sum**," "I think, therefore I am," or "**Dubito, ergo sum**," "I doubt, therefore I am." In other words, the only thing of which he could be certain was his own doubting, which is thinking, which requires a thinker.

Descartes believed only humans had a mind, although many behaviors of both humans and infrahumans (animals) could be explained based upon strictly mechanical principles. For Descartes, the mind is unextended, free, and a nonmaterial set of processes or functions rather than a thing, while the body is limited, extended, and made up of substance. Many human bodily systems are governed by mechanical principles, including the respiratory, circulatory, and even the nervous system. Descartes compared the nervous system of humans and animals to the hidden hydraulic system that was responsible for the surprising and pleasant movement of various statues in the Gardens of the Palace at St. Germain. These wonderful mechanical statues operated by hydraulic pressure so that when a visitor stepped on a pressure plate in a walkway the increased water pressure caused the movement of the statues. Accordingly, Descartes thought the nervous system was made up of hollow tubes containing delicate threads that connected the sense receptors to the brain. The alleged threads were connected to the ventricles or cavities of the brain which were filled with animal spirits. Thus, sensory stimulation such as a candle flame brought near to one's finger caused increasing tension in the threads from the finger and hand to the brain, which in turn caused activation of the animal spirits or then imagined energy forces which flowed through nerves to the appropriate muscles so that the finger is automatically pulled away from the flame before being severely burned.

According to Descartes, automatic bodily movement not supervised or determined by conscious awareness of the mind is an example of **undulatio reflexa**. This foundational idea, the theory of reflex action, is the basis of 20th-century stimulus-response psychology, according to which an external object (a stimulus) yields inevitably an involuntary response. Some bodily actions are automatic, indicating that the body can operate in some spheres without direct involvement of mind, which was considered as essential for all bodily involvement. Mind and body interact and Descartes strengthened the role of the body in the mind–body interaction. According to Descartes, the relationship between mind and body is not unidirectional in which only mind matters, but rather, the body can exert a much greater influence on the mind.

Descartes believed that only humans had a mind while animals do not possess a mind. Animals are automata; they have no free will, no thought processes, and do not experience emotions. According to Descartes, the cries and yelps of animals were comparable to the sounds of the hydraulic hisses and vibrations of machines.

In 1650, Queen Christina of Sweden invited Descartes to serve as her philosopher in residence at her royal palace in Stockholm. Descartes accepted, and lessons began at 5:00 a.m. each day, contrary to Descartes' temperamental preference for starting the day much later in the morning. After about six months of this academic regime, Descartes contracted pneumonia and died.

■ Summary

This chapter focused upon the pursuit of knowledge, and we began the odyssey of learning with a review of the four river valley civilizations, the first of which appeared about 5000 B.C. The beginning of the river valley civilizations was marked by the establishment of agriculture, the development of writing, and the organization of the complex systems to regulate and control the exchange of goods, services, and properties.

We examined the two-stage revolution of major religions and philosophies, namely, Chinese philosophy, Indian religions of Hinduism and Buddhism, Judaism, and Greek philosophy, all of which to varying degrees influence the lives of millions of people across the globe today. These philosophical and religious traditions have endured across time as a consequence of addressing universal issues of the nature of the human condition.

We presented some of the foundational features of Roman philosophy and examined the development of Christianity across Europe and Islam throughout the Middle East and Northern Africa. We examined the contributions of Islamic science and philosophy reflected, in part, in the works of Avicenna and Averröes. We then considered the leading edge of the Renaissance which was heralded by the works of the Judaic philosopher Maimonides as well as the Scholastics such as Thomas Aquinas, both of whom attempted to reconcile the forces of faith and reason.

The Renaissance (from about 1450 to 1600) focused upon the potential power of the individual as the engine of adding value to the world by means of individual discoveries in the arts, religion, philosophy, science, and politics rather than being derived only from dogma or doctrine. The Renaissance presented the foundational idea that human experiences, like the physical world, could also be explained and understood in natural rather than supernatural terms.

We concluded this chapter by examining the life and works of René Descartes, whose work ushered in the modern period (1600 to about 1960) in which rationality and science were championed as the most valid and accurate ways of knowing.

Chapter 4—Philosophical Foundations of Psychology

Discussion Questions

- What were the first four river valley civilizations in the world?
- What are the different ways of knowing?
- How do the foundational ideas of the major religious systems differ from one another?
- What are the foundational ideas of Scholasticism?
- How was the Renaissance influenced by religion, philosophy, science, and politics?
- Who influenced the physiological foundation of psychology? Explain.

Biological Foundations of Psychology

CHAPTER OVERVIEW

This chapter focuses upon the foundational idea that "matter makes mind." Humans have almost always speculated about the relationship, if any, between the soul (immortal part of a person that lives on after death), the mind (psychological functions such as sensing, feeling, thinking, and remembering), and the body, especially the brain. In fact, over thousands of years right up to the present moment, lay persons, religious figures, philosophers, and scientists have sought to understand this relationship. Psychology has focused specifically upon the connection between mind or psychological functions and corresponding specific brain regions and activities. In general, some psychologists have concluded that "matter makes mind," that is, psychological functions are the result of the brain (monism), while others have concluded that the mind and body interact with one another on an equal or near equal footing (interactionism). An understanding of the foundational findings regarding the mind–brain relationship provides an informed context from which you can draw your own conclusions regarding the matter of whether or not "matter makes mind."

We turn first to the work of Thomas Hobbes (1588–1679) and René Descartes (1596–1650), both of whom provided a clear bridge from primarily philosophical speculation to the systematic study of the biological basis of human and infrahuman actions, especially those mediated by the spinal cord. Thereafter, we review empirical studies of the spinal cord reported by Robert Whytt (1714–1766), Charles Bell (1774–1842), and Francois Magendie (1783–1855), which led to the **Bell-Magendie Law**.

The **Law of Specific Nerve Energies**, put forth by Johannes Müller (1801–1858), states that "we are aware directly, not of objects themselves, but only of the resulting activity of our nerves." During the 19th century Müller's law resonated throughout the major laboratories around the globe, and made unequivocally clear that the study of mind need proceed primarily, if not exclusively, through studying the nervous system.

Shifting from early studies of the spinal cord to a discussion of the historical conceptualizations of the brain, the discovery of the early Egyptian medical records known as the **Edwin Smith Surgical Papyrus** provided the oldest written record using the word "brain" as well as describing some of the anatomy of the brain and the cerebrospinal fluid. We then review the writings of Claudis Galen (129–199), who advocated a ventricular model of the human brain according to which humors or fluids flow through the tubes of nerves. The Galenian model remained relatively unchallenged for the next 1,500 years due primarily to the Roman Catholic Church's prohibition against dissection of the human body.

One of the first truly systematic and empirical studies of the role of different brain sites in different mind or psychological functions was conducted by Marie-Jean Pierre Flourens (1794–1867). According to Flourens, the brain operates under the direction of two principles, namely, **action propre** (a specific brain sub-site serves a specific function, e.g., cerebellum—coordination of voluntary movement), and **action commune** (brain sites influence each other). Pierre-Paul Broca (1824–1880) and Carl Wernicke (1848–1905) took brain localization further when they discovered the brain sites for speech production and speech comprehension, respectively.

The first demonstration of the effects of electrical stimulation of the cortex was reported by Gustav Fritsch (1839–1927) and Edward Hitzig (1838–1907). Phantom limb, a clear and unequivocal sense that a limb removed accidentally or surgically is still experienced as present, coupled with the clinical findings from the traumatic brain injury of Phineas Gage (1823–1860), made plain that different mind or psychological functions are localized in different regions of the brain. In fact, in some cases, it appears as if an intact brain is all that is necessary for specific experiences even if the appropriate body part is not stimulated directly or is missing entirely!

We next review briefly some foundational laboratory and clinical findings reported during the 20th century resulting from major technological developments. For example, early studies with the microelectrode afforded the first direct observations of the activities of single neurons **in situ** coupled with the later development toward the close of the 20th century of direct observations of activities of specific brain sites while the person was performing different cognitive tasks, using radiographic imaging techniques such as CATS, PETS, and MRI images and split-brain preparations.

We conclude with a focus upon the development of consciousness or direct experience of the subjective world including sensations, feelings, thoughts, memories, and a sense of self. Recent findings indicate clearly that a sense of self is present at about 2 years of age for the human child while chimpanzees and orangutans share with humans direct access to their subjective worlds, as they too have a sense of self. Thereafter, we identify some of the neuroscientific and health-related challenges facing psychology during the early decades of the 21st century.

LEARNING OBJECTIVES

When you finish studying this chapter, you will be prepared to:

- Define and outline the major issues of the mind–body relationship as well as discuss Thomas Hobbes' influential philosophy of this relationship

- Identify the ideas behind René Descartes' hydraulic model of the neurons system, spinal cord reflexes, the connections between sensory and motor nerves, and the relationship between the spinal cord and the brain

- Discuss the contributions of Robert Whytt, Charles Bell, and Francois Magendie to our understanding of the anatomy and functions of spinal nerves and reflexes

- Define the Bell-Magendie Law and discuss the controversy over the priority and accuracy of the discoveries that led to the formulation of the law

- Define Johannes Müller's law of specific nerve energies and describe the impact of this law in establishing firmly the study of the nervous system in the history of psychology

- Discuss the importance of early Egyptian texts, the **Edwin Smith Surgical Papyrus**, to our initial understanding of brain localization of mind functions such as sensing, perceiving, thinking, and remembering

- Summarize the views of Aristotle (384–322 B.C.) and Claudius Galen (A.D. 129–199) regarding the role of the heart, brain, and humors for control of mind and body functions

- Present the foundational findings of Marie-Jean Flourens on brain localization and his principles of **action propre** and **action commune** derived from systematic investigations with animals

- Identify the location and function of the speech production and comprehension centers of the human brain as first discussed by Pierre-Paul Broca and Carl Wernicke, respectively

- Discuss the early studies of electrical stimulation of the brain, clinical cases of phantom limbs, and the traumatic brain injury of Phineas Gage, all of which provided unequivocal clinical evidence of the localization of different mind or psychological functions in different areas of the human brain

- Identify the issues involved in the Golgi-Ramón y Cajal controversy as well as define the neuron doctrine

- Describe the insights into the functioning of the brain arising from technological advances in techniques and procedures of microelectrodes, such as CATS, PETS, MRI, and split-brain studies

- Discuss the decade of the brain and foundational research findings indicating that chimpanzees and orangutans have a concept of self like humans of two years of age or older and can access their subjective world of feelings, ideas, and intentions

- Identify the key findings describing the relationship between the brain and consciousness and the brain challenges that face psychology and neuroscience in the first decade of the 21st century

- Discuss the changing theories in the relationship between affect and health and provide multiple examples of how affect can influence health

INTRODUCTION

We believe all persons have a mind, although some of us at one time or another may behave mindlessly or as if we didn't have a mind. The list of questions about mind is as endless as it is fascinating. What is the mind? Where is it located? Is it material (i.e., made of matter)? What is the nature of the relationship of the mind to the body, particularly to the brain? Do human infants have a mind? What about infrahumans? Is the brain the mind and is that all that matters? In this chapter, we will focus upon the foundational idea that matter makes mind.

Mind–Body Relationship

The philosophical and biological foundations of psychology are built upon the nature of the relationship between the mind and body and the constructs of mechanism and motion. We define mind as a set of psychological processes including sensing, feeling, thinking, and remembering. The body is made of physical substances such as cells, fluids, tissue, muscle, and bones. Body is material, and according to the monist that is all that matters. For the monist, the brain is the mind. The dualist perspective as championed by René Descartes states that the mind and body are separate realities or entities and the relationship between them is primarily interactive in that they influence each other. The work of philosophers like Thomas Hobbes and René Descartes provides a clear segue or transition from the philosophical to the biological foundations of psychology.

Thomas Hobbes (1588–1679)

Thomas Hobbes earned his bachelor's degree from Oxford University in 1608, and spent the rest of his life as a tutor for the wealthy family of William Cavendish, serving for brief intervals in other tutorial positions and as secretary to Sir Francis Bacon (Urmson, 1960). Hobbes traveled to the European continent on three occasions, visiting with Galileo in 1635 after which he concluded that the universe is made up of only matter (materialism). For Hobbes, humans are machines governed by mechanical laws of motion, and there is no need to postulate a nonmaterial mind. Humans are driven by appetites to maximize pleasure and minimize pain, and, accordingly, social stability and material gain arose as a consequence of the social contract between people and the State, which prescribed acceptable affect or feelings, behaviors, and cognitions or thoughts. Hobbes reasoned that humans are equipped with reason which allowed us to seek an enlightened solution to self-preservation by abandoning the nasty, hostile, and lonely state of nature in favor of a civil order strong enough to suppress civil war and protect all citizens. Hobbes' *Leviathan*, published in 1651, presented the foundational rationale for the enormous power vested in the State (the leviathan) to dictate human conduct arising from rule by an absolute monarch so as to avoid civil wars (Hobbes, 1651/1962). Interestingly, Hobbes believed that knowledge of human nature would promote enlightened actions by the ruling monarch. Accordingly, he began *Leviathan* with a focus upon human psychological phenomena including sensation (all human ideas arise from experience), imagination (decaying motions within the sense organs), and thought processes (motions within us which are relics of those made in the senses). Hobbes' beliefs concerning the nature of mind and human behavior can be described in a number of ways:

- **materialist** because he believed that all that existed is physical
- **mechanist** because humans like everything else in the universe are machines
- **determinist** because all actions including human behaviors are subject to physical laws of motion
- **hedonist** because human behaviors are driven by seeking pleasure and avoiding pain.

Hobbes' philosophical explanation of mind and of human behavior provides a firm basis pointing later researchers and theorists in the direction of a search for a biological basis that would support his ideas.

SPINAL CORD STUDIES

There are many marvelous and complex systems in the human body, including the digestive system that yields energy, the skeletal system that provides structure, and the nervous system that guides our affect, behaviors, and cognitions. The most important system for psychology is the nervous system, which has been studied throughout the history of humanity. The 18th century focused primarily upon systematic study of the spinal cord while the 19th century focused upon the study of the brain. The spinal cord was subjected to systematic observation and experimentation first because it was more readily accessible than the brain.

René Descartes (1596–1650)

The foundation for a systematic study of the spinal cord was provided by René Descartes' hydraulic model of the action of the nervous system and his concept of "undulatio reflexa" or (automatic) movement in the absence of will (Descartes, 1665/1985). Interestingly, a series of systematic experiments and observations of the spinal cord arising from Descartes' philosophical work demonstrated the soundness of his general idea that the spinal cord provided the infrastructure for bodily movement, although his ideas about the mechanical basis of the functioning of the spinal cord were proven inaccurate. For example, Descartes considered the human body a machine and viewed body parts such as nerves and muscles as analogous to pipes and springs. Descartes reasoned that like the fluid that flowed through a closed system of pipes yielding hydraulic pressure that caused movement of the springs of the statues found in many royal gardens of his time, so too was there a fluid that flowed through the nerves that activated movement of muscles and tendons of the body (Jaynes, 1973). The "nervous fluid" or "animal spirits," composed of very minute and fast-moving particles, flowed through the closed or hydraulic system of neural pipes like wind in a tunnel and then terminated in muscles, causing bodily movements. According to Descartes, involuntary movement arose from an external stimulus (such as a candle flame) that when touched activates a tiny neural fiber in the finger which instantly opens a valve in the ventricle of the brain, causing animal spirits to flow rapidly to the muscles of the finger and hand resulting in withdrawal of these body parts from the flame. Descartes reasoned that this complex series of events occurs rapidly and smoothly like pulling a string that closes the many vanes of a Venetian window blind or shade. Although Descartes' explanation of bodily movements was later proven incorrect, it did provide a rich basis for the systematic study of the early foundation of spinal cord reflexes, the linkage between sensory and motor capacities of the nerves, and the potential connections between peripheral nerves and the spinal cord and brain.

Robert Whytt (1714–1766)

Stephen Hales (1677–1761) was the first to demonstrate a spinal reflex by decapitating a frog, then pinching the hind leg of the headless frog, and observing that the frog leapt briefly about. These spinal reflexes remained for many hours, and were only eliminated when the spinal cord of the frog was destroyed (McHenry, 1969). Unfortunately, Hales did not publish his systematic findings regarding spinal reflexes.

Robert Whytt, the personal physician of the King of England and president of the Royal College of Physicians, studied more extensively and systematically spinal reflexes in frogs and published his finding in an *Essay of the Vital and Other Involuntary Motions of Animals* in 1751 (Fearing, 1930). Whytt reported that spinal reflexes remain after decapitation, but when the spinal cord was destroyed such reflexes were eliminated. Accordingly, the matter making up the spinal cord made possible rudimentary yet vital reflex actions. Whytt went on to distinguish between voluntary and involuntary action (e.g., spinal reflexes, respiration, and the pupillary or Whytt's reflex (McHenry, 1969). Lastly, Whytt also emphasized the protective and adaptive nature of reflexes and anticipated the findings of classical conditioning when he noted that the sight or even the thought of food caused an increase in salivation.

Charles Bell (1774–1842)

Charles Bell was a distinguished British anatomist and physiologist educated at Edinburgh University. Most of his professional life was spent working in London; however, in 1836, Bell returned to Edinburgh to assume a professorship in surgery. In 1811, Bell reported his experimental findings based upon sectioning the anterior and dorsal roots of the spinal cord of rabbits, and concluded incorrectly that the anterior or ventral roots were responsible for voluntary movement while the posterior or dorsal roots managed involuntary movements (Gallistel, 1981). Bell summarized his findings in a brief pamphlet titled "**Idea of a New Anatomy of the Brain; Submitted for the Observation of his Friends**," which was circulated privately to about 100 of his friends and close colleagues. Although wrong about the differential functions of the roots of spinal nerves, Bell did correctly demonstrate that cranial nerve V was sensory to the face and motor to mastication whereas the cranial nerve VII controlled muscles involved in facial expression. Each of the twelve pairs of cranial nerves are automatically linked directly to the brain thus bypassing the spinal cord (Table 5-1). He also provided an accurate description of facial paralysis, or Bell's palsy, arising from injury to the thoracic cranial nerve.

Francois Magendie (1783–1855)

Eleven years later and unaware of Bell's earlier paper of 1811, Francois Magendie in 1822 reported his results based upon severing the anterior or ventral and the posterior or dorsal roots of the spinal cord in puppies (Grmek, 1974; Magendie, 1822/1965). Magendie's findings were published in a three-page paper appearing in the French *Journal of Physiology and Experimental Pathology*, and he concluded correctly that the anterior or ventral roots mediate sensations while the posterior or dorsal roots manage movement (Figure 5-1).

TABLE 5-1	The Twelve Pairs of Cranial Nerves
Cranial Nerves	**Function**
I Olfactory	Smell
II Optic	Visual field and ability to see
III Oculomotor	Eye movements; eyelid opening
IV Trochlear	Eye movements
V Trigeminal	Facial sensation
VI Abducens	Eye movements
VII Facial	Eyelid closing; facial expression; taste sensation
VIII Acoustic	Hearing; sense of balance
IX Glossopharyngeal	Taste sensation; swallowing
X Vagus	Swallowing; taste sensation
XI Accessory	Controls neck and shoulder muscles
XII Hypoglossal	Tongue movement

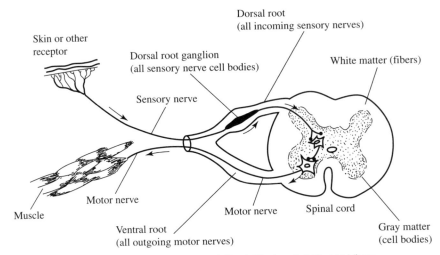

FIGURE 5-1 The Roots of the Spinal Cord: Horizontal Planar View

Bell-Magendie Law

Although Magendie's published spinal cord findings were clear and definitive, John Shaw, Charles Bell's son-in-law, sent Magendie a copy of Bell's 1811 privately circulated pamphlet and challenged the priority of Magendie's findings (Gallistel, 1981). Magendie had not read Bell's paper prior to Shaw sending it to him. Also, Bell and his students began a systematic campaign to discredit the priority of Magendie's discoveries while Magendie concluded that Bell's earlier findings were unclear and incorrect given Bell's assignment of involuntary and voluntary movements to the ventral (anterior) and dorsal (posterior) roots, respectively. The conflict between Bell and Magendie over the priority of the findings of the differential functions of the roots of the spinal cord was never truly resolved during their lifetimes.

Today, we refer to the **Bell-Magendie Law**, which states that sensory information is mediated by the ventral or anterior roots of the spinal cord while the dorsal or posterior roots carry neural information about movement. The Bell-Magendie Law made plain that sensory nerves carry neural information from sense receptors to the brain, and the motor nerves, in turn, carry neural information from the brain to the muscles and glands. Accordingly, inasmuch as the ventral roots of the spinal nerves **always** carry sensory information and the dorsal roots **always** carry motor information, the spinal cord is anatomically and functionally lawful. This finding suggested that there may be further lawful specialization of other nerves and that the brain may also be organized into sensory and motor regions. The Bell-Magendie law supports the foundational idea that mind may be lawful and is rooted in the body.

Johannes Müller (1801–1858)

Johannes Müller was a gifted student at the University of Bonn. He published his magnum opus *Handbuch der Physiologic des Menschen* (*Handbook of Human Physiology*) over the period 1833–1840. Müller extended the work of Sir Charles Bell (Bell, 1811/1965) and introduced his "law of specific nerve energies," consisting of ten components, which stated first and fundamentally—**We are aware directly, not of objects themselves, but only of the activity of our nerves themselves**. Accordingly, Müller made unequivocally clear that the nature of the nervous system rather than the nature of the physical stimulus determines our sensory experiences. Thus, the study of the mind can proceed by studying the nervous system. This theory facilitated Müller's rapid rise to one of the most prestigious academic positions in Europe, namely, the Chair of modern experimental physiology at the University of Berlin in 1833 at the age of 32 (Boring, 1957; Steudel, 1974).

The second component of the law of specific nerve energies stated that there are five kinds of nerves (i.e., auditory, olfactory, optic, gustatory, and tactile) and each imposes its specific quality upon the brain and thus the mind. The third component of the law was that each of the five types of sense organs was maximally sensitive to a certain type of stimulation. Thus, the same stimulus affecting different nerves gives rise to different qualities (sensations) appropriate to the particular nerve, while a different stimulus affecting the same nerve gives rise to the same quality or sensation. The law of specific nerve energies was extended to the notion that there are specific nerve fiber energies corresponding to various psychological qualities. For example, Thomas Young and Hermann von Helmholtz suggested that there are three different optical nerves for the three primary colors of light, namely, red, green, and blue (Herrnstein & Boring, 1966). Likewise, for hearing, Helmholtz suggested that there are thousands of specific auditory nerves each corresponding to a different perceptible tone. The law of specific nerve energies made plain that the contents and activities of the mind are rooted in the body, especially the nervous system and the brain.

Neural Impulses

Johannes Müller believed that neural transmission occurred at a rate too fast to be measurable or as fast or faster than the speed of light (186,000 mps). Helmholtz was the first to measure the velocity of the neural impulse by recording the time lag between stimulation of a nerve and muscle contraction of the leg of a frog (Boring, 1942). The speed of the neural impulse was observed to be around 50 to 100 meters per second, or about 60 miles per hour, nowhere near the speed of light and even much slower than the speed of sound. The mind was subject to time rather than instantaneous and beyond the time boundaries accessible to scientific investigation.

The neuropsychological studies at the beginning of the 20th century made it clear that (a) scientific observations and findings derived from animals could be generalized to humans; (b) there was an emphasis on localization of psychic functions such as sensations, perceptions, and memory in the nervous system, especially the brain; (c) the nervous system is organized in terms of structure and function and so too mind arises from different brain sites and activities; and, lastly, (d) the scientific study of the nervous system is one of the major keys to understanding the human experience.

BRAIN LOCALIZATION

The systematic study of the structure and functions of the spinal cord occupied center stage during the 18th and 19th centuries because it was more accessible than the brain and the brain was not always considered an important part of the body. For example, Aristotle thought the heart rather than the brain was the seat of intelligence and thought. Likewise, the Egyptians did not value the brain, as they removed and discarded it while preserving the heart and other vital organs as part of the mummification process. Despite the Egyptian dispatch of the brain, they provided the oldest written record using the word "brain," and, most importantly, described in an ancient paper-like document (**The Edwin Smith Surgical Papyrus, ESSP**) the anatomy of the brain, the meninges or covering of the brain, and the cerebrospinal fluid. The **ESSP** was written around 1700 B.C. and draws together texts that date back to 3,000 B.C. This document, probably the first written medical text, describes forty-eight patient cases, and is about 15 feet long and 13 inches wide. It derives its name from Edwin Smith, an American Egyptologist, who purchased the text on January 20, 1862, in Luxor, Egypt, from a dealer named Mustapha Aga (Breasted, 1930; Schwartz, 1986). The forty-eight cases of **The Edwin Smith Surgical Papyrus** focus upon twenty-seven head injuries, one spinal cord injury, and various other injuries, all of which most likely resulted from falls or military combat. Fortunately, our understanding of the brain has advanced significantly since 3000 B.C., and we turn now to a brief review of some of the foundational discoveries of the brain right up to the present use of technological brain imaging techniques including **Positron Emission Tomography** (**PET**) and **Magnetic Resonance Imaging** (**MRI**) which provide a direct view into the working brain.

The human brain consists of about 100 billion individual neurons, each of which is a separate cell. Neurons are responsible for sending and receiving neural impulses or signals that underlie sensations (detection of energy or stimuli), motion, regulation of internal processes (e.g., digestion, body temperature), reproduction, and adaptation to the external environment. Interestingly, single-cell organisms as well as many organisms with less complex brains than humans can perform all of the functions identified above. Thus, the question arises, What is the unique function or purpose of the human brain? Accordingly, let us consider the brain as a bodily organ specialized to help individuals carry out major acts of living. The success of an organism in its environment depends on the complexity and capacity of its brain as well as the demands of the environment. Unlike the brains of other animals, the human brain has the capacity for many spoken and written languages, which allows us to examine our ancestors' perspectives about the brain.

Aristotle (384–322 B.C.) speculated that the heart rather than the brain was the site of both nervous control and the human soul. Later, the Greek physician, Claudius Galen (A.D. 129–199) was one of the first to dissect the brains of humans and other animals, and as a consequence he believed that the fluid-filled cavities rather than the brain's substance were the important parts of the brain (Jackson, 1969). We now know these cavities as the cerebroventricular system filled with cerebrospinal fluid. Interestingly, Galen believed that bodily functions and our overall health depended on the distribution of four body fluids or humors, namely, **choler** (blood which carried the animal's vital living spirit), **phlegm** (or mucus which caused sluggishness), **black bile** (melancholy), and **yellow bile** (elevated temper). The ventricular model of the human brain that focused upon the flow of humors or fluids through the tubes of the nerves remained relatively unchallenged for almost 1,500 years. Slowly, the gaseous model came to replace the ventricular model as it was observed that cutting a nerve did not lead to a leak of fluid, so it was suggested that gases rather than humors flowed through the neural tubes. When nerves were dissected under water, no gases bubbled up so the gaseous model ran out of gas, and most importantly, perspectives and explanations about the functioning of the brain were becoming increasingly grounded in systematic observations and experiments rather than philosophical and moral authorities.

Marie-Jean Pierre Flourens (1794–1867)

An important scientific investigator of brain functions was Marie-Jean Pierre Flourens, who was interested in determining the unique functions of different parts of the brain. The adult human brain is about the size of a grapefruit and weighs about three pounds. The brain is divided into the left and right cerebral hemispheres which are joined at the bottom by the corpus callosum. The brain is made up of different parts which are clearly defined and distinct, even to the untrained eye, while at the same time the brain appears as a unified structure. Over 150 years ago, Flourens set out to study scientifically the unique functions of separate anatomical parts of the brain as well as how the brain might function as a unified system (Boring, 1957). Flourens used the method of ablation which involves surgical removal of specific structures in order to assess functions. Flourens observed an animal's pre-operative behavior, surgically removed one of the parts of the brain, allowed time for recovery, and then observed the animal's postoperative behavior. When the cerebral lobes were removed the animal could no longer initiate voluntary movements while still showing reflexes (e.g., pupils of the eyes would dilate in dim light and constrict in bright light). Thus, Flourens concluded that the cerebrum is responsible for perceiving, willing, memory, and judgment. Table 5-2 presents a summary of other brain sites studied by Flourens and the specific function(s) lost when a specific site was surgically removed.

Flourens implemented forever in psychology the importance of the systematic study of the brain when he concluded that perceiving (seeing and hearing) as well as higher mental functions such as willing, memory, and judgment are located in the brain. He concluded that the brain operates under the direction of two principles. **Action propre**, according to which a specific brain subsite serves a specific function while **action commune** indicates that removal of any single brain site reduces the overall expression and vitality of other functions mediated by other brain sites (Boring, 1957). Thus, for example, removal of the cerebellum eliminates coordinated movement and also dampens or lowers the overall functions mediated by other brain sites, such as reduced ability to initiate voluntary movements.

TABLE 5-2	**Functional Levels of the Brain According to Flourens**	
Anatomical Site	**Results of Ablation**	**Function(s)**
Cerebrum	Loss of judgment, inability to initiate voluntary movement, inability to remember	Perceiving, willing, memory, judgment
Cerebellum	Loss of coordination	Coordination of voluntary movement
Corpora quadrigemina	Disturbances in visual and auditory processes	Mediation of visual and auditory reflexes
Medulla	Death of animal	Vital knot-respiration and heartbeat

Pierre-Paul Broca (1824–1880)

In many ways during the 19th century, Paris, France, was the global capital for the experimental and clinical study of the relationships between the brain and psychological functions such as sensing, feeling, thinking, and remembering. However, the brain localization of what was then and is still considered to be one of the most distinguishing features of humans, that is, articulate speech, was first studied by an obscure French physician outside of Paris. In 1836, Marc Dax reported to a medical society meeting in Montpellier that forty of his patients who had speech disturbances exhibited signs of damage to the left hemisphere.

Interestingly, it was not until 1861, when Paul Broca presented his clinical findings to the Anthropological Society in Paris, that the scientific community widely accepted that the speech center is located almost universally in the inferior gyrus of the frontal lobe of the left hemisphere, now known as **Broca's area** (Broca, 1861/1965). Broca worked for only five days, April 12 to 17, 1861, with his now famous 51-year-old male patient, Leborgne or Tan (the only word he could say). In 1831, Tan had been admitted to Bicêtre, a mental hospital near Paris, because he could not talk. Broca examined Tan, and concluded that there was no damage to his throat, tongue, lips, and larynx. Tan died on April 17; Broca performed an autopsy, and found a lesion in the third frontal convolution of the left cerebral hemisphere. Broca's finding was contrary to Flourens' view that the cortex or gray matter covering of the brain acted as a unified whole rather than being divided into specific areas for specific psychological functions.

In 1874, the German neurologist and psychiatrist Carl Wernicke (1848–1905) reported that damage to the posterior third of the superior left temporal gyrus, **Wernicke's area**, interferes with speech comprehension. There is a band of nerve fibers, the **arcuate fasciculus**, that connect Broca's and Wernicke's areas, which when damaged causes conduction aphasia or inability to repeat what is said although patients can still speak sensibly and understand language. Thus, expressive or motor aphasia (speech production) arises from damage or lesions in Broca's area, receptive or sensory aphasia (comprehension of speech) in Wernicke's area, and conduction aphasia (fluent but meaningless speech in response to conversation or questions) arises from damage or lesion in the arcuate fasciculus.

Electrical Stimulation of the Brain

To date, we have examined briefly the findings of brain localization based upon clinical studies of damaged brains or experimental studies involving removal or ablation of different parts of the brain. The first demonstration of the effects of electrical stimulation of the cortex was reported by Gustav Fritsch (1839–1927) and Edward Hitzig (1838–1907), who was a skilled anatomist (Boring, 1957; Clark, 1972). As an army physician, Hitzig applied a mechanical stimulus to different cortical regions which in turn gave rise to different muscular movements. Later, Hitzig teamed up with Fritsch to study the effects of electrical stimulation upon rabbit and dog brains. They found that stimulation in anterior regions of the cerebral cortex generated movements while stimulation of the left cerebral hemisphere produced movement on the right side of the body and vice versa. These findings were soon replicated in many laboratories around the world, and were extended by David Ferrier (1843–1928), who localized or mapped both motor and sensory functions just anterior and posterior of the central sulcus which divides also the frontal from the parietal lobes. The foundational idea that arises from studies of brain localization is that matter makes mind, an idea that is further supported by phantom limbs and causalgia.

Phantom Limbs and Causalgia

After a limb such as an arm or leg has been removed accidentally or by surgery, the person almost always has the clear impression that the limb is still there and not missing at all. The person may feel itching in the missing limb, that he or she can still move the missing limb, and might even momentarily forget it is gone and try to use it. Usually, the older the person at the time of amputation the more vivid the phantom limb sensations, many of which remain throughout the person's life. Although the persistence of sensations in limbs after amputation was known as far back as the 16th century, the well-known Philadelphia physician Silas Weir Mitchell (1829–1914) introduced the term **phantom limb**, a phenomenon that makes plain that psychic functions are located in the brain (Phantom Limb and Causalgia, 1998). Mitchell also was the first to describe **causalgia**, which arises after an injury has healed and there persists intense burning pain and sensitivity to the slightest vibration or touch although at a site some distance from the original wound.

What is responsible for the phantom limb phenomenon? According to Damasio (1999), Damasio and Grosset (1995), and Ramachandran and Blakeslee (1998), the brain gives rise to mind because the brain has a mental map of the body which is a well-formed guide of where every body part is in relation to every other part. This mental map becomes clearly visible with the following exercise. First, write your name with your preferred hand; then close your eyes and write your name again with your preferred hand. Second, repeat this sequence with your nonpreferred hand, that is, write your name with your eyes open and then with your eyes closed. You will notice that your best or typical signature arises with your preferred hand with eyes open, and it gets progressively unclear until the last condition of nonpreferred hand with eyes closed. Our mental maps grow clearer with practice. The sensory and motor experiences of the phantom limb arise from the random firing of the neurons within the remaining mental map of the missing limb. Thus, phantom limb phenomena support further the idea that matter makes mind.

Phineas Gage (1823–1860)

On September 13, 1848, Phineas Gage suffered a catastrophic injury while working on the Rutland-Burlington Railroad in Cavendish, Vermont (Harlow, 1869; MacMillan, 1986). Up to this point in time, Gage was a responsible, well-liked, and friendly young man of 25 years of age. While tamping gunpowder with a 3-foot-13-pound iron rod, an explosion occurred driving the steel tamping rod, about the size of a broom stick, through the orbit of his left eye, and the rod flew out the top of his head—excising his left eye and destroying his left prefrontal cortex. Amazingly, after the accident, Gage walked to his co-workers and was taken to a nearby hotel room attended by the town physician—Dr. John Harlow. Gage was bedridden for two months, then was able to walk unassisted, and he lived for over twelve years after the accident. However, his personality changed dramatically, appearing capricious and irascible, and he behaved irresponsibly, quite contrary to his pre-accident temperament and behavior (MacMillan, 1986).

The damage to Gage's brain dramatically changed his mind and he was unable to find a job with his former employer. He instead exhibited himself and the tamping iron at Barnum's Museum in New York City, and then worked in Chile as a driver of horse-drawn carriages. Gage died on May 21, 1860, and his skull and tamping iron are displayed in the Warren Anatomical Medical Museum at Harvard University.

NEURAL UNITS AND PROCESSES

We turn now to a brief review of some of the major technological advances for the systematic study of the nervous system, beginning with the end of the 19th century and ending with the beginning of the 21st century. The findings indicate that the basic unit of the nervous system is the single-cell neuron, that neurons interact with each other to organize into higher-order structural and functional systems, and that there are specific brain sites for specific mind or psychological functions (e.g., sensing, feeling, thinking, and remembering). As a result of the progress made during the 20th century, we now have a fairly firm understanding of the nervous system and the relationship between the mind and the brain. We begin with the foundational studies of the neuron and the development of the neuron doctrine.

The Golgi–Ramón y Cajal Controversy

In 1906, the Italian Camillo Golgi (1843–1926) and the Spaniard Ramón y Cajal (1852–1934) shared the Nobel Prize for their anatomical studies of the neuron—the basic structural building block of the nervous system in which the human embryonic brain over nine months of development gains neurons at the incredible rate of 250,000 per minute (Gazzaniga, Ivry, & Mangun, 1998; Thompson, 1993)! Golgi, working by candlelight in his kitchen, found that by exposing blocks of neural tissues to silver nitrate solution he could see an individual neuron composed of a cell body, dendrites, and axons. Inasmuch as Golgi's stain exposed only some neurons, he concluded that all neurons are connected together, forming a reticulum or net of cells rather than physically separated simple cells in extremely close proximity to each other. Contrarily, Ramón y Cajal, staining first embryonic rather than adult neural tissue, demonstrated clearly that axons end in dendrites and cell bodies of other neurons and they do not make physical contact, but rather share a minute gap which we refer to as the synapse, affording greater plasticity of neural messages as demonstrated later with chemical and electrical signaling systems. In addition, Ramón y Cajal was not only the first to identify the unitary nature of neurons; he also observed that the transmission of electrical information from one neuron to another is unidirectional from the dendrites down to the axonal terminal branches. Ramón y Cajal, considered by some to be "the father of modern neuroscience," first articulated the **neuron doctrine** including the principles of connectional specificity, according to which the connections between neurons are not random, that is, circuits pass information through specific pathways. The second principle of the neuron doctrine of dynamic polarization means that some parts of neurons are specialized for taking information in while others are specialized for sending it out to other neurons or muscles. Another important component of the neuron doctrine is that each neuronal element has an all-or-none character to its discharge while whole neuronal networks are the fundamental infrastructure of the perception of objects, registering information about the size, distance, shape, and color of the many objects we encounter each moment of our daily lives (Gazzaniga et al., 1998). The foundational idea derived from the neuron doctrine is that individual neurons are the basic computational unit of the brain. Neurons do the logical operations that afford survival in a complex and dynamic world.

Golgi, despite the accumulating evidence to the contrary provided by Ramón y Cajal using the greatest cell stain ever developed for seeing individual neurons (which was developed by Golgi), persisted in seeing blocks of neural tissue as made up of physically connected neurons (i.e., the forest) while Ramón y Cajal saw each neuron as an independent unit, as indeed is the case (i.e., the tree). Thus, two persons looking at the same thing each saw it differently even though the evidence favored unequivocally the individual neuronal unit model. This fundamental discrepancy was reflected in part by Golgi's continued refusal to acknowledge Ramón y Cajal's contributions when he gave his acceptance speech for the Nobel Prize in Stockholm in 1906, followed immediately by a more gracious acceptance speech by Ramón y Cajal.

The Microelectrode

The microelectrode, which delivers discrete electrical or chemical stimulation to a cell and can record the electrical activity from within individual neurons and muscle cells, was invented by Ida Hyde (1854–1945) in 1921. Dr. Hyde was the first woman ever elected to the American Physiological Society (1902) and remained the only woman member for the next twelve years until 1914. Also, she was the first woman awarded a doctorate in physiology from a German university (University of Heidelberg) as well as to do research at Harvard Medical School (Gazzaniga et al., 1998). Ironically, and unfortunately reflecting the failure to recognize the important historical role of women in psychology prior to the 1970s, Ralph Gerard was incorrectly awarded the Nobel Prize in the 1950s for the discovery of the microelectrode!

The early research of Hyde allowed scientists to study the functional features of single neurons and, along with Ramón y Cajal's anatomical findings that were focused upon individual neurons, locked firmly in place the neuron doctrine and the foundational idea that the nervous system in general and the brain in particular is not a big blob of tissue, but rather is built up from discrete neural units. Subsequent anatomical and functional studies of single neurons and specific brain areas using the microelectrode gave rise to the major discoveries of the localization of specific mind functions in the brain (e.g., learning, memory, perception, and speech—Broca's area in the third convolution of the left frontal cerebral hemisphere) as well as the overarching debate of localizationists versus the holistic view of brain function.

In another instance of the asymmetrical and distorted recognition of pioneer women in the early years of psychology and neuroscience, Angelique Arvanitaki employed the microelectrode to study the internal activities of a single neuron and was the first to report that the spontaneous activity of a neuron is an inherent property and not the result of an entire neural circuit. In 1963, Sirs Alan Lloyd Hodgkin and Andrew Fielding Huxley were awarded the Nobel Prize for their findings of the ionic mechanisms of nerve cell membrane, pushing aside the earlier foundational contributions of Angelique Arvanitaki. Fortunately, many women in diverse areas of neuroscience are now rightfully recognized as leading scientists including, for example, Patricia Golddman-Rakic (research in neurophysiology and neuroanatomy of the frontal cortex as well as past president of the Society of Neuroscience), and Rita Levi-Montalcini, the neurobiologist who shared the Nobel Prize in 1986 for the discovery of nerve growth factor (Gazzaniga et al., 1998).

CATS, PETS, and MRI

Computer Assisted Tomography Scanning (CATS) allows us to see deeper and more clearly into the brain, and provides valuable information about the localization of mind functions in healthy as well as damaged brains. A **CAT** scan is a relatively unobtrusive procedure requiring the person to lie supine as a sophisticated X-ray machine scans the head or any other part of the body, yielding a three-dimensional image based upon differential absorption of radiation by biological materials of different densities (bone most dense, blood and air least dense, neural tissue in between these extremes). **CAT** scans are employed to assess neurological damage, particularly but not exclusively to the brain as a result, for example, of tumors, trauma arising from a car accident or diving into the shallow end of a swimming pool, and the advanced stages of neurological diseases such as Alzheimer's, Parkinson's, and Multiple Sclerosis (Gazzaniga et al., 1998; Thompson, 1993). **CAT** scans are also used in combination with angiograms which provide an image of the arteries of the brain to diagnose and treat strokes (disruption of blood flow to the brain which is dependent on 20% of the oxygen we breathe yet accounts for only 2% of total body mass).

Positron Emission Tomography Scanning (**PETS**) and Magnetic Resonance Imaging (**MRI**) do not measure directly neural events like the Electroencephalography (**EEG**) but rather indirectly by detecting blood flow in the brain while the subject is engaged in a cognitive task. In general, **MRI**'s are less expensive than **PETS**, do not use radioactive components, and provide a more detailed image of the functioning part of the brain for a given cognitive task. Both **PET** and **MRI** scans have been instrumental in advancing **cognitive neuroscience**, which focuses upon the neural activity in different brain parts while the subject is engaged in a mental activity.

Cognitive psychology assumes that a cognitive task is composed of a set of mental operations (e.g., The Stroop task in which the subject has to name as quickly as possible the stimulus color regardless of the color word presented). Thus, for example, the subject is presented with a list of color words appearing in the same color (congruent list), random colors, and color words presented in a different color—incongruent list (Gazzaniga et al., 1998; MacLeod, 1991; Stroop, 1935). Thus, one mental operation includes identification of the color of the stimulus and another operation includes the identification of the color concept associated with the word, despite the fact that the stimulus color is irrelevant to the task and produces interference in the incongruent list. Interestingly, the Stroop effect is present even after thousands of trials with healthy adults reflecting the well-practiced mental operation of skilled readers in analyzing letter strings for their symbolic meaning. The interference effect upon color naming is markedly reduced if the required response is a motor response (e.g., a timed key press) rather than a vocal response. Prior to the use of **PET** and **MRI** scans for studying cognitive tasks, reaction times were the primary measures of underlying mental operations. However, with **PET** and **MRI** scans it is now possible to see which brain areas are active or "light up" during different cognitive tasks.

The **PET** scan has been used to study the neural basis of, for example, language and memory. Posner, Petersen, Fox, and Raichle (1988) presented, visually or auditorily, words to subjects who looked or listened to the words or repeated the presented words or associations with words (e.g., noun-verb; cake-eat) while measuring regional blood flow with **PET** scans. When subjects simply looked at the words the regions in the occipital cortex (visual area) exhibited the highest local blood flow so the **PET** scan "lit" for this area compared to other brain areas, and when they heard the words auditory areas "lit up." When subjects repeated the words, a region in Broca's area (i.e., the speech center) as well as primary and supplementary motor areas along with the anterior cerebellum were activated. Lastly, for the semantic association task (noun-verb pairs) the anterior cingulate region (part of the prefrontal cortex) and the right lateral cerebellum were activated or "lit up" with these regions playing a special role in semantics or meaning, the most complex aspect of language.

Interestingly, the association areas of the cerebrum and cerebellum are the most recent to evolve phylogentically and are very elaborated in the human brain!

In a study of human memory, Squire and Zola-Morgan (1991) had some subjects learn a list of words which they later recalled (declarative explicit memory) while other subjects had to say the first word that came to mind upon seeing the first two letters of the words (implicit memory). **PET** scans during the recall tasks indicated that blood flow increased in the right hippocampus for explicit or declarative memory while for the implicit memory task the occipital or visual areas of the right cerebral cortex "lit up" or exhibited increased blood flow. These findings suggest that there may be different brain localizations for explicit and implicit memories.

Recently, Duncan et al. (2000) suggested that general intelligence, or the "g" factor as proposed by Charles Spearman in 1904 as common to all intellectual abilities, may well be located in the lateral frontal cortex in that this brain region was most active during spatial, verbal, and motor tasks as indicated by **PET** scans. Sternberg (2000) has called for caution in interpreting these findings as based on correlational data only and general intelligence tests focused upon spatial, verbal, and motor tasks do not measure talents such as creativity or adaptability. Accordingly, the jury is still out on the "g" factor as common to all intellectual abilities and the precise brain location of general intelligence. Lastly, Maquet et al. (2000) used **PET** scans to assess brain function and found that the same brain areas most activated for subjects who had just learned a reaction time task were also most activated during the Rapid Eye Movement (**REM**) phase of sleep, which some researchers believe is important for strengthening memories. Thus, it appears that the brain areas important for learning the reaction time task may well be "reactivated" during **REM** sleep. Not only may it be valuable to get a good night's sleep before a big test, but it may also prove beneficial to get a good night's sleep after studying or practicing a task. In short, to be at your best while awake it is important to get regular and sound sleep. In summary, all of the above **PET** scan studies clearly support the foundational idea that matter makes mind.

Split Brains

The two cerebral hemispheres of the brain are connected by a number of commissures or neural cables including the corpus callosum, the largest (consists of more than 200 million axons) and the most important of the commissures. In a foundational study of brain function, Sperry (1961/1964) severed the corpus callosum and anterior commissure of cats and found that a visual discrimination learned by one cerebral hemisphere did not transfer to the other hemisphere. In effect, one half of the brain did not know what the other half had just learned, suggesting that two separate conscious states or split minds existed in one, albeit disconnected, brain.

Gazzaniga (1967, 1970, 1995, 1998) and Gazzaniga and Sperry (1967) reported a series of studies of split-brain patients whose corpus callosum had been severed to eliminate otherwise intractable epileptic seizures. When the entire corpus callosum is severed there is little, if any, perceptual and cognitive interaction between the cerebral hemispheres. However, there is no loss of intelligence or any other sign of brain damage and the seizures are eliminated. As is now well known, the left cerebral hemisphere is primary for language, speech, and problem solving while the right hemisphere is critical for visuospatial tasks such as drawing pictures of a wide variety of objects. Accordingly, split-brain patients cannot name or verbally describe visual or tactile stimuli presented to the right hemisphere because the incoming sensory information is disconnected from the dominant left hemisphere containing the speech center. However, the left hand, which is controlled by the right cerebral hemisphere, can be used to point to, select, or draw the visual object presented in the left visual field. Thus, when stimuli and responses are ipsilateral (i.e., on the same side of the mid-line of the body) then split-brain patients can identify accurately objects verbally or motorically (match presented object by pointing to the same object presented in a sample of objects) if the left cerebral hemisphere is activated. On the other hand, only motoric nonverbal responding is possible when stimuli are presented to the left of the mid-line, thus activating the right cerebral hemisphere, because the sensory information cannot be transferred to the left cerebral hemisphere which is the locus of the speech center (i.e., Broca's area).

Interestingly, when only the posterior half of the corpus callosum is severed, transfer of semantic information about a stimulus but not the stimulus itself takes place between the right and left cerebral hemispheres. For example, when the word "knight" is presented to the left visual field thus sending information to the right cerebral hemisphere, a patient with the anterior portion of corpus callosum intact would respond with a definition or description of the meaning of the word, such as "two fighters in a ring wearing ancient uniforms and helmets," but would report not seeing anything when the entire corpus callosum was severed.

In summary, the foundational research findings of Roger Sperry (1913–1994), Michael S. Gazzaniga, and others restored to scientific psychology the systematic study of consciousness, which had been all but totally abolished from psychology because of the rigid emphasis of behaviorism upon materialism (i.e., the primacy of the physical world) at the expense of excluding the subjective world (i.e., consciousness consisting of sensations, thoughts, feelings, and memories). Most likely consciousness is the result of evolution as consciousness is an efficient and unitary process for managing the body and the brain.

MATTERS OF THE MIND

The period of 1990 to 2000 witnessed extraordinary developments in our understanding of the nervous system, mind–brain relationships, and the evolution of consciousness. This progress was fueled, in large part, by enhanced funding of brain research under the banner of the "Decade of the Brain" approved by the U.S. Congress and signed into law by then President George H. W. Bush. As a consequence of the "Decade of the Brain," our enhanced understanding of neurotransmitters led to the introduction of antidepressants such as Prozac and Zoloft, and we determined more clearly that humans along with chimpanzees and orangutans have access to the subjective world of feelings, thoughts, and memories as well as a sense of self. In addition, emerging research with stem cells, the cellular engine for almost all the different cells in the human body, provides promise of perhaps ameliorating and/or possibly curing major illnesses of the nervous system such as Alzheimer's, Parkinson's, and Lou Gehrig's Disease. It is clear that our growing knowledge of the nervous system provides much hope for dealing with serious illnesses that have long plagued humankind.

Decade of the Brain

The recognition of the importance of the brain for psychological and physical well-being is well established in the mind of the public, due in part to the centuries of scientific study of the brain. In fact, in the United States, the 1990s was designated as "The Decade of the Brain" leading to enhanced funding with resultant scientific findings in the areas of neurotransmitters and associated medications for treating various psychological disorders (McGaugh, 1990). For example, antidepressants such as Prozac, Zoloft, Paxil, and Elavil prevent nerve cells from reabsorbing the serotonin that is already in circulation, and, in turn, lead to less anxiety and calmer emotional states. As was stated in the preamble of the Resolution adopted by the U.S. Congress proclaiming the 1990s as "The Decade of the Brain," treatment and rehabilitation of disorders and disabilities that affect the brain represent a total economic burden of $305 billion annually as of the early 1990s. Accordingly, during the 1990s and the early part of the 21st century, great advances, beyond the scope of this chapter, have been made with new instruments that allow direct observation of ongoing brain activities and the use of stem cells that challenge directly the centuries-old believe that neurons could not be regenerated in the central nervous system. In fact, it is now clear that central nervous system neurons can be regenerated or replaced with new neurons. Thus, the potential for new historic findings about the brain in particular and the nervous system in general is vast and challenging in the coming years.

Minds and Monkeys

Inasmuch as monkeys and other infrahumans have a brain, does it then follow that monkeys have minds? The question here is that there may be two fundamentally distinct groups of life: those who know that the mental world exists (e.g., humans) and those who do not. Are humans truly alone and apart from other creatures or are there kindred spirits to us here on Earth or perhaps elsewhere in the universe as well? Accordingly, we turn now to the issue of psychological evolution or the evolution of the mind (Povinelli, 1993).

Psychological evolution focuses upon the question of whether species differ with respect to the presence or absence of basic psychological traits. For example, does a human have access to her or his own mind while primates, cats, dogs, and other animals do not, that is, the capacities for self-recognition, a self-concept, accumulated knowledge, intention, and social attribution? This is the phylogenetic expression of the evolution of mind. Similarly, does a 15-month-old infant compared with a 36-month-old child have access to her or his own mind? This is ontogenetic expression of the evolution of the mind. In humans, it appears as if pretend or symbolic play emerges at approximately 18 months of age, suggesting that such performance is supported by some understanding of mental representation on the part of the young pretender (Povinelli, 1993).

In a series of elegant experiments, Gallup (1970, 1982) demonstrated that chimpanzees are capable of recognizing themselves in mirrors by spontaneously using mirrors to explore previously unknown parts of their bodies such as their heads and anal-genital regions. Orangutans also are capable of self-recognition while gorillas and other primates (rhesus macaque monkeys) are **not** capable of self-recognition. Gallup (1970, 1982) suggested that except for humans, chimpanzees, and orangutans, all other primates are incapable of reflecting on their own experiences. It appears as if the human child's capacity for self-conception or self-awareness arises between 18 and 24 months of age. Self-conscious emotions in young children emerge hand-in-hand with the onset of self-recognition.

Brain Challenges

In an article in *The Atlantic Monthly* titled "The Organization Kid," Brooks (2001) writes that in the domain of contemporary child-rearing practices, biology has displaced psychology and theology as there is now a scientifically discernible pattern or script for human life carried in our genetic code. Basically, the script says that if in the course of human development something goes wrong, it is the result of either a genetic flaw or our brain synapses have not been properly cultivated. Brooks (2001) offers some suggestions for enhancing our brain resources by reference to popular parenting resources such as the book *Baby Minds: Brain Building Games Your Baby Will Love* and the so-called "Mozart effect" (classical music enhances infant and child brain development) reflected in the Compact Disc (CD) *Mozart for Babies' Minds* (featuring the Violin Concerto no. 3). The foundational idea here is that enhancing brain development expressed as dense and plentiful synaptic connections is possible with appropriate environmental stimulation which in turn enhances the development of the mind so that the child is prepared to be among the elite of the Information Age on the Right Side of the Digital Divide. As Brooks (2001) states, "Accomplishment begins with the first breaths of life" (p. 44) to which we add the invaluable and universal principle of functionality "use or lose it," which applies not only at the early but also the later stages of life.

In an intriguing article, Lemonick and Park (2001) report on a group of 678 nuns (the School Sisters of Notre Dame) who live on Good Counsel Hill in Mankato, Minnesota, who have been the focus of a painstaking and systematic longitudinal study of Alzheimer's Disease (**AD**) conducted by David Snowdon and his colleagues of the University of Kentucky. Alzheimer's Disease is associated with aging (average onset between 60 and 65 years of age), will afflict fourteen million Americans by 2050, is characterized by the gradual spread of sticky plaques and tangled fibers that prevent brain cells from communicating with each other, and leads to severe memory loss, inability to care for oneself, and ultimately death. **AD** is a harsh brain disease that takes a serious toll on the patient, family, and other loved ones.

Interestingly, what The Nun Study has demonstrated to date is that a history of strokes and head trauma increase the chances of having **AD** later in life, while having a college education and an active intellectual life may possibly help to prevent one from getting **AD**. Furthermore, Snowdon (2001) found that based upon an examination of autobiographies written by each nun early in their religious careers, the more we express ideas and positive emotions (e.g., love, hope, gratitude) rather than negative emotions (e.g., fear, sadness, shame) the longer we may live and the less likely we are to exhibit symptoms of **AD**. So we can conclude tentatively from the nuns on Good Counsel Hill that it is important that we remain intellectually active throughout life and maintain a positive spirit peppered with positive emotions despite the setbacks and challenges we all face along our journeys.

There are innumerable other brain diseases which afflict many persons including Parkinson's Disease (**PD**) and Lou Gehrig's Disease or Amyotrophic Lateral Sclerosis (**ALS**). Parkinson's Disease is a chronic and progressive disorder of movement, affecting approximately 0.5% of the population of the United States or approximately 1.25 million Americans. Parkinson's varies greatly in severity from one person to another, and is characterized primarily by tremors or involuntary rhythmic movements of the arms and/or legs or difficulty starting or sustaining voluntary movements. Autopsies and histofluorescene of the brains of Parkinson's patients reveal fewer neurons in the substania nigra (midbrain structure) as well as markedly reduced content of dopamine in this and related brain sites compared to normal brains. Fortunately, taking Levo-Dopamine (L-Dopa) medication alleviates temporarily (for up to fifteen-plus years) many of the movement dysfunctions that accompany Parkinson's Disease, although there are risks of some potentially serious side effects especially with increasing time on L-Dopa medication. In effect, to date **PD** can be managed fairly well but not yet cured.

Lou Gehrig's Disease or **ALS** is a much more serious and debilitating disease than **PD**, and involves loss of the use and control of muscles due to destruction of the nerves controlling first voluntary and then involuntary muscle groups. There is, at present, no cure for **ALS** and death usually occurs within two to ten years of original diagnosis of the disease with only about 20% of **ALS** patients living longer than five years.

As always, there are hopes and challenges for understanding, managing, curing, and ultimately preventing **AD, PD**, and **ALS**. The promise of new treatments in the years ahead arises from very preliminary basic brain research using animal models for implanting stem cells in different brain sites to grow new neurons or revitalize existing although not optimally operational neurons. Stem cells from human embryos and fetal tissue have the ability to divide for indefinite periods and to give rise to specialized cells. Thus, stem cells offer the possibility of a renewable source of replacement neuronal cells and tissue to treat by injecting or targeting brain sites involved in different neurological diseases such as **AD**, **PD**, and **ALS**. Hopefully, some of the ethical and moral issues surrounding the harvesting of embryonic and fetal tissue stem cells will be addressed and, perhaps, adult stem cells can replace the use of the above early developmental stem cells, making each of us potentially our own source of healing by cell therapy!

Affect and Health

There have been relatively few systematic research efforts directed toward the study of the effects of emotional experience on physical health mediated by physiological mechanisms until the latter part of the 20th century, specifically 1990–2000. The possibility of a link between emotional experiences and health and well-being moderated by some kind of physiological mechanisms is not new. For example, Hippocrates (Ca. 460–Ca. 377 B.C.), the founder of medicine, was the first to propose the theory that emotions and disease are linked through a common antecedent (Salovey et al., 2000). Although the details were wrong, evidence emerged periodically over the centuries supporting his general theory.

Important scientific advancements of our understanding of the link between emotions and physical health and well-being required a move away from the traditional theory of emotional states and physical health. The traditional theory approached the interaction from the perspective that the onset of physical illness (e.g., headaches, chronic fatigue, colds, etc.), especially those that interfere with pleasurable daily activities, lead to negative affect or emotion (Keefe et al., 1986; Rodin & Voshart, 1986; Turk, Rudy, & Stieg, 1987); whereas, the new theory viewed the interaction as emotions influencing physical health (Cohen & Rodriguez, 1995; Herbert & Cohen, 1993). The movement to this approach facilitated the emerging prominence of the direct effects of emotional experiences on physiology, especially as mediated by the immune system.

The previously mentioned Nun Study (Lemonick & Park, 2001) demonstrated through autobiographies (Snowdon, 2001) that higher frequency of feeling and expressing positive, as opposed to negative, emotions is indicative of longer life span and lower incidence of Alzheimer's Disease symptoms supports Hippocrates' theory. This study exhibits how the emotions have a direct effect on illness.

An extended life span may be a result of healthy patterns of cardiovascular or immune system functioning (Salovey et al., 2000). The physiological mediation between emotion and health can be illustrated specifically in terms of healthy immune system functioning.

The immune system functions in fighting off the common cold by releasing as the first line of defense, the secretory immunoglobulin A (S-IgA), which is highest when negative affect is reduced through substitution with positive affect (Stone et al., 1996).

In addition to the effects of increase in S-IgA being a result of emotion, peoples' perceptions of, and decisions regarding their physical health are also dependent on emotion. For example, those that experience persistent affect have a higher frequency of reporting symptoms independent of actual illness severity (Cohen et al., 1995; Watson, 2000). Emotions can be used to positively affect physical health through the prevention of and coping with physical distress. Such tools as optimism and general positive affect can equip humanity with the capability of maintaining healthy behaviors for prevention of, and resilience from disease through creativity and innovation (Fredrickson, 1998).

These mood regulation strategies and social support systems, which are necessary for a basic level of human functioning, continually illustrate the importance of the emerging field connecting affect with physical health. From its meager start with Hippocrates, to its empirically validated state in the 21st century, it is undeniable that the history, identification, and application of the fundamental ideas of psychology, specifically the effects of affect on physical health, are pertinent to humanity on multiple levels.

◼ Summary

We began this chapter with an outline of the major issues surrounding the mind–body relationship as reflected in the early works of Thomas Hobbes and René Descartes. Philosophers and psychologists have focused upon the nature of the connection between mind or psychological functions (e.g., sensing, feelings, thinking, and remembering) and corresponding specific parts of the nervous system which included first studies of the spinal cord and then different brain sites.

We reviewed the early 19th century empirical results and controversy over the primacy and accuracy of the findings surrounding the anatomy and functions of spinal nerves. These studies culminated in the discovery of the **Bell-Magendie Law**, according to which the ventral roots of the spinal cord always carry sensory information and the dorsal roots always carry motor information. According to Johannes Müller's **Law of Specific Nerve Energies**, we are aware directly, not of objects themselves, but only of the activity of the nerves themselves.

We then turned to a brief review of early Egyptian writings of brain anatomy and the ventricular system as well as Galen's hydraulic model of the nervous system. Thereafter, we focused upon the foundational studies of brain localization by Marie-Jean Flourens and Pierre-Paul Broca. We examined also the findings from brain stimulation studies, clinical case studies of the phantom limb phenomenon, and the traumatic brain injury of Phineas Gage. We reviewed the extraordinary technological advances of the 20th century which provided deeper observations and insights into the nature of the mind–brain relationship. We began with the development of the microelectrode which afforded direct study of the activity of single neurons culminating in the development of **CAT, PET**, and **MRI** techniques, which allowed observation of differential activity among different brain sites while a person was performing specific cognitive tasks. We concluded this chapter by indicating the primacy of brain research as reflected in governmental support of the Decade of the Brain and highlighting the complex issues of the evolution of consciousness.

■ Chapter 5—Biological Foundations of Psychology

Discussion Questions

- ■ Why is the Bell-Magendie Law important to the history of psychology?
- ■ What law had the most impact on the study of the neurons system in the history of psychology?
- ■ How did early Egyptian texts influence our understanding of brain localization of mind functions?
- ■ How did Marie-Jean Flourens further develop our understanding of brain localization?
- ■ Why don't our nervous systems and minds operate instantaneously?
- ■ Where are the centers for speech production and comprehension and what are their functions?
- ■ How did the study of Phineas Gage support the theory of brain localization?

Phrenology, Mesmerism, and Hypnosis

CHAPTER OVERVIEW

Some believe that mind is a product of the brain and thus mind is made of matter. Others believe that although mind is located in the brain, mind is not made of matter, but rather is composed of psychological processes such as thinking, feeling, and remembering. Still others believe that in addition to the brain (body) and mind there is also the matter of soul.

Historically, philosophers, scientists, and religious authorities have debated extensively the nature of mind, body, and soul. Today, many millions, perhaps billions of people around the world believe the soul is unique to humans, and that it is immortal. Despite the prevalence of the belief in the soul, the concept of soul as defined above is absent or barely treated in most versions of psychology and is considered more appropriately the province of religion, spiritualism, and/or psychic phenomena.

The idea of mind, on the other hand, has come (e.g., associationism/cognitive neurosciences) and gone (e.g., behaviorism) in psychological systems of thought, and in general is conceptualized as a set of processes such as thinking, feeling, and remembering. These processes afford knowledge of the finite world and die with the body. Material monists believe that the body or specifically the brain gives rise to mind while mental monists believe that the physical world is the product of the human mind. In contrast, dualists believe mind and body are different yet interact with each other, or the activities of each parallel yet are independent of each other (i.e., psychophysical parallelism).

Baruch Spinoza (1632–1677) thought and wrote a lot about the mind and body and is considered by some to have had a more prominent role in the establishment of psychology as an independent science than has been attributed to René Descartes (1596–1650). Spinoza argued that the mind and body were two features of the same thing yet independent of each other like the peel and fruit of a banana, and they were on an equal footing, thus providing a conceptual pathway to examine systematically psychological interactions with bodily processes. Spinoza distinguished between emotions and passions with only emotions influenced and guided by reason.

The concepts of conscious and unconscious minds grew directly from the work of Gottfried Wilhelm von Leibniz (1646–1716), who was an extraordinary inventor, mathematician, and philosopher. Leibniz gave us the foundational idea of monads, which he conceptualized much like the atom, and he viewed them as units of energy rather than of matter. There were four levels of monads and at the lowest level the monads had insufficient energy to reach awareness. The clarity of the conscious mind varied from distinct vivid experiences, or what he called apperceptions, to petit perceptions which never enter our awareness or conscious mind unless they accumulate, such as hearing the sound of rain but not that of a single rain drop or when a vague sense becomes a clear and distinct feeling or idea. Leibniz's ideas influenced later developments in psychophysics, Freudian psychoanalysis, and the field of hypnosis.

Phrenology was the popular 19th-century practice that established firmly in the mind of the public the idea that the brain and mind are related to each other such that variations in the bumps of the skull represented different amounts of underlying brain tissue, and more importantly, different levels of intellectual and emotional capacities as well as personality traits. Franz Joseph Gall (1758–1832), his student Johann Gasper Spurzheim (1776–1832), and the publishing firm of Fowler and Wells spread phrenology around Europe and America to such an extent that it was almost common practice for everyone to have had a "phreno-logical read" at one time or another. Phrenological findings were reported at prestigious universities and research institutes, and many firms as late as the 1920s insisted that candidates for executive positions submit the results of a phrenological examination. Although based upon shabby science and extraordinary marketing, phrenology did sell the public on the idea that mind and body are connected and "a read of one reveals the other." Today, personality inventories and intelligence tests, which are based on solid psychometric practices and principles, are an extension of the enduring human desire to know more about oneself in terms of capabilities, personality traits, and what may be in one's future. For example, the Five Factor Model of Personality (FFM) includes the factor of conscientiousness. This factor is a valid predictor of a wide variety of job performances in many cultures and countries around the world. Also, over the past fifty years IQ test scores around the globe have increased by more than fifteen points and this rate of increase may be accelerating, a phenomenon known as the Flynn Effect. These are both examples of the value of the practice of indexing psychological capacities, which originated as a by-product of phrenology.

The work of Franz Anton Mesmer (1734–1815) further popularized in the mind of the public the foundational idea that mind matters. He believed that the world was permeated by a force that he called "animal magnetism," which if not properly distributed and flowing throughout the body gave rise to mental and physical illnesses such as, for example, anxiety attacks, memory lapses, blindness, and paralysis. After earning the M.D. in 1766 from the University of Vienna, Mesmer treated Viennese patients presenting symptoms for which there appeared to be no physical basis, and achieved symptom relief for many of his patients by passing and placing specially designed magnets on different parts of their bodies. After he was castigated by the Viennese medical community, Mesmer set up an initially successful practice in Paris where he established schools to train persons in his magnetic techniques. Later, Mesmer was investigated by a scientific commission appointed by the king of France and led by Benjamin Franklin, and was ultimately discredited as a fraud by the commission and the medical-scientific community. He died in Germany in 1815, although his foundational ideas that mind can influence and even repair psychological and bodily functions live on right up to the present. Witness, for example, the popularity of magnetized bracelets and jewelry worn on different parts of the body, and more importantly the many achievements of psychosomatic medicine.

Marquis de Puysegur (1751–1825) was one of Mesmer's more famous students who induced sleep-like states in his patients rather than a crisis or emotional upheaval, which Mesmer thought was essential for a cure. The Marquis de Puysegur called the sleep-like state artificial somnambulism, which later came to be called hypnosis.

The transition from the practice of mesmerism to hypnosis was advanced in England, India, and France. John Elliotson (1791–1868), a famous English physician, used suggestions or mesmerism as a surgical anesthetic as did James Esdaile (1808–1859) working in India. James Braid (1795–1860) provided an explanation of mesmerism which he attributed to fatigue of the elevator muscles of the eyes arising from continuous staring at an object coupled with verbal suggestions of relaxation, giving rise to a sleep-like state that he called hypnosis.

The practice of hypnosis had by then been legitimized within the medical community, and was studied in the Nancy School of hypnosis under the pioneering work of Auguste Ambroise

Liébeault (1823–1904) and Hippolyte Bernheim (1840–1919), according to whom hypnosis was a normal phenomenon representing a sleep-like state somewhere between wakefulness and natural sleep. Contrarily, the Parisian School of hypnosis led by the world-famous neurologist Jean-Martin Charcot (1825–1893) considered hypnosis to be a reflection of an underlying neurological disorder like hysteria. Charcot and Pierre Janet (1859–1947) promoted the foundational ideas that psychological dysfunctions and symptoms of physical illnesses could be treated with hypnosis based upon verbal suggestions, and that the human mind consists of at least two major components, namely, the conscious and the unconscious.

In America in the 1890s, Hugo Münsterberg (1863–1916), director of the prestigious psychological laboratory at Harvard University, initiated laboratory studies of hypnosis which were later extended by Clark Hull (1884–1952) at Yale University in the 1920s and 1930s. Most of the results from both of these laboratories still stand as valid today, and include such findings as no difference in susceptibility to hypnosis as a function of intelligence and little evidence that hypnosis enhances memory. Major outcomes of these laboratory studies were the further legitimization of hypnosis as a sound clinical intervention and a search for a model that could explain the hypnotic mechanism as well as a wide variety of hypnotic phenomena such as hypnotic age regression.

The state model of hypnosis crystallized during the 1960s argued that hypnosis represented a special state of consciousness lying somewhere between wakefulness and natural sleep with the skill of the hypnotist as the primary determinant of the depth and effectiveness of the hypnotic state. The alternative or non-state model proposed that the hypnotic experience arises primarily from cognitive mechanisms under the control of the person being hypnotized. Thereafter, dissociation theories of hypnosis developed, promoting one of two different mechanisms: (1) that during hypnosis consciousness is fragmented such that a part of consciousness is sealed off from the analytical component of consciousness or (2) that hypnotic states are the result of uncoupling of cognitive and behavioral subsystems from control by the executive or analytical component of consciousness.

Studies of hypnotic age regression indicate that there is not a return to previous age as reflected in age appropriate perceptions, physiological responses, and cognitions, but rather a change from an analytical to pre-logical modes of information analyses and thinking. Interestingly, the study of hypnosis and other psychic phenomena (e.g., mental telepathy) by the Boston School of Abnormal Psychology during the period of 1870–1890 is considered by some historians of psychology as the driving force that led to the establishment of clinical psychology.

The results of efficacy and effectiveness studies of hypnosis in particular and other modalities of psychotherapy in general (e.g., cognitive and/or behavior therapies) have yielded the unequivocal findings that these types of psychological interventions work for a variety of specific disorders. Some psychologists have argued that despite the positive remedial value of many modalities of psychotherapy, more emphasis and resources must be provided for the prevention of the conditions such as poverty, discrimination, and lack of educational opportunities that give rise to the stresses and illnesses that afflict many people around the world.

Psychoneuroimmunology (PNI) is beginning to emerge and stake a claim on the field of psychology around the globe. As a paradigm, PNI is presented as the connection between the mind and the body on a biological level at the scientific interface of psychology, neurology, and immunology.

LEARNING OBJECTIVES

When you finish studying this chapter, you will be prepared to:

- Define mind, body, and soul as well as the relationship between them
- Indicate the contributions of Baruch Spinoza (1632–1677) to the establishment of psychology
- Discuss Gottfried Wilhelm von Leibniz's (1646–1716) concept of monads, threshold of awareness, and his suggestion that humans have both a conscious as well as an unconscious mind
- Describe phrenology and how the read of one domain of features (i.e., bumps on the head) can serve as a read of other features, namely, intellectual resources and personality traits
- Discuss the predictive validity of the Five Factor Model of personality for a wide variety of performances as well as the Flynn Effect of human intelligence
- Describe and analyze the contributions of Franz Anton Mesmer (1734–1815) based upon his concept of animal magnetism, as well as other investigators who contributed to a clearer description of hypnotic phenomena, especially the works of the Marquis de Puysegur (1751–1825), influential English physicians, and especially James Braid (1795–1860)
- Describe and differentiate between the Nancy School and the Parisian School of hypnosis and the existence of the conscious and unconscious components of mind
- Describe the early findings of laboratory studies of hypnosis from Harvard and Yale Universities that still stand today, such as hypnosis does not significantly enhance memory
- Define and distinguish between the state and non-state models of hypnosis as well as the two dissociation theories of hypnosis
- Review the results of extensive studies of hypnotic age regression
- Describe the central role of the study of hypnosis for the establishment of clinical psychology as well as the results of efficacy and effectiveness studies
- Discuss the effect of conditions such as poverty, discrimination, and lack of educational opportunities as they potentially relate to stress and illness
- Identify the mechanisms of psychoneuroimmunology and discuss the influence of this paradigm on the practice of psychology and medicine

---

INTRODUCTION

All humans appear to have a brain and a mind. Brain is made of matter such as neural tissue (e.g., neurons and glial cells) and fluids while mind is made of nonmaterial expressed as functions such as sensing, feeling, thinking, and remembering. It is unequivocally clear today that different mind functions are associated with different brain sites. As a result, many psychologists and scientists from related disciplines have concluded that "matter makes mind." However, it would be likewise mindless to conclude that mind or cognitive strategies or interventions (e.g., relaxation techniques, cognitive-behavior therapies, visualization, self-affirmations, self-fulfilling prophecies, and hypnosis) do not influence brain and bodily functions so that we must keep in mind that "mind matters."

Mind and Soul

As you may recall from chapter 4, "The Philosophical Foundations of Psychology," there has been and continues to be a fundamental debate over the meaning and nature of the human mind and soul. This debate is global with mind considered by scholars from many cultures to be the province of primarily moral philosophy, a portion of which has evolved into the psychological and social sciences. The concept of soul has also been treated initially by moral philosophers, and is now the primary province of religion- and faith-based approaches to knowledge. In general, the mind affords us contact and awareness of the finite mortal world. The mind came to be understood as psychological functions, such as, for example, sensing, feeling, thinking, and remembering. Most philosophers, scientists, and thinkers believe the mind dies with the body. The concept of soul or spirit refers primarily to that feature of a human being that many millions of people believe provides access to universal knowledge, and is immortal in comparison to the body and the mind (i.e., the brain). In general, historical as well as contemporary psychology focuses primarily upon brain–mind relationships.

Baruch Spinoza (1632–1677)

There are some historians of psychology who believe Baruch Spinoza had more of an influence upon the founding of psychology as an independent science than René Descartes because of Spinoza's views on the mind–body relationship and the denial of free will (Bernard, 1972). Spinoza was born in the Christian city of Amsterdam, of Jewish parents. After graduating from a Jewish high school in Amsterdam where he followed the usual curriculum of the study of the five books of Moses and the Talmud, Spinoza went to a Dutch teacher to learn Latin and the "new science" including the works of Copernicus, Galileo, Harvey, and Descartes. Spinoza also read the works of Arab and Jewish philosophers, especially Maimonides, but the most important of all of these scholars for the development of his own philosophical system was Descartes.

In accord with Jewish custom, which required all men to learn a trade, he became highly skilled in the art of grinding and polishing lenses. Thus, Spinoza worked at his trade by day and studied at night so as to shed light on his intellectual passion of understanding the human experience and the laws of the physical and psychological worlds. Although Spinoza first embraced Descartes' philosophy that there was a material body and a nonmaterial mind, he later rejected the Cartesian view that God, Nature, and Mind were all separate phenomena. For Spinoza, all three were inseparable, meaning that God was everywhere and in everything, which put him in opposition to the Judaic and Christian teachings that humans are made in the image of God. Accordingly, Spinoza was criticized severely and avoided at all costs by members of both religious communities (Alexander & Selesnick, 1966). For Spinoza, the mind and body were inseparable so that whatever happened to the body was reflected in the mind as emotions and thoughts while emotions and thoughts influenced the body.

The mind and body were on an equal footing providing a clear conceptual pathway to examine systematically the impact of psychological interventions upon bodily processes.

The second important aspect of Spinoza's philosophy for the development of psychology as an independent science was his view that nature is lawful and, as "humans are a part of (Spinoza) rather than apart from (Descartes) nature," it follows that human thoughts and behaviors are determined. According to Spinoza, free will is an illusion even though humans think of themselves as free because they may be conscious of their thoughts, intentions, and emotions at a given moment; yet all of them are caused by prior thoughts, intentions, and emotions that are unconscious because the person is not now aware of them in the present moment (Spinoza, 1677/1955).

Lastly, Spinoza assisted the launching of psychology as a separate science by distinguishing between emotions and passions. Passions, unlike emotions, are not linked to any specific thought or behavior, and therefore they are maladaptive as, for example, when a person is in a state of rage or heightened excitability. An emotion, on the other hand, is related to a specific thought or behavior such as love of a spouse or partner which can be moderated or influenced by reason. Behavior and thoughts that are guided by reason permit adaptation and survival of the person, which is not the case under the influence of the passions. Spinoza believed that by understanding the origins of passion it is possible for reason to gain control over passions.

Conscious and Unconscious Minds

Most people would agree that there are times when each of us may have done something automatically while not aware of what we were doing. Such experiences suggest that our mind is not unitary and consists of a conscious and unconscious component. Another way of expressing this sense of duality is that some of our experiences and actions become dissociated from our sense of conscious awareness. Our current understanding of the conscious and unconscious components of the human mind began with the ideas of Gottfried Wilhelm von Leibniz (1646–1716). Leibniz was born in Leipzig, Germany, the son of a Professor of Moral Philosophy at the University of Leipzig (Urmson, 1967). Unfortunately, his father died when Leibniz was six, and young Gottfried was sent off to school to continue his education that had begun as home schooling under his father's tutelage. He entered the University of Leipzig at the age of 14, completed the standard classical curriculum, and completed his doctoral dissertation for his law degree at 19 years of age. Inasmuch as the university awarded only twelve law doctorates per year with priority determined by age of the candidate, Leibniz did not make the top twelve slots, due to his youthful age. As a result, he left the University of Leipzig in a rage, signed up at the smaller University of Altdorf, and earned his doctorate within the following six months.

Leibniz secured his first position with a Nuremberg alchemical society, and then became a legal advisor to Baron Johann Christian von Boineburg, which afforded him the opportunity to work on projects of interest to his patron as well as on many personal projects (e.g., a cataloging system for libraries and a study of doctrinal differences and similarities between Catholics and Protestants). Leibniz was dispatched on a diplomatic mission to Paris by his patron in 1672 where he remained until 1676, and while there he invented a new kind of watch that functioned more accurately than others in use at the time as well as a mathematical calculating machine that was so advanced that it won him membership in the prestigious

Royal Society as one of the first non-British members. Also, while in Paris he developed binary arithmetic in which all numbers are represented with just ones and zeroes, the system used for representation and calculation in present-day electronic computers. He also invented, independent of a similar discovery by Isaac Newton (1642–1727), the calculus which is still in use today.

Leibniz's third professional position, in which he remained for the rest of his forty-three years of life, was as court librarian and political and technical advisor to the House of Hanover in Germany. However, before starting this position in 1673 he visited London and Amsterdam, met Baruch Spinoza, and observed the dynamic movement of microorganisms through the first microscope invented by Anton von Leeuwenhoek (1632–1723). This observation of the smallest particles of matter convinced Leibniz that the entire world is made up of infinitesimally small entities, all of which are alive and have varying capacities to perceive—to register impressions of the rest of the world. Leibniz considered these tiny entities not to be made of matter but rather as units of energy which he called **monads** after the Greek **monos** which means unit. He conceived of four levels of monads which differed primarily in terms of their clarity, distinctness, and completeness of their perceptions of the world. There was a supreme monad or God, rational monads equivalent to the conscious human mind, sentient monads found in nonhuman living organisms, and, lastly, simple monads that made up the remainder of matter whether organic or inorganic. The level of awareness for the last type of monads was indistinct and unconscious.

According to Leibniz's monadology, consciousness varies from the clear, distinct, and **rational apperceptions** through indistinct perceptions terminating in minute or **petit perceptions** which never enter our consciousness (Aiton, 1985). However, as petit perceptions accumulate their combined force eventually leads to consciousness, much like hearing the sound of rain without being able to hear the sound of a single raindrop as it falls upon a surface. Accordingly, a continuum exists between the unconscious and conscious mind. Most likely Leibniz was the first major philosopher to propose an unconscious as well as conscious mind as well as the concept of limen or threshold. Experiences above a given collection of petit perceptions yield awareness while experiences below this level or threshold remain unconscious.

We turn now to developments in phrenology which provided the platform for the systematic study of the mind, popularized the idea of brain localization of specific mind functions, and represented a simple, straightforward, and seductive although grossly fallacious system of psychological assessment of a person.

PHRENOLOGY

The term *phrenology* was coined by Thomas Foster in 1815 and began in association with the scientific studies of the anatomy of the nervous system by Franz Joseph Gall (1758–1828). Phrenology was built upon the foundational ideas that humans could be studied scientifically and that mind could be studied objectively and explained in terms of natural causes. The key focus of phrenology was upon explaining individual differences between persons, which was of central interest to American psychology and the public from the 1830s to the turn of the 20th century (Bakan, 1966). During a phrenology exam, the client would talk about herself or himself while the phrenologist was examining the client's skull and then the phrenologist would find bumps on the client's head that fit the description. Phrenology, although built upon this correlational database, popularized the foundational idea of brain localization of specific psychological functions. In addition, phrenology made plain the practical value of the newly emerging science of psychology to pragmatic Americans and others from the 1830s to the beginning of the 20th century.

Franz Joseph Gall (1758–1832)

Gall earned his medical degree at the University of Vienna in 1785, and as a skilled anatomist demonstrated that each hemisphere of the brain controls the opposite side of the body (i.e., **contra-lateral representation** of function) and that mental abilities of different species correlated with the size and complexity of the cortex of the brain. He argued soundly that the anatomical convolutions of the brain were stable within a given species, meaning that the surface of the brain or cortex was not a chaotic mix of ridges (gyri) and valleys (sulci) but had a lawful structure and arrangement (Temkin, 1947). Gall's anatomical findings were well received by the medical and scientific communities. Gall became convinced that just as the anatomy or structure of the brain is lawful, so too must the functions of the mind (i.e., psychological functions such as thinking and remembering) be lawful as well. Gall launched the study of the human mind by drawing first upon observations from his childhood that classmates with protruding eyes appeared to have better memories than him. Gall, along with his student and colleague Johann Gasper Spurzheim (1776–1832), by the method of cranioscopy (measurement of the physical shape and bumps and dents of the skull), mapped out the location on the skull, and therefore, by deduction, the brain localization of the thirty-seven faculties which were subsumed under the two overarching domains of the **affective** or **emotional and intellectual faculties** (Sizer & Drayton, 1892). The phrenological movement responded to the enduring human need for knowledge about oneself and the desire to predict one's future personal and professional lives.

Phrenology in America

Gall died in Paris in 1828 and was denied burial in consecrated ground because his work was judged to be deterministic and materialistic and therefore smacked of atheism. As a consequence his books were placed on the Catholic Church's **Index of Prohibited Books**. Spurzheim carried on and visited America in August 1832, where he lectured to the faculty of Yale and Harvard, and was dead by September of that same year (Bakan, 1966). In 1838, George Combe (1788–1858), a Scottish phrenologist, lectured widely to the general public from Boston to Washington, DC, resulting in phrenological societies popping up all over the United States so that by the 1840s it appeared as if the majority of Americans believed in phrenology (Davies, 1955). Interestingly, as a harbinger of things to come, the faculty and president of Brown University declared that mesmerism was more important than phrenology (Pickard & Bailey, 1945), while in the late 1880s the Psychology Department of Cornell University was founded to accumulate evidence regarding the value of phrenology (Dallenbach, 1955).

Orson, Lorenzo, and Charlotte Fowler and Samuel Wells formed the phrenological firm of Fowler and Wells in 1844, which dominated the phrenology business from its inception to the beginning of the 20th century. Thousands of phrenological examinations, including those of celebrities such as Walt Whitman, were conducted in Fowler and Wells parlors in

Boston, New York, and Philadelphia, as well as many other franchises they established throughout the country (Davies, 1955). Interestingly, Ray Kroc (1902–1984) had a phrenological examination when he was 4 years of age predicting that he would work in the food industry. He went on in 1955 in Des Plaines, Illinois, to establish McDonald's restaurants, which in 2001 numbered 28,000 restaurants in 121 countries and served 29 million people per day (Gross, 1997; McDonald's, 2001). Although riddled with shabby science, phrenology popularized the foundational ideas that the brain is the organ of the mind, mental functions can be localized in the brain, and individual characteristics can be measured, while also stressing the importance of individual differences and models of personality.

Personality Assessment

Many businesses at the beginning of the 20th century required a phrenological reading of applicants, especially for leadership or sensitive financial positions in their organizations, and thus they were sent off to phrenological parlors for an assessment of their capabilities and personalities (Davies, 1955). Although phrenological assessments are no longer used today, organizations still need to predict the performance of applicants for high-level executive positions, and they now send such applicants to Executive Assessment Centers for a battery of interviews, personality inventories, and participation in simulated decision-making exercises. In fact, personality inventories are a major component of contemporary assessment processes, due, in part, to the Five Factor Model of personality (FFM) and the robust predictive power of some of the five personality dimensions for a wide range of organizational functions (McCrae & Costa, 1997; Hogan, Hogan, & Roberts, 1996; Mount, Barrick, & Strauss, 1994; Salgado, 1997). The five personality factors can be represented by the acronym of **OCEAN** which stands for **Openness to Experience, Conscientiousness, Extroversion, Agreeableness, and Neuroticism (or emotional stability)**. The evidence indicates clearly that conscientiousness (i.e., a responsible, dependable, persistent, organized, and achievement-oriented person) is the most valid predictor of a wide variety of job performances in many countries around the globe (Hogan, Hogan, & Roberts, 1996; Hurtz & Donovan, 2000; Mount, Barrick, & Strauss, 1994; Salgado, 1997). It has also been clearly demonstrated that emotional stability (i.e., a calm, secure, at-ease person) is also a valid predictor of a wide variety of job performances (Salgado, 1997). Thus, the bottom line when hiring someone is to select a person who is conscientious and calm.

The assessment of intelligence has been a central and at times an extremely controversial issue in psychology and related disciplines throughout the 20th century (Herrnstein & Murray, 1994; Neisser et al., 1996). In a comprehensive report from the American Psychological Association, Neisser et al. (1996) concluded that there are many ways to be intelligent and thus there are many conceptualizations of intelligence. In general, intelligence test scores predict individual differences in academic achievement fairly well, yielding correlations of about 0.50 with grade point average and 0.55 with number of completed years of education. Also, a significant correlation between occupational status and intelligence has been demonstrated even when measures of education and family background have been statistically controlled. They also report one of the most striking findings regarding intelligence test scores, namely, **The Flynn Effect**, or the fact that mean IQ test scores in many countries around the world have increased more than fifteen points, a full standard deviation, in the last fifty years and the rate of increase may be accelerating (Flynn, 1999). It may be that these increases in IQ test scores are driven by improved nutrition, cultural changes, experiences in testing, or some other factors. Although a fair amount is known about the nature and assessment of intelligence, there are many questions that remain unanswered to date such as the pathways of genetic and environmental influences on intelligence and what accounts fully for the differences in IQ scores between blacks and whites (Neisser et al., 1996).

MESMERISM

The development of mesmerism, to be known later as hypnotism, was critical to the future of psychology because mesmerism helped to establish the paradigm that "mind matters" and that psychological factors such as self-concept, moods, and self-management skills, rather than only neuroanatomy, physiology, and brain chemistry, contributed to adaptive as well as maladaptive persons. In addition, the development of mesmerism beginning in the 1770s promoted a naturalistic explanation of mental illness rather than one based upon demonology or evil spirits.

Franz Anton Mesmer (1734–1815)

Franz Anton Mesmer was born in Iznang on the German shore of Lake Constance. He first studied law in 1759 at the University of Vienna before switching to medicine and earning his M.D. in 1766, based on his dissertation titled "On the Influence of the Planets," in which he argued that the planets influenced human health and well-being through a celestial force in much the same way the waxing and waning of the moon influences the tides of the oceans. He called this planetary force "animal gravitation or magnetism," which he believed was like Isaac Newton's (1642–1727) conception of universal gravity, that is, a powerful and ubiquitous force that could operate at distance upon biological processes much like metal filings drawn to a magnet. According to Mesmer, physical and/or mental illnesses were due to the congestion of the animal magnetism in different parts of the body and the appropriate treatment consisted of redistributing and thus balancing the flow of "animal gravitation or animal magnetism" by placing magnets on different parts of the body.

Mesmer, a handsome man with what friends described as a magnetic personality, married a wealthy widow ten years his senior and of noble descent, Maria Anna von Posch, thus affording him access to the wealthy and influential members of Viennese society. He established a respected medical practice in Vienna, and became a patron of the arts and friend of Wolfgang Amadeus Mozart (1756–1791). Mesmer practiced medicine sporadically and his interest in animal magnetism was reawakened when he met a Jesuit priest and professor at the University of Vienna, Maximillian Hell (1720–1779), who told Mesmer of healings he had accomplished by placing magnets on the body of his patients. Thereafter, Mesmer saw as a patient a 27-year-old woman, Fraulein Oesterlin, who presented with a large number of physical symptoms for which there was no observable bodily cause. Mesmer decided to treat her with magnets as he had learned that some English physicians were also treating certain diseases with magnets and he had been very impressed by Father Hell's experiences with magnets as well. Mesmer directed the patient to swallow some preparation containing iron, and then shortly thereafter attached three magnets specially designed by Father Hell to her stomach and legs. Fraulein Oesterlin began to feel streams of a mysterious fluid running downward through her body with many of her presenting symptoms (e.g., dizziness, feelings of weakness, and anxiety) receding for a number of hours. Mesmer concluded that these results were due not to the magnets alone but rather to a magnetic fluid accumulated in the patient with the magnets enhancing the animal magnetism and giving it direction and expressing its influence at a distance (Ellenberger, 1970).

Mesmer focused the rest of his life on the elaboration and use of animal magnetism as a powerful cure for a wide variety of illnesses. He used magnets in the early stages of his medical practice, eventually abandoning the placement of magnets on the body of the patient as he became convinced that he could manipulate the animal magnetism by waving a special wand, laying his hands over the patient's body, and finally realizing his words alone drove the above manipulations. Lastly, Mesmer developed a group technique for manipulating the flow of animal magnetism in his patients by having them sit around a "baquet," a tub filled with magnetized water, with each patient holding onto a metal rod attached to the baquet. He would then encourage by his words and domineering presence one of his patients to have a crisis consisting of emotional outbursts, screaming and sobbing, and eventually convulsing. He observed that, in general, after one patient went into a crisis others around the baquet followed suit. Almost all of the patients experienced some temporary relief of their symptoms, and some even claimed they were cured.

Mesmer's fame spread by word of mouth from his patients as well as by the publicity surrounding two particular incidents. In 1775, he challenged the miraculous healings of a priest named Johann Joseph Gassner (1727–1779) explaining that the healings were a result of the redistribution of animal magnetism rather than, as Gassner claimed, a result of the driving out of demons through his practice of exorcism (Ellenberger, 1970). Mesmer's attribution of theses cures to animal magnetism won the debate since his theory fit more with the Zeitgeist or Spirit of the times and emphasized the power of naturalistic rather than supernatural forces as suggested by Gassner. The second incident that further rocketed Mesmer to notoriety in Vienna occurred in 1777 when he agreed to treat Fraulein Paradies, a 17-year-old pianist, blind since the age of 3 and a favorite friend of then Austrian Empress Maria Theresa (Fancher, 1996). Both Fraulein Paradies and Mesmer claimed that her sight was restored as result of Mesmer's magnetic treatments but the cure was limited as she could see only when alone with Mesmer. This incident caused the Viennese medical community to claim that Mesmer was a fraud and as a consequence his standing in the community toppled, which in turn caused Mesmer to leave Vienna for Paris in 1778.

Once in Paris, Mesmer set up his practice in a private mansion and magnetized patients from the highest social levels for large fees while also having a sliding fee schedule for less-well-off Parisians. His practice grew and he switched to group treatments using the "baquet" mentioned earlier. However, resentment grew within the Parisian medical community as word spread of Mesmer's success, the exorbitant fees collected from his wealthier clients, and his unconventional treatments. In 1784, the king of France appointed a commission consisting of Benjamin Franklin, then U.S. ambassador to France, as presiding officer; Antoine Lasoivier, the great chemist; and Joseph Guillotin, the creator of the guillotine to study objectively the effects of animal magnetism. The commission reported in August 1784 that Mesmer did affect the well-being of some of his clients not by a physical force, but rather by suggestion and there was no evidence found for the existence of animal magnetism, which the commission concluded was a figment of Mesmer's imagination. Despite the report, Mesmer carried on with his practice as well as training mostly wealthy students in mesmerism in his quasi-religious schools, which he had established earlier and called "Societies of Harmony."

Mesmer left Paris in 1792 for London and then Germany where he died in 1815. Right up until his death, he attributed his cures (in most cases the removal of psychological symptoms of anxiety and related bodily responses) to the flow of vital energy (i.e., animal magnetism), while in retrospect it seems more reasonable to identify suggestion, social contagion or influences of others, and self-fulfilling prophecies for generating the crisis which he thought was essential for a cure (Eden, 1984; Merton, 1948). It is interesting that in recent years there have been a number of claims of the curative powers of magnetized bracelets as well as growing popular interest in traditional Chinese medicine, which is centered upon maintaining good health by a harmonious distribution and flow of "Qui" (i.e., a vital energy) along the meridians of the body which do not coincide anatomically with the pathways of the nervous or circulatory systems.

Marquis de Puysegur (1751–1825)

One of Mesmer's students from the "Society of Harmony" schools was Amand-Marie-Jacques de Chastenet, Marquis de Puysegur. The Marquis de Puysegur, a member of one of the most prominent families of 18th-century French nobility, used magnets and reported that his patients did not have to experience a crisis, which Mesmer thought was essential for symptom relief, but instead benefited as well from putting the patient in a peaceful and sleep-like trance which Puysegur referred to as **artificial somnambulism**. Puysegur also found that while treating one of his patients, a servant, during the sleep-like trance there was enhanced suggestibility such that the person reported numbness in different parts of the body and did not feel pinpricks which otherwise would have been painful. He also reported that many of his patients forgot the trance state and only remembered the state when magnetized, which today is referred to as posthypnotic amnesia. Puysegur also found that clients, upon awakening from the trance state, would perform unpredictable acts such as scratch themselves in response to a cue from the therapist even though they had forgotten that they had been so instructed during the trance state, which today is referred to as posthypnotic suggestion (Ellenberger, 1970). It is reasonable to conclude that what was later to be known as hypnotism was inspired by Mesmer while the true founder of hypnotism was Puysegur (Richet, 1884).

HYPNOSIS

The transition from the practice and theoretical accounts of mesmerism to hypnosis took place initially in England, although important developments also arose from clinical and scientific observations in India and France. Sporadic reports from mesmerists of inducing an anesthetic state in some of their clients attracted the attention of some legitimate medical practitioners as chemical anesthetics did not become available until the 1850s.

The transition from mesmerism to hypnosis makes plain the powerful influences of prevailing scientific paradigms and how they serve to dampen innovation while providing some degree of explanation of interesting, although not yet fully understood, phenomena. For example, John Elliotson (1791–1868) was a successful and creative physician at the prestigious London University College Hospital who was the first to use the then newly invented stethoscope to listen to the sounds of the heart (around 1837) and was the first to use suggestions encouraging relaxation or mesmerism as a surgical anesthetic to diminish pain. Elliotson was ridiculed by his medical superiors and colleagues for using mesmerism as well as the stethoscope, neither of which they thought would be of any value in the practice of medicine. Elliotson resigned from the hospital in protest when the university council passed a resolution prohibiting the practice of mesmerism in the hospital, thus precluding him or others from studying further the effects of systematic and focused suggestions as well as an anesthetic agent upon a variety of illnesses. In addition, Elliotson was dismissed from his duties as president of the Royal Medical and Chirurgical Society (Alexander & Selesnick, 1996). Clearly, scientific paradigms can in some cases cause a great deal of professional and personal pain.

James Esdaile (1808–1859), a physician with the British army in Calcutta, performed in the late 1840s more than 250 painless operations using mesmerism or suggestions encouraging relaxation to anesthetize his Indian patients. Esdaile kept meticulous clinical notes and reported that the anesthetic effect was substantial and that for some serious operations the mortality rate was reduced by almost 50% with anesthetized patients. Back in Britain, Esdaile's results were dismissed on racist grounds that his patients really liked to be operated on, his Indian assistants probably colluded in some way with the patients, and what worked for Indians would not work for Europeans (Ellenberger, 1970). Around 1850, ether and chloroform were starting to be used widely for anesthesia and as a consequence interest in mesmerism as an anthesthetic agent waned quickly.

James Braid (1795–1860), a prominent Manchester surgeon, studied systematically the effects of mesmerism upon his patients. He concluded in his book published in 1843, *The Rationale of Nervous Sleep*, that the mesmeric trance states were simply the result of excess muscle fatigue due to prolonged concentration giving rise to physical exhaustion. As a consequence, mesmerism came to be understood as a sleep-like state and was renamed first **neuro-hypnology** which Braid shortened to **hypnosis** (Alexander & Selesnick, 1966). Thus, hypnosis was made acceptable by using an explanation that fit within the medical paradigm, namely, hypnosis was the result of muscular fatigue of the elevator muscles of the eyes which relax causing the eyes to close after prolonged fixation on an object, coupled with relaxing verbal suggestions from the hypnotist. Braid advanced the systematic study of hypnosis by conceptualizing it as a biological phenomenon which could be studied scientifically.

The Nancy School of Hypnosis

From 1860 to 1880, hypnosis fell to the margins of medical and surgical practice, due, in part, to the development of chemical anesthetic agents. However, a modest French physician, Auguste Ambroise Liébeault (1823–1904), after having established a solid medical practice in the small rural village of Pont-Saint-Vincent not far from the city of Nancy, France, started to experiment with hypnosis. He recruited patients, mostly poor people and peasants, by allowing them to choose between standard medical treatments for a fee or treatment by hypnosis for free. After a while his hypnotic practice boomed, he learned a great deal, and he had to set up a sliding fee scale to control the burgeoning number of patients who selected hypnotic treatments. He considered hypnosis the same as natural sleep, which differed only because it was induced by suggestion and concentration on the idea of sleep. Liébeault treated a wide range of illnesses, such as arthritis and ulcers. He attracted the attention of Hippolyte Bernheim (1840–1919) from Nancy, a physician renowned because of his research on typhoid fever, who started using hypnosis in 1882 and published his findings in 1886 (Ellenberger, 1970). Bernheim became the leader of the Nancy School of Hypnosis, according to which hypnosis was not a pathological condition but rather a natural state of heightened suggestibility, that is, the ability to transform an idea into an act induced by the suggestions of the hypnotist. Bernheim used hypnosis less and less as he came to observe that he could obtain the same effects by suggestion alone during the awake state as he could with hypnosis. He called this new treatment strategy "psychotherapeutics" (Ellenberger, 1970). The Nancy School of Hypnosis promoted the foundational ideas that hypnosis was a state of heightened suggestibility, a state somewhere on a continuum between wakefulness and natural sleep, and that susceptibility to hypnosis was a trait that varied from person to person.

The Parisian School of Hypnosis

The Parisian School of Hypnosis, led by the great 19th-century neurologist Jean-Martin Charcot (1825–1893), argued that only people suffering from hysteria (presenting bodily symptoms like paralysis, convulsions, anesthesia, and memory loss without any signs of organic or physical illness) could be hypnotized (Ellenberger, 1970; Fancher, 1996). According to Charcot, susceptibility to hypnosis, like susceptibility to hysteria, was a reflection of some underlying neurological disorder.

Charcot came from a financially modest family, earned his M.D. in 1853, and then became the private physician and traveling companion for a wealthy banker. He married a wealthy widow and returned as a financially secure man to the famous Salpêtrière Hospital in 1862 where he had done his clinical residency as a medical student. Initially, the large Salpêtrière Hospital in Paris housed about 4,500 indigent patients, most of whom were women suffering from a variety of neurological and psychosomatic disorders. Charcot focused his attention upon those female patients who exhibited difficulty remembering events and persons, temporary paralysis of a limb that the patient could not move while awake yet moved freely when the patient was asleep, and anesthesia or insensitivity to noxious and painful stimuli, all of which are the cardinal symptoms of hysteria. Unlike other physicians who thought that hysteria was just a form of malingering, Charcot concluded that hysteria was due to the progressive deterioration of the nervous system. Inasmuch as both hysteria and hypnosis shared the same cardinal symptoms of selective memory loss, paralysis, and anesthesia, Charcot believed that hypnotizability indicated the presence of hysteria. As Charcot's reputation as a premier neurologist grew throughout Europe many came, including Sigmund Freud (1856–1939), to see his spectacular demonstrations of hypnosis, especially when he hypnotized Blanche Wittman, who was one of his most demonstrative patients, exhibiting a wide variety of imaginary sensations and physical states during the hypnotic state.

Although Charcot's theory that hypnosis and hysteria were reflections of an underlying neurological disorder is no longer considered valid, he gave hypnosis further scientific credibility and promoted the foundational idea that hysteria and other psychological ailments such as neuroses and psychoses are as real and in some cases as painful and debilitating as physical illnesses. Charcot helped immensely to put the mind and body on the same footing, and to make plain that "mind matters."

Alfred Binet (1857–1911), who later went on to develop the first systematic test of human intelligence, worked as a laboratory assistant for Charcot at La Salpêtrière from 1883 to about 1890, during which time he assisted Charcot in experimental studies of **transfer and polarization** (Wolf, 1973). For example, during hypnosis the act of moving one leg could be transferred to movement of the other leg by passing a magnet near the patient while polarization yielded opposite or polar emotions or perceptions as a result of the magnet. As another example, while under hypnosis, a patient who first exhibited pleasure for an object would express disgust for the same object when a magnet was presented. Interestingly, neither transfer nor polarization could be demonstrated by other hypnotists including members of the Nancy School. Eventually, Binet and others had to retract their earlier claims and demonstrations of these phenomena and attribute them appropriately to suggestion and the willingness of the patient to please the hypnotist as the patients knew in advance what was expected of them (Wolf, 1973). Thereafter, Binet was forever sensitive to circular arguments like those given by authority figures such as Charcot, who argued that hypnosis reflected an underlying disorder of the nervous system because only patients with neurological disorders such as hysteria could be hypnotized.

Pierre Janet (1859–1947) studied under Charcot at the La Salpêtrière and like Charcot believed that hysteria was due to a weakness of the nervous system. Janet reasoned further that this nervous weakness gave rise to inadequate psychological tension and a lack of psychic cohesiveness of the personality induced by excessive fatigue or some type of traumatic experience, yielding a condition he called **psychasthenia** (Ellenberger, 1970). As a consequence, conscious experiences became split off from each other yielding hysteria and dissociative phenomena such that the individual behaved as if completely motivated by separate, dissociated personalities. Janet hypnotized many patients diagnosed with this psychological disorder, characterized by phobias, anxiety, obsessions, or compulsions, and found that their neurotic symptoms receded when they were able to recall the traumatic event that appeared to have been associated with the onset of their symptoms. Janet concluded that hysterical symptoms arise from the subconscious influence of dissociated aspects of the person's personality. The dissociated parts of consciousness, once remembered, could then be integrated under hypnosis so that eventually the personality became whole again. Thus, unlike Charcot, Janet explained hypnosis and hysteria as the result of psychological rather than organic influences, and anticipated some of Sigmund Freud's foundational ideas of unconscious memories and motives shaping conscious experiences and behaviors.

Laboratory Studies of Hypnosis

In 1892, Hugo Münsterberg (1863–1916), at the invitation of William James, became director of the Psychology Laboratory at Harvard University. Münsterberg enjoyed an excellent reputation as a careful and methodical laboratory-based experimental psychologist, and was very interested in applying psychological ideas derived from the laboratory to assist people with daily living in a wide variety of situations such as the workplace, school, and the courtroom. In effect, Münsterberg was an early example of the scientist-professional model that was adopted widely in psychology in the 1950s and was known as the Boulder Model for training clinical psychologists (Albee, 1970, 2000; Baker & Benjamin, 2000; Benjamin & Baker, 2000). Münsterberg accepted clinical patients in his laboratory only if they presented problems of scientific interest, which was determined through assessment using clinical interviews, observations of their behaviors, and responses to word-association tests. None of his patients paid a fee for his services. He tailored his treatment plan to fit the needs of the individual, although throughout most plans he relied heavily on suggestions, therapist and self-based positive expectations that the patient would get better (self-fulfilling prophecies), and in some cases he used hypnosis (Münsterberg, 1909). He emphasized the facilitative effects of hypnosis for the patient's openness to suggestions for improvement, and his endorsement of hypnosis was important for legitimizing hypnosis as sound and scientific clinical treatment strategy (Münsterberg, 1910).

Clark L. Hull (1884–1952), in his book, *Hypnosis and Suggestibility: An Experimental Approach* (1933), summarized approximately ten years of systematic laboratory studies employing physiological recordings during the hypnotic state as well as standardized techniques for fixation and providing direct suggestions for producing the hypnotic state. Almost all of Hull's findings regarding hypnosis are still considered valid today, including his foundational finding that the personal capacity for hypnosis is distributed normally like other human traits, such as height, weight, and intelligence. This was an important finding because it stressed that the individual rather than "the power of the hypnotist" alone is a key variable for the induction of the hypnotic state (Hull, 1933).

Again based upon objective laboratory findings, Hull reported further that females were slightly more hypnotizable than males, children more susceptible than adults, no differences in susceptibility to hypnosis as a function of intelligence, and likewise no relationship between neurosis or psychosis and susceptibility to hypnosis. In addition, Hull and his colleagues at the Institute for Psychology at Yale University, during the period from approximately 1920 to 1930, found little evidence that hypnosis enhances memory or that posthypnotic suggestions were effective. Hull's overarching conclusion was that the hypnotic state was not qualitatively different from the normal state of consciousness, but rather only differed in degree of openness to follow suggestions accompanied by the temporary suspension of analytical thought processes. Hull's study of hypnosis came to an end when a woman who had been hypnotized as part of Hull's research program sued Yale University because she claimed that the experience caused her to have a mental breakdown. Her case was settled out of court, and Yale suspended further study of hypnosis.

The laboratory-based studies of hypnosis were extremely important because they made plain that hypnotic phenomena such as posthypnotic suggestions could be studied objectively and systematically, and the efficacy of hypnosis as a therapeutic strategy could be evaluated empirically. As a consequence of sustained laboratory studies coupled with systematic clinical case studies, there evolved new models and theories to explain hypnotic phenomena and the mechanism(s) responsible for hypnosis.

The State and Non-State Model of Hypnosis

Hypnosis is now part of mainstream psychology (Kirsch & Lynn, 1995), used by many mental health professionals, and when used in conjunction with cognitive-behavioral and psychodynamic treatments improves substantially their efficacy (Kirsch, Montgomery, & Sapirstein, 1995; Kraft & Rudolfa, 1982). Hypnosis also remains an important research topic (Lynn & Rhue, 1991). Hypnosis is the primary focus of Division 30-Society for Psychological Hypnosis of the American Psychology Association. Division 30 has defined hypnosis as a procedure wherein changes in sensations, perceptions, thoughts, feelings, or behavior are suggested, with this definition embraced by a broad range of practitioners and researchers (Chaves, 1994; Fromm, Hilgard, & Kihlstrom, 1994). It is now well established based upon extensive laboratory and clinical research that hypnosis is not a reflection of weakness or gullibility, not related to sleep. Responsiveness to hypnosis is more dependent upon the efforts and abilities of the person hypnotized than the hypnotist; suggestions are responded to equally with or without hypnosis, hypnosis does not increase the accuracy of memory, and hypnosis does not yield literal reexperiencing of childhood events (Hilgard, 1965, 1975; Kirsch & Lynn, 1995).

Since the earliest demonstrations of hypnotic phenomena the fundamental question still not fully answered is the identification of the mechanism(s) for explaining how hypnotic communication gets translated into behavior. The **State or Special Process Model of Hypnosis**, dominant during the 1960s, attempted to answer that question by proposing that the hypnotic state is a unique form of consciousness somewhere between wakefulness and sleep (Bowers, 1966; Kirsch & Lynn, 1995, 1998). According to this model, the primary agent in the dyadic hypnotic relationship is the hypnotist who, based upon her or his clinical and persuasive skills, could induce the unique hypnotic state. The failure to find systematic and reliable clarion markers for this unique state of consciousness, such as, for example, true age regression as reflected in age appropriate physiological or cognitive changes, caused most researchers and clinicians to reject this model. Furthermore, the fact that hypnotic phenomena can also occur when the person provides self-administered suggestions is not readily accommodated by the state model as well (Kirsch & Lynn, 1995).

On the contrary, the **Non-State or Social Psychological Model** proposes that hypnotic suggestions are translated into behavior when the person being hypnotized engages in two fundamental cognitive processes, namely, (a) sustaining and elaborating upon suggested images, and (b) disregarding other distracting internal and external stimulus intrusions (Barber, 1969; Spanos & Barber, 1974). According to the non-state or social psychological model, hypnotic behaviors are identical to other complex social behaviors arising from ability, expectancy, attribution, and belief (e.g., self-fulfilling prophecies). We turn now to the more recently developed dissociation theories of hypnosis which have evolved out of and replaced the state and non-state models of hypnosis.

Dissociation Theories of Hypnosis

Spanos (1982) introduced the terms **special process** to replace the state model and **social psychological** to replace the non-state model of hypnosis. The special process model included dissociation theories of hypnosis according to which hypnotic behavior is qualitatively different from nonhypnotic behavior because it is produced by either a trance or dissociation. The foundational idea that hypnosis and related hypnotic phenomena arise from the dissociation of consciousness into two or more parts can be traced to the earlier work of Charcot (1887/1889) and Janet (Janet, 1889). However, laboratory findings that there was interference between tasks executed by presumably dissociated parts of consciousness cast serious doubts about the dissociation theory of hypnosis (Hull, 1933; Kirsch & Lynn, 1998; White & Shevach, 1942).

In light of the above difficulties for dissociation theories of hypnosis, Hilgard (1975, 1986, 1994) introduced his neodissociation model of hypnosis which consists of three major components, namely, (a) "**an executive ego**" (i.e., alert, critical, and analytical form of consciousness) that plans and monitors functions but which may not have access to all of the person's consciousness including some thoughts, feelings, and memories due to an amnesic barrier; (b) below the executive ego there are **three relatively autonomous control systems** that deal with movement, pain perception, and memory; and (c) **hierarchically aligned subsystems under the executive ego**. Hilgard (1986, p. 2) defines dissociation as "a division of consciousness in which part of the attentive effort and planning may continue without awareness of it all." Thus, according to Hilgard (1994), hypnotic suggestions yield dissociation between executive monitoring and planning functions that are otherwise integrated. These functions persist during hypnosis although they are less robust, evaluative, and editorial (Kirsch & Lynn, 1995). Thus, the dissociation in cognitive functioning along with the amnesia between the dissociated parts gives rise to the apparent involuntariness of many hypnotic responses.

Hilgard's (1986, 1994) neodissociation theory focuses upon the division of consciousness into parts not immediately available to each other, while other dissociation theories focus upon the dissociation or uncoupling of cognitive and behavioral subsystems from executive control (Bowers, 1992; Bowers & Davidson, 1991; Woody & Bowers, 1994). Thus, according to the dissociation of control theory of Bowers and his colleagues, hypnosis uncouples lower-level functions from the integration of the subsystems normally driven by consciousness.

The evidence in support of either Hilgard's neodissociation theory of the fragmentation of consciousness or Bowers' and colleagues' dissociation of control theory that proposes an uncoupling between the executive control system (i.e., alert, monitoring, critical, and analytical form of consciousness) and subsystems such as movement and memory is slim (Dixon & Laurence, 1992). Accordingly, there are still many unanswered questions regarding hypnosis and the mechanism(s) responsible for it (Hilgard, 1975; Kirsch & Lynn, 1995). Some of the unanswered questions include, for example, What makes responsiveness to hypnosis so stable over time? Does hypnosis give rise to fundamental shifts in information processing? Does hypnosis potentiate other forms of psychotherapy? What are the physiological mechanisms responsible for hypnosis? What changes, if any, occur during hypnotic age regression (Kirsch & Lynn, 1995)?

Hypnotic Phenomena: Age Regression

In hypnotic age regression, a participant is instructed to relive an experience that occurred earlier in life, usually involving an adult reliving some earlier childhood event which in some cases yields dramatic changes in behavior and demeanor. Authentic hypnotic age regression must include three components, namely, **ablation** (the functional loss, similar to amnesia, of knowledge acquired after the regressed age); **reinstatement** (the return to prior patterns of perceptual, cognitive, or physiological performances); and **revivification** (recovery, like hyperamensia, of previously inaccessible memories), with reinstatement having been studied most extensively (Kihlstrom, 1985).

The effects of hypnotic age regression have been studied especially for visual illusions. In some interesting studies, Parrish, Lundy, and Leibowitz (1968, 1969) studied the effects of hypnotic age regression upon the magnitudes of the Ponzo and Poggendorff illusions, which increase and decrease, respectively, as a function of chronological age from childhood to adulthood. These investigators found that when 19-year-old participants were age regressed to 9 and 5 years of age the Ponzo illusion decreased, while the Poggendorff illusion increased in magnitude, respectively. Interestingly, task motivated, nonhypnotized participants were not able to match these performances. Thus, using a within-subjects or repeated-measures design rather than the standard between-subjects design characteristic of developmental psychology, Parrish and colleagues found that under hypnotic age regression magnitudes of these illusions were more like those of younger persons than the actual chronological ages of the participants. Unfortunately, others have been unable to replicate these findings (Asher, Barber, & Spanos, 1972; Perry & Chisholm, 1973).

Nash (1987) reviewed sixty years of hypnotic age regression research and found no systematic evidence for the reinstatement of psychological or physiological functions during hypnotic age regression. Thus, for example, there was no enhancement of recall for significant memories of childhood such as the day of the week when you turned 7 years of age, no reinstatement of infant-like EEG patterns or return of the Babinski reflex seen during the first six months of infancy, or no ablation (i.e., elimination) of recently learned conditioned responses as an adult when regressed to an earlier age (Nash, 1987). It appears as if a wide variety of affective, cognitive, and perceptual responses of hypnotically age regressed persons do not resemble those of children and when they do, waking control subjects do as well on the target measures. What does seem to occur is a shift toward more prelogical modes of thinking so that hypnotic age regression involves more a topographic rather than a temporal shift of thinking, perceiving, and feeling (Nash, 1987).

HYPNOSIS AND CLINICAL PSYCHOLOGY, EFFICACY STUDIES, AND PREVENTION

Recently, Taylor (2000) has argued that the study of hypnosis has played a pivotal role in the establishment of clinical psychology in contrast to the widely received doctrine that Lightner Witmer (1867–1956) established the field at the University of Pennsylvania in 1896. It is indeed the case that Witmer made significant contributions to the development of psychology in the schools, advocated that psychologists and physicians work together, and that he was most interested in the study of mentally defective children (Routh, 1994; Taylor, 2000). It appears as if Witmer did not embrace or practice psychotherapy, or "psychotherapeutics" as it was originally called, at the beginning of the 20th century. Taylor (2000), on the contrary, has suggested that clinical psychology in the United States began, like experimental psychology, within the tradition of the university setting when physiological psychology fused with psychical research to study the paranormal including dissociation and hypnosis. During the period from 1870 to 1890, the physiological and psychological laboratories at Harvard University studied extensively functional rather than organic disorders of the nervous system including comprehensive investigations of hypnotic phenomena. There then developed at Harvard University a graduate specialty called experimental psychopathology, with courses offered by William James, and at Clark University with courses offered by Adolf Meyer, including courses on hypnosis. This period of investigations of hypnosis and other related phenomena is known as the Boston School of Abnormal Psychology, and served as the point of departure for further study of the nature and outcomes of psychotherapy from 1880 to 1920 (Burnham, 1968; Gifford, 1978; Taylor, 2000).

As discussed in chapter 3 and in the present focus on hypnosis, in their foundational study Lipsey and Wilson (1993) provided a meta-analysis of the efficacy of psychological, educational, and behavioral treatments based upon thousands of investigations of reported treatment outcomes. The unequivocal results of this comprehensive study are that well-developed psychological, educational, and behavioral treatments have substantial positive effects on targeted outcome variables. In addition, the above results still stand strong when controlling for studies culled from the data set in the meta-analysis because of weak research designs, oversampling of published studies, or disproportionate representation of very small sample studies. There were fifty-four studies that used hypnosis exclusively as the treatment intervention, and there was a strong positive effect upon the study outcomes (Edwards, 1991). In short, psychotherapy in general and hypnosis in particular work! The next step for treatment effectiveness research is to determine which treatment interventions are most effective, the mediating causal processes through which they work, and the characteristics of the participants, providers, and contexts that most yield positive results (Lipsey & Wilson, 1993).

Also, as presented earlier in chapter 3, and important to review here again in the context of our discussion of hypnosis, there are two fundamental methods to determine if psychotherapy and other psychological interventions work, namely, efficacy and effectiveness studies (Seligman, 1995). In general, the methodology of choice that has served as the gold standard for evaluating the outcomes of psychotherapy has been efficacy studies that contrast some kind of therapy to a comparison group under well-controlled conditions, some of which are outlined in Table 6-1. For example, the results of efficacy studies indicate that cognitive therapy, interpersonal therapy, and medications all provide equally well moderate relief from unipolar depressive disorder; cognitive therapy works very well in panic disorders; and systematic desensitization relieves specific phobias. Unfortunately, efficacy studies are not very realistic because, for example, psychotherapy in the field is not of fixed duration as is the case for efficacy studies. Psychotherapy is self-correcting so if one technique does not work another technique is tried, and clients shop around for the appropriate therapist instead of, as in efficacy studies, being passively and randomly assigned to a predetermined therapy (Seligman, 1995).

Consumer Reports (1995, November) published an article that employed an effectiveness methodology based upon 2,900 returned questionnaires from subscribers who had seen a mental health professional. The findings indicated that clients benefited very substantially from long-term (one year or more) compared to short-term therapy and the combination of psychotherapy and medication was no more effective than psychotherapy alone. Interestingly, no particular modality of psychotherapy (e.g., cognitive, behavioral, and/or dynamic therapies) was better than the other for any reported disorder (Seligman, 1995).

Like the efficacy method, the effectiveness method has limitations such as relying upon retrospective reports rather than concurrent reports of the effects of therapy. However, the

---

TABLE 6-1	**Features of Efficacy Studies of Psychotherapeutic Interventions**

- Patients assigned randomly to treatment and control conditions
- Patients participate only in a fixed number of sessions
- Target outcomes clearly operationalized (e.g., self-reports of panic attacks)
- Only patients with single diagnosed disorder included in the study
- Fixed period of follow-up after completion of therapy

Adapted from Seligman, M.E.P., The effectiveness of psychotherapy: *The Consumer Reports Study*, pp. 965–974. Reprinted by permission of Martin E. P. Seligman, PhD.

combined results of efficacy and effectiveness studies make unequivocally clear that psychotherapy is a valuable treatment for a variety of psychological and physical disorders.

Despite the clearly established positive benefits of psychotherapy and hypnosis, the limited availability of these treatments (due to costs, time, and health insurance limits) indicates the need to shift from a totally remedial to a prevention strategy for dealing with the many mental health problems that are attributable in large measure to poverty, lack of educational opportunities, crime, and discrimination (Albee, 1970, 1990). According to Albee (2000), the social learning stress-related model of mental disorders seeks first and foremost to reduce poverty, discrimination, exploitation, and prejudices because they are major sources of stress causing emotional problems. Furthermore, Albee (1998, 2000) acknowledges that psychotherapy is effective but too expensive to be profitable for corporate health care organizations. As a consequence, according to Albee (2000), clinical psychology has joined with corporate forces and proponents of the organic/brain defect medical model of stress-induced illnesses that perpetuate social injustices. The real issue is to deal directly with the root causes of stress and mental health problems of the "many" rather than focus primarily upon the "few" who can afford psychotherapy (Albee, 1990, 2000).

PSYCHONEUROIMMUNOLOGY

Similar to the other practices related primarily to Eastern cultures, a new field of medicine is emerging on the foundations that dualism is inaccurate. Dualism, the paradigm presented by Descartes that the mind and the body are separate, has been the basis of Western medical practices for centuries; however, the new field of psychoneuroimmunology (PNI) crosses that boundary by integrating the fields of endocrinology, immunology, psychology, and neurology. Presently, no formal definition of PNI exists due to its recent formation and emergence (Pelletier, 1999).

However, a growing body of evidence continues to emerge on the significance of PNI for understanding of the affective, behavioral, and cognitive systems and their interaction, especially in human beings. The nervous system and the immune system both communicate using the same biochemical language with the immune system containing neurotransmitter receptor sites as well as producing and secreting neurotransmitters as a communications tool. Neurons not only communicate with the immune system (the system responsible for detecting and ridding the body of "non-self" cells); neurons also communicate with the brain on multiple dimensions.

The brain is integrated into this system primarily under the domain of stress. Specifically, a new class of PNI chemicals, endogenous opioids and neuropeptides, has been linked to communication between the brain and the immune system as well as in response to stress. Although evidence exists to support the paradigm, for example, the correlation found between stress of medical students on examinations which were significantly and negatively correlated with immune functioning, there is hope that the limited amount of empirical evidence that is beginning to mount in support of the PNI paradigm will further illuminate the association between specific subjective states and neuroendocrine processes and immune function (O'Leary, 1994).

■ Summary

We started this chapter with a brief discussion of the ideas of mind, body, and soul and indicated that psychology has focused primarily upon the nature of the relationship between the mind and body, particularly the brain. Baruch Spinoza played a prominent role in the establishment of psychology as an independent science as a result of his views that mind and body are on an equal footing, thoughts and behaviors are determined, and emotions are driven by reason. Gottfried Wilhelm von Leibniz gave us the idea of monads, and the related ideas of threshold of consciousness and that the mind consists of conscious and unconscious components. Leibniz's ideas influenced later developments in psychophysics, Freudian psychology, and ultimately our understanding of hypnosis.

Phrenology, a popular 19th-century practice, firmly established in the public's mind that the mind and brain are related and that a read of one (i.e., the relative distribution of bumps on the head) reveals the other (i.e., intellectual capabilities and personality traits). Although phrenology was based upon shabby science, it promoted the idea that just as the anatomy of the brain appears lawful so then the functions of mind may also be lawful.

We then reviewed the work of Franz Anton Mesmer, especially his construct of animal magnetism. Mesmer switched ultimately from using magnets to only his words to induce in his patients a crisis which he believed essential for a cure. Mesmer was investigated by a committee appointed by the king of France and chaired by Benjamin Franklin, then U.S. ambassador to France, which concluded that there was no scientific basis for the construct of animal magnetism and that any changes in his patients' conditions were most likely due to suggestions and the patient's unintended desire to collude with him. One of his students, the Marquis de Puysegur, induced a hypnotic sleep-like state, reported symptom relief without the patient experiencing a crisis, and called the induced state artificial somnambulism, which later came to be called hypnosis.

The practice of mesmerism or the use of suggestions was employed successfully as an anesthetic by some prominent English physicians. James Braid explained mesmerism as a state induced by fatigue of the elevator muscles of the eye due to prolonged staring at an object coupled with suggestions to relax. He called this sleep-like state hypnosis.

Hypnosis had now been legitimized in the medical community and was studied by the Nancy School of Hypnosis, which advocated that hypnosis was a natural phenomenon of a sleep-like state somewhere between wakefulness and natural sleep. The Parisian School of Hypnosis, led by the world-renowned neurologist Jean-Martin Charcot, believed that hypnosis like hysteria was a reflection of an underlying neurological disorder. Charcot, and especially his student Pierre Janet, made plain that the human mind consists of at least two major components, namely, the conscious and unconscious minds.

Systematic laboratory investigations of hypnosis and related psychic phenomena were launched by Hugo Münsterberg at Harvard University in the mid-1890s and continued at Yale University under the direction of Clark Hull up until the 1930s. The basic findings of these laboratory studies of hypnosis are still valid today and include the findings of no significant difference in susceptibility to hypnosis as a function of intelligence. As a result of systematic laboratory and clinical case studies the state and non-state models of hypnosis were developed. The former model stressed that hypnosis represented a unique state of consciousness somewhere between wakefulness and normal sleep. The non-state model stated that hypnosis was not a unique state of consciousness, but rather arises primarily from cognitive mechanisms of sustaining and elaborating upon suggestions and ignoring intrusive internal and/or external stimuli. Thereafter, dissociation theories of hypnosis, which proposed that hypnosis was either the result of the fragmentation of consciousness or the uncoupling of cognitive and behavioral subsystems from control by the executive or analytical component of consciousness, rose to prominence. We then briefly reviewed the findings of hypnotic age regression that indicate clearly that there is not a return to the functions of a previous age but rather the appearance of pre-logical modes of information analyses and thinking.

We concluded this chapter by reviewing the contributions of the Boston School of Abnormal Psychology that studied extensively hypnosis and related phenomena from about 1870 to 1890, and is considered by some to be the primary force for the development of clinical psychology. We also presented the extensive results of efficacy and effectiveness studies, which indicate clearly that hypnosis as well as other forms of psychotherapy are sound interventions for a variety of disorders. Lastly, we indicated the importance of promoting prevention programs that focus upon dealing with the stresses and illnesses that arise out of poverty, discrimination, and lack of educational opportunities that challenge many millions of people around the globe. We briefly introduced psychoneuroimmunology, which illustrates further the connection between the mind and the body at the scientific interface of psychology, neurology, and immunology.

■ Chapter 6—Phrenology, Mesmerism, and Hypnosis

Discussion Questions

■ How are the soul, mind, and body related?

■ According to phrenology, how could the assessment of one domain (bumps on the head) inform about another domain (personality traits)?

■ What is the predictive validity of the Five Factor Model?

■ How did the two schools of hypnosis differ?

■ How has psychological research supported or refuted the theory of hypnotic age regression?

■ What is psychoneuroimmunology? Explain.

Associationism

CHAPTER OVERVIEW

This chapter focuses on the intriguing and enduring issue of how the mind acquires content. We begin with a brief treatment of the sources of human knowledge including empiricism, according to which, if you don't experience it you don't know it so, to enrich one's knowledge and one's self, it is important to be open to new experiences. Another source of knowledge is revelation, which is based upon dogma and faith with this source of knowledge widespread today, as we see, for example, in almost all religious movements around the world. We next turn to positivism, according to which true human knowledge is only derived from public, reliable, and consensual observations absent any subjective or metaphysical overlay or assumptions. The last source of human knowledge is associationism, which is the central topic of this chapter. Basically, associationism, considered by some to be the first school of psychology, grows out of empiricism, and represents a set of formal rules for the combination of ideas or experiences in the mind.

As part of our treatment of the sources of knowledge we focus first on the positivism of Auguste Comte (1798–1857), his views on the stages of intellectual development of societies, his hierarchy of sciences, and his twisted journey into the dogmatism in almost all religious systems, which he argued so forcefully against. Thereafter, we present the work of Ernst Mach (1838–1916) who, unlike Comte, stressed the importance of studying the immediate, unanalyzed experiences of an observer as the key to understanding how the human mind acquires content. Comte argued for the study of the products of mind, namely, behaviors (precursor to behaviorism) while Mach argued for the study of immediate experiences (precursor to Gestalt psychology). Both were considered positivist due to their emphasis upon the importance of collecting data from observations rather than speculations or "what ifs."

Our examination of the British empiricists begins with John Locke (1632–1704) and his unequivocal position that the mind acquires content only through experiences, that there are no innate ideas. Locke distinguished between primary (inherent in an object such as size or shape) and secondary (not given in an object but added as an operation of mind such as color or temperature) quality of ideas, and the processes of sensation and reflection. Locke's work continues to have a profound impact not only upon psychology, but also politics, education, government, and public policy.

We next review the work of George Berkeley (1685–1753) who, unlike John Locke, did not distinguish between primary and secondary ideas and thus believed that all we know is our subjective experiences. Thus, a tree in the forest exists even though we may not experience it because it is experienced in the mind of God, and if it falls and we are there at that moment we hear the crashing sound; if we are not there when the tree falls there is no sound, although the tree existed. Berkeley, an Anglican clergyman, was arguing against the rising tide of materialism which rejects the concept of God or any other metaphysical assumptions.

David Hume (1711–1776) continued in the tradition of the British empiricists yet was also the bridge to associationism given his emphasis upon the articulation of the three laws of associationism and its treatment of impressions (sensory stimulation) and ideas. David Hartley (1705–1757) is considered to be "the father" of British associationism, and the first to study the mind or psychological phenomena as a natural science by proposing a physiological model of association. We then turn to a review of the work of James Mill (1773–1836) (the father of John Stuart Mill), who attempted to tie together the motivational and cognitive dynamics of the mind, while his son argued for a science of human nature focused upon associationism. James Mill's psychology had the capacity to yield what he called secondary laws of nature in which description, measurement, and prediction were not as precise as in physics, which was grounded in primary laws that were more precise such as the freezing or boiling points of water.

Alexander Bain (1818–1903) is considered by some to be the first psychologist, the author of the first psychology textbooks, *The Sense and the Intellect* and *Emotions and the Will*, and the founder of *Mind*, which was the first periodical devoted entirely to psychology. Bain integrated mental and biological processes like David Hartley before him so that the laws of associationism applied to both the acquisition of ideas and voluntary behaviors, with the latter retained if followed closely by positive outcomes or rewards. Thereafter, we treat briefly the work of Immanuel Kant (1724–1804), who stands as the continental counterpoint to the British empiricists and associationists because of his emphasis upon innate categories of thought such as the perception of time and space, which impose essential operations on the human mind rather than arguing for specific innate ideas such as the existence of God. Thus, Kant argues that associationism would not be possible if the mind were unable to perceive the temporal or spatial separation between two or more stimuli or events, as they would appear as a bundled conglomeration and cacophony of sensory experiences. Also, we discuss briefly Kant's concept of noumena or "things in themselves," which precludes accurate knowledge of objects of the physical world because the categories of the mind act on the sensory data and render all of our experiences with the subjective imprint of the mind.

We then turn to a series of studies that have extended and confirmed empirically some of the key principles of associationism, as reflected in studies of the operation of memory systems, sensory conditioning, selective deprivation, repressed memories, and "the seven sins of memory," especially absent-mindedness. For example, Hermann Ebbinghaus (1850–1909) conducted almost exclusively, with just himself as the only participant, his foundational studies of human memory with findings that are as accurate today, in general, as when he first reported them over 100 years ago. Interestingly, Ebbinghaus' work made plain, contrary to Wilhelm Wundt's claim, that psychology could study higher mental processes in the laboratory. Therafter, Brogden (1939) studied sensory conditioning in dogs, and was the first to show unequivocally that the simple contiguity of purely sensory events is connected in the mind. Richard Held and his colleagues (Held and Hein,1963) demonstrated the profound, although not always irreversible, effects of selective environments and experiences upon critical perceptual and behavioral capacities, the bottom line of which is that restrictive and degraded environments produce profound and corrosive effects upon organisms, which in some cases are reversible. Lastly, we examine briefly repressed memories and absent-mindedness as important issues facing all of us today.

This chapter makes plain that who we are is in large measure determined by our experiences and where we have been up to the present. Thus, for each of us our future affords the opportunity to expand and develop ourselves through rich, diverse, and challenging experiences and contexts, or to stand still at best.

LEARNING OBJECTIVES

When you finish studying this chapter, you will be prepared to:

- Identify and differentiate the four origins of human knowledge

- Discuss Auguste Comte's approach of studying the mind through behaviors in comparison to Ernst Mach's study of the immediate, unanalyzed experience of the observer as an indication of how the human mind acquires content

- Describe how John Locke's theory of empiricism has influenced diverse arenas such as politics, education, government, and public policy in addition to psychology

- Distinguish the difference between George Berkeley's empiricism and John Locke's in terms of primary and secondary ideas

- Demonstrate how David Hume's differentiation of simple from complex ideas bridged empiricism and associationism, thus calling for the development of psychology as a science

- Identify the four goals of British associationism

- Discuss David Hartley's associationism as physiological parallelism and in terms of contiguity

- Describe how the Mills attempted to combine the psychological processes of motivation and cognition under the umbrella of associationism

- Discuss how John Stuart Mill's and his father John Mill's views differed in regard to sensations and ideas, as well as John Stuart Mill's distinction of ideas as simple or complex

- Identify Alexander Bain as the individual often referred to as the father of psychology for his textbook publications and application of associationism to the study of behavior

- Explain Immanuel Kant's belief that the mind is not passive, but rather active as it adds something to the sensory data before entering consciousness

- Discuss how Hermann Ebbinghaus' systematic study of memory was a critical step in the establishment of psychology as a science

- Discuss sensory conditioning and selective deprivation that demonstrate the critical role of experiences in determining sensory-motor capacities

- Provide arguments against using testimony in trials arising from repressed memories and illustrate how the "seven sins of memory" are adaptive anywhere in today's world

---

INTRODUCTION

Most of us have been blessed with loving and supportive parents or other guardians who have given each of us a priceless foundation of positive experiences that influence our physical and psychological development throughout our lives. In fact, even if our parents are deceased they are still in many ways an important part of us and we carry warm memories and images of them and their love and guidance. How did we acquire the knowledge of the love and caring of our parents, of our selves, and everything else we know about the world? Perhaps all we now know and will know in the future began very simply and quietly. In the first few days and weeks of our lives, when we were hungry and/or in discomfort we were nursed and held gently by our mother, her face was close to ours, her voice may have been soft and melodic, and we had contact comfort with her relaxed and caring demeanor. We learned to associate mother's face, soft voice, and contact so that eventually the sound of her voice brought us some momentary comfort until she picked us up and we could see her face and be close to her. As the years go by, and perhaps we no longer see or hear our mother or other primary caretaker, we can still conjure up in our minds an image of her or him, and even experience a calming effect just from the memory of those earlier, quieter, sweeter, and tender times. In effect, our sensory experiences are the infrastructure of the mind and repeated sensations are knitted together or connected to create simple and complex ideas that may be with us forever.

ORIGINS OF HUMAN KNOWLEDGE

This chapter is about the fundamental issue of how the mind acquires content, and then stores and retrieves that content. Many philosophers and psychologists have answered unequivocally that almost all we know arises from our experiences, that is, what is given to us initially by our senses, especially those of seeing, hearing, touching, tasting, and smelling.

Empiricism

Those who subscribe to empiricism as the sole source of human knowledge state clearly that the mind acquires content as result of experience. Thus, there are no innate ideas such as ideas of space, time, good, evil, or God, all of which we can possibly learn about depending upon our experiences. Observation is the initial gateway to human knowledge so that inductive scientific inquiry (making many specific observations of a given phenomenon and only then reaching some general conclusion based upon the observations) is the preferred method to learn about nature, including human nature. Reason takes a backseat in the drive to acquire knowledge so that deductive scientific inquiry (starting with a general or broad premise or assumption and gathering specific observations relative to the general statement) is the less-preferred method of inquiry. Also, the environment is the primary source of content of the mind, and basically all humans begin life with comparable capacities so that claims of inherent advantage of royalty or the privileged are empty and invalid. Observations rule rather than kings and queens, deities or their spokespersons, and/or politicians.

Revelation

Here knowledge is said to arise only to a special few or under special circumstances. Religious and cult systems rely on revelation as the primary source of truth and ultimate knowledge with designated individuals as those to whom such knowledge has been revealed or made available who in turn become spokespersons for true or expert knowledge. Observation takes a backseat to dogma and faith in particular persons and principles, and only those observations that support or extend the revealed knowledge are considered valid and acceptable.

Positivism

This method for gaining knowledge was introduced by Auguste Comte (1798–1857). Comte was born and raised by his Catholic parents in the French city of Montpellier (Urmson, 1967). He entered the Ecole Polytechnique at Paris in 1816 where he was a good student as well as a troublemaker, and was dismissed along with his classmates in 1816 because they revolted against school policies and practices. In 1817, Comte went to work for Henri Saint-Simons (1760–1825), who influenced Comte to take a more elitist rather equalitarian view of humanity and society, and even though the two parted ways on a bitter note, Saint-Simons' influence lasted a lifetime.

Comte started his publishing career in 1822, married Caroline Massin in 1825, gave public lectures on "positive philosophy" in 1826, and published his six-volume magnum opus, titled *Course of Positive Philosophy*, over the period 1830–1842 (Urmson, 1967). Comte argued that according to positivism the only thing we can be certain about is that which is publicly observable and grounded in our sensory experiences. Positivism was true knowledge provided by our senses while all other knowledge derived by reason or revelation was nonsense (Robinson, 1986). Put simply, knowledge comes only from empirical observations. In effect, for Comte and his followers, science was now the arbiter of truth, taking the place of both religion, which sought true knowledge by recourse to some supernatural force or figure, and metaphysics or the attempt to explain the world of objects and experiences by recourse to some hidden or as yet known natural power or principles. In fact, by the late 1840s, for Comte and some others, science became "scientism," which was to be the new global religion requiring unfaltering faith and adherence to positivism, similar to what was asked of believers in the other global religions, namely, Judaism, Christianity, or Muslim. Comte called his new religion "The Religion of Humanity," with the central focus upon humanity rather than God, with scientists replacing philosophers and priests; and its followers would be drawn from the marginalized working-class men and women. Comte believed that societies passed through three stages of development based upon their explanatory system for the causes of natural events, namely, theological, metaphysical, and scientific explanations (Leahy, 1987). The theological system explained events by relying on invisible gods and spirits while the metaphysical system moved from gods/spirits to abstractions and other unobservable forces as, for example, Leibniz's concept of monads (Urmson, 1967). The third system is scientific and switches emphasis from explanation to description, prediction, and control of natural events, that is, positivism rules. Societies evolve from one explanatory system to another when the wisest members see the next stage of development and lead the way, which usually involves dramatic changes in the thinking and behavior of members of the society. For Comte, science was to seek the lawful relationship between physical events, and only empirically or sensory-based observations were acceptable as scientific as long as they could be publicly confirmed. Lastly, Comte proposed a hierarchy of sciences with the first developed and most basic being mathematics followed by astronomy, physics, chemistry, physiology, biology, and the last developed and most comprehensive, namely, **sociology**. The term *sociology* was coined by Comte to refer to the comparative study of different societies in terms of their development in reference to his three explanatory systems with psychology excluded from his list of sciences as it focused upon the study of the individual, which is much less complex than the study of groups and societies. Comte believed that the individual can be best studied by means of physiology and biology, as reflected in the then contemporary work of phrenology, rather than through introspection, which was private and not directly observable by others and thus not a source of positivistic data (Leahy, 1987). Comte incorporated hierarchy in much of his thinking and writing, both of which became twisted as he became more and more preoccupied with promoting his "Religion of Humanity," outlining details of worship of the Great Being symbolized by the female body in chapels containing the busts of the great benefactors of humankind, and the construction of a positivist calendar.

Ernst Mach (1838–1916) continued the development of positivism, although, unlike Comte, who stressed that science must focus on physical events that could be experienced by any interested observer, the focus for Mach must be upon the immediate experiences of the scientist. Mach's version of positivism, is known as phenomenalism, which influenced the later development of Gestalt psychology that claimed the immediate unanalyzed experiences of the observer as the subject matter of psychology. Comtean positivism influenced the later development of behaviorism, which claimed observable behavior as the appropriate subject matter of psychology. For Mach, sensations were the key positivistic data, so mind could be studied by observing the immediate experiences of the individual; for Comte, behaviors ruled and mind could be studied by observing the products of the mind, namely, behaviors. Both were positivists as they stressed observation while they differed in terms of what needs to be observed—sensations for Mach and behaviors for Comte.

Logical positivism, developed in the 1920s, had a profound influence upon the subsequent development of psychology, especially when combined with the practice of operationalism, which mandates that theoretical constructs (e.g., motivation) be related to observable phenomena (Koch, 1959; Stevens, 1935). Briefly, logical positivism divided science into the observable and the theoretical domains with the former focused upon empirical observations while the latter aimed at providing an explanation of the observed events. Thus, for example, if we observe a human or infrahuman who persists in the pursuit of food and once satisfied engages in other behaviors, and if again deprived of food, now for a longer period of time than before, resumes food-seeking behaviors with greater intensity and increasingly stereotyped behaviors based on previous experiences (the observations), we conclude that the organism is motivated (the theoretical term). Although we don't see motivation directly we infer its existence by operationally defining it as number of hours of food deprivation (independent variable), length of time of food-directed behaviors, and/or intensity of food-related behaviors (dependent variables). Logical positivism and operationalism were embraced enthusiastically by psychologists because they allowed for the study of many unobservable theoretical constructs such as anxiety, hope, learning, intelligence, and motivation in both human and infrahuman organisms without recourse to mentalism, since these and other psychological constructs (e.g., leadership, conflict, cooperation, thinking, decision making, and even love) were measured operationally.

Associationism

Basically, associationism grows out of empiricism and represents a set of formal rules for the combination of ideas in the mind. Aristotle, in his *Concerning Memory and Reminiscence*, presented his theory that memory is a function of three primary associative processes. The first and fundamental process is contiguity (i.e., things that occur close together in time and/or space are linked in the mind), second is the process of similarity, and last is the process of contrast. Thus, if we were to see a roundish red object and hear almost simultaneously the sound "apple" when shown again the same object we might say "apple," which is an almost inevitable outcome if the pairing of these two stimuli are repeated a few times. Our memories are important because they represent our experiences; these are impressed upon our mind, which is a blank slate or tabula rasa at birth so all we have in our mind is given by our sensory experiences.

We turn now to the British empiricists who in turn gave rise to the British associationists, and lastly, we will review some recent later developments of associationism that emphasized the linkage between behaviors rather than strictly focusing primarily upon the linkage of ideas.

THE BRITISH EMPIRICISTS

The powerful intellectual forces of rationalism or the use of reason to develop knowledge rather than relying upon magical or religious systems to explain and understand the natural world (including human nature) in Western European philosophy in the 17th century were articulated by René Descartes (1596–1650), Baruch Spinoza (1632–1677), and Gottfried Wilhelm von Leibniz (1646–1716). Thus, for example, Descartes advocated that the human mind is not made of matter but rather is immaterial and possessed certain innate ideas (e.g., knowledge of God, space, time, and motion). Baruch Spinoza advocated materialistic monism (mind like everything else is made of matter) and determinism or the view that all events in the natural world are determined (free will was an illusion) including our feelings, behaviors, and thoughts. Lastly, Leibniz argued that there is nothing in the mind that is not first in the senses except the mind itself. Thus, no ideas come from experience because ideas cannot be created by anything physical like a brain and what is in the mind is the potential to have ideas, which is actualized by our experiences. All these thinkers and tinkers wanted desperately to establish rational explanations of the natural world rather than to rely upon religious dogma or the revised and received works of Aristotle or Plato that characterized philosophical thought from about 500 to the start of the Renaissance around 1450.

John Locke (1632–1704)

John Locke was born in the small English village of Wrighton, obtained his bachelor's, master's, and medical degrees from Oxford University in 1652, 1656, and 1674, respectively. Locke spent most of his life at Oxford except when he lived in Holland from 1684 to 1689, and he never married. He published his *An Essay Concerning Human Understanding* in 1690 when he was 60 years of age, after working on it for seventeen years and then revising it a number times with the fifth edition appearing posthumously in 1706, and he died peacefully at the home of friends in 1704 (Urmson, 1967). Although Locke wrote on diverse subjects including how the mind gains knowledge, politics, education, child rearing, and theology, he focused upon the core issue of how the mind acquires content.

According to Locke, the mind acquired content or ideas first and foremost by experience. An idea was a mental image that arose from either sensation or direct sensory simulation or reflection, or the mind's ability to remember and think about the residual idea after termination of the sensory stimulus. He wrote that there were no innate ideas as advocated by Descartes, and all of the content of the mind arises from sensory experiences processed by the innate operations of the mind including perception, thinking, and memory, which are part of human nature and thus given before any experience. Locke cited a letter from an Irish scientist, William Molyneux (1656–1696), to further buttress his position that there were no innate ideas. In the letter, Molyneux asked rhetorically: if a person was born blind and had sight restored as an adult, could that person, by sight alone, distinguish between a cube and globe, which he or she had been able to do with only the sense of touch. Both Locke and Molyneux responded "no" at first; however, with subsequent visual experiences the answer became "yes." The foundational ideas here are that the mind features plasticity, is shaped by experience; and that systematic educational experiences enrich and strengthen all minds, not just those of reigning royalty and other privileged members of a society.

Experience is the primary force for liberation of the individual and systematic experience or education can give rise to a just and equal social order for all citizens. Locke's campaign was not only to oppose the innate ideas of the Cartesian philosophical system, but much more importantly, to demonstrate the fallacy of innate moral principles which he considered the foundation of Christian morality and the infrastructure of dogmatism. Thus, those who did not believe in God were morally corrupt, could not be trusted, and were atheists who sought to "rob God" of existence, given the prevailing and dominant religious belief that God had implanted in the soul of all humans the idea of God. Locke argued that only experience brings knowledge and there are no innate moral truths, although a person could come to believe in God depending upon his or her experiences. Accordingly, he was considered by many leading figures of Christianity as dangerous and morally corrupt.

For Locke, experience trumps dogma! All knowledge comes from sensory experiences of external objects registered passively upon the mind as well as from reflection or awareness of the operations of our mind working on previous sensations. Thus, being aware of a bouquet of flowers might give rise to the idea of pleasant while the original sensations of the sight, fragrance, and hearing their name gave rise to the idea of flower. Simple ideas come passively to the mind. However, **complex ideas** arise as a result of the active combination of simple ideas by the mind so that the bouquet is now one of roses. Locke coined the phrase "the association of ideas," although he did not state any laws of association as he thought the variety of associations of ideas was infinite.

Like others before him, Galilei Galileo, René Descartes, and his mentor at Oxford University, Robert Boyle (1627–1691), Locke distinguished between primary and secondary qualities of objects. Primary qualities give rise to ideas that are inherent properties of the object such as solidity, shape, motion, and size, while secondary qualities are not found in the object themselves and include temperature, color, sound, and taste. Locke gave the demonstration of **the paradox of the basins** to distinguish between primary and secondary qualities of objects. Prepare three basins of water with the cold for the left hand, the middle for tepid or lukewarm water, and hot water for the right hand. After a few minutes of soaking of the hands, place them both in the middle bowl of tepid water and observe that now the water feels warm to the left hand and cool to the right hand even though the actual temperature of the water remains unchanged. This demonstration indicates that there can be a difference between appearances and reality, and that the ideas arising from primary and secondary qualities of objects are equally vivid to the mind.

Thomas Hobbes (1588–1679), an earlier British empiricist, whom we discussed in chapter 4, believed in an absolute monarchy (a hereditary sovereign such as king, queen, or emperor with unlimited power) because he had little faith in the capacity of human nature for cooperation and altruism. On the other hand, Locke advocated for a constitutional monarchy which involved a social contract defending the natural and inalienable rights of every individual with the absolute right of the governed to overthrow the government if it violated the rights of the individual. Thus, Locke argued effectively for government by and for the people as well as education to enhance the quality of the citizenry and society as a whole.

George Berkeley (1685–1753)

George Berkeley was born in Kilkenny, Ireland, entered Dublin College at the age of 15, earned his bachelor's and master's degrees when he was 20 and 22 years of age, respectively, was ordained as a deacon (a rank just below that of a priest) in the Anglican church at the age of 24, and published in the same year (1709) his first major work, *An Essay Toward a New Theory of Vision* (Gulick & Lawson, 1976; Urmson, 1967). In 1790, Berkeley published his most important work relative to psychology, titled *A Treatise Concerning the Principles of Human Knowledge*. His scholarly reputation was firmly established by the time he was 30 years of age compared to John Locke, who didn't publish his major work until the age of 60; relatively speaking Berkeley was the hare while Locke was the turtle. Newly married, Berkeley sailed to Newport, Rhode Island in 1728, as part of the first leg of his journey to establish a new college in Bermuda that was intended to educate the natives and colonists in America. It never got off the ground because of a lack of promised government funding and the miscalculation of the geographical access to Bermuda from the mainland. Berkeley was so impressed by his two-year stay in America that after his return to London in 1731, he helped to establish the University of Pennsylvania, contributed books to Yale and Harvard universities, and although he never made it to California, the city of Berkeley and the University of California-Berkeley were named after him. In 1734, Berkeley was appointed Anglican bishop (the highest rank in the priesthood) of Cloyne, Ireland, where he wrote and preached, and championed with unbridled zeal the healthy restorative powers of tar-water! Bishop Berkeley died in 1734 while sipping tea and listening to a sermon read to him by his wife.

Berkeley's writings focused upon three issues, namely, distance perception, dualism, and dogma. We do not directly perceive distance, but rather only become aware of distance as a result of the sensations arising from the movement of our eyes as objects move toward or away from us. It is well known that as an object moves toward an observer, the eyes converge and diverge as the object recedes from the observer (to demonstrate just move this book so it is about 6 inches or 15 millimeters from you and notice the muscular sensations arising from the rectus muscles of the eyes as the object moves toward and away from you). Berkeley stood in opposition to Descartes' view that distance perception and some other ideas were part of human nature and, therefore, innate while standing in agreement with Locke that all the ideas in the mind are the result of experience.

However, it was on the matter of primary and secondary qualities that Berkeley differed with Locke because he believed this distinction created a dualism consisting of the world of objects (primary qualities) and the world of ideas or perceptions. Berkeley concluded that all that exists are our ideas or perceptions of the objects, and that in the absence of the perception objects do not exist, yet when a given object is not perceived by a given individual that object continues to exist because God (the ultimate perceiver) perceives it. In fact, Berkeley wrote that what we perceive are ideas in God's mind so that with experience we perceive accurately the external world! In effect, "**esse est percipi**" or "**to be is to be perceived**." This astounding position is known as mentalism, immaterialism, and subjective idealism and is reflected in part in the later development of Gestalt psychology that emphasized the primacy of the immediate or phenomenal experiences of the observer as the primary subject matter of psychology.

The third focus of Berkeley's philosophy was upon the growing dogma of **materialism**, which leads to the dismissal of God as all in the world is matter that is governed by physical laws and there is no need to turn to supernatural forces. It is important to remember that Berkeley was a man of the cloth, and he wanted to address directly the philosophy of materialism. For Berkeley, all that exists is perceived, and, therefore, there is no need for a physical world. Berkeley is best remembered for his ardent support of empiricism, and making plain that ideas arise from a mixture of sensations that are combined through repetitive associations.

David Hume (1711–1776)

The last of the British empiricists, David Hume was born in Edinburgh, Scotland, attended the University of Edinburgh but left before he graduated. He then went to La Fleche, France, where René Descartes had studied, and completed his most famous work, *A Treatise of Human Nature* (1748). While there, he served as a secretary to an ambassador in Paris from 1763 to 1765, returned to Edinburgh in 1768, and died in 1776.

According to Hume, the content of the mind comes from impressions or sensory stimulation and ideas which are faint copies of impressions. In addition, there are simple and complex ideas: simple ideas arise from actual prior impressions while complex ideas arise from the association of simple ideas and need not reflect any combination of impressions, which can occur in the imagination. Thus, for example, we may have separate impressions of a lizard and a bird (i.e., we actually see a lizard and a bird, or two separate simple ideas) and perhaps later we have an idea of each arising from our memories, which may be combined by our imagination into the idea of a flying dragon that we have not actually perceived. Hume believed that ideas are combined by the three laws of association, namely, **resemblance** (e.g., thinking of an apple gives rise to the recollection of a pear, another fruit), **contiguity** (e.g., remembering a loved one gives rise to the time and/or place when and where you last met), and **cause and effect** (e.g., when we remember an accident we think of the person(s) and or event(s) just before it). Hume came eventually to consider cause and effect as the equivalent of contiguity so that he championed two laws of association, namely, resemblance and contiguity.

Hume concluded that we are only aware of the impressions and ideas in our minds, and thus have no rational proof of external objects that we come to believe exist as a result of the constancy and coherence of our impressions. Hume's position is known as skepticism, which later stimulated the philosophical system of Immanuel Kant. Hume, in arguing that all we know is our own experiences, concluded that we can be certain of nothing and can only expect that future events will follow our past experiences thus giving rise to our sense of certainty. In effect, Hume is calling for the establishment of a psychology that focuses upon the systematic study of our experiences and how we use them through learning to adapt to a wide variety of environments.

THE BRITISH ASSOCIATIONISTS

As we all know from our everyday experiences, ideas come in streams such that one thought or idea usually gives rise to another almost automatically. For example, perhaps you may remember that when in elementary school your teacher or classmate might have produced a screeching noise with chalk on a blackboard and now, years later, when you recall the incident or are in a classroom you may still experience the chills or become squeamish. Perhaps you may even experience a more intense reaction when you think of someone running their fingernails up and down the blackboard! Events derived originally from sensations that give rise to impressions become associated or connected in the mind, even though such events may have taken place years ago, and when now associated give rise not only to ideas but also to bodily and emotional reactions. This is due to associationism, which grew out of and extended British empiricism. According to Misiak and Sexton (1966), British associationism sought the following goals: (a) identify the laws of association, (b) analyze human consciousness and indicate how the contents can be explained by the laws of association, (c) break down the contents of mind into the most elementary components, and (d) identify the anatomical and physiological basis of mental phenomena.

David Hartley (1705–1757)

David Hartley studied initially to become a minister like his father, but could not accept one of the thirty-nine articles of faith required of ministers of the Anglican Church: eternal damnation if not repentant for sins. Accordingly, Hartley turned from the healing of souls to the healing of bodies, earned his medical degree at Cambridge University, and had a successful medical practice. In his spare time over a span of eighteen years, he wrote his *Observations of Man* (1749/1971), which presented ninety-one propositions regarding the nature of the body and the mind. Hartley founded British associationism, and is considered by some to be the first to study the mind or psychological phenomena as a natural science by proposing a physiological model of association (Webb, 1988).

For Hartley, the main law of associationism is contiguity, which he stated in his propositions X for the mind and XI for the physical or bodily side of an experience such that when A, B, and C are presented closely together in time and/or space, A alone can give rise to B, C, or B and C together, especially the more frequently the elements are repeated together. Likewise, on the bodily side (Proposition XI), these three stimuli produce corresponding vibrations in the sensory nerves (i.e., impressions) that are transmitted to the brain yielding miniature vibrations (sensations). For Hartley, after sense impressions cease there remain miniature vibrations that Hartley called "Vibratuncles," which are ideas or weaker copies of sensations. Hartley believed that after-images reflected the residual neural "Vibratuncles" as, for example, after staring for a few minutes at a waterfall and then looking to the rocks on the side and they appear to be moving upward, or looking at a candle flame and then closing the eyes and continuing to see the flame. Hartley extended associationism to account for behaviors that started out as involuntary responses to stimuli, such as when an object is put within the grasp of an infant, producing an automatic grasping response. Grasping then becomes associated with other objects and ideas so that it becomes selective as when reaching for a toy compared to the flame of a candle which has been associated with intense heat and thus neural vibrations. Thus, by association grasping becomes voluntary, according to Hartley, which is the first attempt to explain not only the origin of ideas by association but also behaviors. Lastly, Hartley wrote that excessive vibrations caused pain while mild or modest vibrations gave rise to pleasure, and as a result of our experiences particular events, people, and objects become associated with pleasure and pain. We learn to cherish those things that give us pleasure, hope for them when they are absent, and enjoy them when they are present.

Hartley's model of neural vibrations is obviously inaccurate, yet for his time it represented a solid attempt to "neutralize" associationism; construct a model of the mind that was in accord with Isaac Newton's (1642–1727) law of gravitation, according to which **all** objects in the universe attract each other so that everything is in movement or undergoing vibrations; and he attempted to explain not only how the mind acquired content or ideas, but also voluntary and involuntary behaviors.

The Family Mills

James Mill (1773–1836) was the father, John Stuart Mill (1806–1873) the son, and together their work represented the culmination of British empiricism and associationism. Interestingly, James Mill attempted to fuse together into one system the motivational dynamics of the mind (i.e., **utilitarianism**) and the cognitive dynamics of the mind (i.e., **associationism**). James Mill was born the son of a Scottish village shoemaker and his mother demanded that he devote himself to studying so as to eventually obtain a secure and meaningful career. As a result of his promising academic performances, James Mill entered the University of Edinburgh, studied for the Presbyterian ministry, and was licensed as a preacher in 1799, although he was unsuccessful in finding a parish as no one could understand his sermons. Accordingly, Mill moved to London in 1802 to work as a journalist and editor. In 1806 he began writing the *History of British India*, which was published in 1818 and was an immediate success that won him an administrative position with the East India Company (an extremely successful global trading company set up by the British government to bring luxury items such as teas, silk, and cashmere to England). Mill worked the rest of his life for the East India Company, which provided him with the financial independence and security to pursue his interests in social reform, something he believed would be advanced by a clear understanding of human nature.

James Mill's most important work for psychology was *Analysis of the Phenomena of the Human Mind* (1829), in which he stated that sensations and their copies or ideas are the basic ingredients of the human mind, ideas are associated or connected together exclusively by contiguity, and they are both equally vivid in the mind. Ideas arise from sensations, and the strength of the association of ideas is a function of their vividness and frequency with the latter more important for the linking together of ideas. In addition, Mill had met Jeremy Bentham (1748–1836) in 1808, and accepted his principle of **utilitarianism**, according to which humans are motivated by two sovereign forces, namely, pleasure and pain rather than reason. For Mill, free will is an illusion with the attention of the mind directed mechanically by the pursuit of pleasure and the avoidance of pain, as Bentham had advocated in his *Introduction to Principles of Moral Legislation* (1789). Mill endorsed Bentham's principle that government must pursue policies and practices that assured "the greatest good for the greatest number." In addition, education must assume the responsibility of molding the person's mind. According to Mill, humans were pulled and pushed by the forces of pleasure and pain and our minds populated with ideas that were the result of our experiences with complex ideas arising from the association of simple ideas. James Mill presented a very mechanical and passive view of the mind, sometimes referred to as mental mechanics or mental physics.

John Stuart Mill had a childhood designed by his father to produce a mental machine rather than a boy who would eventually develop into a man. John studied for hours per day, was fluent in Greek and Latin, and wrote his first serious paper about the nature of Roman government siding with the common person rather than the aristocracy or the patricians, all before reaching his adolescence. In 1823, at the age of 17, John took a position as a clerk working for his father at the East India Company. He became severely depressed at the age of 20, began to recover in his mid-twenties, and at 30 he befriended and fell in love with Harriet Taylor, a married woman. He lived with her and her husband until the husband died, and at 43 Harriet and John Stuart married. She died in 1858, and for the remainder of his life John Stuart was an ardent advocate of women's rights including the introduction of a bill in the British House of Commons to guarantee women the right to vote. The bill failed, but John Stuart continued his interests in government and citizen participation as reflected in his important paper, *Considerations on Representative Government* (1861), which still informs debate about the roles of citizens, elected representatives, and public administrators in governmental processes.

In 1843, at the age of 37, John Stuart Mill published his most important work for psychology, *A System of Logic*, which went through eight editions, and included a chapter that, unlike Auguste Comte, advocated that a science of human nature was possible although such a science might not be as exact as physics. Inasmuch as John Stuart Mill was the leading philosopher of science of his day, his work contributed significantly to the establishment of psychology as an independent science because others listened to what he had to say. He believed science consists of primary and secondary laws. Primary laws govern phenomena that can be observed, measured, and predicted precisely, such as the freezing point of water or the orbit of a planet, while secondary laws often interact with primary laws, making measurement and prediction less precise but still possible in general because they are still subject to primary laws. Thus, for phenomena governed by secondary laws, we can describe, measure, and predict them in general rather than specifically as is the case for phenomena governed only by primary laws. Therefore, a science of human nature could not predict with total accuracy how one may think, feel, and act in a particular context or environment because it is impossible to know all previous and future contexts or environments in which one finds oneself. We do know that the context or environment does influence how a person thinks, feels, and acts and thus these phenomena are subject to primary laws (environmental effects) that interact with secondary laws (features of past and present environments). In fact, Mill proposed that the first science of human nature would identify universal laws (primary laws) of the operation of the human mind, and the science he called **ethology** would identify the secondary laws of how the mind develops under specific contexts (i.e., individual differences).

John Stuart Mill identified the laws of the British empiricists and those of associationism as one set of primary laws of human nature. Accordingly, all ideas arise exclusively from our experiences, sensations give rise to ideas which are images that remain in the mind after the external stimulus is removed, ideas become associated as a result of primarily contiguity so that the closest in time and space are more likely associated together, and simple ideas are connected to form complex ideas. These are primary laws because they apply to all persons anywhere in the world. Interestingly, John Stuart Mill, unlike his father, distinguished between sensations and ideas, considering the former stronger than the latter, and he argued that complex ideas are not always an aggregate of simple ideas (mental physics) but could also arise from a fusion of an aggregate of simple ideas even though the simple ideas lose their identity and cannot be identified in the complex idea (e.g., the ideas of stars and sky may give rise to the idea of heaven). This notion of "mental chemistry" was later reflected in the work of Gestalt psychology and its mantra that "the whole is different from the sum of the parts." We turn now to a friend of John Stuart Mill who is considered by some to be the first true psychologist.

Alexander Bain (1818–1903)

Alexander Bain is considered by some historians of psychology to be the first psychologist compared to any of the philosophers and scholars we have presented up to this time. He is thought to have authored the first two textbooks of psychology (1855 and 1859), which stood as the definitive psychology texts for fifty years in European and American universities, and to have founded *Mind*, which was the first periodical focused exclusively on psychology. Bain bridged the 19th and 20th centuries and was indeed the leading psychologist of the pre-scientific period of psychology, which ended in 1879 when Wilhelm Wundt (1832–1920) established the first formal psychological laboratory at the University of Leipzig, Germany.

Alexander Bain was born in Aberdeen, Scotland, to parents of modest means, and, like his father, worked throughout most of his childhood to earn money for books and his education. He enrolled in Marischal College (it later became the University of Aberdeen) which, like other Scottish schools, accepted poor yet gifted students; he graduated with honors, and then moved to London to work as a freelance journalist. While in London, Bain befriended other intellectuals, including John Stuart Mill, with whom he became close friends. As a result of his sustained efforts and the assistance of influential friends, Bain published his two classic psychology texts, *The Senses and the Intellect* (1855) and *Emotions and the Will* (1859). As a consequence of the publication of these two books, Bain won an appointment as professor of logic and rhetoric at the University of Aberdeen where he remained for the rest of his life.

Basically, Bain, like David Hartley before him, integrated mental and biological processes which he believed operated in parallel rather than interacting with each other (i.e., psycho-physical parallelism). Bain endorsed the centrality of the law of contiguity for the association of ideas and added the unique twist that neurological changes were responsible for such associations, although he was not explicit about the nature of such changes. In addition, Bain argued that hedonism or the pursuit of pleasurable events and the avoidance or escape from painful ideas as well as unpleasant events transformed reflexive behaviors into voluntary behaviors under the direction of the same laws of association that applied for ideas. Thus, behaviors followed closely by positive consequences were more likely to be repeated than those followed by negative outcomes, which in many ways anticipates Edward Lee Thorndike's (1874–1949) law of effect, treated later in this chapter. Bain's work focused the laws of associationism upon behaviors rather than limiting the laws only to the association of ideas, and in so doing provided the bridge from armchair philosophical speculation that characterized all other earlier British empiricists and associationists to emphasize observations of behaviors and their associated consequences. Bain is clearly the main philosophical bridge to the beginnings of scientific psychology as well as to the psychologies of the 20th century.

In summary, the British empiricists (Locke, Berkeley, and Hume) liberated us, in part, from our biological roots and the tyrannies of unchecked imperial forms of government, and pointed the way out of the major forces that compromise human potential, namely, ignorance and poverty, by indicating the importance of systematic educational opportunities for all citizens. These developments are due to the foundational idea that the human mind acquires content **only** through experiences rather than through biology alone or privileged ancestry. This foundational idea has had a profound impact upon the subsequent developments in psychology but also on how we construct our governments and the instruments of government as well as our educational institutions around the world. Likewise, the British associationists (Hartley, the family Mills, and Bain) provided the laws of associationism that explained how the mind comes, albeit passively, to possess simple and complex ideas, thus liberating humans from minds that are tethered solely to sensations and their faint copies or ideas, giving rise to an unbounded human mind. In addition, the incorporation of utlilitarianism into their philosophical systems allowed the associationists to extend their laws of the mind to account for voluntary behaviors arising from their consequences, which informed much of psychology during the 20th century.

Counterpoint—Immanuel Kant (1724–1804)

Immanuel Kant was born in Konigsberg, Prussia, the son of a saddler, where he spent his entire life except for a few modest excursions. He enrolled in the University of Konigsberg in 1740, earned his doctorate in 1755, and lectured as a Privatdozent (private tutor) there for many years. He assumed the chair of logic and metaphysics in 1770, resigned from the university where he spent his entire professional life in 1797, and died of poor health in 1804. Kant never married nor traveled; his universe consisted of thoughts, and he wrote his famous books *Critique of Pure Reason* and *Critique of Practical Reason* in 1781 and 1788, respectively. Interestingly, students flocked to his classes and found Professor Kant to be an excellent lecturer despite the difficulty they had in reading his books. His influence upon German psychology has been profound and is most clearly reflected in Gestalt psychology (chapter 11).

Kant synthesized rationalism and empiricism, and believed, unlike David Hume, that some truths of the universe and the mind were certain and not based solely on subjective experience. Kant argued that certain **categories of thought rather than specific ideas** (unlike René Descartes, e.g., idea of God) were innate, given, or exist a priori (independent of experience). For Kant, sensory data were important but the mind did not just passively receive such data that were then mechanically cobbled together into different associative patterns driven by the laws of association; rather, the mind acted or added something to the data before they became conscious knowledge. The perception of time was one of the categories of thought, according to which the concept of time is added to the sensory data. For example, we see a person running down a road, which yields a stream of sequential images on our retina, yet in any given retinal image there are no data that indicate it came before or after any other image in the sequence. Thus, according to Kant, the mind adds time to the sensory data. Likewise, for two or more sequential events to be associated it is essential that they be perceived as appearing at different times, otherwise they just appear fused as a single sensation. The perception of space is also another categorical idea that is essential for the perception of two or more simultaneously presented sensations, which likewise can only be associated if the mind adds space to the sensory data. Hence, the empiricists were correct in asserting that sensations are essential for knowledge, although their position is incomplete because they failed to acknowledge, as did the rationalists, that the mind acts upon the sensory data to supply missing features from the sensations, such as the perception of time and space.

Kant believed that we could never achieve true knowledge of objects of the physical world, that is, "things in themselves" or **noumena**, because the categories of the mind act on the sensory data and render all of our experiences with the subjective imprint of the mind. All we know are "appearances," and our mind creates the universe at least as we experience it. Inasmuch as the mind is not a physical thing, Kant argued that the study of the mind or psychology can never be a science. In addition, when we introspect upon our experiences we change the nature of our consciousness, and thus do not give an accurate picture of the mind. Kant presented a philosophical system that integrated empiricism and rationalism, a process that is still ongoing in psychology today, as reflected, for example, by the study of the integrative roles of nature and nurture in developmental or cognitive processes.

ASSOCIATIONISM: LATER DEVELOPMENTS

We now review briefly some extensions of the foundational ideas of associationism as reflected in the systematic study of human memory, animal learning, selective environmental studies, and repressed memories. In effect, these relatively more recent studies represent a transition from a focus upon the association of ideas to human memory, the association of behaviors, and the robust impact of the environment for our understanding of animals and humans.

Hermann Ebbinghaus (1850–1909)

Ebbinghaus was the first to measure systematically human memory, as a result of the inspiration arising from reading Gustav Fechner's (1801–1878) *Elements of Psychophysics*, which was published in 1860. He worked essentially alone, extending associationism by focusing upon the serial recall of **lists of nonsense syllables** with which he or others had little if any experience and therefore few prior associations, which afforded an unencumbered opportunity to study empirically **the associations** between the elements within the list. He argued that psychology could be considered a natural science and devised the completion test to measure the cognitive capacities of school children. He also determined the most effective operating hours for schools, and authored one of the most famous one-liners in the history of psychology, namely, "Psychology has a long past, yet its real history is short" (Ebbinghaus, 1908, p. 3). He was a cooperative, social, and engaging individual; his original findings have stood the test of time, and he did much to help to expand the development of psychology beyond the restrictions of laboratory psychology (Roback & Kiernan, 1969).

Hermann Ebbinghaus was born in Barmen near Bonn, Germany, graduated from the Barmen **Gymnasium** (high school), entered the University of Bonn when he was 17 to study history, and then switched to philosophy. He spent a year in the Prussian army, earned his doctoral degree in 1873 from the University of Bonn, and then spent the next three years traveling in England and France. Ebbinghaus purchased a copy of Fechner's *Elements of Psychophysics* in a bookstore in London and became convinced that he could study higher mental processes (i.e., memory), experimentally as Fechner had studied the intensities of sensations and, contrary to Wundt's position, that higher mental processes such as memory and language could only be studied from a cultural rather than a laboratory-based perspective. Ebbinghaus completed the bulk of his studies of memory in 1880, yet did not publish his findings in *Concerning Memory: An Investigation in Experimental Psychology* until 1885 so as to be certain of the validity of his results, since he had served as both experimenter and participant in collecting his data.

Ebbinghaus was a cofounder, along with Arthur König (1856–1901), of the *Journal of Psychology and Physiology of the Sense Organs* published in 1890, which provided an opportunity to publish a broad range of scientific psychological findings compared to Wundt's journal, *Philosophical Studies*, which published almost exclusively findings from his laboratory at the University of Leipzig. Ebbinghaus was appointed to a professorship at the University of Breslau in 1894, and in 1902 he published his *Principles of Psychology*, which quickly became very popular because it was readable and thus introduced many to scientific psychology. In 1905, Ebbinghaus assumed a professorship at the University of Halle, and died suddenly in 1909 from pneumonia. Throughout his career Ebbinghaus argued and demonstrated through his research that psychology is a science, that higher mental processes could be studied experimentally, and that from the most ancient subject of philosophy there will arise the newest science, namely, psychology. Although Ebbinghaus had no followers, did not establish a school of psychology, and worked pretty much alone in his classic studies of human memory, his work makes plain the foundational idea that psychology is a science that can study systematically a wide variety of phenomena (beyond simple sensations) and their relation to physiological structures and it is on an equal footing with other sciences such as chemistry and physics.

Prior to Ebbinghaus, memory was studied after it had been developed, primarily using introspection. He studied memory from start to finish and thus was able to look at its formation, as well as any changes in memory with the passage of time. For example, Ebbinghaus found that he could learn a list of seven nonsense syllables in one repetition while a list of twelve nonsense syllables required seventeen repetitions before he could recall the entire list correctly in the order in which they were presented. Generally, the longer the list, the greater the number of repetitions required. Likewise, in general, spaced, active, and whole rather than massed, passive, and piecemeal learning yields better recall. Thus, the more one has to learn the more time will be required, the more active the learning needs to be, and it is best to avoid breaking the material into small segments or packets that need at some time to be tied together. Remembering is not automatic or easy but is facilitated by the above practices. In terms of forgetting of nonsense syllables, forgetting proceeds rapidly for the first two days after original learning and then slows down over the next few days. As is well known from Ebbinghaus' work and most likely from our personal experiences, over 50% of material learned is forgotten after sixty minutes and roughly 66% after twenty-four hours. If you want to remember something, always remember to repeat the material to be remembered.

In addition to his carefully controlled laboratory studies of psychological phenomena, Ebbinghaus also systematically investigated applied psychological problems. For example, in the 1890s German children were in school from 8:00 a.m. to 1:00 p.m. without any breaks, and visible signs of fatigue appeared widespread as the day wore on. Ebbinghaus was commissioned to study the problem and unlike prior investigators of the fatigue problem, he employed cognitive rather than sensory tests (e.g., the two-point threshold) of changes in performances during different intervals of the school day. Thus, Ebbinghaus devised the sentence completion test (e.g., _____ are always younger than their fathers) and analogy tests (e.g., July is to May as Saturday is to _____). Although the initial question of the best hours for school got lost, because most German schools still start at 8:00 a.m. and go without any interruption until 1:00 p.m., Ebbinghaus found that based upon test results he was able to distinguish between children with good, average, and poor grades and interestingly, he thought his work was a measure of general intellectual abilities and his tests were employed as part of the tests of intelligence devised later by Alfred Binet (1857–1911).

Ebbinghaus advanced significantly the scientific study of associationism which many considered as the fundamental mechanism for the construction of ideas, although his work has been considered by some as eventually limiting the study of memory to restrictive laboratory conditions focused upon artificial materials rather than natural everyday conditions (Kintsch, 1985; Neisser, 1982; Slamecka, 1985). Interestingly, the nature of the changes of science over time informs us that with many pioneers in any field of study, early innovations are seen first as opening up new perspectives and methods for studying a given phenomenon while at some later time they are considered limiting and need to be expanded or abandoned.

Sensory Conditioning

In 1939, W. J, Brogden reported evidence of sensory conditioning in a three-phase study with dogs. In Phase I, a bell and a light were presented simultaneously for 200 times or pairings. Then in Phase II one of these two stimuli (e.g., the bell) served as the conditioned stimulus for conditioning forelimb extension with a mild electric shock, serving as the unconditioned stimulus. After a conditioned response was obtained, Phase III began, in which the other stimulus (i.e., the light) that had never been paired with the unconditioned stimulus but in Phase I had been paired with the bell now elicited the conditioned response, namely, forelimb extension. This experiment is significant because it makes plain the fundamental importance of cognitive associative learning and provides clear evidence, almost 2,000 years after Aristotle and more than 200 years after the associationists, that simple contiguity of purely sensory events are connected in the mind. Subsequent studies of sensory conditioning in humans were first disappointing, but later studies using a voluntary response (i.e., key pressing) rather than an involuntary response (i.e., galvanic skin response) yielded unequivocal evidence of sensory conditioning (Brogden, 1947; Chernikoff & Brogden, 1949; Karn, 1947).

Selective Deprivation Studies

In a series of animal studies, Richard Held and his colleagues examined the impact of selective environments upon developmental competencies and learning (Hein & Held, 1967; Held & Bauer, 1967; Held & Hein, 1963). In one study, Held and Hein (1963), working with 10-week-old kittens, exposed them to a selective environment for three hours per day for forty-two consecutive days while for the remainder of each day they were housed individually in comfortable home cages with dim illumination. Normal everyday kittens at 10 weeks of age exhibit eye blink responses to rapidly approaching objects and duck their heads as well to avoid collision with such a moving target. In addition, such kittens also extend their front legs when jumping from surfaces of differing height. In the Held and Hein (1963) study, kittens were paired in teams of two with one the "active kitten" and the other the "passive kitten" and both were placed in the same circular environment (like a huge metal drum) with the circular walls painted with vertical black and white strips. The active kitten was in a yoked harness attached at one end to a revolving bar overhead while the passive kitten rode in a gondola suspended from the overhead revolving bar. Thus, the active kitten could move in a circular path (i.e., walk in circles) with both kittens exposed to the same basic visual environment. At the end of forty-two days of three hours per day or a total of 126 hours or 5.25 days of the above selective environmental experiences the active kitten could perform easily and rapidly all of the visual-motor functions described above, while the passive kitten was unable to perform these previously present and critically important functions of interacting appropriately with rapidly moving visual targets such as eye blink and head ducking or extension of forelegs to assure a smooth landing when jumping from one surface to another. Interestingly, when the passive kitten was allowed to move around freely for about ten days the above visual motor responses were reinstated and appeared indistinguishable for the most part from comparable responses of the so-called "active kitten." The above findings make plain the profound effect of the environment or context upon basic psychological capacities.

Repressed Memories

For the early British associationists, conscious memory was an essential psychological process for understanding how the mind comes to acquire content and construct complex ideas while little treatment was given to the possibility of unconscious memories. The concept of repression assumes that something happens that is so shocking that the mind pushes the memory into the inaccessible unconscious mind and the memory of the event is banished from consciousness for a long time and perhaps even for a lifetime.

An important legal case went to trial in 1990 in which the jury returned a verdict of guilty of first-degree murder after one day of deliberations. The defendant was convicted of murdering, twenty years earlier, an 8-year-old girl, with the major evidence provided by his daughter whose memory of witnessing the murder had been repressed for more than twenty years. The above case made national headlines and represented the first instance in which a person was tried and convicted of murder on the basis of a freshly unearthed repressed memory.

Many clinical psychologists believe that repression operates for early traumatic memories (Bruhn, 1990), even though there is no controlled laboratory support for the concept of repression so it is important to be cautious in the use of repression as an interpretative concept for behaviors and experiences (Holmes, 1990). Loftus (1993) has studied systematically the concept of repressed memories, and has suggested that honestly believed repressed memories might be influenced by external factors in addition to internal psychological forces that impact memories. For example, one possible external factor is popular books about childhood sexual abuse readily available in bookstores, such as *The Courage to Heal* (Bass & Davis, 1988). Interestingly, this book was implicated in hundreds of alleged cases of sexual abuse in families (Wakefield & Underwager, 1992). Another potential external force that may influence recall of earlier abusive events comes from the work of Blume (Blume, 1990), who observed that many individuals who enter therapy without such memories appear to acquire them during therapy. Some therapists probe persistently for traumatic memories while others inquire about sexual abuse during every intake of a new patient. Thus, if discussion of incest goes on during the day, and day residue gets into one's dreams at night then it would not be surprising to observe that dreams of incest might result.

Lastly, Loftus (1993) has speculated that it may be possible to inject a whole event into someone's mind (memory injection) for something that never happened. In the "lost in the mall" protocol, a 14-year-old boy was convinced by his older brother (who served as a confederate in the study) that when he was 5 years old he was lost in a shopping mall even though there was no evidence that he in fact had ever been lost in a mall. Further studies by Loftus and Hyman and their colleagues (Hyman & Pentland, 1996; Loftus & Pickrell, 1995; Mazzoni & Loftus, 1998) have established that although it is possible to implant false memories of different types of childhood experiences in a significant number of experimental participants there may be limits to the kinds of memories that can be implanted in such studies (Pezdek, Finger, & Hodge, 1997). It is important to be open to the possibility of the existence of repressed memories which may be very real in the privacy of the therapeutic session, yet it is also important to continue to systematically study repressed memories when we are dealing with the reality of the courtroom.

The Seven Sins of Memory

Memory makes possible a sense of personal history, knowledge of facts and concepts, and the learning of complex skills. The systematic study of the darker side of memory moved to center stage in the 1990s as noted above, with the public and legal focus upon the accuracy of recovered memories of childhood sexual abuse (Read & Lindsay, 1997; Schacter, 1996). There is good reason to believe that although some recovered memories have been corroborated and appear to be valid, there are also good reasons to believe that many such memories are inaccurate (Schacter, 1996). Schacter (1999) has recently attempted to provide a broader framework for the study of human memory with his focus on what he terms "the seven sins of memory." The first three sins all arise from different types of forgetting, namely, **transience**, or the decreasing accessibility of information over time; **absent-mindedness**, or the inattention or shallow processing at the time of encoding or during attempts to retrieve stored information; and **blocking**, or the temporary inaccessibility of information stored in memory. These are all sins of omission such that when individuals need to remember the desired information it is inaccessible or unavailable. The other three sins involve distortions or inaccuracy of memory, and include **misattribution**, or attributing a recollection or idea to the wrong source; **suggestibility**, or memories that are implanted as a result of leading questions or comments when attempting to recall a previous experience; and **bias**, involving retrospective distortions and unconscious influences that are related to current knowledge and beliefs. The seventh and final sin is **persistence**, or remembering information that we cannot forget even if we would like to forget.

Inasmuch as each of us is subject to absent-mindedness, we present here a few studies of this frequent, at times frustrating, and fascinating form of forgetting in which we pay insufficient attention as a stimulus is encoded or because attended information is processed superficially. For example, the well-known depth-of-processing studies have found that divided attention at the time of encoding yields poor later memory for target information (Craik & Lockhart, 1972). Thus, when a person is asked to perform shallow encoding by counting, for example, the number of vowels in a list of words, rather than deep encoding such as putting each word in the list in a category, then memory is significantly better for deep processing. Likewise, shallow encoding seems to be responsible for an interesting phenomenon called "change blindness" (Simons & Levin, 1998). Change blindness arises when people fail to detect any altered features in a scene or object. Thus, for example, Levin and Simons (1997) showed a movie in which an actor performed a simple action, and unbeknownst to the participants, the original actor was replaced by a new person. Interestingly, only one third of the participants noticed the change. In a follow-up study, using a naturalistic setting, an experimenter asked a person on a college campus for directions, then two persons carrying a door passed between them such that the door momentarily occluded the first questioner while a new person was substituted and continued asking for directions. Incredibly, only seven out of fifteen participants noticed the change of person asking directions!!

In summary, Schacter (1999) and others (see, for example, Bjork & Bjork, 1988; Schooler & Anderson, 1997) have suggested that memoric lapses may be reflections of an adaptive memory system that is keyed into present contexts. Thus, for example, it may well be that it is no longer functional to remember old telephone numbers from weeks, months, or years ago or what outfit I wore on the first Tuesday of January in 1998 unless, of course, this information continues to be adaptive in present contexts. In short, you need to use stored information or otherwise you are most likely to lose it. There is only so much stuff we can cart around before we become bogged down and unable to act adaptively to present and future environmental demands.

■ Summary

This chapter focused on the intriguing and enduring issue of how the mind acquires content. We began with a brief treatment of the sources of human knowledge including empiricism, revelation, positivism, and associationism. As part of our treatment of the sources of knowledge we focused first on the positivism of August Comte, his views on the stages of intellectual development of societies, his hierarchy of sciences, and his twisted journey into the dogmatism in almost all religious systems, which he argued so forcefully against. Thereafter, we presented the work of Ernst Mach, who, unlike Comte, stressed the importance of studying the immediate, unanalyzed experiences of an observer as the key to understanding how the human mind acquires content. Comte argued for the study of the products of mind, namely, behaviors (precursor to behaviorism) while Mach argued for the study of immediate experiences (precursor to Gestalt psychology). Both were considered positivist due to their emphasis upon the importance of collecting data from observations rather than speculations or "what ifs."

Our examination of the British empiricists began with John Locke and his unequivocal position that the mind acquires content only through experiences. We next reviewed the work of George Berkeley, who, unlike John Locke, did not distinguish between primary and secondary ideas and thus believed that all we know is our subjective experiences.

David Hume continued in the tradition of the British empiricists, yet he also bridged the gap to associationism by emphasizing the articulation of the three laws of associationism and its treatment of impressions (sensory stimulation) and ideas. We then studied David Hartley, who is considered to be "the father" of British associationism, and the first to study the mind or psychological phenomena as a natural science by proposing a physiological model of association. Thereafter, we turned to a review of the work of James Mill, (the father of John Stuart Mill), who attempted to link the motivational and cognitive dynamics of the mind. John Stuart Mill argued for a science of human nature focused upon associationism.

We were introduced to Alexander Bain, considered by some to be the first psychologist, the author of the first psychology textbooks, *The Sense and the Intellect* and *Emotions and the Will*, and the founder of *Mind*, which was the first periodical devoted entirely to psychology. Thereafter, we briefly discussed the work of Immanuel Kant as the continental counterpoint to the British empiricists and associationists because of his emphasis upon innate categories of thought. Also, we discussed Kant's concept of noumena or "things in themselves," which precludes accurate knowledge of objects of the physical world because the categories of the mind act on the sensory data and render all of our experiences with the subjective imprint of the mind. We then turned to a series of studies that have extended and confirmed empirically some of the key principles of associationism, as reflected in studies of the operation of memory systems, sensory conditioning, selective deprivation, repressed memories, and "the seven sins of memory," especially absent-mindedness.

■ Chapter 7—Associationism

Discussion Questions

- How do the four origins of human knowledge relate to one another?
- How has John Locke's theory of empiricism influenced fields outside as well as inside psychology?

■ What key differentiation did David Hume make to help develop psychology as a science?

■ How did the "father of psychology" influence the study of behavior?

■ By whom and through what method was memory first measured?

■ How do the "seven sins of memory" contribute to inaccurate memories?

Voluntarism and Structuralism

CHAPTER OVERVIEW

Psychology has gradually evolved into a science over the past 125-plus years. In the early formative years of psychology, it was the work of a few German scientists that launched the discipline as a separate science from biology, chemistry, physics, and the extensive influences of philosophy. Ernst Heinrich Weber (1795–1878) focused his psychological experiments upon **psychophysics and consciousness** by studying systematically the just noticeable difference (JND). The JND was defined as the difference between two stimuli detected accurately on 75% of the presented trials. Weber's work demonstrated that the JND between two stimuli depended upon the ratio of the difference between the stimuli regardless of the physical intensities of the stimuli, which is expressed mathematically as $K = (\Delta I)/I$.

Gustav Fechner (1801–1887) argued for psychophysical parallelism, according to which the mental and physical worlds run parallel to each other but do not interact. Fechner developed the Weber-Fechner law, according to which the perceived intensity of a stimulus increases arithmetically as a constant multiple of the physical intensity of the stimulus or $S = K \text{ Log } R$. In other words, changes of physical intensity gallop along at a brisk pace while the corresponding changes of perceived intensity creep along. The Weber and the Weber-Fechner laws were the first laws to provide a mathematical statement of the relationship between the mind and the body. Also, Gustav T. Fechner introduced three psychological methods that were very important in establishing psychology as an independent, laboratory-based science, variations of which are still used today. Another significant contribution to the psychophysical foundations of psychology was made almost 100 years later when S. S. Stevens (1906–1973) demonstrated that psychological intensity (experiences of physical magnitudes) grows as an exponential function of physical stimulus intensity, that is, equal stimulus ratios always produce equal sensory ratios although different ratios hold for different sensory modalities $(S = K\Phi^b)$.

Wilhelm Wundt (1832–1920) used Weber and Fechner's work on the relationship between subjective and physical intensities as a key component in the establishment of psychology as an independent science. **Voluntarism**, as Wundt's new psychology became known, focused upon the specific subject matter of **immediate conscious experiences** of an adult studied by systematic introspection. According to Wundt, our immediate conscious experience is composed of **sensations** that have reference to some "external things" (stimuli) and **affect** or **feelings** (experiences more general than sensations that accompany intense sensations and fall on continua of pleasant to unpleasant, relaxed to strained, and calm to excited). Ideas arise from combinations of sensations derived from memory or previous associations of sensations. The active combination of these components of consciousness was referred to as **apperception** in Wundt's laboratory. This mental process, apperception, allowed individuals to yield complex, unified conscious experiences as opposed to merely a conscious array of unorganized elements. The use of systematic introspection or the more specific strategy known as **internal perception**, a narrow focus on verbal immediate responses to precisely controlled stimuli by trained observers, was an attempt to avoid committing the stimulus error. The stimulus error arises when the person focuses primarily upon a description of the stimulus instead of the conscious experience evoked by a stimulus.

Wundt's interests were widely diversified and included topics such as mental chronometry and cultural psychology or Völkerpsychologie. Mental chronometry was a systematic laboratory method for measuring the speed of mental processes that included measurements of **discrimination** and **choice reaction times**. The primary objective of mental chronometry was to demonstrate that psychological or mind functions could be measured, studied scientifically, and yield consistent findings indicating that mind or psychological processes follow identifiable laws.

Some of Wundt's contemporaries differed with him not only about the subject matter of psychology, but also the primary methods of study of psychological phenomena. For example, Franz Brentano (1838–1917) envisioned an alternative subject matter for psychology that focused upon the study of the activities or acts of the mind consisting of recall, feelings, and judging, his **act psychology**. Brentano thought that psychology needed to focus upon mental acts as opposed to the contents of consciousness. For Brentano, the systematic study of what the mind does was more critical for the emerging discipline of psychology than understanding what was in the mind. Likewise, Oswald Külpe (1862–1915) focused upon the study of imageless thought. Külpe argued that some thoughts or ideas arose in consciousness without specific images, which ran directly opposite to Wundt's psychology that consciousness always consisted of some combination of the three elements of consciousness (i.e., sensations, feelings, and images).

Edward Bradford Titchener (1867–1927) was responsible for introducing Wundt's voluntarism to the United States under the name of **structuralism**. In addition, Titchener developed his Core-Context Theory of Meaning that explained the derivation of meaning of sensations (core) depending upon the context or fringe images in which the sensation was located or embedded.

Wundt's conceptualization of the psychological experiment was the first in a series of three specific models that have been integral steps in the construction of the current psychological experiment as we know it today. The **Leipzig** or **Wundtian model** was characterized by the lack of distinction between the ideas of experimenter and subject as they were interchangeable roles. The **Parisian model** did not permit the interchange of roles between the experimenter and the subject as in the Leipzig model, but rather established rigid experimenter–subject (or doctor–patient) roles considered critical for objective experimentation. Finally, the **American model**, the most recent model, introduced the study of populations, samples, and groups of persons rather than only the study of individuals, leading to an emphasis on keeping individual subjects anonymous and constructing experimental protocols requiring relatively brief experimenter–subject contacts.

Recently, psychologists taking the lead from Wundt's analysis of consciousness into three components (sensations, feelings, and images) have studied systematically human love and identified three components of love. Specifically, the triangular theory of love describes the three elements of love: **intimacy, passion**, and **decision** or **commitment**. According to this theory, it is possible to have combinations of some or all of these three elements that yield different types of love. Love that is referred to as liking is the combination of experiences of the intimacy component of love in the absence of passion and decision commitment, while romantic love is the combination of intimacy and passion causing lovers to be drawn not only physically to each other, but also with an emotional bond yet without necessarily a long-term commitment. The combination of all three elements of love is consummate love and is very difficult to maintain once it is reached.

LEARNING OBJECTIVES

When you finish studying this chapter, you will be prepared to:

- Define the relationship between the mental and physical worlds as described by the psychophysical laws proposed by E. H. Weber, G. T. Fechner, and S. S. Stevens.
- Identify and define Fechner's three psychophysical methods
- Describe the role that psychophysics played in the development of Wundt's psychology of voluntarism
- Explain the challenges that psychology faced in the early years as an independent science
- Identify the subject matter (immediate conscious experience) and method of study (systematic introspection of conscious experiences) of Wundt's new psychology, voluntarism
- Describe the elements of consciousness according to Wilhelm Wundt
- Explain and define simple, discrimination, and choice reaction times as expressions of mental chronometry
- Compare and contrast the work of Franz Brentano and Oswald Külpe to that of Wundt
- Describe E. B. Titchener's study of consciousness and his core context theory of meaning
- Define and distinguish between Wundt's voluntarism and Titchner's structuralism
- Explain the social development of the psychology experiment
- Identify the three components of the triangular theory of love

INTRODUCTION

The majority of what we take for granted today in the field of psychology in many respects is the direct result of pioneers such as Ernst Heinrich Weber, Gustav Theodor Fechner, Wilhelm Maximilian Wundt, and Edward Bradford Titchener. The foundation of the current field of psychology, not even considering the subfields and clinical practices, are based on findings from their early basic research utilizing laboratory experiments. The psychophysicists such as Weber and Fechner and much later S. S. Stevens introduced the strategy of examining the relationship between the physical and mental worlds by deriving mathematical equations that arose from empirical laboratory-based experiments.

Wundt was then successful in introducing this view of rigorous study of psychological phenomena into somewhat controlled laboratory experiments. Accordingly, Wundt defined the subject matter of psychology and established the first laboratory and method of study for psychology. Although his early methods have changed and have been expanded greatly as the science has grown, his was the first step toward the empirical basis of laboratory research in psychology.

PSYCHOPHYSICAL LAWS AND CONSCIOUSNESS

Psychophysics set out to describe and understand how the intensity of sensory experiences related to the physical intensity of stimuli, and to determine if a lawful relationship existed between the physical and subjective worlds. In the beginning, psychophysics provided laboratory-based tools to determine the relationship between the mental and physical worlds, and also set the stage for the importance of defining the subject matter and methods of study in the subsequent schools of psychology, beginning with Wundt's voluntarism.

Weber's Law

Ernst Heinrich Weber (1795–1878) was a professor of anatomy at the University of Leipzig where his earlier studies in anatomy, biology, physiology, and physics prepared him, along with his brother, to discover the utility of excitatory and inhibitory functions of the central nervous system. Later his interests shifted toward the study of sensations arising from the skin and muscles, which led him to publish a classic in experimental psychology in 1834, *The Sense of Touch* (Weber, 1978).

Weber was interested in determining how we detect or become aware of the difference in intensities between two stimuli which we do automatically on a daily basis when, for example, we lift objects and notice one just heavier than another, or when we turn up the volume on our radio or television so we can hear it just a little more loudly. Weber found that the judgments we make of the intensive differences between two stimuli are relative rather than absolute. For example, if we had one canister or box filled with sand and this standard stimulus weighed 120 grams, the question then becomes how much do we have to change (increase or decrease) the weight of another canister or box (the comparison stimulus) to just notice the difference in weight between these two stimuli. In this example for lifted weights, Weber found consistently that he had to add (or subtract) 3 grams to the comparison stimulus for the difference to be just noticed reliably (i.e., on 75% of the test trials). Thus, the relative difference between two weights had to be 1/40 to detect reliably the difference between the weights of the two objects.

Put another way, **K** = $\Delta I/I$, where **K** is the experience of the just noticeable difference (**JND**), ΔI is the amount of change of the physical intensity of the comparison stimulus over the standard stimulus or **I** (Weber, 1978). Thus, to just notice the difference consistently between a standard stimulus, say, of 200 grams, the other lifted weight (the comparison stimulus) had to weigh now 5 grams more (205 grams) to be perceived consistently as just heavier or 5 grams less (195 grams) to be perceived consistently as just lighter than the standard. Ratios between the intensities of stimuli matter rather than the absolute differences between the intensities of the stimuli. **K** = $\Delta I/I$ is known as Weber's Law and was the first mathematical statement that described the relationship between the physical and psychological worlds!

In general, the Weber fraction varies from one sensory system to another, and is valid only over the middle of the intensive continuum for any sensory system. Thus, for example, the Weber fraction is 1/50 for length so if the length of a line (the standard stimulus) was 100 millimeters (just a little more than 3¾ inches) then the comparison stimulus or other line would have to be 104 millimeters long (just a little more than 4 inches) to be perceived consistently as just longer, while the comparison would have to be 96 millimeters to be perceived consistently shorter than the standard of 100 millimeters. However, the just noticeable differences for very heavy or very light weights or very long or very short lines would yield Weber fractions much larger than the above 1/40 and 1/50, respectively. Albeit, Weber's findings were all that some others needed to make the case that the mind or psychological functions could be measured and psychology could be considered a separate discipline distinct from philosophy and biology although arising from and related to both of these disciplines.

Weber-Fechner Law

Gustav T. Fechner (1801–1887) was a trained physician who argued for **psychophysical parallelism**, according to which the mental and physical worlds run parallel to each other but without direct interaction. After graduating with his M.D. in 1822, he focused his work strictly on physics. His interest in a demonstrable relationship between the mind and body emerged following his resignation from his position as the chair of physics at the University of Leipzig in 1838, as a result of severe emotional exhaustion. His emotional disturbance was a reaction to what he perceived as permanent blindness; however, when he regained his sight his emotional health improved as well. He resumed his faculty position at the University of Leipzig in 1848 as a professor of philosophy rather than as professor of physics.

His program of work in psychophysics began with the publication of *Zend Avesta, On Concerning Matters of Heaven and the Hereafter* (Fechner, 1851). This magnum opus contained the psychophysical law that bears his name, which came to him in a dream on the morning of October 22, 1850, when he had an insight that there must be a measurable relationship between sensory and physical intensities. According to the Weber-Fechner Law, the **perceived intensity** of a stimulus increases arithmetically while physical intensity gallops along as a constant multiple of physical intensity, or $S = K \log R$. In this equation, **S** is the perceived intensity, **K** is a constant, and **Log R** is the logarithmic function of the physical intensity of the stimulus. The logarithmic function describes sensation as growing in equal steps (arithmetically) while the corresponding stimulus intensity continually increases as a function of a constant multiple (geometrically). Thus, larger and larger outputs of stimulus energy are required to obtain corresponding sensory incremental effects, or, as eloquently described by Woodworth (1938, p. 437), "The sensation plods along step by step while the stimulus leaps ahead by ratios." This means that as a stimulus gets larger there must be a larger change in stimulus intensity for a change to be detected (Fechner, 1966/1860).

Let us take, for example, lifted weights that have a Weber fraction of 1/40, and start with a standard stimulus weight of 120 grams (R1) shown on the x or horizontal axis in Figure 8-1. We already know that for a comparison weight to be perceived as just heavier, it has to be 123 grams (R2), as shown in Figure 8-1. Now, for a comparison stimulus to be judged just heavier than R2 of 123 grams it has to be 126.07 grams (R3); for another comparison to be perceived as just heavier than R3 (126.07 grams) it has to weigh 129.22 grams (R4); for comparison stimulus to be perceived as just heavier than R4 (129.22) it has to be 132.45 grams (R5), and so on, with stimulus intensity along the x axis increasing as a constant multiple of 1/40

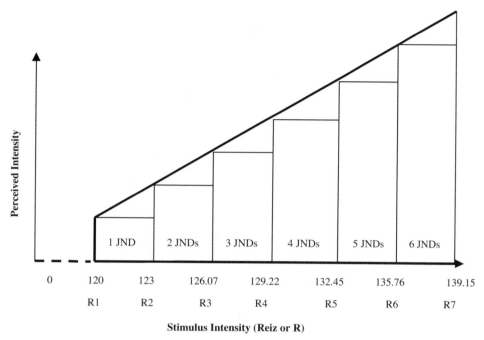

FIGURE 8-1 A Visual Representation of the Weber-Fechner Law—S $=$ K Log R

(the Weber fraction) and perceived intensity increasing along the vertical or y axis increasing as a constant addition of JNDs. Fechner argued that the perceived intensities of a stimulus as indicated by the JND are additive such that a weight of 126.07 would be perceived as twice as heavy as the original standard stimulus of 120 grams, while a weight of 129.22 would be perceived as three times heavier than the original standard. Although the argument was elegant, the data did not fit precisely the predictions of the Weber-Fechner Law as JNDs are not additive. Thus, as in the above illustration of the progression of physical and perceived intensities, R4 is not perceived consistently and therefore lawfully as three times heavier nor is R3 perceived consistently as twice as heavy as the standard stimulus, R1. In addition, the Weber-Fechner Law required a true zero for the perceived scale, the absolute threshold, which is variable, depending upon how it is measured, and changes slightly over time during measurement.

Gustav T. Fechner also introduced three psychophysical methods into psychology that were very important to Wilhelm Wundt when he launched psychology as a laboratory-based experimental science in 1879. The **method of just noticeable differences** or the **method of limits**, as it is called today, requires a person to compare two stimuli with the intensity of one varied (the comparison stimulus) until the person notices the comparison as just different from the other or standard stimulus. The data described earlier in this section and the data presented in Figure 8-1 have been collected using the method of limits. The **method of average effort or adjustment** was Fechner's second method and requires the person to adjust or change continuously a variable stimulus until it matches a standard stimulus or appears just different. This method can be used to measure both the difference limen or threshold (DL, the just noticeable difference) and/or the absolute limen or threshold (AL, that stimulus energy that is detected on 50% of the trials with this statistical value set somewhat arbitrarily by the experimenter and thus can yield different ALs). In the **method of constant stimuli or right and wrong** cases, comparison stimuli are paired randomly with a standard stimulus and the person reports whether the comparison stimulus is greater than, equal to, or less than the standard stimulus or, alternatively detected or not detected. This method is used to measure both the difference and absolute thresholds, respectively. In all three of Fechner's psychophysical methods, repeated measures are taken yielding average values such that both the difference and absolute thresholds are best thought of as statistical values rather than fixed immutable values. Some variations of Fechner's original three psychophysical methods are still used today, for example, to measure air quality or how much sweetener needs to be added to a cereal so that it appears just sweeter than unsweetened cereal, which can save the manufacturer large sums of money when tons of cereal are produced. Lastly, as any seasoned cook well knows, we use some of Fechner's methods when adding just the right amount of herbs, condiments, and/or oils to produce our favorite dishes.

The Weber and the Weber-Fechner laws were the first laws to provide a mathematical statement of the relationship between the mind and the body based upon systematic psychophysical methods employed in a laboratory setting. Weber and, especially, Fechner were revolutionary in their thinking and methods of study pointing psychology in the direction of examining potential lawful relationships in the field. These laws, along with Fechner's three psychophysical methods, the advances in brain localization, nerve physiology, and philosophy stressing empiricism and associationism, provided the fundamental calculus to launch the new science of psychology (Fechner, 1966/1860).

Stevens' Law

We now move ahead to a scientist who was very much influenced by the work of E. H. Weber and Gustav Fechner but not in agreement with their proposed laws. S. S. Stevens (1906–1973) presented yet another set of principles by which the mind–body relationship could be measured in his paper "**To Honor Fechner and Repeal His Law**" (Stevens, 1961). In this paper, Stevens respectfully demonstrated that the Weber-Fechner law was incorrect because it does not apply at the extreme ends of any intensive continuum; for example, weight, brightness, length, and JNDs are not equal and cannot be added one to another. Accordingly, Stevens believed sensory or psychological intensity (experiences of magnitude) grew as an exponential function of physical stimulus intensity by which equal physical ratios always produce equal sensory ratios. **Stevens' Law** is written as $\mathbf{S} = \mathbf{K}\emptyset^{\mathbf{b}}$ in which **S** is equal to sensory intensity, **K** is equal to a constant, Ø is equal to physical intensity, and **b** is the exponent for the relationship between sensory and physical intensities.

Examples of this relationship can be seen in length, brightness, and electric shock. In terms of **length**, for a line to appear twice as long as another (double sensory intensity), we must increase the length of a line by 100% (i.e., double the length). Thus, the exponent describing this sensory continuum is 1.0. **Brightness**, on the other hand, requires an increase in physical intensity of the light by 900% for the light to appear twice as bright; thus, the exponent is 0.33. Turning to **electric shock**, we learn that for an electric shock to appear twice as intense as another electric shock we only need to increase the stimulus intensity by 20%. Thus, the dynamic range of perceived intensities of brightness is very broad allowing us to see under very dim and extremely bright conditions. On the other hand, the dynamic range of perceived intensities for electric shock is very narrow such that small changes in the intensity of electric shock are perceived as very large, thus protecting us from potential tissue damage and possible electrocution.

Stevens came to these conclusions by utilizing magnitude and cross-modality estimations. With magnitude estimation the subject estimates directly the sensory intensity of a stimulus relative to a modulus or referent, whereas with cross-modality estimation the subject is asked to measure directly sensory intensity by matching one sensory intensity (e.g., hand-grip intensity) against another sensory intensity (e.g., line length). In general, both of these psychophysical methods yield consistent and reliable results.

The initial two theorists, Weber and Fechner, and later Stevens made a significant contribution to the field of psychophysics by exploring the relationship between the existential duality of nature, the physical and mental worlds, and paved the way for the progress of deciphering lawful relationships in psychology for years to come. The successful implementation of methods of measuring mental processes in general was notable, but we must also remember the passion that drove these scientists to achieve that point, and that is the desire to understand the relationship between mind and matter, sensation and stimuli, and internal and external environments.

WILHELM WUNDT (1832–1920)

Wilhelm Wundt formally founded a laboratory-based experimental psychology in 1879 when he established the first experimental laboratory at the University of Leipzig with the intent to "mark out a new domain of science." It was Wundt who took the psychophysical tools and findings reported by Weber and Fechner and launched psychology as a separate scientific discipline, and in so doing transformed psychology from a branch of philosophy into a science. His desire to move psychology away from unsystematic introspection employed by philosophers toward the use of the scientific method was directly influenced by his medical background. His interest in laboratory work began with the realization that the practice of medicine was not for him and thus he initially pursued research in physiology, which later came to include a growing interest in psychology and psychological research. The combined interest in physiology and psychology led Wundt to write (1969/1910) *Principles of Physiological Psychology* in 1910. His position at the University of Leipzig teaching sensory physiology, psychology, anthropology, and physiology afforded him the opportunity to establish himself as one of history's most productive research scientists by publishing an average of two journal publications per month in the journal he created, *Philosophische Studien* (*Philosophical Studies*) during his first four years at Leipzig.

Establishment of Psychology as an Independent Science

In many ways it is surprising yet fortuitous that Wilhelm Wundt established psychology as an independent science. First off, Wundt, for a variety of reasons, had a relatively lackluster academic career prior to entering medical school at the University of Heidelberg where he devoted himself totally to his studies and earned his medical degree in three years in 1855. He then turned to developing his research skills primarily in physiology at the prestigious University of Berlin, studying with prominent scientists including Johannes Müller and Emil Dubois-Raymond. Thereafter, he returned to Heidelberg, instructing medical students in the required course of sensory physiology, and in addition taught some courses of his own including one dealing with psychology as a natural science. From about 1862 to 1874, the year that he joined the University of Leipzig due to his growing and solid reputation in psychology, Wundt taught a variety of courses in physiology and philosophy, lectured on the need for the development of experimental psychology, did not make much money, married Sophie Mau in 1872, and all along continued to refine his ideas about the systematic study of consciousness (Bringman, Balance, & Evans, 1975). Although Wundt was immersed initially in the materialistic sciences of his day, such as physiology, he was not a materialist and believed that consciousness does not arise from "a thing or substance." Therefore, a new science was needed to identify the composition of and the psychological laws that govern conscious experiences via a laboratory-based science (Blumenthal, 1975). Accordingly, Wundt established a one-room psychological laboratory in 1879; directed as well as participated actively in student research in the laboratory; published voluminously; established a journal, *Philosophical Studies*; and from these developments the field of psychology as an independent scientific discipline expanded rapidly and widely thereafter. The academic dean who had recruited Wundt to the University of Leipzig in the latter part of 1864, with the expectation that Wundt would make a difference in the area of psychology, saw that Wundt was indeed a great intellect and organizer, and a hard worker, and only after Wundt threatened to move to another university did resources begin to flow his way in the mid-1880s, including the move to a multi-room, well-equipped laboratory facility.

Voluntarism: The Subject Matter and Method of Study

Wundtian laboratory-based psychology is the systematic study of immediate conscious experiences and the identification of the psychological laws that govern dynamic or changing conscious experiences. The psychological process of attention and volition or choice are central to Wundt's psychology, and accordingly he named his psychology **voluntarism**, which was the first formal school of psychology and is very different in many respects from E. B. Titchener's school of psychology known as structuralism (Blumenthal, 1975). Wundtian psychology focused upon the immediate conscious experience (e.g., actually tasting an apple) rather than the mediated conscious experiences (reading about the taste of an apple) of the person. In the laboratory, the subject or participant focused upon the internal perception, that is, what the person was actually experiencing in response to highly controlled stimuli, rather than defining the properties of the stimulus which is known as the stimulus error. In other words, internal perception focused on what the highly trained person was perceiving, rather than his or her awareness of the external stimulus, with attention paid to the size, intensity, duration, quality, and affect of the experience rather than properties of the stimulus.

The Composition of Consciousness

Immediate conscious experiences were thought to be composed of two fundamental components or elements. The first element was **sensation** or the basic mental process or experience that has reference to some "external thing" (the stimulus). The modality of a sensation is determined by the sensory nerve activated (e.g., the visual or auditory nerve), and could be differentiated by quality, intensity, clearness, and duration of the sensation. **Affect** or

feelings were the second component of immediate consciousness. This element was conceptualized as experiences that accompany sensations and are perceived as more general than sensations. Feelings varied along three dimensions from pleasant to unpleasant, relaxed to strained, calm to excited. The intensity of a sensation yields changes in the nature of a feeling as, for example, slight tickling might be experienced as pleasant while more intense and protracted tickling is perceived as unpleasant. An **idea**, another component of consciousness, arises from combinations of sensations derived from memory or previous sensations. Ideas are retrospective and historical while sensations and feelings are given in the immediate conscious experience related to an external stimulus (Bringmann & Tweney, 1980).

Apperception

The systematic study of immediate human consciousness, which included sensations, feelings, and ideas, stressed the total perceptual experiences derived from the elements of consciousness. The combination of these elements of consciousness was thought to arise from either passive or active combinations. Passive combinations produced by perceptions were referred to as **associations** while active combinations were the result of **apperception** or what we call today selective attention. The mental process of apperception involving what the person chooses to attend to allows the individual to yield a complex unified conscious experience as opposed to an array of unorganized elements, that is, sensations, feelings, and ideas. Just as chemical elements react to yield compounds, apperception results in a total perceptual experience which is inherently different from the sum of the individual experiences. The dynamics of apperception are illustrated by the attentional processes of **blickpunt** and **blickfeld**. The blickpunt is a glance point in which elements are the focus of attention (i.e., apperception) and blickfeld (i.e., perception) is a field of consciousness in which elements are not in the range of immediate attention or awareness. Thus, for example, you may be focused on reading the sentences on this page yet not aware of the pressure sensations from your watchband, shoes, or the chair in which you are seated until you shift your attention voluntarily to these sensations and feelings. Apperception yields new experiences similar to chemical interaction of molecules to form a whole different from the parts as, for example, water which arises from the gases of two parts hydrogen to one part oxygen.

Mental Chronometry

Mental chronometry, based upon the measurements of reaction time (RT), was developed by Franciscus Cornelius Donders (1818–1889) and imported into Wundt's laboratory as a method for measuring various mental processes. Donders and Wundt concluded that RT could be used as a measure of mental activity, which is composed of nerve impulses that had been measured as a result of the earlier work by Hermann L. F. von Helmholtz (1850), one of Wundt's mentors. Thus, if the mind was made of nerves and nerve impulses that could be measured, it followed deductively that mental activity could also be measured. Mental chronometry in Wundt's laboratory consisted of measuring **simple, discrimination, and choice reaction times**, which are progressively more complex mental operations. Discrimination reaction time (DRT) is the amount of time it takes, for example, to respond to a green light compared to simple reaction time (SRT), which is the time it takes to respond to any light as no discrimination between the color of the light stimuli is required. Thus, the duration of the mental process of discrimination could be measured as follows:

$$\text{Discrimination Time} = \text{DRT} - \text{SRT}$$

Therefore, using the subtractive process of first measuring simple reaction time and then subtracting that time from the time for discrimination reaction time provided a laboratory-based measure of the psychological process of discrimination. It then followed that perhaps more complicated psychological processes could also be measured using the subtractive process. Choice time (CT), a more complicated psychological process than discrimination time, involves the time that it takes to make a choice such as releasing one key for a green light and releasing a different key for a red light. It was believed that the mental process of choosing could also be measured as the difference between choice reaction time (CRT) and discrimination reaction time (DRT). Following our above example this relationship exists because the CRT is essentially a DRT in addition to the time to make the choice response of which key to release.

$$\text{Choice Time} = \text{CRT} - \text{DRT} - \text{SRT}$$

Many studies were conducted in Wundt's laboratory by many of his students utilizing both discrimination reaction time and choice reaction time in experiments referred to as **complication experiments**. Unfortunately, the reaction time method was abandoned because the additive premise that was the foundation of this work was found invalid. Specifically, choice reaction time did not always exceed DRT plus SRT, so it failed to support the additive time expectations of the mental chronometry model.

Völkerpsychologie or Cultural Psychology

The ten-volume *Völkerpsychologie*, published by Wundt in 1916, encompassed his work on group or cultural psychology over the last twenty years of his life. Wundt believed that higher mental processes such as thinking, memory, and motivation could not be studied experimentally in the laboratory but could be studied by historical analysis and naturalistic observations of members of different cultures. The *Völkerpsychologie* described Wundt's belief that cultures could be understood as points on a continuum from those then considered as primitive (e.g., Australian aboriginal) to advanced (e.g., Germany) cultures. This theory was developed through addressing topics such as anthropology, the psychology of religion, and group social psychology. Wundt's studies of the variety of subjects contributing to his model of cultural psychology were strongly influenced by Darwinian thought that identified evolution as an underlying mental process (Wundt, 1916). The comparison of different cultures along an evolutionary continuum allowed Wundt to better understand consciousness as an organized whole rather than focus only upon the individual parts of consciousness as identified by systematic yet relatively simple laboratory studies.

ALTERNATIVES TO VOLUNTARISM

Clearly, Wundt was the first to present a comprehensive psychology, voluntarism, grounded in laboratory experiments of immediate conscious experience employing the method of systematic introspection and later other methods such as reaction time experiments. Interestingly, his program of psychology did not go unchallenged especially regarding the issue of the primary subject matter of psychology and the content of consciousness.

Franz Brentano (1838–1917) and Act Psychology

Shortly after Wundt defined immediate conscious experience as the subject matter for the new discipline of psychology, Franz Brentano envisioned an alternative subject matter, namely, the systematic study of the mental acts of consciousness. In essence, Brentano took a step away from Wundt's work, which studied what was immediately in the mind, and a step toward the study of the activity of the mind in the mental processes consisting of recall, feeling, and judging. Brentano earned a doctorate in philosophy in 1862 from the University of Tübingen and two years later was ordained into the Roman Catholic priesthood. His success as a teacher was his ability to influence and inspire his students, one of whom was Carl Stumpf (1848–1936), who was an important influence on the founders of Gestalt psychology.

Specifically, Brentano thought that psychology needed to focus upon mental acts of consciousness as opposed to the contents of consciousness. Accordingly, **what the mind does** or the activity of the mind was more important for psychological study than understanding **what was in the mind** or the content of the mind. He insisted that the mind be studied through the concept of activity as the fundamental base of empiricism in his book *Psychology from an Empirical Standpoint* (Brentano, 1874). Brentano used the term *empirical standpoint* to distinguish his consistent and reasoned account of the mind from Titchener's and Wundt's descriptive nature of the mind. Brentano's work on mental acts, known as **Act Psychology**, emphasized three key mental acts; recall, judging, and feeling. The first of these, recall, is remembering or having an idea of an object. The second act is in judging the object, which can also be thought of as the affirmation or the denial of the object, while the third act of feeling is forming an attitude toward the object. Brentano used the method of internal perception to study mental phenomena, which differed from Wundt's method of inner observation (or introspection) in that it was a perception of psychological experiences that contain an object in themselves that is identical to an object outside itself. For example, a psychological experience consists of the first step, the act of seeing, and then the second step, the content of the seeing. In Wundt's view only the second step was crucial, the content of the seeing; thus, it could only be studied through introspection. Although both Brentano's and Wundt's methods rested on the foundation of inaccurate human memory, Brentano justified its use by arguing that all science consults memory; thus, psychology is no different.

As Brentano continued his studies he struggled with the question of unity of experience. He was unsure if the total experience was a sum of the three key mental acts or if it was the relationship between the parts that created the experience. He concluded with some reservation, knowing that there was more work to be done in the area, that the mental acts or consciousness were unified, unique to the individual, and composed of all three (and even more as he later discovered) key mental acts. His work on these three specific types of mental acts and the formation of the self as a result of the integration of past, present, and intentions about the future became an inspiration for Gestalt psychology as well as psychoanalysis.

Oswald Külpe (1862–1915) and Imageless Thought

Oswald Külpe established the theory of imageless thought as another alternative to the psychology of Wilhelm Wundt. Külpe believed that some thoughts could be imageless in the absence of a sensation, feeling, or image as required by Wundtian psychology (Lindenfeld, 1978). Interestingly, Külpe earned his PhD under Wundt in 1887 and later became one of Wundt's major critics.

Once in his laboratory at Würzburg, Külpe pursued testing his theory by asking persons how they solve problems in terms of mental operations such as searching, discriminating, and categorizing information through the use of scrambled pictures, in hopes of developing an alternative to Wundt's work utilizing the elemental building blocks of consciousness. Külpe believed that the ability to form a mental image was fundamentally different from the ability to remember an experience or recognize something. Examples of this concept include recognizing an individual when one is unable to form a mental image of the individual from memory alone, and the understanding of words such as philosophy and empiricism that have no direct mental image associated with them. Research on problem solving using **mental set** or **einstellung** illustrated a predisposition to respond in a given way. When subjects are made aware of certain elements of a problem to be solved, although other elements are present, the variability in the method of problem solving is greatly reduced. The mental set provided for an individual through instructional communication significantly impacts the method by which a person solves the problem at hand. Thus, for example, if instructed up front to listen primarily to what women say in a meeting rather than men, the accuracy of recall for the contributions of women speakers would be much higher than if no mental or einstellung was activated.

Külpe had a large influence on the field of psychology through the research conducted in his many laboratory studies of mental processes. He was successful in using experimental methods to decipher a difference between the elemental mental processes of Wundt and his study of the higher-order mental processes, such as problem solving, using mental sets.

Edward Bradford Titchener (1867–1927) and Structuralism

E. B. Titchener's psychology evolved from his two years of doctoral study under Wilhelm Wundt, which earned him a PhD in 1892. He was the primary force that introduced the Titchenerian brand of Wundtian psychology utilizing introspection in the United States. After completing his doctoral studies with Wundt in Leipzig, Titchener was offered a position at Cornell University in a relatively rural part of New York State, where he spent the remainder of his life as an Englishman who never became a U.S. citizen or immersed in American society. Titchener referred to his brand of psychology as **structuralism** as did William James (1842–1910). Titchner's structuralism was a system of psychological thought intended to be modeled after more established sciences such as chemistry that employed observation or **introspection** as the method to search for the same three basic elements of consciousness as Wundt (i.e., sensations, feelings, and images or ideas).

Titchener's **Core-Context Theory of Meaning** explained the assignment of meaning to sensations which were the core of the experience while the elicited **fringe images** from prior sensations and associations were the **context**. The context in which the sensation is experienced determines the meaning of the sensation; for example, a particular fragrance may elicit images of particular flowers thus giving meaning to the individual. This context or fringe image is necessary for the sensation to acquire meaning; thus, in the case of rapid speech in which a sensation is experienced but the context is not assessed it is possible to have sensation without meaning. It is also possible for meaning to be associated with meaningless sensations; for example, learning a new language. In this instance, meaning is associated with the currently meaningless sensation of vocalizing a new pattern of syllables.

Titchener's view on the fundamental question of the basic elements of consciousness was one component of his work; he also studied the differences in levels of primary (involuntary) and secondary (voluntary) attention. His experimental studies on association that included the core-context of meaning theory also examined emotion and its relation to the James-Lange theory of emotion. Titchener did not agree with the James-Lang theory, which argued that emotions were a result of an organic or physiological experience. On the contrary, Titchener thought that affect was associated with earlier memories or images and that emotion was the result of a much more complex psychological process rather than primarily an organic cause.

Titchener, like Wundt, had many of his works published, namely, two books: *Outline of Psychology* (Titchener, 1896) and *Experimental Psychology* (Titchener, 1905), and many journal articles that he presented at meetings of the **Society of Experimental Psychologists**, which he established in 1904. Although he never attended a meeting of the American Psychological Association (APA) he established the Society of Experimental Psychology to concentrate on laboratory psychology as opposed to the APA's focus upon both laboratory-based and applied psychology. Titchner served as the doctoral mentor for Margaret Floy Washburn (1871–1939), the first woman PhD psychologist, who studied comparative psychology.

THE ORIGINS OF THE PSYCHOLOGICAL EXPERIMENT

The early psychophysicists such as E. H. Weber and G. T. Fechner pioneered the conceptual framework for an experimental psychology while Wilhelm Maximilian Wundt built upon their work and established the first psychology laboratory in a university setting. Over the years other changes have occurred in the protocol of the psychological experiment, such as providing participants with more information about the nature and purpose of the research they are involved in, the development of status differentials between the researcher and the subject, and an elaborate set of rules created to govern the permissible interactions among the researcher and participants.

There are three main models of psychological experimentation that have been employed over the years in the evolution of the psychological experiment; the **Leipzig**, the **Parisian**, and the **American models**. Danziger (1985) found that during the period 1875–1890, the Leipzig model was dominant, which basically involved no distinction between the roles of researcher and subject in an experiment. For example, the subject and researcher were often roles filled by the same person; this type of research was conducted in Wundt's laboratory.

The hypnotic experiments conducted in Paris, France, by Charcot and others were different from the Leipzig model and the current American model. The Parisian model did not permit the interchange of roles between the experimenter and the subject as did the Leipzig model. This distinction by the Parisian model established the rigid patient–doctor relationship roles that are considered by some as critical for objective experimentation.

The American model of the psychological experiment differed from both the Leipzig and Parisian models by studying populations, samples, and groups of persons rather than focusing on individuals. In addition to this focus on aggregated data as opposed to individual data, the American model kept individual subjects anonymous and included only brief experimenter–subject contacts. Both the Parisian and the American models were modified from the original Leipzig model so that there is a strict difference in the function of the subjects (mainly as a data source) and the researcher (theoretical conceptualization, task administration, and publication of the study) to remove possible confounds from the experimental process, while the American model made it possible to identify psychological characteristics that could be applied across populations instead of being applicable primarliy to individuals.

THE ELEMENTS OF LOVE

Regardless of what the subject matter of psychology was according to Wundt, Brentano, Külpe, or Titchener, one thing is certain: they all experienced love. Although feelings were studied extensively in Wundt's laboratory, the uniquely human experience of love was not studied. Thus, it was not until many years later that, like consciousness, some proposed that love consists of three elements that can be combined into different patterns yielding different types of love. Human love, which is a sought-after and desirable experience, is thought to be composed of three main elements, namely, **intimacy, passion**, and **decision or commitment** (Sternberg, 1986). According to the triangular theory of love (Sternberg, 1986), the element of intimacy is characterized by feelings of closeness, connectedness, and bondedness in loving relationships while passion is characterized by drives that lead to romance, physical attraction, sexual consummation, and related phenomena in loving relationships. Although both intimacy and passion lead to love, love is not complete without the final element of decision or commitment. In the short term this element is the decision to love someone else besides oneself and in the long term it is the commitment to maintain that love. In a relationship two of these three components tend to be stable, intimacy and decision; however, passion tends to be unstable and comes and goes over the course of a loving relationship.

Loving relationships cover a wide variety of experiences other than consummate love, which is the result of the combination of all three elements but rather can include liking or romantic love as well. In **liking** one experiences the intimacy component of love in the absence of passion and decision-commitment, whereas in **romantic** love the combination of intimacy and passion coexist, causing lovers to be drawn to each other not only physically but also with an emotional bond without commitment. Although it may appear that once **consummate** love is reached one has reached the pinnacle of love, yet it must be noted that reaching consummate love is easier than maintaining it. A beautiful piece by Louis de Bernieres described the phenomenon of maintaining consummate love, in his book *Captain Corelli's Mandolin* (1994), as roots that have grown so intertwined that it is inconceivable to ever part even after the passion has burned away, whereas when the petals fall away and the roots have not intertwined the consummate love falls apart as well.

Summary

In this chapter we have seen the influence of German psychologists on the development of psychology as an independent science. Ernst Heinrich Weber studied systematically the just noticeable difference (JND) which is summarized in his law $\mathbf{K} = \Delta\mathbf{I}/\mathbf{I}$. Gustav T. Fechner's work, building upon Weber's Law, is captured concisely by his psychophysical law that states that the correspondence between the perceived intensity of a stimulus increases by the addition of a constant (i.e., the JND) while the physical intensity must increase by a constant multiple or $\mathbf{S} = \mathbf{K\,Log\,R}$. Later psychophysical studies by S. S. Stevens demonstrated the limitations of Fechner's Law.

Wilhelm Wundt built upon the earlier work of Weber and Fechner on the relationship between the mind and the physical world as a key component in the establishment of psychology as an independent science. Wundt, in the first psychological laboratory at Leipzig University, began the study of scientific psychology by focusing upon the subject matter of **immediate conscious experiences** composed of sensation, affect or feelings, and images. Wundt also studied mental chronometry, which measured the times of discrimination and choice mental processes.

Franz Brentano envisioned an alternative subject matter for psychology known as act psychology and Oswald Külpe studied imageless thought. Edward Bradford Titchener was responsible for introducing laboratory-based psychology to the United States under the name structuralism as well as developing his Core-Context Theory of Meaning.

As we have seen, Wundt's conceptualization of the psychological experiment was a crucial first step in a series of three specific models that have been integral in the construction of the current psychological experiment. The Leipzig, the Parisian, and the American models were all derived from Wundt's original protocol for the psychological experiment. We concluded this chapter by reviewing briefly the triangular theory of love. According to this theory, there are three elements of love: intimacy, passion, and decision or commitment, with different combinations of some or all of these three elements yielding different types of love.

Chapter 8—Voluntarism and Structuralism

Discussion Questions

- How did Gustav Fechner's theory of psychological parallelism build on Ernst Heinrich Weber's work in "just noticeable difference" (JND)?
- When studying immediate conscious experiences, what is the particular error that Wundt identified as being necessary to avoid?
- How did Wundt's predecessors envision a different subject matter and method of study to understand psychophysics and consciousness?
- Who introduced structuralism to the United States and how did it draw upon Wundt's voluntarism?
- What were the three key steps in developing the modern-day psychological experiment?
- According to the triangular theory of love, how do the three elements of love interact to produce the feeling of love?

Functionalism

CHAPTER OVERVIEW

The functional school of psychology or functionalism demonstrated that psychology could and should study all humans in an attempt to understand the adaptive value of human affects, behaviors, and cognitions. Functionalism demonstrated the importance of adaptability for the organism, and the psychologists of the functional school generalized this theme of adaptability to the discipline as a whole by founding several subdisciplines of psychology, including clinical and industrial psychology.

The **Theory of Evolution** demonstrated to the world that species evolve in response to environmental stimuli and that to survive, evolution must prove adaptive and functional to members of a species. Without adaptive evolution an individual or an entire species would not survive in an ever-changing environment. Each organism is not simply reacting to its environment, but also attempting to change the environment in a dynamic fashion, thus incorporating the adaptive functions of the individual organism into the evolutionary equation. Evolutionary theory gave rise to an interest in individual differences and provided a basis to argue that psychology must be a discipline for all people as all individuals strive to adapt to their environment. In addition, by clearly indicating that species evolve, psychologists further argued that other species could be studied and the findings generalized to humans, as animals represented a different stage of development in the evolutionary process.

Near the end of the 19th century and the beginning of the 20th century the United States was a frontier country devoted to democracy and the belief that through hard work the strong survive. Accordingly, a growing number of psychologists at this time believed that psychology should study only human adaptive processes including motivation, consciousness, and interactions with the environment. The insistence of the early functionalists that psychology study the functional and adaptive capacities of the individual resulted in the school of psychology known as functionalism, which has inspired legions of psychologists right up to the present.

We first examine the foundational ideas of the "forerunners of functionalism," namely, Charles Darwin (1809–1882), Sir Francis Galton (1822–1911), and Herbert Spencer (1820–1903). We then study two famous and influential American psychologists, William James (1842–1910) and Granville Stanley Hall (1844–1924). Next we examine the "founders" of functionalism, John Dewey (1859–1952) and James Rowland Angell (1869–1949), followed by several psychologists who promoted a more polished version of functionalism, namely, Harvey Carr (1873–1954), James McKeen Cattell (1860–1944), Edward Lee Thorndike (1874–1949), and Robert Sessions Woodworth (1869–1962). Lastly, we look at Hugo Münsterberg (1863–1916) and Lightner Witmer (1876–1956), both of whom promoted the continuation of functionalism in psychology. Each individual discussed in this chapter focused upon the foundational theme that organisms evolve, work, think, and pursue goals in the relentless pursuit of adapting to changing environments.

LEARNING OBJECTIVES

When you finish studying this chapter, you will be prepared to:

- Describe the role of evolutionary theory in the development of psychology as a scientific discipline

- Describe the development of comparative or infrahuman psychology

- Discuss the importance of individual differences within psychology and describe how examining individual differences gained popularity at the beginning of the 20th century

- Explain the social and economic forces in the United States around the beginning of the 20th century which promoted a functional psychology

- Discuss why subdisciplines such as clinical, industrial/organizational, forensic, and comparative psychology developed and prospered in the United States

- Explain the adaptive role of consciousness for the individual and understand the importance of studying the adaptive psychological functions of adults, children, and infrahumans

- Elaborate on some contemporary functional issues in psychology and provide examples of how the functional approach remains central today in psychology and related disciplines of inquiry

INTRODUCTION

The future of psychology as a science and a profession requires the applications of scientifically harvested findings to a wide variety of practical problems at the local and the global levels. At the beginning of the 20th century, there were three systematic schools of thought namely, structuralism, functionalism, and behaviorism. As schools of psychology and individual research and applied interests of psychologists developed, a narrowing of the focus of the subject matter and acceptable methods of study for psychology began to evolve. This maturation arose in part as a consequence of the need to develop expert knowledge of specific and easily recognized psychological phenomena of interest and value to the public, such as the causes and treatment of dysfunctional or abnormal behaviors, thoughts, and emotions. Accordingly, psychology, especially during the middle and latter part of the 20th century, became somewhat of a dichotomous discipline consisting of either clinicians or academic psychologists who were loyal to their modes of training. Psychologists were not often afforded opportunities to branch out until much later in their careers, perhaps after earning tenure in an academic setting or establishing a secure clinical practice.

Today, however, psychology is broadening as both clinicians and academicians address a wide range of applied problems and opportunities such as, for example, productive employment, health care, environmental issues, and ethnic conflict resolution. This expansion is due to the fact that many of the problems facing global and local communities are moderated significantly by a systematic application of psychological interventions grounded in a sound understanding of human and infrahuman affective, behavioral, and cognitive systems. For example, near the end of the 19th century and the beginning of the 20th century many health problems were the direct result of poor sanitation, poor nutrition, and the lack of appropriate medication for infectious diseases. As we enter the 21st century, many health concerns and challenges are now due primarily to affective states (rage, depression), behaviors (substance abuse, personal health care), and cognitions (stereotypes, racism, and ethnic conflict), although many people around the world still suffer from poor sanitation, nutrition, and lack of basic medical care. The current barriers to health and psychological well-being now result more from unequal distributions of resources stemming from growing economic and income disparities, asymmetrical or uneven balancing of basic human rights, and the failure of some to appreciate fully the assets and liabilities of differing cultures and societies. Accordingly, psychology can play an increasingly central role in addressing the challenges facing us today because psychologists are educated to not only address, in general, the specific issues identified above, but also almost all issues concerning the functions and consequences of affects, behaviors, and cognitions.

SETTING THE STAGE FOR FUNCTIONALISM

The turn toward studying the various functional capacities of all humans and infrahumans (or other species) in psychology began in earnest near the beginning of the 20th century. This emerging focus on a more broad and applied discipline of psychology was an abrupt challenge to the 19th-century, primarily laboratory-based psychologists like Wilhelm Wundt (1832–1920) and Edward B. Titchener (1867–1927), who began what they hoped would be a tradition of psychological science by focusing almost exclusively upon studying white adult males while ignoring persons of color (the global majority), women, children, persons with psychological disorders, and other species (i.e., comparative psychology). It is hard to imagine this early phase of psychology as it is so alien in terms of guiding principles, methodologies, and aspirations of the current state of psychology. A psychology, such as structuralism, that ignored the above subjects was not adaptive or functional in America in the late 1800s or early 1900s, and accordingly, did not survive in the United States. While scientific psychology was born in Europe, a group of primarily American psychologists developed a school of psychology, functionalism, to make psychology an applied and pragmatic discipline to serve the practical needs of the greatest number of people.

Functionalism was the first truly American school of psychology because many of the foundational ideas and applications of functional psychology were crafted first in America and then elaborated upon by American psychologists. Interestingly, much of what functionalism has to offer can be applied to the world as a whole because it promotes pragmatism and embraces a problem-solving orientation. In fact, it may be said that as Charles Darwin was out discovering the world he also discovered the true basis behind functionalism, which is the idea that psychological, physical, and physiological manifestations of an organism are purposeful in that they promote the adaptive capacities of the organism as well as the species of which the organism is a member. For the functional psychologist, psychological processes were studied primarily to promote the adaptive functioning of an organism to the environment.

We begin our examination of functionalism with a brief synopsis of the life of Charles Darwin (1809–1882). Although not necessarily the first to suggest the concept of the evolution of species in response to environmental imperatives, at the time Darwin conducted the most systematic and comprehensive research program in support of the idea that a species evolves and in so doing develops the ability to adapt to its environment.

Charles Darwin: Evolution Is Adaptive and Functional

On the Origin of Species by Means of Natural Selection (1962/1859) is one of the most important books ever written because it causes us to think of the creation and development of humanity and other species in ways that are primarily naturalistic rather than divine and theological. In short, Charles Darwin's work makes plain that humans are not the product of divine design nor do we necessarily have some ultimate purpose or goal, but rather, like all other creatures, we try constantly to manipulate, react to, and adapt to our diversified environments. Darwin's work suggests clearly that life is shaped more by fortuitous forces than divine intervention, thus calling for the systematic observation of adaptive processes rather than reliance on theological principles to explain the development of an individual as well as the species of which the individual is a member.

Prior to his voyage around the world on the **HMS** *Beagle* (1831–1836), Darwin showed very little promise in life, which caused his father to worry that Charles would end up being of little consequence to family and colleagues (DeBeer, 1971). Accordingly, Darwin was sent by his father to the University of Edinburgh to study medicine, but soon decided that life spent in the practice of medicine would be dull. His father then directed that Charles should study for the clergy, a respectable profession, and he thus stayed three years at Cambridge University where he passed much of his time socializing, hunting, drinking, and playing cards rather than studying theology. Interestingly, however, Darwin spent a good deal of his time collecting and categorizing beetles, which coincided with an earlier interest in collecting shells and minerals.

John Stevens Henslow (1797–1861), a noted botanist and one of the only instructors at Cambridge that Darwin admired, was first offered the position of naturalist aboard the HMS *Beagle* but had to decline because of family commitments. Henslow suggested Darwin be appointed naturalist on the *Beagle,* and after debating the issue with his family and arranging for his uncle to meet his expenses Charles Darwin set out on what many consider to be one of the most important voyages ever. An interesting point to note is that the captain of the *Beagle,* Robert Fitzroy (1805–1865), was a staunchly religious man. In fact, Fitzroy hoped that a trained naturalist would be able to find scientific evidence for the biblical account of creation that God created Earth and all the creatures on Earth with a specific purpose. In addition, Darwin himself believed in the biblical account and as a result faced a lot of personal as well as societal turmoil when he later made claims for evolution over creation.

The *Beagle* left England on December 27, 1831, when Darwin was 23 years old. The expedition sailed first to South America, then Tahiti, New Zealand, the Azores, and back to England for a journey time of five years during which the formative steps of an intellectual project grew into a valuable understanding of the nature of all living organisms. As Fitzroy had planned, Darwin often left the ship to travel inland and explore in hopes of defending the biblical account of creation. During his on-shore excursions Darwin often wondered why God had created so many species and why some survived and some did not. In addition, Darwin made the astute yet obvious observation that it would be nearly impossible to fit all of these different species on Noah's Ark as presented in the Bible. Finally, he observed that the fossil and rock formations he found along his journey were much older than the approximately 6,000 years that had been established as the age of the earth according to biblical accounts.

It was in 1835, while in the now famous Galapagos Islands, that Darwin was able to study lizards, sea lions, several species of finch, and the famous huge tortoises which inhabit the islands. At this time, the *Beagle* had been gone from England for nearly three and a half years, and Darwin was perhaps starting to become tired such that while on the Galapagos Islands he did not observe and categorize as diligently as earlier in the journey. However, he did notice subtle differences in species, birds in particular, from island to island within the Galapagos chain. Most importantly, he noticed differences in the shapes of the beaks of **Darwin's finches** and although he did not think much of it at the time, he later believed that the different environments of the islands caused the changes he saw in the birds.

In 1836, Darwin arrived back in England with an enormous collection of specimens and observational data, which he immediately set out to catalogue. He also returned a changed man, as he was no longer the fun-loving chap he was when he left, but was now a dedicated scientist anxious to develop his idea of evolution. Furthermore, he arrived a celebrity among zoologists and geologists, as he had been sending specimens home to Henslow and many were well aware of his careful and comprehensive work. Darwin's reputation impressed even his father, who provided him with a healthy living allowance so he could continue his work without the worries of earning a steady income (Desmond & Moore, 1991). Despite the focus on the evolution of many different species, perhaps the most important and dramatic example of evolution in his father's eyes was Darwin's development into an important man of science.

Darwin and Psychology

Darwin's impact upon the development of science, especially biology, zoology, and geology, is well known while his impact upon psychology is less well known. Darwin clearly was not a psychologist and much of his work and life occurred before the establishment of any formal psychological laboratories. Darwin paved the way for functional psychology as well as comparative and evolutionary psychology as a consequence of demonstrating that all species evolve by adapting to ever-changing environments, and reasoning that there is a structural and functional continuity between humans and infrahumans.

After returning to England he married his cousin Emma Wedgwood and moved to London. In the next section we shall see how another cousin, Sir Franics Galton (1822–1911), was a firm believer in eugenics and the thought of marrying one's cousin may have been considered by Darwin and others as a way to enhance and keep good genes in the family. Charles and Emma had ten children and Emma often had to care not only for the children but also for Charles, as he was chronically ill for the balance of his life after returning from his travels.

Darwin's *Theory of Evolution* began as reflections he had while on the *Beagle* as he began to reject the biblical account of creation while still maintaining some of his religious beliefs by allowing that God created a set of principles that guide evolution, although he was still stuck with the question as to why species evolve. He began to answer this question for himself after reading some works of Thomas Malthus (1766–1834), who argued that welfare for the poor in Britain would only increase the number of poor people thereby reducing the overall quality of life for the more fortunate members of British society. Malthus further argued that only those best suited for survival would survive, leading Darwin to postulate that the adaptive functions of an organism would survive while nonadaptive functions would perish and most likely the organism as well. Accordingly, Darwin concluded that species evolve over several generations by adapting to changing environments similar to the process of selective breeding. In fact, Darwin considered evolution a natural example of adaptive selection. By the late 1830s, Darwin had an outline of the essential features of his theory, yet it wasn't until 1859 that *On the Origin of Species* was published.

There are a number of reasons why Darwin delayed the publication of his ideas besides being quite ill upon his return from the voyage on the *Beagle* (Richards, 1983). First, Darwin devoted this time to publish in 1839, shortly after his return, his journal titled "The Voyage of the Beagle," which went through two printings and a second edition in 1845. Second, Darwin was busy organizing his collection of specimens as well as conducting other studies to further develop his ideas on evolution. Lastly, and perhaps most importantly, Darwin was well aware of the intense public reaction that might ensue after he published his ideas stressing evolution while questioning seriously the biblical account of creation and the uniqueness of human beings compared to other animals. Darwin had seen how the scientific community had attacked other controversial ideas and he wanted to be certain of his argument before opening himself up to such intense scrutiny.

It was not until he received a letter on June 18, 1858, from the naturalist Alfred Russel Wallace (1823–1913) that Darwin decided it was time to publish his theory of evolution. Wallace had asked Darwin to review his paper titled "On the Tendency of Varieties to Depart Indefinitely from the Original Type." Darwin read the paper and noticed quickly the similarities to his own theory including the credit Wallace gave to Malthus for inspiring his beliefs about evolution. At first Darwin wanted to let Wallace publish his account, but after further reflection and after receiving advice from several close friends he decided to submit his paper along with Wallace's to the July 1, 1858, meeting of the Linnean Society. Neither paper received much attention and evolution was essentially passed over until November 1859, when Darwin's *On the Origin of Species by Means of Natural Selection or the Preservation of Favoured Races in the Struggle for Life* was published. All 1,250 copies of the first printing sold out on the first day of publication! Darwin was correct; the public reaction, both favorable and unfavorable, was going to be intense.

Members of the clergy as well as some fellow scientists were quick to criticize Darwin for arguing that humans descended from apes and accused him of basing his entire theory on shoddy scientific work. Other scientists and members of the public embraced his ideas and were awed by the genius of this seemingly simple theory. Darwin removed himself from many of the ensuing debates and allowed others to defend his work. To this day many believe that Darwin's ideas present an attempt to destroy many religious beliefs while others believe it accurately represents the natural order of the world. Whatever your personal beliefs it is difficult to debate the enormous impact that Charles Darwin has had on science, religion, and the law. Darwin died at his home (Down House) on April 19, 1882, and although he would have preferred a quiet burial at his home, he lies buried along with other British notables at Westminster Abbey in London, England.

The Legacy of Charles Darwin

Darwin's work provided a refreshing framework for addressing the persistent and nettlesome questions about the utility, purpose, and function of human consciousness. Accordingly, consciousness and other psychological functions such as thinking and behaving could now be reasonably and scientifically studied for their adaptive and functional utility as they promote survival in ever-changing situations. Darwin's work further provided the rationale for studying animal behavior to gain a better understanding of human behavior. His findings seriously questioned the gap or discontinuity that was believed to exist between humans and infrahumans (all other animals), and helped develop the idea that if a continuity of species does exist then perhaps we may be able to identify some functions of animals similar to some psychological functions of humans.

Most importantly for psychology, Darwin paved the way for American functional psychology that stressed the **utilities of consciousness**, which promotes adaptation as a consequence of awareness of internal needs and the demands of the external environment. Darwin further impacted psychological inquiry by making plain that infrahumans, nonadaptive or dysfunctional adults, and children could be studied systematically and that such studies can inform us about normally adaptive organisms as well as organisms with problems of adaptation. Darwin also set the stage for the study of individual differences within and across cohorts or groups as well as the study of individuals or groups across time or longitudinally. As a result, American psychologists became interested in a broad range of topics, as they were no longer forced to look at psychological phenomena through either a physiological lens or the restrictive and controlled, laboratory-based method of introspection that focused upon the contents rather than the functional utilities of consciousness.

Sir Francis Galton: To Quantify Is to Know

There were a number of similarities between many of the founders of functionalism in terms of background, family history, and professional life. Two of the most important figures from which the functionalists gained insights had similar backgrounds, namely, a similar gene pool. Francis Galton (1822–1911) and Charles Darwin were half cousins and Galton, like Darwin, did much to influence future functional psychologists.

Francis Galton was born just outside of Birmingham, England, to a wealthy family that made a fortune during England's Industrial Revolution. Galton was a precocious child who could apparently read some French and tell time by the age of 4 and by the age of 5 could read any book in English put before him. He was also very well versed in mathematics although he had difficulty during his mathematics examinations at Cambridge. While at Cambridge he also studied medicine, but quit his studies before graduating. Despite a nervous breakdown, Galton earned a degree in mathematics and returned, at his father's insistence, to the study of medicine. After his father's death, however, Galton again quit studying medicine, as he disliked it immensely, and began to forge his own path in life.

As a consequence of his wealthy family background, Galton had the luxury to delve into various personal interests regardless of potential financial or career ramifications. His first professional interest was that of explorer and traveler. In the mid-1840s and early 1850s, Galton traveled to several regions of Africa and published the accounts of his journeys, for which he won a gold medal from the Royal Geographical Society. As he had been intrigued throughout his travels with how humans adapted to their environments, *On the Origin of Species* was especially interesting to him because it demonstrated how one's environment can alter both physical and mental functions (Pearson, 1924).

Although some of the subject matter of Galton's work appears to have no apparent functionality or utility, it does serve to illustrate how he thought about various subjects and it reflects his incisive ability to examine and quantify almost anything. For example, shortly after his return to England he made a "beauty map" of Britain and found that women in

London ranked highest in beauty while the women of Aberdeen, Scotland, ranked last in beauty. These findings could be related to class issues, which Galton often overlooked, or such findings could be based on actual objective criteria. While Galton's research on presumed beauty does seem a bit frivolous, it demonstrates clearly Galton's belief that almost any phenomenon, no matter how uniquely individual, can be quantified, counted, or "operationally defined" (Diamond, 1977).

Galton and Psychology: Individual Differences

In 1869, Galton published *Hereditary Genius,* in which he sought to demonstrate that greatness was inherited because it appeared to him that great or eminent men had great sons. Daughters were excluded from Galton's study as they had little means for eminence at this time as indexed by education and business ownership both of which were culturally and legally limited to men. He believed that humans are inherently different from each other and that each infant is born with a set of hereditary traits that account for more than can be explained through environmental influences upon the developing child and mature adult. Galton proposed that mental characteristics fall along a continuum comparable to what we now term the **bell curve** or **normal distribution**. In other words, approximately 67% of a population or sample (segment of the population) fall within plus or minus one standard deviation of the mean (i.e., the average). Additionally, 95% of a population or sample fall within plus or minus two standard deviations of the mean and 99% of the population or sample fall within plus or minus three standard deviations of the mean. For example, if an IQ (Intelligence Quotient) test has a mean of 100 and a standard deviation of 15, most people (67%) would fall within the range of scores between 85 and 115. The range 70–130 would encompass 95% of the population or sample and the range 55–145 would encompass 99% of the population. These statistical criteria help scientists determine the "normal" and "abnormal" ranges of various physical and cognitive abilities. As a result of these ideas, Galton developed the statistical concept of the "average man" which can be used to determine the characteristics of a population. This appears to be the beginning of Galton's study of eugenics as he could now determine which segments of a population were seemingly superior and those seemingly inferior. Unfortunately, many cognitive or intelligence tests are biased for or against certain groups, and examining only results or numbers without considering the context or background of the tested person promotes biased reporting and decisions.

In 1884, Galton established an anthropometric laboratory at the International Health Exhibition in London. In 1884, nearly 10,000 people were tested and measured with an additional 7,000 individuals tested over the next several years (Johnson et al., 1985). The measurements included height, weight, strength, visual acuity, and lung capacity. Galton assessed mental ability using physical measures such as visual reaction times, as he believed there was a substantial relationship between sensory and mental acuities. This type of relationship was formally derived mathematically in 1896 by Karl Pearson (1857–1936), a student of Galton's, who developed the product moment correlation coefficient or **correlation** (Pearson, 1896). This test allows researchers to demonstrate a linkage or relationship between two variables, although it does not indicate causality or a cause-and-effect relationship between the measured variables. For example, let us say that we found that violence and ice cream consumption are positively related, as they both increase during a hot summer. However, ice cream consumption most likely does not cause violence and violence most likely does not cause ice cream consumption. There are other factors that impact each dependent or measured variable, such as an increase in temperature, yet the two are related as they both increase during the hot summer months.

Many of Galton's sexist and elitist views are seen clearly in the selective reporting and interpretations of his quantified findings. For example, he argued that women were intellectually inferior to men and believed their inadequacies may be traced to deficient sensory capacities as, for example, longer reaction times than males. He further cited as evidence the fact that men were employed in the jobs that required sharp sensory capacities, such as piano tuners and wine tasters. Of course, we see today that women would not then have had the opportunity to be employed in these positions due to prevailing stereotypes and prejudices, which Galton and many others of his time chose to overlook.

Galton advocated the birth of fit individuals while discouraging the birth of what he considered as unfit individuals based on his ideas of the distribution of mental abilities. He argued that if great people (those at the high end of the bell curve) mated generation after generation there would result a race of great people. In *Hereditary Genius*, Galton presented data that he had collected from what he considered to be 977 eminent individuals drawn from 300 families also deemed eminent by Galton. He had established statistically that in the normal population eminence was achieved in one out of 4,000 people, while in his sample he found that 31% of fathers and an amazing 48% of sons were eminent. This finding, he argued, was due solely to genetic transmission and was not influenced by the environment or opportunities available to such privileged persons. Clearly, his sample was gifted primarily because they were privileged and thus afforded many more opportunities for advancement than those in lower socioeconomic classes. It is important to note that Galton's work makes plain that science can be used to address social issues and that statistics can be manipulated or presented in ways to support several different ideas or theories about a given phenomenon. The foundational idea here is that the methods of science are neither intrinsically right nor wrong; however, the purposes and the potentially biased interpretation of such findings may very well be wrong and unethical.

In addition to his physical and sensory testing of individuals, Galton also pioneered the use of surveys to collect data as well as the methodological breakthrough known as **twin studies**. To further examine his ideas about hereditary traits he sent surveys to ninety-four pairs of identical or monozygotic twins and found that even after long separations the twins had many physical and mental similarities. Galton interpreted these findings as clear support for his ideas about the robust influence of heredity upon individual capacities and accomplishments. These findings led Galton to coin the term *eugenics*, which is the movement toward improving the human species by controlling heredity through selective human reproductive practices (i.e., selective breeding). He further believed that encouraging certain exceptional individuals to reproduce would result in "positive" eugenics while also noting that "negative" eugenics mandates that the intellectually inferior and poor must be discouraged from reproducing. Lastly, in 1908, Galton founded a Eugenics Society and spent many of his remaining years advocating for a eugenics-based society. Although Galton is perhaps most remembered for his elitist and controversial ideas about eugenics, he did provide psychology with statistical analyses, new methodologies still used today, and the belief that almost anything can be quantified.

Herbert Spencer: Social Darwinism

Herbert Spencer (1820–1903) is the man responsible for popularizing Darwin's theory of evolution in America. He coined the phrase "survival of the fittest" at a time when some Americans, such as Andrew Carnegie (1835–1919), the wealthy oil entrepreneur who came to the United States in 1848, were becoming accustomed to winning and surviving economically while others faltered. While Darwin was most interested in biological evolution and the idea that fitness was the result of selective adaptation to the environment, Spencer advocated **Social Darwinism**, which focused upon social evolution and the idea that fitness was the result of winners beating out others for limited resources. Social Darwinism can be seen, for example, in an open-market economy where in general the most adaptive person or business survives as the result of beating others for limited resources and the losers are eliminated because they are not fit enough to survive.

Social Darwinists impacted the political and social beliefs of their times in the late 19th and early 20th centuries. They believed that evolution represented natural and robust forces shaping adaptation, and thus any attempt by humans or social programs to alter these forces were considered misguided. Hence, successful business enterprises should not be "punished" with taxes as their success was simply an indication of their fitness. This rationalization made it easier for many to explain the widening gaps in wealth, power, and opportunities in America between themselves and others not of European descent. The argument of the Social Darwinists was circular in that, although not empirically validated, the belief persisted that being fit meant being successful while being successful meant being fit. Those who held to this circular and closed-minded belief system obviously did not want to consider the idea that being successful meant having greater opportunities rather than solely some biologically endowed advantage of one group compared to other groups.

In some respects, eugenics and Social Darwinism are still with us as reflected in the practices of some humans who can reproduce sexually but who can afford, and opt for, in-vitro fertilization "to get the right offspring" (Ridley, 1999). For example, since 1978 approximately 100,000 test tube babies have been born in the United States. Technological advances make it possible to select and eliminate certain genetic characteristics in an attempt to produce genetically superior offspring. Additionally, it is predicted that by the year 2025 human cloning may well be feasible, thus allowing individuals to clone themselves and to literally build children in the parents' predetermined image.

FORERUNNERS OF FUNCTIONALISM

William James (1842–1910) is considered America's first psychologist, although he preferred to be called a philosopher, especially near the end of his career. William James was one of the most distinguished contemporary psychologists of his time, and even now, more than ninety-five years after his death, he is still considered a distinguished psychologist and philosopher. His widespread popularity then and now is attributable, in part, to his wonderful abilities to communicate clearly, mostly through his writings, and his extensive practical knowledge of human behavior and experience as well as his willingness to study phenomena that many outside of psychology find interesting and important.

William James: Psychologist, Philosopher, and Pragmatist

William James was raised in a wealthy Irish-American family and spent much of his youth traveling, studying, and being indulged by his parents. Barbara Ross (1991) and Lightner Witmer (1909) both referred to James as "the spoiled child of psychology." However, the fact remains that contemporary psychology and philosophy are still influenced by the fertile and insightful ideas of William James.

William James' father, Henry James Sr. (1811–1882), was raised in a very strict environment and when it came to raising his own family he decided to do so in a manner opposite his own upbringing. Accordingly, Henry James Sr., placed few boundaries on his children thus allowing them to study what they pleased when they pleased. The James family traveled extensively throughout Europe and the children met many of the great thinkers of their time including Henry David Thoreau (1817–1862), Ralph Waldo Emerson (1803–1882), and John Stuart Mill (1806–1873).

Perhaps, in part, as a result of these varied travels, meeting different people, and being allowed to engage in several different pursuits, William James had difficulty determining his path in life. In 1861, James entered Harvard to become a scientist but soon found that the life of science was not for him after first studying chemistry, which required tedious and obsessive laboratory work. Still attempting to discover his place in the world, William James next tried comparative anatomy, although his interest in studying comparative anatomy did not last long and his ruminations about his place in the world persisted. In 1864 he enrolled in Harvard Medical School but his interest soon shifted to an Amazon expedition that was headed by the biologist and geologist Louis Agassiz (1807–1873). Again he hoped the trip would provide him with a place in the world, but he soon became disillusioned with Agassiz and the trip because although the sights along the Amazon river were fascinating, the physical labor and tedium of the work proved overbearing. James found Agassiz a dedicated and experienced researcher; he also found him rigid in his beliefs, especially Agassiz's view that Darwin's theory of evolution was wrong because Agassiz firmly believed that all species were created by God rather than evolutionary processes. Furthermore, James became ill during the Amazon river journey and decided to return home, with the firm belief that the life of a collector was not for him as his interests were more speculative than afforded by collecting and classifying things. Although he was able to get over his Amazon illness, he was plagued by all sorts of real and imagined health problems for the remainder of his life.

While travelling in Europe, William James spent much of 1867 and 1868 at health spas as well as the laboratories of such 19th-century notables as Gustav Fechner, Emil du Bois-Reymond, and Hermann L. F. von Helmholtz. James was still trying to reconcile his scientific education with his more reflective and philosophical personality. Likewise, psychology was attempting to define itself as a science although much of the discipline had grown out of philosophy and much of the focus of the emerging discipline of psychology was still philosophical. What was needed was someone who could sort out and make plain the connection between science and philosophy in psychology.

James returned to the United States in 1868, and soon thereafter discovered an essay by the French evolutionary philosopher Charles Renouvier (1815–1903). William James decided to accept Renouvier's view that humans have free will, since we can sustain a thought when we choose to or even when other spurious thoughts involuntarily invade our minds (Myers, 1986). This was a very pragmatic way of thinking about free will, and he decided, as his first act of free will, to believe truly in free will. From this point on he believed in the pragmatic nature of ideas and further believed that he must take philosophy seriously for the remainder of his life.

Although James earned his medical degree (M.D.) in 1869, he vowed to never practice medicine because he hated the details and was disturbed by the materialistic orientation of the profession. In 1872, James was offered a position by his former chemistry professor and then president of Harvard University, Charles William Eliot (1834–1926), to teach physiology and anatomy at Harvard. In 1874, he offered his first course on the relationship between physiology and psychology. As there were no courses offered in psychology when James attended Harvard as a student, it was likely that the first psychology course William James ever attended was his own. Much of what James knew about psychology at that time was self-taught and to assist his students' understanding of the material he set up a small demonstration laboratory in 1875. Some have argued that this was the first psychological laboratory in the world. Although James' laboratory was used primarily for lecture demonstrations, it produced no original research, unlike Wundt's laboratory, which generated original psychological data. Although Wundt's laboratory was established four years later in 1879, it is considered the first psychological laboratory in the world.

James as a Psychologist

In 1878, at the age of 36, William James married Alice Howe Gibbons, a Boston schoolteacher whom his father had decided two years earlier that he should marry. Shortly before their wedding, William James had signed a contract with the publisher Henry Holt (1840–1926) to write a manual of psychology. The correspondence between the two men must have been fanciful as it took James twelve years to complete the book. Luckily, William and Alice shared many of the same interests and were very devoted to each other. In fact, it was on their honeymoon in the Adirondack Mountains that she helped him begin writing his classic text, *The Principles of Psychology*, which would become one of the greatest psychological texts ever written in terms of both scope and content. Finally, in 1890, the 1,393-page *The Principles of Psychology* was completed and became an instant success. The book was immediately a best seller and in 1892, Henry Holt published a shorter, 478-page version titled *Psychology: The Briefer Course*.

In *Principles* and in the varied and lively lectures given by James, it is clear that he was as ill-suited for the psychological laboratory as he was for the chemistry or anatomy laboratory. However, William James was a brilliant psychologist and had the uncanny ability to express his ideas in ways that most people could readily understand and use in their everyday experiences. While the general public may have appreciated James' clear and direct writing style, several of his contemporaries, including Wilhelm Wundt and G. Stanley Hall, believed that James was more a literary figure than a psychologist. James probably considered these criticisms as compliments rather than intended pejorative statements.

James' disdain for laboratory work is made clear in his *Principles* by his reference to such work as **brass instrument psychology** (James, 1961/1892). Although James gave a thorough explanation of research methods such as psychophysical and reaction time methodologies, he could not help but express his personal views that these laboratory-based methodologies were boring. James was clearly an eclectic, and, accordingly, as a result welcomed initially psychological findings derived from any methodological approach that appeared valid and yielded practical and useful results. This attitude of openness to methodology and psychological content as well as a growing appreciation for applied psychological findings signaled clearly James' break with structuralism. The structuralists believed there was only one method of psychological experimentation, namely, highly controlled laboratory studies grounded in systematic and rule-bound interpretations of the contents or structures of consciousness. James, on the other hand, believed firmly that the best approach for studying psychological phenomena often depended on the needs of the situation. Although he supported the use of a variety of methods for collecting psychological data, James rarely used any systematic techniques, preferring instead to write about psychological phenomena rather than collect psychological data. James, however, was very clear that **introspection** or rich and fluid reports of consciousness was the best overall methodology to study psychological experiences and mental life. His brand of introspection involved careful self-examination and reflection on the states and transitions among states of consciousness requiring mental activities such as thinking and remembering.

James believed that consciousness must have biological utility because it had survived generations of evolution. In fact, he spoke of the **stream of consciousness**, which he considered personal and ever-changing with respect to discrete situations while simultaneously and paradoxically remaining continuous so as to yield stability of personality. Consciousness, according to James, was composed of four separate yet related characteristics in that (1) it is personal, (2) it is constantly changing, (3) it remains continuous, and (4) it is selective (James, 1961/1892).

William James was opposed to the belief held by structural psychologists that consciousness could be understood by breaking it down into its individual structures or elements (sensations, feelings, and images). The structuralists' attempt to piece together the individual elements into a meaningful state of consciousness was meaningless as they represented distinct points in time without considering the contextual events that led up to each individual element over time. In fact, James reasoned that piecing these elements together would be like piecing together puzzle pieces without a sense of awareness of the overall picture of the puzzle. Pieces may be put together but afterwards does the overall picture make sense? James argued that consciousness could not be studied one piece at a time because it is continuous (the stream of consciousness) and all the prior events leading to any single event must be considered relative to the individual. For James, consciousness is a cascading awareness rather than a rigidly constructed phenomenon. Accordingly, consciousness serves an adaptive function by allowing the individual to adapt quickly to new situations through rapid cascades of awareness while maintaining a continuous sense of self and purpose.

Much of James' work in psychology was laced with paradox with a focus primarily upon empowering the individual, rather than a search for normative laws. For example, he reasoned that whenever an individual is thinking he or she must at the same time be aware of **the self** or of one's personal existence. James defined the self as partly known and partly knower, and partly object and partly subject (James, 1961/1892). James further separated the self into the material self, the social self, and the spiritual self. The material self has at its center the body of the individual and certain parts of the body seem to belong more to the individual than others (i.e., those parts of the body that each individual truly understands on a more intimate level). The material self is further composed of the clothes we wear, our immediate family, our possessions, and our home. All these aspects of the material self represent the instinctive preferences of the individual and when coupled with the practical interests of our lives illustrate the goods, goals, and possessions which define the self. "We all have a blind impulse to watch over our body, to deck it out with clothing of an ornamental sort, to cherish parents, wife, and babes, and to find for ourselves a house of our own which we may live in and 'improve'" (James, 1961/1892, p. 45).

The social self rests on the recognition or opinions one receives from others. We are social beings and have an innate drive to be with others, to be recognized by others, and to be recognized favorably by others. With each person we meet we give off an image of ourselves. Accordingly, James stated that a person has as many social selves as there are individuals who recognize and have an opinion about the person or about the group of which the person is a member. The social self is functional as it allows the individual to adapt to any given situation so that an individual may fit the role of a loving mother at home while also fitting the role of a demanding CEO at work.

The spiritual self represents the entire collection of an individual's states of consciousness. At any moment we have the ability to make concrete in our minds any thought we desire and in so doing can bring about emotions related to the other aspects of the self. At the very core of the spiritual self lies the states of consciousness which involve activity. Thus, we actively seek to collect goods and associate with others. This sense or need for activity is at the root of our soul and the self is defined not simply by one or another of these selves but by all of them working and actively seeking together.

William James was responsible for elaborating the **James-Lange theory of emotion**. Although many of the ideas behind this theory were originally proposed by Carl Lange (1834–1900), a Dutch physiologist, William James is best remembered for the theory which is often illustrated using a hypothetical encounter with a huge bear in the wilderness. According to James-Lange theory, if you were to stumble upon such a bear you would first run to escape the bear and second, you would feel fear. The theory postulates that we feel different emotions because the body has specific physiological arousal states that precede or come before each emotion. Thus, in this context we run and become afraid while in a different context we may cry and then feel sad. Although similar, fear and anger are not the same emotion because the body produces a distinct arousal set for each emotion. Accordingly, we run to escape, physiological changes occur, and we interpret or process those bodily changes as representing fear. Emotion is the result of feeling distinct physiological changes within the body (Reisenzein, Meyer, & Schützwohl, 1995). Emotions are biologically based and amendable to scientific study like other bodily and psychological functions. James succeeded in centering the scientific study of emotions in psychology by means of the James-Lange theory.

James as a Philosopher

Toward the end of his life James concentrated on philosophy and turned away from psychology. As a true sign of his times, his philosophy was pragmatic, down-to-earth, and lacked many of the esoteric frills of other philosophies. In two books, *Pragmatism* (1907) and *The Meaning of Truth: A Sequel to "Pragmatism"* (1909), he presented his pragmatic philosophy (James, 1975a, 1975b). His central theme was that pragmatism could be used to establish truth. In essence, ideas and beliefs are true because they work as they promote adaptability of the individual or group. Accordingly, if a belief helps an organism to adapt to environmental demands then that idea works for that individual. If the belief works then it is true and the organism should continue with the belief as long as it fosters adaptability. If an individual believes something will work to relieve stress or pain in a given situation then it is valid for that individual but perhaps may not be adaptive (i.e., valid) for another individual in the same situation. In short, truth is personal and facile depending upon the particular individual and environment. James intended his philosophy, as well as his psychology, to be both individualistic and relative. A belief that works for one person may not work for another and depending on how a belief is framed it can mean one thing for you yet something entirely different for me. Thus, a pragmatist judges all beliefs by their outcomes for the individual.

Granville Stanley Hall: Scientific and Professional Psychology

G. Stanley Hall (1844–1924) was not only an important forerunner to functionalism but also remains to this day one of the most influential American psychologists. Like many of his contemporaries, Hall had varied interests (which helped foster psychology in America) many of which were similar to the broad range of interests held by William James. Despite this similarity G. Stanley Hall and William James were different in many ways, as for example, Hall was raised in a strict parental environment while James had much less restrictive parents. Hall firmly believed in experimentation and the role of psychology as a science, admired hard work and discipline in education, and never had any doubts about the merits of a scientific experimental psychology, unlike those expressed periodically by William James.

While Hall was an important psychologist, his legacy may well rest upon his efforts and abilities to promote psychology as a profession rather than primarily as a science. Hall was the major architect of the establishment of the American Psychological Association in 1892, founded laboratories and journals, and either trained directly or oversaw indirectly the graduate studies of many well-known and influential psychologists of the early part of the 20th century. Hall was also instrumental in creating an outstanding psychology department at Clark University and bringing Sigmund Freud to the United States for the first time in 1909 to give a series of lectures at Clark University in celebration of the 20th anniversary of the university.

Granville Stanley Hall was born in a small western Massachusetts town. His mother was a teacher and his father was foremost a farmer, although he did teach some and was elected to the state legislature from 1855 to 1856. Hall gained an appreciation for hard work early in his life as well as the value of education for the improvement of self and society. In 1862, at the age of 18, Hall enrolled in Williston Seminary, remained there for a year, and then in 1863 enrolled in Williams College where he earned his bachelor's degree in 1867. While at Williams, Hall studied history and philosophy, and he had envisioned traveling to Europe upon graduation to seek a higher degree. Unfortunately for Hall, he could not afford to study in Europe and decided that given his interest in philosophy the only real option left would be to study for the clergy in the United States. Accordingly, he enrolled in Union Theological Seminary in New York City immediately following his graduation from Williams. Moving to the city was quite a change for this farm boy from western Massachusetts, yet he made the most of his time in New York by taking advantage of the social, cultural, and educational opportunities of the city. In 1869, he finally had enough money to travel to Europe and stayed there until 1871, when he returned to Union Theological Seminary.

While in Europe, Hall planned to study theology and philosophy but also discovered physiology while studying with Emil du Bois-Reymond (1818–1896) at the University of Berlin. Hall ran out of money and thus never earned a degree while in Europe. He returned to the United States and completed his theological studies at Union but was never ordained as a minister, in part because the president of Union thought less than highly of Hall's trial sermon (required of all senior theological students before graduation) (Ross, 1972). After graduation, Hall found a job at Antioch College in Ohio; he discovered and read Wilhelm Wundt's *Principles of Physiological Psychology* (1874/1904) and decided to head to Germany to study psychology.

Hall Entering Psychology

Prior to leaving for Europe, Hall attended Harvard University as a graduate student and earned a modest income by teaching English at the university. While at Harvard, he took some graduate courses with William James and conducted experimental research on perception with the physiologist Henry Pickering Bowditch (1840–1911). He also completed his doctoral dissertation on the muscular perception of space in 1878. His dissertation stood as the first PhD ever awarded by the psychology department at Harvard University and the first American doctoral degree focused solely upon a psychological topic (Benjamin, Durkin, Link, Vestal, & Accord, 1992; Bringmann, Bringmann, & Early, 1992). In 1879, Hall was back in Germany and ready to begin his studies with Wundt at Leipzig. Hall claimed at the time that he was the first American student to study with Wundt, although it appears that he had little contact with Wundt, did not think highly of Wundt, conducted no publishable research while there, and left one year after his arrival in Leipzig.

After leaving Leipzig he traveled to Berlin to study with Hermann L. F. von Helmholtz (1821–1894) and conducted some research with Helmholtz on the speed of neural responses but discovered that Helmoltz was at the time more interested in physics than physiology. Hall's second trip to Europe was seemingly a disappointment; however, while in Germany he encountered a woman he knew from Antioch, Cornelia Fisher, and before returning to the United States in 1880 they were married in Berlin in 1879 (Ross, 1972). Hall was 36 years old at this time, was poor and unemployed, was extremely well educated, valued hard work, and was now more confident in expressing his own views of the appropriate subject matter and practices of psychology.

After returning to Boston in 1880 with his new wife, Hall was invited by President Eliot of Harvard to give a series of twelve public lectures on education. His lectures were a success and caught the attention of several prominent individuals including President Daniel Coit Gilman of Johns Hopkins University. President Gilman asked Hall to give a similar series of lectures at Johns Hopkins in 1882, and he was so impressed that Gilman offered Hall a part-time lecturer position in philosophy. In 1884, Hall was offered a full-time professorship at Johns Hopkins for the amazingly generous sum of $4,000 per year. Hall accepted the position of Professor of Psychology and Pedagogy, and at the age of 40, G. Stanley Hall had his first real full-time job!

In 1887, while still a professor at Johns Hopkins, Hall received $500 from an anonymous donor interested in supporting a journal focused on psychological research conducted at Johns Hopkins University. The *American Journal of Psychology* was born, and in the first issue Hall criticized psychical research saying it was nothing more than illusion and deception. He learned later that the anonymous donor was keenly interested in psychic phenomena and demonstrated her or his dislike of the initial issue by providing no further funds to support the journal. Thus, Hall had to raise additional money to keep the journal alive and in so doing founded the first English-language journal devoted entirely to psychology. As the journal gained financial backing, Hall did include articles on spiritualism and psychical research but only to ridicule the lack of scientific basis of the research. Hall supported the journal until 1920 when he sold it to E. B. Titchener then of Cornell University in Ithaca, New York. The *American Journal of Psychology* is still published today.

Hall as an Established Psychologist

By 1888, Hall had distinguished himself as a psychologist and an industrious person who embraced rather than shied away from hard work. For these reasons, Professor Hall received an invitation that year to be the president of a new university in Worcester, Massachusetts. The university, Clark University, had been established by Jonas Gilman Clark (1815–1900), a man who had made a fortune selling mining supplies to prospectors during the California gold rush and now wanted some philanthropic recognition and respect as well as personal posterity by opening a university in his hometown of Worcester. In fact, Clark wanted to create a school for the youth of Worcester, but Hall convinced him that a graduate rather than solely an undergraduate institution similar to Johns Hopkins University was the path for them to pursue. Hall believed that the university should focus on science and that an undergraduate division could be added once the graduate division was established. Clark was ultimately convinced, and when the school opened in the fall of 1889 it offered only graduate programs in biology, chemistry, mathematics, physics, and psychology.

In the first three years of Clark University's existence, many of the faculty and students produced cutting-edge research, which led to an international reputation for Clark University and attracted students from all over the world. However, Jonas Clark had poorly gauged how much money was needed to support a university, and as a consequence Clark University was under constant economic stress. In addition, at the end of the first year of Hall's presidency, his wife and child were killed in an accident, and during the second year faculty began to leave for better positions, especially to the University of Chicago. Finally, in 1892, after several disagreements with the faculty and the pressures of working at a financially unstable university, almost two thirds of the faculty and students left Clark University. Psychology remained the only viable academic department at the university in large part because Hall was deeply involved in the work of the department and many of the faculty members and students in the department remained loyal to Hall and Clark University (Ross, 1972).

The psychology laboratory and the university ultimately survived the trying first three years and the psychology laboratory remained a state-of-the-art facility. In fact, the laboratory flourished, and under Hall's reign the psychology department at Clark University conducted research on developmental psychology, comparative psychology, and eugenics; it also promoted the introduction of psychoanalysis in America during the Clark Conference to celebrate the 20th anniversary of the university in 1909. This latter development symbolized, in part, by Professor Sigmund Freud's 1909 Clark lectures is very important as the lectures represented a very applied model of psychology, namely, psychoanalysis, and a theory that emphasized sexual development throughout the lifespan, which was then considered a very controversial view of infancy and childhood.

Hall and Scientific/Applied Psychology

In 1883, Hall began a series of studies in which he gave questionnaires to more than 200 Boston schoolchildren. He had hoped to establish an empirical description of the mind of a child by asking children questions about nature, religion, stories they knew, immortality, and death. Based on these initial questionnaires, Hall and the other members of the psychology department at Clark developed a host of additional questionnaires targeted at adolescents on topics such as anger, envy, jealousy, dreams, and play. Hall compiled this wealth of information into a 1,373-page book titled *Adolescence* (1904), which was the first book dedicated to the study of teenagers. Accordingly, Hall was the first person to mark adolescence as a distinct stage of lifespan development with some even suggesting that this book marks the beginning of developmental psychology.

Adolescence further illustrates the value Hall placed on evolutionary processes and the role of genetics in human and species development. Hall described his theory of **recapitulation** based on a theory originally formulated in 1866 by Ernst Haeckel (1834–1919), a German anatomist. According to this theory, the development of an organism can be seen as a recapitulation of the evolution of the species. Thus, a human fetus is said to go through a morphological or bodily stages of development resembling fish, reptiles, and non-primate mammals before emerging as a full-fledged human. The theory of recapitulation or ontogeny recapitulates phylogeny and also embraces functional development such that children crawl before they are able to walk upright and babble or baby talk before meaningful speech emerges.

Evolutionary theory and genetics formed a foundational theme for much of Hall's work in psychology casting Hall as an ardent supporter of eugenics. Hall believed that individuals of a species inherited attributes and it is reasonable to assume that once "higher" or "lower" traits were acquired they were readily passed down from one generation to another. In fact, he believed that there were higher and lower human races and saw it as a social obligation for him and other members of the "higher" white race to educate female and black students. While this belief is recognized today as clearly sexist and racist, an ironic twist occurred in that this belief led G. Stanley Hall to mentor, advise, and educate several women (Diehl, 1986) and more black students in the early decades of the 20th century than any other psychologist (Guthrie, 1976).

G. Stanley Hall was a firm believer in and proponent of psychology as a science and a profession. He founded several journals, was the president of an acclaimed university, brought Sigmund Freud to the United States for the first time, founded the American Psychological Association, and was elected twice as president of the association. While he is best remembered for his professionalization of psychology, he was also a gifted researcher and insightful teacher. Hall saw value in the theory of evolution and incorporated these beliefs into much of his professional and scientific work. His dual emphasis on genetics and the applied aspects of psychology mark him as the last important bridge between the early theorists such as Charles Darwin and Francis Galton, and the psychologists such as John Dewey and James Rowland Angell, who founded the psychological school of functionalism.

THE FOUNDING OF FUNCTIONALISM

For functional psychology, the subject matter of psychology was clearly consciousness and behavior in the service of adaptation to changing environments. For the functional psychologists, the overriding question for psychology became: What are the functions and utilities of consciousness? rather than What are the contents of consciousness as pursued by the Wundtian and Titchnerian approaches to psychology? The functionalists answered that the purpose of consciousness was to mediate between the demands of the external environment and the needs and desires of the internal environment of the organism. Consciousness is beneficial because it helps an organism adapt to the environment and is therefore functional. For functional psychologists, the validity of an idea or an action arises from the extent to which a given idea or action promotes the adaptability of the organism.

Darwin, Galton, Spencer, James, and Hall shaped and provided a path for functional psychology with each providing his own original ideas while building and expanding on those who had also earlier addressed topics of interest to the founders of functionalism. As William James was one of the most immediate forerunners to those now considered functional psychologists, a passage from his *Pragmatism* (1981/1907) is an appropriate summary of the work of the above forerunners of functionalism as well as an introduction to the beliefs of the founders of the functional school of thought. Although this was published after the "founding" of functionalism, James' thoughts on pragmatism had been maturing for years and quite nicely represent how truth is established as seen through the eyes of a functionalist.

> Any idea upon which we can ride, so to speak; any idea that will carry us prosperously from any one part of our experience to any other part, linking things satisfactorily, working securely, simplifying, saving labor; is true for just so much, true in so far forth, true **instrumentally**. This is the "instrumental" view of truth taught so successfully at Chicago, the view that truth in our ideas means their power to "work." (James, 1981/1907, p. 30)

John Dewey: A Vermonter and Functionalist

John Dewey (1859–1952) was born in Burlington, Vermont, and was infused with the values of individual liberty, democracy, and simplicity. Dewey had a relatively undistinguished academic career and appeared to learn more from travelling through Vermont than from the classroom. It is most likely that this early interest in "nontraditional" education influenced Dewey's later beliefs about education and psychology.

Dewey attended the University of Vermont (UVM) from 1875 to 1879 and received a broad education focused around his strong interest in philosophy and psychology. Despite his average educational attainment during his first two years at UVM, he decided to take seriously his studies during his junior year and improved his academic standing enough to graduate Phi Beta Kappa in 1879. After graduation he taught high school for three years, two in Pennsylvania and one in Vermont, before he decided that he had had enough of teaching in the then rigidly prescribed curriculum emphasizing memorization and passive learning styles. At the time there were no national or local standards for education and students were often disciplined using physical force. These pedagogic or educational practices did not coincide with Dewey's philosophy for educating children grounded in the belief that for America to become a truly inclusive democracy all citizens must be afforded a quality education.

The next stop for John Dewey was Johns Hopkins University where he entered graduate school in 1882 to study psychology and philosophy. He studied psychology under G. Stanley Hall and earned his PhD in psychology in 1884. His doctoral dissertation was titled "The Psychology of Kant," reflecting clearly his dual interests in philosophy and psychology similar to, for example, the broad interests of William James. Importantly, his keen interests in both psychology and philosophy shaped much of his later work and contributed substantially to the founding of functionalism.

After graduating from Johns Hopkins, Dewey accepted a faculty appointment to teach philosophy at the University of Michigan. While at Michigan he wrote one of the early American textbooks in psychology which was a mix of philosophy and psychology and was aptly titled *Psychology*. The book was published in 1886 and thus precedes the publication of James' *The Principles of Psychology* by four years. Dewey's *Psychology* did not receive the recognition that James' *Principles* did; however, it was relatively popular for the four years prior to the publication of James' book and was used to teach many notable psychologists including James Rowland Angell (1869–1949).

In 1896, while still at the University of Michigan, Dewey published the foundational journal article of the system of psychology we know today as functionalism. The paper, titled "The Reflex Arc Concept in Psychology," was published in the *Psychological Review*, and was John Dewey's greatest achievement in psychology as well as his first and last purely psychological manuscript. In this paper, Dewey struck at the heart of some of the then foundational and structural concepts of psychology; for example, the prevailing explanatory model of the reflex arc. It was fairly widely accepted that the reflex arc could be broken down into the components of a stimulus and a response thus forming an arc or a bridge where a behavior simply ends with a response to a stimulus. John Dewey used the example of a child touching a flame to illustrate the restrictive and mechanical features of this conceptualization of the reflex arc. According to the original conceptualization, a child sees a flame (stimulus), reaches for it (response), feels pain from the flame (stimulus), and then withdraws the hand (response). Behavior is a series of responses to stimuli with much of it running off mechanically with little conscious attention to the constantly changing relationship between the organism and the environment.

On the contrary, Dewey suggested that the mechanistic description of the reflex arc, as described above, is more adaptively considered as a circle including the entire conscious organism. He argued that as a result of the active rather than the passive engagement of the organism, the current and future perceptions of candle flames or similar stimuli change so that it is too simplistic to break down behavior into stimulus and response elements. As Dewey pointed out, the entire behavioral sequence does not begin with the child seeing the flame and end with the child withdrawing her hand after she has been burned by the flame. Dewey said simply yet profoundly that there must be a place for the adaptive organism in psychology rather than focusing solely on the mechanistic stimulus and response elements of the reflex arc. Thus, for example, because the child had previously experienced pain, the child may now well approach the situation differently, reflecting the active and adaptive engagement of the organism arising from the similar prior experience. In other words, Dewey argued that behavioral sequences must be thought of in terms of how they are adaptive to the organism, which includes past experiences, present needs, and future expectations of the organism rather than just the mechanistic, closed, and lifeless elements of the reflex arc (Dewey, 1896). It is precisely here that Dewey broke with the ideas of Wilhem Wundt and Edward B. Titchener by emphasizing that behavior and consciousness cannot be meaningfully separated into parts, but rather must be examined as a whole in relation to the adaptability of the organism to the environment. For Dewey and other functional psychologists, it is how an organism functions within its environment that is more important than simply what it reacts to in a vacuum. An organism's experiences and reactions to an environment are psychological rather than mechanical as they incorporate thoughts, feelings, and behaviors. John Dewey argued for a psychology focused on the functions of, rather than the elements of, consciousness and behavior.

Dewey and Education

John Dewey is remembered more readily as a pioneer in American education than in psychology because, although he is considered one of the founders of functionalism, his only psychological works were *Psychology* and "The Reflex Arc Concept in Psychology." As was discussed previously, John Dewey spent time teaching in public schools and did not like what he experienced. He believed that the emphasis on rote learning, drills, and strict discipline made the classroom a place to avoid rather than a place to learn. Dewey also believed that education was a means for survival, and that if America was to survive as an inclusive democracy, as many citizens as possible must be included in every phase of American life, especially education. This meant reforming the American educational system so that all could have the opportunity to receive an education and prosper instead of reserving that "right" to a privileged few. John Dewey began the movement known as **progressive education**, centered on the foundational idea that every student is to be considered an active learner, that a student learns best by doing, and that education is for the adaptation to challenging and changing environments.

The University of Chicago had been an attractive academic appointment to John Dewey most importantly because of the inclusion of pedagogy or the art and science of teaching along with psychology and philosophy. Thus, while at Chicago he was afforded the opportunity to work extensively with children of all ages. Dewey believed that **to learn was to do**, and he applied this philosophy to himself as well as the school-aged children with whom he worked. In 1896, he began a "laboratory school" to examine how children learn and think and to help children learn by learning from other children. Drills and memorization were not part of his progressive educational program and instead, Dewey encouraged his students to participate in their own education rather than depend solely upon the teacher as the engine for education. This represented a new way of educating children and Dewey's laboratory school served as a model for several others, mostly on other university campuses around the country.

In 1899, Dewey wrote *The School and Society*, which firmly established his reputation as a leading philosopher of education. He used much of what he had learned through psychology and his laboratory school at the University of Chicago as the focus for this influential book. He argued that children learn by meeting the needs of conversation, construction, curiosity, and artistic impression. This marked a distinct movement away from traditional education and emphasized the progressive education movement. Thus, John Dewey began two schools of thought, namely, functionalism and the progressive education movement by articulating the limitations he identified with prior ideas and practices focusing upon psychology and education, respectively.

John Dewey left Chicago for Columbia University in 1904, subsequently giving departmental leadership to another Burlington, Vermont, native, James Rowland Angell. In 1892, Dewey became a charter member of the American Psychological Association and was elected president in 1899. While at Columbia he focused primarily on philosophy and education and made no further formal contributions to psychology. He continued to write and to support education and other liberal causes such as the American Civil Liberties Union, the National Association for the Advancement of Colored People, and women's suffrage (Hilgard, 1987). He was also one of the founders of the American Association of University Professors.

James Rowland Angell: Popularizing Functionalism

The similarities between John Dewey and James Rowland Angell (1869–1949) extend much further than the fact that both were the cofounders and initial leaders of the functional school of psychology. Like Dewey, Angell was born in Burlington, Vermont, and his ancestry can be traced back to original New England settlers. Angell's early life was more focused on academics than Dewey's, as his father, James Burrill Angell (1829–1916), served first as president of the University of Vermont and then the University of Michigan.

James Rowland Angell earned his A. B. degree from the University of Michigan where he took a course in psychology taught by John Dewey and read Dewey's text *Psychology*. Thereafter, Dewey encouraged Angell to remain at Michigan and work toward his master's degree, which he earned in 1890. Angell enrolled in Harvard in 1891 where he studied with such notables as William James and Hugo Münsterberg, and earned his second master's degree in 1892. While at Harvard, William James put Angell to work on research focused upon psychical or psychic phenomena such as clairvoyance and mental telepathy. Angell was unable to draw any sound conclusions about the validity of psychical phenomena although, more importantly, he did have the opportunity to work with William James. Although he received a number of honorary doctoral degrees in his lifetime, the two master's degrees were his highest earned academic degrees.

After Harvard, Angell traveled to Europe to work with Wilhelm Wundt at Leipzig. Unfortunately, Wundt notified him that his laboratory was fully staffed and could not support another student. Although Wundt invited Angell to attend his lectures, Angell decided to move on because he was already familiar with Wundt's psychology.

After leaving Leipzig, Angell studied with Hermann Ebbinghaus, Hermann L. F. von Helmholtz, and finally Benno Erdmann at the University of Halle, Germany. He remained at the University of Halle and based his dissertation on Immanuel Kant's perceptions of freedom, which focuses on duty as the highest human obligation. Angell's dissertation was accepted with the condition that it be rewritten in better German. He planned to remain at Halle, albeit with no income, to finish the dissertation but shortly thereafter was offered a salaried position teaching philosophy at the University of Minnesota. The lure of an income was too much, and he thus decided to return to the United States and forego completion of his dissertation.

James Angell spent a year in Minnesota and then accepted a position in the philosophy department at the University of Chicago under John Dewey in 1895. Angell spent twenty-five years at the University of Chicago and was promoted to Dean of the Faculty of the university in 1911. James Rowland Angell, like John Dewey, was also elected president of the American Psychological Association, in 1906, served as president of Yale University for most of the 1920s and 1930s before retiring in 1937, and thereafter served as president of the Carnegie Corporation in 1939. When Angell left the University of Chicago, he passed the chair of the department to another one of his students, Harvey A. Carr.

Angell gave an outline of his view of functionalism, in his 1906 presidential address for the American Psychological Association, titled "The Province of Functional Psychology" (Angell, 1907). In this address he asserted that the earliest versions of psychology, dating back to Greek, Roman, and Arabian cultures, were relatively functional in nature and that it was the structural psychologists who departed from this earlier conceptual foundation of psychology. In the address, Angell summarized three foundational ideas of functionalism.

First, functionalism was the study of mental operations while structuralism was the study of mental elements. A functionalist is interested in how the mind operates, what it is used for, and how it helps an organism to adapt while a structuralist is interested in identifying the basic elements of mind (i.e., sensations, feelings, and images). Second, functionalists view consciousness as an adaptive process to meet the actual demands of life events. Consciousness is adaptive as it mediates between the demands of the external environment and the internal needs and desires of the organism to allow the organism to function effectively within ever-changing environments. To further highlight the adaptability of consciousness, Angell argued that consciousness is always changing and thus performing an adaptive service for the organism. Much like William James' idea of a stream of consciousness, the conscious mind is always at work shifting and forming itself to meet the demands of the ever-changing environment. If consciousness did not have the ability to always change it would not prove itself effective and functional for the organism. The third foundational idea is that functional psychologists are concerned with the entire organism and its relationship to the environment. Functional psychology makes no distinction between mind and body as they are considered as one and the same. Thus, the interchange from one to the other flows easily and constantly and promotes the adaptability of the organism. This flow between mind and body allows the organism to use the most adaptive process for the situation. Solely examining one or the other would inherently neglect an important and necessary system within each and every functional organism.

In addition to his presidential address and obvious support of functionalism, Angell conducted research at the University of Chicago on topics such as reaction times, sound localization, and maze learning by rats. Comparative psychology grew rapidly at Chicago under the guidance of Angell and one of his students, John B. Watson (1878–1958), who is considered to be the founder of the school of psychology known as behaviorism.

Harvey A. Carr: A Mature Functionalism

Harvey A. Carr (1873–1954) was born on a farm in Indiana and remained there until the age of 26 when he enrolled at the University of Colorado. While at Colorado he earned his bachelor's and master's degrees, and then in 1901 he enrolled in the University of Chicago as a psychology graduate student. The first class Harvey Carr took at the University of Chicago was taught by James Rowland Angell, and in his second year of graduate studies he worked as an assistant to John B. Watson, the founder of behaviorism. While working with Angell and Watson, Carr developed two interests that remained with him throughout his professional career. His first interest was the perception of space as represented by his dissertation, titled "A Visual Illusion of Motion During Eye-Closure," and his second interest was represented by the bulk of his publications focused upon maze learning.

In 1905, Carr graduated with the third doctoral degree in psychology awarded by the University of Chicago and as there were no positions immediately available in academia, he left to teach high school in Texas. However, in 1908, John B. Watson left the University of Chicago for Johns Hopkins University and Carr subsequently returned to Chicago to replace him as a faculty member in the psychology department. During Carr's time at Chicago, functionalism became more widely accepted and as a consequence was no longer considered an unfocused and incompletely developed theoretical alternative to structuralism. Carr, like so many functionalists, protested against being labeled with any sort of limiting intellectual tag reflecting a functional attitude of openness to new ideas, methods of inquiry, and content. Despite his objections to being labeled a functionalist, Carr did influence the functional school of thought by overseeing an estimated 130 dissertations and chairing the psychology department at the University of Chicago for many years.

Carr's most direct influences upon psychology are his textbook *Psychology: A Study of Mental Activity*, published in 1925, and the vast number of graduate students he was involved with during their graduate studies and beyond. In his textbook, Carr defined psychology as the study of mental activity, a generic term for activities such as perception, memory, judgments, and will or decision making. In addition, he believed that mental activities are concerned with the acquisition, retention, organization, and evaluation of experiences along with their subsequent utilization in guiding conduct (Hilgard, 1991). Thus, an organism uses mental activities to adapt or to guide conduct in the environment. Adaptation, according to Carr, involves a motivating stimulus, a sensory stimulus, and a response that alters the situation to satisfy the motivating conditions. For example, a motivating stimulus such as hunger or pain disrupts one of the senses of an organism until the motivating demand (eating or pain removal) is addressed. The organism uses its mental activities to perceive the stimulus and to take subsequent steps to alleviate the disturbance, proving functional to an organism's ability to adapt (Hilgard, 1991). Carr was elected president of APA in 1927 and remained at the University of Chicago until his retirement in 1928, during which time functionalism was further refined as a school of psychology.

FUNCTIONALISM AT COLUMBIA UNIVERSITY

Functionalism was never established as a formal school of psychology consisting of a uniform set of methods of inquiry, a fixed definition of the subject matter of psychology, and clearly identified followers. Paradoxically, functionalism is conceptualized as flexible in thought, methods, and subject matter while at the same time fixed in the insistence on conceptual flexibility that allows for broadening the scope of psychology. Accordingly, functionalism focused on the utilities of consciousness and behaviors for a wide variety of organisms in a variety of environments rather than rigid methods of study and precise definitions of the subject matter of psychology. Features of functionalism can be found in almost all areas of contemporary psychology, making plain that the functionalist perspective easily grew beyond the walls of the University of Chicago.

James McKeen Cattell: A Quantifiable and Functional Psychology

James McKeen Cattell (1860–1944) was raised in a family environment similar to that of James Angell in that his father was president of Lafayette College in Eaton, Pennsylvania, a Presbyterian clergyman, and a professor of Greek and Latin. His mother was from a wealthy Irish-American family. Cattell was schooled at home until the age of 16 when he was sent to Lafayette College. While at Lafayette, he was inundated with Scottish Realist philosophy, which stressed that humans have an intuitive understanding that reality exists and is in direct opposition to David Hume's view that a sense of permanent reality violates common sense given our continuously changing perceptions of the world around us. The Realists believed further that the mind is more than a collection of associated ideas and thus has its own existence in reality. Cattell was particularly impressed and influenced by one of his professors at Lafayette College, who believed that by exhaustively collecting data one would begin to see patterns in any problem at hand and viable conclusions would soon follow. This belief in precise data collection remained with Cattell throughout his life and greatly influenced his beliefs about psychology and research. He graduated from Lafayette with honors in 1880 and, using part of his inheritance, he traveled to Europe to further his formal education.

His first stop in Europe was at the University of Göttingen where he studied with Rudolph Hermann Lötze (1817–1881). His actual studies with Lötze are not as important in a historical sense as is the essay he wrote about Lötze, which earned Cattell a fellowship to Johns Hopkins University. He entered Johns Hopkins in 1882 and conducted promising research on reaction times to various stimuli. Although his research went well, his fellowship was not renewed after his first year because it appears that Cattell did not get along well with Daniel Coit Gilman, who was then president of the university. Another and perhaps more accurate reason for his lack of renewed funding may have been the studies he conducted using only himself as a subject. Cattell wanted to test the effects of various drugs on consciousness and behavior so he frequently took large doses of alcohol, nicotine, caffeine, hashish, opium, and morphine. Later in life Cattell remarked that the doses he took must have been the highest possible without suicidal intent (Sokal, 1971). It is interesting to note that the person awarded Cattell's old fellowship at Johns Hopkins was John Dewey, ironically, the candidate Cattell beat out for the position when they both originally applied to Johns Hopkins University.

In 1883, Cattell went back to Europe to study with Wilhelm Wundt at Leipzig, Germany. Interestingly, Wundt typically assigned his students both research topics and protocols or specified procedures for the assigned research project of investigation, so it must have been surprising to Cattell when Wundt let him continue the work he had begun at Johns Hopkins. While at Leipzig, Cattell built several instruments that improved not only his work, but became standard in many psychology laboratories including, for example, a "gravity chronometer," which was used in his reaction time research and allowed materials to be presented for a controlled and predetermined amount of time. His research at Leipzig went very well and he found that reaction or reading times for unconnected words and letters were much slower than for connected words or letters. Much of this early research was published in Wundt's own journal *Philosophische Studien* (*Philosophical Studies*).

Cattell completed his doctoral dissertation, "**Psychometric Investigations**," in 1886, the first American to complete a dissertation with Wundt. For the dissertation, Cattell conducted research on individual differences in attention and the effects of fatigue upon attention and other mental processes. Cattell was the first of thirty-three Americans to earn their doctoral degrees with Wundt, and despite the tart flavor of their personal relationship Cattell owed much professionally to the support that Wundt provided him while at Leipzig (Benjamin, Durkin, Link, Vestal, & Accord, 1992).

After completing his dissertation, Cattell secured a fellowship at St. John's College, Cambridge, England. While at Cambridge, Cattell met Sir Francis Galton and the similarities between them in their outlook on life and science had an enormous impact on Cattell. Most importantly, both loved to count or quantify everything they did or saw. They both believed that the more one measured the more one was able to know about the measured phenomenon. Although Cattell did not work directly with Galton, the few times they did meet and their brief correspondence affirmed Cattell's early education at Lafayette College on the importance of measuring phenomena as an essential ingredient for psychology.

Cattell returned to the United States to an appointment as professor of psychology at the University of Pennsylvania in 1889. He established a laboratory there and quickly resumed his studies on reaction times. In addition, he set out to use the Galtonian strategy of measuring psychological processes (i.e., intelligence and attention span) using physical measurements. In an article in the journal *Mind* in 1890, Cattell described the tests, both his and Galton's, and in doing so coined the term *mental test* (Cattell, 1890). Thus, he believed that psychological processes could be measured using physical measures such as reaction times and sensory thresholds or sensitivities. The basic idea was that if you have a very fast reaction time coupled with high sensitivity to sensory stimuli then you are probably smarter than a person exhibiting a lower profile of such physical measures.

Cattell remained at the University of Pennsylvania for two years and then in 1891 accepted a position as professor of experimental psychology at Columbia University in New York City. He established another laboratory at Columbia and resumed his studies on reaction times and other mental tests. Many of the mental tests used in both his University of Pennsylvania and Columbia laboratories were physical tests such as reaction times, which he believed would readily assess psychological processes. Often his tests were not conducted to test a specific hypothesis but only to accumulate more data. For example, he began testing incoming first-year students although his tests had nothing to do with admission to the university and were not utilized initially for any predictive purposes. In 1901, Cattell asked Clark Wissler (1870–1947), one of his graduate students, to use Galton's newly developed correlational technique to determine if his mental tests were indicative of academic achievement (Wissler, 1901). Wissler did not find a strong correlation or relationship between Cattell's tests and academic achievement, and, in fact, he found that one's grade in physical education was as predictive of other grades as any of Cattell's tests. This project obviously ended the emphasis on physical tests such as reaction time as a measure of mental abilities, and Cattell concluded that to measure psychological processes one needed psychological rather than physical measures.

Cattell was enthusiastic about quantifiable results in psychology, and his focus and insistence on "hard" facts promoted psychology as a science in the early years of the development of psychology. After his tests were found not to be predictive of psychological processes, Cattell turned his attention from measurement projects to a sustained campaign to professionalize the field of psychology. In 1894, he helped James Mark Baldwin (1861–1934) establish the *Psychological Review* and remained as an editor until 1904. He was a charter member of the APA and in 1895 was elected president. Also in 1895, Cattell bought the rights to *Science*, a journal that had previously been backed financially by Thomas Edison and Alexander Graham Bell. Cattell quickly turned it into one of the most prestigious journals published in the United States, and in 1900 it became the official journal of the American Association for the Advancement of Science (AAAS). Cattell served as president of the AAAS in 1924, was the first psychologist admitted to the National Academy of Sciences in 1901, and had a hand in publishing several scientific journals. Cattell's academic career at Columbia and elsewhere was cut short in 1917 when the president of Columbia accused him of treason because he publicly opposed sending conscripts (most likely conscientious objectors) to fight in World War I. He was fired from his position at Columbia and although Cattell sued the university for libel and won, he never received back salary compensation during the legal process. He also never held another academic position anywhere.

Thereafter, Cattell founded the Psychological Corporation, which today remains an active force in applying psychological knowledge to educational and organizational settings and is an important source of psychological tests. While at Columbia, Cattell supervised more than fifty doctoral dissertations and established Columbia's reputation for having one of the best psychology programs in the country. Two of his most famous students, Edward Lee Thorndike and Robert Sessions Woodworth, both shaped significantly the future of functionalism in particular and psychology as a science in general.

Edward Lee Thorndike: Animal Behavior and Connectionism

Similar to many of the early functional psychologists, Edward Lee Thorndike (1874–1949) was born in Williamsburg, Massachusetts, to a Victorian homeworker and a Methodist minister. His family moved often, usually every two or three years, as his father was assigned to different congregations. Thorndike was always seen as the new kid in the neighborhood and he became painfully shy because of the necessity of starting his life over again every few years. However, he also learned to become very resourceful, which helped his studies, and as his mother was a strict teacher, he also became an exceptional student. He entered the Methodist-affiliated Wesleyan University in Connecticut in 1891, and quickly excelled. During his junior year he was required to take a psychology course and to read William James' *Principles* to be eligible for an academic prize. Like most psychologists of his generation, Thorndike was enamored with the James text because of its sheer magnitude and engaging style. After graduating from Wesleyan with honors in 1895, Thorndike enrolled at Harvard for graduate studies in order to study psychology directly with William James.

Thorndike began his graduate studies by conducting research examining the psychic phenomenon of mind reading; however, when his experimental hypotheses were consistently rejected he turned to the experimental study of animal learning. One of his first experiments used chickens and mazes made out of stacked books, reflecting the resourcefulness cultivated during his childhood and adolescent years. He initially placed a chicken in the crude maze and waited for the chicken to find its way out through an exit which contained food, water, or other chickens. After each trial in the maze, the chicken subsequently ran increasingly faster to the exit. This reduction in time to run the maze, a latency measure according to Thorndike, indicated that the chicken had learned how to escape from the maze. He realized that reading behavior was more accurate than reading minds, and introduced the study of animal learning into psychology. While Thorndike is best known for his animal research he did not begin this line of research out of a profound interest in either animals or comparative psychology. Originally, he most likely began working with animals to satisfy requirements needed to graduate. His decision to use chickens probably came about as the result of a series of lectures he attended by C. Lloyd Morgan at Harvard in 1896. During these lectures Morgan described how chickens learned to discriminate between different-colored kernels of corn. The kernels of corn were dipped in either a bitter-tasting quinine or sweet-tasting sugar water. The chickens subsequently learned to peck only at the sweet-tasting kernels. Again, the foundational idea is to read behaviors (not minds) using a number of measurable and observable phenomena such as, for example, latency and food preferences, which can be applied to study the learning capacities of a wide variety of organisms.

Thorndike decided to leave Harvard in 1897 even though his experiments were going well there and he received a great deal of support from William James (e.g., when Thorndike could not find a place to house his chickens James allowed him to keep them in his home). Actually, he left as a result of a romantic relationship that seemed to be going nowhere at the time (Jonçich, 1968). He then won a fellowship to attend Columbia University to study with Cattell. Thorndike arrived in New York with his two most highly trained chickens and set out to study the formation of associations using these chickens along with other species, most notably, cats. A lab was provided for him after an incubator he was using for his chickens caught fire in his apartment and his landlady insisted that he get rid of the chickens. Cattell found space for Thorndike's animal laboratory in the attic of a building on campus so he could study systematically his thirteen new kittens and cats.

Thorndike disdained the anecdotal strategy of assessing animal intelligence, which attributed higher learning to any act an animal made such as clawing at a door seemingly as a signal to get outside. As a result he set out to examine animal learning scientifically and built a series of puzzle boxes to test his animals (Jonçich, 1968). When the cats were initially placed in the puzzle boxes they exhibited random acts and a great deal of hit and miss or "trial-and-error" learning. Eventually, often by accident, the cat would perform the correct responses and the box would open allowing the cat to escape. Each time the cat was placed in the box it more rapidly performed the correct behavior and reduced the amount of incorrect behaviors preceding the correct target functional behavior. This progressive refinement of behaviors or trial-and-error learning was determined primarily by what Thorndike termed the **Law of Effect**. He proposed that the connections between appropriate external stimulus conditions and pleasurable behaviors are strengthened and "stamped in" whereas the connections between stimuli and annoying or nonpleasurable behaviors are "stamped out." This is not to say that animals do not learn about nonpleasurable events; in fact, they learn about both as they learn what behaviors to perform and what behaviors not to perform.

Thorndike also observed that cats progressively became better at learning to escape from different boxes. While they were not able to learn a sequence of behaviors, they did become more apt at figuring out what was required in each situation. They became more "box wise" and learned new escape behaviors more rapidly. A point to remember is that these experiments were conducted in less than a year and before Thorndike had earned his doctorate. The results were published in *Science* in June of 1898, and presented at the January meeting of the New York Academy of Science. They were further written up for his doctoral dissertation, "An Experimental Study of the Associative Process in Animals," which was accepted by Columbia University in 1898.

Following his presentation at the 1898 meeting of the APA, Thorndike's findings were criticized as arising from unnatural learning situations thus invalidating his conclusions. His most vocal opponent, Wesley Mills (1847–1915), was a comparative psychologist from McGill University in Montreal, Canada. Mills criticized Thorndike for not respecting the work of those who had come before him, and because his puzzle boxes represented unnatural situations in which cats must perform unnatural acts. Mills published an article illustrating his opposing views in the May 1899 edition of the *Psychological Review*. Unphased by the criticism, Thorndike provided a sound response in the next issue of the *Psychological Review*. However, then as well as now, we find that some still believe that understanding fully animal (as well as human) behavior is not only possible within the controlled confines of the laboratory environment and yields the most accurate data about cause and effect relationships while others believe that studying organisms in their natural environments produces the more valid and reliable conclusions about animal and human behavior. This mode of systematic field-based observation and data collection is known as **ethology** and is well known in a large part due to the work of Konrad Lorenz (1903–1989) and Niko Tinbergen (1907–1988).

After earning his doctorate, Thorndike went to Cleveland, Ohio, and taught at Case Western Reserve for a year. This was a relatively unhappy year for him, and he was delighted when he received a message from James McKeen Cattell asking him to return to Columbia University. He remained at Columbia for the rest of his academic career, which spanned forty-three productive and lucrative years. While at Columbia he averaged between ten and twelve publications a year and focused much of his time on educational psychology instead of the animal learning for which he is best known in psychological circles. One of his most famous publications on educational psychology was a three-volume textbook, aptly named *Educational Psychology* and published in 1913, based upon his detailed lecture notes, which he distributed over the years to students in his classes and which he eventually coalesced into textbooks. Thorndike's publications made him a relatively rich man. In 1924, for example, his book royalty earnings were an amazing $68,000, roughly five times what he made as a professor (Jonçich, 1968)!

Thorndike was elected president of the American Psychological Association in 1912, and in 1933 he was elected president of the American Association for the Advancement of Science (AAAS). Even during the nine years between his retirement and death, Thorndike continued to publish at a rate of over five publications a year. Although he is mostly remembered for his animal learning research, Thorndike contributed greatly to our understanding of educational psychology as well.

Robert Sessions Woodworth: Author and Educator

Robert Sessions Woodworth (1869–1962) was born in Belchertown, Massachusetts. His family was of traditional New England stock and included Robert Sessions, who participated in the Boston Tea Party. Woodworth's father was a stern and disciplined minister while his mother was a teacher who had graduated from Mount Holyoke College. During his youth he spent time in other parts of New England, Iowa, and Ohio as his father held pastorates in each location. He attended high school while in Massachusetts and decided to enroll in Amherst College to become a teacher, although his parents wanted him to become a minister.

He graduated from Amherst with an A.B. degree in 1891 and taught high school math and science for a couple years, then spent two years teaching at a small college in Topeka, Kansas. During this time he discovered the works of both G. Stanley Hall and William James. He had heard Hall lecture and was fascinated with the idea of studying scientifically the then new field of psychology, including phenomena such as learning and perception. He also read *The Principles of Psychology* and was intrigued and captivated by William James. Accordingly, he decided to pursue a career in either philosophy or psychology and left for Harvard in hopes of studying with William James in the fall of 1895. While at Harvard, Woodworth worked with William James and met Edward Lee Thorndike and Walter B. Cannon, with whom he would maintain lifelong friendships. Also while at Harvard, James directed Woodworth's research on topics such as time perception, language, and thought. In addition, as James was interested in the nature and purpose of dreams at this time, they attempted to correlate Woodworth's dreams with the content of his day. They were not successful, although they did notice that Woodworth often dreamt of things he had not completed during the day.

Woodworth spent three years at Harvard and during that time he received another bachelor's degree along with a master's degree in psychology. In addition to his studies and research with James, Woodworth also served as a research assistant at the Harvard Medical School. He left Harvard to study psychology at Columbia under Cattell, who had offered him a fellowship, possibly at the persistent request of Thorndike. Cattell was interested in precise testing in psychology and this appealed to Woodworth so he accepted the offer. He earned his PhD in 1899 and was immediately offered a faculty position in physiology at Columbia University, which he accepted.

Early in his career Robert Sessions Woodworth spent much time conducting research on learning with Edward Lee Thorndike. One of the areas they focused upon was the phenomenon of "transfer of training" or how improving one mental function impacts the efficiency of another mental function. Near the turn of the century Harvard had developed an "elective" curriculum which allowed students to avoid certain classical subjects such as Latin if they chose. Interestingly, others had begun to follow Harvard's lead and a debate inevitably ensued as to whether learning the so-called classical subjects did in fact enhance the learning of other subjects. The foundation of the transfer of training research arose from the education doctrine or belief that studying certain disciplinary subjects—"the Classics" such as Latin, Greek, literature, and mathematics—strengthens the functional infrastructures of the mind such as synthetic thinking or putting together disparate subjects into meaningful relationships.

In a series of experiments Woodworth and Thorndike (Thorndike & Woodworth, 1901) tested subjects on relatively easy tasks to determine if they would improve their ability to perform other similar tasks. They initially trained subjects, for instance, on how to estimate the area of a rectangle and then had subjects either estimate the area of different shapes or estimate the weight of an object. They found very little transfer of knowledge between the tasks, even between the relatively similar tasks of area estimation. They did find, however, that there was more transfer between similar tasks, yet not enough based on their data to support the pervasive classical educational doctrine of the time. In fact, their findings provided little if any support for the notion that learning about truly divergent subjects increases the transfer of knowledge from one domain to another. What we know today indicates that learning strategies are applicable across disparate knowledge domains while the domain content is not as transferable as the strategy.

In 1902, Woodworth spent a year in England on a fellowship in Charles Sherrington's laboratory at the University of Liverpool, studying physiology in hopes that his psychology background would advance his career in physiology. At the end of the year he was offered a position by both Cattell and Sherrington and decided to accept the offer to return to Columbia and to psychology full-time. Upon returning to Columbia, Cattell put Woodworth to work on a project requested by the organizers of the 1904 St. Louis Exposition. The organizers wanted Cattell (and subsequently Woodworth) to conduct tests on people of different races, and over 1,000 people were tested during the exposition. Unlike some of the forerunners of functionalism, such as Sir Francis Galton, Woodworth had a relatively objective and fair-minded opinion of racial differences (Woodworth, 1910). He believed that many of the classifications that psychologists use such as skin tone and brain size were not indicative of the mental capacity, status, or standing between different racial groups. He pointed out that such characteristics, like many other personal or dispositional features (e.g., height, weight, and sensory sensitivities), vary in any population as indicated by the classic bell curve. Thus, he concluded that culture and educational opportunities must be considered as the primary determinants of differences between and within racial and cultural groups. Many in Woodworth's time did not accept what he advocated because they were concerned about the cost of social changes needed to repair past social injustices.

In 1914, Woodworth was elected president of the American Psychological Association (APA), and during his presidential address he discussed a topic he first visited during his dissertation, namely, imageless thoughts or thinking of something in the absence of an image such as the ideas of justice or beauty. The likelihood of imageless thoughts was not possible, according to some psychologists like, for example, E. B. Titchener, who argued that sensations and images were always present in consciousness when one was thinking. On the contrary, Woodworth argued that while most thoughts involved sensations and images, not all did, especially complex thoughts such as beauty. In contemporary psychology it has been argued that thoughts such as stereotypes impact an individual without the individual being consciously aware of the stereotypical thoughts. Thus, while thoughts may have sensations and images associated with them, they are not necessary to promote or initiate some ideas such as stereotypical thoughts.

Woodworth was critical of the belief in a simple stimulus-response (S-R) model for psychology, and echoed what the Chicago functionalists proposed, namely, a stimulus-organism-response (S-O-R) model for psychology. For the "O" or organism part of the S-O-R model, Woodworth stressed the motives or drives of the organism. In two of his books, *Dynamic Psychology* (1918) and *Dynamics of Behavior* (1958), Woodworth discussed and defined what he saw as the motivational drives impacting organisms. Some of the drives were basic drives such as hunger, thirst, and sexual needs. Still other drives involved cognitive evaluations of needs and values as manifested in professional and personal ambitions. Regardless of the drive, Woodworth believed that psychology must take into account the motivational state of the organism rather than just the stimulus and response features of an action or set of actions, otherwise such a psychology would be incomplete.

Many of Woodworth's contributions to psychology are due to his extensive teaching program and published writings. His most influential book began as handouts for his course on experimental methods in psychology. By 1920 the handouts had grown to a 285-page reader and by 1938 had grown to 823 pages of his book titled *Experimental Psychology*. The book was revised in 1948 and again in 1954; it was considered the definitive text for many years and was the introduction to experimental psychology for thousands of psychology students. Woodworth made plain that the experimental method in psychology must include the determination of the systematic manipulaton of one variable, the independent variable (IV), upon the measured or the dependent variable (DV). Woodworth argued that there is no independent or manipulated variable in correlation studies so that only studies employing the above experimental methodology could provide information about cause-and-effect relationships. Today, this perspective is still endorsed by almost all psychologists around the globe. In 1931, Woodworth published a history of psychology titled *Contemporary Schools of Psychology*. In this text he wrote that all schools of psychology were valuable and that no then current school was sufficiently complete to embrace all of psychology. Although Woodworth's research program complements the functionalist position, he did not place himself firmly into one school of psychology or another. Ironically though, the functionalist school stresses adaptability, which is what Woodworth proposed by not aligning himself with any one school of psychology.

THE LEGACY OF FUNCTIONALISM AND CONTEMPORARY ISSUES

We have already discussed how the American Zeitgeist was fertile ground for the founding of functionalism at the beginning of the 20th century. However, there were other, seemingly more practical reasons why functionalism took off in America. While more traditional textbooks may like to focus on the theoretical and philosophical roots of all new movements, we think that in a chapter about functionalism it is just as important to examine the practical reasons why psychologists were looking to apply what they knew. As you read this section remember some of the issues and think about them again as we discuss the contemporary reasons for the push toward more applied psychology. It is interesting to note how patterns of history do repeat themselves and thus how learning about history can be helpful for adapting to present and future environments.

While the number of research facilities and universities offering psychology was increasing rapidly near the end of the 19th century, the number of psychologists earning doctoral degrees was increasing even more rapidly. Thus, jobs in the traditional settings were not increasing with demand and those without independent sources of income had to look toward less traditional places to survive economically. Many psychologists were employed by the military during times of war; however, these positions were rarely permanent or lucrative. Therefore, many psychologists looked toward more popular writing as a way to not only inform the public about the new psychology but to also supplement their incomes. In addition, many psychologists sought out positions where they could readily apply their knowledge. One of the most lucrative and inviting areas to work in was the American corporation. One of the most influential psychologists to enter the applied world of psychology was Hugo Münsterberg.

Hugo Münsterberg: Popularizing Applied Psychology

We have already described some of the laboratory findings of Hugo Münsterberg (1863–1916) in chapter 2, focusing upon spiritualism (Benjamin, 1993; Coon, 1992) and in chapter 6 on hypnosis (Münsterberg, 1909, 1910). Interestingly, Münsterberg is also important in the context of functionalism because he popularized psychology for the American public by writing hundreds of articles published in many widely read magazines and newspapers such as *The Atlantic Monthly* and the *Boston Globe*, both of which are still published today. Münsterberg was for a time a widely celebrated psychologist who was respected for both his ideas and his ability to express his ideas to the public at large. Although Münsterberg popularized psychology in the United States, his German heritage and his continued promotion of Germany prior to and during World War I jaundiced his name and the recognition that the scope of work deserved.

Hugo Münsterberg was born in Danzig, Germany, and remained there until he left for the University of Leipzig to study medicine at the age of 19. While at Leipzig he took a course with Wilhelm Wundt and was so charmed by psychology that he changed his focus and earned his PhD with Wundt in 1885. Two years later he completed his initial academic endeavor and earned his M.D. from the University of Heidelberg, Germany. While at Leipzig it appears that Wundt and Münsterberg did not always agree on either research topics or the interpretation of the results of their research. Such disagreements became more pronounced, even after Münsterberg went to the University of Freiburg and set up a laboratory. Although Wundt continued to criticize Münsterberg's work because it dealt with the cognitive contents of the mind, Münsterberg was able to attract students as well as acclaim from such notables as William James because of the applied orientation of his laboratory.

In 1892, the same year that Titchener arrived at Cornell, William James offered Münsterberg the chance to become director of the psychology laboratory at Harvard. This was a highly paid position and James flattered Münsterberg saying that Harvard needed a genius to run this laboratory. Despite the desire to stay in Germany he accepted the offer, stayed at Harvard for three years, and then returned to Germany, attempting to secure a professorship at home. After realizing that he would not be offered a good position in Germany, he returned to Harvard and remained in the United States until his death in 1916.

Upon arriving in the United States he could barely understand English and it wasn't until two years after his arrival that he could lecture adequately in English. His transition from traditional German professor to head of a psychology laboratory at one of America's leading universities was not an easy one for Münsterberg. In fact, it may be said that he never made the transition and died partly as a result of his reluctance to let go not only of the strict German academic tradition but also his complete faith in all things German. In the beginning, Münsterberg criticized American psychologists for writing popular articles, attempting to apply their services to businesses, and accepting fees for giving lectures. His ideas about these issues would change and it is interesting to note that much of his greatness in American psychology is directly attributed to his excellence in these areas he once criticized.

In 1901, Münsterberg wrote *American Traits*, a cultural and psychological analysis of American society, which was widely received and marked the turning point in Münsterberg's career. Thereafter, he concerned himself more with writing for the public and less with academic writing projects intended primarily for his peers and colleagues. While at Harvard he grew increasingly interested in psychology in the courtroom, clinical psychology, forensic psychology, and industrial psychology. He was willing to examine a broad range of topics, which allowed his students to do the same. Despite his belief that graduate studies were too difficult for most women, he worked with and encouraged female students including Mary Whiton Calkins (1863–1930; see chapter 12). Most importantly, Münsterberg possessed the ability and willingness to examine and support sensational and often unpopular topics. Two of the most important were his support of Germany during World War I and his opposition to prohibition or the manufacturing, distribution, and sale of alcohol during the period from 1919 to 1933.

Before his unfortunate and untimely death due to a massive stroke during a lecture at Harvard in 1916, Münsterberg served as president of both the American Psychological Association and the American Philosophical Association. However, he is most widely remembered for his applied work and his ability to take psychology to the public, especially forensic, clinical, and industrial/organizational psychologies.

Forensic Psychology

Forensic psychology deals with psychology and the law. Münsterberg was an early founder of forensic psychology and he wrote articles on crime prevention, the use of hypnosis and mental tests to interrogate and test suspects, and some of the problems of using eyewitness testimony. He wrote *On the Witness Stand* in 1908, which focused on the problems of eye-witness testimony and also examined false confessions, the power of suggestion during questioning, and the use of physiological measurements obtained from the lie detector to detect guilt. The power of the book and his ideas are evident in that the book was reprinted as recently as 1976 and many contemporary psychologists are still investigating some of his seminal ideas, especially the use of eyewitness testimony (Loftus, 1979, 1992; Shaw, 1996). Furthermore, as a result of renewed interest in many of these ideas the American Psychology-Law Society was established as Division 41 of the American Psychological Association.

As with many of his other writings, most of Münsterberg's publications on forensic psychology were intended more for popular than strictly scientific audiences. Also, in typical Münsterberg fashion, he was able to induce changes in courtroom procedures while also upsetting a large section of the populace. For example, in what has become a series of foundational investigations in group processes, Münsterberg found that when making independent judgments of the number of white dots arranged on a gray board individuals were correct only 52% of the time. However, after the individuals discussed their initial judgments as a group, the group was then correct 78% of the time thus illustrating the usefulness of the jury system (as cited in Moskowitz, 1977). Münsterberg's original studies were conducted using Harvard undergraduates. When he employed Radcliffe students in his studies he found no differences between the initial independent judgments and the final group judgments. As a result, Münsterberg decided that the jury system was satisfactory as long as women were kept out of it. Fortunately, most of the public and legislators chose to listen to his ideas about the usefulness of juries while ignoring or downplaying his ideas about keeping women out of juries.

Clinical Psychology

In 1909, Münsterberg wrote a book called *Psychotherapy*, which described the outcomes and procedures of his various clinical interventions. The book was written for the general physician and was most likely read by the general public as well. Münsterberg saw patients as a clinician in both Germany and the United States, and of the hundreds he saw he never accepted a fee. He met and treated patients in his laboratory and would only accept patients he considered to be of scientific interest. His approach to clinical work was very direct and he absolutely disagreed with others such as Freud, who believed that patients have a subconscious mind which the clinician must uncover (Landy, 1992). Accordingly, Münsterberg and Freud did not agree on therapeutic approaches to the treatment of clinical cases.

Primarily as a result of his medical background, Münsterberg believed that mental illness had a physiological basis and manifested itself in behavioral maladjustment. Thus, his dominant approach to therapy was to impose his will on the patient primarily by employing direct suggestions to encourage the patient to expect to get better. He believed that if he told patients they would get better they would believe this and would indeed get better. In psychology today, many would term this approach as having specific "demand characteristics," meaning that there is an expectation from the researcher or therapist as to how the participant or client will react. The client or participant realizes this expectation and attempts to behave in a manner consistent with the expectation. In addition, Münsterberg assured his patients that they would behave in the manner that was consistent rather than contrary to their own standards of conduct (Moscowitz, 1977).

Industrial/Applied Psychology

Münsterberg may be considered America's first industrial psychologist. In 1913, he wrote *Psychology and Industrial Efficiency*, which dealt with the best way to select new employees as well as increase job satisfaction, productivity, and efficiency. He noted that the best way to accomplish several of these objectives was to hire workers for positions that matched their cognitive and emotional abilities. In order to do so he argued that companies need to use psychological tests and job simulations to ensure the best fit between an employee and any given job. Accordingly, Münsterberg was hired as a consultant by several companies to conduct an array of research focused upon topics such as personnel selection, advertising and marketing, display of products, equipment design, and industrial efficiency.

Münsterberg also conducted research on a wide variety of job occupations including, for example, salesperson, telephone operator, and railroad motormen (Moscowitz, 1977). He was determined to demonstrate that industrial psychology was a scientific discipline. For example, to assess the attention, judgment, and reaction times of railroad workers, Münsterberg devised a laboratory game that simultaneously measured all three constructs in a "real world" situation. He showed the motormen a series of cards that had a set of railroad tracks and various obstacles (e.g., pedestrians and horses) that were moving at various speeds either alongside or toward the railroad trolley. The workers had to identify the objects that were about to cross the tracks of the railroad trolley that they were "driving." The scores obtained by Münsterberg showed high agreement with the company's own ratings of the motormen. Thus, he was able to show not only that industrial psychology could be studied scientifically but also that laboratory studies could be analogous to real-life situations.

A foundational theme of Münsterberg's work in industrial psychology stressed the importance of assessing work conditions and the psychological conditions of the worker. Specifically, he argued that the motivation of the worker to perform his or her task day after day was at least as important as either the physical work conditions or the fit between worker and job. Most of the industrial topics that Münsterberg was interested in or laid the initial groundwork for are still being examined today. There can truly be no doubt that Hugo Münsterberg was the founder of industrial/organizational psychology. He was not, however, the only psychologist interested in applied aspects of psychology, as the next psychologist we will discuss, Lightner Witmer, is considered to be the first clinical psychologist.

Lightner Witmer: The Beginnings of Clinical Psychology

Although Hugo Münsterberg was an early influence on the field of clinical psychology, Lightner Witmer (1876–1956) founded and coined the term *clinical psychology*. Similar to Münsterberg, Witmer's accomplishments in the field of psychology have been overshadowed by some of his contemporaries (e.g., Sigmund Freud) and although he is the founder of clinical psychology, he is less well remembered than founders of the other specialized disciplines of psychology. Witmer belongs among the functionalists because he believed that psychology should be applied in the campaign to solve real-world problems.

Witmer spent much of his life in and around his native city of Philadelphia. He earned his bachelor's degree in 1888 at the University of Pennsylvania and while teaching at a local preparatory school he took classes in psychology and served as a laboratory assistant for James McKeen Cattell, who was then director of the new psychology laboratory at the University of Pennsylvania. When Cattell left for Columbia, Witmer left for Leipzig and earned his doctorate under Wundt.

Trained as an experimental psychologist, he returned to the University of Pennsylvania as the head of the psychology laboratory. Witmer resumed his laboratory work but gradually his interests shifted and he focused more on his belief that psychology should be applied and practical. The formal founding of clinical psychology occurred when Witmer examined and treated a 14-year-old boy who had been referred to him by the boy's teacher. The teacher informed Witmer that the boy appeared quite intelligent yet he could not learn to read. Witmer worked with this boy, to whom he gave the pseudonym Charles Gilman, and concluded that he had what was later termed dyslexia (McReynolds, 1996). Witmer continued to work with Charles for several years and yielded some perceptible improvements in the boy, thus validating his "clinical" approach.

During the summer of 1896, Witmer offered a three-week course in child psychology and later in the fall wrote "Practical Work in Psychology" for the journal *Pediatrics*. During 1896 it is estimated that he saw an additional twenty-four clients, most between the ages of 3 and 16 years, presenting such symptoms as speech and learning difficulties, chorea, hydrocephalus, and hyperactivity (McReynolds, 1996). In December of the same year, Witmer presented a paper titled "The Organization of Practical Work in Psychology" at the annual American Psychological Association (APA) meetings, which marked the formal introduction of his "psychological clinic" to psychology.

Over the next several years the clinic grew as Witmer further developed his clinical skills. He often consulted with physicians and began using various tests, but often abandoned them as useless in clinical settings. In 1907, Witmer founded *The Psychological Clinic*, a new journal, and in its first edition he provided some history and outlined the new field of "clinical psychology." Following this introduction, Witmer's University of Pennsylvania clinic grew rapidly and became a prototype for clinics around the country, mostly headed by psychologists in university settings.

The clinic, and therefore clinical psychology, began with a relatively narrow focus on children and adolescents. More often than not the children had school-related problems, thus it is easy to see how Witmer is also considered a pioneer in **school psychology** (Fagan, 1996). By 1909, the clinic had grown not only in size but also in the conceptualization of how to treat clients. A team approach had developed where a child was likely to see a physician, a social worker, and either Witmer or one of the psychologists (master's and doctoral level) or graduate students he had trained. The team approach was designed to identify the problem, determine the cause, and make recommendations for treatment. Thus, both physicians and social workers were part of the team, so as to examine both the medical and social history of each client. Although a child was sometimes seen for several sessions the dominant approach was to structure the child's entire environment in a manner that would bring about behavioral change. While Witmer did not develop a theory of therapy like Sigmund Freud or Alfred Adler and while no contemporary psychologists can directly trace their therapeutic roots back to Witmer, his approach is very similar to that employed by many contemporary behaviorists and clinicians. He emphasized the importance of a child's background along with direct observations, and although he developed formal tests (e.g., Witmer Formboard and Witmer Cylinders) he was not quick to use any particular type of test. He believed that each child was an individual with various strengths and weaknesses and the overarching purpose of an individual psychologist of a team was to be helpful.

Lightner Witmer was not the most influential clinical psychologist, but he was the first! Although educated as a laboratory psychologist, he believed that psychology must have a purpose and must help individuals. While most of the individuals he helped were children and adolescents, he did treat adults directly in his clinic and indirectly by providing a model for the development of other psychology clinics (Sexton, 1965). In addition to his contributions to the field of clinical psychology, his approach also influenced other clinics, such as one for vocational counseling (Vocational Guidance Clinic) developed by Morris Viteles (1898–1996), who was also at the University of Pennsylvania (Thompson, 1998). The field of clinical psychology has become the most widely recognized area of psychology and has thus taken on a life of its own. Witmer's contributions to psychology as a whole were clearly influenced by the pragmatic, functional, and applied beliefs of the functional school of psychology.

A FUNCTIONAL FUTURE

Many of the specialty areas of psychology that were founded or popularized by those in the functional school of psychology, including industrial/organizational, clinical, counseling, and school psychology, are still developing and prospering today. In addition, new subdisciplines that can trace their ancestry back to those related to functionalism, such as evolutionary psychology, are gaining recognition within the field of psychology. Functionalism was more a state of mind than a school of psychology and it can be said that any psychologist who is interested in focusing on the organism, adaptation to the environment, or applying his or her knowledge beyond the laboratory is either a functional psychologist or interested in functional ideas.

The functional school of thought within psychology opened the field to new methods of inquiry, new topics to examine, new participants to work with, and a new, more adaptive and applied focus. While the formal school no longer exists, the ideas and methods developed are still used today. Examples of functional topics or disciplines include global and indigenous psychologies (see chapters 1 and 18), positive psychology, creativity, health psychology, prevention, population control, war, famine, environmental psychology, and a plethora of other topics and disciplines.

■ Summary

We began this chapter by focusing on the foundational idea that organisms not only react to but also act on their environment and in so doing functionally adapt to their dynamic environments. We first examined the work of Charles Darwin, who developed his theory of evolution after returning from an epochal trip during which he discovered that organisms of the same species had developed different biological capacities in response to the demands of their local environments. This line of thinking led to the investigation of individual differences personified by the work of Darwin's cousin, Sir Francis Galton. Herbert Spencer then popularized the notion of Social Darwinism in the United States by arguing that successful individuals, as indicated by social standing, wealth, and professional status, had adapted more readily to their environments and, therefore, must be encouraged to have multiple offspring.

Evolutionary theory provided a foundation for psychologists, mostly those born and raised in the United States, to move beyond examining only the contents of consciousness in a restrictive laboratory environment. One of the forerunners of functionalism in America, William James, believed that psychology had the ability and the responsibility to examine issues that were of immediate interest among the general public. Granville Stanley Hall worked to make psychology a scientific profession and stressed the importance of scientific inquiry over all other methods of inquiry.

We next focused on the founding of the school of functionalism, which began at the University of Chicago with John Dewey. Dewey provided the initial conceptual break with structuralism by stressing that a psychology focused solely on the contents of consciousness without considering the adaptive capacities of the organism was an incomplete psychology. James Rowland Angell extended the original ideas of functionalism and promoted its foundational themes in his 1906 presidential address to the American Psychological Association. In his address, Angell emphasized the three functional themes of studying mental operations, not contents; casting consciousness as adaptive for an organism; and appreciation of the entire organism and the interactive relationship to the environment. Harvey A. Carr further developed functionalism as a mature school of psychology and is best remembered as a gifted writer and teacher.

We then moved to Columbia University, and described the work of James McKeen Cattell, who believed that quantifiable results yielded valid psychological knowledge. Edward Lee Thorndike stressed the systematic examination of animal behavior over the anecdotal accounts that once populated the field and conducted foundational studies of animal learning under controlled laboratory conditions. Robert Sessions Woodworth promoted the importance of including the organism in the S-O-R model of psychology and not limiting the model to a simple stimulus-response or S-R model of psychology.

Hugo Münsterberg had the keen ability to take psychology to the public. He wrote for both scientific and general audiences and also founded both forensic and industrial psychology while advancing the field of clinical psychology. We next examined the contributions of Lightner Witmer, who coined the term *clinical psychology*.

■ Chapter 9—Functionalism

Discussion Questions

- ■ Why have subdisciplines such as clinical, industrial/organizational, forensic, and comparative psychology prospered in the United States?
- ■ What is the significance of the bell curve in defining the term *normal*?
- ■ What is the relationship between functionalism and structuralism?
- ■ What is the functional approach to psychology? Describe some examples.
- ■ What was the first contribution to the theory of individualism?
- ■ What are two examples of contemporary issues that illustrate the continued legacy of functional thought in contemporary psychology?

Behaviorism

CHAPTER OVERVIEW

Learning theory is often thought of as the backbone of psychology and on a broader basis, it is life itself. From the day life begins to the day that it ends, learning never ceases. There is no doubt that humans and many other varieties of organisms learn to walk or locomote, think, and interact with each other although there continues to this day a controversy concerning the model or theory of learning that explains fully the mechanism(s) of learning.

We begin our treatment of learning with a brief look at the roots of behaviorism and three overarching models employed in the study of learning, namely, stimulus-response (S-R), stimulus-organism-response (S-O-R), and response (R). All of the theories of learning presented in this chapter develop one of the above models of learning as determined by the focal mechanism identified as primarily responsible for the production of learned behavior.

We continue our inquiry into learning theory with a discussion of John B. Watson (1878–1951) who, in 1913, proclaimed that psychology is a division of the natural sciences in which objective study rules over earlier subjective methods of study in psychology, especially introspection or verbal self-reports of the contents of consciousness as championed by Wilhelm Wundt (1832–1920) and Edward B. Titchener (1886–1927). Watson viewed psychology as the measurement of glandular secretions and muscular movements, which gave rise to behaviors and three fundamental emotions expressed through hereditary pattern reactions. All other emotions arose from these three hereditary pattern reactions, which were mediated by learned experience following the rules of Pavlovian or classical conditioning. Karl Lashley (1890–1958) furthered Watson's strict behaviorist theory by mapping levels and types of learning across the cortex of the brain. Lashley used the paradigms of empiricism and stimulus-response learning to illustrate that specific regions of the brain follow the rules of **mass action** and **equipotentiality** for simple learned tasks, while for complex learned tasks such as **shape discrimination**, very specific parts of the brain mediate responses which in this case were the occipital cortices. Thereafter, we examine basic and applied Pavlovian conditioning, especially regarding contemporary studies of treatment strategies for addictions and anxiety.

In general, Watsonian behaviorism and Pavlovian learning exemplify a S-R model while most of the neobehaviorists that follow embrace a S-O-R model of learning. The neobehaviorists are distinguished by many features including their total commitment to positivism (knowledge derived only from systematic observation and carefully controlled experimentation), and their belief that all psychological phenomena could be studied and understood through scientific inquiry. Although many psychologists fall under this heading, we focus upon Clark Hull (1884–1952), whose interests spanned far beyond neobehaviorism including, for example, systematic studies of concept formation and hypnotism. Hull created a complex mathematical system of learning known as the **hypothetico-deductive theory of behavior**, which incorporated numerous operationally defined bundles of variables into relatively complex equations or general principles with the intent of understanding, predicting, and controlling all behaviors. Hull's work served as a major impetus for numerous studies of animal learning during the period from about 1940 to 1960.

Edward C. Tolman (1886–1959) embraced behaviorism, although he used a different perspective to explain learning as contrasted with some of his contemporaries and predecessors. He thought Watson's view of behaviorism was too mechanistic, which caused him to include cognitive mechanisms such as cognitive maps, thinking, memory, and reward expectations as central concepts to explain human and infrahuman learning. Tolman's cognitive molar (versus Clark Hull's mechanical molecular view of learning) led him to distinguish between place as compared to response learning.

We examine next another behaviorist who studied learning from a point of view much like Tolman's as both subscribed to the learning model of Stimulus-Organism-Response. Orval Hobart Mowrer (1907–1983) believed that learning was mediated by two types of responses, namely, autonomic emotional responses and instrumental behavioral responses. In Mowrer's theory, there are two fundamental emotions, fear and hope, that arise from drive induction and drive reduction, respectively.

The concept of learning, especially operant learning, was addressed at length by Burrhus Fredric Skinner (1904–1990). Operant conditioning differs from Pavlov's classical conditioning most notably because with operant conditioning the response is emitted (action arises in the absence of a specific stimulus) while Pavlov's respondent conditioning requires a specific stimulus to elicit a specific response from the organism.

Martin Seligman's (1942–   ) work is then examined in relationship to biological predisposition to conditioning particularly in terms of learned helplessness and learned optimism. Seligman thought that both of these learned behaviors, as well as others, were conditioned at a faster rate because of the biological predisposition to learn these specific behaviors. In addition, we briefly touch upon Seligman's work on explanatory style and his contributions to the recent emergence of positive psychology stressing a focus upon the scientific study of ordinary human strengths and virtues.

We examine next the research of Albert Bandura (1925–   ) and his foundational work focused upon perceived self-efficacy. Bandura is a major advocate of social learning theory, which generated a great deal of initial attention especially arising from his famous study known as the Bobo Doll Study. In this study, Bandura showed that the modeling of a learned behavior without specific overt response learning during observation of the behaviors to be learned was sufficient for learning, although the addition of reinforcement increased the speed of learning. Bandura's work has a great deal of clinical application through the use of modeling, exploring a client's levels of perceived self-efficacy, and providing the skills for self-regulation, another area he investigated extensively. We conclude this chapter with a brief treatment of positive psychology, which is built in large measure upon the fundamental psychological mechanism of learning.

LEARNING OBJECTIVES

When you finish studying this chapter, you will be prepared to:

- Identify the three overarching paradigms of learning and the specific theories of learning derived from them

- Describe the conflict in psychology between subjective and objective methods of study and how this controversy gave rise to the school of behaviorism

- Distinguish between mass action and equipotentiality and how these concepts contributed to early studies of the mapping of the cerebral cortex

- Understand the benefits of a molar versus a molecular approach to the study of learning and performance and the distinction between "place" (molecular-mechanical model) versus "response" (molar-cognitive model) learning

- Differentiate between drive reduction and drive induction and the effects they exercise upon the acquisition and maintenance of learned behaviors

- Describe the four defining features of neobehaviorism and how they shaped Clark Hull's hypothetic-deductive theory of learning

- Distinguish between respondent (classical) and operant (instrumental) learning

- Identify behaviors that organisms are biologically prepared to learn

- Understand the effect that learning has on self-referential process such as perceived self-efficacy and explanatory style

- Give specific examples of the application of Pavlovian conditioning in clinical settings

- Identify the defining characteristics of positive psychology and how this 21st-century school of psychology is shaping current and future psychological research and interventions

INTRODUCTION

The influence and impact that behaviorism has had and continues to have on the field of psychology is profound and extensive. From the beginning, behaviorists set out to move away from the methodology of introspection and focus primarily upon consciousness toward objective scientific methods, stressing the operational definitions of independent and dependent variables while measuring muscular motions and glandular secretions. The main goal of behaviorism, as outlined by the founder, John B. Watson, was to predict a response when given a stimulus and the stimulus when given a response. After almost sixty years, starting with the 1940s, the systematic behavioral study of human and nonhuman or animal learning began to reach this goal with a new challenge emerging today, namely, to establish a link between findings from laboratory studies and the application of these findings to add value for people from varied cultures around the globe in the domains of education, health, and productive lives.

There were many repercussions within psychology after Watson's formal introduction of behaviorism in 1913 given the temporary derailment and loss of primary emphasis on the systematic study of the content (voluntarism and structuralism) and the utilities of consciousness (functionalism). In short, some said that "behaviorism caused psychology to lose its mind." Psychology was depersonalized because of the focus upon measuring muscular and glandular secretions rather than studying verbal self-reported consciousness. To further increase the knowledge base about learning and adaptability of organisms to a variety of environments or contexts, behaviorists began systematically testing and studying animal behavior in the search for translational applications to understanding human behavior. As a result of the translational applications, scientists began to understand further the functioning of the human brain rather than subjective perceived experiences derived only from the cumbersome and restrictive verbal reports of adult humans.

MODELS OF LEARNING

Multiple models of learning are presented in this chapter, each of which is unique, although some common features can be identified that yield a meaningful grouping or taxonomy of the models of learning. Although there may seem to be a limitless range of explanations of learning, they can be broken down into three types of models or theories. The models of learning revolve around the emphasis upon some combination of three variables, namely, **stimulus, organism**, and **response variables**. The stimulus is the object in the organism's environment that elicits a behavior while the response is an observable behavior. The understanding of learning is not only about the systematic study of the presence and/or absence of a particular stimulus eliciting a particular response (S-R model), but also, according to some, the host of internal cognitive and emotional activities that take place between a stimulus and an observable response, the S-O-R model. Lastly, some investigators have focused only upon the response(s) of the organism (R-model). Thus, the three models of learning include the stimulus-response (S-R), stimulus-organism-response (S-O-R), and response (R) models.

Stimulus-Response (S-R)

This model, as its name implies, is concerned strictly with the stimulus and the subsequent response. The first name that may come to mind when speaking of a stimulus-response model of learning is Ivan P. Pavlov (1849–1936). The S-R model took off with Watson's (1913) *Psychological Review* article in which he threw down the gauntlet by defining the goal of psychology to achieve a model of learning by which "given the response the stimulus can be predicted; given the stimuli the response can be predicted." Watson proclaimed the uselessness of studying consciousness by introspection and he sought to describe higher psychological processes such as thinking as merely a complex chain of stimuli and responses.

Stimulus-Organism-Response (S-O-R)

Many learning psychologists came to view the S-R model of learning as too simplistic, reductionistic, and mechanistic, and argued for a Stimulus-Organism-Response model of learning. They believed that understanding only the stimulus-response relationship is not sufficient because in almost all cases of drive reduction, cognitive and emotional states of the organism intervene between the stimulus and response. The S-O-R model of learning was championed by psychologists such as Hull, Tolman, Mowrer, Seligman, and many practitioners of behavior therapy. Tolman factored into his S-O-R model of learning cognitive processes intersecting between the stimulus and response. Likewise, Mowrer's theory of learning was similar to Tolman's in that he believed that the emotional state of the organism was important and he developed his two-factor theory of learning including emotional and instrumental responses. Seligman's theory of biological predisposition to learning and his studies of explanatory style, learned helplessness, and learned optimism are also presented in the context of a S-O-R model of learning.

Response (R)

A strict response-based model of learning is the most reductionist view of learning. B. F. Skinner promoted this model of learning advocating the primary focus only upon the consequences that follow a response or chain of responses by an organism. Skinner believed strongly that Type R (response) conditioning, also known as operant conditioning, was the dominant type of conditioning or learning over Type S (stimulus) conditioning, also known as classical or Pavlovian conditioning in which a specific stimulus elicits a specific response. Operant conditioning is exemplified, for example, when a food-deprived rat presses a lever to receive a food pellet and the frequency of this emitted action increases as a consequence of the contingent reinforcement. The Skinnerian R-based model of learning aims to predict and control behavior, and excludes the existence of intervening variables such as cognitive processes or emotional states because they contribute to explanatory fictions (hypothetical internal factors that serve as non-causal-explanation of learned behaviors).

MIND, MOTION, AND MAPPING: THE BEGINNING

The mind takes a different form for the behaviorist than it did for the earlier introspective psychologists. Those who employed the introspective model to study consciousness frame the mind to be much like a black box. Accordingly, it was argued that the mysterious contents of mind could be studied only through the verbal reflections and reports derived from detailed descriptions of conscious experiences in response to specific stimuli. This method-ological perspective stands in direct opposition to the behaviorist view of psychology, which embraces objective methodology to study publicly learned behaviors as indexed exclusively by alternate muscular movements and glandular secretions. For the behaviorist, mind does not matter while what matters is the systematic study of behavior or bodies in motion.

Watson saw psychology as a science equivalent to physics because both study scientifically **bodies in motion**, which for psychology were muscular movement and/or glandular secre-tions. If overt behaviors can be explained and quantified by muscular movements and/or glandular secretion, then it follows, according to Watson, that even highly private and personal responses can be studied scientifically and objectively. In effect, an organism, human and/or infrahuman, is nothing more than a bundle of muscular twitches and glandular secretions shaped primarily by the environment and refined further through the mechanism of classical conditioning.

John Broadus Watson (1878–1958)

Watson was born in Greenville, South Carolina to Pickens Butler Watson and Emma Roe, who had visions of her son becoming a Baptist minister. However, luckily for the field of psychology, Watson directed his future goals away from his mother's. Watson earned his undergraduate degree from Furman University without exhibiting much enthusiasm for his studies. Surprisingly, he continued his education at the University of Chicago where he graduated magna cum laude in 1903 with a PhD alongside distinguished peers such as John Dewey and Henry Donaldson.

Watson began his academic career at Johns Hopkins University, and his controversial paper, "Psychology as the Behaviorist Views It," which attacked the current method of intro-spection used in psychology, was published in *Psychological Review* (1913), although further advancement of his work was cut short by the calling of World War I. Upon his return to Johns Hopkins University, Watson's career in academia came to an abrupt end due to his intimate affair with one of his graduate students, Rosalie Rayner, while he was married to Elizabeth Watson, a noted philanthropist and socialite. After leaving Johns Hopkins, Watson began a new career in business that provided him with a large amount of wealth serving as the vice president of the J. Walter Thompson Company. Although Watson's career in academia as an academic-research psychologist was cut short, his contributions to the field as a whole, and specifically to the field of learning as the founder of behaviorism are immeasurable.

Historically, up until Watson's **Behaviorist Doctrine**, as his 1913 paper is often called, psychology focused upon studies of adult human consciousness utilizing the method of introspection that was grounded in the verbal reports of highly trained participants. Watson outlined a series of criticisms of introspection and the focus upon consciousness, and, accordingly, proposed a change of subject matter and method of study for psychology to the behaviorist view of human behavior as bodies in motion studied through the scientific method utilizing objective observations (Watson, 1924). Watson proposed a reductionistic analysis of responses to stimuli. As a reductionist, he asserted that complex behavior patterns such as food preferences, and even thinking as well as almost any learned behavior could arise from classical, respondent, or Pavlovian conditioning reflected by muscular movement and/or glandular secretions. This reductionist view of responses including only muscular movement and/or glandular secretion allowed Watson to systematically study behavior in quantifiable terms. Behavioral analysis could be applied to all animals as well as humans, easily replicated, and yield specific hypotheses not possible from introspective psychology.

Emotions, Thinking, and Instinct

When behaviorism began to win over its opponents there were still many who were hesitant to embrace it because they found it difficult to see the translation of findings derived from animal studies of learning as applicable to improving the quality of life of humans. Although Watson had made claims about the capacity of behaviorism to improve the quality of human life, the animal studies he conducted had yet to link the findings from these studies to enhancement of the well-being of humans. Watson saw an opportunity to sway the skeptics, including university administrators who were reluctant to supply him with adequate funding, and, accordingly, he accepted an invitation to set up a laboratory in Adolf Meyer's clinic at Johns Hopkins University (Buckley, 1989).

At his new laboratory, Watson studied primarily reflexes and basic emotional responses and conditioned emotional responses of infants in search of the fundamental emotional responses that we all have in common. He identified three fundamental unconditioned emotions: **fear, rage**, and **love**. Fear was defined as a response including catching of the breath, clutching of the hand, blinking of the eye, puckering of the lips, and crying with the stimulus being a sudden loud noise and/or loss of support or any abrupt change in a pattern of stimulation (Watson & Morgan, 1917). The second emotion, rage, is a response characterized by crying, screaming, stiffening of the body, and slashing movements of the arms and hands in response to hindering or restricting severely an infant's movement. Love, the third identified emotion, is smiling, gurgling, and/or cooing resulting from gently stroking or rocking an infant. These three emotions were observed in newborn infants while studies with slightly older persons made plain that there was a much wider range of experienced emotions. Watson conducted the famous **Little Albert Study** in an attempt to understand the expanding range of emotions associated with increased age. The subject of Watson's study, Albert B., was a good candidate for this particular study because he was reared from birth in a "stable environment" allowing a clean pallet, if you will, for conditioning, which culminated in the fundamental finding that classical or Pavlovian conditioning was the process by which previously neutral stimuli could give rise to additional emotions.

The Little Albert Study as well as the balance of Watson's work rested on the presumption that psychology exists without attention to subjective mental events and only muscular movements and/or glandular secretions verified through objective observation are the true subject matter of psychology. This presumption could pose a problem in explaining the phenomenon of thinking, something that is inherently intangible and mental; however, Watson even had an explanation for thinking. He conceptualized both speech and thought as forming through the association of thought patterns resulting from each experience over a lifespan (Watson, 1924). When one learns to speak he or she learns the associated muscular habits ranging from the larynx to the rest of the body (e.g., hands, shoulders, tongue, facial muscles, and throat). To further illustrate the view that thinking and speech are paired with muscular movements, he pointed out that the young, deaf, and speechless use bodily motions and talking to themselves when executing thinking patterns and that there are bodily movements such as the shrug of the shoulders that can replace words themselves. Watson then believed that eventually overt speech or movement of the lips and other laryngeal muscular movements became implicit or not readily observable, with thinking still taking place in the absence of overt movement of the human body.

Instinct, as well as emotion and thought, was a topic to which Watson paid attention over the years. To illustrate his changing views concerning the existence of instincts, Watson redefined an instinct as a hereditary pattern reaction composed primarily of movements of the striped muscle. He observed that animals have visibly identifiable instincts; however, human instincts are not as easily defined. Human habit quickly becomes the director of actions and it is in this way that instincts and emotions are similar in that both are hereditary modes of actions.

Watson was a determinist who interpreted all behavior in physical terms, that is, that behavior is essentially bodies in motion, in contrast to William McDougall's view that instincts were key to understanding human behavior. McDougal (1871–1938), an English psychologist who came to the United States in 1920, believed that all human behavior arose from innate tendencies of thought or action. This instinctual theory, as presented in his book titled *An Introduction to Social Psychology*, directly opposed Watson's objective and scientific view of behaviorism (McDougall, 1908). The two different explanations of behaviorism continued to develop independently until the two men were asked to discuss their differences in a public debate. The Psychology Club of Washington, DC, brought the two men together on February 5, 1924, to debate their differences (Watson & McDougall, 1929). The debate, which occurred at a time when there were only 464 members of the APA, attracted 1,000 persons and when it was all said and done the judges sided with McDougall. The judges decided in favor of McDougall's position because they focused upon the negative social consequences associated with Watson's views that people are not responsible for their actions, but rather that they are determined by the environment. Thus, Watson argued that criminals should not be punished but reconditioned, making plain a shift of control from the individual to the environment with learning identified as the most important psychological process to shape and explain away behavior, including criminal behavior. The social costs affiliated with Watson's behaviorism presented yet another challenge to the widespread acceptance of behaviorism, especially given the switch from assigning the responsibility for behaviors from the individual to the social developmental environment.

Karl Lashley (1890–1958)

Lashley, a psychologist who earned his doctorate from Johns Hopkins in 1914 and served as the APA president in 1929, spent the majority of his career between the Yerkes Laboratory of Primate Biology at Orange Park, Florida, and Harvard University studying the relationship between brain functioning and behavior. More specifically, he studied brain localization in rats from a behaviorist perspective. Lashley succeeded in bringing behavioral techniques together with physiological techniques, and used these two techniques to study the effects of cortical ablation or removal on learned behaviors both in mazes and discrimination tasks so as to better understand the acquisition, retention, and reacquisition of learned behaviors.

Mass Action and Equipotentiality

Two main concepts emerged from Lashley's systematic program of research examining the effects of cortical ablation upon leaning in rats, namely, mass action and equipotentiality. Mass action, simply stated, means that the more cortical tissue available the more rapid and accurate specific task learning. Equipotentiality states that learning does not depend on a particular patch of cortical tissue, thus making "all cortical tissue equal" with such equality moderated only by task complexity. Thus, for "simple tasks" any cortical tissue is satisfactory to mediate learning while for "complex tasks," such as language production or speaking, specific cortical localization is critical (e.g., Broca's area for speech production); as task complexity increases, equipotentiality or substitutability of one location of cortex for another particular location decreases. However, almost regardless of task complexity, mass action holds so that the more cortical tissue the faster and more accurate the learning.

Lashley's (1929) work, reported in *Brain Mechanisms and Intelligence*, showed findings focused upon the study of brain localization and maze learning. Three different mazes were created, namely, Mazes I, II, and III, for the study of equipotentiality and mass action (Figure 10-1). He found that there was a positive relationship between the magnitude of cortical removal or injury and learning capacity for mazes of varying task difficulty. For example, he found that the more cerebral cortex removed or injured the lower the learning for all three mazes and especially for the relatively difficult task (Maze III). Although for complex mazes the rate and accuracy of learning was positively related to task difficulty, acquisition as well as retention of learned maze behaviors was not influenced by the locus of cortical lesions for relatively **simpler tasks** (Mazes I and II; Lashley, 1929). Thus, a 50% reduction in the **anterior** portion of the cortex produces the same result as a 50% reduction in the **posterior** cortex for a relatively simple task (Mazes I and II) but not for more complex maze learning tasks only (Maze III). Put simply, the cerebral cortex exhibits mass action for all levels of task complexity and equipotentiality primarily for relatively simple tasks (see Figure 10-2).

The principles of mass action and equipotentiality explain well the neurophysiological components for simple learning tasks yet leave unanswered questions about more specific and **complex tasks**. Accordingly, Lashley set out to identify the limits of equipotentiality for more complex learning tasks such as the acquisition and retention of brightness and shape discrimination compared to maze learning. Lashley first turned to the study of the relationships between brain localization and brightness discrimination. He (1929) found that rats whose occipital cortices were destroyed before they learned a brightness discrimination task

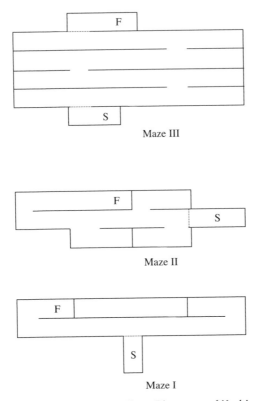

FIGURE 10-1   Floor Diagrams of Karl Lashley's Three Mazes
Maze I: least complex (only one choice point to reach food (F) from start box (S); Maze II: three choice points; and Maze III: most complex, involves eight choice points.

From Lashley, K. S. (1929). *Brain mechanisms and intelligence.* Copyright © 1929. Reprinted by permission of The University of Chicago Press.

showed only a decrement in the speed and accuracy with which they learned the task. However, if a rat had learned brightness discrimination before experiencing cortical insult the original learning was destroyed temporarily so that the rat was able to relearn the task. This is to say that if an insult occurs before learning then the speed of acquisition of the learned behaviors (i.e., brightness discrimination) is reduced although the capacity to learn the brightness discrimination endures. Likewise, if learning occurs after an insult the learned behavior is temporarily lost although the ability to relearn is retained. These findings indicate that the occipital cortex, although involved in the acquisition of brightness discrimination, is not essential to such a learning task. Rather, there are other brain mechanisms (i.e., the superior colliculi) that mediate the acquisition, and retention of brightness discrimination (Lashley, 1929). The findings on brightness discrimination supported Lashley's theory that habits (simple and perhaps complex ones as well) could be relearned utilizing different cortical and subcortical mechanisms following a brain injury.

Lashley found that rats lacking the striate occipital cortex could not learn or acquire form or shape discrimination (i.e., distinguish between a circle or triangle). Unlike with brightness

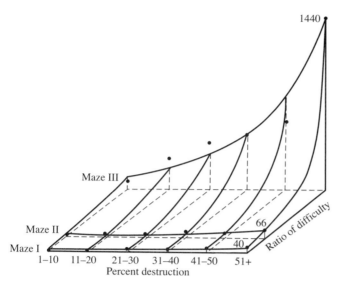

FIGURE 10-2 Karl Lashley's Three-Dimensional Surface Showing the Relationships Among the Percent of Destruction, Ratio Difficulty, and Errors in the Maze

From Lashley, K. S. (1929). *Brain mechanisms and intelligence.* Copyright © 1929. Reprinted by permission of The University of Chicago Press.

discrimination, when the animal learned form or shape discrimination before the cortical lesion was imposed, permanent postoperative amnesia resulted indicating that no amount of retraining could reestablish the learned form discrimination. These findings make plain that there was obviously no other brain mechanism that could mediate form discrimination other than the striate cortex. Thus, equipotentiality did not hold for form discrimination although it did hold for brightness discrimination learning tasks. When partial rather than complete lesions of the striate occipital cortex were employed after discrimination learning then form or shape discrimination was only partially abolished. Thus, unlike the findings for brightness discrimination, not all learned behaviors can always be reacquired after brain injury. Task complexity moderates equipotentiality whereas mass action applies across task complexity in that the larger the cortical insult the slower and less accurate the learning.

PAVLOVIAN OR CLASSICAL CONDITIONING

We suspect that most of our readers have some fundamental understanding of Pavlov's work or classical conditioning; however, there may not be an immediate understanding of how Pavlov supported Watsonian behaviorism. As a young boy growing up in the small Russian town of Ryazan, Ivan P. Pavlov (1849–1936) was greatly influenced by his mother, who was the daughter of a Russian Orthodox priest, his paternal grandfather, who was the village sexton, and his father, who was the parish priest. Pavlov grew up with the intent of following in his family's footsteps by becoming a priest until he read Darwin's (1899/1859) *On the*

Origin of Species and Sechenov's (1965/1866) *Reflexes of the Brain*. These two works influenced him to enroll in the University of St. Petersburg in 1870. Pavlov earned his M.D. in 1883 and his career leapt forward when he was appointed to the chair of pharmacology at the St. Petersburg Military Academy in 1891, where he organized the Institute of Experimental Medicine in St. Petersburg. Thereafter, he was appointed professor of physiology at the University of St. Petersburg in 1895. Pavlov (1902/1897) was awarded the Nobel Prize in physiology for his *Lectures on the Work of the Digestive Glands*, and finally in 1907 was elected a full member of the Russian Academy of Science. (See chapter 16 for further details about I. P. Pavlov).

Basic Pavlovian Conditioning

For his Nobel Prize address, Pavlov, rather than describe his research on the digestive tract, for which he was awarded the prize, focused upon his latest work on what he called **psychical stimuli**. Pavlov came to realize through his studies concerning the pairing of neutral stimuli with feeding that he was working with two types of salivary reflexes, both of which were caused by physiological responses of the nervous system. The foundational physiological response was the unconditioned response (UCR) caused by the natural stimulation of the oral cavity. The second reflex, conditioned responses (CR), could activate areas other than the oral cavities (i.e., eyes, ears, and/or nose; Pavlov, 1955). The next step was to explain the relationship between the two types of responses. He described the paradigm in terms of an unconditioned stimulus (US), a biological stimulus that has the capacity to elicit automatically a reflex activity that yields the UCR, whereas a conditioned stimulus (CS) is a stimulus that was at one time a neutral stimulus but through repeated pairings with the US elicits a CR similar to the UCR. This basic paradigm, as we will see, has been applied to many learning phenomena to explain phenomena such as delayed conditioning, trace conditioning, stimulus conditioning, extinction, spontaneous recovers, disinhibition, stimulus generalization, discrimination, and temperament.

Applied Pavlovian Conditioning

Pavlovian conditioning or classical conditioning is no longer viewed strictly as the pairing of a conditioned stimulus with an unconditioned stimulus, but rather involves circumstances around the learning, that is, the context of the learning and other pertinent variables (Rescorla, 1988). An area of psychology that has undergone major changes as well as flourished as a result of the systematic application of the principles of Pavlovian conditioning is psychotherapy. In fact, the work of Rescorla (1988) and others has extended Pavlovian conditioning so that we now have a better understanding, treatment, and even prevention of pathology, especially in the areas of anxiety disorders and drug addiction.

Recent theories of panic disorder (PD) with and without agoraphobia (fear of going out of the home) have been based in classical conditioning. Pavlovians argue that the conditioning of anxiety and/or panic to interoceptive (i.e., increased heart rate or lightheadedness) and exteroceptive (i.e., physical location) cues upon exposure to an episode of a panic attack can be understood as **emotional conditioning**. Anxiety is the emotional state that prepares one for the next panic, and panic is the emotional state that is designed to aid coping with a trauma in progress. After the exposure to a panic attack, a previous neutral stimulus (now the

CS) such as a place (e.g., a room, in a car, and/or in an airplane) or an interoceptive cue becomes paired with the panic attack (US and UCR) for which anxiety is the CR (Bouton, Mineka, & Barlow, 2001). After the conditioning of the stimulus has occurred, the mere presence of the conditioned stimulus may evoke anxiety and lead to a panic attack that spirals the subject into the development of a panic disorder (PD). The classical conditioning perspective of PD, by taking both the emotions and the contextual cues into consideration, provides an excellent illustration of how the evolution of Pavlovian conditioning has led to broad and useful application of this specific learning paradigm.

Another solid example of the application of Pavlovian conditioning is in the process of understanding drug addiction. The ingestion of a drug constitutes a US and it may be paired with other stimuli such as objects, behaviors, or emotions present at the time of taking the drug (CS). The CR (conditioned response) to the conditioned stimulus is often opposite of the unconditioned response, that is to say that when the ingestion of morphine, which usually elicits a decrease in pain sensitivity, is paired with a CS, the CR is an increase in pain sensitivity (Siegel, 1989). This phenomenon has been illustrated with other drugs such as alcohol and is thought to be the body's compensatory reaction: the body is preparing to neutralize itself against the drug.

The conditioned stimulus (CS) can act as a motivator in instances of drug dependence and panic disorder. In the case of drug dependence, the CS can increase tolerance to the drug through the compensatory nature of the CR. The compensatory CR (e.g., feeling more pain) may also be adversive and motivate the user to take the drug again. In the case of anxiety, the CS may increase the vigor of the instrumental behavior of avoidance of the US (unconditioned stimulus) because fear motivates avoidance behavior. With this understanding, it is possible to alter behaviors to free the client from this vicious cycle. Thus, for example, if increased heart rate is the CS with anxiety it may be possible to free the client from the CR by exposing him or her to the CS under alternative conditions. In this case increased heart rate (CS) is paired with the response of exercise instead of a panic attack.

There are significant implications for classical conditioning in the treatment of pathology using behavioral therapy. For learning to occur it is thought that the CS must supply **new information** about the US; for example, if there is a second CS present that already predicts the US then there will be no new conditioning (Kamin, 1969). This may limit the number of CSs that will elicit anxiety or other CRs. Pavlov also discovered two phenomena that have clinical implications, namely, extinction and counterconditioning. **Extinction** can reduce the CR if the CS is repeatedly presented in the absence of the US after conditioning, and **counterconditioning** can eliminate the effects of the CS by pairing the CS with a significantly different US and UCR. Counterconditioning is the basis of the common clinical tool, systematic desensitization (Wolpe, 1958). Although these forms of behavior therapy illustrate promise in treating persons with psychological disorders such as panic attacks or drug dependence, it is important to remember two points. The first point is that the original learning is not destroyed but only lies dormant, and in or with the correct context or timing there is potential for relapse (Bouton, 2002). The second key point is that the treatment of anxiety disorder can be challenging when identifying the CS because emotional learning can occur without any conscious recollection or awareness of the process, making it difficult for the subject to remember the initial panic attack and the details around the conditioning of the CS (LeDoux, 1996; Ohman, Flykt, & Lundqvist, 2000). Although there are still challenges to be overcome in improving behavioral therapy as a treatment for pathology, Pavlovian conditioning and its potential for enhancing the effectiveness of behavioral therapy can be expected to grow in the future.

NEOBEHAVIORISM

Watson's behaviorism and the S-R model of learning finally established the systematic study of behavior, especially learned behavior, as the subject matter of psychology. Neobehaviorism developed further a coherent set of four key principles to guide the study of learning under the S-O-R model of learning. First, the neobehaviorists believed that data derived from animal learning are applicable to our understanding of human learning, and, second, that an explanatory system to account for all learning data could be developed. Third, neobehaviorists endorsed completely the concepts of operationism, according to which all variables (i.e., independent, intervening, and dependent variables) must be expressed in a manner that could be measured. In effect, the neobehaviorist embraced positivism, according to which all knowledge is based on the systematic study of natural phenomena whose unique properties and relations must be verified unequivocally through empirical science without recourse to metaphysical assumptions or concepts. Finally, like Watson, the neobehaviorist focused on learning as the core of psychology. Many of these principles and future developments in neobehaviorism, which spanned the period from about 1930 to the early 1960s, were grounded in the work of Hull, Tolman, Mowrer, and Skinner.

Clark Hull (1884–1952)

Hull was marked as a man of perseverance from the time he was a young boy growing up in rural New York, as he had to overcome the ravages of typhoid fever and poliomyelitis. He quickly expressed other uses for his perseverance by graduating from the University of Michigan in 1913 with a bachelor's degree and then from the University of Wisconsin at Madison in 1918 with a PhD. He remained in Madison for ten years focusing his research and teaching primarily on aptitude testing before moving to Yale University's Institute of Human Relations. It was at Yale that he pursued in earnest new interests in suggestibility and hypnosis as well as methodological behaviorism.

Hull, while at Yale University, published a total of thirty-two papers and one book on hypnosis. These works described the nature of hypnosis as a state of hypersuggestibility that facilitates the recall of earlier memories more so than the recall of more recent ones, and the posthypnotic state as one in which suggestions are ineffective (Hull, 1933). In addition to describing the nature of hypnosis, Hull went on to describe the susceptibility to hypnosis as normally distributed although it has been assumed that children and women were more susceptible to hypnosis than men. Unfortunately, as a consequence of litigation surrounding an alleged incident of sexual harassment associated with one of his studies of hypnosis, which was settled out of court, Yale University mandated that Hull discontinue his excellent work on hypnosis and focus upon new research interests in psychology. Throughout Hull's tenure at Yale University, his theories, such as the frustration and aggression hypothesis, were applied by the university to a number of internal problems.

Methodology and Learning

Hull, despite the change of research program, had a long-standing commitment to the importance of systematic methodology in psychology. Accordingly, Hull's quantitative skills and their application to behaviorism emerged as a natural transition to the study of learning. Hull's behavioral approach became more and more evident as the years progressed, as reflected clearly in his APA presidential address in 1937, "Mind, Mechanism, Adaptive Behavior," which many refer to as Hull's **Principia**. Sir Isaac Newton (1642–1727) was Hull's hero, and he had all of his graduate students read Newton's *Principia*, which he kept on his desk at all times so that they would understand that his work mirrored Newton's mechanistic theory of the physical world (Newton, 1999/1687). Newtonian theory, translated in terms of behaviorism, stated that human beings are merely machines and the relationships between the variables generating behaviors could be described mathematically. Following his APA presidential address, Hull (1943, 1951) published his *Principles of Behavior* and *Essentials of Behavior*, indicating clearly his intent to pursue the application of his quantitative skills to the field of learning to better understand human behavior. Hull, like his hero Newton, was considered a fundamental force in the science of psychology as reflected by the fact that his work became so well respected that 40% of all experimental papers between 1941 and 1950 in the *Journal of Experimental Psychology* and *Journal of Comparative and Physiological Psychology* made reference to his work and 70% of all articles dealing with learning cited his work (Spence, 1952).

In the style of a true neobehaviorist, Hull agreed with Watson in his reductionist view that when studying behavior there is no need to consider consciousness, purpose, intentionality, or the emotional state of the organism. Instead, an organism is viewed as being in a continuing state of interaction with the environment in which specific biological needs must be met for survival, and when they are not met the organism behaves in a manner to reduce the specific need. Accordingly, from this view of animal and human learning, drive reduction or essentially a reinforcement theory was marked as the key mechanism for explaining all of infrahuman and human learning.

Hypothetico-Deductive Theory of Behavior

Hull developed his hypothetico-deductive system based on Newton's work. This system entailed the development of sophisticated postulates or principles which were then tested, modified if needed, revised, and then the revisions were tested again. This series of forming hypotheses and then testing them through experimental observations was conducted on Hull's set of eighteen postulates, which are mathematical statements about behaviors shaped by the operation of three sets of variables (Hull, 1951). Inasmuch as the postulates could not be directly tested themselves, specific hypotheses that could be tested were developed and from the experimental results the postulates were then modified if necessary as dictated by the data. This hypothetico-deductive theory focused on studies conducted using three major sets of variables, namely, **input or stimulus variables, intervening or organismic variables**, and **response or output variables**. Each of these three variables was operationally defined so that input or stimulus variables are defined as the number of reinforced trials and/or the amount of reward. For the second set of variables, the **intervening variables**, three are presented here. First, **habit strength** ($_SH_R$) is defined as the tendency for **particular**

or specific response and varies directly as a function of the number of reinforced trials of a particular response. Second, **drive** (D) is defined as the number of hours of deprivation (e.g., 24 hours food deprived). Finally, **reaction potential** ($_SE_R$) is defined as the tendency of any response to occur which was a function of $_SH_R$ and D minus any **negative reaction tendencies** ($_SI_R$). In other words, one's reaction potential (the probability of any response) could be mathematically defined as a function of the number of reinforced trials for a particular response ($_SH_R$) combined multiplicatively with level of drive. The final set of variables was the response variables. Hull believed that there were four different measures of output or response variables; **latency** ($_ST_R$), **amplitude** (A), **number of responses to extinction** (N), and **probability** (P). These three sets of variables and their operational definitions allowed Hull to create a hypothetical quantitative connection between intervening variables such that all human and nonhuman behavior could be explained through equations linking the three variables together and, in particular, one equation that we now examine briefly.

Drive Reduction Theory of Learning

Hull believed finally that he could, by means of his hypothetico-deductive system, explain all instances of animal and human learning grounded in the mechanism of drive reduction. For example, Hull's drive reduction theory proposed that the **readiness to respond** for any behavior ($_SE_R$) is a direct function of **habit strength** for a particular behavior ($_SH_R$), an acquired habit or specific learned response, multiplied by the **drive state** of the organism (D), which energizes behavior and transforms response readiness to behavior through a defined number of hours of deprivation.

$$_SE_R = {_SH_R} \times D$$

This equation indicates that habit strength and drive combine multiplicatively to determine reaction potential. According to Hull's model, the pairing of a stimulus with a particular response that leads to positive reinforcement increases habit strength ($_SH_R$), in which the reinforcement serves to reduce drive (e.g., food) but with each pairing drive is reduced while habit strength is increased so that habit strength and drive state are inversely related. Learning then can be defined as an increase in habit strength that is incremental in nature, not abrupt, and mathematically defined by the number of reinforced trials also known as the **learning curve**. Drive reduction theory of learning makes plain that response readiness or tendency for any response is most likely if habit strength and drive are both at heightened levels, while if either the drive or habit strength (also known as learning) are zero then there will be no reaction or expressed behaviors.

Although Hull's work and theory of drive reduction were referenced in a large number of publications at one point in time, many believe that the complexity and number of assumptions required by his hypothetico-deductive theory of behavior limited the widespread adoption of his model.

EDWARD CHACE TOLMAN (1886–1959)

Tolman grew up in Newton, a suburb of Boston, Massachusetts, in a middle-class family. After graduating from Massachusetts Institute of Technology in 1911 with a degree in electrochemistry, he continued his education at Harvard University and eventually earned a PhD in

1915 under the imminent psychologist E. B. Holt (1873–1946). At the start of his career at Harvard University, Tolman became intrigued with Watson's work, although Tolman disagreed with Watson's mechanistic stimulus-response system to account for animal and human learning. Tolman believed that learned behavior is purposeful and goal-directed and can be understood by the operation of **intervening cognitive variables** studied under carefully controlled experiments. Tolman, following his graduation from Harvard, taught at Northwestern University before moving to the University of California at Berkeley where he remained for the balance of his professional career (Crutchfield, 1961).

Fundamental Ideas

Tolman promoted a psychology in the S-O-R model that respected the objective nature of behaviorism while at the same time including cognitive components of thinking, remembering, and goal-directedness as mediators of behavior because he found Watson's mechanismic behaviorism too restrictive and unable to account for some important types of learning such as latent and insight learning. Tolman stressed five main points in his work. First, he studied behavior from a molar perspective. He defined his **molar** perspective as large units of behavior directed toward a goal as opposed to Watson's **molecular** focus upon muscular movements and glandular secretions as the initial engines for learning. Second, Tolman believed behavior was **purposeful**. He argued and later demonstrated that goal-directed behavior of human and infrahumans involves expectancy of a reward which can be operationally defined and measured in laboratory-based studies of learning. Third, Tolman employed the concept of **intervening variables** to demonstrate that learning cannot be attributed exclusively to stimulus-response connections (as Watson proposed) without considering what may be going on inside the organism. Cognitions, expectancies, purposes, hypotheses, and appetite were, for Tolman, all examples of intervening or mediating variables reflecting psychological processes going on within the organism. Thus, he promoted a stimulus-organism-response model to explain learning (S-O-R model). Fourth, Tolman thought that there were two distinctive types of learning, namely, **place** and **response learning**. **Place learners** learn by means of cognitive maps, which are mental representations of the relative position of stimulus objects in their environment, while **response learners** were thought to learn through repetition and reinforcement of specific responses. Finally, Tolman saw behavior as arising from five independent variables. Regardless of which type of learning, place or response, Tolman thought that environmental stimuli (S), physiological drive (P), heredity (H), prior training (T), and age (A) all ultimately contributed to the acquisition and retention of learned behavior (B). He expressed this through a simple equation:

$$B = F (S,P,H,T,A).$$

Theory and Experiments

As previously mentioned, Tolman did not support a strict stimulus-response model of learning that stressed the primacy of the modification of a set of rigid and specific mechanical responses as the responsible mechanism for learning. On the contrary, he argued that **cognitive maps** were created through an overall knowledge of the structure and spatial patterns of elements in the learning environment of the organism. For example, Tolman,

Ritchie, and Kalish (1946a, 1946b) demonstrated in a series of experiments that rats learned faster when utilizing place learning versus response learning. In the prototypical experiment, Tolman created a maze in which the rats started from points S_1 and S_2 while place learners always found food in the **same** place. Now with the response learners regardless of starting from S_1 or S_2 rats found food by **always** turning to their right (Figure 10-3). Tolman and his colleagues found that place learners learned more rapidly than response learners. In 1948, Tolman published his final paper, titled "**Cognitive Maps in Rats and in Men**," describing the application of these findings to human behavior by arguing that environments that are too limited have negative effects upon learning due to the inability of the learner to perceive the entire environment and consequently determine a path to the goal. On the other hand, comprehensive or complex environments are preferred because they also facilitate the creation of complex cognitive maps that connect different place elements in the learning environment. The environment was a key variable in Tolman's concept of cognitive maps; consequently, it may come as no surprise that the concept of cognitive maps has been highly utilized in the field of environmental psychology.

In addition to his systematic studies of learning through cognitive maps, Tolman also studied extensively the impact of **reward expectancy** upon learned behaviors and **latent learning**. Using a T-maze, both Elliott (1928) and Tolman (1932) were able to study objectively the phenomenon of reward expectancy (see Figure 10-4). Tolman believed that reward expectancy was an important intervening variable that had a significant effect on animal (i.e., appetitive bran mash versus aversive sunflower seeds) and human learned behaviors (i.e., expecting a $100 reward versus a $10 reward). Thus, for example, Tolman found that the experimental group of rats that were rewarded with mashed bran for nine consecutive days and then on the tenth day were rewarded with sunflower seeds exhibited disrupted behavior over the following six-day period (number of errors increased on the eleventh and subsequent days) while the control group that received sunflower seeds throughout the entire experiment experienced no disruptive changes in behavior (Figure 10-4). Tolman explained the rats' change of behavior in the experimental group by means of the intervening, mediating, or organismic variable of reward expectancy such that the rats expected a specific appetitive

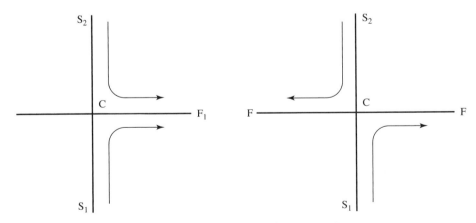

FIGURE 10-3   Mazes for Studying Place and Response Learners

Adapted from Tolman, E. C., Ritchie, R. F., and Kalish, D. (1946a). Studies in spatial learning. II. Place learning versus response learning. *Journal of Experimental Psychology, 26,* 221–229.

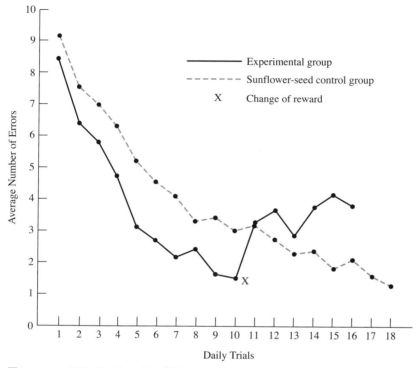

FIGURE 10-4 Results of Tolman's Study of Reward Expectancy

Adapted from Tolman, E. C. (1932). *Purposive behavior in animals and men*. New York: Century. Copyright © 1932 Appleton Century Crofts.

reward and upon changing the reward to one less appealing there was a decremental change in learned behavior.

Latent learning involves reinforcement, and the expression of learning in performance. Latent learning can be defined as hidden learning that is only revealed under specific conditions. In this instance, Tolman and Honzik (1930) employed two groups of rats in which one group received a food reinforcement at the end of running a maze while the other group received no food reinforcement after running the same maze. Over time, the first group improved significantly both their accuracy and time of running the maze and the second group showed modest although not significant improvement on both measures. Such findings would lead one to believe that the first group had learned and the second group had not learned to traverse quickly and smoothly through the maze, although Tolman saw something else in the data. He believed that the second group of rats had learned but had no motivation to perform as there was no reward in the goal box. He decided to test this hypothesis by putting the second group of rats back in the maze with a food reinforcement and to his excitement there was a dramatic decrease in the time to complete running the maze and an increase of the accuracy by the rats who previously had not been reinforced when they had run the maze. These startling results indicated that there had been previous learning by these rats that had not been expressed in performance due to a lack of reinforcement.

Tolman succeeded in crafting an objective behaviorism coupled with cognitive mechanisms that related more closely to everyday learning situations for animals and humans. As a result, he helped psychology "find again its mind," which was temporarily lost during the reign of Watson's revolution focused only on mechanistic behaviorism. The Tolmanian consideration of cognitive mechanisms with methodological behaviorism changed dramatically the field of learning and set the stage for the emergence of many subfields that would later develop into modern psychology, including motivation, neuropsychology, and mathematical theories of learning.

ORVAL HOBART MOWRER (1907–1983)

Mowrer approached the explanation of learning from a different perspective compared to Watson and Tolman. Throughout his study at the University of Missouri, where he earned his PhD in 1932, and during his work with Hull at Yale University, Mowrer came to believe that there was much more to learning than merely the mechanical pairing of stimulus-response units as promoted by Watson, Lashley, and Pavlov. His S-O-R theory, unlike Tolman's, incorporated the emotional state of the organism rather than the cognitive processes of the organism as central to the acquisition and retention of learned behaviors.

Two-Factor Theory of Learning

Mowrer developed a two-factor theory of learning which explained learning as contingent upon reinforcement of instrumental responses mediated by the central nervous system coupled with emotional responses mediated by the autonomic nervous system (Mowrer, 1947).

Mowrer (1960) introduced his emotional learning theory in his book *Learning Theory and Behavior*. Although Mowrer spent a significant portion of his career studying the conditioning of emotions as the foundation of learning, he outlined two types of learning. One type of learning, which Mowrer referred to as **sign learning**, is that which arises when the conditioned stimulus precedes drive induction or drive reduction. In effect, sign learning is classical or Pavlovian conditioning. Sign learning is mediated by the autonomic nervous system and represents an automatic elicited response of the organism to a stimulus. The second type of learning that Mowrer focused upon was **solution learning**, which involves a voluntary or instrumental response leading to a reduction of a drive, for example, to avoid shock (aversive learning) or to seek food (appetitive learning).

Emotional Conditioning

Mowrer's learning theory focused primarily upon the emotional state of the organism during learning and he studied extensively drive induction and reduction. Mowrer believed that there were two basic emotions: **fear** arising from drive induction, and **hope** arising from drive reduction, and it was these two foundational emotional states that were conditioned or linked to specific stimuli and responses, respectively. Drive induction causes an increase in a drive and gives rise to the emotional experience of **fear**, while drive reduction causes a diminution of drive and is associated with the emotional state of **hope**. An example of drive induction would be sitting in the dental chair and the dentist saying, as she starts the drilling, "this will only take a few" seconds; or at an extreme, realizing that you may not have a safe place to sleep the next night if you are unfortunately a homeless person. Drive reduction, on the other hand, is exemplified when the dentist says, "just another few seconds and I am done," or a person finds a secure place to be safe, sleep, and rest. Drive induction promotes fear and the organism will learn instrumental responses to attenuate or reduce this fear, which is an engine for learning. For example, when a stimulus precedes an increase in drive then that stimulus serves as a cue or signal to elicit fear and appropriate avoidance behavior to the unconditioned stimulus (US). Likewise, if a stimulus precedes or signals a decrease in drive then that stimulus serves as a cue to elicit hope and the appropriate instrumental response. Mowrer's study of positive emotions like hope has been examined along with other positive emotions more recently in a field known as "positive psychology." We will discuss in more detail positive psychology and other contemporary S-O-R theorists after a brief look at Skinner's work as a response (R) theorist.

BURRHUS FREDRIC SKINNER (1904–1990)

B. F. Skinner was and still is a foundational force in psychology as a result of his high intelligence, creativity, and hard work. Having grown up in a small town in Pennsylvania during the Progressive era (1940–1950s), his mother instilled in the young Skinner the so-called Protestant ethic or the value of hard work. He went to Hamilton College in New York where he read Watson's *Behaviorism* and Pavlov's *Conditioned Reflexes*, both of which motivated Skinner to move to Cambridge, Massachusetts, where he studied psychology at Harvard University under E. G. Boring and earned his PhD in 1931. Skinner began his professional career at Harvard, moved to the University of Minnesota in 1936, and then was appointed as chair of the psychology department at Indiana University in 1945. After a three-year stay at Indiana he moved back to Harvard (Lattal, 1992). Skinner spent the majority of his career developing a descriptive and atheoretical system of behaviorism influenced greatly by the contributions of such notable scholars as C. Lloyd Morgan, C. Darwin, E. L. Thorndike, I. P. Pavlov, and J. B. Watson. Skinner, reflecting his commitment and love of psychology and hard work, addressed the 1990 annual meeting of the American Psychological Association in Boston, Massachusetts, a few days before his death from leukemia, pleading with his colleagues to move closer to descriptive behaviorism or an R model of learning and away from the misguided field of cognitive psychology (Holland, 1992).

Types of Conditioning

Skinner presented his theory of experimental descriptive behaviorism in his 1938 book *The Behavior of Organisms: An Experimental Analysis,* which described two types of conditioning: **Type S** and **Type R**. Type S conditioning is the same as **Pavlovian** or **classical conditioning** or what he called **respondent conditioning**, according to which the unconditioned stimulus elicits the specific unconditioned response and pairing a neutral stimulus (CS) with the UCS could eventually, after a few pairings, elicit the conditioned response by the CS alone. Skinner thought that this type of conditioning could not explain all behaviors. He thought that most behaviors are emitted by the organism and controlled by the immediate consequence of the response. Type R conditioning, also known as **operant conditioning**, arises when an emitted behavior occurs and the immediate consequences affect the likelihood of the repetition of that behavior. Skinner studied extensively this form of conditioning devoted entirely to the study of responses (R), in direct opposition to the stimulus-organism-response (S-O-R) models advanced by Hull, Tolman, Mowrer, and their students. Skinner's emphasis on responses was apparent in his definition of an operant as a behavior operating on the environment thus producing a given consequence. Skinner was not interested in the study of intervening variables because they left the door open to pseudo-explanations of learned behavior while responses could be observed and measured. He believed that the subjective states of "feeling" could be expressed only through verbal reinforcement contingencies and are thus nothing more than additional behavior (Delprato & Midgley, 1992).

Schedules of Reinforcement

Skinner studied different schedules of reinforcement because they increase or decrease the rate of response, depending upon the particular schedule of reinforcement. He identified two broad categories of reinforcement schedules: **continuous reinforcement** (CRF) and **intermittent reinforcement** (IRF) schedules. CRF is used with contingent reinforcement to condition or acquire a specific operant; while IRF is used to maintain the operant behavior once learned. In CRF, reinforcement always follows the target response to be learned or never follows such response (i.e., extinction). Within the intermittent reinforcement schedules there are two subsets: interval and ratio schedules, which are further divided into two types of schedules of reinforcement. With an **interval schedule** the critical element is **time**. Interval schedules consist of a **fixed interval** schedule that delivers reinforcement at a constant interval of time, say every two minutes; and a **variable interval** schedule that delivers reinforcement aperiodically, but when averaged over the experimental session it is delivered on average at a specific interval of time, say every two minutes. **Ratio schedules**, on the other hand, focus upon **response rate** as the critical variable for delivery of reinforcement rather than the pairing of time, as in the case of interval schedule reinforcement. Ratio schedules consist of a **fixed ratio** that delivers reinforcement at a constant proportion of rate of response, and a **variable ratio** that delivers reinforcement aperiodically, but when averaged over the experimental session it is delivered on average at a specific proportion of rate of response. According to Skinner, the types of reinforcement schedules are critical as they govern the rate of acquisition, maintenance, and extinction of all learned behaviors with fixed schedules employed during the initial acquisition stage of learning and then using intermittent schedules to maintain the newly acquired behavior (Lattal, 1992).

Law of Acquisition

Skinner thought that psychology should have two main goals: the prediction of behavior and the control of behavior through the experimental analysis of behavior. In an effort to achieve this goal he invented the operant chamber for bar pressing with rats (Skinner, 1956), and eventually light pecking by pigeons (Skinner, 1960). He believed that these two inventions, which would later be referred to as the **Skinner Box**, would facilitate progress toward the above two goals. According to Skinner, these learning environments allowed the identification of laws determining first animal and ultimately human learning because they required, for example, relatively easy responses, the target response is not crucial for the organism's survival, and the target response is unambiguous. For example, a rat will on average press a bar about six times per hour in the chamber, which is an ideal base for operant conditioning. Rate of response was the key measurement (dependent variable) in the process of operant conditioning. For example, to document that learning occurred the rate of responding must increase over time while for extinction of the learned behavior the rate of response must approach or equal zero over time. Skinner observed that after a few reinforced trials the rate of operant responding, bar pressing or pecking at an illuminated circular disk, is extremely rapid, which spawned the development of the law of acquisition. This law stated that if the occurrence of an operant is followed by a reinforcing stimulus the rate of response is increased exhibiting learning (Lattal, 1992).

Behavioral Technology

Finally, Skinner's interests turned toward an integration of his earlier love for writing and his then current passion for the study of behavior. As a college student, he aspired to be a writer and sent copies of his work to Robert Frost, receiving much praise for his pieces; however, he changed fields after feeling as though freelance writing was a dead-end career choice. As his interests in learning moved more to applied research he desired to create a technology of behavior based on his extensive findings regarding the impact of reinforcement and especially schedules of reinforcement for modifying behaviors, believing that a society could be engineered thus creating a utopian community. Throughout his career his interests continued to evolve causing him to branch out into studies of language, parenting, education, and military applications of learning principles. However, his most notable works in social engineering focused upon applied behavioral technology and included *Walden Two* and *Beyond Freedom and Dignity* in which he argues for the translation of his behavioral research findings to individual and societal living situations (Skinner, 1948, 1971). He described the present order of living where it is assumed that the person will rationally choose between right and wrong by means of directive laws. However, Skinner argues that because the law stresses individual autonomy and freedom rather than survival of the human species, the laws of our society need to be reoriented to stress the survival of the species rather than focus solely upon the freedom and choices of the individual. The reorientation of the social value system would arise from education thereby creating a society in which basic materialism, arts, and the sciences necessary for a decent life would flourish while factors such as individualism, rampant technology, and individual greed would be reduced by the application of the principles of operant conditioning.

MARTIN SELIGMAN (1942–)

Martin Seligman is a foundational leader in the field of contemporary psychology. His work, like many other modern psychologists, does not fit neatly into the category of neobehaviorism, although it has evolved from it with a S-O-R model of learning. Seligman (1970) found that not all behaviors could be conditioned equally well, through either Pavlovian or operant conditioning, but rather that animals seemed best able to learn using what they were biologically prepared to learn.

Learned Helplessness

Seligman (1975) investigated the types of learning that animals were biologically prepared to learn, one of which he titled **learned helplessness**. In his studies, he observed that many of the lab animals learned that if the consequences of a behavior seemed to be independent of their behaviors then they learned to be helpless in that situation. Thus, for example, as applied to learning in the classroom, if one worked extra hard for a semester by going to every class, every review session, completing all of the assigned readings, and even the supplemental readings, to meet one's goal of earning a 4.0 grade point average (gpa), and at the end of the semester received one's usual 3.2 (gpa), one may learn rather readily that there is probably no systematic connection between the extra behaviors one engaged in to earn a higher grade and one is thus helpless. This type of learning, learned helplessness, has been applied to the study of depression and has yielded effective clinical interventions by minimizing noncontingent reinforcement conditions.

Learned Optimism

On a more positive note, Seligman is also well known for his work on **learned optimism** (Seligman, 1991). He has argued that psychology in recent years is finally turning to the systematic study of positive emotions such as hope, which have been left out of psychology for too long. Seligman has focused upon the study of **explanatory style**, which is an individual's interpretation of events and naturally occurring reinforcement schedules in our daily lives, to explain the origins of learned optimism and pessimism. Learned optimism involves the **partial reinforcement extinction effect** (PREE), a reinforcement schedule related to that of the previously discussed continuous reinforcement (CRF) and partial reinforcement (PRF) schedules. As mentioned before, CRF is particularly useful in the extinction of previously reinforced behaviors of animals. For humans, not only is the reinforcement schedule important in determining human behavior, but also the relationship between the reinforcement schedules and explanatory style. For example, a person who thinks that a naturally occurring reinforcement schedule may be an extinction schedule without any further reinforcement is likely to give up immediately in the absence of reinforcement, while a person who thinks the absence of reinforcement, is temporary continues to respond. The optimist is inclined to take a chance and persist somewhat longer at a task than a pessimist and most likely but not always gains access to reinforcement.

Explanatory Style

Explanatory style as a concept can be broken down into three important components; permanence, pervasiveness, and personalization. The first dimension, **permanence**, states that those who believe that the cause of bad events is permanent give up more easily than those who are more optimistic and believe that the cause of bad events is only temporary. Examples of this include a permanent or pessimistic explanatory style in which one might say, "You are always mad at me" or "I always do poorly in school." Whereas, an optimistic explanatory style might sound like the following, "You get mad at me when I don't respect your space" or "I don't do well in school when my priorities lie elsewhere." Here setbacks or negative outcomes are stated specifically and focus on actions. The take-home message concerning the two types of explanatory style in this category is that if one tends to use statements such as **always** or **never** one most likely has a pessimistic style; whereas if one tends to use statements such as **sometimes** or **lately**, blaming bad events on temporary conditions, one has an optimistic explanatory style.

The second component of explanatory style, **pervasiveness**, is further divided into two dimensions, namely, specific and universal pervasiveness. Pervasiveness in general is concerned with space or range of affected area as opposed to time. Universal explanations of failures tend to yield pessimism, and the person is most likely to give up on everything when something in one area goes awry. However, those persons who construct **specific** explanations of setbacks in one area of their lives and see them as temporary will most likely tend to carry on with the rest of their lives, being challenged or incapacitated in only one area, and will tend to be optimistic.

Personalization, the third and final category of explanatory style, can also be broken down into the dimensions of internal versus external causation of a setback. The pessimistic assessment of blaming oneself (**internalization**) when bad things happen tends to lead to low self-esteem, while the optimistic view of realistically identifying other people or circumstances (**externalization**) for negative events does not lead to a low self-esteem. Imagine the impact of this attribution process practiced regularly, as it means the difference between a self-image of being increasingly worthless, talentless, and unlovable compared to a self-image of enhanced worthiness, talent, and lovableness.

Although personalization controls how one feels about oneself, the other two factors, permanence and pervasiveness, control what one does and how long and across what specific or universal dimensions an explanation of both positive and/or negative events endures. Seligman's view was that helplessness, which in this discussion can be thought of as being similar to pessimism, and optimism are both behaviors with biological predispositions to be learned. Seligman thought that by studying positive concepts, such as hope, in the laboratory, the field of psychology could be expanded to not only focus upon disheartening subjects such as depression and suicide, but also in part upon uplifting features of the human spirit such as hope and love.

ALBERT BANDURA (1925–   )

Professor Albert Bandura, another contemporary S-O-R theorist and foundational psychologist, graduated from the University of Iowa in 1952 with a PhD in clinical psychology. His first and last full-time position, which he received only a year after his graduation, was and is still at Stanford University. Bandura has become noted for his opposition to radical behaviorism, reflected in his emphasis upon cognitive factors as important controlling influences on human behavior. His primary interests focus on the study of the three-way interaction between cognition, behavior, and the environment as the determinants of learned behavior and personality developments.

Social Learning

Bandura has spent the majority of his career studying social learning, which involves observational learning. Social learning combines the theories of cognitive and behavioral psychologies anchored upon the three-way interaction of cognitive processes, the environment, and behavior as the determinants of learning (Bandura, 1986). As a result of the inclusive nature of social learning, it is often considered as the most integrative explanation of learning, and has been applied in clinical settings to address a variety of psychological problems.

Social learning focuses upon the operation of four psychological processes essential for understanding learning, namely, attention, retention, reproduction, and motivation. In the first step, **attention**, an individual notices something in his or her environment and thus focuses on features of some particular behaviors exhibited by the model. This stage can vary depending on the characteristics of the observer, the modeled behavior, and competing stimuli. For example, an individual learning to shoot a basketball may pay attention to the trajectory used by the model or instructor (i.e., shooting right for the hoop or basket or using the backboard). The second step in the process of social learning, according to Bandura, is **retention**, in which an individual remembers the observed modeled behaviors during the attention phase. In this step, imagery and language aid retention by facilitating the recall of mental images and verbal cues associated with the behavior to be learned. For example, the individual who paid attention to the trajectory of a basketball shot in the first step now remembers a mental image and words associated with that basketball shot. **Reproduction** is the third step in Bandura's social learning model, in which an individual produces the behavior that was modeled. This step involves the conversion of a symbolic representation of the modeled behavior into actual performance of that behavior. Thus, after observing and retaining information about the trajectory of the basketball shot the individual produces the behavior and shoots the basketball. The fourth and final step in the social learning process is **motivation**. Here, the environment presents a consequence that changes the probability that the targeted behavior will be emitted again. Consequently, the key determinant to subsequent attempts to continue shooting basketballs (and hopefully making a basket or scoring points) is motivation.

Bandura's research indicates clearly that the process of modeling plays a significant role in the formation of thoughts, feelings, and behaviors. An extremely important feature of Bandura's social learning theory is that learning that arises through actual execution of the target behavior during the acquisition phase of learning can also be learned through modeling. Importantly, Bandura has argued that the exposure to a model performing a target behavior to be learned can yield learning **without** reinforcement. This is a bold position because it directly opposes the principles behind Hullian, Skinnerian, and Pavlovian models of learning, not to mention the fourth step of Bandura's learning theory (i.e., motivation). Bandura does not deny that reinforcement and/or punishment is not required for learning; however, he recognizes that the presence of reinforcement or punishment changes the speed or rate at which the modeled behavior is learned. Bandura's theory of social learning provides a framework for understanding and learning that arises in the absence of explicit rewards or punishment, especially the acquisition of learned behaviors by children.

Bandura's studies of modeling are perhaps his most well-known work (Bandura, 1973). In a series of studies known as the **Bobo doll** studies (inflated doll of approximately four feet high, weighted at the bottom so that when struck the Bobo doll falls over and then returns to the upright position as a result of the weight), Bandura found that children would change their behavior without directly experiencing reinforcement simply by watching others perform a behavior that the observer attends to in a given situation. In these experiments, children were asked to watch a video in which a child behaved aggressively toward a Bobo doll. The participant children were randomly assigned to one of three groups with each group viewing a different ending to a brief video associated with the model acting aggressively toward the doll. The first group saw the child in the video get praised for his aggressive behavior, the second group saw the child in the video get punished for hitting the Bobo doll by having to sit in a corner without any toys, and the third (the control) saw the child receive no response to aggressive behavior toward the Bobo doll. Upon completing the video, the participant children were then allowed to play with toys including the Bobo doll and their behaviors, especially acts of aggression, were recorded. The results indicated that the children who watched the video in which the child was rewarded for aggressive behaviors emitted significantly more acts of aggression than did the children who saw the video where there were no consequences associated with the aggressive behavior.

Self-Efficacy

Bandura extended his social learning theory that arose originally from the Bobo doll study by introducing the concept of perceived self-efficacy (PSE) to the field of psychology (Bandura, 1982). Bandura (1986) not only introduced the concept of PSE but continued to research and extensively analyze the concept as reflected in his important work titled *Social Foundations of Thought and Action* (1986). Perceived self-efficacy is defined by Bandura as a person's judgment of her or his capabilities to execute a specific task.

Self-Regulation

As Bandura's interests changed over time he studied social learning, then perceived self-efficacy, and lastly self-regulation. He proposed that human personality is an interaction between the environment and psychological processes. One such process was self-regulation or the process by which humans are able to control their own behavior (Bandura, 1997). To regulate one's own behavior Bandura outlined three relatively simple steps: **self-observation, judgment**, and **self-response**. The first step, self-observation, is executed through the use of a journal or some other tool that can aid in keeping track of one's behaviors. In the second step, judgment, the behavioral observations made in the first step are compared to standards set by another person, group, or organization. Self-response, the third and final step, requires the individual to give him- or herself a reward if behaviors were at or above the standard and no reward if behavior(s) were below the standard. Bandura's research on self-regulation has been adapted in the clinical setting, especially the use of self-control therapy for smoking cessation. For example, in an attempt to quit smoking, smokers observe their behavior by tracking the number and times a day cigarettes are smoked as well as the triggering events. Then their behavior is measured up against a goal (e.g., two rather than ten cigarettes per day) defined by the individual. Finally, the patients will reward or not reward themselves in response to how well their actual behavior measured up to their goal behavior.

POSITIVE PSYCHOLOGY

Positive psychology also belongs to the S-O-R model of learning because of the presence of the organism as an intervening variable between the stimulus and response. Positive psychology is unique because it focuses upon the systematic study of human strengths and virtues as opposed to human weakness, including negative emotions and behaviors. Thus, positive psychology focuses upon subject matter such as hope, perseverance, future-mindedness, well-being, contentment, optimism, responsibility, and tolerance (Seligman & Csikszentmihalyi, 2000).

The history of the evolution of the unique field of positive psychology began with the changes that the field of psychology experienced shortly after World War II. Although some preliminary work had been conducted in the field before World War II, such as Terman's (1939) work on giftedness and marital happiness (Terman et al., 1938) as well as Jung's work on the search for discovery and the meaning of life (1933), no one thought that the field would move so far away from this type of positive, strength-based, affirmative subject matter. In 1946 the Veterans Administration (now Veteran's Affairs) was established to aid veterans of World War II returning home and it was through this organization that many psychologists realized that they could enjoy full-time employment in the clinical field aiding veterans. Then, in 1947 the National Institute of Mental Health (NIMH) was established, which was more focused on the disease approach rather than the maintenance of already healthy behaviors. One of the major consequences of this development was that psychologists studying these diseases had a stable source of funding through NIMH grants. With this publicity psychologists began flocking to the field of mental disease and pathology with few remaining to study the positive strengths of humans.

Instead of believing that humans lived passive lives directed by instincts and tissue, needs reinforced only through a stimulus-response reinforcement schedule, positive psychologists decided that they would study human strengths and virtues using scientific method designs (Seligman & Csikzentmihalyi, 2000). Accordingly, positive psychology has addressed such issues as happiness, materialism, and flow. For example, positive psychologists argue that happiness cannot be found solely through material possessions or power when we consider the following sociocultural and psychological factors. For example, the first sociocultural factor is the growing disparity between the rich and the poor. As the disparity increases measurements of relative deprivation, that is, how much less of an item (in this case money) one has in comparison to another continues to increase. Relative deprivation remains robust and persists because the culture has all but eliminated other measures of success and well-being. Two psychological factors that explain in large measure why happiness cannot be found in money is that the human mind has a tendency to escalate or raise the bar whenever a goal is reached. In this fashion, one may never reach one's goal because it has been set at an unattainable level thus leading to unhappiness. The second factor that prevents money or material possessions in general from creating true happiness is that the more energy that is invested in acquiring material goods the less energy remains to invest in social, religious, physical health, and other realms of life that are necessary for true happiness (Seligman & Csikzsentmihalyi, 2000). Material goods cannot lead to happiness and ironically after a threshold, which varies according to other variables, the acquisition of material goods does not increase or decrease happiness but is irrelevant.

Flow is another key concept in positive psychology. This concept is understood as an experience that becomes so engrossing and enjoyable that it becomes autotelic (worth doing for its own sake; although there may be no material consequences arising from the activity or experience itself). Unfortunately, no one ever reaches the stage of being truly autotelic, that is, one never possesses flow regardless of what he or she is doing because it is humanly impossible to act in a way that is without regard for any intrinsic or extrinsic motive. With that in mind one can understand happiness not as "**what** one does," but rather "**how** one does it." To have these autotelic-like experiences one must become involved in life; an involvement that is not dependent upon monetary rewards but rather on finding enjoyment and opportunity in social contexts (Seligman & Csikzsentmihalyi, 2000).

■ Summary

Let us review what we have learned in our reading on behaviorism. First, we recognized that learning theory is often thought of as the backbone of psychology and on a broader basis it is life itself. There is no doubt that organisms learn to walk, think, and interact with each other; however, controversy concerning the most complete and accurate model that explains learning still exists. We examined first three models of learning, namely, stimulus-response (S-R), stimulus-organism-response (S-O-R), and response (R) models.

We utilized these models as a framework for examining learning theories beginnings in 1913 with John Watson's introduction of the concept of framing psychology as a division of the natural sciences in which objective study rules over the subjective methods of study such as interospection. Watson viewed psychology as the measurement of glandular secretions and muscular movements. Karl Lashley's work furthered Watson's strict behaviorist theory as discussed in relationship to the mapping of the brain. Pavlov's work was discussed as it carried on the S-R theory of behaviorism set forth by Watson and illustrated in depth how classical conditioning is applied in modern-day settings, specifically in terms of addictions and anxiety disorders.

There followed another group of psychologists who studied learned behaviors, known as the neobehaviorists. The neobehaviorists (C. Hull, E. C. Tolman, and O. H. Mowrer) were distinguished by four main characteristics. We focused first upon Clark Hull, who created a complex mathematical system to understand learning, known as the **Hypothetico-Deductive Theory of Behavior**.

Edward Chace Tolman thought that Watson's view of behaviorism was too mechanistic, which led him to include cognitive process in his theory of learning. Tolman's molar versus molecular view of the learning experience led him to distinguish two types of learning, place and response learning, and focus upon cognitive mechanisms such as reward expectancy, latent learning, and cognitive maps.

We then examined briefly the work of O. H. Mowrer, another neobehaviorist who believed that emotional learning occurred through the two types of responses, namely, instrumental and emotional responses.

We next distinguished between B. F. Skinner's form of **operant conditioning**, which differs from Pavlov's form of **classical conditioning** because the organism's response is emitted in Skinner's paradigm (action is engaged in without specific stimuli) while Pavlov's paradigm requires a stimulus to elicit a response from an organism.

Martin Seligman's work was also addressed in relation to a biological predisposition to conditioning, particularly learned helplessness and learned optimism. In addition to these topics we briefly touched on Seligman's work on explanatory style.

The work of Albert Bandura was then discussed. His interests in perceived self-efficacy and social learning were then described with specific attention to one particular study known as the Bobo Doll study. In this study, Bandura showed that the modeling of a behavior without reinforcement was sufficient for learning, although the presence of reinforcement increased the speed at which learning occurred. Bandura's work has a great deal of clinical application through the use of modeling, exploring a client's levels of perceived self-efficacy, and providing the skills for self-regulation.

Lastly, we reviewed briefly positive psychology. We focused upon the unique subject matter of positive psychology, studying human strengths and virtues such as hope, perseverance, future-mindedness, well-being, contentment, optimism, responsibility, and tolerance. We discussed the influence of sociocultural factors on happiness and the flow or autotelic experience. In summary, happiness is found neither in money, other material possessions, nor what one does; rather, it is found in how one does what one does.

■ Chapter 10—Behaviorism

Discussion Questions

- What are three models of learning and what distinguishes each model?

- How do basic and applied Pavlovian conditioning differ between themselves and Skinnerian conditioning?

- How does O. H. Mowrer's theory of emotional conditioning compare to Pavlov's classical conditioning?

- What is neobehaviorism and who are some of the psychologists who fall in that school of thought?

- Identify the contributions of M. Seligman and A. Bandura to our understanding of learning and personality development.

- Why has psychology historically focused on negative subject matter and what caused the movement toward positive psychology?

CHAPTER 11

Gestalt Psychology

CHAPTER OVERVIEW

This chapter discusses the roots of Gestalt psychology and presents the work of some of the more prominent early Gestalt theorists and the influence of that work on psychology as a whole. Gestalt psychology was another product of psychologists working in Germany during the early 20th century that was then imported and further developed in the United States. The early roots of Gestalt psychology began outside of psychology in the disciplines of philosophy and the natural sciences. Immanuel Kant's (1724–1804) idea that phenomenological experiences are not reducible to an elemental state, Edmund Husserl's (1838–1916) proposal of the existence of two new types of sensation, **space form** and **time form**, and Christian von Ehrenfels' (1859–1932) development of the concept of **Gestaltqualitaten** (or **form qualities**), are described herein as providing the groundwork upon which Gestalt psychology was built. The emergence of work within psychology inspired by some of these early theorists was initially undertaken by researchers and theorists dissatisfied with the structuralists who dominated German psychology during that time period.

The work of Max Wertheimer (1880–1943) is discussed as the first evidence of research within psychology employing Gestalt concepts. His research into the subject of apparent movement, a phenomenon Wertheimer called **phi phenomenon**, is discussed. Wertheimer further influenced the development of Gestalt psychology through his description of the concept of **isomorphism**, and his research leading to the development of the Gestalt Principles of Perceptual Organization.

Two psychologists, Kurt Koffka (1886–1941) and Wolfgang Köhler (1887–1967), collaborated with Wertheimer in his initial research into the phi phenomenon and became, along with Wertheimer, the premier researchers and theorists on Gestalt psychology. The high degree of their influence on Gestalt psychology is evident from the nickname earned by the threesome—the Gestalt Triumvirate.

Each of these three prominent figures in psychology played a slightly different role in Gestalt psychology's development. Wertheimer was the acknowledged founder and inspirational leader, Kurt Koffka popularized Gestalt psychology and was influential in its spread beyond Germany's borders to America's shores. Wolfgang Köhler rounded out this productive threesome as Gestalt psychology's primary theorist and researcher. He expanded the application of Gestalt ideas from the area of perception to learning research in his influential work with apes, described in his text *The Mentality of Apes* (1925). Some of the concepts Köhler developed from this research include **insight learning**, and **Umweg (or detour)** problems.

Another influential Gestalt psychologist discussed in this chapter is Kurt Lewin (1890–1947). Some of Lewin's contributions include his development of **field theory**, in which he incorporated the concept of the life space. Lewin also conducted influential research on the impact of different leadership styles, authoritarian and democratic, on child development, as well as what he called "action research," in which he explored such issues as leadership and group problem solving in an industrial setting.

Other researchers have contributed to the development and expansion of Gestalt psychology and this chapter concludes with a discussion of some of their works, including Kurt Goldstein's (1878–1965) work with brain damaged World War I veterans, Karl Duncker's (1903–1940) work on problem solving providing the basis for our understanding of the concept of functional fixedness, and Hedwig von Restorff's (1906–1962) memory research.

Frederick S. Perls (1893–1970) described a psychotherapeutic approach that he derived from some of the concepts employed in Gestalt psychology. The general goals and concepts of Perls' Gestalt therapy are discussed, although Perls' work is not acknowledged by many Gestalt psychologists as a true extension of Gestalt psychology. While Gestalt psychology's level of influence in Perls' development of Gestalt therapy has been questioned, there is no question concerning the influence Gestalt ideas and concepts have had on psychology as a whole. Despite early beginnings arising from the work of a small group of German psychologists primarily focused on research in perception, Gestalt psychology expanded its influence to such widely diverse areas of study as learning, motivation, child development, and problem solving.

LEARNING OBJECTIVES

When you finish studying this chapter, you will be prepared to:

- Discuss the early roots of Gestalt psychology in philosophy and the natural sciences
- Define and describe the following concepts: elementism, phenomenology, Gestaltqualitaten, space form/time form
- Discuss the significance of Max Wertheimer's research on phi phenomenon
- Describe some of the Gestalt principles of perceptual organization
- Discuss the different roles played by Max Wertheimer, Kurt Koffka, and Wolfgang Köhler in the early development of Gestalt psychology
- Describe the differences between insight learning and trial-and-error learning
- Discuss Kurt Lewin's contributions, including: field theory, action research, and his work on leadership styles and prejudice
- Define functional fixedness and the Von Restorff Effect
- Describe the general principles of Gestalt therapy

INTRODUCTION: THE FIGURE AND THE GROUND

American psychology began, in large measure, as a European import. However, once the seeds of European psychology were planted in American soil this import, fertilized by American ambition and cross-pollinated with an indigenous spirit both utilitarian and pioneering, began to grow in ways that brought American psychology farther away from its European roots. While American psychology was evolving and changing, European psychology itself did not remain stagnant and Germany was one of the intellectual centers of this evolving European psychology during the early years of the 20th century.

Often acknowledged as the birthplace of the scientific psychology that found its way to American shores, German involvement in the growth and development of psychology did not end with the pivotal works of Wilhelm Wundt at the University of Leipzig. Another later contribution to psychology that in many ways was a deep reflection of the German psyche was the development of Gestalt psychology which, ironically, began as a revolution against Wundtian voluntarism and Titchenerian structuralism.

At the root of this revolution were Gestalt psychologists' objections to the Wundtian focus on **elementism**, "the thesis that all psychological facts . . . consist of unrelated inert atoms and that almost the only factors which combine these atoms and thus introduce action are associations" (Köhler, 1959, p. 728). In its place the Gestaltists proposed a different thesis, namely, that "the whole is different from the sum of its parts." Rather than take a Wundtian elementist approach, the Gestalt approach was **phenomenological**; that is, involving the study of meaningful intact experience not analyzed or reduced to elemental parts. For example, an introspective study of the experience of holding a cup of hot coffee in the morning would be broken down, by a structuralist, into individual component parts, such as the sensation of heat, the texture of the cup's outer surface, and the visual experience of the color of the coffee and of the mug. No attempt would be made to integrate these experiences. In contrast, a phenomenologist would attempt to study the experience as an integrated whole. For example, the Gestalt approach would include all of the above sensory elements, as well the phenomenological experience of the feelings of refreshment and even of bracing oneself for the day ahead.

At the helm of this phenomenological revolt were three men who came to be known as the Gestalt Triumvirate: Max Wertheimer, Kurt Koffka, and Wolfgang Köhler. What evolved as a result of their combined efforts was a Gestalt movement that accepted the centrality of some key principles, namely, that psychological awareness cannot be understood simply by breaking experiences down into what appear to be component parts, and that physical and psychological contexts and past experience are important factors in our psychological experiences. While these principles were first identified through studies in visual perception, these and other Gestalt principles were later extended to the areas of problem solving, learning, intra- and interpersonal relationships, and psychotherapy.

Laying the Groundwork for Revolution

Historians have debated the relative importance of the Zeitgeist as opposed to the Great Person as the cause of significant events in history. This debate is particularly relevant to the history of Gestalt psychology. Proponents of "Great Person" historical theories would argue that Max Wertheimer's insight into perceptual mechanisms in 1910 was fundamental to the development of Gestalt theory and that Gestalt psychology would never have developed without his contribution (Seaman, 1984). However, Zeitgeist theorists would disagree, arguing that at the time of Wertheimer's insight, many antecedents had already laid significant groundwork making the development of Gestalt theory inevitable (O'Neil & Landauer, 1966).

One of the earliest contributors to the Gestalt approach to studying psychological phenomena was the German philosopher Immanuel Kant, who reasoned that when we **first perceive a novel object**, we experience mental states that appear to be reducible to the kinds of sensory elements proposed by empiricists and associationists as the building blocks for simple and complex ideas. When past experience with an object is lacking, our experience of that object is reduced to one of raw "elemental" sensations. Kant argued, however, that these phenomenological experiences are not reducible to an elemental state, and furthermore, they are meaningfully organized not through some mechanical associative process, but rather in a priori fashion. The mind, in the process of perceiving, seeks to create a meaningful and organized whole. For Kant, the mind is not the passive recipient of sensations but is instead an active agent coordinating sensations into perceptions. Our experience of the outside world, which Kant called the **noumenal world**, is filtered by our minds to give us the **phenomenal world**. The noumenal world consists of "things-in-themselves" and can never be experienced directly, while the phenomenal world is created by the intuitions and conceptions of our minds and is therefore directly experienced. For example, if we were to ski down a hill and hit a tree our experience of the tree would have been described by Kant as noumenal in nature, as it is obtained through our sensory systems and thus is not one of direct knowledge. We do not "become one with the tree"; instead we experience the tree as something separate from the self, an external object actively constructed by the mind from the various sensory phenomena coupled with our own preexisting mental conceptions.

Kant's concept of perception as an organized unified experience was in opposition to Wundt's later focus on breaking down consciousness into basic elements as practiced in the Wundtian form of introspection. Psychologist Franz Brentano (1838–1917) criticized the Wundtian introspective method of analyzing perceptual awareness into elements such as sensations, feelings, and images, arguing that it was artificial and yielded a derived or constructed version of consciousness. Instead, Brentano favored a more Kantian phenomenological form of introspection with the direct observation of experience as it occurred without further analysis of consciousness into elemental parts.

At the same time that elementism and phenomenology were debated in philosophy and psychology, a similar shift was occurring in the natural sciences, including physics. With the discovery and acceptance of the notion of **fields of force**, that is, regions or spaces crossed by lines of force, such as electricity or magnetism, these fields allowed the exertion of physical forces at a distance and without direct contact between objects or matter. Accordingly, the notion of elementism was being reconsidered and physicists began to think of the physical world in terms of fields and organic wholes.

Ernst Mach (1838–1916), a professor of physics at the University of Prague, made observations concerning perceptions of space and time in his book *The Analysis of Sensations* (1885), which later had a significant impact on the Gestalt movement. In this book, Mach proposed the existence of two new types of sensation—**space form** and **time form**, and argued that these sensations exist independently of their elements. As an example of a space form, a triangle can be made large or small or can be painted any color while still retaining its basic triangular nature. A time form, such as a melody, can be played on different instruments or in different keys yet the melody remains recognizable and distinct. Similarly, Mach observed that our perception of an object does not change regardless of our spatial orientation to it. You can look at a table from the front, from the side, or from above, without changing your unified perception of it as a table.

Christian von Ehrenfels expanded on Mach's ideas, and, in 1890, published a critique of Wundt in which he noted Wundt's failure to include what Ehrenfels considered to be a key element of consciousness in addition to sensations, images, and feelings. Ehrenfels dubbed these elements of consciousness **Gestaltqualitaten (form qualities)** and described them as qualities of experience that cannot be explained in terms of associations of elementary sensations. Ehrenfels considered these form qualities to be new elements created by the mind as it operated on sensory elements, and, therefore, these Gestaltqualitaten are phenomenological as opposed to noumenal in nature. Ehrenfels, like Mach, used a musical melody as an example of such Gestaltqualitaten. According to Ehrenfels, a melody is more than individual notes, and thus can be transposed to different keys or played on different instruments while remaining recognizable. The melody has form quality (Gestaltqualitaten) even when the expression of the melody varies across different musical instruments.

Philosopher Edmund Husserl also played a role in laying the groundwork for Gestalt psychology. While working at the lab of G. E. Müller in Göttingen, Husserl and his contemporaries expanded on an idea popularized by Georg Wilhelm Friedrich Hegel (1770–1831) in his most important work, *The Phenomenology of Mind*. According to Husserl, **phenomenology** is the scientific examination of the data of conscious experience. Although his understanding of phenomenology in fact closely resembled William James' conception of psychology, Husserl did not consider phenomenology as a type of psychology but rather as a separate science altogether (Thorne & Henley, 1997). For Husserl, phenomenology and psychology could be of mutual benefit in that phenomenology offered a methodology for analyzing the data of consciousness and a structure with which to guide such an analysis. In turn, psychology could provide new discoveries and collect the data about the nature of conscious experience that could aid in refining phenomenology (Thorne & Henley, 1997). Despite Husserl's separation of phenomenology and psychology, there are many similarities between his theories and the Gestalt movement leading to the possibility that one may have influenced the other. The direction of this influence, whether phenomenology inspired the Gestalt movement or the reverse, is unclear (Henley, 1988). Against this backdrop of a growing discontent with elementism within psychology as well as other scientific disciplines, most notably physics, Max Wertheimer was inspired to lead a revolution within German psychology.

MAX WERTHEIMER (1880–1943)

Born in Prague to a family of intellectuals and artists, Wertheimer attended local schools until the age of 18 at which time he attended the University of Prague. He was a multitalented young man, gifted in mathematics, philosophy, literature, and music. Although he started at the university as a law major, Wertheimer soon changed his major to philosophy and attended lectures by the aforementioned Christian von Ehrenfels. Later, Wertheimer studied philosophy and psychology at the University of Berlin as a student of Carl Stumpf (1848–1936) and then earned his doctoral degree in 1904 at the University of Würzburg under the direction of Oswald Külpe (1862–1915).

Phi Phenomenon

Between 1904 and 1910, Wertheimer worked at the Universities of Prague, Vienna, and Berlin. His fateful revelation that sparked the formal development of Gestalt psychology came to him while on a vacation trip from Vienna to the German Rhineland. As the story goes, while riding on a train Wertheimer came to a sudden and dramatic realization concerning the perception of **apparent movement** (the phenomenon in which the perception of movement is experienced when no actual physical movement has taken place, e.g., the perception of movement experienced when watching a videotape or an I-Max movie projected upon a stationary screen). Wertheimer's inspiration was that this perceived movement must mean that perception does not necessarily have a one-to-one correspondence with sensory stimulation as assumed by the structuralists. Instead, Wertheimer proposed that perceptions have properties that are not predictable based on the analysis of elemental sensations that comprise them, and that, indeed, the whole of perception may be different from the sum of its sensory parts!

Eager to test his hypothesis, Wertheimer abandoned both the train and his vacation plans! When the train stopped in Frankfurt, Germany, Wertheimer left to purchase a **stroboscope**— an early precursor of the motion picture camera that allowed still images to be projected on a screen in a time sequence giving the figures in the image the compelling and unmistakable appearance of movement. The stroboscope was a popular toy at the time; in fact, Wertheimer purchased his from a toy store in Frankfurt. In his experiments using the stroboscope, Wertheimer did what no one had thought to do before, namely, to ask the question: Why does apparent movement occur? Many people had used the stroboscope before Wertheimer and seen the same apparent movement, yet none had thought to inquire systematically regarding the conditions that give rise to apparent movement. After experimenting with the toy stroboscope in his hotel room, Wertheimer went to the Frankfurt Academy (which later became the University of Frankfurt) where he could conduct more extensive research on the phenomenon of apparent movement.

While researching his hypothesis at Frankfurt, Wertheimer recruited the assistance of two other former graduates of the University of Berlin, Kurt Koffka and Wolfgang Köhler, both of whom were then working in Frankfurt, and the Gestalt Triumvirate was born. Using Koffka, Köhler, and Koffka's wife, Mira, as subjects, Wertheimer conducted a series of experiments. Wertheimer selected the **tachistoscope** over the stroboscope for his experiments because it afforded him the ability to control selectively individual features of a visual stimulus while holding other factors constant. Using the tachistoscope, which was a device that flashed lights on and off for brief intervals, Wertheimer was able to project light through two narrow slits, one vertical and the other tilted 20° to 30° from the vertical. If the light was projected first through one slit and then the other with a relatively long time interval between projections (an inter-stimulus interval, ISI, greater than 200 milliseconds), subjects saw two discrete successive lights appearing first at one slit and then at the other. When the ISI was shortened (to less than 50 milliseconds), the subjects reported seeing two discrete lights shining continuously. When a moderate ISI was utilized (approximately 60 milliseconds), the subjects reported the perception of apparent movement, specifically, the subjects saw **a single line of light which moved back and forth from one slit to the other**. This simple but effective demonstration could not be explained using the logic of the Wundtian elementists because this appreciation of movement where none in fact existed in the raw sensory data could not be broken down into individual elements of consciousness. Given that the lights themselves were always stationary and therefore no movement was provided by the sensory data, Wundtian psychologists would have predicted that introspection of the light stimuli used in this experiment would have produced two successive lines rather than the perceptual experience of one line in continuous motion.

In his 1912 paper titled "Experimental Studies on the Seeing of Motion," Wertheimer gave this perceived movement the name **phi phenomenon**. He reasoned that explaining this phenomenon in elemental terms, as resulting from sensations of movement derived in consciousness from eye movements experienced when watching an object in apparent motion, was futile and unnecessary as the stimulus duration time was below the experience threshold for eye movements. Instead he reasoned that phi phenomenon existed just as perceived or experienced and was not reducible to sensory elements compounded by consciousness. In this same paper, Wertheimer was also the first of the three original Gestaltists to describe the concept of **isomorphism** (which literally means identical shape or form). This principle assumes a direct correspondence between brain processes and mental experiences. This is not to say that brain processes and perception are identical in form, for example, when you see a cube it is not the case that somewhere in your brain a neural pattern develops in the shape of a cube. Gestalt psychologists illustrate the concept of isomorphism using the analogy of a map. The relationship between neural processes and corresponding perceptions is similar to that of a map and the region it depicts. Although the map is not a literal recreation of the countryside, we are able to equate features (such as lakes, rivers, and mountains) on the map with corresponding features in the landscape.

Wertheimer remained at the University of Frankfurt until 1916 and during World War I became a German army captain conducting research for the military on sound localization, which led to the later invention of an early type of sonar. Between 1916 and 1929, Wertheimer reestablished his working relationship with Koffka and Köhler while a **Privatdozent** (the approximate German equivalent of a postdoctoral fellow) at the University of Berlin. While at the University of Berlin, the threesome established the journal *Psychologische Forschung* (*Psychological Research*) which provided the primary publication forum for the developing Gestalt movement.

Wertheimer's career as a psychologist was unfortunately hampered by two key factors, namely, his Jewish heritage and his own perfectionist tendencies. The anti-Semitic atmosphere in Germany at the time made appointment to a full professorship an unlikely achievement for Wertheimer, particularly given the fact that budgetary decisions and professorial appointments at the twenty-one universities in the German Empire were strongly controlled by educational and financial officials of the German government (Ash, 1998). Wertheimer's career was also hampered by his lack of publications. A noted perfectionist, Wertheimer apparently found it very difficult to release manuscripts for publication (Thorne & Henley, 1997, p. 377). Through the influence of non-Jewish friends and supporters in academic circles, Wertheimer finally was appointed to a professorship at the University of Frankfurt in 1929.

Despite this overdue acknowledgment of his research contributions and abilities, Wertheimer found the growing anti-Semitic influence of the Nazi regime increasingly intolerable and finally left Germany in 1933 to seek refuge in the United States. Along with a group of scholars from various fields seeking refuge from Nazi Germany, Wertheimer came to work at the "University in Exile" (later known as the New School for Social Research) in New York City. This institute was founded to create a haven for academic freedom with a mission "to follow the truth wherever it leads, regardless of personal consequences" (Hothersall, 1995, p. 230). During the 1920s and 1930s the New School was responsible for rescuing over 170 scholars, scientists, and their families from fascist Europe.

Gestalt Principles of Perceptual Organization

After completing his initial studies on the subject of apparent movement, Wertheimer expanded his research into perceptual organization, and, in 1923, published a paper summarizing his position that we perceive all objects in much the same manner in which we perceive apparent motion, namely, as unified wholes and not as clusters of mechanically or passively associated elemental sensations. Contrary to the associationists' belief that we learn to form patterns through the building of associations between elemental sensations,

Gestalt theory proposed that perceptual organization occurs spontaneously and that the brain functions as a dynamic system in which all elements present in a given stimulus and its context at a given time interact with each other. Gestalt organizational mechanisms aid in organizing this dynamic system, and are triggered in some cases by stimulus features and in others as inherent neural processes. Elements that are similar or close together tend to be processed in combination while dissimilar elements or elements that are far apart are not. On the basis of research into this premise, Wertheimer delineated several of the basic principles summarized in Figure 11-1 by which the brain organizes sensory elements.

Wertheimer's early contributions to Gestalt theory were heavily focused in the area of perception, which proved both a blessing and a curse for the developing Gestalt movement. Since Gestalt psychology began as a revolt against Wundt and the structuralists with their use of introspection and focus upon perception, it was necessary for proponents of Gestalt psychology to also focus on perception to gain acceptance through the direct refutation of Wundtian introspective methodology. This early focus, however, also meant that Gestalt psychology was unfairly categorized as dealing only with perception.

Productive Thinking

After immigrating to the United States, Wertheimer remained at the New School for Social Research until his death in 1943. His American colleagues' recognition of his significant research is evident from their invitation to him to join the prestigious Society of Experimental Psychologists in 1936. His American career, however, proved stressful for Wertheimer due to the need to adapt to both a new language and a radically different culture.

A great deal of Wertheimer's research in the United States was focused on his interest in education. In addition to his collaboration with John Dewey (1859–1952) on a radio program, Wertheimer was involved in writing a book on productive thinking in which he sought to expand the scope of Gestalt psychology by applying Gestalt principles of learning to creative thinking in humans. Written as a series of case studies, *Productive Thinking* (1982/1945) included cases involving children solving simple geometric problems as well as interviews with Wertheimer's close friend Albert Einstein concerning the more complex thought processes that led Einstein to the development of his famous theory of relativity. In writing these cases, Wertheimer found evidence supporting his theory that learning and problem solving proceed in a top-down or deductive fashion from perception of the whole problem downward to its parts. This approach contradicted the prevailing model, namely, Thorndike's trial-and-error learning in which the whole problem is not necessarily evident to the solver and thus problem solving must proceed from the bottom-up through inductive reasoning. Although *Productive Thinking* became Wertheimer's best-known work, he never knew of its impact, as he died of a coronary embolism on October 12, 1943, in New Rochelle, New York (two years before the book's publication).

Each of the three members of the Gestalt Triumvirate played a slightly different role in the development of Gestalt psychology. Wertheimer is considered the founder and inspirational leader of the Gestalt movement with his program of research into the significance of phi phenomenon and the discovery of organizational principles that operate for perception and learning. However, because of his limited publications, Wertheimer was unable to function as the movement's popularizer, a role that belonged to Kurt Koffka.

Principle	Example
Proximity Elements close together in time or space appear to belong together and tend to be perceived together. Figure (a) is seen as three double columns of circles instead of one large unified collection of circles. **Continuity** Perception tends to follow a direction and to connect elements in a way that makes them appear continuous. In Figure (a) we tend to follow columns of circles from top to bottom in continuous lines.	**(a)** o o o o o o o o o o o o o o o o o o o o o o o o o o o o o o
Similarity Similar parts tend to be seen together as a unified group. In Figure (b) the circles appear to form one group while the dots form another separate group organized in rows instead of columns.	**(b)** o o o o o o • • • • • • o o o o o o • • • • • • o o o o o o
Closure We have a perceptual tendency to fill in the gaps in incomplete figures. In Figure (c) you perceive three squares despite the fact that the figures are incomplete. **Simplicity or Pragnanz** We tend to see figures as being as good as possible given the stimulus conditions. Gestalt psychologists termed this Pragnanz, or "good form." A good Gestalt is symmetrical, simple, and stable and cannot be reduced to a simpler form or made more orderly. The squares in Figure (c) are good Gestalts because they are perceived as both orderly and complete.	**(c)** [] [] []
Figure/ground We tend to organize into two separate components: the object being looked at (the figure) and the background against which it appears (the ground). In Figure (d) the figure and the ground are reversible and you may see either two faces or a vase depending on how your perception is organized.	**(d)**

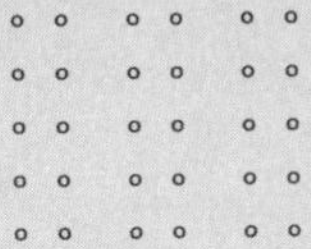

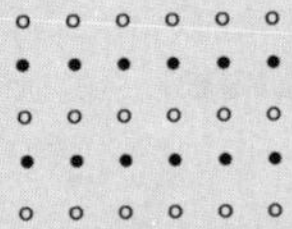

FIGURE 11-1 Gestalt Principles of Perceptual Organization

KURT KOFFKA (1886–1941)

Kurt Koffka was born and educated in Berlin and earned his PhD there in 1909 as a student of Carl Stumpf. In addition to his studies in Berlin, Koffka also spent one year at the University of Edinburgh in Scotland where he developed his strong fluency in English, a skill that later served him well in his efforts to spread Gestalt psychology beyond German borders. Koffka was already working at the University of Frankfurt when Wertheimer arrived in 1910 and invited Koffka to participate as a subject in his research on the phi phenomenon.

Koffka left Frankfurt in 1911 to take a position at the University of Giessen, forty miles from Frankfurt, where he remained until 1924. Putting his English fluency to the test, Koffka then traveled to the United States where he was a visiting professor at Cornell University from 1924 to 1925, and two years later at the University of Wisconsin-Madison. Eventually, he accepted a position at Smith College in Holyoke, Massachusetts, where he remained until his death in 1941.

While at the University of Giessen, Koffka wrote an article for the American journal *Psychological Bulletin*, which introduced American psychologists to the new Gestalt psychology that was taking shape in Germany. Unfortunately, his article, titled "Perception: An Introduction to Gestalt-Theorie" (1922), may have reinforced the misconception that Gestalt psychology focused exclusively on perception (particularly visual perception) and that it had marginal, if any, relevance for other areas such as learning or developmental psychology, which were of great interest to American psychologists and the public as well.

In fact, the scope of Gestalt psychology was far broader than simply the systematic study of visual perception. The primary Gestalt concern was a search to identify a priori or innate mechanisms that might serve to organize and direct **all** mental experiences including learning, thinking, and feeling, in addition to perceptual experience. As Gestalt psychology's most prolific writer, Koffka made great strides, after the publication of his 1922 *Psychological Bulletin* article, in expanding awareness and understanding of the breadth of Gestalt psychology. His major works to that end included a book on child psychology from the Gestalt perspective, *The Growth of the Mind* (1924) and his most ambitious work, *Principles of Gestalt Psychology* (1935). In the latter work, which Koffka dedicated to Wertheimer and Köhler, he sought to apply Gestalt psychology systematically to diverse areas such as perception, learning and memory, social psychology, and personality. Although Koffka intended the text for a lay audience, it never achieved the level of popularity he hoped for and, according to Henle (1987), "was probably read only by professional psychologists." (p. 14).

While Koffka was working to popularize Gestalt psychology both in Germany and in the United States, the third member of the triumvirate, Wolfgang Köhler, was functioning as Gestalt psychology's primary theorist and researcher.

WOLFGANG KÖHLER (1887–1967)

Born in Reval, Estonia, Köhler grew up in northern Germany. Like Wertheimer and Koffka, Köhler attended the University of Berlin, earning his PhD in 1909 under the direction of Carl Stumpf. Interestingly, although Stumpf directed the early academic careers of all three members of the Gestalt triumvirate, none of the three attributed any influence on Stumpf's part to their later development of Gestalt psychology. Indeed, Stumpf himself denied having any influence on the Gestalt school (Thorne & Henley, 1997, p. 376).

In addition to his Berlin studies, Köhler spent some time studying at the Universities of Tübingen and Bonn. He also studied under physicist Max Planck who heavily influenced Köhler's thinking about **Gestalten** (forms or patterns). After earning his PhD, Köhler went to work with Koffka at the University of Frankfurt where his 1910 reunion with Max Wertheimer led to his involvement in Wertheimer's phi phenomenon research.

The Mentality of Apes

In 1913, Köhler's career took an interesting turn when he accepted the invitation of the Prussian Academy of Science to head an anthropoid research station on Tenerife, one of the Canary Islands off the northwest coast of Africa. Six months after Köhler's arrival on the island, World War I began and he was reportedly unable to leave the island. A controversial theory proposed by psychologist Ronald Ley (1990), and challenged by historians and Gestalt psychologists alike, suggests that Köhler's assignment on Tenerife involved more than the supervision of anthropoid research and that Köhler was also engaged in espionage activities for the German government. Ley (1990), based on archival research and interviews, charged that Köhler concealed a radio transmitter on the top floor of his home, which he used to broadcast information to the German navy concerning allied naval activities. Ley (1990) published a highly readable account of his search for information about Köhler's alleged espionage activities titled *A Whisper of Espionage*; however, this account builds a case that is primarily based on circumstantial evidence and Ley was unable to find a "smoking gun."

Whether or not he was engaged in espionage, Köhler spent seven years at the research station studying the behavior of chimpanzees assisted by his first wife, Thekla Köhler. The product of that research was his 1917 publication of *Intelligenz prufunge an Menschenaffen* (*Intelligence Tests with Anthropoid Apes*), which was published in English in 1925 as *The Mentality of Apes* (Köhler, 1976/1925). The work became a classic text in psychology.

Just as Wertheimer (1982/1945) challenged trial-and-error learning in his *Productive Thinking*, Köhler raised his own challenges in his research studies described in *The Mentality of Apes*. Thorndike's theory of trial-and-error learning was based on the premise that an animal makes a specific response that is either rewarded or not rewarded and those rewards serve to strengthen the bond between a stimulus and a response. Learning, according to Thorndike, proceeds in a trial-and-error fashion and the subject eventually learns to prefer responses that most reliably lead to a reward. Thorndike formed his theory on the basis of research using animals in puzzle boxes. One of Köhler's main arguments against trial-and-error learning was that the puzzle boxes utilized in Thorndike's experiments made it difficult for the animals to see the whole problem or situation, forcing them to rely on random activity and trial-and-error learning to solve the problem.

Köhler reasoned that this problem situation was artificial and instead tried to create a problem situation for his chimpanzees in which the animals were able to see all of the problem elements but not necessarily the sequence or structure of elements that would lead to a solution. In order to solve the problem, the animal would need to restructure the perceptual field in some way. Put simply, the animal would need to see first the Gestalt, or the relationship between the elements of the situation, that would then yield a solution. Thereafter, the execution of that solution would proceed as a smooth pattern of actions rather than in a discontinuous and extended trial-and-error fashion.

For example, in one study a piece of fruit was placed outside of a cage just beyond the chimpanzee's reach. If a stick was placed near the bars of the cage in front of the fruit it would be easy for the animal to perceive the relationship between the stick and the fruit and the animal would readily use the stick as a tool to bring the fruit within reach. However, if the field were rearranged so that the stick was placed at the back of the cage, the animal would then need to restructure the perceptual field in order to solve the problem. In both cases, **awareness of the solution of the problem preceded the execution of the solution** plainly revealing that learning and problem solving may be more fruitfully cast as cognitive rather than solely behavioral phenomena. Köhler's work can be seen as an early expression of the cognitive movement that swept through all areas of psychology beginning in the late 1950s, and that continues to the present moment.

On the basis of these and similar studies using a variety of problem situations, Köhler derived the concept of **insight learning**, to describe the apparently spontaneous apprehension or understanding of the relationship between stimulus elements in a problem. The animals appeared to make an insightful discovery or to experience a kind of "A-ha moment," which led to a sudden behavioral change that resulted in accomplishing the target task. Köhler concluded that insight learning involved certain characteristics including the fact that it often occurred suddenly, there were no partial solutions to a problem (it was either solved completely or not at all), and that learning did not depend on reinforcement. Unlike Thorndike's trial-and-error learning, reward provided an incentive for learning but learning was not dependent upon this reinforcement. Later research by Birch (1945) indicates that the boundary between insight learning and trial-and-error learning may not be as clearly defined as Köhler originally thought. Instead, in order for insight to occur, subjects must have at least acquired experience and/or skill in one aspect of the problem's solution.

Köhler also created tasks involving what he termed **Umweg** or detour problems. In an Umweg problem situation, the goal is visible but cannot be reached directly so that the animal must make a detour, initially traveling away from a goal in order to obtain it.

Coming to America

In 1920, Köhler returned to Germany where his career progressed rapidly, due in part to the critical acclaim of the high level of scholarship evident in his second book, *Static and Stationary Physical Gestalts* (1920). Despite the fact that Köhler was relatively young by German academic standards, he succeeded G. E. Müller at the University of Göttingen in 1920 and two years later took over Stumpf's coveted position as professor of psychology at the University of Berlin where he remained until 1935.

Described as the exact opposite of the warm and friendly Max Wertheimer, Köhler appeared cold and aloof and apparently experienced some interpersonal difficulties. In the mid-1920s he divorced his wife, marrying his second wife, Lili Köhler, a young Swedish student. After his remarriage, Köhler apparently had little contact with the four children from his first marriage. In addition, his students were quick to note his development of a tremor in his hands, which became noticeably worse whenever Köhler was stressed or annoyed. Indeed, his laboratory assistants were said to have taken care to observe Köhler closely every morning to see how badly his hands were shaking as a way of gauging his mood (Ley, 1990).

Despite the sometimes negative comparisons with Wertheimer, Köhler had distinct advantages over Wertheimer when it came to the advancement of his career. Köhler, not being Jewish, was not hampered by the anti-Semitic leanings of some German political officials who were in control of professorial appointments. In fact, Köhler may have used his influence to help Wertheimer achieve his Frankfurt professorship. When Köhler later immigrated to the United States, his fluency in English meant that he also did not share Wertheimer's difficulty in adjusting to the language barrier presented by his new professional environment.

Köhler made brief forays across the Atlantic, first as a visiting professor at Clark University in 1925, then as William James Lecturer at Harvard in 1934, and as a visiting professor at the University of Chicago in 1935. Yet each time, Köhler returned to his native Germany. A staunch opponent of Nazi political policy who openly condemned the dismissal of Jewish and anti-Nazi professors, Köhler wrote the last anti-Nazi article published in a German newspaper in 1933. Despite his own fears that his action would lead to his immediate arrest, Köhler was in fact not arrested, possibly due to his high position in German academia and the relative newness and subsequent cautiousness of the Nazi regime. His status, however, became increasingly precarious over time and he finally immigrated permanently to the United States in 1935.

Köhler taught at Swarthmore College in Pennsylvania until his retirement in 1958, at which time he moved to New Hampshire where he continued researching and writing at Dartmouth College. Of the members of the Gestalt triumvirate, Köhler had the longest "American" career and as a result garnered the most American recognition for his contributions. In 1947, he received the Warren Medal for his studies of figural after-effects and a general theory of perception. The American Psychological Association (APA) honored Köhler with the Distinguished Scientific Contribution Award in 1956 and elected him president of APA in 1959. His final recognition from the APA, however, arrived too late. Köhler was selected to receive the APA Gold Medal Award in 1967 but, unfortunately, died before he could accept it and the award is not given posthumously.

FROM STRUCTURALISM TO BEHAVIORISM

We have already discussed the origin of Gestalt psychology as a revolt against structuralism. When Gestalt psychologists first made their way to the United States, however, they found themselves operating in a very different environment, one in which Wundtian psychology had already given way to new and different approaches. The behaviorist school presented a new challenge to Gestalt psychology. Again, the issue that concerned proponents of the Gestalt approach was that of reductionistic and elementist qualities that they considered to be equally present in behaviorism and structuralism. Gestalt psychologists were also critical of behaviorism's total rejection of consciousness as an appropriate subject for scientific psychology. As Koffka argued, it was senseless to develop a psychology devoid of consciousness, as the behaviorists proposed, since that would reduce psychology to little more than a collection of animal research studies. Perhaps one Gestalt psychologist whose work most strongly reflected a move away from atomistic thinking was Kurt Lewin, and through this work he expanded Gestalt psychology far beyond the scope of the first three Gestalt psychologists.

KURT LEWIN (1890–1947)

Kurt Lewin was born in Mogilno, in what is now part of Poland, and moved to Berlin in 1905. He was raised in a warm and affectionate middle-class Jewish home and was educated at the universities of Munich, Freiburg, and Berlin, where he completed studies toward his PhD in psychology as a student of Carl Stumpf by 1914. However, Lewin did not actually receive his degree until 1916 due to the outbreak of World War I. While a student at Stumpf's Berlin Psychological Institute, Lewin was intrigued by the potential of a scientific psychology but found the Wundtian approach in the coursework at Berlin to be both irrelevant and dull (Hothersall, 1995). His goal was to develop a more useful and meaningful psychology.

Lewin distinguished himself as a German soldier during World War I and by the time the war ended he had risen through the ranks from private to officer and was awarded the Iron Cross (one of Germany's highest military decorations) before being wounded and hospitalized in 1918. After the war, Lewin returned to the University of Berlin where he was welcomed into the ranks of the Gestalt Triumvirate. While at the University of Berlin, Lewin conducted research on association and motivation and began to develop the system for which he later became famous, namely, field theory.

Field Theory

Field theory, as defined by Lewin, borrowed from physics the concept of fields of force to explain behavior within the context of the individual's total physical and social context. An important concept of Lewin's field theory was that of the **life space**, which Lewin presented as a kind of psychological field encompassing all past, present, and future events that affect an individual. Lewin first described this concept in a paper written in 1917, while he was a soldier on furlough, under the title "The War Landscape." In this paper describing the soldier's experience of war, Lewin referred to the soldier's "life space" and used such terms as boundary, direction, and zone which later became central concepts in his field theory. Seeking a mathematical model to represent his concept of the life space, Lewin used a form of geometry called topology to diagram the life space and to represent symbolically at any given moment an individual's goals and the strategies to achieve them (Figure 11-2).

Lewin incorporated into these "topological maps" arrows or vectors to represent the direction of movement toward a goal, and used valences or weights to quantify the positive or negative value of objects within the life space. For example, objects attractive to the individual would be given a positive valence while objects that were threatening or prevented achievement of a desirable goal carried a negative valence. Lewin reasoned that it was possible to represent all forms of experiences and behaviors with such topological maps thus yielding a powerful tool for describing subjective experiences and associated behaviors relative to psychological forces in a given environment or context.

In the process of expanding his field theory, Lewin was focused sharply upon applied aspects of Gestalt psychology, more so than the three Gestalt founders. Criticizing the work of industrial engineers and industrial/organizational psychologists, who were at that time heavily focused on time and motion studies and increasing efficiency, Lewin argued that work is something more than producing maximum efficiency. Instead, work has "life value" and should be enriched and humanized (Hothersall, 1995).

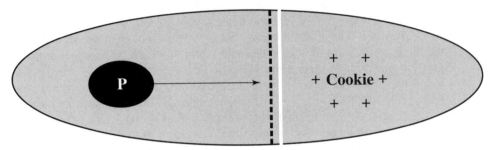

FIGURE 11-2   Life-Space Diagram of a Child Desiring an Out-of-Reach Cookie

Pursuing his own life's work, Lewin was appointed a Privatdozent at the University of Berlin in 1921 where he quickly attracted students with the applied focus of his lectures and research programs. Lewin enjoyed notably close relationships with many of his students, often meeting with them as a group for informal discussions at the Swedish Café across the street from the Berlin Psychological Institute. Included in this group was one young woman who made her own significant contribution to Gestalt psychology, namely, Blyuma Zeigarnik.

The Zeigarnik Effect

During a regular meeting with his students at the Swedish Café, Lewin made an observation that led him to hypothesize that attaining a goal relieves tension. One of the members of the group at the café had called for the bill and their waiter demonstrated exact recall for what everyone had ordered despite the fact that he had not written down any of the orders. Later, Lewin asked the waiter to write down the check again, at which time the waiter responded that he no longer knew what the group had ordered because they had already paid the bill. Lewin reasoned that the unpaid bill (an incomplete task) created psychological tension that was relieved when the bill was paid (and the task completed), creating closure and dissipating the tension, thus erasing a no longer needed memory.

To test Lewin's theory one of his students, Blyuma Zeigarnik, devised a study in which a large number of subjects were given a variety of cognitive and mechanical tasks. The subjects were allowed to complete some of the tasks but not others and then a few hours elapsed before a recall test was administered. Zeigarnik demonstrated that subjects remembered many more of the incomplete rather than the completed tasks. She concluded that a subject, when given a task, feels the need to complete it, and if prevented from doing so this need for completion creates psychological tension, which in turn facilitates recall of the incomplete task. In a further extension of her original classic study, Zeigarnik hypothesized that if the recall test were delayed for longer than two or three hours the state of tension would be decreased and recall of incomplete tasks would likewise decrease. When she tested subjects after waiting a full twenty-four hours after the task period, she indeed found that recall of the interrupted tasks was considerably reduced (Köhler, 1947, p. 304). Zeigarnik completed this research as part of her dissertation, published in 1927 under the title "Uber das Behalten von erledigten und unerledigten Handlungen" ("On the Retention of Completed and Uncompleted Tasks").

Modern television and advertising writers have managed to take clever advantage of this phenomenon, known today as the Zeigarnik Effect. For example, end-of-season cliff-hanger episodes are produced in the hope that tension resulting from lack of closure will compel you to tune in for the next season. Some of you may also recall advertising campaigns in which a series of commercials build on a single story line with each commercial segment ending with a lack of closure, which the advertisers expect will create psychological tension thus compelling viewers to buy the product.

Lewin in America

In addition to the young European students who were flocking to learn more about Lewin's ideas, he also attracted American psychology students studying in Germany. English-speaking psychologists first became acquainted with Lewin's field theory and research following the publication of an article by one such student. In 1929, J. F. Brown published an article in the *Psychological Review* titled "The Methods of Kurt Lewin in the Psychology of Action and Affection," in which Brown outlined Lewin's theories and described experiments performed by Lewin and some of his students. In this article, Brown (1929) emphasized Lewin's focus on total acts or Gestalts, and warned psychologists not to dismiss Lewin simply because he had not discovered any absolute psychological laws. Brown likened Lewin's theories to some of the work done by physicists during the early phase of the development of physics as a science, saying:

> Like all pioneers, rather than dictate finished laws, Lewin's aim has been to indicate directions and open new paths for experiment from which laws must eventually come. (Brown, 1929, p. 220)

Lewin further developed his American following when he presented a paper titled "The Effects of Environmental Forces" at the Ninth International Congress of Psychology at Yale University in 1929. A particularly powerful feature of the presentation was Lewin's use of a brief film of an eighteen-month-old infant that served as an illustration of his concepts. This film, along with Lewin's use of diagrams and illustrations, allowed him to convey his concepts across a language barrier. As social psychologist Gordon Allport, who attended the lecture, later wrote, "to some American psychologists this ingenious film was decisive in forcing a revision of their own theories of the nature of intellectual behavior and of learning" (Allport, 1968, p. 368).

This presentation along with a later article of Lewin's, titled "Environmental Forces in Child Behavior and Development," secured Lewin's reputation in America. He was invited to spend six months as a visiting professor at Stanford University in California. On his way home, Lewin visited former students in Japan and in Russia giving lectures to psychologists in both countries. Riding the Trans-Siberia Express on the final leg of his trip home, the news came of Hitler's rise to political power as Chancellor of Germany. While his status as a decorated World War I veteran protected Lewin from Nazi law mandating the removal of Jewish professors, Lewin was not immune from persecution. He resigned from the University of Berlin in 1933 after making a public statement that he had no desire to teach at a university that would not accept his own children as students.

Seeking assistance from his American colleagues, Lewin's situation came to the attention of Robert Ogden, dean of the School of Education at Cornell University, who presented Lewin's case to Cornell's president, Livingston Farrand. A psychologist, Farrand was also chairman of the Emergency Committee in Aid of Displaced German Scholars and Scientists, established to assist academics who were victims of Nazi persecution (Freeman, 1977). With the support of the Emergency Committee, Ogden offered Lewin a nonrenewable two-year faculty appointment at Cornell in the School of Home Economics rather than the department of psychology.

Lewin left Germany in August 1933, followed by two of his Berlin students, Tamara Dembo and Jerome Frank, who both joined him at Cornell. During his two years at Cornell, Lewin published two major works, *A Dynamic Theory of Personality* with co-authors Fritz and Grace Heider, and *Principles of Topological Psychology* with Donald Adams and Karl Zener. Unfortunately, both books received mixed reviews partly because of the difficulty of the material and partly due to a continued lack of familiarity with Lewin's work on the part of most psychologists in America.

When his two years at Cornell were completed, Lewin attempted to secure financial backing to organize a psychological institute at the Hebrew University of Jerusalem where he hoped to conduct research on Jews immigrating to Palestine as well as on the roots of anti-Semitism and ways to combat it. He was unable to secure adequate funds, and instead found a position at the Child Welfare Research Station at the University of Iowa in Ames, Iowa.

The Child Welfare Research Station

Lewin went to work at the Child Welfare Research Station accompanied by his former student Tamara Dembo. Again, Lewin proved to be very popular with the student body and revived his Berlin tradition of informal discussions in what came to be known as "the Iowa, Tuesday-at-Noon, Hot Air Club." In one important series of experiments, Lewin and his students investigated the effects of authoritarian and democratic leadership styles on the behavior of children (Lippitt, 1939). In this series of experiments, Lewin divided 10-year-old boys into groups who then engaged in various activities while being exposed to different leadership styles, namely, **authoritarian** and **democratic**. In the authoritarian group, the adult leader exercised absolute authority over decision making and imposed these decisions on the group, while in the democratic group the adult leader allowed the children to participate in decision making yielding to the desires of the majority. In each of Lewin's experiments, authoritarian leadership led to increased aggression both in terms of overt acts and more subtle hostility. The boys also evidenced a general preference for democratic leadership. As Lewin later said:

> There have been few experiences for me as impressive as seeing the expression on children's faces during the first day under an autocratic leader. The group that had formerly been friendly, open, cooperative, and full of life, became within a short half-hour a rather apathetic-looking gathering without initiative. The change from autocracy to democracy seemed to take somewhat more time than from democracy to autocracy. Autocracy is imposed on the individual. Democracy he has to learn! (Lewin, quoted by Marrow, 1969, p. 127)

Action Research

Beginning in 1939, Lewin returned to an earlier interest, conducting what he called "action research" in an industrial/organizational setting. Using various techniques including group problem-solving sessions, Lewin worked as a consultant both in industry and later during World War II as part of the American war effort (Marrow, 1969). During the war years, Lewin also founded the Society for the Psychological Study of Social Issues, serving as the society's president from 1942 to 1943. From its inception, the society has been active in conducting research and in producing publications on a variety of social issues including peace, war, poverty, prejudice, and family matters (Perlman, 1986). Many psychologists today consider Kurt Lewin as the founder of social psychology.

As a consequence of working in such varied settings, Lewin realized the restrictive nature of his position in Iowa so he decided to move on. He organized the Research Center for Group Dynamics, which he established on the campus of the Massachusetts Institute of Technology (MIT). One of the most significant achievements of this research group was the development of the concept of "Training or T groups." These T groups were designed to develop effective leadership skills, improve communication techniques, and combat prejudice and destructive attitudes. The techniques developed have been widely used in a variety of educational, counseling, industrial, and clinical settings.

Lewin also became involved in a series of studies on prejudice that he conducted as part of a second research institution, the Commission on Community Interrelations (CCI) for the American Jewish Congress, headquartered in New York City. Under Lewin's leadership, this institute was involved in research that significantly impacted such social problems as racial discrimination in employment and the effects of segregated and integrated housing on racial attitudes. One particular study, which Lewin called "Ways of Handling a Bigot," used role-playing in a series of vignettes presenting different versions of a single incident. In each case, an actor would express a prejudiced or bigoted opinion, which would be answered differently in each vignette. In one such vignette, the bigoted remark would be unanswered while in the second it would receive a quiet response, and in the third vignette the remark would be met with an emotionally fused and angry reply. When an audience was polled regarding their perception of these different ways of handling a bigot, the calm answer was preferred as the best way to respond to the depicted situation 65% of the time, while 80% of the audience stated that they wanted to see the bigot challenged. Rationality rather than emotionality was preferred as the appropriate mode of handling bigotry suggesting that educational strategies could be deployed to manage major racial problems.

Lewin died of a heart attack on February 1, 1947. Edward Tolman gave a memorial address at that year's APA convention in which he said:

> Freud the clinician and Lewin the experimentalist—these are the two men whose names will stand out before all others in the history of our psychological era. For it is their contrasting but complementary insights which first made psychology a science applicable to real human beings and real human society. (Tolman, 1947, in Marrow, 1969, p. ix)

EXPANDING GESTALT'S INFLUENCE

Even if Gestalt psychology never expanded beyond the efforts of Lewin and the influential threesome of Wertheimer, Koffka, and Köhler, their combined efforts alone would have constituted a significant contribution to psychology as a whole. Although Gestalt psychology began with the efforts of the above four influential individuals, it did not end with them as well. Many others have contributed to an expansion of the scope of Gestalt psychology and others have brought ideas from Gestalt psychology into more recent movements such as humanism and cognitive psychology.

For example, Kurt Goldstein (1878–1965) was an editor of *Psychologische Forschung* as well as a pioneer in clinical neuroscience whose work with brain-damaged veterans of World War I expanded our understanding of the relationship between neurology and behavior within the context of a Gestalt framework (Thorne & Henley, 1997). Karl Duncker (1903–1940) was a student of both Wertheimer and Köhler and followed in their footsteps as a Gestalt psychologist with a particular interest in thinking. His 1945 work on problem solving provided the basis for our current understanding of the concept of **functional fixedness**, defined as the opposite of creativity or the inability to use objects to attain a goal in ways that differ from the objects' previously established usage (Thorne & Henley, 1997).

Another Gestalt psychologist who studied under the founders of Gestalt psychology and who followed them to the United States to escape the Nazi regime was Hedwig von Restorff (born in 1901, although the precise date of her death is not known). Her name has become synonymous with the phenomenon she discovered as part of her research, namely, the **Von Restorff Effect**. Von Restorff was involved in memory research with subjects who were asked to learn lists of nonsense syllables with a three-digit number imbedded in the list. Subjects invariably evidenced better recall for the three-digit number than for any of the syllables. Expanding on the concept of the figure–ground relationship, von Restorff hypothesized that the number provided a sharp figure against the background of nonsense syllables (Baddeley, 1990). This phenomenon, in which any stimulus in an information array stands out in some fashion and is recalled better than any other element in the array, is known as the Von Restorff Effect.

More recently, individuals such as Rudolph Arnheim (1904–   ) and Mary Henle (1913–   ) have continued to identify themselves as Gestalt psychologists and to extend the scope of Gestalt psychology. Rudolph Arnheim has written concerning classical Gestalt topics in such articles as "The Trouble with Wholes and Parts" (1986) and has also tried to dispense with misconceptions of Gestalt psychology so as to expand the range of applications of Gestalt principles. A particular area of interest for Arnheim has been in the area of visual perception and his works, including *Visual Thinking* (1969) and *Art and Visual Perception* (1974), helped develop the fields of the psychology of art and of architecture (Thorne & Henley, 1997).

Mary Henle has been one of the primary historians of Gestalt psychology in addition to her contributions to the Gestalt research enterprise. A Professor Emeritus at the New School for Social Research, Henle has compiled several essay collections and written articles on some of the many contributors to the development of Gestalt psychology. One controversial question that Henle has sought to answer concerns the relationship between Gestalt psychology and a later movement that professed to be an extension of Gestalt psychology, namely, the Gestalt therapy approach developed by Frederick S. Perls.

GESTALT THERAPY

In his 1951 book *Gestalt Therapy* (co-authored by Ralph Frank Hefferline and Paul Goodman), Perls first described an approach to psychotherapy that he claimed, in one of his later works, derived its perspective "from a science which is neatly tucked away in our colleges; it comes from an approach called Gestalt psychology" (Perls, 1969, p. 61). In all of his books on his therapeutic approach, Perls made use of terminology and concepts from Gestalt psychology and continued to lay claim to a link with Gestalt psychology; however, he acknowledged that he was never accepted by Gestalt psychologists and admitted to never having actually read any of their books.

In her article analyzing Perls' claim to a relationship between Gestalt therapy and Gestalt psychology, Mary Henle firmly denied any basis for Perls' attributions:

> What Perls has done has been to take a few terms from Gestalt psychology, stretch their meaning beyond recognition, mix them with notions—often unclear and incompatible—from the depth psychologies, existentialism, and common sense, and he has called the whole mixture gestalt therapy. His work has no substantive relation to scientific Gestalt psychology. To use his own language Fritz Perls has done "his thing," whatever it is, it is not Gestalt psychology. (Henle, 1978, p. 31)

Fritz Perls' "thing," whether it may rightly be referred to as an extension of Gestalt psychology or not, does make use of basic Gestalt principles in deriving an understanding of the nature of human beings and of behavior, including the Gestalt principles of closure, projection, and figure/ground, conceptualizing behavior as an integrated whole, which is more than a summation of component behaviors, and viewing behavior within the person's environmental context. Gestalt therapy holds at its core basic assumptions about human nature:

- That a person **is**, rather than **has**, emotions, thoughts, and sensations, all of which function in union giving rise to the whole person
- That a person is an integral part of her or his environment
- That a person behaves **proactively**, not reactively
- That a person is capable of self-awareness, is able to make choices, and is therefore responsible for behavior and capable of self-regulation
- That the fundamental drive for behavior is the need for **self-actualization**
- That a person is neither intrinsically good nor bad
  (Passons, 1975, pp. 12–15)

The goal of Gestalt therapy was to increase self-awareness and to work toward integration of the person into a systemic whole. Metaphorically, it may be said that Gestalt therapy did not, itself, achieve integration with Gestalt psychology as a similar systemic whole.

GESTALT PSYCHOLOGY TODAY

Gestalt psychology has managed to influence a broad selection of areas within psychology including perception, learning, cognitive psychology, personality, social psychology, and motivation. One of Gestalt psychology's most significant contributions has been the sustained fostering of interest in conscious experience as legitimate subject matter for psychological study during the years in which the dominance of behaviorism threatened to remove consciousness entirely from the domain of psychology. Without the Gestalt movement as a counterpoint to behaviorism, the current rejuvenated interest in the areas of humanistic and cognitive psychology would have been less likely. In turn this resurgence of humanism and cognitive psychology has given new relevance to the research of the early Gestalt psychologists such as Wertheimer, Köhler, and Lewin.

Wolfgang Köhler (1959) addressed the question of Gestalt's legacy or place within psychology in his presidential address to the American Psychological Association. In this address, Köhler traced Gestalt psychology from the work of Wertheimer to the then current work of social psychologists Solomon Asch and Fritz Heider. Köhler proposed that the next step would be the gradual disappearance of competing individual schools of psychology such as Gestalt psychology and behaviorism and the emergence of a single unified psychology. Thorne and Henley (1997) have pointed to modern cognitive-behavioral therapies and the latest advances in cognitive science related to learning theory as evidence that Köhler may have been correct in his prediction as these developments exemplify the combining of disparate areas of psychology.

In the course of the development of Gestalt psychology and through its continued influence in a wide variety of areas within psychology it is possible that Gestalt psychology has come close to approaching the vision for the movement that was summarized by Kurt Koffka:

> The hopeless error which the materialists committed was to make an arbitrary discrimination between these three concepts (matter, life, and mind) with regard to their scientific dignity. They accepted one and rejected the two others . . . whereas each of them may, as a conception, contain as much of the ultimate truth as the others . . .
>
> I have implied the kind of solution our psychology (will) have to offer. It cannot ignore the mind-body and the life-nature problem, neither can it accept these three realms of being as separated from each other by impassable chasms. . . . To be truly integrative, we must try to use the contributions of every part for the building of our system. (Koffka, 1935, pp. 11–12)

■ Summary

Gestalt psychology arose from the dissatisfaction of a rising group of young German psychologists with the elementism characteristic of the ideas of the structuralists who dominated psychology during the early 20th century. This chapter discussed some of the ideas of German philosophers and natural scientists, including Immanuel Kant, Ernst Mach, Christian von Ehrenfels, and Edmund Husserl, that formed the philosophical groundwork from which Gestalt psychology arose. These philosophers and theorists contributed the concepts of fields of force and Gestaltqualitaten.

The work of three key figures in psychology who became known as the Gestalt Triumvirate (Max Wertheimer, Kurt Koffka, and Wolfgang Köhler) was discussed. Accordingly, we presented Max Wertheimer's research on phi phenomenon and the Gestalt principles of perceptual organization, Kurt Koffka's efforts to popularize Gestalt psychology, and Wolfgang Köhler's influential research on insight learning.

Kurt Lewin's broad influence brought Gestalt psychology to bear on such diverse areas as social psychology, industrial/organizational psychology, and child development. Some key contributions of Lewin include his development of field theory and T (training) groups and his research on the effects of different leadership styles on child development and his work on prejudice.

Many other individuals have contributed to the expansion of the scope of Gestalt psychology and some of their contributions were also described in this chapter, including, Kurt Goldstein, Karl Duncker, Hedwig von Restorff, Rudolph Arnheim, and Mary Henle. Frederick Perls' Gestalt therapy was also discussed, since Perls presented his psychotherapeutic technique as having been derived from basic principles of Gestalt psychology.

■ Chapter 11—Gestalt Psychology

Discussion Questions

■ Was the development of Gestalt psychology more in keeping with the "Great Person" theory or the "Zeitgeist" theory of history and why?

- According to Kant, what is the difference between the "noumenal world" and the "phenomenal world"?
- What effect did anti-Semitism have on Max Wertheimer's career and why?
- Why did early Gestalt theory focus on the area of perception and what, if any, impact did this focus have on Gestalt psychology's later development?
- How do Wertheimer's and Köhler's theories on learning and problem solving differ from Thorndike's theories of trial-and-error learning?
- What personal experiences or historical events may have contributed to Lewin's theories on the impact of leadership styles on childhood development and his research on prejudice?
- What, if any, relationship exists between Gestalt psychology and Gestalt therapy?

Psychoanalysis

CHAPTER OVERVIEW

In this chapter we break away from our discussion of the more experimentally focused areas of scientific psychology to explore the school of psychoanalysis. Psychoanalysis, the early framework of which was the inspiration and life's work of Sigmund Freud (1865–1939), was influenced by earlier ideas on the nature of psychopathology.

As a means of providing a conceptual framework for a systematic discussion of psychoanalysis, we begin with an overview of the history of attitudes and ideas concerning psychopathology including pre-Hippocratic mystical and surgical approaches to the treatment of pathological behavior. Thereafter, we present Hippocrates' more holistic approach to the treatment of psychopathology. Our discussion of the history of psychopathology then progresses through the Middle Ages and the reemergence of practices reminiscent of pre-Hippocratic belief systems along with a discussion of the emergence of the first mental asylums, which began soon after the Middle Ages. With the institutionalization of the mentally ill there also developed the first systematic study and categorization of types of psychopathological behavior leading to two divergent theoretical views of the etiology of psychopathology, namely, the **psychic** view and the **somatic** view.

Hysteria, a common disorder of the 1800s, characterized by sensory and/or motor disability not attributable to an actual physiological dysfunction, provided a proving ground from which to test out and further develop the conflicting ideas and theories of the psychics and the somatics. The somatic model argued that abnormal behavior had a physical cause such as a brain lesion or impaired nerve function whereas the psychic model argued that mental or psychological causes gave rise to abnormal behavior. Sigmund Freud's theory of psychoanalysis emerged initially from his pursuit of a psychic explanation for the development of hysteric symptoms and developed further into a general theory of personality development.

Many of the more significant ideas and accomplishments of Sigmund Freud are herein described, including, his first published work on hysteria, co-authored by Josef Breuer and titled *Studies on Hysteria*. This inaugural book introduced the technique of having the patient talk about experiences surrounding the onset of symptoms and the patient's resultant experience of catharsis. Other contributions made by Freud in later works include: his proposal of the seduction theory, which attributed the development of neuroses to the experience of childhood sexual abuse; Freud's self-analysis through the technique of dream analysis, which Freud published as *The Interpretation of Dreams*; and his early emphasis on the unconscious mind as a major influence on behavior. Freud expanded psychoanalytic theory from the focus on hysteria and psychoneuroses to a more general behavior theory with his publication of *The Psychopathology of Everyday Life*, which included his conceptualization of a psychosexual theory of human development.

Throughout the course of his professional career, his work and efforts in developing psychoanalysis, and his founding of the Vienna Psychoanalytical Society, Freud emerges as an often uncompromising and controlling individual, personality traits which influenced heavily both his personal and his professional relationships. We discuss the work of some of Freud's followers who further developed psychoanalysis, some of whom proceeded with their own theoretical contributions while maintaining a strict adherence to the theoretical framework established by Freud (such as Sigmund Freud's daughter Anna Freud and Freud's biographer Ernest Jones), while others (including Carl Jung, Alfred Adler, and Karen Horney) developed ideas divergent from those of Sigmund Freud.

Anna Freud and Ernest Jones are discussed further in terms of their influence as Freud's biographers and propagandists in developing the Freud "myth," which in some ways was as influential in the developing course of psychoanalysis as the actual "facts" of Freud's life and work. Carl Jung, who early on was a close disciple of Sigmund Freud, diverged from Freud's theories, particularly regarding the nature of libido, and went on to develop his own theoretical contributions to psychoanalysis including a theory of psychological types as well as his development of what Jung called analytical psychology.

We conclude this chapter with the contributions of another follower of Freud, namely, Alfred Adler (1870–1937), who ultimately diverged from Freud to develop his individual psychology, which included the concept of the inferiority complex. Adler's individual psychology, unlike Freudian psychoanalysis, de-emphasized the unconscious mind and instead focused on the conscious and on the role of social urges in determining human behavior.

LEARNING OBJECTIVES

When you finish studying this chapter, you will be prepared to:

- Describe early attitudes and ideas concerning psychopathology
- Describe and contrast the psychic and somatic models of psychopathology
- Identify three key differences between psychoanalysis and other schools of psychology
- Discuss the theories and contributions of Sigmund Freud to the development of psychoanalysis
- Discuss the influence of the work and ideas of Sigmund Freud on popular culture
- Discuss the roles of Anna Freud and Ernest Jones in influencing the developmental course of psychoanalysis
- Compare and contrast the ideas of Sigmund Freud with those of Carl Jung, particularly regarding libido, personality structure, and the unconscious mind
- Compare and contrast the ideas of Sigmund Freud with those of Alfred Adler, particularly with regard to their ideas concerning the importance of the unconscious mind

INTRODUCTION

Psychoanalysis differs in several important ways from the other schools of psychology discussed previously in this text. These schools of psychology arose within universities with the emphasis upon scientific practices including the centrality of laboratory- and field-based research. In contrast, psychoanalysis developed and continues to exist primarily in the clinical setting with some ties to academia, although not closely bound. Another key difference between psychoanalysis and other schools of psychology is their primary focus.

Previously described schools of psychology such as behaviorism were focused on explanations of behavior in general, and emphasized quantification of phenomena and experimentation. The scope of some of these schools of psychology was quite broad and encompassed both normal and abnormal behavior of humans as well as infrahumans. In contrast, psychoanalysis, at least in its initial development, was more narrowly focused on the causes and treatments of abnormal human behavior.

While other schools of psychology have waxed and waned in popularity, few have experienced the intensely divisive debate that has characterized psychoanalysis from its inception right up to the present. Psychoanalysis gives rise to intense responses ranging from dogmatic devotion to critical castigation. Regardless of what any individual may think or feel concerning psychoanalysis, the impact of psychoanalysis and its founder Sigmund Freud (1865–1939) on psychology and on popular culture is undeniable, pervasive, and enduring. Perhaps more than any other school of psychology, psychoanalysis has become an integral part of Western culture and many of its terms and ideas, often in poorly understood and misinterpreted form, have filtered into daily usage. Id, ego, superego, regression, repression, anal retention, penis envy, Freudian slip, catharsis, free association, wish-fulfillment, and Oedipus complex are only a few of the ideas attaining the status of common usage that have their roots in psychoanalysis.

SETTING THE STAGE: ANTECEDENT INFLUENCES ON PSYCHOANALYSIS

While Sigmund Freud is credited as the founder of the psychoanalytic school, he did not give birth to psychoanalysis from within a void. Indeed there are many antecedent practices and theorists whose influence is evident in Freud's creation. Given the focus on abnormal human behavior, psychoanalysis was particularly influenced by earlier ideas about the nature of psychopathology.

Psychopathology or mental illness is a term that can be quite difficult to define, and while at first one might think that it could be defined by purely objective criteria, upon further analysis it becomes evident that psychopathology is determined by social factors as much as it is by physiology. While no perfect criteria have as yet been devised for determining that a behavior is psychopathological, several currently agreed-upon criteria include the following: statistical infrequency, unexpectedness, violation of norms, personal distress for the sufferer, or resulting in disability or dysfunction (Neale, Davison, & Haaga, 1996).

The History of Attitudes/Ideas Concerning Psychopathology

Since the dawn of time humankind has made subjective judgments concerning normative human behavior, but over time such judgments have varied considerably regarding what constitutes normal versus abnormal behavior as well as both the cause(s) and the treatment for abnormal behavior. At times, possession by demons or evil spirits was considered to be the cause and there is evidence that as early as prehistoric times a form of primitive psycho-surgery called trephining, which involved cutting a hole in the skull, may have been performed for the purpose of releasing these demons or spirits (Maher & Maher, 1985). In addition to such early surgical interventions, a variety of treatments including physical torture and administration of potions or tonics were attempted with the common aim of all such treatments to make the human "host" an uncomfortable environment for the demon or spirit.

Hippocrates (c. 470–410 B.C.) attributed all illness, physical as well as mental, to natural rather than metaphysical causes and prescribed remedies involving rest as well as moderation in both diet and physical activity. This approach was accepted by both Greek and Roman practitioners at least until the time of Galen (A.D. 129–210). During the middle ages, treatment of mental illness in Europe in some cases was more reminiscent of pre-Hippocratic practices. While less violent than earlier treatments for "demonic possession," medieval attempts to remedy dysfunctional behaviors were often times conducted by members of the clergy and involved prayer and the application of holy water and religious relics, and, in some cases, ritualistic insults or threats. Once again the goal of these practices was to make the "host" environment unpalatable and drive out the demon or spirit deemed to be the cause of the abnormal behavior.

"Therapeutic" practices changed somewhat by the mid-13th century, during the Inquisition, when the mentally ill were frequently caught up in campaigns conducted by the church to root out heresy and the practice of witchcraft. Again abnormal behavior was thought to have been the result of demonic possession but with a new element in that the person possessed by a demon was considered to be the victim of witchcraft (Thorne & Henley, 1997). Accordingly, the focus was then shifted more toward finding the guilty witch who had cursed the victim rather than on treating the afflicted individual.

In general, the common perceptions of medieval treatment of the mentally ill often paint a bleak and brutal portrait; however, the reality of medieval practices may be considerably different. Neugebauer (1978), in reviewing manuscripts from medieval and early modern England, found evidence that mental illness may have been measured during this time period in terms of the practical impact of abnormal behavior on the community. Furthermore, when deemed warranted, the Crown appointed a supervised guardian for the disturbed individual.

The collectivization of the mentally ill into asylums was an essentially unknown practice until around the 15th century when many of the first asylums emerged from institutions that had previously been used to house people with leprosy. As the disease of leprosy gradually disappeared from Europe, leprosariums were re-tooled to house the mentally ill. The function of these early asylums, however, was frequently not the treatment or improvement of the mentally ill but rather their segregation from society. The conditions in the earliest institutions were often filthy, brutal, and degrading. One of the worst of such asylums was at St. Mary of Bethlehem in London, which achieved such a level of notoriety that its name was later shortened colloquially to Bedlam, a word that became synonymous with madness and uproar. The existence of these early asylums may well have represented the first systematized stigmatization of the mentally ill. Ironically, even today society is still struggling with issues of segregation and stigmatization in our treatment and attitudes toward the mentally ill. Social change is often slow, and some consider the standard of treatment of the mentally ill as an index of the overall health and functionality of the larger society.

Toward the end of the 18th century the mentally ill began to experience more humane treatment, most notably as a result of the actions of Philippe Pinel (1745–1826). One of the first to advocate for the possible treatment of mental illness, Pinel radically improved the care of individuals at La Bicêtre asylum in Paris in 1793 and a year later at Salpêtrière, another renowned Parisian public hospital.

Similar improvements in the treatment of the mentally ill were made in England by the English Quaker, William Tuke (1732–1822) and in the United States by Benjamin Rush (1745–1813). Another American to impact radically the care of the mentally ill was Dorothea Dix (1802–1887), whose efforts to reform conditions at asylums in the United States are further described in the chapter on women in the history of psychology.

Changes in treatment of the mentally ill were accompanied by changing ideas concerning the etiology or basis of mental illness. Two different models of thought, the **somatic** and the **psychic**, began to emerge in psychiatry during the 19th century. The somatic model argued that abnormal behavior had a physical cause such as a brain lesion or impaired nerve function. In the mid-19th century, the German physician Wilhelm Griesinger suggested that mental illness was indicative of an underlying physiological problem, an idea proposed earlier by Hippocrates (Thorne & Henley, 1997). Emil Kraepelin (1856–1926), one of the most famous of Wilhelm Wundt's students, further subdivided mental illness into two major categories, dementia praecox or schizophrenia and manic-depressive psychosis, attributing different physiologic causes, chemical imbalance, or metabolic disorder, respectively, to these two categories (Thorne & Henley, 1997).

In contrast, the psychic model of thought argued that mental or psychological causes gave rise to abnormal behavior. Practitioners of the psychic model began to explore the role of emotional factors instead of physiological problems as a possible cause of abnormal behavior. Psychoanalysis evolved initially as a part of this exploration into the role of emotional or psychic factors, particularly in the disorder known as **hysteria**.

The term *hysteria* was used as a label for one of the most common disorders in late 19th- and early 20th-century Europe. The major symptoms of hysteria included sensory or motor problems such as a lack of sensation in a limb or impaired sight or hearing without a known anatomical cause. The famous Parisian neurologist, Jean Martin Charcot (1825–1893) initially believed the cause of hysteria to be physiologic in nature, but after experimenting with the response of the symptoms of hysteria to treatment with hypnosis, Charcot came to believe in a psychic or emotional origin instead. The work of Charcot on the use of hypnosis in cases of hysteria is further described in chapter 6, Phrenology, Mesmerism, and Hypnosis.

Building on the foundation of earlier theorists such as Charcot, Sigmund Freud began in the late 19th century to build his school of psychoanalysis initially to address treatment of individuals exhibiting symptoms of hysteria. From this limited initial focus, Freud's psychoanalytic theory and techniques have grown to encompass the full range of human behavior and have revolutionized psychotherapy as well as our understanding of human behavior to a degree not unlike the impact of Einstein's Theory of Relativity on our understanding of the universe.

SIGMUND FREUD (1856–1939)

Early Life

Sigmund Freud was born in the town of Freiberg, Moravia (now known as Pribor and part of the Czech Republic), the son of a Jewish wool merchant Jacob Freud and his third wife Amalie. Freud's father was forced by financial and business setbacks to move the family to Leipzig, and later, when Sigmund was 4 years old, to Vienna. Freud remained in Vienna for the majority of his life before he was forced to leave Austria to escape Nazi persecution in 1938.

Early on, Sigmund Freud demonstrated great intellectual abilities and his academic efforts and ambitions were strongly encouraged by his parents. Although not the eldest of his father's eight children, Sigmund was Amalie's first born and her favorite, a position which secured him certain privileges in the household. Freud was first in his class at school for several years in a row and graduated with distinction from the local Gymnasium (high school) a year earlier than normal, at the age of 17. His exposure during his high school years to the work of Charles Darwin (1809–1882) awakened in Freud an interest in biological science. In 1873, Freud began to study medicine at the University of Vienna, not with the intention of becoming a practicing physician but instead as a way of pursuing a career in scientific research.

Freud took longer than usual to complete his medical training due to his interest in a broad range of course work including subjects such as philosophy in addition to his more physiologically related courses in physiology and neurology. Freud's earliest work in the experimental sciences was in the fields of biology, dissecting the genital structure of eels, and physiology, conducting a detailed examination of the spinal cord of fish.

While studying medicine in Vienna, Freud began to experiment with the drug cocaine. In addition to using it himself to treat his own enduring problem with depression, Freud became a cocaine enthusiast, advocating its use to his fiancée and family as a cure-all for a variety of complaints. A medical colleague of Freud's, overhearing Freud's enthusiastic endorsement of the drug, conducted experiments on the use of cocaine as an anesthetic to facilitate eye surgery and thus introduced the use of cocaine into medical practice.

Freud published six papers on the benefits of cocaine in the period between 1884 and 1886. Following their publication, the use of cocaine became popular in both Europe and the United States and Freud was criticized by his professional peers for his role in introducing the drug along with its negative physiological and social side effects to the world. Although his personal papers reveal continued use of the drug for several years, over time Freud became less vocal in his advocacy of cocaine to the extent of omitting reference to his papers on cocaine's benefits from his own bibliography. Freud's decreasing advocacy of the use of cocaine may have been in part related to the tragic death of his friend Ernst von Fleischl in 1891, from cocaine addiction; Freud had initially prescribed the drug ironically as a treatment for Fleischl's addiction to morphine (Breger, 2000).

Although Freud's earliest ambition was to become a scientific researcher, his medical professor Ernst Brücke (1819–1892), the director of the physiological institute where Freud worked, discouraged Freud from pursuing his goal because of financial concerns. To begin with, few academic positions were available to scientific researchers in general and Freud's ambitions were likely to be hampered even further by his Jewish heritage, due to the growing anti-Semitism in Europe and particularly in Austria.

Finances were much on Freud's mind at this time since he had become engaged to an attractive young woman named Martha Bernays, whom he met while visiting one of his sisters. Some measure of financial security was essential if Freud was ever to establish the kind of respectable bourgeois household that he believed would be acceptable to Martha Bernays' family. Reluctantly, Freud put aside his dreams for more practical and potentially lucrative pursuits and completed his medical examinations in 1881, taking a post at the Vienna General Hospital a year later. Freud left this post four years later to open a private practice as a clinical neurologist. Freud and Martha Bernays married about five months later.

The Development of Psychoanalysis

For a brief period prior to his marriage, from October 1885 to February 1886, Freud traveled to Paris to work with the French neurologist Jean-Martin Charcot (1825–1893). His acquaintance with Charcot, and his observation of Charcot's use of hypnosis to treat symptoms of hysteria, stimulated Freud's interest in the study and treatment of mental illness. Freud saw in the treatment of mental illness a possible road to greatness, which was something that always appealed to him. Previously, Freud thought his discovery of the "miracle drug" cocaine might give him the fame he sought, but when controversy over cocaine's effects made it more likely cocaine would lead to Freud's infamy, he moved on to other interests. Freud's interest in mental illness was developed through his acquaintance and correspondence with two individuals who later became his close personal friends and exerted a major influence on his career, two nose-and-throat specialists, Wilhelm Fliess (1858–1928) from Berlin and another physician, Josef Breuer (1842–1925).

Breuer and the Case of Anna O., Studies on Hysteria

Josef Breuer was a well-respected Viennese physician who first met Freud in the late 1870s. In late 1882, Breuer told Freud of his work with a young woman from a wealthy Jewish family named Bertha Pappenheim. Pappenheim suffered from a variety of strange physical symptoms which she first experienced while caring for her gravely ill father. These symptoms included a nervous cough, which first brought her to Breuer as a nose-and-throat specialist, in addition to limb paralysis, impaired tactile sensation, distorted vision, anorexia, vivid hallucinations, and a bizarre language disorder. At one point, Pappenheim was only able to speak English and not her native German language, although she appeared able to understand when addressed in German. Since no physiological basis could be determined for her symptoms, Breuer's diagnosis was hysterical neurosis.

Throughout the period of her treatment, from November 1880 to the summer of 1882, Breuer found that Pappenheim's symptoms were improved after getting her to talk about the subject matter of her various symptoms. Pappenheim called this process her "talking cure" or "chimney-sweeping" (Freud & Breuer, 2000). Each evening, the two would meet to discuss her symptoms, focusing in particular on Pappenheim's memories of when each symptom first appeared, with hypnosis often used to assist Pappenheim's recall. While frequently a very difficult and emotional process, Pappenheim would usually feel calm and her symptoms improved as a result of this release of tension, a process Breuer referred to as **catharsis**, which was a term first employed by Aristotle (Hothersall, 1995).

According to Freud (as later reported by Ernest Jones), as Breuer's treatment of Pappenheim continued, Breuer's wife became increasingly concerned about the relationship between her husband and Bertha Pappenheim and she therefore insisted that Breuer end his treatment of her. Breuer acceded to his wife's wishes and Pappenheim responded to Breuer's termination of treatment by going into hysterical childbirth, crying out that she was "Giving birth to Dr. Breuer's baby" (Breger, 2000). Again according to Freud, Breuer fled in horror taking his wife with him to Venice where they conceived their daughter Dora (Jones, 1953).

Interestingly, there is little or no evidence to support the Freud/Jones account of the events surrounding Breuer's termination of Pappenheim's treatment. In fact, Breuer continued to function as Pappenheim's physician for several years. In addition, Breuer and his wife did not travel to Venice at the time suggested by Jones and their daughter was in fact conceived prior to Breuer's termination of Pappenheim's treatment (Breger, 2000).

Another Freudian myth concerning Anna O. is the presentation of Breuer's treatment of her resulting ultimately in a permanent cure of her symptoms. In actuality, Pappenheim was institutionalized for a year following her therapy with Breuer. However, Pappenheim fell in love with the superintendent of the institution, causing her mother to remove her from the institution and take her back to Germany. She later recovered and returned to public life, going on to a successful career as Germany's first social worker, an author of short stories, a playwright, and as a champion of women's rights (Ellenberger, 1972). Later in life Pappenheim was reticent to comment on her relationship with Breuer, and out of respect for her privacy and for the fact that she was a friend of Freud's fiancée, Breuer always referred to her in discussions with Freud as Fraulein Anna O. This was the name later used by Freud and Breuer when in 1895 they published her case as part of their work "Studien über Hysterie (Studies on Hysteria)."

Freud had been intrigued by Breuer's discussion of the case of Anna O. and increasingly his own private medical practice became specialized in the treatment of hysteria. Initially, Freud used conventional methods including baths, massage, electrotherapy, and rest, but by 1889 he had found these methods to be ineffective and turned instead to hypnosis. After returning to France to study hypnotic techniques of Liebault and Bernheim at the Nancy School of Hypnosis, Freud came back to Vienna and began to incorporate the use of hypnosis in his treatment of hysteric patients.

Freud, however, became increasingly dissatisfied with hypnosis as a therapeutic technique due to his discovery that not all patients were even susceptible to hypnotic suggestion and those who could be hypnotized were susceptible to different degrees. Some patients were totally unaffected by the use of hypnosis while others were only temporarily relieved of their symptoms. As a result, Freud concluded that the patient–therapist relationship was more important than the actual technique used in therapy.

Inspired by Breuer's work with Anna O., Freud began to treat his patients by engaging them in a dialogue during which Freud instructed them to try to recall events associated with the first appearance of hysterical symptoms. As was the case with Pappenheim, Freud found that his patients often were able to recall and describe memories of events they had apparently repressed for years. Freud gradually developed the use of a process involving **free association**, in which he asked patients to describe everything that came to mind during their session. He first referred to his new therapeutic process as "Breuer's method," while later describing it as "physical analysis," and finally "psychoanalysis."

After using this method with several patients, Freud implored Breuer to collaborate with him in publishing the case of Anna O. Initially reluctant, Breuer was finally convinced and **Studies on Hysteria** came to fruition, presenting the "talking cure" and catharsis as described and analyzed in the context of case studies of five hysteria patients including Anna O. In the process of writing *Studies on Hysteria*, Freud and Breuer increasingly began to disagree on key points in the treatment of hysteria, particularly Freud's emphasis upon the patient–therapist relationship. As described by Christopher Monte in *Beneath the Mask* (1980):

> Breuer could not have known, but his patient viewed him, as all future analytic patients were to view their therapists, as father, lover, confessor, friend, rival, villain, and hero, calling up emotions for these changing perceptions of the therapist from previous relationships to important people in her life. (Monte, 1980, pp. 44–45)

Freud coined the term *transference* in reference to this process of the patient projecting emotions and images from past relationships onto the therapist, and later developed the term *counter-transference* in reference to a similar process occurring in the therapist's response to the patient. Freud described the presence of both transference and counter-transference in

Breuer's relationship with Anna O., stating that Anna O. had transferred her feelings for her father to Breuer and that Breuer in turn had counter-transferred his love to her. According to Ernest Jones, Freud's biographer, Freud attributed Breuer's inability to accept Freud's analysis of his relationship with Anna O. as the cause of the permanent rift between these two formerly close colleagues (Breger, 2000; Jones, 1953). Freud may have suggested this as the cause of the rift as a means of presenting himself in a more favorable light regarding the dissolution of their relationship. The real reasons for the break are doubtless more complicated as is true of most intense relationships be they personal, professional, or both.

Despite the break in their professional relationship, Freud always acknowledged Breuer's influence on his development of psychoanalysis and Breuer in turn referred to Freud with both admiration and awe. This pattern of intensely close relationships ending in permanent and irreparable disaffections appeared frequently in Freud's life. However, Freud's break with Breuer may have been one of the most amicable of the many subsequent separations between Freud and some of his key future colleagues.

Freud's Seduction Theory

In addition to his focus on the patient–therapist relationship, Freud was increasingly convinced of the importance of sex in the development of neuroses. Although he was the first to popularize such a theory, Freud was not the first to suggest a sexual etiology for mental disorder. Indeed, Freud later claimed to have been inspired in this belief after hearing both Breuer and Charcot discuss their observations that neuroses could always be traced to sexual problems. Freud took this idea even further when, in an 1896 address to the Viennese Society of Psychiatry and Neurology titled "The Etiology of Hysteria," Freud first acquainted the psychiatric community with his **seduction theory**, namely, the idea that neuroses are the result of childhood sexual abuse. Freud was influenced in this belief by observations that the majority of his neurotic patients reported traumatic sexual experiences in childhood often involving a family member. In his 1896 address, Freud reported that such experiences appeared to involve some form of seduction, usually by an older relative, often the patient's father.

Freud's seduction theory proved controversial and was received with some skepticism, revealing another personal tendency of Freud's that appeared repeatedly throughout his career, namely, his intense and often heated response to criticism. In the case of his seduction theory, when the president of the Society of Psychiatry and Neurology, Krafft-Ebing, was quoted as saying it sounded like a "scientific fairy tale," Freud responded by saying that his critics were asses and could all go to hell (Jones, 1953).

A year later, however, Freud was himself questioning or at least modifying his earlier claims of childhood sexual abuse in the experiences of his patients. He instead felt that in the majority of these cases the childhood seduction experiences described were not real but rather his patients were actually reporting fantasies. This new stance appeared to be a compromise between Freud's earlier seduction theory and a complete rejection of any sexual basis of neurosis. Freud stated that, while not based in reality, such sexual fantasies were indeed quite real to these patients, and since such fantasies focused on sex, sex still lay at the root of their neuroses.

Historians have voiced differing opinions regarding the reason for this seeming reversal on Freud's part regarding this critical feature of his theory of the etiology of neuroses. Most notably, Jeffrey Masson, one-time director of the Freud Archives, claimed in 1984 that Freud lied about the reality of his patients' experience of childhood sexual abuse. Masson claimed the reports of abuse from Freud's patients were real and that Freud knowingly decided to promote his sexual fantasy theory so as to make his system more acceptable to his peers and to the public who would have been reluctant to believe in the possibility of the widespread childhood sexual abuse implied in Freud's earlier seduction theory (Masson, 1984).

Most Freudian scholars have refuted Masson's claims citing evidence that Freud never denied that childhood sexual abuse sometimes took place but only stated that it had not actually occurred as frequently as reported by many of his patients. As Freud stated in a letter to his friend Fliess in 1897, "I no longer believe in my neurotica [the seduction theory]," giving as his reasons his inability to cure his patients with interpretations based on this theory, and the belief that "there are no indications of reality in the unconscious" and that too many respectable fathers would have to be accused of being perverse (Breger, 2000). In addition, Masson's critics stress Freud's own self-analysis as a significant contributing factor for his changing views on childhood sexual abuse as it related to his seduction theory (Storr, 2001). More recent analyses have suggested a more complicated scenario, namely, that Freud did not deliberately suppress the truth as Masson claimed, but that he instead underestimated the true incidence of childhood sexual abuse and that "more of Freud's patients were telling the truth about their childhood experiences than he was ultimately prepared to believe" (Crewsdon, 1988, p. 41; Krüll, 1986).

The Interpretation of Dreams

Sex may have continued to play a prominent role in Freud's theories regarding psychopathology due, in part, to his own difficulties and issues around sex. While emphasizing the role of sex in determining the behavior of others, Freud seemed to go to great pains to emphasize his own ability to rise above his personal sexual needs, stating that we should try to rise above such a "common animal need" and that "Sexual excitation is of no more use to a person like me" (Freud, 1954, p. 227).

Many of Freud's personal sexual difficulties appear related to his concerns about birth control and his dislike of both condoms and coitus interruptus. Freud, in a 1908 essay titled "'Civilized' Sexual Morality and Modern Nervous Illness," related his personal belief that all known methods of birth control impair sexual enjoyment and that contraceptive devices can "even actually cause illness." There is evidence that the Freuds practiced abstinence periodically as a means of preventing pregnancy. During one such period of abstinence, Sigmund Freud developed a number of symptoms, migraine headaches, urinary problems, spastic colon; and anxiety about travel, heart disease, and death, all of which he diagnosed as anxiety neurosis resulting from accumulated sexual tension.

Freud undertook his own treatment through a process of self-analysis focused primarily on the method of **dream analysis**. He was inspired to attempt dream analysis by his observation that a patient's dreams often provided significant clues to underlying emotional causes for disturbed behavior. He did not believe that standard free association would be possible in a self-analysis due to the difficulty of splitting into the roles of patient and therapist simultaneously. Accordingly, because he believed that events in dreams must have meaning that reflect something from within a person's unconscious mind, Freud saw dream analysis as a means of accessing his own unconscious.

Each morning, Freud would write down any remembered content from his dreams of the night before and would then free-associate about the recalled context of these dream stories. This self-analysis was one of the lengthiest analyses undertaken by Freud and lasted for two years. The entire self-analysis was published in 1900 as *The Interpretation of Dreams* and is considered by many to be Freud's most influential and groundbreaking work; it was the first published work in which Freud introduced a psycho-developmental process that he later termed the **Oedipus complex**.

In the course of his self-analysis, Freud discovered what he sensed was a universal process in child development in which children feel sexual attraction for the parent of the opposite sex coupled with fear of the same-sex parent who is now perceived in the role of rival. He later called this the Oedipus complex in reference to the Greek legend in which Oedipus, separated early in life from his birth parents, as an adult unwittingly kills his father and marries his own mother.

Although it took a while for the full impact of *The Interpretation of Dreams* to be realized, and Freud in his correspondence with his friend and biographer Ernest Jones expressed his belief that the book had been unfairly overlooked or poorly perceived by his professional peers, the actual evidence reveals that the book was in fact extensively and quite favorably reviewed in Germany and was well known to educated Germans (Decker, 1971). One individual greatly influenced by this book was a young physician from Zurich, Switzerland, named Carl Jung.

The Psychopathology of Everyday Life

While *The Interpretation of Dreams* introduced many of the key ideas in his developing psychoanalytic theory, the theoretical portrait was incomplete. Freud expanded his psychoanalytic theory with another book called *The Psychopathology of Everyday Life* (1904), which was published a year after *The Interpretation of Dreams*. In this new work, Freud suggested that in the course of our everyday lives our behavior is modified by the influence of unconscious ideas struggling to be expressed. The term *Freudian slip* was coined to describe "mistakes" such as slips of the tongue or the pen, the inability to remember a name, or forgetting a task. Freud considered such "mistakes" to be reflective of some unconscious idea struggling for expression and believed them to be a source of information to be analyzed as a means of understanding the unconscious mind of the patient. Freud's proposition, that one's behavior could be potentially outside of one's conscious control and that one might instead be following the dictates of a sometimes almost primal unconscious mind, was revolutionary! Other previous theorists had touched on the possible existence of the unconscious mind, but none had delved into it as deeply or with such frankness as Freud.

Building a Legacy: Freud and His "Naughty Boys"

With the publication of *The Interpretation of Dreams* and *The Psychopathology of Everyday Life*, Freud's reputation began to grow and he found himself at the center of an expanding circle of admiring individuals, mostly young doctors, all interested in learning how to practice this new psychotherapy called psychoanalysis. By 1902, a small group of men including Freud, Alfred Adler, Rudolf Reitler, and Wilhelm Stekel had begun meeting on a regular basis every Wednesday evening in the waiting room of Freud's office at Berggasse 19 in Vienna, which was also the location of Freud's private residence and is now a museum open to the public. This group came to be known as the Wednesday Psychoanalytical Society. By 1908, it had expanded to twenty members and had changed its name to the Vienna Psychoanalytical Society.

While Freud continued to develop his psychoanalytic theories and technique he also became increasingly rigid and controlling concerning the developmental path of psyhoanalysis. His attitude toward the Vienna Psychoanalytical Society was that of master to disciples and Freud was intolerant of challenges from even his most favored followers. What resulted from this developing Freudian orthodoxy was a series of bitter defections and estrangements of former Freud supporters. Two of the first to defect were Wilhelm Stekel and Alfred Adler. Adler resigned from the Vienna Psychoanalytical Society in 1911, taking nine of the then thirty-five members with him, after bitter disagreements with Freud over Adler's critique of Freud's sexual theory of hysteria. Stekel left the Society in 1912. The most bitter defection, however, was yet to come.

In 1906, Carl Jung had sent a copy of one of his papers to Freud and there followed a friendship and correspondence that lasted seven years. At first Jung was, at least on the surface, just another eager and unquestioning student, but Freud soon recognized the potential to expand interest in psychoanalysis beyond his mostly Jewish circle of Viennese adherents by fostering the interest of the Christian-Swiss Jung. The Freud–Jung correspondence became increasingly intimate and intense and by 1909, Freud was referring to Jung as "my dear friend and heir." In a letter to Jung written in April of 1909, Freud wrote of the time, "when I formally adopted you as eldest son and anointed you, in the land of the unbelievers, as my successor and crown prince" (Breger, 2000). However, by 1912, Jung and Freud were disagreeing more and more as Jung began to immerse himself in studies of mythology and in the development of what he called a collective unconscious, pursuits that were deemed unacceptable to Freud. Finally, in 1914 the two split irrevocably and Freud expelled Jung, along with a number of Swiss colleagues he had enticed into the Vienna Society, from membership.

Freud in America

During this same period between 1900 and 1914, in which Freud was establishing and maintaining his position of unquestioned authority within the Viennese psychoanalytical community, his reputation was spreading beyond Vienna. In 1909, he achieved international recognition after accepting an invitation from G. Stanley Hall to speak at Clark University in Massachusetts, where Freud was awarded an honorary doctorate in psychology. Freud's trip to America proved to be a tremendous success and he found himself warmly received by such eminent American psychologists as William James, E. B. Titchener, and James McKeen Cattell. His lectures presented a clear and concise discussion of psychoanalysis and Freud's conception of the existence and nature of an unconscious mind fell on fertile ground. Some of this reception had been cultivated by the writings of Canadian psychologist H. Addington Bruce who, between 1903 and 1917, had written numerous books and magazine articles on the subject of the unconscious (Dennis, 1991).

Despite the overall success of Freud's appearance at Clark University in engendering an interest in psychoanalysis within the American psychological community, he did not look favorably on this trip. Freud was not fond of traveling and on his trip to America he was particularly plagued by a variety of physical complaints, mostly digestive, as well as general complaints about the quality of American cooking, the lack of sufficient public toilets, and his distaste for the American tendency toward informality. He never returned to the United States and was quoted by his biographer Ernest Jones as having said that "America is a mistake; a gigantic mistake, it is true, but nonetheless a mistake" and "is it not sad that we are materially dependent on these savages, who are not a better class of human beings?" (Gay, 1988, pp. 563–566; Jones, 1955, p. 60).

Even though Freud never returned to America, his first and only trip established a psychoanalytic presence in the new world that continued to survive and thrive despite, or perhaps because of, the absence of his personal influence. For example, A. A. Brill and Ernest Jones began planning psychoanalytical societies in the United States—Brill founded the New York Psychoanalytic Society and Jones founded the American Psychoanalytic Society, both in 1911.

Theory of Personality Development

Over the period between 1895 and 1940, Freud published numerous books and papers developing and explaining his ideas about the unconscious and about the development of personality. He was a prolific and engaging author as evidenced by a 1929 initiative of several of his supporters to nominate Freud for a Nobel Prize in literature, although he never received this award.

A number of key psychoanalytical concepts were proposed and explained by Freud in his impressive body of written works. Throughout all of his writings he reiterated his belief in the operation of unconscious dynamic forces within an individual personality and more and more saw himself as an explorer of this unconscious. At first, Freud described personality as comprised of the **unconscious** (the locus of material not easily accessible to the awareness of an individual often as a result of repression), the **preconscious** (the locus of material more readily accessible to conscious perception but still at the border of full consciousness), and the **conscious** (that level of mind of which we are readily aware). He later shifted his explanations of personality from a focus on levels of consciousness to the separation of consciousness into three subsystems: the **id, ego**, and **superego**. The nature and details of these three subsystems are described in Table 12-1.

Freud considered the mind of the healthy individual as exhibiting an effective and adaptive working balance and interchange in the three subsystems. An imbalance or discord between subsystems would result in the kind of maladjusted behavior that would interfere with the individual's ability to lead a happy and productive existence in society.

In his theorizing on the subject of personality development, Freud continued to give center stage to the importance of sexuality. He believed that all aspects of our lives are driven by the psychic energy that derives from our deepest animal instincts. Freud further believed that over the course of an individual's development, although the basic aim of an individual instinct is unchanged, our method of achieving this aim and the experiences that satisfy an instinct evolve and change. The sexual instinct was believed by Freud to be one of the most important of these instincts.

Freud described the evolution of an individual's sexuality over the course of childhood development by advocating the radical idea that sexual development, began not with puberty but rather much earlier, in infancy. The concept of an infant as a sexual being was one of Freud's most controversial proposals, particularly given the social mores prevalent in Europe during the

TABLE 12-1	Freud's Three Subsystems of Personality

Sub-System	Description and Features
Id	■ Only system present at birth
	■ Satisfies the first principle of life which Freud called the **pleasure principle**—the goal of the pleasure principle is to eliminate tension or to at least reduce it to acceptable levels—tension causes discomfort whereas relief from tension is satisfying and pleasurable
	■ Function is to discharge psychic energy released in the organism in response to external or internal stimuli
	■ Primitive reservoir of energy, undifferentiated and derived from instincts (for example, hunger, thirst, and sex)
	■ Completely unconscious
Ego	■ Functions according to the **reality principle**—the goal of which is to prevent discharge of psychic energy until the source of tension reduction is accessible (the hungry child learns to postpone eating until it can find food)
	■ Develops as the result of the Id's growing inability to deal effectively with the external environment
	■ To be effective, must function on all three levels of consciousness (unconscious, preconscious, conscious)
Superego	■ The moral component of personality
	■ Develops from the ego through the incorporation of parental and societal standards of behavior
	■ Primarily unconscious, like the id
	■ Exerts control over the ego by rewarding or punishing it

early years of the 20th century. It is important to appreciate that through his sexual theory of personality development Freud expanded the concept of sexuality from the purely reproductive functions that had been the focus of earlier theorists. Freud's "sexual instinct" was in many ways more of a "sensual instinct" in that he considered not only the genitals but rather any part of the body where sensations could be focused, creating psychic tension that could somehow be relieved through an action such as stroking or suckling, to be an erogenous or sexual zone.

Freud proposed that all children proceed through stages in their psychosexual development in which the sexual instinct is focused at each stage within a different bodily erogenous zone. Freud gave each of these stages a name reflecting the bodily area he considered to be central at each stage of psychosexual development: the **oral stage**, the **anal stage**, the **phallic stage**, and the **genital stage**. The details of each stage are described in Table 12-2.

Critics of Freud often point to his stages of psychosexual development as incorrect or incomplete due to their focus primarily on male sexuality. The substance of some of these criticisms and the debate about psychosexual development in psychoanalytic theory is presented in more detail in the chapter on women in the history of psychology as part of the discussion of the work of Karen Horney (1885–1952), a disciple of Freud.

TABLE 12-2	Freud's Stages of Psychosexual Development	
Phases	**Stage**	**Description**
Pre-Genital (Sexual gratification is self-directed and not focused on reproduction)	Oral Stage (~birth to age 2 years)	■ Stage of infant sexuality in which all the infant's energy is centered around obtaining satisfaction through the oral zone
		■ Five modes of satisfying orally include: taking in, holding on, biting, spitting out, and closing. These five modes are prototypes for different personality traits
		■ Frustration or overindulgence of any functional mode may result in fixation of the personality into one of these prototypes with resultant consequences for later adult behavior. Ex.: biting is the prototype for adult "biting" behavior in the form of sarcasm and cynicism
		■ Adult manifestation may take the form of the opposite of what would be dictated by the prototype
	Anal Stage (~age 2 to 4 years)	■ Becomes central at about the age of 2 and lasts until end of the 3rd or beginning of 4th year of life
		■ Satisfaction is derived from pressure on the anal sphincter and its release through defecation
		■ Toilet training represents the child's experience of external authority. Overly harsh or overly lax toilet training can result in fixation at the anal stage of development
	Phallic Stage (~age 4 to 6 years)	■ Satisfaction is focused on the genitals
		■ Beginning development of Oedipus complex
		■ Ends typically around age 6
	Latency (~age 5 or 6 years to 12 years)	■ Temporary period during which sexual development is static or regresses to earlier stages
Genital	Genital Stage (~age 12 years onward)	■ Focus of sexual gratification begins to turn outward and becomes centered on reproductive functions
		■ Period of socialization and of social activities such as marriage and starting a family which support reproductive functions
		■ Activities that were satisfiers in previous stages are all incorporated into adult behavior. For example, sexual gratification may be derived from kissing even though it does not lead to reproduction because it stimulates the erogenous zone that was the focus in the oral stage

Interestingly, Freud admitted to his lack of understanding of female sexuality. As early as 1905, he wrote, in his paper "Three Essays on the Theory of Sexuality," that while his research had resulted in an understanding of male sexuality, "(the sexuality) of women—partly owing to the stunting effect of civilized conditions and partly owing to their conventional secretiveness and insincerity—is still veiled in an impenetrable obscurity." He had progressed no further in his understanding by 1926 when he described female sexuality as "the dark continent" in psychology (Freud, 1926).

Freud in Exile

In 1923, Freud who had been a long-time tobacco addict was diagnosed with cancer of the mouth. Although he lived for another 16 years, he was plagued throughout the remainder of his life by almost constant pain as a result of the cancer and the numerous operations required to remove portions of his palate and upper jaw.

In addition to his physical suffering, Freud's life was also marred by the increasingly hostile environment surrounding him in Vienna as a result of the Nazis' rise to power. In 1933, the Nazis officially condemned psychoanalysis as signaled by a rally in Berlin in May of that year during which Freud's books were publicly burned. Freud's comment on the event was to say, "What progress we are making. In the Middle Ages they would have burnt me; nowadays they are content with burning my books" (Freud as quoted in Jones, 1957, p. 182). This was an ironic comment given the acts of genocide committed by the Nazis in their concentration camps, but at the time of his comment, Freud was not aware of these events, which were yet to come.

Freud remained in Vienna until March of 1938 when German troops arrested and detained his daughter Anna. After intervention by the American government, Nazi officials agreed to allow Freud and members of his immediate family, including his wife and daughter, to leave Vienna and travel to London. He unfortunately was forced to leave other members of his family behind including four of his sisters, all of whom died in Nazi concentration camps.

The Last Year

Freud's final year spent in England was marked by his increasingly failing health as a consequence of his spreading cancer, although he remained mentally alert and continued working to his last days with the help of others, including most of all his daughter Anna. Finally on September 21, 1939, Freud could no longer stand the pain and requested that his physician Max Schur put an end to his suffering. Schur fulfilled Freud's wish by administering an overdose of morphine over a twenty-four-hour period. The father of psychoanalysis was gone.

FOLLOWING IN FREUD'S FOOTSTEPS

Freud's tight control over the development of psychoanalysis during his lifetime led to a schism in the school's development. Freud's followers in general took one of two paths, strict adherence or strong divergence from a purely Freudian psychoanalysis. One of the strongest of Freud's adherents was his daughter Anna.

Anna Freud: Child Psychoanalysis

Anna (1895–1982) was the youngest of Freud's six children and the one most involved in her father's work. As Freud began his long battle with cancer, he became increasingly reliant on Anna's support. Anna often would be responsible for reading Freud's papers for him at international professional meetings, and later, as his health progressively failed, she became his private nurse.

During his lifetime, Anna remained much in her father's shadow, her main contribution to psychoanalysis deriving from her role as supporter of the "Great Man." Freud's death in a sense freed Anna to take a more active role in developing her own contributions to the discipline. Her theoretical developments, in particular her development of child analysis and her explication of the ego and its mechanisms of defense, were Anna's own inspiration. Her contributions are described in detail in chapter 14, Women in Psychology.

Perhaps one of the most controversial elements of Freud's relationship with his daughter Anna was his psychoanalysis of her. Her formal analysis as conducted by her own father, began when Anna was twenty-three years old and lasted a full four years. For some reason Anna's analysis was not publicized, whether to preserve his daughter's privacy or because of concerns about public perceptions of a father's analysis of his own daughter, especially his analysis of her sexuality. Reference to this father–daughter analysis was made in disguised form in Freud's 1919 paper, "A Child Is Being Beaten," and again in Anna's own 1922 paper, "Beating Fantasies and Daydreams"; however, the fact of their patient–therapist relationship was not publicly revealed until the 1960s.

After emigrating to England with her father in 1938, Anna was instrumental in building a British branch of the school of psychoanalysis that over time developed its own unique flavor much in the same way American psychoanalysis developed in ways that distinguished it from its European cousin. Anna, together with Freud's disciple Ernest Jones, also contributed a great deal to the Freud legend and mythology. Jones at one time was rumored to have been interested in marrying Anna, possibly as a means of achieving his ambition to become Freud's acknowledged successor (Breger, 2000; Ferris, 1997).

Ernest Jones

Jones (1879–1985) was born in Wales and received a medical degree from the University College Hospital in London. He was very interested in neurological research and initially encountered Freud's work as a result of this interest. The two developed a friendship beginning in 1908 and Jones became increasingly involved in facilitating the spread of psychoanalysis beyond Vienna. He was the first to introduce psychoanalysis to Great Britain and founded the British Psychoanalytical Society in 1913. He also brought psychoanalysis to North America while teaching there as a professor of psychiatry at the University of Toronto from 1909 to 1912.

While Jones may have been ambitious to become Freud's successor, his role arguably was more that of Freud's publicist. Jones wrote a three-volume biography of Freud that was considered for a long time to be the definitive text on Freud's life and works. A great deal of this biography presented Jones' secondhand account of the version of events as presented to Jones by Freud through their conversations and correspondence.

Jones' biography of Freud, however, may be more of a testament to the old adage that "history is written by the victors." In many instances, the Jones/Freud account of events tended to present Freud in the most favorable light possible, particularly in recounting his disagreements with former friends and disciples. Jones' biography of Freud was also written as a primarily retrospective recounting of events according to Freud and many discrepancies are revealed when comparisons are made with descriptions of the same events in the context of private correspondence of Freud and others written at the time of the actual occurrence of these events.

In addition to writing Freud's biography, Jones and Anna were both in control of editing and censoring the release of Freud's personal papers after his death. Scholars attempting an analysis of Freud's life and his work are now able to benefit from greater access to some of Freud's personal correspondence, shedding a light that often times illuminates the contradictions in the portrait of the man as painted by Anna Freud and Ernest Jones. Their creation of the Freud myth presents a central paradox that arises in attempts to write a "true" biographical account of Freud and of psychoanalysis. The paradox is that the "facts" of Freud cannot be totally separated from the "myths" since they both were instrumental in setting the course of the development of psychoanalysis.

CARL JUNG (1875–1961)

Carl Gustav Jung was born in Kesswil, Switzerland, the son of a minister of the Swiss Reformed Church who married a minister's daughter. Most of his early childhood was spent in the town of Klein-Hüningen, where he attended the local school until he was 11 years old. At that time, he transferred to the Gymnasium in the nearby town of Basel.

As a child, Jung was deeply impacted by his mother's mental illness. She had been hospitalized for several months in a mental institution when Jung was only 3 years old. This separation was a defining moment for Jung, who was deeply troubled by his mother's being away. From then on, he always felt mistrustful when the word "love" was spoken. The feeling he associated with "women" was for a long time that of innate unreliability. "Father," on the other hand, meant reliability and—powerlessness (Breger, 2000). Jung described his mother as an uncanny creature with two different personalities. By day she appeared to him a seemingly ordinary village woman, by night a "strange and mysterious" creature (Hayman, 1999, p. 8). She exposed her son at an early age to her interest in spiritualism and claimed that she could see ghosts and communicate with the dead.

Jung went on to study medicine at the local University of Basel from 1895 to 1900, where he exhibited an interest not only in medicine but also in philosophy and theology. Jung had previously been interested in pursuing a career in archeology but settled on a medical career when it became clear that his family could not afford to send him away to a university that had an archeology program. In 1900, after reading a textbook of psychiatry written by Krafft-Ebing, Jung became interested in psychopathology. In studying the human mind, Jung saw the potential to blend his dual interests in objective science and in philosophy. He also, perhaps, saw an opportunity to better understand both himself and his mother.

Later that year, Jung moved to Zurich to become the assistant of Dr. Eugen Bleuler at the Burghölzli mental hospital where he later rose to the position of Senior Staff Physician. Bleuler was a student of Charcot and was regarded as an expert on schizophrenia. From 1902 to 1903, Jung studied psychopathology at the Salpêtriére in Paris under the tutelage of Pierre Janet. While there Jung wrote a paper on his experimental research with word association in addition to his doctoral dissertation, "On the Psychology and Pathology of So-Called Occult

Phenomena" (1902). Jung's life progressed on a personal as well as a professional level. In 1903, he married a very wealthy young woman named Emma Rauschenbach with whom he had five children.

While working with Bleuler, Jung was asked to review Freud's *The Interpretation of Dreams*. Reading this book was Jung's first introduction to the concept of repression, and to the potential existence of an unconscious. Freud's ideas struck a chord with Jung as a result of observations he had been making while conducting research, at Bleuler's request, in the use of **word association**. Using the method earlier introduced by Galton, Jung asked individuals to respond to words presented singly with the first word that came to mind (Thorne & Henley, 1997). Jung then recorded both the content of their response as well as the latency between presented word and a subject's response. Jung believed that a slower than average response to a given word indicated that the word had special significance for the person. This special meaning could be found in a unified cluster of ideas in the unconscious, which Jung referred to as a "complex." These complexes were relegated to the unconscious as a result of repression.

In 1906, struck by the similarity between his conclusions and those of Freud, Jung sent a paper he wrote on his word association work to Freud. A year later he also sent Freud a copy of his book on schizophrenia, titled *The Psychology of Dementia Praecox*. On the basis of Jung's friendly overture, the two embarked on a seven-year correspondence that included over 300 letters. Their first face-to-face meeting occurred in 1907 and Jung reported that the two "met at one o'clock in the afternoon and talked virtually without a pause for thirteen hours" (Jung, 1961, p. 149).

Jung differed from the majority of Freud's disciples in two very important ways: he was not Jewish and he was also an established physician with ideas of his own concerning psychopathology that pre-dated his first exposure to Freud's work. For many of Freud's other disciples, their exposure to Freud's psychoanalysis represented their first serious involvement in the study of psychopathology. Instead of impeding any relationship between Jung and Freud, these differences were central to its development. In reading Jung and Freud's correspondence, as well as letters written by Freud to others such as Ernest Jones, Freud reveals political motives in cultivating his relationship with Jung. Namely, Freud saw "winning the Swiss" and bringing "Zurich" into his camp as important to the advancement of psychoanalysis (Breger, 2000).

Despite their rapport, Jung and Freud from the very beginning were not in universal agreement. Jung in fact disagreed with Freud on at least two key points regarding psychoanalysis: Jung's belief that Freud neglected the importance of personal rapport as a healing force in the patient–therapist relationship, and that Freud overemphasized sexuality. Although Jung raised these criticisms early in their relationship, they remained mostly unaddressed and in the background until their personal relationship began to falter. The first real difficulties between the two arose during Freud's trip to America in 1909, in part as a result of Jung's growing interest in mysticism.

Despite their differences, in 1911, Freud established Jung as the first president of the International Psychoanalytic Association, against the objections of many of its Viennese members who were jealous and distrustful of Jung and accused Jung of being anti-Semitic. The cracks in Freud and Jung's splintering relationship grew following Jung's lecture tour to America in 1912, during which Jung presented his own theories, disagreeing with Freud on several points, most particularly on the definition of **libido**.

Jung believed that Freud overly defined libido in sexual terms whereas Jung regarded libido as more generalized life energy, only a part of which was sexual. For Jung, libido expressed itself in a variety of creative impulses including growth and reproduction. Jung also rejected the Oedipus complex, explaining maternal attachment in terms of dependency needs stemming from the mother's ability to provide food rather than sexual gratification. According to Jung, it was only later in life when a child has matured and developed sexual functioning that nourishing activities attain sexual nuances.

To a great extent, the differences in opinion between Freud and Jung regarding sexuality no doubt stemmed from the differences in their respective relationships with their mothers and their differing personal attitudes toward sex. While Freud, during his self-analysis, found evidence within himself of his own sexual attraction to his mother, Jung's own self-analysis revealed no such tendency. Jung described his mother as both fat and unattractive and expressed his inability to believe in Freud's persistent claim that every little boy harbors sexual desire for his mother. His objections to Freud's focus on sexuality were also partly a result of the differences between the types of patients typically seen by the two men. In his general practice, Freud saw primarily highly functional neurotics whereas Jung's patients were more commonly hospitalized schizophrenics. In one letter to Freud, Jung wrote, "The loss of reality function in schizophrenia cannot be reduced to repression of libido—defined as sexual hunger. Not by me at any rate" (Jung, as cited in Breger, 2000, p. 227).

Jung also did not share Freud's slightly prudish attitude toward sex. In addition to his active sexual relations with his wife Emma, Jung indulged what he called his "polygamous nature," engaging in a number of affairs with other women including at least two documented affairs with female patients (Breger, 2000). The importance of sexuality to Freud and Jung's respective theories appeared to be in inverse proportion to the frequency with which each of these men actually satisfied their own sexual needs.

In addition to their clashes on sexuality, Jung and Freud differed significantly in their views concerning determinism. Freud presented the adult personality as largely predetermined by childhood events while Jung was much less pessimistic. Jung instead believed that we are shaped both by our past and by our hopes and aspirations for the future. As such, Jung saw the potential to change behavior throughout one's lifetime.

The Final Break

In 1912, Jung published *The Psychology of the Unconscious* in which he openly expressed opinions that were divergent from those of his mentor, Freud. While writing this book, Jung expressed in his correspondence to friends and colleagues his concern that when this book was published it would damage his standing with Freud. He in fact delayed publication of this book for several months because of his concerns about Freud's reaction. His concerns proved to be well founded as their correspondence thereafter became increasingly angry. After Freud criticized Jung for his differing opinions, Jung replied in one letter by quoting Nietzsche: "One repays a teacher badly if one remains only a pupil" (Breger, 2000). In November of 1912, the two met at the Park Hotel in Munich, Germany, to attempt a reconciliation. Their reconciliation was short-lived. A few weeks later, Jung expressed anger over Freud's refusal to consider any of Jung's ideas on the basis of their merits as well as his feelings of always being diagnosed and interpreted by Freud.

Freud responded to this criticism by doing exactly what Jung accused him of, that is, diagnosing him: "One who while behaving abnormally keeps shouting that he is normal gives ground for the suspicion that he lacks insight into his illness. Accordingly, I propose that we abandon our personal relations entirely. I shall lose nothing by it, for my only emotional tie with you has long been a thin thread—the lingering effect of past disappointments." To which Jung replied, "I accede to your wish that we abandon our personal relations, for I never thrust my friendship on anyone. You yourself are the best judge of what this moment means to you. 'The rest is silence.'"

Jung was devastated by the break. As he wrote later in his autobiography: "After the parting of the ways with Freud, a period of inner uncertainty began for me. . . . It would be no exaggeration to call it a state of disorientation" (Jung, 1961, p. 170). In much the same way that his personal struggles had prompted Freud to undertake his own self-analysis, Jung also began a period of intense self-analysis that led to the development of his own personality theory, later known as analytical psychology. After this period of mental turmoil, Jung published *Psychological Types or the Psychology of Individuation* (1921).

Psychological Types

Rejecting Freud's restrictive presentation of libido as purely sexual in nature, Jung further depicted libido as potentially directed by a person in two ways, either inward or outward. Jung called the tendency of inwardly directing libido **introversion** and outwardly directing it **extroversion**. The introvert is focused on the inner subjective world of ideas and tends to be self-sufficient, whereas the extrovert is focused on the external objective world of objects and people and needs to have people around. Jung stated that while both tendencies were present in everyone, one tendency is usually more dominant for a given individual. Jung also identified four psychological functions, each utilized to differing degrees in a given individual: thinking, feeling, sensation, and intuition. The **Myers-Briggs Type Indicator** (MBTI) was developed years later as a personality assessment device and incorporated Jung's personality type theory (Thorne & Henley, 1997).

Personality Structure

Jung also rejected Freud's division of personality into the three structures of id, ego, and superego. For Jung, the major part of personality consisted of three different structures, which he called the ego, the personal unconscious, and the collective unconscious.

In Jung's system, the **ego** was comprised of the conscious mind including all of perception, thought, feeling, and memory. The **personal unconscious** was the superficial layer of the unconscious and contained experiences at one time conscious that have been repressed, suppressed, or forgotten as well as experiences too insignificant to affect the ego. The personal unconscious was the realm of **complexes**, which Jung described as "autonomous groups of associations that have a tendency to move by themselves, to live their own life apart from our intentions" (Jung, 1968, p. 81).

The final structure of personality as described by Jung was probably the most radical departure from Freud's work and it reflected, in part, Jung's long interests in both archeology and mysticism. Jung called this structure the **collective unconscious**. He believed that the collective unconscious existed at a deeper level than did the personal unconscious and that it was composed of "contents and modes of behavior that are more or less the same everywhere and in all individuals" (Jung, 1939, pp. 52–53).

The collective unconscious contained so-called **archetypes**, universal thought-forms that transcend the individual's experience; archetypes are unconscious and inherited predispositions to perceive or respond in certain ways (Thorne & Henley, 1997). Jung, as a result of his travels and readings in anthropology, which compared different cultures around the world, found that all cultures included what appeared to be universal symbols and that their rituals often seemed similar in terms of the experienced thoughts and emotions. For example, a family's and community's great joy and hope expressed directly and symbolically at the time of a birth and their sadness and loss surrounding someone's death. Accordingly, it is the similar underlying emotional and cognitive experiences across disconnected and even isolated cultures that Jung believed were a reflection of inherited dispositions for all humans.

Jung reasoned that archetypes revealed themselves symbolically in a variety of ways in myths, fables, dreams, visions, and even works of art. Examples of such archetypes include birth, death, power, magic, God, and the hero. In addition, Jung felt that some archetypes are so developed that they function as separate systems within the personality. These higher-level archetypes include: the **persona**, the **shadow**, and the **anima** and **animus**, all of which are described in Table 12-3.

Jung also proposed an overall integrating archetype, which he called the "self." His "self" arises through individuation, the process that makes a person a unique entity (Thorne & Henley, 1997). According to Jung, the ultimate goal of life is self-realization or the full development of the "self."

Until his death in 1961, Jung wrote extensively on his system of personality development; however, he did not achieve the same level of influence within psychology as his mentor Freud. This may be due in part to the difficulty of his writing style. Freud was a highly skilled writer with the ability to communicate difficult concepts both clearly and concisely. In contrast, Jung's writing was not as logically structured and could be very difficult to understand. Jung also tended to deal with concepts from such diverse and often mystical sources as religion, astrology, and alchemy, all of which would have been viewed with a jaundiced eye by most of his professional peers. These same mystical overtones, however, were responsible for a brief resurgent interest in Jung's work during the 1970s and 1980s.

TABLE 12-3	Jung's Higher-Level Archetypes
Archetype	**Description**
Persona	■ The role a person assumes in society for public consumption, which may or may not reveal a person's true nature.
Shadow	■ The residue of our animal nature. The dark side of human nature assumed to be responsible for socially unacceptable thoughts, feelings, and actions. A source of creative energy.
Anima/Animus	■ Recognizes the importance of human sexual duality. The anima represents the feminine aspects existing within a man while the animus represents male aspects existing within a woman.

ALFRED ADLER (1870–1937)

Alfred Adler was born in a suburb of Vienna, the second child of a wealthy grain merchant. Adler suffered from a series of physical complaints including rickets and pneumonia, which prevented him from competing successfully with his older brother and also inspired his early determination to pursue a career in medicine.

Adler attended the University of Vienna and received his medical degree in 1895. Two years after graduation, he married a young Russian woman named Raissa Timofejewna. At first Adler specialized in ophthalmology, but later moved on to practice general medicine before developing an interest in psychiatry. This was due in part to the difficulty he experienced in coping with the death of his patients, particularly younger ones. By this time, Adler had children of his own, three girls and a boy.

In the autumn of 1902, Freud invited Adler, along with Reitler and Stekel, to join him in forming the Vienna Psychoanalytic Society. Adler succeeded Freud as president of the society in 1910. Although during the early years of the Vienna Psychoanalytic Society the majority of its members appeared to express an almost total agreement with Freud, their meetings featured frequent personal attacks and squabbles over hierarchy within the society. Interestingly, such attacks often took the form of psychoanalytic interpretations of one anothers' behaviors and hidden motivations.

By early 1908, Adler was sufficiently discontented with such behavior to propose a reorganization of the meetings to devote more time to free and open discussion, the abolishment of the rule requiring that everyone speak, as well as the proposal that all new members be elected by secret ballot. His intention was to make the society both more open and more democratic. His proposal was only partly accepted by the group because of Freud's concern that a more open membership process might dilute his control of the society.

As early as 1906, Adler had also begun to express ideas that diverged from Freud's. In his 1907 book, titled *Study of Organ Inferiority and Its Psychical Compensation*, Adler began to develop his concept of the inferiority complex based on the idea that persons with inferior organs or physical disability—poor eyesight, impaired locomotion, deafness, speech defects—were driven to overcome their handicaps in compensation for the disability and that this compensatory mechanism explained both healthy development as well as neurosis (Breger, 2000). Adler further developed this theory to include what he called an "aggressive drive" defined as: "Fighting, wrestling, beating, biting and cruelties . . . (the refinement of which) lead to sports, competition, dueling, war, thirst for dominance, and religious, social, national and race struggles" (Breger, 2000, p. 199). Adler also reasoned that this aggressive drive could be turned inward as shown by a subject exhibiting traits of humility, submission and devotion, subordination, self-flagellation, and masochism (Breger, 2000).

Adler spoke, in a 1908 paper, of what he termed the "need for affection" as a basic drive. He felt that this drive was exhibited in childhood through a child's desire to be fondled and praised, and a child's tendency to want physical closeness to loved ones. Later in life, Adler saw evidence of this same drive in adults striving for loving relationships and friendship. While Freud also left room for the concept of love in his system, it was always intertwined with the sexual instinct. Freud did not look favorably on what he perceived to be Adler's rejection of the importance of the sexual instinct.

Tensions were further heightened between the two when Adler introduced his concept of the "masculine protest" as an extension of his "aggressive drive." This masculine protest was defined by Adler as the wish to be strong and powerful in reaction to things that make one feel "unmanly," manliness being imbued with qualities of power, strength, and aggression, and femininity being equated with weakness. Adler made it very clear that these concepts were not reflective of fixed biological characteristics, but instead arose from the way in which men and women were treated in European society (Breger, 2000). As he stated in 1910, taking a stance that starkly disagreed with that of Freud:

> To this is added the arch evil of our culture, the excessive pre-eminence of manliness. All children who have been in doubt as to their sexual role exaggerate the traits which they consider masculine. . . . All neurotics have a childhood behind them in which they were moved by doubt regarding the achievement of full masculinity. The renunciation of masculinity, however, appears to the child as synonymous with femininity, an opinion which holds not only for the child, but also for the greater part of our culture. (Breger, 2000, p. 200)

Adler also began to differ from Freud in his methodological approach to psychotherapy. Abandoning what had become by this time "classical Freudian" psychotherapy, with its focus on the analysis of transference reactions, Adler would first strive to diagnose the individual's "life plan" or "personal myth," the patient's personal style, conflicts, and "mistaken" neurotic path, and then communicate this to the individual as a means of helping him or her to gain understanding and insight (Breger, 2000). Treatment was usually brief, results being expected as quickly as within three months, in contrast to more traditional Freudian psychoanalysis that often lasted years.

By the end of 1910, members of the Vienna Psychoanalytical Society were openly critical of Adler's theories, claiming that he had diverged too far from "the Professor"; a view apparently shared by Freud who, in his private correspondence, was beginning to refer to Adler as "paranoid," "neurotic," and a danger to psychoanalysis (Breger, 2000). Four meetings of the Vienna Psychoanalytical Society were devoted to a discussion of Adler's ideas between January and February of 1911. During these meetings, Adler tried to communicate what he saw as evidence that underlying what Freud and his followers perceived as a purely sexual instinct were much more important connections, namely, the "masculine protest" (Breger, 2000). Freud was very critical in his response, formulating his critique in a personal attack in which he attempted to discredit Adler's ideas by interpreting them as symptoms of Adler's ambition to step out from behind Freud's shadow. As Freud, Adler, and the other members of the society became further embroiled in the debate, the climate became increasingly tense for Adler. He survived it for about four months before resigning to form his own group, originally called "The Society for Free Psychoanalytic Research," and later named "The Society of Individual Psychology." Nine other members of the Vienna Psychoanalytical Society resigned in support of Adler and joined his new organization.

Individual Psychology

The key differences between Adler's personality theory and that of Freud include the following: Adler de-emphasized sexuality and in particular rejected the idea of infantile sexuality; Adler's psychology was ego-oriented and made consciousness, not the unconscious, the center of personality; Adler also stressed human social urges as playing an important role in molding personality. Also, unlike Freud, who oftentimes was perceived as having little actual interest in his patients as anything more than subjects for study, Adler was concerned with improving the lives of his patients and evidenced an interest in combating some of the basic problems of existence. Freud also treated mostly upper-class patients whereas Adler worked with the middle class and working poor.

After World War I, Adler became interested in attempting the early prevention of neurosis and established child-guidance centers in Vienna's public schools. Individual psychology attracted a growing number of followers before reaching the height of its popularity in the early 1930s. Adler wrote and lectured extensively on individual psychology, making regular trips to America before moving there permanently in 1932 to become Professor of Medical Psychology at the Long Island College of Medicine in New York City. Adler died of a heart attack in 1937, while on a lecture tour to Aberdeen, Scotland.

▉ Summary

In this chapter we discussed the development of the school of psychoanalysis, which differs from other schools described previously in this text in a number of key ways, that is, psychoanalysis was clinically based and focused on explaining and treating abnormal human behavior while other schools were laboratory- and/or academically based and focused on experimentation and on explanation of general human and infrahuman behavior. Inasmuch as psychoanalysis was initially developed as an exploration of abnormal human behavior, we began this chapter with an overview of the history of attitudes and ideas concerning psychopathology, beginning with pre-Hippocratic approaches to the treatment of pathological behavior, proceeding with Hippocrates' more holistic approach incorporating prescriptions for physical activity as well as dietary recommendations, followed by our discussion of the Middle Ages and the reemergence of practices reminiscent of pre-Hippocratic belief systems along with the post–Middle Ages emergence of the first mental asylums.

We then discussed the impact of institutionalization of the mentally ill with the concomitant development of the first systematic study and categorization of types of psychopathological behavior, leading to two divergent theoretical views of the etiology of psychopathology, namely, the **psychic** model and the **somatic** model. We also discussed the ideas and accomplishments of some of the psychic and somatic models' earliest respective proponents, including Wilhelm Griesinger, Emil Kraepelin, and Jean-Martin Charcot.

Hysteria, a common disorder of the late 1800s and early 1900s, characterized by sensory and/or motor disability not attributable to an actual physiological cause, was frequently the subject of study for these early theorists and provided the initial inspiration for Sigmund Freud's development of psychoanalysis. Sigmund Freud's theory of psychoanalysis emerged initially from his pursuit of a psychic explanation for the development of hysteric symptoms and developed further into a general theory of personality development.

We discussed many of the more significant ideas and accomplishments of Sigmund Freud including: his work with Josef Breuer in using first hypnosis and later "the talking cure" for the treatment of hysteric symptoms; his proposal of the seduction theory, which attributed the development of neuroses to the experience of childhood sexual abuse, later modified by Freud to focus on childhood sexual fantasy as opposed to the real experience of childhood sexual abuse; Freud's self-analysis through the technique of dream analysis and his early emphasis on the unconscious mind as a major influence on behavior; his expansion of psychoanalytic theory from the focus on hysteria and psychoneuroses to a more general behavior theory; and his conceptualization of a psychosexual theory of human development.

Throughout the course of his professional career and his work and efforts in developing psychoanalysis and his founding of the Vienna Psychoanalytical Society, Freud emerges as an often uncompromising and controlling individual, which influenced heavily both his personal and his professional relationships. We discussed the work of some of Freud's followers who further developed psychoanalysis either in strict adherence to Freud's original psychoanalytic framework or in conflict with and divergence from Freud's ideas. Our discussion included the roles of Sigmund Freud's daughter Anna Freud and Freud's biographer Ernest Jones in developing the Freud "myth" and the influence of their efforts on the developmental course of psychoanalysis. We also discussed the work of two individuals who diverged radically from Freud in the development of their own ideas, namely, Carl Jung and Alfred Adler.

Carl Jung, who early on was a close disciple of Sigmund Freud, diverged from Freud's theories, particularly regarding the nature of libido, and went on to develop his own theoretical contributions to psychoanalysis including a theory of psychological types as well as his development of analytical psychology.

We concluded this chapter with the contributions of Alfred Adler, who diverged from Freud to develop individual psychology, which included the concept of the inferiority complex. Adler's individual psychology, unlike Freudian psychoanalysis, de-emphasized the unconscious mind and instead focused on the conscious and on the role of social urges in determining human behavior.

■ Chapter 12—Psychoanalysis

Discussion Questions

- ■ What are the differences and/or similarities between early and modern attitudes and ideas concerning psychopathology?

- ■ What are the key differences between the psychic and somatic views of psychopathology?

- ■ In what way did Philippe Pinel, William Tuke, Benjamin Rush, and Dorothea Dix contribute to the treatment of mental illness?

- ■ How did the development of psychoanalysis differ from the development of other schools of psychology?

- ■ What role did the disorder known as "hysteria" play in the development of psychoanalysis? Why was "hysteria" important to the debate surrounding the psychic and somatic theories of psychopathology?

- ■ According to Freud, which was more important: the patient–therapist relationship or the therapeutic technique used? Why?

- ■ How did Freud's thoughts regarding his "seduction theory" change over the course of his career? What reasons have been proposed for this change?

- ■ What role did Freud's personal difficulties play in his development of dream analysis?

- ■ How did C. G. Jung's theories diverge from those of Sigmund Freud? How did Alfred Adler's diverge from Freud?

Beyond Psychoanalysis: Continuing Developments in Psychotherapy

CHAPTER OVERVIEW

Following Freud's development of psychoanalysis during the late 1800s and early 1900s, psychotherapeutic techniques and theories continued to evolve, sometimes as an expansion of Freud's work, and at other times in direct refutation of some of Freud's most fundamental concepts. In this chapter, we continue with some of the key developments in the growing field of clinical psychology, focusing primarily upon the history of psychotherapy.

We begin with object relations theory and examine briefly the theories and contributions of two of the most prominent object relations theorists: Melanie Klein (1882–1960) and W. R. D. Fairbairn (1889–1964). We turn next to some of the key figures in the history of psychotherapy who refined and extended psychoanalytic and object relations theories; for example, British pediatrician D. W. Winnicott (1896–1971), who diverged from the paths of Freudian psychoanalysis and Kleinian object relations to develop concepts such as transitional objects, holding environments, and the "good enough" mother.

Other theorists broke new ground in psychoanalysis including Heinz Hartmann (1894–1970), who diverged from Freudian psychoanalysis to develop his own ideas concerning "ego psychology"; Margaret Mahler (1897–1985); and Heinz Kohut (1913–1981). Social psychologist Erich Fromm (1900–1980) expanded further the scope of psychoanalytic theory from a focus on individual development to an improved understanding of processes at work in societal development. His groundbreaking work on the concepts of narcissism and symbiosis influenced many subsequent theorists within psychology and psychoanalysis.

Our discussion of theorists who presented extensions or alternatives to psychoanalysis and object relations continues with the work of developmental psychologist Erik Erikson (1902–1994), who developed the first detailed model tracing human development across the lifespan; Gordon Allport (1897–1967), who was instrumental in gaining within the academic setting, acceptance of the formal study of personality, which had previously been exclusively focused in the clinical setting; and Henry Murray (1893–1988).

Beginning in the early 1960s a new movement emerged in opposition to what were then the two most influential theoretical forces in psychology, namely, behaviorism and psychoanalysis. This new movement, known as humanistic psychology or the "third force," emphasized the operation of conscious, not unconscious, experience and focused on the creative power of the individual, as opposed to psychopathology. We describe the work of some of the more prominent proponents of humanistic psychology, including Abraham Maslow (1908–1970), Carl Rogers (1902–1987), and Rollo May (1909–1994).

LEARNING OBJECTIVES

When you finish studying this chapter, you will be prepared to:

- Describe object relations theory and the contributions of Sigmund Freud, Melanie Klein, and W. R. D. Fairbairn to its development
- Define and describe Winnicott's concepts of the "transitional object," the "holding environment," and the "good enough" mother
- Compare and contrast Hartmann's "ego psychology" with Freudian psychoanalytic theory

- Describe Mahler's Stage Model of Infant Development

- Explain why and how Kohut transformed psychoanalysis from a Freudian drive/structure model to a relational model

- Discuss Fromm's theories concerning sociocultural development including the concept of the "escape from freedom" and his model of personality types

- Discuss Erikson's eight-stage model of human psychological development

- Discuss Allport's contributions to personality theory

- Compare and contrast Murray's "personology" with Freudian psychoanalytic theory

- Discuss why humanistic psychology was considered a third force in psychology

- Discuss the contributions of key figures in humanistic psychology including: Abraham Maslow, Carl Rogers, and Rollo May

- Discuss factors contributing to the ultimate failure of humanistic psychology to succeed as a separate school of psychology

INTRODUCTION

In the preceding chapter, we presented an overview of the history of psychoanalysis with a particular focus upon the foundational work of Sigmund Freud. While Sigmund Freud was instrumental in establishing the basic theoretical and methodological framework for psycho-analysis, subsequent practitioners have frequently taken psychoanalytic theory and psychotherapy in new and different directions. In this chapter we review some of these devel-opments in psychotherapy and their implications in terms of our evolving understanding of such issues as the motivation for behavior, the nature of the psychotherapeutic relationship, the etiology or precipitating factors in abnormal or pathological behavior, and even the con-cept of what constitutes abnormal behavior.

While psychoanalysis represents only one approach to psychotherapy, there is no denying the overall impact of psychoanalysis on psychotherapy as a whole (Westen, 1998). New approaches to psychotherapy were sometimes proposed as an expansion or further development of ideas originally present in Freud's own work, while at other times such developments arose from a perceived failing or internal inconsistency within Freudian theory or through attempts to apply psychoanalytic techniques to different clinical populations (e.g., children or schizophrenics). For example, object relations theory was one modified branch of psychoanalysis that emerged primarily in England before becoming popular in the United States in the 1960s. Object relations theory is a complex psychodynamic approach to understanding human behavior which evolved as both an expansion of and a deviation from Freudian ideas.

OBJECT RELATIONS THEORY

In its broadest sense, the term *object relations* refers to the process by which the self-structure forms early in life out of our relationships with objects. Objects, in psychoanalytic theory, do not adhere to the traditional definition of an object as an inanimate thing. Instead, an object can be truly anything, that is, while an inanimate thing can be an object, so can a person or even a part of a person. Additionally, objects can be both external and internal to an individual.

The use of the term *object* originally appeared in Freud's work to refer to anything toward which an individual directs drives for the purpose of satiation, with drives categorized into two types: libidinal and aggressive. However, in Freud's drive/structure model of the human psyche, the role of the object, while important, is also somewhat limited and secondary.

Freud's drive/structure model includes four basic assumptions relevant to a discussion of objects and object relations:

1. The unit of study in psychoanalysis is the individual as a discrete entity.
2. The essential aim of the individual is to achieve a state in which the level of stimulation within the individual is as close to zero as possible.
3. The origin of all human behavior can be ultimately traced to the demands of drives.
4. There is no inherent object; rather, the object is "created" by the individual out of his or her experience of drive satisfaction and frustration (Greenberg & Mitchell, 1983).

In reviewing particularly the fourth assumption, it becomes clear that in Freud's model drives took center stage with object creation occurring as a secondary process. For Freud, objects are created by drives and object relations are therefore a function of drive. Although Freud introduced the use of the word "object," the full development of a theory of object relations was primarily the accomplishment, not of Freud, but of his followers, in particular Melanie Klein and W. R. D. Fairbairn.

Melanie Klein

Melanie Klein (1882–1960) is important to discuss within the context of this chapter for her role as one of the primary theorists in the development of object relations theory.

Prior to the appearance of Klein's first psychoanalytic publication in 1919, a gap existed between psychoanalytic theory and practice. Freud had initially constructed his theory of psychoanalysis on the basis of clinical work with young adult hysterics; however, Freud subsequently expanded psychoanalytic theory into a general theory of psychosexual development. Freud's system elaborated a number of hypotheses concerning the inner emotional and psychological life of children, even though his theories remained largely based on extrapolations from adult recollections of childhood events and fantasies. Prior to 1919, no psychoanalyst had attempted to apply psychoanalytic techniques directly to children either to improve their emotional and psychological well-being or to test out Freud's developmental theories firsthand (Greenberg & Mitchell, 1983).

Encouraged by her mentor and analyst, Freud's friend Sandor Ferenczi, Klein began to address this gap by applying psychoanalytic principles and techniques to the treatment of children. In the course of her work with children, Klein became increasingly focused on the relationship between the child and the maternal nurturing figure, particularly during the first years of a child's life. This focus on the mother–child relationship was somewhat tragically ironic given the very troubled relationship between Melanie Klein and her daughter Melitta, also an analyst, who maintained that her brother Hans, killed during a mountain climbing accident in 1934, had actually committed suicide because of his poor relationship with their mother (Grosskurth, 1986).

As Klein began developing object relations theory she maintained that her work was not a contradiction but rather an expansion of Freudian orthodoxy. However, she did deviate from Freud, particularly regarding the relative impact upon development of the psyche of internal forces versus such external forces as the individual's social milieu. Freud's early description of objects de-emphasized the role of environment in development of the psyche. Freud centered the struggles and dramas of relationship *within* each individual in contrast to the usual location of human relating in the social realm of interaction *between* individuals (Cushman, 1992).

Like Freud, Klein presented the major components of the psyche as originating in the individual organism and developing in a maturational sequence, at which time they begin to be modified and transformed through interactions between the individual and others in his or her environment (Greenberg & Mitchell, 1983). This process relied heavily on Klein's concept of "**phantasy**." Klein's use and understanding of "phantasy" was unique enough that subsequent object relations theorists have used the unconventional spelling phantasy to differentiate Klein's use of the term from theories including a more conventional concept of fantasy. For Klein, phantasy constitutes the basic substance of all mental processes. Klein emphasized the child's unconscious phantasies about objects and gave little weight to the significance of environmental experience in determining an infant's basic outlook other than to the nature of her or his unconscious phantasy.

In a series of papers, Klein depicted a child's mental life as filled with increasingly complex phantasies, particularly concerning primary objects, such as the mother, and often specifically focused on the mother's "insides." The child desires to possess the goodness that she or he imagines is contained, for example, in the mother's body. The child imagines a similar interior to his or her own body, containing good and bad substances and objects, and is preoccupied with the need to grasp or obtain "good" substances and objects and to suppress the action of "bad" objects and substances.

In imagining this internal world of objects the child internalizes or **introjects** whole or partial objects and a complex set of internalized object relations are established, with phantasies and anxieties concerning the state of one's internal object world forming the basis for one's behavior, moods, and sense of self (Greenberg & Mitchell, 1983). In this sense, phantasy serves as the vehicle for introjection and the creation of internal objects. Klein theorized that as early as between 6 and 12 months of age infants are able to internalize whole objects with the first whole object usually being the mother in keeping with Klein's emphasis on the particular intensity of the maternal–infant relationship.

While developing further her basic theory of object relations, Klein elaborated several key concepts that remain fundamental to current psychotherapeutic theory and technique. One such key concept is that of **splitting**, which emerged in Klein's 1946 paper, "Notes on Some Schizoid Mechanisms" (Hughes, 1989), and was tightly intertwined with Klein's concept of phantasy. In the course of interacting with external objects in the environment, whole objects are internalized, which in turn form the basis of psychic life. A conflict arises within the individual psyche, however, when it attempts to reconcile the conflicting good and bad aspects of a whole object and these good and bad aspects are split off and internalized as separate good and bad internal objects which cannot be amalgamated (Greenberg & Mitchell, 1983). Another key concept developed by Klein is that of **projective identification**, an extension of splitting in which parts of the ego are separated from the rest of the self and projected into objects.

While Klein retained Freud's overall drive/structure model and presented Freudian instincts as the motivational force for object relations, she also understood instincts as being related to others' responses. This modification was the first transition from a pure drive/structure model to more of a relational/structural model of the human psyche. In some ways, Klein's insistence on her lack of contradiction with Freudian orthodoxy may have hindered her developing a truly cohesive object relations theory.

Critics of Klein have often presented her theories as highly speculative and too heavily focused on descriptions of primitive fantasy material. In addition, many critics point out major shifts in basic principles and areas of emphases over the course of Klein's career as a theorist as well as the unique forcefulness in Klein's writing style. This blend of focus on fantasy material, her theories' internal inconsistencies, and her tendency toward overgeneralizations and hyperbole have resulted in a body of work which is also extremely rich, complex, and, unfortunately, only loosely organized (Greenberg & Mitchell, 1983). This loosely organized quality of Klein's work has contributed to the frequent crediting of the development of a systematic and comprehensive object relations theory to someone other than Klein, namely, W. R. D. Fairbairn.

W. R. D. Fairbairn

Fairbairn (1889–1964), who was from Edinburgh, Scotland, and therefore maintained some physical distance from the influence of Melanie Klein at the British Psychoanalytic Society, is frequently acknowledged as a central figure in the development of object relations theory. His accomplishments toward that end may hinge, in part, on his willingness to make a more radical departure from Freudian theory than did Klein.

Fairbairn first introduced the essential elements of his theory of object relations in his paper "Endopsychic Structure Considered in Terms of Object-Relationships," first published in 1944. One of the biggest points of departure Fairbairn made from Freud's theories concerned the nature of libido. For Freud, libido was primarily pleasure-seeking whereas for Fairbairn libido was object-seeking. By taking this stance, Fairbairn actually questioned two separate but related Freudian claims, that first, the need for gratification of sexual and aggressive drives is the primary motivation for all behavior; and second, our interest in and relation to objects is based primarily on the object's role in serving this need (Eagle & Wolitzky, 1992).

One of Fairbairn's most important contributions to object relations theory was his shift in emphasis away from Freud's focus on the id and toward the ego. In Freudian theory, the ego was regarded as a relatively superficial modification of the id, designed specifically for the purpose of impulse control and adaptation to social reality demands. In contrast, Fairbairn envisioned the ego at the core of the psyche as the real self. By elevating the status of the ego and de-emphasizing the id, instinctual drives that reside in the id lost their importance and human behavior and the human psyche became instead an effect of ego-functioning (Meissner, 2000). Healthy development thus requires an intact and integrated ego.

Fairbairn's radical departure from Freudian theory may have been partly stimulated by the difference between Fairbairn's and Freud's respective patient populations; Fairbairn developed his object relations theory primarily on the basis of his experience with schizoid patients, in contrast to Freud's clinical experience working primarily with neurotics. One of Fairbairn's greatest criticisms of classic psychoanalytic theory was his perception of the failure of psychoanalysts to apply their clinical experience with patients to even their most basic theoretical principles.

Fairbairn theorized object relations as containing a number of basic points that differentiate object relations from classical psychoanalysis:

1. The ego is conceived of as whole or total at birth, becoming split and losing integrity only as a result of early bad experiences in relationships with objects, particularly the mother object.
2. Libido is regarded as a primary life drive and the energy source of the ego in its drive for relatedness with good objects.
3. Aggression is a natural defensive reaction to frustration of libidinal drive and not a separate instinct.
4. The psyche evolves as ego unity is lost and a pattern of ego-splitting and the formation of internal ego–object relations ensue.

In developing his object relations theory Fairbairn collided with adherents of Melanie Klein as well as orthodox Freudians. In particular, Fairbairn's conception of the original primitive ego was very different from Klein's. Klein presented the primitive original ego as split either at the very beginning of life due to opposing attachment and death instincts or relatively early in infancy. According to Fairbairn, however, there exists at the outset a "whole, pristine, unitary ego" that only splits as a consequence of environmental failure. As a consequence of this particular aspect of his theory, Fairbairn is frequently criticized for a perceived overemphasis on the role of parents and their early interactions with the infant as the root of all later difficulties in living. But even his critics acknowledge Fairbairn's work as providing a starting point for the accomplishments of later theorists, including Bowlby's work on attachment, Kernberg's work in the treatment of severe personality disorders, and Mitchell's relational theory. Fairbairn's work has been increasingly influential in research on infant development, child abuse, and the borderline, schizoid, and narcissistic disorders. One of Fairbairn's most influential written works was *Psychoanalytic Studies of the Personality* (1953).

ALTERNATIVES TO CLASSICAL PSYCHOANALYSIS AND OBJECT RELATIONS

D. W. Winnicott

Donald Woods Winnicott (1896–1971) was born into a prosperous middle-class family in Plymouth, England. Winnicott studied medicine in Cambridge but interrupted his education to serve as a surgeon on a British destroyer in World War I. He completed his medical studies in 1920 and in 1923 he married and took a position as a physician at the Paddington Green Children's Hospital in London.

A contemporary of W. R. D. Fairbairn, Winnicott was an early enthusiastic supporter of Freud and was heavily influenced by Freud's work. Winnicott first became aware of Freud and of psychoanalysis in 1919 when he read Freud's *The Interpretation of Dreams* (Jacobs, 1995). In 1923, Winnicott's involvement with psychoanalysis became deeper and more personal when he entered into analysis with James Strachey, who had himself been analyzed by Freud and had functioned as Freud's English translator.

In 1927, Winnicott was accepted for training by the British Psychoanalytical Society, qualifying as an adult analyst in 1934 and as a child analyst in 1935. He was still working at the children's hospital, and commented later that "at that time no other analyst was also a pediatrician so for two or three decades I was an isolated phenomenon" (Jacobs, 1995). Winnicott's work was heavily influenced by his experiences as a psychiatric consultant to the Government Evacuation Scheme during World War II. His work in treating psychologically disturbed children and working with their mothers gave Winnicott the basis upon which he would later build his most original theories. In particular, his work with evacuated children in Oxfordshire (in collaboration with his second wife Clare, who was a psychiatric social worker) dramatically shaped Winnicott's thinking as a psychoanalytic theorist.

Over six million people, many of them urban working-class citizens, were evacuated from England's cities to the countryside during World War II, particularly following the blitz of September 1940. In many cases, these evacuations resulted in the separation of children from their parents; fathers were frequently off serving in the military while mothers were required to leave the home and seek employment either for financial reasons or in support of the war effort. Despite these evacuations, nearly 8,000 children were killed in Great Britain (Holman, 1995).

We can now only imagine the stress and resultant psychological problems experienced by these children as a consequence of separation from their homes and often from their parents, even in some instances a parent's death. To give some perspective to the situation, contrast it with the stress and anxiety experienced by children in the United States, particularly in New York City, following the tragic events resulting from terrorist attacks on the World Trade Center and the Pentagon on September 11, 2001.

Many of Great Britain's child evacuees were unwelcome in the private middle-class homes that were required to accept them. Many children brought with them psychological problems, and social work services throughout the country set up programs to meet the needs of these children. In cases where home placements were unavailable or unsuccessful, these children were placed in hostels or group homes established for the purpose of providing specialized care. Clare Britton (Winnicott) worked with these evacuated children in Oxfordshire and it was there that she met D. W. Winnicott, who came on a weekly basis as a consultant to work with the children in these hostels.

The Winnicotts' work in Oxfordshire became well known across Great Britain; their paper on the Oxfordshire program was the lead article in the premier issue of *Human Relations*, an interdisciplinary journal published by the Tavistock Institute of Human Relations (Winnicott & Britton, 1947). The Winnicotts were also influential in the institution of significant changes in the structure of child welfare services in Great Britain. Subsequent to the experience of many families with the trauma of child–family separation during World War II, and particularly following the 1945 well-publicized death of a foster child, the British Home Office established the Curtis Committee in 1946 to investigate and report on the state of child welfare services. The committee interviewed 229 witnesses including John Bowlby, Susan Isaacs, and D. W. and Clare Winnicott. Their final published assessment, known as "The Curtis Report," was well received and the majority of their recommendations were implemented as part of the Children's Act of 1948 (Kanter, 2000).

When Winnicott first completed his studies to become a psychoanalyst, the British Psychoanalytical Society was in the process of being torn apart by controversial collisions between subgroups within the movement who considered themselves either "Freudians" or "Kleinians." Winnicott himself chose to belong to a third splinter group known simply as the "middle group."

From his experience at Paddington Green Children's Hospital, Winnicott became convinced of the importance of the behavior and state of mind of the mother (or other primary caretaker) in the healthy psychological development of the child. A particularly well-known quote of Winnicott's concerns the importance of relationship in the development of self during infancy:

> There is no such thing as a baby—meaning that if you set out to describe a baby, you will find you are describing a *baby and someone*. A baby cannot exist alone, but is essentially part of a relationship. (Winnicott, 1964, p. 88)

This notion of the infant, not simply as a discrete, individually functioning unit but rather in terms of its relationship to others, is a key feature of Winnicott's work and differentiated his theories from those of both the Kleinian and the Freudian camps. Winnicott believed that it is not instinctual satisfaction that causes an infant to begin to feel real and that life is worth living, but rather relational processes that lead to these feelings.

One of Winnicott's most influential written works was his paper "Transitional Objects and Transitional Phenomena" (1953). Winnicott later expanded upon the ideas presented in this paper in his book *Playing and Reality,* published in 1971, the year of his death. One of the key concepts presented in these works was that of a **transitional object**, described by Winnicott as an object used by the child as a bridge between subjective and objective reality. The transitional object is used by the child to control anxiety when threatened and in early development of play.

Another key concept of Winnicott's is that of the "**holding environment**." While Winnicott argued that the self was developed as a consequence of the parent (usually maternal)–child relationship, he also described a conflict that arises between the child's need for intimacy and the urge for separation or individuation (Cushman, 1992). According to Winnicott, the maternal figure plays a critical role in infant development by providing a "holding environment" that psychologically contains and protects the child and within which the infant can begin to integrate the "bits and pieces" of her/his experience into a more cohesive sense of self. In a psychotherapeutic relationship, the therapist is also seen as an actively holding and nurturing figure—not just in fantasy but also in reality. Winnicott used the term *good enough mother* to refer to any ordinary woman whose maternal instincts are not deflected by personal disability or by faulty "expert" advice and who is capable of providing the above described holding environment.

In the years following World War II, Winnicott was the physician in charge of the Child Department of the Institute of Psychoanalysis for twenty-five years; president of the British Psychoanalytical Society for two terms; a member of study groups convened by UNESCO and the World Health Organization (WHO); and he continued to lecture widely and produce publications while simultaneously maintaining a private practice as a pediatrician. Winnicott also continued his work at the Paddington Green Children's Hospital into the 1960s. He died in 1971 following a series of heart attacks.

Heinz Hartmann

Heinz Hartmann (1894–1970) was another prominent figure in the psychoanalytic community whose work diverged from that of Freud. Hartmann is particularly known for his theories on "**ego psychology**." Another branch of psychoanalysis, ego psychology, so called because of its focus upon ego structures and functions, was primarily developed by Anna Freud and her followers and became the primary American form of psychoanalysis from the 1940s to the 1970s. Ego psychologists translated, simplified, and operationally defined many Freudian constructs and encouraged experimental investigation of psychoanalytic hypotheses (Steele, 1985).

Born in Vienna, Hartmann was an intellectual aristocrat and the product of a long family tradition of scientific and academic achievement. An ancestor from his father's side of the family was noted astronomer and historiographer Adolf Gans (1541–1613), who was a personal acquaintance of Johannes Kepler (1571–1630). Hartmann's paternal grandfather was a well-known professor of literature and also a politician who served as a deputy in the German parliament; Hartmann's father, Ludo Hartmann, was a famous historian and professor of history at the University of Vienna as well as Austrian ambassador to Germany after World War I (Greenberg & Mitchell, 1983). Hartmann's maternal grandfather, Rudolf Chrobak, was a professor of obstetrics and gynecology who was described by Sigmund Freud in his *On the History of the Psychoanalytic Movement* as "perhaps the most eminent of all our Viennese physicians" (Freud, 1914, p. 13). With such an esteemed academic lineage, Hartmann would seem to have been destined for greatness.

Hartmann began work at the Vienna Institute of Psychiatry and Neurology in 1920. He moved to the United States in 1935 to become director and later president of the Psychoanalytic Institute of New York. He also served as president of the International Psychoanalytical Association from 1951 to 1957.

Hartmann's ultimate goal was to develop psychoanalysis into a "general psychology" rather than a theory limited by a focus on psychopathology, as evidenced by his statement that "in order fully to grasp neurosis and its etiology, we have to understand the etiology of health, too" (Hartmann, 1951, p. 145). Hartmann approached psychological development as a problem of evolution and adaptation to reality. According to Hartmann, actions (from infancy onward) are always undertaken in an attempt to adapt to one's physical and psychological realities; his reality principle took precedence over Freud's pleasure principle. Instead of Freud's conceptualization of fantasy as regressive and pathological, Hartmann believed fantasy furthered an individual's relation to reality. His psychotherapeutic strategy shifted from an interest in the examination of intrapsychic conflict and the defensive functions of the ego to an examination of the ego's adaptive functions to an average environment. Environmental failure became the key causal element in psychopathology.

Hartmann's most important and influential publication was his work, *Ego Psychology and the Problem of Adaptation* (1958/1939), in which he introduced the idea of the ego as autonomous from the instinctual drives of the id. He also emphasized the central role of the ego in the adaptation of the psyche to the individual's environment and the relevance of cognitive functions in learning about reality for the purpose of ego adaptation.

Throughout his career he remained committed to Freud's drive/structure model and, while he was aware of the many radical alternatives to drive theory proposed in the 1930s and 1940s by such theorists as Harry Stack Sullivan, Erich Fromm, Karen Horney, and others, he was unwilling to abandon drive as the conceptual center of psychoanalysis. Recognizing the validity, however, of some of their criticisms of strict orthodox Freudianism, Hartmann sought to create a blended theory incorporating their modifications within the framework of a drive/structure model. For this reason he has been referred to as an accommodation theorist or a mixed model theorist. The end result of his efforts was to open psychoanalysis to possibilities never before considered (Greenberg & Mitchell, 1983).

Margaret Mahler

Margaret Schonberger Mahler (1897–1985) was born in a small district on the border of western Hungary. Educated in Hungary and Germany, she studied medicine, eventually specializing in pediatrics, and gained a reputation for her work with severely disturbed and psychotic children. While working in Heidelberg, Germany, Mahler became more deeply interested in psychology and trained as a psychoanalyst. Her particular area of interest was in gaining a better understanding of early childhood development both in normal as well as disturbed children (The Margaret S. Mahler Psychiatric Research Foundation, 2002).

Mahler emigrated from Europe first to London and later to New York where she continued her work in psychoanalysis. She established a therapeutic nursery at the Masters Children's Center in New York City, which later expanded to include a mother–child center for neighborhood families. The center provided a setting in which Mahler and her colleagues could further their observational research into child development.

Mahler, like Hartmann, followed an accommodation approach in her modification of orthodox Freudian theory. In her work she presented the problem of development and adaptation as a coming to terms with the human environment. She presented successful development as a process she called "separation-individuation," which involved movement through different levels of relatedness, beginning with a state of embeddedness within a symbiotic child–mother dyad to the achievement of a stable individual identity. The various stages of development delineated and described by Mahler are summarized in Table 13-1.

TABLE 13-1	Mahler's Stages of Infant Development
Stages and Ages	**Primary Features**
Normal Autism: 0–2 months	Infant unaware of the mother.
Normal Symbiosis: 1–4 months	Awareness of the need to depend on another for satisfaction.
Differentiation: 4–10 months	Child begins to realize that there is a difference between him/herself and the primary parenting figure.
Early Practicing: 10–18 months	"The height of the child's love affair with the world." (Greenacre, 1957)
Rapprochement: 18–36 months	Continued exploration by the child of the environment, combined with a growing fear of loss of the object and the love of the object. Child begins to realize that love object is a separate individual, and surrenders her/his feelings of infantile grandiosity.
Object Constancy: 3 years on	Internalization of a constant inner image of the mother. Mother is clearly perceived as a separate person in the outside world, and at the same time has an existence in the internal representational world of the child. The ability to tolerate delayed gratification signifies the beginning of ego (only possible after mother is internalized).

From Mahler, M. S. (1975). *Psychological birth of the human infant.* Copyright © 1975 by Margaret S. Mahler. Reprinted by permission of Basic Books, a member of Perseus Books, L.L.C.

From the beginning of her interest in psychology until her death in 1985, Margaret Mahler conducted research, wrote, taught, and supervised analysts in training in New York and Philadelphia. A prolific author, her publications continue to serve as a resource for clinicians and researchers (The Margaret S. Mahler Psychiatric Research Foundation, 2002).

Heinz Kohut

Heinz Kohut (1913–1981) was born in Vienna, the only child of a concert pianist who had married the daughter of a wealthy merchant family, the Lampls. His father ended his music career during World War I when he served as a soldier on the Russian Front and after the war he went on to become a successful businessman. His military service meant that Heinz Kohut was separated from his father for a good portion of his early years. Kohut's relationship with his mother, whom he once described fondly as "crazy," was very close, perhaps in part as a result of his early separation from his father (Strozier, 1985).

Kohut attended the Doblinger Gymnasium where he excelled academically. In addition, his family hired a young university student who tutored him from the time Kohut was 8 until he reached the age of 14. Goldberg (1982), in his obituary of Kohut, recounted a story Kohut used to tell concerning a game he and his tutor would often play. The object of the game was to imagine how history might have been changed if a particular event had not taken place or a particular historical figure had not lived. For example, imagine how the world might be different if Caesar had not been assassinated or if the British had won the American Revolution? In addition to greatly expanding Kohut's knowledge of history, this game also doubtless instilled in Kohut at an early age a deep understanding of relationship and the interrelatedness of all human activity.

Kohut entered university at the age of 19 and at the same time had his first exposure to psychoanalysis when he entered therapy with psychoanalyst August Aichhorn. Kohut studied medicine at the University of Vienna, graduating in 1938, at the age of 24. Already a fan of Sigmund Freud, Kohut once poignantly described going to the train station in 1938 to pay tribute to "the Great Man" as Freud departed Vienna to live in exile in England (Strozier, 1985).

Kohut followed Freud into exile when he fled Vienna for England in 1939, and served as a medical intern. He then traveled to the United States, landing on his new country's shores, despite his family's wealth, with only $25 to his name. Kohut had connections in Chicago through a childhood friend as well as acquaintances within the psychoanalytic community that enabled him to obtain an internship there followed by a residency in neurology. By the time he was 31, Kohut had advanced to the position of assistant professor in neurology and psychiatry. He also began training as a psychoanalyst and upon completion of his studies in 1949 he joined the staff of the Chicago Institute of Psychoanalysis.

Through the 1950s and early 1960s, Kohut remained quite orthodox in his approach to psychoanalysis and in later years jokingly referred to himself during this time period as "Mr. Psychoanalysis." He even served as president of the American Psychoanalytic Association in 1964, a testament to the orthodoxy of his beliefs and his consequent acceptability to the "establishment" within the psychoanalytic community.

Kohut, however, began to find his own voice and used it to express what he and many fellow psychoanalysts were beginning to perceive as problems in orthodox Freudian psychoanalysis. Psychoanalytic theory and practice were reaching a crisis point; many orthodox beliefs were being called into question as anachronistic and/or overly focused on personal insight at the cost of empathy, overly obsessed with guilt, and overly valuing autonomy and individualism.

In the late 1960s, Kohut began to focus on issues in the treatment of severely disturbed patients who had previously been considered unsuitable for psychoanalytic technique. It became clear to Kohut at this time that psychoanalysis needed revision because many of the disorders commonly diagnosed by Freud and his contemporaries, such as hysteria, were no longer prevalent due to changes in society and family. New disorders such as borderline and narcissistic personality disorders were emerging which did not easily lend themselves to treatment using orthodox Freudian methodology. For this reason, Kohut did not see himself as diverging from orthodox Freudian psychoanalysis, but rather as attempting to modernize it and to keep it sociohistorically relevant. He presented himself as the "new voice of psychoanalysis."

Beginning in the mid-1960s, Kohut experienced a burst of creativity lasting for the next fifteen years of his life and resulting in a theoretical model that Kohut called his "psychology of the self." His reformulation of psychoanalysis is frequently regarded as the pivotal event transforming the field from the Freudian emphasis on the drive/structure model into a true "relational psychoanalysis." At the center of Kohut's self psychology lies his concept of the self, to which he ascribes functions previously attributed to the id, ego, and superego in the classical Freudian drive/structure model. The self is no longer a representation or by-product of ego activity but is itself an active agent.

For Kohut, the infant is born into an empathic and responsive human environment and relatedness with others is as essential for the infant's psychological survival as oxygen is for physical survival (Greenberg & Mitchell, 1983). The infant's self cannot stand alone—it requires the participation of others to provide a sense of structure. The early self emerges at the point where "the baby's innate potentialities and the [parents] expectations with regard to the baby converge" (Kohut, 1977, p. 99). The emergent infant self, however, is weak and amorphous and cannot stand alone as it requires the participation of others, termed by Kohut as "**self-objects**," to provide a sense of cohesion, constancy, and resilience (Greenberg & Mitchell, 1983). An object is a self-object when it is experienced within the psyche as providing functions in a relationship that evoke, maintain, or positively affect the sense of self. Self-objects serve functions that will later be performed by the older individual's own psychic structure.

A key concept of Kohut's self-psychology is that of "**mirroring**." Kohut presented the infant as seeking two fundamental types of relationship with self-objects. First, the infant needs to display his or her evolving capabilities and to be admired for them, and second, the infant needs to form an idealized image of at least one of her or his parents and to experience a sense of merger with an idealized self-object (Greenberg & Mitchell, 1983). Failures to mirror or to idealize self-objects are termed empathic failures, and they lead to slow internalization of self-object relations. Chronic empathic failures lead to pathology.

Empathy was a critical process in Kohut's approach to psychotherapy. The therapeutic psychoanalytic process involves creation of an empathic interpersonal field in which the participation of the analyst is essential, in contrast to the traditional psychotherapeutic approach in which the therapist is a neutral observer interpreting drive and defense processes within the patient. Like Winnicott, Kohut believed that disorders of the self could be generally understood as environmental deficiency diseases; the parents have failed to allow the child to establish and then dissolve the requisite self-object relationships that allow the generation of healthy structures within the self (Greenberg & Mitchell, 1983).

Heinz Kohut was not the only psychoanalyst to consider social and historical factors in terms of their relevance to psychopathology and to psychoanalytic theory. However, while

Kohut broadened the scope of psychoanalytic theory to make room for such considerations, the primary aim of his self-psychology was the better understanding of **individual development** and not, necessarily, a better understanding of **societal development**; Kohut was a psychoanalyst first and foremost and not a social psychologist. In contrast, Erich Fromm stands as someone who, while he identified himself primarily as a psychoanalyst, was also a social psychologist.

Erich Fromm

Erich Pinchas Fromm (1900–1980) was born in Frankfurt, Germany, the only child of an orthodox Jewish wine trader named Naphtali Fromm and his wife Rosa. Unlike Sigmund Freud whose family, while Jewish, did not actively practice their faith, Fromm's father came from an old rabbinical family and the Jewish faith had a profound effect on Erich Fromm.

In his book *Beyond the Chains of Illusion: My Encounter with Marx and Freud* (1962), Fromm described a couple of events from his childhood that deeply impacted him and affected the nature and scope of his later work as a theorist. The first event occurred when he was 12 years old. At that time Fromm was quite fascinated by an attractive young woman who was a friend of the Fromm family; this fascination stemmed in part from the fact that she was the first painter he had ever met as well as from her physical beauty, which appealed to the adolescent male Fromm.

This attractive young woman, who at that time was 25 years old, remained unmarried and was frequently in the company of her widowed father. When her father died, Erich Fromm was shocked when the young woman committed suicide immediately afterwards, leaving a will stipulating that she be buried with her father. Her suicide had a dramatic impact on Fromm, as he described in *Beyond the Chains of Illusion*:

> I had never heard of an Oedipus complex or of incestuous fixations between daughter and father. But I was deeply touched. . . . I was hit by the thought "How is it possible" . . . that a young woman should be so in love with her father, that she prefers to be buried with him to being alive to the pleasures of life and of painting? Certainly I knew no answer, but the "How is it possible" stuck. And when I became acquainted with Freud's theories, they seemed to be the answer to a puzzling and frightening experience at a time when I was beginning to develop into an adolescent. (Fromm, 1962, p. 4)

Fromm also describes, in the same book, being profoundly impacted by his experiences as a young teenager in Germany during World War I. His early exposure to occasional evidence of racial hatred toward himself and his family as Jews in Germany had not prepared him for what he described as the "hysteria of hate against the British which swept throughout Germany" in the years surrounding World War I. Again Fromm found himself asking "How is it possible?" "How is it possible that millions of men continue to stay in the trenches, to kill innocent men of other nations, and to be killed and thus to cause the deepest pain to parents, wives, friends?" (Fromm, 1962, p. 8). By the time the war ended in 1918, Fromm was obsessed by the need to understand how war is possible, and with a questioning and critically appraising attitude toward individual and social phenomena.

It was with this same questioning and appraising attitude that Fromm first encountered and studied the teachings of two individuals who deeply influenced his work in psychology: Sigmund Freud and Karl Marx. The extent of their influence is suggested by the subtitle of Fromm's intellectual autobiography *Beyond the Chains of Illusion*. As a young student at the University of Frankfurt, his preoccupation with the problem of understanding the seeming irrationality of human mass behavior naturally drew him to the study of psychology, philosophy, and sociology. After two semesters at the University of Frankfurt, Fromm went to Heidelberg in 1919 to study under sociologists Alfred Weber, Karl Jaspers, and Heinrich Rickert. In 1922, Fromm obtained a doctorate and proceeded with further studies in psychiatry and psychology in Munich, during which time he also underwent psychoanalysis with therapist Frieda Reichmann. He then embarked on his own career as a psychotherapist. Fromm's personal life progressed apace with his academic and professional career and he married Frieda Reichmann in 1926. Their marriage, however, was brief; they were separated by 1931 yet remained friends.

In 1929, Erich Fromm cofounded the South German Institute for Psychoanalysis in Frankfurt, together with Karl Landauer, Frieda Fromm-Reichmann, and Heinrich Meng. In 1930, Fromm became a member of the Institute for Social Research in Frankfurt, which held sway over the fields of both psychoanalysis and social psychology. At the same time he completed his training as a psychoanalyst at the Psychoanalytic Institute in Berlin.

Fromm's gradual divergence from Freud stemmed from Fromm's greater focus on political and cultural issues and their impact on individual personality. His interest in the effects of culture brought him into the intellectual orbit of like-minded figures in the psychoanalytic community, including Karen Horney, with whom Fromm engaged in a brief but intense love affair in addition to their intellectual collaboration, and psychiatrist Harry Stack Sullivan.

In 1934, Fromm fled Germany and immigrated to the United States, settling in New York City where he worked at the Institute for Social Research until 1939. Throughout much of his adult life, Fromm's professional career was frequently interrupted by health problems resulting from tuberculosis, which he had initially contracted in 1931. His work was also impacted by his own personal losses, including the failure of his marriage and the death of his father in 1933. In 1941, Fromm began teaching at the New School for Social Research in New York where he remained for several years and also published one of his most well-known books, *Escape From Freedom*. In addition to his work at the New School for Social Research, Fromm also held part-time positions and guest lectured at various institutions such as Bennington College in Vermont and Yale University in Connecticut.

In the 1950s, Fromm and his second wife, Henny Gurland, moved to Mexico City where Fromm was very instrumental in the development of psychotherapy in Mexico. He served as Professor Extraordinary at the Medical Faculty of the National Autonomous University of Mexico where he taught Mexico's first course in psychoanalysis, and in 1956 founded the Mexican Psychoanalytic Society. In 1963, he also opened the Mexican Psychoanalytical Institute.

During the 1960s, while he maintained his primary residence in Mexico, Fromm continued lecturing in the United States. He also became increasingly involved in politics, participating in a peace conference in Moscow in 1962 and becoming actively involved in protests against the Vietnam War. Fromm remained professionally active throughout the 1970s, although his health became progressively fragile and he moved to Tessin, Switzerland, where he found the climate and atmosphere more restful. He suffered a series of heart attacks over a period of several years and finally died of a heart attack on March 18, 1980.

Fromm's Theory

Fromm based his synthetic Freudian-Marxian model on the premise that the inner life of each individual draws its content from the cultural and historical context in which he or she lives (Greenberg & Mitchell, 1983). We each institute and perpetuate social values and processes as a means of individually solving the problems posed by the human condition. Despite the breadth of Fromm's contributions to psychoanalysis and social psychology, his dual emphasis on psychodynamics and sociohistorical factors contributed to the frequent dismissal of his importance by critics who view him more as a social philosopher than as a psychoanalytic theorist (Greenberg & Mitchell, 1983).

According to Greenberg and Mitchell (1983), Fromm believed the major flaw in Freud's psychoanalytic theory was Freud's failure to place his observations of human behavior within a larger context of historical and cultural evolution. In his 1970 book, *The Crisis of Psychoanalysis*, Fromm argued that the central insight of Freud's theory concerned the importance of hypocrisy in that Freud's patients thought of themselves, and to a large degree acted, as the proper Victorian ladies and gentleman their society dictated they be, but at the same time Freud discovered lurking underneath this façade or "false consciousness" a host of sexual and aggressive fantasies and motives. For Fromm, Freud's key discovery was that of humankind's capacity for distorting the reality of one's experience to conform to socially established norms.

Where Freud erred, according to Fromm, was in focusing on the sexual and aggressive content and extrapolating from such content a motivational theory for all human behavior thereby ignoring the process and structure of self-deception. In effect, Freud shifted the focus of analysis away from the relationship between the individual and the world of other people to a focus on forces arising within the individual. Fromm saw a potential solution to "Freud's error" in Marx's ideas concerning history and cultural transformation. Both Freud and Marx, however, developed theories that were deterministic in their view of human behavior: Freud's theory postulated that behavior and the individual psyche were largely determined by biology; Marx saw human behavior as determined by society, particularly by economic systems (Boeree, 1997a). In contrast, Fromm allowed for the possibility for people to transcend determinism by centering a great deal of his theory on the idea of **freedom**, making it the central characteristic of human nature.

According to Fromm, the concept of the individual with unique thoughts, feelings, moral conscience, freedom, and responsibility has evolved over the centuries. Thus, for example, in contrast to the modern individual, a person living during the Middle Ages led a life largely determined by socioeconomic realities. If your father was a peasant, you would grow up to be a peasant; a prince would eventually become a king, all predetermined by the fate of one's birth. Given this relative lack of freedom, however, life is made easier and simpler because an individual's life has structure and meaning and there is no need for doubts or soul-searching (Boeree, 1997a). As the modern individual evolved, the consequences of increased individual freedom emerged, such as isolation, alienation, and bewilderment, thus making freedom a difficult challenge. Fromm described three ways, summarized in Table 13-2, in which we seek to escape the difficulties and associated pain of freedom through an "**escape from freedom**"; one's particular choice of method of escaping from freedom has a great deal to do with what kind of family one grew up in. In particular, Fromm outlined two kinds of family structures lending themselves toward particular choices in method of escape from freedom, namely, symbiotic families and withdrawing families. In a symbiotic

TABLE 13-2	Fromm's Three Methods of "Escape from Freedom"
Authoritarianism	We avoid freedom by fusing ourselves with others and becoming a part of an authoritarian system. Two ways to approach this are, (1) to submit to the power of others by becoming passive and compliant or (2) to become an authority by applying structure to others. Either way, the individual escapes his or her separate identity.
Destructiveness	We escape what is a painful existence by essentially eliminating ourselves: If there is no me, how can anything hurt me? Alternatively, we can respond to personal pain by lashing out at the world: If I destroy the world, how can it hurt me? These approaches lead to destructive behavior (destructive of self or of others): suicide, drug addiction, self-abuse versus crime, terrorism, brutality, humiliation.
Automaton conformity	Another means of escape from freedom is to hide in our mass culture. If I look like, talk like, think like everyone else in my society, then I disappear into the crowd. I no longer have to struggle with decisions and I don't need to either acknowledge my freedom or take personal responsibility for my actions.

Adapted from Boeree, C. G. (1997a). *Erich Fromm: 1900–1980*. [Online]. Available at http://ship.edu/~cgboeree/fromm.html.

family, some members are "swallowed up" by other members so that they fail to develop personalities of their own, for example, the parent "swallows" the child so that the child's personality becomes a mere reflection of the parent's wishes. Symbiotic families tend to promote an authoritarian method of escape from freedom. Withdrawing families, the more recently evolved type of family structure, manifest themselves in two ways: parents are either demanding, holding high expectations of their children and maintaining very high, well-defined standards, or parents tend to be overly controlling of their own emotions, presenting a façade of cool indifference. The most common method of escape from freedom in a withdrawing family structure is automaton conformity (see Table 13-2). Fromm expressed particular concern regarding automaton conformity as he felt that the withdrawing family structure was becoming increasingly prevalent embodied by the modern, shallow, television family (Boeree, 1997a).

Fromm further believed that our families are mostly a reflection of our larger society and culture. We have absorbed our cultures so well that they have become unconscious—the social unconscious, to be precise. This "social unconscious" is very different from Jung's concept of a "collective unconscious." Fromm believed that the social unconscious could be best understood through an examination of our economic systems. Erich Fromm, beyond his reputation as a psychoanalyst, is frequently acknowledged as an important social philosopher and humanist and is considered by some to be one of the truly important figures of 20th-century humanism. He wrote over forty books, at least forty million copies of which have been sold worldwide.

Erik Erikson

A number of theorists described thus far in this chapter have focused the bulk of their theorizing on issues relevant to human behavior and human development during the first half of the lifespan from infancy through the early phase of adulthood. Erik Erikson developed the first detailed model tracing human development beyond these early phases reaching across the continuum of the lifespan.

Erik Erikson (1902–1994) was born in Frankfurt, Germany, the son of Danish parents. His father was protestant and his mother Jewish and the two actually separated prior to his birth. Erikson's mother, Karla Abrahamsen, lived in Karlsruhe, Germany, raising Erikson as a single mother prior to marrying her son's pediatrician, Dr. Theodor Homberger, when Erikson was three years old. For the majority of his childhood Erikson was raised as Erik Homberger and was in fact unaware that Theodor Homberger was not his biological father. He changed his name to Erik Erikson much later in his life, after he immigrated to the United States, and no one knows for certain why he chose Erikson as his new surname.

Erikson attended the Humanistiche Gymnasium in Karlsruhe where he was unfortunately constantly treated as an outsider (Hunt, 1993). He graduated at the age of 18 but was uninterested in pursuing higher education at that time, following instead his interest in art and traveling about the German countryside reading, drawing, and making woodcarvings (Top Biography, 2002). As Erikson himself once said, "I was an artist then, which is European euphemism for a young man with some talent but nowhere to go." Erikson returned home after a year and decided to try pursuing formal studies in art, first in Karlsruhe and later in Munich and then Florence, Italy. In 1927, a former classmate and friend, Peter Blos, invited Erikson to Vienna to become an art teacher at a psychoanalytically oriented school for children founded by Dorothy Burlingham and Anna Freud where, in addition to his work as an art teacher, Erikson also obtained a certificate from the Maria Montessori School, becoming one of the few men to hold membership in the Montessori Lehrerinnen Verein (Top Biography, 2002).

At first, Erikson had difficulty merging his artistic style with his intellectual efforts, but gradually, with the mentoring of Anna Freud, he was able to use his artistic talent for keen observation in the psychoanalytical observation of children's play. While in Vienna, Erikson met and married Joan Serson, a Canadian-born, American-trained sociologist with an interest in modern dance and psychoanalysis. She became an English teacher at the school where Erikson worked and also one of his closest professional collaborators.

Erikson became a psychoanalyst after completing training at the Vienna Psychoanalytic Institute in 1933. By that time fascism was already becoming a concern for anyone with a Jewish heritage, and after considering several options the Eriksons decided to take advantage of an invitation from Hans Sachs, a disciple of Freud, to come to Boston. Erikson was the first child psychoanalyst in the Boston area and he joined the faculty of Harvard Medical School, becoming part of a research team working on personality under the leadership of Henry Murray, who was then director of the Harvard Psychological Clinic. While there, Erikson was influenced and inspired by Henry Murray as well as by a number of anthropologists including Margaret Mead, Ruth Benedict, and Gregory Bateson, all influential figures in the field of anthropology.

During World War II, Erikson conducted research relevant to the war effort, including studies on submarine habitation and on the interrogation of prisoners of war. He also wrote psychobiographical essays on Adolph Hitler and published *Hitler's Imagery and German Youth* (1942). Another, later, psychobiographical work, his book *Gandhi's Truth: On the*

Origins of Militant Nonviolence (1969), earned Erikson both a Pulitzer Prize and the National Book Award, a unique achievement for a psychologist.

Although Erikson was offered a professorship at the University of California at Berkeley his tenure was broken as a result of the activities of Senator Joseph McCarthy and the Committee on Un-American Activities. McCarthyism had infiltrated academia and professors were being forced to sign loyalty oaths establishing that they were anticommunist. Erikson was fired for being one of the few individuals who refused to sign. Although later reinstated, he chose to resign in 1950 in support of his peers who had been fired for the same reason but had not been reinstated to the faculty. Erikson then accepted Robert Knight's invitation to join him at the Austen Riggs Center in Stockbridge, Massachusetts, a center devoted to psychotherapy and research with severely disturbed adolescents and young adults.

From 1960 until his retirement in 1970, Erikson taught as a Professor of Human Development at Harvard University. However, even after his so-called retirement, Erikson undertook his first research efforts in the area of gerontology in collaboration with his wife Joan Erikson and Helen Kivnick. The trio studied twenty-nine people in their eighties, all of whom were parents of children Erikson had earlier studied as part of the Guidance Study at the Institute of Human Development at the University of California at Berkeley. The results of this research were published in 1986 as _Vital Involvement in Old Age_. Erikson's career finally came to an end when he died at the age of 92 in Harwich, Massachusetts on May 12, 1994.

Gordon Allport

Professor Gordon Allport (1897–1967) more than any other theorist played a vital role in bringing the formal study of personality into academic acceptance from out of its previously exclusive focus in the clinical setting. Allport, unlike Freud and many Freudian followers, led a relatively happy and unremarkable childhood. Both Gordon and his brother Floyd Allport pursued the study of psychology at Harvard University. Gordon Allport earned his PhD in psychology from Harvard in 1922.

Allport took time off to travel between his undergraduate and graduate years at Harvard, and visited Sigmund Freud in Vienna. Years later he described this single encounter as traumatic and voiced the opinion that psychoanalysis focused too greatly on unconscious forces and motives and neglected conscious motives (Allport, 1967). Hence, Allport proceeded to develop his own theory of personality that differed dramatically from that of Freud. Allport minimized the role of the unconscious in mentally healthy adults arguing that they instead function in a more rational conscious mode. Allport also disagreed with Freud concerning the impact of childhood experiences on conflicts in adult life and insisted that we are more influenced by the present and by our plans for the future than by our past. Allport also insisted that personality could only be investigated through the study of normal adults and not the study of neurotics. In fact, Allport argued that there were no similarities between normal and neurotic persons. In particular, Allport attributed a more significant degree of influence to the unconscious in the mind of the unhealthy neurotic.

Allport's personality theory centered on the concept of motivation. A key concept in his theory is that of **functional autonomy** or the idea that a motive is not functionally related to any childhood experience and is independent of the original circumstances in which the motive first appeared. Allport envisioned the adult human being as self-determining and independent of childhood experiences. For Allport, motives change over time.

In the course of formulating his own theories concerning personality and the development of the self, Allport reviewed hundreds of definitions of the term *self*. He concluded that the variety of definitions and the very different connotations and ways of interpreting the term *self* made it difficult to conduct research on the concept without engendering confusion. Allport thus decided to dispense with the common word "self" and substituted instead the word "**proprium**" taken from the Greek root meaning appropriate. The term *proprium*, however, never came into popular usage in psychology. For Allport, the "proprium" or self is what belongs to or is appropriate for the individual and this self develops through seven stages from infancy to adolescence. The key element in the course of the development of this self is not the psychosexual issues so important to Freudian theory, but rather social relationships.

A primary area of study for Allport was personality traits, beginning with his doctoral dissertation. He distinguished between **traits**, which can be shared by any number of individuals, and **personal dispositions**, which are traits unique to each individual. He further described three different kinds of traits, including:

- Cardinal traits, which define and dominate every aspect of life
- Central traits, which are more generalized behavioral themes; for example, aggressiveness or sentimentality
- Secondary traits, which are displayed less frequently and consistently than other traits.

Lastly, Allport contributed significantly to research examining such social issues as prejudice. He received the Gold Medal Award from the American Psychological Foundation and the Distinguished Scientific Contribution Award from the American Psychological Association (APA), and also served as a past president of the APA. He remained professionally active until his death in 1967 in Cambridge, Massachusetts.

Henry Murray

Henry Murray (1893–1988) began undergraduate studies at Harvard majoring initially in history. After completing his B.A., Murray transferred to Columbia, earning his M.D. in 1919. Murray then studied embryology at the Rockefeller Institute for four years, followed by further doctoral studies at Cambridge University in England where he completed a PhD in chemistry.

Murray's interest in psychology was prompted initially by a personal crisis. He had fallen in love with a married woman named Christiana Morgan while he himself was also married at the time. Morgan suggested that Murray seek the advice and counsel of Carl Jung, who at the time was also openly having an affair with a younger woman while maintaining his relationship with his wife and family. Jung advised Murray to follow his example and to openly maintain both relationships, which Murray did for the next forty years.

This initial contact on a personal level led to Murray's professional interest in psychology. In 1927, he decided to pursue studies in psychology and returned to the United States to become the assistant to Morton Prince at Harvard's new psychological clinic (Thorne & Henley, 1997). Murray remained at Harvard for the majority of his career with the exception of a period of time during World War II when he worked for the Office of Strategic Services (OSS), which is the prototype for today's Central Intelligence Agency (CIA). His work for the OSS centered on observation of subjects in stressful real-life situations, an approach that evolved into the assessment-center approach now widely used in executive selection in the arenas of business and government.

His work in the area of personality led to his development, in collaboration with Christiana Morgan, of the **Thematic Apperception Test (TAT)** in 1935. The TAT consists of thirty pictures depicting ambiguous social situations, and administration of the test typically consists of the presentation of a subset of these pictures to the subject with the instruction that the subject must then create a story about each picture. The story contents are then analyzed for the presence of common themes giving insight into the personality of the subject. This psychodynamic approach to personality assessment is very reminiscent of Freud's use of dream analysis to reveal unconscious processes. While enthusiastically received at first, the TAT subsequently declined in popularity due to the difficulty in developing valid and reliable scoring methods for interpreting results. It should be noted at this time that for many years it was assumed that the TAT was primarily Murray's work with Christiana Morgan functioning strictly in an assistive role; however, in 1985, Murray himself wrote that Morgan in fact had the main role in developing the test and noted that the original idea came from a woman student in one of his classes (Bronstein, 1988).

Murray's varied background and his exposure, through Jung, to the ideas of Freud both influenced the nature of Murray's own theory of human personality, which he called **personology**. Following the Freudian tradition, Murray's model stressed the concept of tension reduction as well as the importance of the unconscious and the impact of early childhood experience on adult behavior. Murray also incorporated into his model a somewhat modified version of Freud's id, ego, and superego (Murray, 1938). His modification to the id involved his inclusion of positive, socially desirable tendencies such as empathy, identification, and love in contrast to Freud's focusing of the id on more primitive and sexual impulses. While Freud focused on the need for suppression of these dark id impulses, Murray's system allowed for the need to foster or to express fully the more positive aspects of the id as critical for normal development to occur.

Murray also modified Freud's concept of the ego, giving the ego a more active role as the conscious organizer of behavior and not simply as the servant of the id. Murray also expanded the sphere of social influences impacting the development of the superego. Freud focused primarily upon parental influence as the key to development of the superego whereas Murray included one's peer group and exposure to cultural vehicles such as literature and mythology as also influential. Unlike Freud, who felt that the superego was essentially fixed by the age of 5, Murray believed that the superego continued to develop across the life span.

Although he incorporated Freud's structures of id, ego, and superego, Murray's personality theory differed from Freud's in that it centered on motivation. One of Murray's most fundamental contributions to psychology remains his development of a classification of needs to explain motivation and this aspect of his personality theory is heavily influenced by his own background in medicine and chemistry. In Murray's theory, needs, including for example the need for achievement, affiliation, and dominance, involve chemical forces in the brain that organize intellectual and perceptual functioning. Need leads to arousal and increased tension levels in the body which are then only reduced through satisfaction of the need. Need thus activates behavior, the purpose of which is need satisfaction.

A THIRD FORCE IN PSYCHOLOGY: HUMANISTIC PSYCHOLOGY

Beginning in the early 1960s a new movement arose within American psychology known as humanistic psychology or the "third force." Humanistic psychologists emerged in opposition to what were at that time the two most influential theoretical forces in psychology, namely, behaviorism and psychoanalysis. Humanistic psychology was known by the name "third-force psychology" to signify its presence as a third alternative to these two powerful rivals. The basic underlying assumptions separating humanistic psychology from behaviorism and psychoanalysis include:

■ An emphasis on conscious (not unconscious) experience
■ A belief in the wholeness of human nature
■ A focus on free will, spontaneity, and the creative power of the individual
■ The study of all factors relevant to the human condition.

The roots of the humanistic movement in psychology can be found in the work of earlier psychologists including Franz Brentano (1838–1917) and William James (1842–1910), both of whom criticized the mechanistic/reductionistic approach to psychology; Oswald Külpe (1862–1915), who demonstrated that not all conscious experience was reducible or explainable in terms of simple stimulus-response relationships; and the Gestalt psychologists, who believed in taking a holistic approach to the study of consciousness. Psychoanalysts such as Adler, Horney, Erikson, and Allport also contributed to the development of the third force by contradicting Freud's focus on the unconscious and focusing instead on the individual as a conscious being possessing free will and capable of active self-creation and not just passive development in response to external forces. The creative and self-generative aspects of third-force psychology struck a chord with the 1960s American counterculture, expressed primarily by college-age youth.

Abraham Maslow

Abraham Maslow (1908–1970) was one of the leading groundbreakers in humanistic psychology. Maslow was born in Brooklyn, New York, and led a rather unhappy childhood. He was the eldest of seven children born to parents who were both uneducated Russian-Jewish immigrants. His father, an alcoholic and a womanizer, frequently disappeared for long periods of time and Maslow's mother was frequently abusive toward Maslow, openly rejecting him and favoring his younger siblings. Maslow never forgave his mother for her treatment of him, and refused to attend her funeral when she died. He once wrote: "The whole thrust of my life-philosophy and all my research and theorizing also has its roots in a hatred for and revulsion against everything she stood for" (Maslow, as cited in Hoffman, 1988, p. 9).

As an adolescent, Maslow tried to compensate for feelings of inferiority stemming from his scrawny build and large nose by excelling in athletics. When he failed to succeed as an athlete, however, he turned to academics. Maslow enrolled at the City College of New York (CCNY) where he studied law before becoming interested in psychology. He then transferred to Cornell University where Edward B. Titchener (1867–1927) taught Maslow's first course in psychology. Maslow found that psychology as presented by Titchener was "awful and bloodless and had nothing to do with people, so I shuddered and turned away from it" (Maslow, as cited in Hoffman, 1988, p. 26). Fortunately, he did not turn away from psychology for very long. In 1928, he married his first cousin, Bertha Goodman, against his parents' wishes and the couple moved to Wisconsin where Maslow transferred to the University of Wisconsin, earning his B.A. (1930), his M.A. (1931), and a PhD in psychology (1934). While at the University of Wisconsin, Maslow worked with Harry Harlow, who was famous for his experiments with rhesus monkeys and attachment behavior.

A year after graduation, Maslow returned to New York to work with E. L. Thorndike at Columbia where Maslow became interested in research on human sexuality, motivation, personality, and clinical psychology. He also began teaching full-time at Brooklyn College. Initially an enthusiastic behaviorist, Maslow became convinced, on the basis of personal experiences including the birth of his children and his experiences in World War II, that behaviorism was too limited to be of relevance to real human issues.

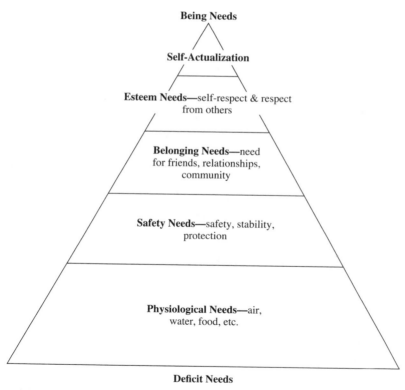

FIGURE 13-1 Maslow's Hierarchy of Human Needs

Adapted from Boeree, C. G. (1997b). *Abraham Maslow: 1908–1970*. [Online]. Available at http://ship.edu/~cgboeree/maslow.html. Frager, R. D., & Fadiman, J. (Eds.), Abraham H. Maslow. *Motivation and personality* (3rd ed.). Copyright © 1987. Electronically reproduced by permission of Pearson Education, Inc., Upper Saddle River, New Jersey.

Maslow's initial attempts to develop humanistically oriented theories within psychology met with resistance from the influential behaviorist establishment. Considered by his peers to be highly unorthodox, Maslow was unable to get any of the major psychology journals to publish his work. After leaving Brooklyn College, he took a position at Brandeis University in Waltham, Massachusetts, where he remained from 1951 until 1969. He was elected president of the American Psychological Association (APA) in 1967 and died of a heart attack on June 8, 1970.

While he was working at Brandeis University, Maslow met Kurt Goldstein, who introduced him to the concept of **self-actualization**, which is a state of achieving the full development and realization of one's abilities and potential (Boeree, 1997b). Maslow was convinced that humans have needs beginning with basic physiological and practical needs, and progressing in hierarchical fashion through higher-order levels of need. Needs at any given level within this hierarchy could not be addressed unless lower-level needs had been satisfied. At the apex of this hierarchical structuring of human needs, Maslow believed that humans have a deep need to achieve the state of self-actualization. Perhaps one of Maslow's most influential and popular contributions was his creation of this **hierarchy of human needs** (Figure 13-1).

Carl Rogers

Carl Rogers (1902–1987) was born in Oak Park, Illinois, a suburb of Chicago. His father was a civil engineer and his mother was a housewife, and Carl was the fourth of their six children. Carl Rogers was an academic achiever even in early childhood and entered school directly into the second grade, having already learned to read before he was old enough for kindergarten. When Rogers was 12 years old, the family moved from the suburbs to a rural farm.

Rogers enrolled at the University of Wisconsin as a major in agriculture but later switched his major to religion with the intention of studying for the ministry. He was selected to join nine other students who traveled for six months to Beijing, China, as part of the "World Student Christian Federation Conference." As is well known, travel to other countries frequently stimulates a broadening of one's thinking and this was no less true for Carl Rogers. His experiences in Beijing caused Rogers to begin to doubt some of his most basic religious views and assumptions. His academic career was also interrupted at this time when he was hospitalized for six months for treatment of an ulcer (Boeree, 2002).

After graduating from the University of Wisconsin, Rogers married Helen Elliot and moved to New York City where he began attending the Union Theological Seminary, a famous liberal religious institution (Boeree, 1998). While there he took a seminar titled "Why am I entering the ministry?" and in the course of taking the class, made the decision not to pursue the ministry. He left the seminary to enroll in the clinical psychology program at Columbia University where he earned his PhD in 1931. His decision to make the transition from theology to psychology was in part stimulated by a course Rogers took at Columbia in clinical psychology taught by Leta Stetter Hollingworth (1886–1939). While still enrolled at Columbia, Rogers began clinical work in psychology, first at the Institute of Child Guidance, and later, after completing his Doctor of Education (EdD) from Teachers College, at the Rochester Society for the Prevention of Cruelty to Children. While there Rogers learned about the clinical theories and therapeutic techniques of Otto Rank (1884–1939), a psychoanalyst and disciple of Sigmund Freud.

Rogers then left New York to take a position as a full professor at Ohio State in 1940. While at Ohio State, he published his first book, *Counseling and Psychotherapy: Newer Concepts in Practice* (1942). In 1945, he went to work at the University of Chicago where he established a counseling center and remained until 1957. While at the University of Chicago, Rogers published his most popular and influential work, *Client-Centered Therapy: Its Current Practice, Implications and Theory* (1951), in which he outlined the bulk of his clinical theory (Gendlin, 1988).

Client-centered (or what is now called person-centered) therapy is distinguished by certain qualities or characteristics including an environment in which the therapist provides unconditional positive regard and empathic understanding toward the client as well as a sense of genuineness or authenticity on the part of the therapist. The therapist displays empathic understanding by listening to what the client is trying to communicate and then sharing his or her understanding with the client as a means of validating the client's communication (Boeree, 2002).

In addition to promoting a very different therapeutic technique as an alternative to psychoanalytic techniques that had previously dominated the clinical setting, Rogers and his colleagues also were instrumental in promoting the idea that psychotherapy could be studied objectively. Rogers was elected president of the American Psychological Association (APA) in 1946 and in 1956 and, along with Wolfgang Köhler and Kenneth Spence, was selected to receive the first Distinguished Scientific Contribution Award by the American Psychological Association (APA).

Rogers eventually returned to the University of Wisconsin; however, interdepartmental conflicts caused him to become disillusioned with academia and in 1964 he left to take a research position in the private sector in La Jolla, California. Although no longer working in the academic setting, Rogers continued to practice as a clinical psychologist and to write about his clinical theories until his death in 1987.

Rollo May

Rollo May (1909–1994) was born in Ada, Ohio. May's childhood was marred by his parents' divorce as well as his sister's psychotic breakdown. He briefly attended Michigan State but was asked to leave after he became involved with a radical student magazine (Boeree, 1998). May then attended Oberlin College in Ohio, and after graduating from Oberlin he traveled to Greece where he taught English at Anatolia College for three years and also studied briefly with Alfred Adler, a protégé and later defector of Sigmund Freud.

Perhaps coincidentally, May shared Carl Rogers' early interest in religious studies, and after obtaining his B.A. from Oberlin College (1930), May earned a divinity degree from Union Theological Seminary (1938) before earning a PhD in clinical psychology granted by Columbia in 1949 (Boeree, 1998). Also like Rogers, May's academic progress was somewhat slowed due to personal illness, in May's case, tuberculosis.

May spent three years in a sanatorium for the treatment of tuberculosis and this experience had a significant impact on him as a psychologist. Forced to face the possibility of death at an earlier age than most, he spent many of his hours reading philosophy and religion and was greatly influenced by the writings of Søren Kierkegaard, a Danish religious writer and philosopher who was influential in the existentialist movement (Boeree, 1998). Before undertaking graduate studies at Columbia, May also studied psychoanalysis at the White Institute where he met influential figures in the psychoanalytic community including Harry Stack Sullivan and Erich Fromm.

May's dissertation had an existentialist orientation as it focused on the meaning of anxiety. He became, over the course of his career, perhaps the most celebrated American existential psychotherapist of his era and he drew heavily on the ideas of existentialist philosophers including Kierkegaard and Heidegger. In 1958, he co-edited the book *Existence: A New Dimension in Psychiatry and Psychology* with Ernest Angel and Henre Ellenberger, in which the trio introduced existential psychology to the United States. He died in Tiburon, California, in October of 1994.

Existential psychology was heavily influenced by the earlier work of existential philosophers such as Søren Kierkegaard (1813–1855), Friedrich Nietzsche (1844–1900), and Martin Heidegger (1889–1976). Two themes in existentialism were particularly appealing to humanistic psychologists, namely, subjective meaning rather than "objective" third-person observations of brain and behavior must be the central focus of psychology. Second, humans have free will and thus must take responsibility for their choices.

The formalization of the humanistic movement in psychology was evident in several events: the founding of the *Journal of Humanistic Psychology* in 1961, the establishment of the American Association for Humanistic Psychology in 1962, and the establishment of the Division of Humanistic Psychology of the American Psychological Association in 1971. Humanistic psychologists sought to promote their theories, methods, and terminology; however, by 1985 even humanistic psychologists were agreeing that while "humanistic psychology was a great experiment . . . it is basically a failed experiment in that there is no humanistic school of thought in psychology, no theory that would be recognized as a philosophy of science" (Cunningham, 1985, p. 18).

■ Summary

The history of psychotherapy has proceeded in many ways as an ongoing dialogue and argument with Sigmund Freud. We presented an overview of the key developments in the history of psychotherapy beginning with a discussion of object relations theory and the work of its primary theorists: Sigmund Freud, Melanie Klein, and W. R. D. Fairbairn.

We continued with an examination of some of the key figures in the history of psychotherapy who in various ways refined and extended psychoanalysis and object relations theory so as to approach new problems and/or deal with old problems in new ways including: D. W. Winnicott's concepts of transitional objects, holding environments, and the "good enough" mother; Heinz Hartmann's "ego psychology" that focused upon ego structures and their functions; and Margaret Mahler's stage model of infant development as an evolutionary process of "separation-individuation." We then discussed Heinz Kohut's pivotal role in exchanging the Freudian drive/structure model focused on processes occurring within an individual for a relational model emphasizing the responsiveness of the developing human psyche to external influences.

We presented the work of social psychologist Erich Fromm in expanding further the scope of psychoanalytic theory from a focus on individual development to an improved understanding of processes at work in societal development. We continued our discussion of theorists who presented extensions or alternatives to psychoanalysis and object relations, including: Erik Erikson's development of the first detailed model tracing human development across the lifespan; Gordon Allport's instrumental role in gaining acceptance within the academic setting for the formal study of personality; and Henry Murray's contributions to personality theory and research.

We discussed the emergence in the early 1960s of a new movement known as humanistic or "third-force" psychology which emerged in opposition to both behaviorism and psychoanalysis. We described some of the key features distinguishing humanistic psychology, including the emphasis on conscious processes and the focus on creative and positive aspects of the individual as opposed to psychopathology. We also discussed the work of some of the more prominent proponents of humanistic psychology, including Abraham Maslow, Carl Rogers, and Rollo May as well as the ultimate fate of humanistic psychology as a separate school of psychology.

■ Chapter 13—Beyond Psychoanalysis: Continuing Developments in Psychotherapy

Discussion Questions

- In what way did Melanie Klein's object relations theory deviate from Freud's theories? How are the theories similar?

- How did the object relations theory of W. R. D. Fairbairn deviate from the work of both Freud and Klein?

- How did the theories of D. W. Winnicott diverge from Freudian psychoanalytic theory? How did Winnicott's theories diverge from Kleinian object relations theory?

- What are some of the key differences between the Freudian drive/structure model and Kohut's relational model?

- According to Fromm, what was the most basic error in Freudian theory? What did Fromm propose as a possible solution for this error?

- Did humanistic psychology develop fully into a separate school of psychology and, if not, why?

- What were the key contributions of Abraham Maslow, Carl Rogers, and Rollo May to humanistic psychology?

- What are three major issues or trends in the organizational and professional development of clinical psychology? Based on current sociocultural and political events, what do you predict will be a future trend in the development of clinical psychology?

Women in the History of Psychology

CHAPTER OVERVIEW

History is often thought of as a final, definitive recording of past events. This idea fails to consider that history is more than a record of past events and people long dead; it is a living and changing entity. While the "facts" of history such as dates, names, and places are for the most part immutable once known, our understanding of those facts and the meaning that we give them is often less certain and more subject to change. History is more than a record of events, it is also a "story." Accordingly, this chapter is more than a simple listing of the historical facts about women who have contributed to psychology's past, as it also tells their "story" by setting the "facts" (the dates, the names, and the places) within a context that helps us understand the meaning of those facts.

We begin with a brief discussion of the functions of history, and then proceed with the 12th-century German nun Hildegard von Bingen (1098–1179). We examine Hildegard's practice of the medieval equivalent of psychotherapy as well as her writings which provide a rich example of psychological theory during the medieval period.

We then fast-forward to the 19th century to discuss some of the earliest acknowledged women contributors to psychology, including Dorothea Lynde Dix (1802–1887), Mary Whiton Calkins (1863–1930), Margaret Floy Washburn (1871–1939), Christine Ladd-Franklin (1847–1930), and Lillien Jane Martin (1851–1943). We describe some of the unique challenges these women faced because of their gender, especially their struggle to break down the educational barrier that prevented women from enrolling in graduate programs in psychology.

We then discuss some of the sociocultural factors influencing the movement of women out of the academic setting and into the applied areas of psychology. We focus upon the groundbreaking work of Leta Stetter Hollingworth (1886–1939), who employed the scientific method to debunk two widespread yet misinformed beliefs about women's intellectual abilities, namely, the variability and menstruation hypotheses. Thereafter, we turn to the work of Maria Montessori (1870–1952), who developed and promoted an innovative and influential pedagogical system, the Montessori Method, and Lillian Moller Gilbreth (1878–1972) who made significant contributions to the field of industrial/organizational psychology.

Many women working in psychology have made significant theoretical contributions to our understanding of gender difference including the work of Karen Horney (1885–1952), Janet Spence (1923–   ), Sandra Bem (1944–   ), and Florence Denmark (1932–   ). Other prominent women in psychology have enlightened both the discipline of psychology and society itself by challenging biased beliefs. Two such women include Evelyn Hooker (1907–1996), who radically challenged beliefs about homosexuality, and Mamie Phipps Clark (1917–1983), whose work in collaboration with her husband, Kenneth Clark, provided pivotal evidence in the landmark 1954 *Brown v. Board of Education* case in which the U. S. Supreme Court ruled to abolish school segregation.

We then present an examination of the contributions of women in developmental psychology. This includes the work of Anna Freud (1895–1982) in the area of child psychoanalysis and the use of play therapy, the multiple contributions of Mary Cover Jones (1896–1987), and Mary Salter Ainsworth's (1913–   ) work on attachment theory.

Looking at more recent contributions of women in psychology, we turn to the work of Anne Anastasi (1908–2001) in the development of the field of differential psychology, Carol Gilligan's work on female moral development, and Elizabeth Loftus' (1944–   ) controversial work on the topic of eyewitness memory. Thereafter, we briefly visit two prominent women leaders in psychology, Dorothy Cantor (the 1996 president of the American Psychological

Association) and Ingrid Lunt (elected in 1993 to the presidency of the European Federation of Professional Psychologists' Associations) to illuminate the challenges of women serving in leadership roles in contemporary psychology.

This chapter concludes with an overview of demographic shifts in the gender composition of psychology and a discussion of the implications of these changes for the future of women in psychology.

LEARNING OBJECTIVES

When you finish studying this chapter, you will be prepared to:

- Describe the four functions of history and their implications for the history of women
- Discuss the early contributions to pre-scientific psychology by Hildegard von Bingen and Dorothea Lynde Dix
- Discuss the challenges encountered by women first trying to break educational barriers, including Mary Whiton Calkins, Margaret Floy Washburn, Christine Ladd-Franklin, and Lillien Jane Martin
- Discuss the sociocultural trends/forces that contributed to the shifting of women from the academic to the applied setting
- Examine the issue of gender difference in terms of the impact of prevailing theories of gender difference on women's ability to contribute as well as the contributions of individual women to a more complete understanding of gender difference, including Karen Horney, Janet Spence, Sandra Bem, and Florence Denmark
- Discuss the work of women psychologists in combating bias in areas other than gender discrimination, including Evelyn Hooker's work on homosexuality and Mamie Phipps Clark's work on race and self-esteem
- Discuss the contributions of women in the area of developmental psychology, including Anna Freud's contributions to psychoanalysis; Mary Cover Jones' work on systematic desensitization, maturation, and drinking behavior; and Mary Ainsworth's work on attachment theory
- Discuss the contributions and challenges of recent women leaders in psychology, including Anne Anastasi, Dorothy Cantor, and Ingrid Lunt
- Summarize the controversial work of Carol Gilligan on moral development and Elizabeth Loftus on the subject of eyewitness memory
- Present a general overview of current demographic changes in psychology and the implications of these changes for women entering psychology

INTRODUCTION: WHY DO WE NEED A CHAPTER ON WOMEN IN PSYCHOLOGY?

This may seem an odd question at first but let us consider it carefully. What purpose is served by devoting a separate chapter to women's contributions in a textbook on the history of psychology? Why are women in psychology's history not simply integrated into the chapter to which their work is most relevant with no distinction made between their contributions and those of the men in psychology's past? We can begin to address these questions by considering why we need to study history in the first place.

Historian Gerda Lerner presented four functions of history in her 1982 address to the Organization of American Historians. History, according to Lerner (1997), serves as memory and as a source of personal identity, provides individuals with a sense of collective immortality, forms the basis for cultural traditions, and provides an explanatory framework for the present.

These functions of history apply equally to the history of a scientific discipline and to the history of a culture or of a person. Studying the history of psychology establishes our collective memory in the discipline and gives each of us a sense of personal identity as psychologists. The study of psychology's past helps give psychology a sense of collective immortality and establishes our cultural tradition within the discipline while it also helps us to explain where we are now as a discipline. These functions of history, however, have implications for women practitioners in the discipline.

Women have often been defined in history by their absence from the written record, thus implying a lack of active involvement in activities of historical importance. This absence is as true of the history of psychology as it has been of the study of history in general. As a result, in the past women students of psychology may have found it difficult to appreciate fully all the uses of history: How could the history of psychology help women psychologists find a personal sense of identity within the discipline if no women appeared in the history texts? How could women psychologists overcome the prejudice of male (and often other female) peers when a failure to acknowledge women's presence in psychology's past legitimized the exclusion of women from the power structure of the discipline?

Since the mid-1960s, there has been a growing effort by historians to rectify the general historical record of humankind by examining the experiences of previously marginalized groups (including women, African Americans, and other minorities) and incorporating those experiences into our general understanding of the past. This trend has affected the history of psychology and is reflected in the most recent generation of texts on the history of psychology, which have begun to incorporate the experiences of these underrepresented groups into our understanding of the discipline's past by devoting chapters specifically to their history. This separation of the experiences of women and minorities from the discussion of the history of psychology in general presents the opportunity to discuss the challenges uniquely experienced by these previously neglected practitioners from psychology's past and its present.

It is also true, however, that the challenges facing women and other minorities have not remained the same throughout psychology's history. For example, the barriers and challenges facing a woman in psychology in 1890 were not the same as those of a woman entering the discipline in 1940 or even in the 1990s. Accordingly, this chapter approaches the history of women in psychology by considering the context (both of psychology as a discipline and of the larger surrounding culture) in which these women were working and the impact of that context on their experience. This approach differs slightly from what readers may have come to expect in a history text. "History" is more than a simple listing of dates, names, and accomplishments. To appreciate fully how and what an individual has achieved requires an understanding of the complex interaction between the ideas and skills of an individual and his or her environment. This "experiential" approach to history (of describing the context in which a person developed and in which his or her ideas were born) will hopefully leave the reader with a richer understanding of the people described and at the same time stimulate personal reflection on the forces shaping each and every one of us as a psychologist.

Does this mean that this chapter holds interest and relevance only for female readers? Definitely not! We hope that the male reader will appreciate the opportunity to gain a better understanding of this interplay between the person and his or her context. Also, as women have made advances in the struggle against cultural barriers, the experiencies of men and women are in many respects becoming more similar, and men may be finding themselves faced with many of the struggles that, until now, have been more often faced by women, such as, for example, the need to reconcile work commitments with the demands of family life.

WHEN DID WOMEN FIRST CONTRIBUTE TO PSYCHOLOGY?

The next question is where (and when) to begin our discussion of women's participation in the history of psychology. Most texts on the history of psychology, this one included, trace the origins of psychology far back to its pre-scientific and philosophical roots. Even before we had a separate discipline of **psychology**, our human interest in a greater understanding of the nature and purpose of human existence found expression in a variety of ways through philosophical discourse, religious belief, and the early practice of medicine and science. Historians of psychology have long acknowledged that a full discussion of the history of scientific psychology needs to include an understanding of the ideas of individuals considered influential in Western as well as Eastern culture such as Socrates, Plato, Hippocrates, Galileo, Comte, Descartes, Locke, Confucius, Siddhartha, and many others. These ideas established the infrastructure leading to the development of the field of study that we know today as psychology.

These same historical texts, however, usually do not include the names of any female contributors until long after the aforementioned infrastructure of psychology was firmly established. In fact, this intellectual and sociocultural structure or context was constructed and then dominated primarily by males, leaving women and other minority practitioners to develop and present their ideas outside the bounds of accepted knowledge and thinking and therefore making their ideas easily dismissable and labeled as irrelevant. Open a text on the history of psychology, start scanning through the pages and it is likely that the first time you will encounter a woman in the story of psychology's past will be sometime in the late 19th century. This is understandable, but no longer acceptable, since it was not until the 1890s that women were allowed access to advanced training in most fields of study, including psychology.

One of the first women's names you come across might be Margaret Floy Washburn (1871–1939) or Mary Whiton Calkins (1863–1930) since they were among the first women to break the above rigid and restrictive barriers to educational access. However, their contributions were made after psychology had a name and after Wilhelm Wundt (1832–1920) formalized the use of science as the primary method of "knowing" in psychology. But were they, indeed, the first women to contribute significantly to psychology's past? This chapter challenges this assumption by beginning the discussion of the role of women in the history of psychology starting in the 1090s! First, however, let us briefly discuss that thousand-year period of history (approximately A.D. 475 to 1492) known to us today as the Middle Ages.

The Middle Ages are not a time period often considered in discussions of the history of psychology. Beyond the work of Simon Kemp in his text *Medieval Psychology*, most historians of the discipline have shared the opinion expressed by Edwin G. Boring (1886–1968) in his classic text, *A History of Experimental Psychology* (1929–1957):

> We are inclined to condemn the Middle Ages for their lack of science, their acceptance of unprovable dogma, their failure to advance what we call civilization; yet *men* (italics added) of intelligence equal to that of today's Nobel Prize winners held these dogmatically determined attitudes toward truth as vehemently as any scientist defends his modern version of reality . . . and our interest in the medieval in this book lies only in the fact that it furnished the kind of thinking from which modern science had to emerge. (p. 7)

Thus, Edwin G. Boring (1929) set the tone for the way in which the medieval era was to be addressed by every historian of psychology from the 1930s onward. Paradoxically, history of psychology texts appear to make light of the fact that the time period in question was no minor flash in the pan, as the Middle Ages encompassed a thousand years! The events often considered as marking the beginning and end of the Middle Ages are the fall of the Roman Empire (A.D. ~475) and the "discovery" of the new world by Christopher Columbus in 1492. A lot happened in between! Imagine if historians of psychology were equally brief in describing what happened between the years 1000 and 2000 (A.D.).

Regarding the history of psychology, certain advances during the Middle Ages gave birth to the academic structure within which scientific psychology developed. The invention of the printing press, the founding of the first universities, and the beginning of the separation of church and science, as divergent authorities on true knowledge of the universe and human experience, all took place during the Middle Ages.

Although it was a period of rapid intellectual and sociocultural change, the Middle Ages were not kind to women. Since history relies heavily on the existence of a written record, it has been difficult to piece together an accurate picture of what it was like to be a woman in medieval Europe as women rarely had access to education, and, therefore, were often unable to leave behind a firsthand written record of their experiences. Information that has survived comes primarily in the form of chronicles, tax rolls, legal and estate records, private account books, diaries and letters and, though sporadic, this record does afford us a clear representation of the marginalized status and diminished opportunities presented to women (Gies & Gies, 1978).

Women's lives, in any historical setting, have been influenced by several factors, including survival issues, conditions of marriage, property rights, legal rights, education and work issues, and political and religious roles. Try thinking about all of these factors as you read about the various women described throughout this chapter. First, however, let us look at each of these factors in terms of women in Europe at the height of the Middle Ages; women living at the start of this millennium, around A.D. 1000.

Female children were often victims of infanticide, because their alleged weakness (physical, moral, and intellectual) meant that a daughter's value was only perceived in terms of the cost of raising her and then providing a dowry (i.e., resources legally transferred to the husband at the time of the marriage), weighed against the potential value obtained by the parents from her marriage, both in material gains and in the allegiances formed between families. An unmarriageable daughter was therefore without value! Marriage often kept European women confined to the home, segregated from the spheres of influence in business, politics, and religion, which were considered men's domain. Often, women were denied property rights; could not inherit, bequeath, or sell property; conduct business in their own name; or even control the assets contributed to the marriage by their parents in the form of dowries. Women could not take legal action, sue, plead in court, or even give evidence. Literacy, which was restricted primarily to the upper class and the clergy in medieval Europe, was even rarer for women than it was for men.

This pattern of male privilege and female restriction was also evident in work roles that were broken down into categories of "outside" and "inside" jobs. The so-called important jobs, the "outside" work, were considered primarily the province of men. Activities within the home (such as child rearing and household management) were considered feminine and of lesser importance. Politically, a few women were able to reign as queens or queen-consorts but usually did so either with no effective power or by aligning themselves with powerful men. These same hierarchical patterns were evident in the Christian church, as women were given limited power, not allowed to preach, and not perceived as authority figures.

Although the above describes briefly the general experiences of women during the Middle Ages, individual women found ways to break every last one of these cultural, economic, and social barriers. Hildegard von Bingen was such a woman!

Hildegard von Bingen

Hildegard von Bingen (1098–1179), the tenth child of a noble family, was born in Bermersheim, Germany, and was given to the Catholic Church by her parents at about the age of 8 (Flanagan, 1998). Sometime between the ages of 8 and 14, Hildegard was placed in the care of an anchorite named Jutta. An anchorite was a person who chose a life of physical confinement to a small cell, usually attached to a larger church, monastery, convent, or castle, where time was spent in prayer and work separated from the general religious community around them (Gies & Gies, 1978). Jutta's cell was attached to a Benedictine monastery at Disibodenberg and it is there that Hildegard spent the majority of the first half of her life.

Little is known of Hildegard's life between about 8 and 38 years of age except that she was educated by Jutta and possibly some of the Benedictine brothers, that she was formally dedicated as a Benedictine nun at the age of about 15, and that when Jutta died in 1136, Hildegard took over leadership of a small convent of Benedictine nuns that had grown as an extension of the original anchorite cell (Flanagan, 1998; Lachman, 1993).

Hildegard, after taking over the leadership of the convent at Disibodenberg, probably reached the highest level of achievement of any of the great medieval abbesses. Inspired by her experience of visions and supported by her male peers in the church, Hildegard began to share her own ideas and over the last half of her life created an impressive body of work that included three religious texts, a scientific and medical encyclopedia (which included works on botany and biology), a medical text, and at least seventy-seven musical compositions (including the world's first opera). It is in these works and through her vast correspondence with a number of prominent religious and political figures of her time that Hildegard shared detailed descriptions of her views on cosmology (the nature of the universe), her ideas concerning epistemology (the origin of knowledge), as well as practical and insightful descriptions of the nature of disease (both physical and spiritual/mental).

Hildegard managed to achieve very high stature during her lifetime and remained influential for centuries after her death at the age of 81. Veneration of Hildegard as a saint began immediately after her death and canonization proceedings were initiated in 1233. However, the canonization process was not concluded and, despite other abortive attempts in 1243,

1317, and 1324, Hildegard was never officially canonized as a saint of the Roman Catholic Church (Bowie & Davies, 1990; Gies & Gies, 1978; Newman, 1987).

It is Hildegard's beliefs concerning epistemology and her concept of the nature of disease that hold particular relevance to the history of psychology. Medieval scholasticism was centered around a principle that all learning began with past authority and that it was, therefore, essential to read and understand the works of previous masters (Baldwin, 1971). In the case of Hildegard, evidence of this approach to learning can be seen in the influence of some of the classical Greek and Roman texts (such as the works of Hippocrates, Galen, and Cassius Felix's *De medicina*) that can be traced in her scientific and medical works, *Physica* and *Causea et Curea*.

Like Galen, Hildegard's concept of disease involved a humoral system that cited imbalance in four bodily fluids (or humours) as the source of illness (physical, spiritual, or mental; Kemp, 1990). According to Kemp (1990), Hildegard's humoral system differed significantly from previous ones in several ways: (a) her system was more sophisticated and complex than any previous or later ones, (b) she distinguished temperaments based on four kinds of phlegm (dry, moist, frothy, and lukewarm), and (c) her system included frank and lengthy discussion of human sexuality. Other systems also tended to assign different planets to each humour and blamed any imbalance on their influence, while Hildegard considered the moon as the main cause of change in the humours and hence in behavior (Kemp, 1990). Also, in *Physica* and *Causea et Curae*, Hildegard presented many ideas that were advanced for her time, including recommending the treatment of diabetes by omission of sweets and nuts from the diet as well as her discussion of the human circulatory system which presaged the model presented by Harvey in the 1600s (Achterberg, 1991).

In her correspondence and in her biographical writings there is evidence that Hildegard may have been practicing a medieval forerunner of psychotherapy. For example, in 1167 the monks of another monastery asked Hildegard to cure a noblewoman they believed to be possessed by a demon (Bowie & Davies, 1990). Unable to travel at the time due to her own personal illness, Hildegard, after expressing her own disbelief at the possibility of demonic possession, first attempted to cure the woman by a unique means; she wrote a therapeutic drama for her reminiscent of shamanic practices in its use of symbolic ritual (Bowie & Davies, 1990). This apparently led to a temporary improvement in the woman's condition, but after she suffered a relapse the monastery again asked for Hildegard's help. The woman was brought to Hildegard's convent at Rupertsberg where she was treated with communal prayer and ascetic practices, which provided the woman a secure and supportive environment in which she could give her behavior full expression (Bowie & Davies, 1990). According to Bowie and Davies (1990), this treatment was successful and the woman's mental instability subsided and her health returned.

While it is true that over 800 years separate Hildegard from the first acknowledged female contributors to psychology, it is interesting to note some similarities between Hildegard's efforts and those of her later "daughters" in psychology. Both Hildegard and many of the other women you will be reading about exhibit a strong applied focus to their work. Hildegard seems to have been particularly adept at generating work that had both a broad theoretical base as well as very focused applications. Many women in psychology have worked primarily in the more applied areas of the discipline. Whether this apparently long-standing tendency for the work of women in psychology to have an applied focus reflects some inherently feminine trait or is simply the result of the working environment of these women is a question deserving some further systematic exploration. In examining the work of some of the women psychologists of the late 19th and 20th centuries we will identify some of the contextual issues that contribute to the clustering of women into the more applied areas of psychology.

Keeping in mind the applied focus of early women practitioners in psychology, we now take a giant leap forward in time to the life of a woman who also had a very applied focus to her work. Interestingly enough, she is another woman her contemporaries often called a saint—Dorothea Lynde Dix. Although one might conclude that women were effectively doing little of relevance to psychology in the intervening 800 years, the lack of information regarding women's work in psychology during that time simply reflects the fact that there is work still to be done in uncovering the role of women in psychology between the 11th century and the mid-19th century.

Dorothea Lynde Dix (1802–1887)

Born in the small settlement of Hampden, Maine, Dorothea Lynde Dix was the daughter of a farmer and Methodist evangelist preacher named Joseph Dix and his wife Mary Bigelow Dix. After the birth of her second son, Mary Dix became a semi-invalid and the burden of caring for the household and her two siblings fell to Dorothea (as the oldest daughter). At the age of 12, Dorothea sought to escape this situation by running away to Boston to live with her wealthy and widowed grandmother.

Like Hildegard, the details of Dorothea's early education are unknown, although she is believed to have attended a village school in Hampden. While in Boston, she completed two years of formal education before an apparent clash of wills with her grandmother led her grandmother to send Dorothea to live with relatives in Worcester, Massachusetts.

While in Worcester, Dorothea decided to open what became a successful school for little children when Dorothea was only 14! In 1819, her career was interrupted when Dorothea returned to Boston to reconcile with her grandmother and to "complete" her education. Dorothea took advantage of whatever private and public courses were open to females but her education was again cut short, this time by the death of her father in 1821. Dorothea then revisited her teaching career and opened a school in part of the Dix Mansion in Boston to help support her still invalid mother. This school remained in operation from 1821 to 1835 and was both successful and respected; it served the educational needs of many socially prominent families. In addition to the Dix Mansion School, Dorothea started a second "charity" school in a carriage house behind the Dix stables to serve children of the poor families in the surrounding area.

Thus, from about the mid-1820s to the mid-1830s, Dorothea Dix was administrator of two schools, prepared and taught lessons, studied to complete her own education, and served as housekeeper and companion for her grandmother! As if all that was not enough, she also began writing prolifically, usually late at night. She published her first book in 1824, an encyclopedia for children called *Conversations on Common Things*. This book was very successful, appeared in its sixtieth edition in 1869, and maintained its popularity for forty-five years!

She also became romantically involved with a cousin from Worcester, Massachusetts, who proposed marriage. Dorothea's life began to fall apart in 1826 at age 24 when her engagement to a distant cousin was broken off and her health failed. The exact nature and cause of her illness is unclear; however, it did not seem to incapacitate her. Although she did cut down significantly on her teaching activities, she continued to write from her sickbed and most of the work she produced during this period was published. After a long period of convalescence, Dorothea Dix converted a large portion of her grandmother's mansion into a new day and boarding school for the education of young women called the Dame School.

Dix suffered a second "nervous and physical collapse" in 1836, and was apparently not expected to survive. The Dame School was closed, and, unable to teach, she spent the next several years travelling in Europe and the eastern United States living on royalties from her writing and some income inherited from her grandmother. However, five years of relative leisure was apparently enough for Dix because when asked to help locate a Sunday School teacher for the East Cambridge jail, Dix emerged from her semi-retirement and took on the job of teaching the class of twenty women inmates.

This decision launched Dix into what was to become her second and probably most widely remembered career activity, namely, as a reformer. In the course of working as a teacher at the jail, Dix observed the poor conditions under which the prison inmates were maintained. In addition, the jail was also used to house individuals considered, by the standard of the times, to be insane. Her concern for the condition of these psychologically disturbed inmates led Dix to start a relentless campaign of lobbying efforts to improve the conditions in which they were housed. Her detailed journal of observations at numerous prisons, almshouses, workhouses, and hospitals were used to draft a series of "memorials" to state legislatures in which Dix also offered practical solutions to some of the problems she had witnessed. This campaign was highly successful and led to an increase in the number of hospital beds in existing hospitals and asylums as well as the establishment of thirty-two new state hospitals in Rhode Island, New Jersey, Pennsylvania, and the South. Dix even went beyond national borders when she launched similar reform campaigns in Canada and Europe.

Dix died on July 18, 1887, in Trenton, New Jersey, at the age of 85. Although never a member of any psychological association or a graduate of any psychology program, Dix had a significant impact on the practice of clinical psychology in the United States. By successfully improving the conditions for the treatment of the mentally ill, she paved the way for the development of the present-day mental health profession. Other than her early efforts to include more academic courses such as math and science in women's curriculum, Dix did not challenge any of the educational barriers that women faced during her lifetime. This was one campaign that she left to other women.

BREAKING THE EDUCATIONAL BARRIER

Mary Whiton Calkins

Mary Whiton Calkins (1863–1930) was born in Hartford, Connecticut, the eldest of five children. Her family then moved to Buffalo, New York, while Mary was still a young child. Wolcott Calkins appears to have been very involved in his children's education: he designed and supervised their early education and, after the family moved to Newton, Massachusetts, he arranged for Mary to enter Smith College in the fall of 1882 with advanced standing as a sophomore. Calkins' collegiate career was interrupted by the death of her sister Maud a year later and Mary spent that year at home taking private lessons. She was able to reenter Smith College in the fall of 1884 as a senior and graduated with a concentration in classics and philosophy.

In 1887, after returning from a sixteen-month family trip to Europe, Calkins' father Wolcott arranged an interview with the president of Wellesley College, a liberal arts college for women. As a result of this interview Mary Calkins was offered a position as Greek tutor at Wellesley, a position that she held for three years, during which time a professor in the Department of Philosophy noticed her skill as an instructor.

Wellesley's founder, Henry Fowle Durant, envisioned an all-woman faculty and a woman president for his establishment, and in the interest of promoting and preserving this vision, Wellesley took an unusual step. Specifically, the Department of Philosophy was planning to introduce coursework in experimental psychology to its curriculum and was in need of an instructor to fill the newly created position. In recognition of her teaching ability, Mary Calkins was asked if she would be interested in the job. Calkins accepted on the condition that she be allowed time to seek formal training in the relatively new field of scientific psychology.

Calkins was then left with the problem of finding a place in which to get her formal training. In the 1890s, few psychology departments or laboratories existed (especially in the United States) and the few departments that did exist did not accept women students! Calkins sought out some of her former instructors to ask their opinions concerning which programs she should apply to for admission. Much of their advice was peppered with reservations related to her gender. For example, in answer to Calkins' questions concerning the merits of studying in Germany, one of her former instructors from Smith College wrote: "Germany is a good place to study if only you can find the teacher you want there. . . . Whether you could have the privilege of attending lectures or obtaining private instruction in psychology and philosophy at any of the German universities outside of Zurich, I do not know" (Gardiner, 1890, as cited in Furumoto, 1980b, pp. 57–58).

Calkins did receive some positive responses to her inquiries about the possibility of studying with John Dewey at the University of Michigan or with G. T. Ladd at Yale. Apparently taking into consideration either the desire to remain close to her family and/or the fact that neither of these two institutions had a psychological laboratory, Calkins decided to forego instruction at both Michigan and Yale and looked instead toward Harvard in her home state of Massachusetts. She wrote Harvard asking for permission to attend the seminars taught by William James and Josiah Royce.

James and Royce were both amenable to Calkins attending their seminars but Harvard's president, C. W. Eliot, refused, fearing a negative reaction from Harvard's governing body if they were to discover that women were allowed to attend Harvard seminars. Mary Calkins' father, Wolcott, came to his daughter's defense, however, and, armed with a petition and a letter of support from the president of Wellesley College, he was able to obtain permission for Mary to attend the seminars of James and Royce. It was carefully noted in the university records, however, "that by accepting this privilege Miss Calkins does not become a student of the University entitled to registration" (Harvard University, 1890, as cited in Furumoto, 1980b, p. 59).

Calkins' experience in attending her first seminar with William James was quite memorable (1930, p. 31):

> I began the serious study of psychology with William James. Most unhappily for them and most fortunately for me the other members of his seminary in psychology dropped away in the early weeks of the fall of 1890; and James and I were left . . . quite literally at either side of a library fire. The Principles of Psychology was warm from the press; and my absorbed study of those brilliant, erudite, and provocative volumes, as interpreted by their writer, was my introduction to psychology.

In addition to her studies with James and Royce, Calkins studied experimental psychology as a private pupil of Edmund Sanford at Clark University. She was also able to take advantage of Hugo Münsterberg's move from the University of Freiburg, Germany, to Harvard in 1892. She appears to have made a very strong impression on Münsterberg, as is evident from his letter in October of 1894 to the president and fellows of Harvard College asking that Calkins be admitted as an official candidate for the PhD:

> With regard to her ability, I may say that she is the strongest student of all who have worked in the laboratory in these three years. Her publications and her work here do not let any doubt to me that she is superior also to all candidates of the philosophical Ph.D. during the last years. More than that: she is surely one of the strongest professors of psychology in this country. . . . The Harvard Ph.D. attached to the name of Mary W. Calkins would mean not only a well deserved honor for her, but above all an honor for the philosophical department of Harvard University. (Münsterberg, 1894, as cited in Furumoto, 1980b, p. 62)

Harvard refused Münsterberg's request! Despite their refusal, in the spring of 1895, Calkins presented her thesis, which was approved by the members of Harvard's Department of Philosophy. An unauthorized PhD examination was held for Calkins on May 28, 1895, in front of Professors Palmer, James, Royce, Münsterberg, Harris, and Santayana, and afterwards those present unanimously voted that Calkins had satisfied all the customary requirements for the degree. Although a written communication of this event was noted in the Harvard records, her degree was never acknowledged or officially sanctioned by Harvard University.

While still completing her graduate studies at Harvard and Clark, Calkins returned to Wellesley in the fall of 1891 as an Instructor in Psychology in the Department of Philosophy, and within months also established a psychological laboratory at Wellesley. Considering the fact that less than a dozen psychology laboratories existed at that time within the United States, this was quite a remarkable achievement and the Wellesley laboratory went on to earn a reputation as a very productive and respected scientific psychology laboratory.

Also, while still a student at Harvard, Calkins had already started to involve herself in all four aspects of what later became her professional life in psychology: (a) the conduct of laboratory experiments using the facilities at Harvard and Clark Universities, (b) the development of her own global theory of psychology, (c) involvement in the political structure of the new psychology, and finally, (d) writing prolifically such that before her retirement Calkins published four books and 105 papers (68 in psychology and 37 in philosophy; Stevens & Gardner, 1982).

This strong involvement in the professional and experimental aspects of psychology did not prevent Calkins from demonstrating her primary interest in teaching and her strong commitment to Wellesley. In all, she remained at Wellesley a total of forty-two years.

As a teacher, Calkins was very involved both as a lecturer and in the direct supervision of her students in the new laboratory at Wellesley. She wrote two popular undergraduate textbooks: *An Introduction to Psychology* (1901) and *A First Book in Psychology* (1909); however, she gained the most attention from fellow psychologists for her work in two areas, namely, her development of the Method of Right Associates and her theoretical model of psychology as a Science of Selves.

In 1892, Calkins published an article in *Philosophical Review* titled "A Suggested Classification of Cases of Association," in which she described a procedure she later called the Method of Right Associates (which later came to be referred to in the experimental literature as the Method of Paired Associates). This was the procedure, now well known to all beginning psychology students, in which pairs of items are presented and the learner learns to anticipate the second item in a pair after presentation of the first item, much in the same way students use flashcards to learn new material. With this paper Calkins became the first psychologist to report and use systematically the Paired Associates methodology.

Calkins used this methodology in her research to demonstrate the influence of primacy, recency, frequency, and vividness on memory. Edward Bradford Titchener (1867–1927) and G. E. Müller (1850–1934) were particularly impressed by Calkins' Method of Right Associates, especially since she was still a student at the time of its publication. Titchener included Calkins' experiment in his 1905 "Student's Manual" and Müller did a series of studies using her method. Unfortunately, although it was probably not Müller's intent when he did so, this may have facilitated Calkins' authorship of the method being lost from the historical record. In 1927, Eleanor Gamble performed an experiment similar to the one used in Mary Calkins' original research, but described the method she used as being "exactly that which was elaborated by Müller and Pilzecker and is familiar to all investigators in the field of memory" (Gamble, 1927). Calkins' original claim to the method was further lost in 1929 when Edwin Boring, in what was to become the textbook of the history of psychology for several generations of psychologists, gave credit for the original idea to Adolph Jost. Calkins herself did not refer to her method by its now more common name of the Method of Paired Associates until 1930 when she wrote an autobiographical piece for publication.

The turn of the 19th century found psychology in the middle of a heated battle between different schools. Two of the most vigorous combatants to take the field were the schools of structuralism and functionalism. At the root of the science of psychology lies the goal of addressing the concept of the self. The structuralists, preoccupied with identifying the elements of consciousness, and the functionalists, who considered the "self" nothing more than a tool facilitating adaptation to the environment, had both relegated the self to the background in terms of its' being of scientific interest. Calkins, on the other hand, had reached the conclusion that the "self" was more than an assembly of elements or a tool, but rather the essence of the individual.

In 1900, Calkins published her first attempt at describing her self-psychology, which attempted to reconcile structuralism and functionalism with what she began to call the "science of selves." She described this "self" as a totality, an integral unit, not separable into component elements, unique, individual, and consistent through time, yet ever-changing. With the release of her textbook, *An Introduction to Psychology*, a year later, Calkins continued to develop her self-psychology, and when in 1905 she was elected president of the American Psychological Association (APA), she again described her theory within the context of her presidential address, "A reconciliation between structural and functional psychology" (Strunk, 1972, p. 199).

Her attempts at integration and synthesis were not successful, probably because she was voicing them at a time when the psychological schools of structuralism and functionalism that she sought to reconcile were most at war with one another. Calkins also failed to defend her theory successfully when she attempted to integrate it with psychoanalysis. In 1930, she published a paper titled "The Self-Psychology of the Psychoanalysts" as a direct attempt at this integration. In that paper she claimed that self-psychology could interpret all of the facts discovered by psychoanalysis, but that she found it necessary to discard the concept of the "unconscious" on the grounds that it was "illogical and untenable." This was the last paper published by Calkins before her death on February 16, 1930 (of inoperable cancer), rendering unavailable to us a clearer understanding of the direction she planned to take in her attempt to reconcile psychoanalysis with her "self-psychology." Although we can never know whether, if given more time, Calkins could have eventually succeeded in her attempts to bring all of psychology together within her Science of Selves, it is an interesting postscript to her work that many of the ideas she expressed in her theory are givens in the later theories of "third-force" and personality psychologists like Gordon Allport, discussed in chapter 13.

Although there was a period of time, from shortly after her death until about the 1960s, during which historians of psychology mostly ignored Calkins, she was quite respected during her lifetime. Her highest honor was her election to the office of president of the APA in 1905 and of the American Philosophical Association in 1918, making Calkins the first woman to hold either of these posts. When a list was created in 1903 of fifty leading psychologists in the United States, in order of their distinction in the field, Calkins was ranked twelfth on the list.

In 1902, Calkins and three other women who had done graduate work at Harvard, yet were considered ineligible for a Harvard PhD because of their gender, were recommended by Radcliffe and approved by Harvard as candidates for the PhD from Radcliffe College. Despite the urging of her peers to accept the Radcliffe PhD, and despite the fact that the other three candidates accepted, Calkins refused the offer. In her reply to the dean of Radcliffe College she explained her reasons as follows:

> I sincerely admire the scholarship of the three women to whom it is given and I should be very glad to be classed with them. I furthermore think it highly probable that the Radcliffe degree will be regarded . . . as the practical equivalent of the Harvard degree and finally, I should be glad to hold the Ph.D. degree for I occasionally find the lack of it an inconvenience; and now that the Radcliffe degree is offered, I doubt whether the Harvard degree will ever be open to women.
>
> On the other hand, I still believe that the best ideals of education would be better served if Radcliffe College refused to confer the doctor's degree. You will be quick to see that, holding this conviction, I cannot rightly take the easier course of accepting the degree. (Calkins, 1902, cited in Furumoto, 1980b, p. 66)

Just three years before her death, a group of her peers, both in psychology and philosophy, sent a petition to the president of Harvard requesting that the university grant her the PhD. The thirteen signers of the petition, all graduates of Harvard, included such prominent psychologists as R. S. Woodworth, R. M. Yerkes, and E. L. Thorndike. In response, Harvard concluded, "there was no adequate reason" to grant their request.

While previous texts on the history of psychology have paid the most attention to Mary Whiton Calkins for her invention of the Method of Right Associates and for her presidency of the American Psychological Association, growing recognition is being given to her proposal of a "self-psychology."

The "Myth of Meritocracy"

Two factors related to the general position of women in psychology, particularly at the beginning of the 20th century, may explain why many women were left out of the historical record of the discipline, and may also explain why Mary Whiton Calkins and Margaret Floy Washburn were more influential and more remembered than many of their sisters in psychology. These two factors include access to publication and the ability to pass on an intellectual legacy to the next generation of psychologists.

The "myth of meritocracy" in science would have us believe that success in science relies solely on the ability of the individual to produce research and scholarly works of sufficient quantity and quality in order to gain the reputation and respect of one's peers. Accordingly, one's race, age, gender, social class, and ethnicity should have no impact in determining who succeeds in science. Analyses of the careers of individuals who have been "successful" in gaining the recognition of their peers in psychology show that all of these factors have an impact.

Put simply, in order to gain a reputation and the respect of one's peers one first needs to gain their attention; otherwise one is in danger of being like the tree that falls in the forest with no one around to hear. In science, the way to get attention is to publish. In order to publish, one needs to submit manuscripts to the editorial boards of journals. As an editor of a major scientific journal one is in the influential position of gatekeeper for a discipline; editorial boards control what ideas are published and control who has the opportunity to gain the attention, admiration, and respect of their peers. Until as recently as 1995, women continued to remain less represented than men on editorial boards of the majority of journals in psychology (APA, 1995). However, there is evidence to support a dramatic shift in gender representation on editorial boards in the period between 1996 and 2004, at least in certain subfields within psychology; for example within the field of education psychology, in 2004, women's representation as editors (70%) exceeded their representation as members in both education (60%) and psychology (52%) (Evans, Hsieh, & Robinson, 2005). This was even more so in psychology at the turn of the century. However, Margaret Floy Washburn very strategically placed herself on the editorial boards of several major psychological journals, all of which still exist today. Accordingly, Washburn's ability to impact the published record of psychological science was much greater than that of many of her contemporary sister (and brother!) psychologists.

In 1924, Washburn led a committee within the American Psychological Association that lobbied successfully for the APA's purchase of several psychological journals. Since personal friends of Professor Washburn owned many of these journals, it is not surprising that she was soon given the honor of serving on their boards. She was an editor for the *Psychological Bulletin* (1909–1915); the *Psychological Review* (1916–1930); the *Journal of Animal Behavior* (1911–1917), which later became the *Journal of Comparative Psychology* (1921–1935); and the *American Journal of Psychology* (1903–1939).

Another way in which to gain influence in psychology was to establish a school of thought or to have students/followers who identified themselves with your theories. Unfortunately, this was something that neither Calkins nor Washburn achieved, partly because of their gender. Many of the prominent women in the early days of scientific psychology found themselves restricted from teaching psychology at the more respected universities because of their gender and that the only teaching posts available were at women's colleges or at small, state-funded, co-educational institutions. Since most of these organizations were given limited access to operational funds they were unable to afford the expense of graduate programs and therefore lacked many of the potential research and scholarly benefits that accompany graduate-level studies. This meant that even if a woman was able to act as a mentor and inspiration for students at the undergraduate level, most of her students who did go on in psychology did their graduate-level work at other institutions with male instructors. Since most psychologists do not begin to gain recognition until they are working at the graduate level, their careers were then identified with their male graduate-level instructors. The names of their undergraduate instructors have been forgotten, despite the critical role these instructors may have played in introducing their students to psychology and in inspiring the desire to pursue psychology as a lifelong career.

Washburn came closer than Calkins did to breaking this important barrier preventing recognition of the contributions of women instructors of psychology. As one of her biographers described her efforts as an instructor at Vassar (a women's college): "Professor Washburn soon made Vassar one of the most active psychological centers in America. She attracted many students, and a good number of them went out to psychological careers all over the country" (Stevens & Gardner, 1982, p. 99).

What separated Margaret Floy Washburn from her peers that allowed her to achieve such a high level of influence? Her secret probably lies in the combination of her engaging personality, her remarkable intellect, and her political acumen.

Margaret Floy Washburn

Margaret Floy Washburn (1871–1939) was born in New York City, the only child of Francis Washburn (an Episcopal minister) and Elizabeth Floy (an heiress). Her mother's wealth played a significant role in Washburn's family life because it left the family free to relocate frequently in the interests of advancing either Margaret's or her father's careers. These frequent relocations coupled with Washburn's own shyness meant also that she was somewhat socially isolated from her peers while growing up.

Washburn entered high school in Kingston, New York, at the age of 12 and then entered Vassar three years later (in 1886) when she was only 15! At the time, Vassar did not have actual "majors," but rather a broad range of courses such as English, Latin, math and sciences, philosophy, psychology, and ethics were available with no opportunity to specialize in any one subject. By the end of her senior year at Vassar, Washburn's intellectual interests began to focus on two particular areas: science and philosophy. An introductory course in psychology taught to all Vassar's first-semester seniors caught her attention because it seemed to combine these two interests. Hearing of a new psychological laboratory being established at Columbia by Leipzig alumni James McKeen Cattell, Washburn set out to be his graduate student. Columbia, however, had never admitted a woman graduate student and the most it was willing to allow was for Washburn to attend lectures as a "hearer" meaning she could audit courses but was not allowed to receive academic credit toward completion of a degree program. In the months before starting to attend these lectures, Washburn prepared for her studies by reading Wilhelm Wundt's article on psychological methods in the first volume of *Philosophische Studien*. When Washburn presented herself to Cattell as his student, she impressed him with her knowledge of scientific psychology as a result of her independent study.

Cattell, recognizing the inequity in Columbia University's restriction of Washburn to hearer status, encouraged her to transfer to Cornell University where she could enroll as a doctoral student. She did so in 1892, starting out as E. B. Titchener's first (and for a while only) graduate student. At that time, the 25-year-old Titchener was one of the most powerful figures in psychology. However, he appears to have been more ambivalent than his forward-thinking colleague, Cattell, when it came to the subject of giving women equal opportunities in psychology. His ambivalence did not, however, prevent him from supporting Washburn's intellectual and professional efforts while she was his graduate student. For example, a paper that Washburn submitted as her doctoral dissertation so impressed Titchener that he sent the manuscript to Wundt who then published the dissertation in his then highly regarded journal, *Philosophische*

Studien. Washburn completed her doctoral studies under Titchener in 1894, the first woman to achieve the PhD in psychology.

Unlike Mary Whiton Calkins, who had her first job lined up before even starting her studies in psychology, Washburn found that finding a job as a psychologist was not easy for a woman, even armed with the PhD. She finally accepted a job as an instructor at a small college for women (Wells College in Aurora, New York). After six years, dissatisfied with her position at Wells College, Washburn eagerly accepted a position as "warden" (supervisor) of the women's dormitory at Sage College of Cornell University. At Cornell she continued to take an occasional seminar with Titchener as her instructor and taught some special courses she developed in social psychology and genetic (animal) psychology. In 1902, Titchener was apparently instrumental in helping Washburn obtain a new position as assistant professor and head of the psychology department at the University of Cincinnati, Ohio.

Washburn only stayed at the University of Cincinnati for one year before she decided to take advantage of a better offer of an associate professorship at her alma mater, Vassar. Although laboratory facilities were already present at Vassar, they were inadequate and Washburn expanded and renovated the Vassar lab to such a degree that she is credited as the lab's "founder." Like Calkins, Washburn encouraged the direct involvement of her students in research. Sixty-nine of the research studies conducted during Washburn's thirty years at Vassar reached publication with 119 students as co-authors (Goodman, 1980).

Despite her tutelage under the strict structuralism of Titchener, Washburn began fairly early in her career to criticize introspection as the primary method of scientific psychology, as well as the restrictive interests and attitudes of the structuralists. Accordingly, Washburn's personal research interests focused on the areas of learning, perception, memory, and aesthetics. Her best-known contributions, however, were in comparative psychology even though she did not perform many experimental studies of animal behavior. A major reason for this lack of firsthand animal research was the unfortunate fact that developing a first-rate animal lab required funds that Vassar lacked due to its status as a women's college.

Therefore, Washburn's major contribution to comparative psychology came from her integration of then-current research studies performed by other investigators. Her work, published in 1908, titled *The Animal Mind: A Textbook of Comparative Psychology*, became a classic in the field. Many of the functional psychologists who later embraced the new school of behaviorism eagerly embraced Washburn's early work with its rejection of introspection and her emphasis on observation of real-life behavior. Washburn included some of her own controversial ideas in *The Animal Mind*, such as her belief that sensory experiences and memory in animals can be inferred from research with human subjects, and that experimental results from research in humans could be extended and verified through experiments in animal behavior.

Washburn's second book focused more on her personal research interests and was called *Movement and Mental Imagery: Outline of a Motor Theory of Consciousness* (1916). In contrast to the theories of the influential behaviorists, and foreshadowing some of the ideas of cognitive psychology, Washburn suggested that in human social relationships (and to a lesser degree animals) we do not react solely to the overt behavior of others but more importantly to what we "conceive their mental states to be" (Stevens & Gardner, 1982, p. 102).

One of the reasons that Washburn's Motor Theory of Consciousness did not develop a following was her insistence that consciousness and higher mental processes could not be ignored, which was clearly at odds with the ideas of the behaviorists, who were becoming a dominant force in American psychology. In short, the behaviorists were advocating the removal of the study of consciousness from the domain of psychology and focusing strictly on observable behavior, while Washburn sought to integrate the study of consciousness and behavior as both central components to the emerging science of psychology. Accordingly, Washburn voiced her disagreement with the ideas of the behaviorists quite openly in her presidential address to the American Psychological Association in 1921; an address that was a direct rebuttal of renowned behaviorist John B. Watson's criticism of her work.

Washburn gained significant recognition from her peers during her lifetime; for example, she was elected president of the American Psychological Association in 1921, she founded the National Institute of Psychology in 1928, she was the second woman elected to the National Academy of Science, and she served on the editorial boards of several influential journals in the field of psychology. One honor that holds particular significance is her 1929 election, after the death of founder and leader E. B. Titchener, to the Society of Experimental Psychologists (a selective, all-male group of then leading psychologists). This holds such significance because it was overdue given her long and distinguished career as an experimentalist; an honor that she had been denied by her own mentor, E. B. Titchener, who would not allow women to become members.

Washburn died of a cerebral hemorrhage in Poughkeepsie, New York, on October 29, 1939. Like Calkins, the influence that she exerted during her lifetime dissipated after her death and she suffered relative neglect from historians of psychology. Despite the challenges she faced, Washburn's authorship of *The Animal Mind* (1908), her rise to the presidency of the American Psychological Association (1921), and her strong female presence as a "gatekeeper" (through her activities on a variety of editorial boards of major psychological journals) stand as significant accomplishments for a woman psychologist working at the end of the 19th century.

Neither Washburn nor Calkins ever married and, while both of them led academic careers somewhat restricted by their gender, they succeeded in a man's world. While both were active in the advancement of their own careers, neither can be described as an active feminist and their success may partly lie in the fact that they learned to succeed within the restrictions of a system without challenging that same system in the name of their gender. Washburn, in particular, is described as the "favorite sister" who managed to develop strong friendships with many powerful male figures in psychology, and while this in no way diminishes her intellectual accomplishments or her research capabilities, it certainly did not hurt her career. In contrast, Christine Ladd-Franklin, during her career, expressed her feminist beliefs as strongly as she did her beliefs about psychology.

Christine Ladd-Franklin

Born in Windsor, Connecticut, Christine Ladd-Franklin (1847–1930) was the daughter of Eliphalet and Augusta Niles Ladd, a prominent and politically well-connected couple. Her mother died when Christine was only 12 and she lived, thereafter, with various relatives, attending school for a while in Portsmouth, New Hampshire. Intellectually precocious, she spent two years studying at a co-educational academy in Wilbraham, Massachusetts, taking the same college-prep courses as the boys who were preparing for places like Harvard University.

A predecessor of Calkins and Washburn, Christine Ladd-Franklin entered Vassar College during its second year of operation (1866–1867) and it took a great deal of persuading, on her part, to secure her father's permission to attend Vassar. Letters from Eliphalet Ladd to his daughter indicate that, though very loving and supportive of his daughter, he was somewhat traditional in his views, occasionally voicing the then commonly held belief that excessive mental activity could be harmful to a female's health and well-being. Christine was able to win her grandmother over to her side with the argument that given the excess of females in New England and her own decidedly plain appearance she (Christine) would be unlikely to find a husband. Therefore, she would need to find a way to support herself and doing so would require an education. Although her diaries do not indicate how she was able to win her father's support, Christine's arguments to her grandmother are rather ironic given that she was one of the first prominent women in psychology to combine successfully career, marriage, and family life.

While achieving success at Vassar, Ladd-Franklin came under the tutelage of another great woman of American science, professor of astronomy Maria Mitchell (1818–1889). Described as "the most important woman scientist in America in the nineteenth century," Mitchell became an inspiration for Ladd-Franklin and was instrumental in turning her interest toward a life in science. It was Mitchell's belief that women's self-definition and experience contributed to their limited role in science and she worked directly with her female students to overcome these handicaps. She felt that "the integration of women into professional circles could come only after women had gained, within a supportive environment, both confidence and expertise" (Mitchell, cited in Kohlstedt, 1987, p. 146).

After graduating from Vassar, Ladd-Franklin worked as a high school teacher for almost a decade. She left teaching in the fall of 1878 when she moved to Baltimore to study mathematics and logic for four years at the newly established Johns Hopkins University. Although Johns Hopkins, after her first year, voted to pay her the equivalent of a fellow's stipend, the university withheld the title of fellow that usually came with the stipend due to her gender. One of Johns Hopkins' reasons for restricting the enrollment of women was the fear of romantic relationships developing between male and female students, ironic in Christine Ladd-Franklin's case, since in the summer of 1882 she married Fabian Franklin, an associate faculty member in the Johns Hopkins Department of Mathematics. Throughout their marriage, Fabian Franklin appears to have taken great pride and interest in his wife's scientific career even providing economic support for her study, research, and writing, as well as taking over primary child-care responsibilities for their daughter, Margaret, when parenting needs conflicted with Ladd-Franklin's career needs.

Ladd-Franklin's early scientific interests were focused on the area of mathematics and physics and, although Johns Hopkins refused to award her the degree of doctorate because of her gender, she had completed the requisite work by 1882. For a period afterwards the newly married Ladd-Franklin seemed to have given up career for family: she had two children, one of whom died soon after birth, and she never held a "full-time" job, choosing instead to relocate whenever Fabian's career required it. However, her involvement in science was far from over and her career as a psychologist was about to begin after this brief hiatus.

Around 1886, Ladd-Franklin began conducting research on the subject of vision, beginning with a study of the **horopter** (the point in space at which the images of an object are formed on identical points on the retinas of both eyes such that these two images are seen as one in binocular vision). Her publication of an article on the subject, titled "A Method for the Experimental Determination of the Horopter" (1887) in the first volume of the new *American Journal of Psychology*, marked her entry into the new field of scientific psychology.

When Fabian went on sabbatical in 1891–1892, Christine traveled with him and baby Margaret to Europe and took advantage of the opportunity to conduct research and to study psychology at the lab of G. E. Müller in Göttingen, Germany. When Ladd-Franklin was denied permission to attend university lectures at Göttingen because she was a woman, Müller not only allowed her full access to his lab facilities; he also repeated his lectures for her in private sessions. Ladd-Franklin also took the opportunity when traveling to Berlin to work with Arthur König, a physicist interested in color vision, at the lab of the legendary physiologist Hermann von Helmholtz. At that time there were two competing theories of color vision: Ewald Hering's theory of three component color pairs supported by Müller and his colleagues in Göttingen, and Helmholtz's three-primary-color theory being advocated by König in Berlin. Ladd-Franklin, working from both labs, leapt right into the middle of the controversy by developing her own theory of color vision, which she presented at the International Congress of Psychology in London and published in *Zeitschrift für Psychologie* (1892) under the title "A New Theory of Sensitivity to Light."

In 1926, four years before her death, Johns Hopkins finally granted Ladd-Franklin the doctorate she had earned 44 years earlier! Although this event may have helped to soothe any hard feelings Ladd-Franklin held toward Johns Hopkins, it could not allay her resentment toward Columbia University. Despite the fact that she lectured part-time in psychology and logic at Columbia for almost twenty years, Ladd-Franklin was neither counted as a faculty member nor did she receive a salary! Although she frequently voiced her resentment toward Columbia in her personal correspondence to her husband and her colleagues, Ladd-Franklin remained at Columbia to benefit from the institutional affiliation and the prestige as well as the access to library and laboratory facilities.

Lillien Jane Martin

"She died as young as she was born. Age ninety-one. And all through those years, she was born every morning" (epitaph of Lillien Jane Martin: Walter Pitkin, cited in DeFord, 1948, p. 119). Although she was born well before both Calkins and Washburn, Lillien Jane Martin (1851–1943) did not become interested in psychology until late in life, entering the field after both of these women had already begun opening doors for women in the discipline.

Born in Olean, New York, Lillien Jane Martin was the daughter of Russell Martin (a prominent merchant) and his wife Lydia Hawes Martin. Unlike many of her women contemporaries in psychology, Lillien Jane Martin did not grow up in a middle-class household nor did she have the benefit of a supportive father. Despite the economic hardships of single motherhood, Lydia Hawes Martin was an enterprising woman with a strong commitment to her children's education. Lillien Jane began school at Olean Academy at the age of 4 because she wanted to attend school, "that marvelous place where older children learned the mysteries of reading and writing and ciphering" (DeFord, 1948, p. 13). When Martin graduated from Olean Academy at age 16, she and her family moved to Racine, Wisconsin, where her mother took a job as matron in a private preparatory school for boys. At that time Lillien Jane began her first career, as a teacher, initially at a nearby girls' school and later in Nebraska. While her mother's job helped to pay for her brothers' further education it did not leave any financial resources for Lillien Jane's educational goals. Thus, her dream of attending college at Cornell University in her home state of New York was one that she would have to struggle with and achieve on her own.

Finally, in 1876, the 25-year-old Lillien Jane Martin had managed to save enough money from her teaching job in Nebraska to afford pursuit of her collegiate goals. When she sent her application to Cornell University, she received the reply: "We have not yet received an application for a female, but we see no reason to oppose it" (DeFord, 1948, p. 22). Lydia Hawes Martin became concerned at the implication that her daughter would be the only young woman at Cornell; and this, coupled with the fact that Lillien Jane would not have been able to afford Cornell's fees without the additional funding of a scholarship, led Lillien Jane to choose instead to attend Vassar College.

Martin graduated from Vassar in 1880 (only six years before Margaret Floy Washburn), and she immediately renewed her teaching career, securing a job teaching physics and chemistry at a high school in Indianapolis, Indiana, with the help of a family friend, David Starr Jordan. It was also during her tenure in Indianapolis that Martin began her second career, as a scientific writer, and also gave lectures to educational associations. While speaking at an educational convention in San Francisco in 1889, Martin was offered the position of vice principal and head of the science department at Girls' High School in San Francisco. After taking this position, Martin spent about five years in San Francisco (c. 1889–1894), spending summer vacations back in Indianapolis with her mother. Also during the early 1890s, Martin began reading the work of Wilhelm Wundt and developed a growing interest in the field of psychology. In 1894, during a summer vacation, she discovered the writings of Theodule Armand Ribot (1839–1916), a French psychologist instrumental in the establishment of psychology as a scientific discipline in France who held views similar to Martin's and inspired her to pursue further study in psychology. No longer bound by family ties since the death of her mother, the 43-year-old Martin was free to pursue this new goal and, after consulting with professors at the University of California, decided that Germany was the best place to study psychology. After resigning her teaching position, she immediately set off to do just that.

Somehow, despite her own lack of proficiency in German and Germany's reputed inhospitality toward women in higher education, Martin managed to gain acceptance at the psychological laboratory of G. E. Müller in Göttingen. Martin stayed at Göttingen for four years (c. 1894–1898), attending classes and conducting research on a variety of topics including aesthetics, perception, imageless thought, and humor. Her ties to German psychology continued long after her return to San Francisco, as she published extensively in German over the next fifteen years and returned to Germany every summer for several years to study and do research in Göttingen as well as in Würzburg, Bonn, and Munich. The esteem with which the German psychological community held Martin is evidenced by the fact that she was granted an honorary PhD from the University of Bonn in 1913 for her research in the areas of imageless thought, hypnotism, memory of visual images, and aesthetics. This honorary title was her only claim to the doctorate since she never received an earned PhD in the United States or in Germany.

In 1899, Martin's old friend David Starr Jordan again helped further her career. As the president of Stanford University, Jordan sent a telegram inviting Martin to join Professor Frank Angell (1857–1939) on the psychology faculty at Stanford. Her extraordinary teaching ability coupled with her administrative and organizational skills allowed her to rise quickly through the academic ranks. Starting as an assistant professor in 1899, she was promoted to associate professor in 1909, and to full professor in 1911. She then became the first woman to head a Stanford department (psychology) in 1915. She "retired" at age 65, in 1916, as Professor Emeritus.

Age, at both ends of the continuum, became an important area of interest for Martin. Beginning with more personal concerns about her own aging process, Martin began to systematize the regime she developed to help elderly persons "beat" old age (Stevens & Gardner, 1982). In 1929, at the age of 78, she founded the Old Age Center, which was the first counseling center established for senior citizens. As a recognized international authority on gerontology, she then opened a farm in Alameda County, California, in 1937, to "give employment and restore self-confidence to a group of elderly men" (Stevens & Gardner, 1982).

However, Martin did not focus exclusively on gerontology, a field of study she helped to establish. Four years after her retirement from Stanford, Martin founded the world's first mental hygiene clinic for "normal preschoolers" at Mount Zion Hospital, San Francisco, where she was also the head of the mental hygiene clinic, and at Polyclinic Hospital. Her dream was for such clinics to exist eventually in every hospital for the dual purpose of the prevention and cure of mental illness (Martin, 1917). Her work with young children and with the aged continued until her death from bronchopneumonia in 1942. As her friend, Walter Pitkin, so eloquently described in his epitaph of Lillien Jane Martin, she spent her entire life re-inventing herself.

OUT OF ACADEMIA

When psychology first reached American shores, it was unusual for women to be allowed access to graduate education in any discipline. As a new field of study, scientific psychology was anxious to establish itself as a distinct academic discipline and needed new recruits in order to achieve this goal (Scarborough & Furumoto, 1987). The fact that during this early period women were more strongly represented in psychology than in any other science in America may be attributable, in part, to this need to build numbers in the new discipline.

This early openness to women's endeavors in the field of psychology began to change, however, as the membership in psychology, particularly at the doctorate level, grew rapidly at the turn of the century. As a result, competition intensified for prestigious positions in the still limited but expanding number of American universities. Riding on an American wave of optimism, and bolstered by psychology's contributions to the war effort in World War I, psychologists began to develop diverse areas of applied psychology, including the mental health movement, the child study movement, the development of mental tests, and educational psychology. This change in psychology from primarily a laboratory science to an applied science presented new career opportunities, particularly for women. Finding themselves excluded from full and equal participation in the academic ranks of psychology, women thus began to seek new employment opportunities in applied psychology outside of the academic setting.

Several of the first women in psychology began in academia and moved into the applied setting after they married. This migration was due in part to academic policies in many American colleges and universities that prohibited married women from teaching on the grounds that such activity would negatively impinge upon their socially accepted primary roles as wives and mothers. For those women psychologists who chose a spouse who was also an academic, employment in academia was often further complicated by anti-nepotism policies that made it difficult for women to obtain positions, or to advance, at institutions that also employed their husbands. Interestingly, a 1976 study by Bryson et al., found that husband-and-wife teams of psychologists who were allowed to work together at the same institution were collectively more productive, in terms of publications and grants, than couples employed by different institutions.

Two other constraints on the academic careers of women identified in the 1970s, by the Bryson et al., study were equally true for women decades earlier, namely, the placing of differential value on husbands' and wives' careers (of course favoring the former) and the inequitable division of responsibility for domestic activities such as housekeeping and child care. These factors, in conjunction with institutional anti-nepotism practices, may have been less of an issue for women who chose employment in the applied setting. The tendency for women to seek employment in the applied sector began to be reflected in the demographics of the discipline in the period between the First and Second World Wars. Specifically, for example, between 1916 and 1938 the number of APA members in academia grew from 233 to 1,229 (a slightly greater than fivefold increase), while the number of members in the applied sector increased nearly twenty-nine-fold (from 24 to 694).

The shifting of women from academia into the newly developing applied areas may have contributed significantly to the loss of many women's contributions from the historical record of psychology. In much the same way medieval women's contributions were lost to history due to the lack of women's acknowledgment in a lasting written record, early work in the applied areas of psychology also often failed to gain recognition in the academic settings or in the established journals of the discipline that were the informational sources for judging individual prominence in psychology.

Leta Stetter Hollingworth is one woman whose life and career provide a clear model of the gender-related challenges facing women psychologists. She also stands as a model psychologist who became one of the first to use the methods of psychology to question some of the deeply rooted sociocultural barriers preventing the full and equal participation of women in scientific endeavors.

Leta Stetter Hollingworth

Unlike many of the other women described thus far, Leta Stetter Hollingworth (1886–1939) was not a native New Englander, but rather a child of the plains. Born in Chadron, Nebraska, she was the daughter of John G. Stetter, a migrant farmer and his wife Margaret Elinor Danly Stetter, who died when Leta was only three. Leta's early childhood was spent with her three sisters living on the farm of her maternal grandparents and going to school in a one-room schoolhouse. The relative stability and happiness of this environment was disrupted when Leta's father remarried in 1898 and Leta and her sisters moved to Valentine, Nebraska, to live with John Stetter and his new wife.

From her early educational experience in a one-room schoolhouse, Leta attended high school in Valentine, Nebraska. Encouraged by her high school teachers and eager to leave her father's house, Leta went off to college at the age of 15, enrolling at the University of Nebraska at Lincoln. She graduated in 1906 with a major in English, equipped with a teaching certificate. Before graduating Leta had also become engaged to one of her university classmates, Harry Hollingworth, who had left Nebraska to obtain his PhD in psychology from New York's Columbia University. She married Harry Hollingworth on December 31, 1908.

Leta Stetter Hollingworth's early years in New York as the wife of a struggling graduate student were frustrating ones. Her attempts to renew her teaching career were unsuccessful since at that time married women were not allowed to teach in New York. She then tried to establish a career as a writer, an ambition fostered from her college days in Nebraska, but to no avail. The opportunity to return to school seemed impossible when the couple already found it difficult to manage financially on Harry Hollingworth's meager salary as an instructor of psychology and logic at Barnard College, Columbia University.

To help support his wife's eagerness to further her own education, Harry Hollingworth made what was for that time period a great professional sacrifice by taking consulting jobs outside of academia in applied areas of psychology. He found great success in the applied setting, becoming one of the leading consulting psychologists in America. With the extra income from Harry's work as a consultant, Leta enrolled at Columbia, and earned her M.A. in 1913 and her PhD in Education in 1916.

As she was finishing up her M.A. in 1913, Leta first became involved in the area of psychology that was one of the major focuses of her later career, namely, mental testing. At the turn of the century, the term *clinical psychology* did not have the same meaning as it does today. Instead, clinical psychology was nearly synonymous with mental testing and the early practitioners of clinical psychology primarily made assessments and diagnoses but did not function in a counseling capacity (Stevens & Gardner, 1982).

In 1913, Emily T. Burr, one of the early practitioners in the mental testing field, went on leave from her position at the Clearing House for Mental Defectives in New York. Leta Hollingworth quickly trained herself to administer and interpret the mental tests used at that facility, and accepted the temporary position as mental tester. Her work during the subsequent year was highly regarded and she was able to retain her position even after Emily Burr's return to the Clearing House. In 1914, Leta Stetter Hollingworth became the first civil service psychologist in New York State as a consequence of legislation that re-categorized mental testers under Civil Service in the state of New York.

She then transferred to the Psychopathic Service at Bellevue Hospital where she quickly advanced to the new position of chief of the psychological laboratory. She achieved this post the same year that she earned her PhD, in 1916. This proved to be a landmark year for Hollingworth in terms of career opportunities since that same year the death of Dr. Naomi Norsworthy left a faculty opening in Columbia University's Teacher's College; an opening quickly offered and eagerly accepted by Leta Hollingworth.

For the remainder of her professional career, Leta divided her time between her clinical activities at Bellevue and teaching courses in educational and clinical psychology at Columbia University. She was instrumental in establishing the Classification Clinic for Adolescents at Bellevue and also acted as principal for the School for Exceptional Children. An acknowledged expert on "subnormal children" and the author of two important books on the subject, *The Psychology of Subnormal Children* (1920) and *The Problem of Mental Disorder* (1934), Leta Hollingworth contributed significantly to the understanding, assessment, and treatment of mental illness and mental retardation/learning disabilities. Although her contributions in these areas are significant, two other areas are the hallmarks of her career, namely, her research on the mentally gifted, and, first and foremost, her research in the scientific study of the psychology of women.

Leta Hollingworth was a prominent advocate for mentally gifted children, and believed that while time and funds should be spent for the education and benefit of "subnormal" children, this should not be done at the expense of education of the gifted. She strongly disagreed with the common assumption of the time that "the bright can take care of themselves" and in the interest of supporting the needs of both the "mentally deficient" and the mentally gifted, she established the Speyer School, P.S. 500, in New York City, in 1936. Hollingworth served as director of the Speyer School, which provided special education for children at both ends of the intellectual continuum, from 1937 until her death in 1939. She wrote two books on the gifted: *Gifted Children* (1926) and *Children above 180 IQ* (published posthumously in 1942).

Although women psychologists before Leta Hollingworth had questioned sociocultural myths of gender difference, Hollingworth was the first to approach the issue scientifically rather than philosophically. While philosophers had been addressing the topic of the nature of women as an academic and social issue for centuries, the so-called "woman problem" (i.e., establishing what was the "proper" role and place of women in society) was not recognized or addressed in the early days of scientific psychology. Wundtian psychologists considered the issue to be primarily a social one and, therefore, outside the limits of psychology. The rise of functionalism in the United States and the incorporation of evolutionary theory into scientific psychology opened the door to the study of gender differences, given the strong biological component inherent in evolutionary theory. The prevailing thinking of the time, however, tended to present as a given the evolutionary supremacy of the Caucasian male with the female role portrayed only in terms of its complementarity and subordination to the male role.

The quality of research on gender differences at the turn of the century was described by Hollingworth's contemporary and sister psychologist, Helen Bradford Thompson Woolley in 1910:

> There is perhaps no field aspiring to be scientific where flagrant personal bias, logic martyred in the cause of supporting a prejudice, unfounded assertions, and even sentimental rot and drivel, have run riot to such an extent as here. (Woolley, 1910, p. 340)

Gender differences and similarities were topics imbued then, and to some extent still today, with emotionally loaded, unfounded assertions and claims with little, if any, empirical evidence to either support or refute such statements. What was needed then, as well as now, is an objective, scientifically grounded approach to the study of the psychology of women. We owe a debt to Professor Leta Stetter Hollingworth for her pioneering spirit and work in this important area of psychology.

Three topics in particular figured prominently in the study of the psychology of women at the turn of the 19th century: (a) structural brain differences between men and women and the implications for differences in intelligence and temperament, (b) the variability hypothesis which attributed greater variability to males in social and intellectual issues, and (c) the maternal instinct and its impact on female "nature." Leta Hollingworth was particularly instrumental in addressing the second topic, the variability hypothesis.

Charles Darwin's theory of evolution did not address initially the question of gender differences in intelligence in any depth. However, Darwin's cousin, Francis Galton (1822–1911), began investigating intellectual differences in his laboratory, concluding that women tended to be inferior to men in all capacities. The fact that women were not seen to excel was used by Galton and his fellow male psychologists as support for the argument that they were incapable of excelling due to a lack of natural ability (Galton, 1907).

Darwin took up the issue of variability in *The Descent of Man* (1874), determining, with the support of data collected by anatomists and biologists, that physical anomalies occurred with higher relative frequency in males than in females across species (Shields, 1975b). Since it was already accepted that variability in traits was the means by which evolutionary progress was made, it was concluded that the male, being more variable than the female, was the progressive agent in a species. Soon this conclusion was translated into an explanation for the greater frequency of male as opposed to female eminence (i.e., financial, political, and social status):

> That men should have greater cerebral variability and therefore more originality, while women have greater stability and therefore more "common sense," are facts both consistent with the general theory of sex and verifiable in common experience. (Geddes & Thomson, 1890/1901, p. 271)

Havelock Ellis (1859–1939), sexologist and social philosopher, popularized the use of the variability hypothesis as evidence of a greater range in intellectual ability in males as opposed to females in his book *Man and Woman* (1934). Noting that there were more men than women in homes for the mentally deficient, as well as more men than women who had achieved eminence, he concluded that greater male variability held for all traits and that women's "tendency toward the average," while it did not imply inferiority, did limit female expertise to "the sphere of concrete practical life" (Ellis, 1934, p. 436).

Statistician Karl Pearson (1857–1936) was one of the first to present the variability hypothesis as an example of "pseudo-scientific superstition," and to suggest that the "woman question" deserved impartial scientific study. The debate between Pearson and Ellis raged back and forth with Pearson criticizing what he labeled as the "erroneous" quality of investigations into relative gender variability and Ellis concluding that Pearson failed to define "variability" and that Pearson's data collection in support of his arguments was highly subject to environmental influence! In the United States, the debate raised by these two Englishmen was taken up by clinical psychologists (the "mental testers" of that time period), at which time the variability hypothesis came face-to-face with eminent mental tester Leta Stetter Hollingworth.

While working at the Clearing House for Mental Defectives, Hollingworth argued that there was no reason to resort to a biological explanation for the greater incidence of male eminence and the greater number of men institutionalized for feeblemindedness; instead, a more parsimonious explanation lay in social fact. On the question of feeblemindedness she concluded that:

> Women have been and are a dependent and non-competitive class, and when defective can more easily survive outside of institutions, since they do not have to compete mentally with normal individuals, as men do, to maintain themselves in the social milieu. (Hollingworth, 1914, p. 515)

To support this argument, she analyzed age and sex ratios in New York institutions and concluded that the ratio of females to males increased with the age of the inmates, supporting her hypothesis that women would be more likely to be institutionalized at an older age than men because these women had become too old to be "useful" or self-supporting. Regarding the issue of gender differences in eminence, Hollingworth argued again for a social as opposed to biological causation. Leta Hollingworth and Helen Montague examined 1,000 male newborns and 1,000 female newborns (to control for socialization effects), and found no gender differences in demonstrated ability. They concluded that:

> The lives of men and women are lived under conditions so different as to constitute practically different environments. . . . We should expect to find adult males more variable than adult females, because the males are free to follow a great variety of trades, professions, and industries, while women have been confined to the single occupation of housekeeping, because of the part they play in the perpetuation of the species. Thus variability has had comparatively little survival value for women. (Montague & Hollingworth, 1914, p. 343)

While still a graduate student at Columbia, studying under anti-feminist learning psychologist E. L. Thorndike (1874–1949), Leta Hollingworth wrote her doctoral dissertation on another issue of concern to the psychology of women: the menstruation hypothesis. A common assumption at the turn of the 19th century, the menstruation hypothesis argued that women perform poorly on mental and motor tasks during menstruation. For three months, Hollingworth tested the ability of men and women on a variety of mental and motor tasks at various times of the month and concluded that there were no demonstrable differences between the women and men on any of the tests at any time during the month. Again, Leta Hollingworth employed her keen mind and critical thinking, coupled with sound methodology, to illuminate the study of the psychology of women (Shields, 1975a).

A professor, clinician, author, feminist, and activist, Leta Hollingworth also became very involved in the larger political and professional scene of psychology, and was instrumental in the development of ethical standards in clinical psychology and in establishing a cooperative working relationship between clinical psychology and psychiatry. These developments were instrumental to the establishment of the American Association of Clinical Psychologists in 1917 (which later became the Clinical Division of the American Psychological Association—Division 7). Although respected by colleagues and students, Leta Hollingworth was denied the professional recognition that her efforts deserved. Lewis Terman (1877–1956; another prominent mental tester) said of Hollingworth's contributions that comparable productivity by a man would have been rewarded by election to the presidency of the American Psychological Association or membership in the National Academy of Science (Terman, 1944, p. 358).

Hollingworth's professional legacy includes her work on adolescents, which helped to shift attention away from strict reliance on biological factors to include consideration of the impact of the environment upon adolescent development. This same thinking is evident in her groundbreaking contributions to the psychology of women. Through careful scientific study, Hollingworth disproved commonly believed, biologically based theories of gender difference (the variability hypothesis and the menstruation hypothesis), and again advocated for environmentally based causes for understanding and explaining potential and performance.

Maria Montessori

Maria Montessori (1870–1952) was born in Chiaravelle in the province of Ancona, Italy, the daughter of Alessandro Montessori (a civil servant and former soldier) and Renilde Stoppani, "a well-educated woman from a landed, old family" (Stevens & Gardner, 1982, p. 107). Maria's family moved to Rome when she was 5.

An apparently conservative man regarding the women's rights movement, Alessandro Montessori was less than supportive of Maria's wish to attend technical school at the Regia Scuola Tecnica Michelangelo Buonarroti (the "Michelangelo School"). Despite his objections, Maria entered the Michelangelo School in 1883 and the poor opinion she formed of that institution while a student apparently led to the later development of some of her many ideas for educational reform. She then went on to become one of a handful of young female students who attended the Regio Instituo Tecnico Leonardo da Vinci. Although her initial career ambition when she enrolled was to become an engineer, Maria abandoned this goal in favor of a less conventional one for a young woman: she decided to become a physician.

This decision met with everyone's disapproval, from her family, friends, and especially university officials. The determined Maria Montessori managed, nonetheless, to enter the University of Rome in 1890 where she completed satisfactorily its equivalent of a "pre-med" curriculum. How Montessori overcame the next challenge, gaining acceptance to the Medical College, is not clearly explained in the historical record. However, "legend" claiming papal intervention is partly supported by a quote from an interview given by Montessori in 1913 that "the fact that a woman was studying medicine caused such a furor in Rome that at last Pope Leo XIII came to my rescue. . . . That changed matters considerably" (Stevens & Gardner, 1982, p. 108)

Montessori apparently achieved some sense of reconciliation, both with her fellow students who had ostracized her and with her own father, when she gave a lecture that was a final requirement of all students at the Medical College. With her father in the audience, Montessori received a standing ovation!

Montessori decided to specialize in pediatrics and was offered her first position, at the San Giovanni Hospital affiliated with the University of Rome. After beginning private practice in pediatrics, Montessori became a volunteer assistant at the psychiatric clinic where she first came in contact with "feebleminded" children. From this experience she developed an intellectual interest in education of so-called mentally defective children.

After spending considerable time between 1897 and 1900 publishing articles and addressing professional audiences on special education for mental defectives, environmental causes of delinquency, and feminism, a league to which Montessori belonged founded a medical-pedagogical institute (the Scuola Magistrate Ortofrenica) to train teachers in the education of feebleminded children. Maria Montessori co-directed this institute with an old colleague, Giuseppe Montesano. While there Montessori developed her "**Montessori Method**," which emphasized the importance of an enriched environment in which the child is free to select learning experiences as well as the incorporation of play as an integral part of learning. The Montessori Method also promoted the concept of "sensitive periods" during which it is particularly appropriate to introduce specific motor and cognitive skills, and that learning should include sensory training to nurture the child's developing perception of reality. As a consequence of the Montessori Method many children who had been labeled as mentally deficient were successfully taught to read and write at a level high enough to pass government-run primary school examinations. This success prompted Montessori to conclude that normal children were receiving an inadequate education in government-run schools and she embarked on an educational reform program shortly thereafter. This campaign was interrupted when Montessori withdrew briefly from the public eye, apparently because her relationship with her co-director, Giuseppe Montesano, had become more than a professional relationship. Montessori had become pregnant and she left the institute to give birth to her and Montesano's son, Mario. Montessori and Montesano never married, and although she provided financially for Mario's care she apparently had little personal involvement in his life, leaving him in the care of a family she knew who lived in the country. Montessori went back to the University of Rome and took courses in pedagogy, experimental psychology, and anthropology. She presented a paper at an educational conference in Naples in 1902 in which she described her fully developed Montessori Method for educating the "unteachable." In 1904, she was appointed to the faculty of the University of Rome's Pedagogic School.

In 1907, Montessori established The Casa in a tenement project in Rome, which was the first school to implement her educational program. As a consequence of her successes at The Casa, Montessori gained recognition for her methods and Montessori schools began to spread rapidly through Italy and then throughout the world. Montessori devoted the rest of her life to the cause of spreading her ideas about education and political reform. She was an idealist who believed that by "freeing education from arbitrary and autocratic control she could free society and all humankind . . . believing that this would lead to human and social perfection" (Stevens & Gardner, 1982, p. 112).

In 1926, Benito Mussolini, an early fan of Montessori, was organizing a fascist state in Italy (Stevens & Gardner, 1982). Mussolini officially recognized the Montessori Method and, by 1929, Maria Montessori was essentially the "head" of Italian education. Although her relationship with the fascist government was initially a favorable one, the increasing interference of the government in her schools coupled with Mussolini's pact with Hitler led to Maria Montessori's disenchantment with fascism. The government began closing the Montessori schools when the loyalty of the teachers became suspect and Maria left Italy. She first fled to Spain, but with Franco's rise to power in 1936, Maria had to leave Spain and take refuge in England. The Montessori Movement lost popularity and by the time Maria Montessori died at the age of 81 of a cerebral hemorrhage, she had lost her status as the darling of the press.

WORK AND MARRIAGE

While it is possible that the lack of a psychology degree may have contributed to Montessori's relative absence from history of psychology textbooks, other women with PhD's in psychology found themselves equally lost to history. Ironically, one factor often contributing to the loss of women's names in the annals of psychology was their choice of spouse. Generally, marriage was not a common choice for women PhD's in any of the sciences toward the end of the 19th century. The marriage rate for women in psychology at that time was actually unusually high for women scientists. About half of the first twenty-five women to seek the PhD in psychology were married, while 75% of the women earning PhD's in all fields between 1877 and 1924 chose not to marry (Scarborough & Furumoto, 1987, p. 162). Several of the eminent women in psychology who chose to marry chose a psychologist as their spouse. An unfortunate occupational hazard existed for these women due to the manner in which journal citations are presented. Specifically, the common usage of first initial and full last name not only makes it impossible to judge the gender of an author; the practice can be doubly hazardous for the female psychologist married to a male psychologist, since it can lead to the mistaken attribution of the work of these women psychologists to their husbands.

Regardless of whether they married a fellow psychologist or someone outside of psychology, women psychologists often found themselves faced with another career challenge: managing both career and child-rearing responsibilities. As mentioned earlier, twelve of the first twenty-five women to earn a PhD in psychology were married. In addition, all twelve of these women had children. While our discussion of Maria Montessori describes how she managed to cope with child-rearing and career management (by leaving her child in the care of trusted friends for the majority of his childhood), the next woman psychologist we describe went to the opposite extreme by combining career with the raising of not one but **twelve** children!

Lillian Moller Gilbreth

Lillian Moller Gilbreth (1878–1972) was born in Oakland, California to William and Annie Moller. As the eldest of nine children, it was her father's expectation that Lillian would forego college and remain at home to help manage the household. Lillian, however, had other ideas. Majoring in English, she attended the University of California, graduating in 1900 and earning distinction as the university's first woman commencement speaker. After obtaining a master's degree (in literature) in 1902, she began to work toward a doctorate in psychology with the goal of becoming a college professor. This plan changed, however, in 1904 when Lillian met and married Frank Gilbreth, a successful building contractor. Frank Gilbreth made no secret of the fact that he strongly wanted a large family and insisted on six girls and six boys. This left the challenge for Lillian Gilbreth to decide if, and how, she could possibly combine pursuit of a career with management of such a large household.

In collaboration with her husband, who was an efficiency expert, Lillian began to develop efficiency techniques that the couple marketed as management consultants. As the Gilbreth household began to achieve the proportions Frank Gilbreth had asked for, these same efficiency techniques began to be put to use in managing the Gilbreths' family life. Life in the Gilbreth home was later immortalized by two of the Gilbreths' children, in the book *Cheaper by the Dozen* (1948).

Frank Gilbreth, however, did not want his desire for a large family to get in the way of his wife's career goals and persuaded her to resume her work in applied psychology. The family moved to Providence, Rhode Island, where they founded Gilbreth, Inc. (a management consultant firm), and Lillian Gilbreth returned to school completing her PhD in 1915, in industrial psychology, at Brown University. Her doctoral dissertation was published as a book titled *The Psychology of Management* (1914), the first of four books that Lillian Gilbreth wrote independently, along with five other books written in collaboration with her husband.

Family and corporation both moved to Montclair, New Jersey, where the Gilbreths prospered from consultation contracts with major firms such as Eastman Kodak, Lever Brothers, Remington Typewriter, and U.S. Rubber. Lillian Gilbreth's thriving collaboration with her husband came to an end, however, when Frank Gilbreth died suddenly in 1923, leaving behind the 45-year-old widow and their twelve children. Lillian Gilbreth continued working as a consulting engineer and management expert, conducted research, and continued to publish and participate at conferences. Looking for new areas to which she could apply her techniques, other than the world of business and manufacturing, she began to interview housewives. In 1927 she published a book titled *The Homemaker and Her Job*, bringing her efficiency techniques into the household to help the average housewife.

It was not until 1935 that Lillian Gilbreth fulfilled her ambition of becoming a college professor. From 1935 until 1948 she not only held a professorship at Purdue University; she also taught courses at Bryn Mawr College in Pennsylvania and at Rutgers University in New Jersey. From 1941 until 1943 she taught industrial relations and was the chair of the Department of Engineering at Newark College, New Jersey. Expanding her influence beyond academia, Lillian Gilbreth served on the President's Emergency Committee for Unemployment in the 1930s. During World War II, she was a consultant to a U.S. naval program for rehabilitation of the disabled, and served on several advisory committees for the war effort (including the War Manpower Commission and the Office of War Information). At the age of 73 she was selected to serve on the Civil Defense Advisory Council and became chair of the national personnel division committee for the Girl Scouts of America. Anyone, male or female, currently struggling to manage career and family life would have to acknowledge that Lillian Gilbreth and her accomplishments stand as an incredible model of efficiency!

Anne Anastasi

Anne Anastasi (1908–2001) was born, raised, and educated in New York City. Her father died when she was only 1 year old and her mother, Mimi, her grandmother, and her maternal uncle raised her. As a consequence of her grandmother's unfavorable attitudes toward the public school system, Anne Anastasi did not attend school until she was 9, instead receiving private tutoring at home until that time. Apparently, Anne's experience in elementary school was not a happy one since she dropped out after only several weeks and was subsequently privately tutored by a woman named Miss Ireland. She returned to public school in 1918, long enough to graduate at the top of her elementary school class.

Anastasi then entered Evander Childs High School in New York City but again dropped out when she found the school to be overcrowded and populated with impersonal teachers. One evening, a family friend made the bold recommendation that what Anastasi really needed was to forego high school entirely and instead attend college. After successfully completing College Entrance Examination Boards she was admitted to Barnard College, the Women's College of Columbia, in June of 1923, at the age of 15.

Anastasi's original intention was to major in mathematics with minors in physics and chemistry, but during her sophomore year two events influenced her to switch to psychology: first, she was impressed by a course she took in developmental psychology taught by Harry Hollingworth, and second, she read an article on statistics written by British psychologist/statistician Charles Spearman (1863–1945). These two experiences led her to conclude that she could successfully combine the best of both worlds, she could "remain faithful to (her) first love, mathematics, and espouse the newcomer (psychology) as well" (Anastasi, 1972, p. 7). She completed her undergraduate degree in psychology in 1928, at the age of 20, graduating Phi Beta Kappa.

In only two years, Anastasi completed her PhD in psychology at Columbia at a time when the university was very active in psychometrics; her doctoral dissertation was titled "A Group Factor in Immediate Memory." She then took a faculty position at Barnard, where she remained until 1939, when she founded the Department of Psychology at New York's Queens College. While at Barnard, Anastasi married fellow Columbia graduate and psychologist John Foley. Anastasi has described being married to a fellow psychologist as almost like having a second degree:

> In many ways, John's experiential background complemented and thereby enriched mine. His Indiana upbringing and I.U. degree certainly provided the much needed broadening of my ultra-limited New York City environment. . . . John not only stimulated my exploration of Kantor's ideas, but also encouraged my interest in areas in which I had had limited preparation . . . as a graduate student at Columbia and for several years in his own subsequent research and teaching, he worked largely in animal psychology, a specialty I had touched upon only lightly in my own training. Similarly, his studies in anthropology and his research with Franz Boas strengthened my own interest in a field that is most relevant to differential psychology. Professionally, my marriage has thus meant that I had the benefit of not one but two PhD's in psychology. (Anastasi, 1972)

In 1947, Anastasi moved to Fordham University (in New York), where she remained until her retirement in 1979. Many of her contributions to psychology were made in psychological testing, and included work on test construction, validation, and reliability. A major underlying theme of much of her research is her interest in the nature and origins of individual differences and in devising ways to measure such differences. With the publication of her book, *Differential Psychology* (1937), the area of psychology that had previously been called "individual differences" came to be commonly referred to as differential psychology. In addition to this influential text, Anastasi also wrote *Psychological Testing* (1954) and *Individual Differences* (1965) as well as a widely used survey text of the various fields of applied psychology titled *Fields of Applied Psychology* (1964).

While her gender did not prevent Anastasi from achieving the presidency of the American Psychological Association in 1970, it is interesting to note that she was only the third woman to hold this position, leaving almost a fifty-year gap between Anastasi and the previous woman president of the APA, Margaret Floy Washburn (who held the post in 1921). This gap may simply reflect general cultural trends rather than a trend specifically within psychology. For example, it is noteworthy that Mary Calkins (who held the post in 1905) and Margaret Washburn served their terms in office during a period when women's roles, women's rights, and the issue of women's suffrage were prominent social and political issues. In addition, a general Zeitgeist of progressiveness and experimentation reached its peak during the so-called "Roaring Twenties." When Anne Anastasi took office as APA's president in 1970, America was once more experiencing a renewed interest in women's rights as well as a general spirit of freedom from social constraints, particularly amongst American youth.

GENDER DIFFERENCE: ARE FEMALE AND MALE SCIENTISTS CREATED EQUAL?

Our discussion of the challenges faced by women in psychology has thus far focused primarily on the practical and structural barriers impeding women's full participation in the discipline, including, for example; (a) educational barriers, (b) structural barriers such as lack of advancement to leadership positions in academia, in professional organizations, and editorships of professional journals; and (c) role conflicts encountered when juggling work and family obligations. Recent research and theory, however, have begun to identify some ideological barriers as well.

Rosser's Stages of Women's Participation in Science

Dr. Sue Rosser, director of the Center for Women's Studies and Gender Research at the University of Florida, has written several books on the subject of women in science, including: *Re-Engineering Female Friendly Science* (1997), *Teaching the Majority* (1995), *Biology and Feminism: A Dynamic Interaction* (1992), *Female-Friendly Science* (1990), and *Feminism within the Science and Health Care Professions: Overcoming Resistance* (1988). In the course of writing these books, Rosser proposed a model that presents women's involvement in different scientific disciplines as evolving through six phases, summarized in Table 14-1.

Although Rosser's model is interesting, it is not easily applied to the participation of women in the discipline of psychology. If you look back over the experiences of the women described in this chapter thus far, it is evident that women's experience in psychology, as a whole, does not neatly progress through Rosser's six phases in a stepwise fashion. One reason for this may be that psychology has not been a unified discipline, but rather a conglomeration of different approaches (theoretical versus applied, structural versus functional, behavioral versus cognitive, and so forth).

As psychology branched out into different areas of study (e.g., developmental psychology, social psychology, and industrial/organizational psychology) and individual practitioners became more specialized, the experience of women practitioners within each of these

TABLE 14-1	Sue Rosser's Model of the Six Phases of Female Participation in Science
Phases	**Characteristics**
1. Absence of Women Is Not Noted	Many scientists in the field would suggest that science is by nature objective and gender neutral. They do not realize that gender can influence science through theories, data collection, subjects chosen for experimentation, or questions asked.
2. Recognition that Most Scientists are Male and that Science May Reflect a Masculine Perspective	Most scientists in a given field are aware that women are underrepresented in all natural science fields. Some scientists believe that since women are not present in the decision-making levels of science, current science views the world from a male perspective. Scientific theories, practices, and approaches, therefore, reflect a masculine approach to the natural, physical world and to science curricula.
3. Identification of Barriers that Prevent Women from Entering Science	Topics of research suggest that women are viewed as anomalies or face problems as a direct result of their gender. Questions are raised about value neutrality in male-led research (for example, exclusion of females as experimental subjects, focus on problems primarily of interest to males, faulty experimental design, and data interpretation based on gender-biased language or ideas).
4. Search for Women Scientists and Their Unique Contributions	It is acknowledged that women have been present in science throughout history and attempts are made to search for examples of women scientists whose work has been credited to others, brushed aside and misunderstood, or classified as nonscience.
5. Science Done by Feminists/Women	Attempts are made to incorporate more "feminine" styles into the "doing" of science. As a result "feminine" science may produce theories/hypotheses that are more relational, interdependent, and multicausal rather than hierarchical, reductionistic, and dualistic.
6. Science Redefined and Reconstructed to Be All Inclusive	Science benefits and "survives" by embracing diversity. More people of varying backgrounds and perspectives become scientists, increasing the likelihood that the scientific method will function optimally, and suffer fewer flaws and biases.

subfields of psychology may have developed at a different evolutionary pace. For example, areas in which there have historically been fewer female participants (applied experimental and engineering psychology, philosophical psychology) may have made less progress through Rosser's six phases than areas that have seen a high level of female participation (psychology of women, developmental psychology). This suggestion of a differential rate of change in female participation in different areas of psychology is supported, in part, by the demographic profiles of the different divisions of the American Psychological Association (APA) in terms of gender composition.

The Psychology of Women

The APA division with the highest percentage of women participants (98.6% in 1995) is Division 35-Psychology of Women. Although APA did not officially establish Division 35 until 1973, the history of the psychology of women as a unique area of study stretches back to the beginnings of scientific psychology. The work of Leta Stetter Hollingworth and her impact on psychology's understanding of women (particularly her debunking of the variability and menstruation hypotheses) stand as hallmarks of the embryonic questioning of assumptions about women and about science as practiced from a predominantly male perspective (evidence of Rosser's Phase 2). As the percentage of women participating in psychology began to increase (post–World War I), interest in the psychology of women began to increase as well. The psychoanalytic school was one of the first to debate feminine psychology in a serious manner and was one of the first to use the term *psychology of women* to designate a unique area of study within psychology.

Mari Jo Buhle, in her book *Feminism and Its Discontents: A Century of Struggle with Psychoanalysis* (1998), describes the historical relationship between feminism and psychoanalysis as having developed "dialogically, that is, in continuous conversation with each other." Her description emphasizes the point that neither feminism nor psychoanalysis remains static and as each continues to develop and change so does their relationship with each other. This relationship has, in turn, had its impact on developing interest in the psychology of women and nowhere is this more evident than in the contrast between the early psychoanalytic theories on the psychology of women as presented by Sigmund Freud and his followers, compared with, for example, the divergent theories of Karen Horney.

As founder of the psychoanalytic school of psychology, Freud constructed his personality theory on the basis of his own self-analysis and his analysis of a series of individual case studies (on almost exclusively female clients). One of the central tenets of his personality theory was the importance of sexual drives in the personality development of both men and women; successful satisfaction of sexual drives, while remaining within societal norms and physiological capacity, led to healthy development while failure to satisfy these sexual drives resulted in neurosis.

Freud proposed little psychological difference between the female and male at birth, with infants of both genders viewing the mother as the primary love object. Psychosexual development remained similar for both genders, through the "oral" and "anal" stages, up until the "phallic" stage. At approximately 3 years of age, according to Freud, the boy's sexual impulses centered on the penis while the girl's centered on the clitoris (considered analogous to the male penis). Boys and girls both have "active" or "masculine" sexual aims, with the implication that active sexual aims are somehow inappropriate for females. From the phallic stage of development onward, Freud's theory of psychosexual development centered on male psychic development and described female development only in terms of what was "lacking" in comparison with the male.

The key features of female psychology as described by Freudian psychoanalytic theory include: (a) the perception of anatomical differences as causal factors in psychological and social differences, (b) the transformation of "active" sexual aims into "normal" passive feminine sexuality, and (c) a tendency for women, by virtue of their anatomy, to be less morally mature and acculturated than men and to exhibit more unsatisfactory personality characteristics. It should be noted, however, that Freud himself acknowledged that his ideas about women were the weakest part of his theory of psychosexual development in that, in 1924, he stated that the psychology of women was extraordinarily obscure to him and he frankly admitted having little clinical support for his hypothesis (Garrison, 1981). Despite his own admissions, however, Freud remained highly resistant to criticisms of his theories. One of the first psychoanalysts to seriously question Freud's theories on the psychology of women has been described as the most important woman in the history of psychology, namely, Karen Horney (Stevens & Gardner, 1982, p. 144).

Karen Horney

Born in Blankensee, a suburb of Hamburg, Germany, Karen Horney (1885–1952) was the daughter of a sea captain, Berenth Henrick Vackels Danielson, and his second wife, Clotilde von Ronzelen. Her parents' marriage was frequently troubled and one major source of conflict between Berenth and Clotilde Danielson was their disagreement over Karen's education. In fact, Berenth, a traditional authoritarian who saw no value in education for females, clashed with Karen's more progressive mother whose persistence and supportiveness were critical to Karen's pursuit of higher education.

After the German equivalent of elementary and high school, Karen developed an interest in studying medicine, and after completing coursework at the Realgymnasium for Girls (which gave Karen the equivalent of two years of college) she began her medical studies. It was common at that time for medical students to attend several different schools for their basic medical education and Karen followed form, completing her medical studies at universities in Freiburg, Göttingen, and Berlin. Her main area of interest was neuropsychiatry, as reflected in her doctoral dissertation, which presented a case study of head injury psychosis.

While studying medicine, Karen met and married a young lawyer, Oskar Horney, and while Karen was completing her medical education the couple had their first child. The stress of medical school, motherhood, and the loss of her own mother resulted in a serious depression that led Horney to the newly founded school of psychoanalysis. Sometime during the early part of 1910, Horney began therapy with Karl Abrahams, a prominent practitioner in the new field, who used very orthodox psychoanalytic methodology with its strong emphasis on early childhood experiences (Quinn, 1987, p. 143). This personal encounter with psychoanalysis had a profound impact on Horney's own later work since one of her primary criticisms of her own psychoanalysis was its constant focus on childhood issues and its de-emphasis of important influences in one's current life situation.

When Karen completed her medical studies and began practicing as a neuropsychiatrist, she employed psychoanalytic technique as a part of her own practice. Horney practiced at the Berlin-Lankwitz Sanitarium (1911–1914) and at a neurological institute run by Dr. Hermann Oppenheim, a prominent Berlin psychiatrist who had gained a reputation as the author of a widely used text titled *Diseases of the Nervous System*. During World War I, Horney worked at a military neuropsychiatric hospital and, in 1911, she also became a member of the Berlin Psychoanalytic Society headed by her own therapist, Karl Abrahams, who described Horney as one of "his most gifted analysands" and who praised her to Sigmund Freud (O'Connell, 1980, p. 84). However, her first important paper, published in 1917, was titled "The Technique of Psychoanalytic Therapy" and was the first sign of Horney's critical stance toward orthodox psychoanalysis. Her criticisms, at that time, were not related to issues of gender, but were rather a refutation of Freud's concept of an unchangeable and instinctive constitutition. In its place, Horney advocated a more affirmative position, introducing the concept of growth as a constructive force in personality development.

At the International Congress held in Berlin in 1922, Horney issued her first challenge to Freudian theory, criticizing orthodox theories on the psychosexual development of women in a paper titled "The Genesis of the Castration Complex in Women." The boldness of her presentation can only be appreciated when one realizes that Freud himself chaired the session. This presentation signaled the growing chasm between Horney's developing personality theory and orthodox Freudian psychoanalysis. Thereafter, Freud began to defend his theories more actively against Horney's criticisms as reflected, for example, in "Some Psychical Consequences of the Anatomical Distinction Between the Sexes" (1925) and "Female Sexuality" (1931).

Freud was not alone in presenting an orthodox psychoanalytic interpretation of the psychology of women. In particular, Karl Abrahams, in 1922, had written an article titled "Manifestations of the Female Castration Complex," which he wrote as a psychological explanation for the wish for sexual equality frequently expressed by his female patients. Dismissing the explanation presented by the women themselves—that their desire for equality arose from situational factors that afforded females less freedom than males and restricted females from choosing a profession or extending their sphere of influence outside the confines of home and hearth—Abrahams instead argued that his female patients' wish for sexual equality was the result of "rationalization," which hid an unresolved unconscious maladjustment that led to the development of a "masculinity complex" (Garrison, 1981).

In contrast to the orthodoxy of Abrahams, Horney began to expand her criticisms of psychoanalysis, accusing orthodox practitioners of being androcentric (male centered) and overly concerned with male sexual anatomy while giving insufficient attention and appreciation to the importance of women's capacity for pregnancy, childbirth, and motherhood. Using her own clinical data to support her arguments, Horney asserted that womb envy was at least as likely to present a problem for men as penis envy could for women. Another radical thread that began entering into her arguments, and which she began to emphasize in her work after 1926, was the importance of cultural factors in psychological development.

In her paper titled "The Problem of Feminine Masochism" (1935), Horney challenged previous theories on feminine psychology by demonstrating that cultural factors and socially approved sex roles encouraged women to be dependent upon men for love, wealth, care, and protection. She wrote:

> Cultural factors exert a powerful influence on women; such, in fact, that it is hard to see how any woman may escape becoming masochistic to some extent, from the effects of the culture alone without any appeal to contributory factors in the anatomo-physiological characteristics of women and their psychic effects. There may appear certain fixed ideologies concerning the "nature" of women; that she is innately weak, emotional, enjoys dependence, is limited in capacity for independent work and autonomous thinking. It is obvious that these ideologies function not only to reconcile women to their subordinate role, but also to plant the belief that it represents a fulfillment they crave, or an ideal for which it is desirable to strive. (Horney, 1935, p. 241)

In *The Neurotic Personality of Our Time* (1937), Horney outlined her model of psychological development in which the underlying cause of neurosis did not vary based on gender, but rather from basic anxiety as a result of a disturbed parent–child relationship and the repression of basic hostility as a means of survival and security. In an attempt to combat this anxiety, the child develops various coping strategies that become permanent parts of the personality structure, including strategies that involve: (1) "moving toward others" in a self-effacing solution of love and compliance, (2) "moving against others" through mastery and aggression, or (3) "moving away from others" through freedom and detachment. Horney viewed "normal" behavior as spontaneously arising from the integration of all three strategies, foreshadowing the work of later theorists such as Sandra Bem (1944–   ) and Janet Spence (1923–   ) and such concepts as androgyny (a blending of traits stereotypically perceived as female or male) and sex-role transcendence (adaptive behavior that steps outside the boundaries of socially predetermined gender role appropriateness). Likewise, subsequent personality theorists are indebted to Horney for her definition of a "person" as someone with unlimited potential for growth and positive interpersonal relationships. Abraham Maslow's concept of self-actualization and Carl Rogers' concept of the fully functioning person expanded on Horney's concept of self-realization (O'Connell, 1980).

Horney's positive impact in describing a more realistic and social-based theory of personality development was not immediately appreciated nor embraced by her peers. Rather, her deviation from orthodox Freudian concepts led to disruption in the New York Psychoanalytic Society, culminating in her resignation in 1941 in response to the society's restriction of her teaching activities on the grounds that she was "disturbing the students with her deviationist' ideas" (O'Connell, 1980, p. 90). That same year in New York City, she founded the Association for the Advancement of Psychoanalysis and the American Institute for Psychoanalysis. Despite her continued activities within psychoanalytic circles, however, her contributions to the psychology of women were effectively suppressed until the rise of the women's movement in the 1960s and 1970s brought with it a revived interest in her personality theory. Unfortunately, Horney died of cancer on December 4, 1952, before the impact of her work on personality theory and on the psychology of women was fully realized.

In keeping with Rosser's six-phase model of women's participation in science (see Table 14-1), a shift began to occur in the study of the psychology of women as the number of women participants in psychology likewise increased. Particularly during the 1970s, the feminist movement and the increasing interest in courses on women's studies had an important and sustained impact on the field of psychology. For example, research opened up exploration of the possibility that women might be viewed as anomalies or face problems as a direct result of their gender. Questions were raised about value neutrality in male-led research through such mechanisms as the exclusion of females as study participants in almost all psychological studies, focusing on problems primarily of interest to males, faulty experimental design, and data interpretation based on gender-biased language or ideas.

Re-Defining Gender Difference

As a growing field, the psychology of women expanded its interests beyond simply the exploration of biological gender difference. As proposed by Nancy Russo at the 1975 APA conference titled "New Directions for Research on Women," the new field of "psychology of women" might best be described as the study of behavior as mediated by the variables of female sex (XX persons) or gender (roles associated with XX persons). This foundational definition of the psychology of women led to the exploration of both biologically and sociologically determined behaviors. From a focus on primarily the study of gender differences, the psychology of women matured to embrace a variety of topics, including: pregnancy, childbirth, motherhood, and menopause; women's health, violence against women (including sexual harassment, rape, battered women); and the mediating effect of female gender in areas such as workplace issues, substance abuse, communication patterns, leadership, and a host of other subjects. Russo's proposed new definition of the psychology of women also made clear that general laws of behavior did not necessarily have to differ for males and females. Several eminent women psychologists participated at this landmark 1975 conference, including Janet Spence, Sandra Bem, and Florence Denmark.

Janet Spence

The name Janet Spence is a prominent one in psychology for many reasons, but most particularly for her contributions to the study of gender difference. Born in Toledo, Ohio on August 29, 1923, Spence obtained her undergraduate degree from Oberlin College and then spent one year at Yale studying clinical psychology before entering the University of Iowa where she completed her graduate studies in psychology in 1949.

From 1949 until 1956 Spence taught at Northwestern University where she conducted her now famous research on anxiety. One of her many achievements in this area of research included her development of the Manifest Anxiety Scale in collaboration with her husband, Kenneth Spence, to test their theory concerning the interaction of task difficulty with arousal level in determining task performance.

In 1960, Spence abruptly left Northwestern to return to Iowa where she accepted a position at the Veterans Administration. There she collaborated with her husband in researching a variety of topics, including concept formation in schizophrenia and in brain-injured subjects, learning, anxiety, and eyelid conditioning. By the time the couple again moved in 1964, this time to the University of Texas-Austin (UTA), Janet Spence had developed a reputation as one of America's leading authorities on learning theory. Unfortunately, while at UTA, anti-nepotism rules slowed the advancement of Janet Spence's career, making appointment to a tenured faculty position unreachable.

Shortly before her husband's death in 1967, Kenneth and Janet Spence published Volume 1 of a two-volume series they co-edited, titled *The Psychology of Learning and Motivation*, followed by the publication of Volume 2 a year after Kenneth Spence died. Janet continued to remain active as a faculty member at the University of Texas and continued to publish several more books, as editor and/or co-author, including: *Masculinity and Femininity* (1978), Volume 3 of *The Psychology of Learning and Motivation* (1969), *Elementary Statistics* (1976), *Contemporary Topics in Social Psychology* (1976), and *Essays in Neobehaviorism* (1971). In recognition of her major contributions, Janet Spence was elected president of the APA in 1984 and received the Gold Medal Award for Life Achievement in the Science of Psychology from the American Psychological Foundation in 2004 (American Psychological Association, 2004a).

After her move to the University of Texas, these interests came to include the examination of gender differences. In collaboration with Robert Helmreich, Spence developed the **Personal Attributes Questionnaire** (PAQ, 1978). In working with this assessment tool, Spence and Helmreich began to question traditional views of gender that tended to present the sexes as bipolar opposites. Their research results using the PAQ found that for high school students, college students, and many other groups, masculinity and femininity were essentially independent, but not opposing, constructs.

This work had a significant impact on theories of gender difference and of feminine psychology. Spence's and Helmreich's research using the PAQ was pivotal in re-defining gender difference in two key ways: first, by questioning the value judgment that was inherent in previous theories that presented masculine behavior as normative and feminine behavior as oppositional to this norm, and second, by raising the possibility for so-called "masculine" and "feminine" traits to be considered, instead, as "human" traits independent of gender. This important work, which contributed to developing theories of gender difference, was expanded upon even further by another attendee at the 1975 APA conference, namely, Sandra Bem.

Sandra Bem

Sandra Ruth Lipsitz Bem was born on June 22, 1944, in Pittsburgh, Pennsylvania, the daughter of working-class parents, Peter and Lillian Lipsitz. After earning her bachelor's degree in psychology from Carnegie-Mellon University in 1965, where she also met and married her husband Daryl Bem, Sandra went on to complete doctoral studies in developmental psychology at the University of Michigan. Her doctoral dissertation was titled "The Role of Task Comprehension in Children's Problem Solving" (O'Connell & Russo, 1990).

As a husband-and-wife team of academics, Sandra and Daryl Bem both had to compromise in making career moves. Daryl left his teaching position at Carnegie-Mellon University to accompany Sandra when she went to Michigan for her graduate degree, and in return Sandra moved with him to Carnegie-Mellon to begin her career in psychology and remained there as an assistant professor in psychology until 1971. At that time, they were both offered one-year positions at Stanford University as part of that institution's initiative to see what it would be like to have a married couple on staff. At the end of the trial year both Sandra and Daryl Bem were offered full-time faculty positions. Sandra remained at Stanford until 1978, at which time her failure to receive tenure in the Psychology Department of Stanford caused her to take a position at Cornell University as an associate professor of psychology and director of Cornell's women's studies program. Continuing with their established pattern of mutual compromise, Daryl Bem moved to Cornell as well.

Sandra Bem's most well-known contribution to psychology is her creation of the **Bem Sex Role Inventory** (BSRI, 1976), which is a widely used scale describing the degree of an individual's conformity to traditional sex-role stereotypes. What was new and unique was that the BSRI allowed individuals to be scored as both feminine and masculine at the same time, unlike previous tests that restricted the respondent to only one of these two sex-roles. An individual scoring high on both feminine and masculine traits is considered "androgynous" which, by Bem's definition, means that the individual applies both sets of traits based on their appropriateness in a given situation. According to Sandra Bem, androgynous individuals are "truly effective and well-functioning"(O'Connell & Russo, 1990, p. 33).

Bem followed the creation of the BSRI with the publication of her book, *Lenses of Gender: Transforming the Debate on Sexual Inequality* (1993), which presented an in-depth look at masculinity and femininity. In this book Bem described three "lenses": (1) "androcentrism," (2) "gender polarization," and (3) "biological essentialism," all of which are taught through the socialization process and are the lenses through which we view gender. Looking through an "androcentric" lens, male experience is seen as the norm or standard by which psychological health is judged, while female experience is seen as not the norm. Through a lens of "gender polarization," the perceived differences between men and women are used to structure society with the masculine way of doing something usually seen as the correct way. In "biological essentialism," both of these lenses, androcentrism and gender polarization, are viewed as natural and based on biological difference. In her work, Bem makes it clear that she considers the focus on biological difference in the study of gender to be misguided and that social change, or what Bem calls "cultural invention," can transform the situational context in which biology operates so radically as to liberate humankind from social constraints and faulty belief systems that had previously appeared to be the result of intrinsic biological limitations (Bem, 1999).

Sandra Bem and her work have received significant professional and popular attention. At the age of 31 she received the APA's Distinguished Scientific Award for an Early Career Contribution to Psychology "for her studies of sex roles, androgyny, and the ontogyny of psychosexual identity and maturity." She also received the Distinguished Publication Award of the Association for Women in Psychology in 1977 (for *Lenses of Gender*) along with the Young Scholar Award of the American Association of University Women in 1980.

Another attendee at the 1975 APA conference, "New Directions for Research on Women," who has had a profound impact on professional psychology and on the study of women is Florence Denmark.

Florence Denmark

Another Pennsylvania native, Florence Denmark was born in Philadelphia on January 28, 1932. Both her undergraduate and graduate degrees were earned from the University of Pennsylvania where she completed a PhD in social psychology in 1958. Her research comparing female and male leaders yielded interesting results that were contrary to expectations in that women leaders were found by Denmark to be less authoritarian than male leaders, and women followers were less likely to conform to their leaders' position than were male followers. After graduation, Denmark moved from Pennsylvania to New York where she was hired as a lecturer at Queens College and held a position as counselor at Queens' Testing and Counseling Center. She also held a simultaneous position at Hunter College, CUNY, beginning in 1964.

Denmark's interests, like those of Janet Spence, have been broad and she has written extensively on the psychology of women. Her list of publications includes an influential text in this area titled *Psychology of Women: A Handbook of Issues and Theories* (with co-editor Michele Paludi, 1993) as well as *Woman: Dependent or Independent Variable* (with co-author R. Unger, 1975). Her other areas of interest include minority group achievement, locus of control, and urban conflict. She is also well known for her political activities and has been described as the consummate politician and activist (Stevens & Gardner, 1982, p. 193). In addition to holding the presidency of the American Psychological Association (APA) in 1979, she has been president of APA Division 35 (Psychology of Women), chair of the psychology section of the New York Academy of Sciences (1975–1977), National President of Psi Chi (1978–1979), and received the Gold Medal Award for Life Achievement in Psychology in the Public Interest from the American Psychological Foundation in 2004 (American Psychological Association, 2004b).

Denmark attributes much of her interest in and contribution to feminism and feminist mental health to early childhood influences. Her family's strong emphasis on achievement, particularly her mother's encouragement and support, helped to spur Denmark along her educational and professional path. As a graduate student, she unfortunately found few female mentors or role models, and, accordingly, it became very important to Florence Denmark to empower other women both through active mentoring and by personal example. As she herself so clearly states:

> It is my lasting hope that I can continue to inspire others (students, women, and minorities) by advisement, instruction, and example to reach their highest potential. I am supportive of the creation of new areas of study within psychology as well as in assisting students and colleagues to achieve their own personal visions within the discipline. I hope my students and younger colleagues will in turn reach out to help other women. (Denmark, 1995, p. 168)

While women psychologists like Horney, Spence, Bem, and Denmark, and some male contributors as well have made great strides in the study of the psychology of women, such work has not been the only focus of women in psychology since the end of the 19th century. While Denmark has written concerning some of the career struggles she and other women encountered as a result of gender, such struggles have not prevented women from contributing to a variety of major subfields within psychology. In fact, some of Denmark's own most noteworthy contributions in psychology have been in the study of leadership qualities and gender-related differences in leadership styles. These scholarly contributions are indeed truly fitting given Denmark's own achievements as a leader in psychology.

WOMEN CHALLENGING BIAS

To date we have described the careers of several women who have made lasting contributions to psychology through the discovery of innovative methodology or through their generation of new theories. The following woman made her contribution to the discipline of psychology and to society by radically redefining perceptions of homosexuality.

Evelyn Hooker

A fearless pioneer on the frontiers of psychology, it is fitting that one of Evelyn Hooker's favorite childhood memories was of herself, as a young child named Evelyn Gentry, perched on the front seat of a covered wagon with her parents and eight siblings on their way to Sterling, Colorado. Evelyn Hooker (1907–1996) was born in North Platte, Nebraska, in her grandmother's house right next door to the home of Buffalo Bill, an icon of the American West. Her childhood was spent on a series of impoverished farms and in a succession of one-room schoolhouses that afforded her only source of books. Despite these challenges, Evelyn's family had a strong belief in and commitment to the value of education as a positive and liberating force. As her mother would constantly say, "Get an education and they can never take it away from you" (Hooker, as cited in APA, 1992, p. 501).

Evelyn Hooker attended Sterling High School where her teachers encouraged her to pursue a college degree, and as a result she enrolled at the University of Colorado at Boulder in 1924 with a full tuition scholarship. As a psychology major, Hooker earned the attention of Professor Karl Muenzinger; she earned her bachelor's degree as his student in 1928 and a master's degree in 1930 with a thesis on vicarious trial-and-error (VTE) learning in rats. On Muenziger's recommendation, Hooker then enrolled in the graduate psychology program at Johns Hopkins University to study with Knight Dunlap (1875–1949). Although Dunlap generally disapproved of women doctorates, he directed Evelyn's pursuit of a doctoral degree in experimental psychology, which she earned in 1932.

After obtaining the PhD, Hooker taught at Maryland College for Women (in Sutherville, MD) from 1932 to 1934 and then at Whittier College in California from 1936 to 1939. Her time at Whittier was interrupted by a year (1937–1938) spent in Europe on an academic fellowship for the purpose of studying psychotherapy (mostly spent at the Institute for Psychotherapy in Berlin). While in Berlin, Hooker lived most of the time with a Jewish family and this experience, occurring as it did within the social and political atmosphere of the Austrian Anschluss (i.e., the forced political union of Austria with Nazi Germany in 1938), proved eye-opening for Hooker and intensified her conviction that she would make her life count by helping to correct social injustices.

On her return to the United States, and after spending 1938–1939 teaching at Whittier, Hooker applied for a position at the University of California, Los Angeles (UCLA) where she became a research associate in psychology. She taught experimental and physiological psychology at UCLA for thirty-one years (1939–1970), with only two interruptions; one was a two-year interval spent teaching at Bryn Mawr College (1947–1948) and the other a period spent convalescing from tuberculosis at a sanatorium in Arizona. While at UCLA, she also trained herself in clinical psychology, obtaining a diplomate from the American Board of Professional Psychology in 1962. At the end of one of her classes at UCLA, a student, Sam From, suggested that Hooker should conduct research on homosexuality. Hooker did not take up his suggestion at first, but finally did some exploratory research several years later. The project, still in its infancy, was put on hold as a consequence of her divorce in 1947 from her first husband, freelance writer Donn Caldwell, and her subsequent remarriage in 1951 to Edward Niles Hooker, a professor of English at UCLA.

In 1953, Hooker applied for a six-month grant from the National Institute of Mental Health (NIMH) to conduct a study that was to be her groundbreaking contribution to psychology. Her proposal to the NIMH was to study two comparable groups of thirty homosexual men and thirty heterosexual men matched in terms of age, socioeconomic status, and intelligence level (as scored using the Wechsler Adult Intelligence test). None of the proposed participants had been hospitalized for mental problems or had been in psychotherapy. Her proposal was considered quite extraordinary, coming as it did at the height of the McCarthy era when legal penalties for homosexual behavior were severe and homosexuality was classified as a severe and pervasive emotional disorder (a diagnostic opinion based mostly on scientific data collected on homosexuals who were imprisoned or were psychiatric inpatients). Accordingly, after receiving her application John Eberhart, chief of the Grants Division of NIMH, quickly flew out to meet with Hooker. As Eberhart told Hooker at the time, "We are prepared to give you the grant, but you may not receive it, and you won't know why and we won't know why" (Eberhart, as cited in APA, 1992, p. 503). Eberhart was proven wrong; Hooker not only received the grant in response to her initial application, but the NIMH also continued to renew her funding until 1961 at which time she received an NIMH Research Career Award.

Finally, with the funding necessary to proceed with her study, Hooker engaged Bruno Klopfer, Mortimer Meyer, and Edwin Shneidman to make blind adjustment ratings of the study participants, who were recruited from the Southern California homosexual community. With the results of her careful and meticulously controlled study, Hooker demonstrated that heterosexual and homosexual men were indistinguishable from each other in terms of social and psychological adjustment. As Judd Marmor has stated, Hooker demonstrated unequivocally that "traditional views of psychologists and psychiatrists that homosexuality . . . was an illness or a 'perversion' were totally without merit" (Marmor, cited in Shneidman, 1998).

Immediate public reactions to her research findings and conclusions were less than favorable and Hooker even found herself occasionally harassed by police, presumably for her work on the then taboo subject of homosexuality (Shneidman, 1998). However, the reaction from the psychological community and from the NIMH was much more supportive. Hooker became chair of the NIMH Task Force on Male Homosexuality (in 1967), and she was given the Award for Distinguished Contributions by the Division of Clinical Psychology of the American Psychological Association (APA) in 1974 as well as awards from several gay and lesbian rights groups. In 1991, she was honored by the APA with an Award for Distinguished Contributions to Psychology in the Public Interest. An American Psychological Foundation fund was started to continue her research on homosexuality and there is to this day an Evelyn Hooker Center for the Mental Health of Gays and Lesbians at the University of Chicago.

Evelyn Hooker was described by many as a strikingly handsome woman with a wonderfully full voice and a room-filling laugh; the life of this charismatic and courageous woman has been immortalized on film. In 1992, David Haugland and Richard Schmiechen made a documentary film titled *Changing Our Minds: The Story of Dr. Evelyn Hooker*, which was nominated for an Academy Award for best documentary. As her friend Edwin Shneidman (1998, p. 481) wrote in Evelyn Hooker's obituary, "Many homosexual men have stated that they owe improvements in the attitudes of society and in their acceptance of themselves directly and indirectly to the work of Evelyn Hooker. Thus, one can say that, in relation to the gay rights movement in America, she was their unrivalled diva."

One husband-and-wife team of psychologists deserve recognition here for their pivotal research in the area of racial bias, namely, Mamie Phipps Clark (1917–1983) and her husband Kenneth Clark (1914–   ).

Mamie Phipps Clark

Mamie Phipps Clark was born in Hot Springs, Arkansas. Her father, Harold Phipps, was a native of the British West Indies and maintained a practice as a physician, assisted by his wife Katie. Encouraged by her parents to strive for high goals, Mamie attended Howard University after graduating from high school. When she first enrolled at Howard, Mamie held a double major in physics and mathematics, but after meeting her future husband, Kenneth Clark, she was persuaded to switch to his major, psychology. She and Kenneth both benefited from the experience of learning psychology under the tutelage of Francis Cecil Sumner (1895–1954). After graduating magna cum laude in 1938, Mamie spent the summer working in the law office of William Houston, a civil rights lawyer, which gave Mamie some early insight into the psychological effects of racial segregation.

Mamie returned to Howard University to obtain her master's degree and then enrolled in Columbia University's doctoral program, by which time she and Kenneth Clark were married and had already begun collaborating in research on the effects of segregation. Mamie Clark's master's thesis was titled "Development of Consciousness of Self in Negro Preschool Children." She earned her PhD from Columbia in 1943, the only African-American student in the psychology program. It was difficult enough for a woman psychologist to find positions after graduation, while for an African-American woman, it was even tougher.

Mamie Clark worked in a series of research and clinical jobs, as a research psychologist with the American Public Health Association (1944–1945), with the Armed Forces Institute Examination Center at Columbia (1945–1946), and with the Riverdale Children's Association (1945–1946) before she and her husband founded the Northside Center for Child Development in Harlem in 1946. Mamie was executive director of the center from 1946 to 1979, and her husband Kenneth was research director (1946 to 1966) and later chief psychologist.

In the late 1930s and 1940s, both of the Clarks conducted a series of studies on the negative self-images of black school children using coloring tests and dolls, and their findings indicated clearly that these young African-American children had developed negative self-images and experienced emotional anxiety regarding the color of their skin. Thus, for example, both black and white children, when given their choice of doll, would select a white doll as their preference with which to play. These studies were cited as evidence when the U.S. Supreme Court ruled to abolish school segregation in the landmark *Brown v. Board of Education* case of 1954. Mamie Phipps Clark died on August 11, 1983, leaving behind two children and three grandchildren. She and her husband also left behind a research legacy that must not be forgotten.

WOMEN IN DEVELOPMENTAL PSYCHOLOGY

As Florence Denmark described psychology in the late 1950s and 1960s: women were scarce in academia; there were relatively few women in graduate programs in psychology; they were clearly encouraged to avoid areas considered more "masculine" such as industrial psychology, and to focus their interests in areas of psychology considered "more natural" for women, such as developmental psychology. One woman who made significant advances in the analysis of children was inspired, like Karen Horney, by the work of Sigmund Freud, namely, his daughter Anna.

Anna Freud

Anna Freud (1895–1982) was the youngest of Sigmund Freud's six children and the only one to follow in her famous father's footsteps as a psychoanalyst. Anna Freud has been described as "her father's daughter" and the two shared an extremely close bond.

Anna Freud's professional education was unconventional and, although a serious student, she never finished Gymnasium (the equivalent of a high school education) and received no formal scientific training. Her first professional role was as an elementary school teacher, a position she held while attending her father's lectures at the University of Vienna and informally attending meetings of the Vienna Psychoanalytic Society. After undergoing analysis, reportedly with her father in the role of analyst, Anna became a member of the Vienna Psychoanalytic Society in 1922 and began practicing as a child analyst the following year. When his own battle with cancer of the jaw made it impossible for Freud to continue his speaking career, Anna took on the responsibility of reading her father's papers at international psychoanalytic meetings. This allowed Freud to continue publicizing his own theories while it also exposed Anna to the psychoanalytic community. Toward the end of his life, Anna was her father's private nurse.

After her father's death, Anna went on to become his successor as a major force in the psychoanalytic movement. Many of her most noteworthy contributions were in the area of child analysis. For example, it was Anna Freud who systematized an approach to child therapy that differed from the approach used with adults. She published her first book on this technique, *Introduction to the Technique of Child Analysis*, in 1928. It was her belief that the main distinction between child analysis and that of the adult was that children were too young to shift their emotional focus away from the original family members and were, therefore, incapable of an adult form of transference. Children thus required a different psychoanalytic technique, which Anna Freud then introduced and refined over the course of her career. Interestingly, this belief in a need for different psychoanalytic techniques when working with children was the basis for long-standing struggles between Anna Freud and Melanie Klein (1882–1960) which, after Anna Freud's immigration to London during World War II, led to deep schisms in the British Psychoanalytic Association. In contrast to Anna Freud, Melanie Klein believed that the technique used when working with adults, of analyzing their transference-resistance reactions to the therapist, could also be used effectively with children.

Instead of confining herself to the use of orthodox adult techniques that focused on "talking" therapy, Anna Freud was an innovator in the use of play materials in child analysis and in working with children in their own home setting. Although child analysis is the area of practice most identified with Anna Freud, she also was one of the first Freudian psychoanalysts to stress ego psychology.

While her father had mentioned the term *defense mechanisms* in 1894, it was Anna Freud who described these mechanisms in detail in her best-known work, *The Ego and the Mechanisms of Defense* (1937). These defense mechanisms are used by the ego when it is threatened by conflict between the id and the superego and include repression, regression, rationalization, projection, reaction formation, displacement, and sublimation, as described in Table 14-2.

TABLE 14-2	Psychoanalytic Defense Mechanisms Used by the Ego
Defense Mechanisms	**Description**
Repression	Removal from consciousness of unacceptable ideas, memories, and impulses.
Regression	A retreat to an earlier stage of development as the result of trauma.
Rationalization	The ego attempts to account for failures by providing reasonable, but untrue explanations for behavior.
Projection	The attribution of unpleasant or disturbing desires to others while denying the presence of these desires in the self.
Reaction formation	The individual expresses a desire for the opposite of what it is he or she really wants.
Displacement	Emotion is shifted away from its true object to one that appears "safer."
Sublimation	Displacement in which the object to which emotion is displaced is one that is socially approved.

Adapted from Thorne, B. M., & Henley, T. B. (1997). *Connections in the history and systems of psychology.* Copyright © 1997 by Houghton Mifflin Company, Boston, MA. Adapted with permission.

After her immigration to London, Anna Freud established the Hampstead Child Therapy Clinic, which became her best-known professional achievement. The clinic offered facilities for the treatment of children, research, analytic training, and education. Largely supported by American funds, provided with the stipulation that American students would be given preference, the Hampstead Clinic trained many American child psychologists who then returned to the United States to continue child therapy, research, and training at various places across the country.

During the years she spent establishing the clinic, Anna Freud's disagreements with Melanie Klein continued, causing a division within the British Psychoanalytic Association. An arrangement was made separating this group into three subgroups of equal size, Freudian (led by Anna Freud), Kleinian, and middle (composed of analysts who disagreed with both Anna Freud and Melanie Klein). These equal proportions were maintained as new students were admitted to the Association. The powerful impact these two women had on psychoanalysis as it developed in Great Britain is evidenced from the fact that the British school remained a "house divided" until both of these eminent figures died (Anna Freud died on October 9, 1982). Only then were the British able to become more unified, though even today some old divisions still remain between the more orthodox followers of Anna Freud and Melanie Klein.

Other major contributions have been made by women working in the area of developmental psychology, including Mary Cover Jones, another alumna of Columbia University.

Mary Cover Jones

Mary Cover (1896–1987) was born in Johnstown, Pennsylvania, a fairly industrialized mining town east of Pittsburgh. She grew up there, graduated from Johnstown High School, and then left Johnstown in 1915 to attend college at Vassar. It was the dawn of the Jazz Age and feminism was a growing force on college campuses across the country. Skirt hems were getting higher, women's hair was getting shorter, and women were lobbying across the country for the right to vote (finally obtained nationwide with ratification of the nineteenth amendment to the U.S. Constitution in 1920).

During the spring of her senior year at Vassar, Mary Cover took advantage of relaxed restrictions at Vassar and attended a lecture in New York City. The speaker was none other than John B. Watson (1878–1958), who was presenting the results of a study conducted by Watson and Cover's friend, Rosalie Raynor, in which fear was conditioned in a young child named Albert (Logan, 1980). As is well known, Watson and Raynor found that by coupling presentation of a noxious stimulus with the child's reaching for a white rat, they had successfully conditioned the child to fear the rat, a fear that eventually was generalized by the child to a fear of other furry objects. Intrigued by Watson's presentation, Mary Cover then wondered whether the conditioning approach used in their study could also be used to remove rather than instill fears.

Mary Cover graduated from Vassar and went on to Columbia University to work toward her PhD in psychology. While there, she met and married fellow student Harold Jones, who was later her frequent collaborator. The newly wedded Mary Cover Jones also began a series of experiments to try to answer the question that had been raised in her mind when attending Watson's lecture in 1919.

Her friend Rosalie Raynor, a Vassar classmate of Mary's, introduced her to John Watson, who had recently left academia following his highly public and sensationalized affair with Rosalie Raynor and his resultant divorce from his first wife (Watson later married Rosalie Raynor). In an unofficial capacity, Watson advised and supervised Mary as she undertook her series of experiments to attenuate or eliminate fears. At first her attempts met with little success. Working with several children who feared a variety of objects, Jones found no reduction in fear as a result of (a) the simple passage of time, (b) through verbally appealing to the child that its fears were groundless, or (c) by having peers ridicule the child for its fears. Finally, using a method suggested by Watson and Raynor, Jones was successful in de-conditioning fear in a young boy named Peter. She reduced Peter's fear of rabbits by placing a rabbit at a distance from the boy while he was eating and gradually moving the rabbit closer and closer to Peter. Jones theorized that the pleasurable sensations Peter associated with eating grew to replace the fear the child had associated initially to the rabbit. This study has been cited as a pioneering example of the behavior therapy technique now known as **systematic desensitization**.

A very nurturing person by nature, Mary Cover Jones was to say in her later personal recollections, "It has always been of the greatest satisfaction to me that I could be associated with the removal of a fear . . . I could not have played the role of creating a fear in a child, no matter how important the theoretical implications" (Jones, 1974, p. 581). Despite the fact that the Peter study later became a classic, it was given little attention at the time of Jones' original experiments. In fact, it was dismissed as unsuitable for Jones to submit as her dissertation because of the limited number of cases. The Peter study finally gained public attention when Watson included it in his book *Behaviorism*, which was written for a mass audience and published in 1924.

While completing her PhD, Mary taught emotionally disturbed children in the New York City public school system (1920–1921), lectured at Women's Medical College in Philadelphia (1921–1922), and resumed work she had begun after her undergraduate degree administering mental tests. Her first publication, in 1921, was a study comparing three group intelligence tests administered to children in New York City. In 1923, Harold Jones earned his PhD and joined the faculty at Columbia, and Mary obtained a position at Columbia's Institute of Child Welfare as a research associate. She remained at the institute for four years.

After obtaining her PhD in 1926, family obligations and her status as the wife of an older and more established male psychologist had their impact on Mary's career. As an example, by that time the Jones were parents of two small children and, although Mary opted to employ full-time in-home help both for child care and general household chores, she insisted on not working full-time while her daughters were still at home. In 1927, the couple moved to California so that Harold Jones could take a highly advantageous position as Director of Research on the staff at the University of California, Berkeley. Unfortunately for Mary, this move was not so advantageous for her career since anti-nepotism policies at Berkeley restricted her to low-status jobs; she worked at Berkeley for twenty-five years before she was offered an assistant professorship in the education department, which at that time was considered to have lower status than the psychology department. As further evidence of the conflict Jones experienced between her roles as mother and as psychologist, she postponed accepting an academic appointment at Berkeley for two years because the department demanded a full-time commitment that she was unwilling to make due to her sustained responsibilities as the mother of two children. Such personal conflicts, however, did not prevent her from continuing to make significant contributions to psychology.

In 1928, Berkeley hired Nancy Bayley and Jean Macfarlane as administrators of two longitudinal studies, the Berkeley Growth Study and the Berkeley Guidance Study. At that time, Mary Jones was involved primarily in setting up a nursery school at Berkeley. In 1932, a third longitudinal study was undertaken at Berkeley's Institute of Human Development and Mary Jones was to be a major participant. The Adolescent Growth Study (later called the Oakland Growth Study) followed the transition through puberty of 200 fifth and sixth graders from five elementary schools in the Oakland area. Another of Mary Jones' major contributions to developmental psychology emanated from her research as a part of that study, namely, her research on the effects on personality development of early and late maturation in adolescence.

Through careful study over a number of years, Jones was able to show that measurable group differences in personality development exist among adolescents who mature earlier or later than their peers (Jones & Bayley, 1950; Jones & Mussen, 1958; Mussen & Jones, 1957). She further documented that late-maturing males and early-maturing females, both of whom were less popular than their peers, developed coping strategies that remained well after maturation (Logan, 1980). Although the generalizability of these results has come into question due to the fact that the study sample was composed of a relatively small group of white, urban, middle-class volunteers from the western United States, the research has become a standard topic in textbooks on developmental psychology.

In 1960, after working at Berkeley's Institute for Human Development for thirty-three years, Mary Jones and her husband retired. Tragically, what began as their first retirement vacation, a trip to Paris, came to an unforeseen end when Harold Jones died suddenly of a heart attack. Mary Jones abruptly found herself devoid of two of the primary focuses of her life, her career and her husband. In a healthy response to her personal grief, she came out of retirement and joined her friend Nevitt Sanford at Stanford University's Institute for the Study of Human Problems. During her four years there, Jones made a third lasting contribution to psychology, combining the investigation of alcohol problems with the ongoing longitudinal studies at Berkeley.

For her research, Jones interviewed in depth the now adult participants of the Oakland Growth Study regarding their drinking behavior. Personality characteristics of the different drinking pattern groups were then compared looking back, retrospectively, at three different ages: junior high, senior high, and adulthood. Although individual group sizes were small, patterns emerged and Jones demonstrated that adult male and female problem drinkers had exhibited patterns of instability, unpredictability, and impulsivity in their youth. She further documented that as adolescents, male problem drinkers seemed to overemphasize the masculine role and began their drinking careers as a means of defying authority. As described by Nevitt Sanford (Sanford, 1968), this research stands "as one of the best studies of its kind."

As professors, Mary Cover Jones and her husband Harold earned reputations as stimulating teachers as well as being very supportive and encouraging of young colleagues. Together the married team of psychologists produced the first educational television course on developmental psychology, and Mary Jones participated in a similar course at the University of Minnesota (Mussen & Eichorn, 1988). This is an interesting and noteworthy accomplishment, particularly in this day and age of technological innovation in educational techniques such as Web classes and distance learning programs.

During her lifetime Mary Cover Jones authored over seventy publications; she was a president of Division 7 of the APA (Developmental Psychology), a Fellow of both the APA and the Gerontological Society, and a recipient of the G. Stanley Hall Award (the highest honor given in developmental psychology). In 1954, *The American Psychologist* listed Mary Cover Jones as one of the twenty-six authors most often cited in introductory psychology textbooks

(Logan, 1980). She remained professionally active until only a few months before her death on July 22, 1987.

Many women psychologists have made significant contributions in the study of children. Many have also been longtime collaborators with husbands also working as professional psychologists. But not all long-term collaborations have been cemented by marriage bonds; some intellectual collaborations have withstood the test of time on their own. One example is the long, collaborative relationship between Mary D. Salter Ainsworth and John Bowlby.

Mary D. Salter Ainsworth

Mary Dinsmore Salter was born in Glendale, Ohio, in 1913, and by the time she was 4 years old her family moved to Toronto, Canada, where she received all of her formal education. Her bachelor's (1935), master's (1936) and doctorate (1939) were all earned at the University of Toronto. While completing her graduate training, Ainsworth became interested in the security theory developed by her professor, W. E. Blatz.

According to Blatz (1966), there are several kinds of security, of which the first to develop is what he termed **immature dependent security**. At this early stage of development, infants or young children feel secure only if they can rely on parent figures to care for them and to take responsibility for the consequences their actions. At the same time, children are curious about the world around them and feel the need to explore, which often involves feelings of insecurity. The child is nevertheless secure if it can retreat to the safety of the parent figure whenever it becomes uneasy as a result of its exploratory activities, and thus requires comfort and reassurance. In short, the primary role of the parent is to provide the child with a secure base from which to explore and learn about the surrounding environment.

With age and experience, the child becomes increasingly self-reliant, building the basis for **independent security**. At this point, usually achieved by young adulthood, the person is fully emancipated from her or his parents and Blatz viewed any continued dependence on them at this point to be undesirable. Blatz saw the emergence of **mature dependent security** through a mutually contributing and give-and-take relationship with someone of one's own generation. Each partner in this mature relationship provides a secure base for the other.

For her doctoral dissertation research, Ainsworth developed two self-report scales intended to assess the degree to which a person felt secure or insecure. After earning the PhD, Ainsworth held a position as lecturer in the University of Toronto's psychology department until 1942 at which time she was commissioned in the Canadian Women's Army Corps (CWAC).

Although her primary interest while at Toronto had been in the area of personality development, her work as director of personnel selection at CWAC and as superintendent of women's rehabilitation in the Department of Veterans Affairs led her to clinical psychology. When Ainsworth returned to the University of Toronto as an assistant professor in 1946, she began work in diagnostic assessment techniques and taught a range of courses (including introductory experimental psychology and personality theory and assessment). She also began to revisit her earlier work on security research with W. E. Blatz.

After marrying fellow psychologist Leonard Ainsworth, Mary Ainsworth accompanied her husband to England where she first encountered John Bowlby. In 1950, responding to his advertisement for a research assistant, Ainsworth took the position at the Tavistock Clinic in London where Bowlby was directing a team investigating the effects of separation from the mother during early childhood on personality development. In contrast to followers of

Melanie Klein, who attributed emotional problems in children to fantasies generated from internal conflict between aggressive and libidinal drives, Bowlby had come to believe that actual family experiences were a much more important and basic cause of emotional disturbance in childhood and in later adulthood. Bowlby's commitment to the value of direct observation in a real-life environment had a profound impact on Mary Ainsworth.

In 1954, Ainsworth accompanied her husband to Kampala, Uganda, where she conducted longitudinal research on mother–infant interaction and the development of infant–mother attachment at the East African Institute for Social Research. Assembling a sample of twenty-eight Ugandan babies and their mothers, Ainsworth undertook in-home visits every two weeks over a period of nine months. Her research yielded rich data, which she shared with John Bowlby, aiding in the identification of attachment behaviors and of phases of attachment as well as individual differences in attachment and their relationship to differences in maternal caregiving practices.

In late 1955, the Ainsworths moved to Baltimore, Maryland, where Mary was appointed as a clinical psychologist at Johns Hopkins University. There she taught courses in personality and assessment and provided clinical experience and research supervision through a part-time appointment at a private psychiatric hospital. She also maintained a private practice in diagnostic assessment, primarily with children. Ainsworth was appointed associate professor at Johns Hopkins in 1958, professor in 1963, and fellow at the Center of Advanced Study in the Behavioral Sciences, Stanford University (1966–1967). The Ainsworths divorced in 1960.

In 1962, Mary Ainsworth's teaching and research interests shifted to developmental psychology and she began planning her now famous Baltimore longitudinal study of mother–infant interaction and the development of attachment during the first year of life (Bretherton, 1992). Although the sample was small (only twenty-six mother–infant dyads), the study was intensive including home visits covering about seventy-two hours with each dyad. Data collection was not completed until 1966 and the data analysis required an additional ten years to complete! The study was truly pioneering as Ainsworth was the first researcher in America to make extensive, systematic, naturalistic observations in the home setting (American Psychologist, 1998). Although Ainsworth herself attaches more importance to the data collected from this home visit study, she is most noted in psychology texts for devising the "strange situation" technique.

In the "strange situation," the mother and her infant (usually about 10 to 12 months of age) are introduced to a laboratory playroom where an unfamiliar woman later joins them. While this stranger plays with the baby, the mother leaves briefly and then returns. Later, the baby again is separated from the mother but the stranger leaves as well, leaving the baby alone. Then the stranger returns, and finally the mother rejoins her baby. Children exposed to the "strange situation" exhibit different patterns of behavior that reveal insight into their attachment relationship with the mother (Bretherton, 1992). When this "strange situation" was used to study children from the Baltimore study, a few of the 1-year-olds were surprisingly angry or ambivalent when the mother returned from the separation period. Another group seemed to snub or avoid the mother, even though they had searched for her while she was gone. When analyses were done on the home data collected earlier, it was revealed that those infants who had been ambivalent toward or avoided the mother on reunion in the "strange situation" had a less harmonious relationship with her at home. Ainsworth's first use of the "strange situation" has inspired significant follow-up research into infant attachment and expanded attachment research to other phases of the life span.

When Ainsworth first published the results of the Baltimore Project, her conclusions were not immediately embraced by all of her professional peers. Indeed, many psychologists strongly criticized her claims regarding the meaning of behavior patterns exhibited by infants exposed to the "strange situation," with most of their critique centering on concerns that the "strange situation," utilized as it was in a laboratory setting, was artificial and that behavior patterns could be interpreted in many different ways. For example, critics argued that seemingly avoidant behavior exhibited upon the mother's return to the room could be interpreted as independence rather than disrupted bonding (Bretherton, 1992).

In 1974, Ainsworth moved to the University of Virginia first as a visiting professor and later as Commonwealth Professor (1975–1984). She retired as Professor Emeritus in 1984 although she remained professionally active until 1992. Always active in professional organizations, Ainsworth served as president of the Society for Research in Child Development (1977–1979), and has been honored over the course of her career with a number of awards from such organizations as the American Psychological Association (APA), the Society for Research in Child Development, the American Academy of Pediatrics, and the American Academy of Arts and Sciences. Several of these awards were shared with John Bowlby who continued to exchange ideas and research data with Ainsworth despite their geographic separation. In 1998, Ainsworth was the recipient of the American Psychological Foundation's Gold Medal Award for Life Achievement in the Science of Psychology.

GROUNDBREAKERS AND NEWSMAKERS

Looking at some more recent contributions to psychology, women continue to steadily expand their active participation in the discipline and at times their work has resulted in controversy. Two women whose work has sparked a radical reconsideration of previous foundational theories are Carol Gilligan and Elizabeth Loftus.

Carol Gilligan: *In a Different Voice*

Early in the 1970s, Carol Gilligan was working as an assistant professor at Harvard University and as a research assistant to Lawrence Kohlberg. It was then that she came to a realization that caused her to question previously held beliefs concerning standards of moral human behavior. In what stands as a fine example of the kind of research efforts Rosser (see Table 14-2) describes as occurring in phase two of her stages of women's participation in science, Gilligan noticed that the majority of studies of psychological and moral development, including those on which Lawrence Kohlberg based his six stages of moral development, had involved only privileged white men. By analyzing subjects' responses to a series of hypothetical moral dilemmas, Kohlberg had constructed a six-stage model by which to measure ethical maturity (Kohlberg & Kramer, 1969).

Taking a controversial stance, Gilligan asserted that Kohlberg's moral development theory was biased against women and began conducting research on female subjects to investigate female moral development. The result of this research was Gilligan's landmark book titled *In a Different Voice: Psychological Theory and Women's Development* (1982). Theories on moral development prior to Gilligan's research had conceptualized moral decision making primarily using an ethic of **justice**. Based on her research on female responses to moral dilemmas, Gilligan concluded that this was a more "masculine" approach and that, in contrast, females tend to base their moral decision making more on an ethic of **care**. Gilligan believes that these gender differences in moral decision making are due to contrasting images of self (Gilligan, 1982).

Although it would be easy to cast Gilligan's theory in terms of a dichotomous "we versus them" approach to gender differences, Gilligan herself does not do so. She instead sees an ethic of justice and an ethic of care as two separate but noncompeting ways of conceptualizing moral problems, with one more frequently associated with men while the other is more typical of women. Both genders are capable of using either ethical perspective, although they tend to select one focus over the other based on their image of self (Gilligan, 1982). Criticisms have been raised of Gilligan's theory of moral development on the grounds that the data used to support her theory did not sufficiently control for the effects of occupation and level of education (Colby & Damon, 1983).

How do these two ethical perspectives compare? Gilligan views the quantity and quality of relationships as key to separating the two perspectives. An ethic of justice is not relational, but rather based on values such as individual rights, equality before the law, and fair play, all of which can be pursued without ties to others (in fact they may be more easily pursued in the absence of the need to consider relationships). In contrast, an ethic of care is a relational orientation and requires consideration of interpersonal involvement and connection. Important values are sensitivity to others, loyalty, responsibility, self-sacrifice, and conciliation. Gilligan (1982) believes that women's greater need for relationships, and thus their greater tendency to utilize an ethic of care in moral decision making, is due to distinct feminine identity formation early in life.

In support of this latter conclusion, Gilligan points to the work of Janet Lever, a sociologist at Northwestern University (Gilligan, 1982). In her research studies of children's play styles, Lever (1976) found distinct gender differences such that boys tend to prefer games with lots of intricate rules and when disputes arise over how the rules are to be interpreted, such arguments do not break up the game. In fact, Lever (1976) noted that some boys appear to enjoy this debate over rules. In contrast, girls play shorter and less complex games and, when disagreements arise, will usually bend the rules to avoid hurting an individual. Gilligan believes these patterns continue in adulthood with women showing a tendency to change rules in order to preserve relationships while men abide by the rules and view relationships as replaceable (Gilligan, 1982, p. 16).

Prior to Gilligan's landmark research, it was the consensus in the scientific community that findings from studies on male subjects could be generalized to women and, furthermore, a concern existed that to argue otherwise would be detrimental to women in that it would provide ammunition to those opposing women's rights and arguing against equal treatment for both genders. Gilligan courageously went beyond these concerns and opinions to ask the question: "What are we missing by not listening to half the population?" Gilligan was also one of the first researchers to reconceptualize gender differences in a way that did not imply a value judgment (i.e., one gender is inherently better than the other), but instead approached difference from a "different-but-equally-valuable" standpoint.

Elizabeth Loftus: Eyewitness Memory

While Carol Gilligan caused psychology to question assumptions about the generalizability of research derived almost exclusively from white male subjects to females, Elizabeth Loftus caused us all to question our own beliefs about what is true. While Gilligan's work stirred the pot, Loftus caused it to boil over! Although some of Professor Loftus' research has been presented in chapter 7, Associationism, we emphasize here her foundational ideas regarding eyewitness testimony.

Born in Los Angeles, California on October 16, 1944, Loftus is the daughter of Sidney and Rebecca Fishman. Although she initially planned a career as a math teacher, Loftus changed her mind while a student at the University of California, Los Angeles (UCLA) and earned her bachelor's in psychology and mathematics in 1966. In 1968, she married Geoffrey Loftus and continued graduate studies in psychology at Stanford University where she earned her master's degree in 1967 and her PhD in 1970. Thereafter, Elizabeth Loftus spent three years working at the New School for Social Research in New York (1970–1973) before accepting a position as assistant professor at the University of Washington in Seattle. Professor Loftus is now on the faculty at the University of California, Irvine.

Beginning in the 1970s, Loftus' interest in memory research led her to study traumatically repressed memories, eyewitness memory, and most recently false memories (Loftus, 2003, 2004). At that time, the media were featuring a growing number of stories in which individuals were reporting memories of childhood sexual abuse that had been allegedly repressed for many years. These recovered memories resulted in legal actions against alleged perpetrators often twenty, thirty, or even forty years after the remembered events were said to have occurred. In Loftus' opinion, such increasing reports gave rise to four questions: (a) How common is it for memories of child abuse to be repressed? (b) How are jurors and judges likely to react to these repressed memory claims? (c) When repressed memories surface, what are they like? and (d) How authentic are the memories (Loftus, 1993)?

As a result of the publication of her work, Loftus was asked to testify as an expert witness in over 200 trials, giving her opinion on the unreliability of eyewitness testimony based on false memories. Loftus' opinion concerning the authenticity of repressed memory accounts is probably best described by Loftus herself:

> There are those with extreme positions who would like to deny the authenticity of all repressed memories and those who would accept them all as true. As Van Benschoten (1990) has pointed out, these extreme positions will exacerbate our problems: "Denial fosters overdetermination, and overdetermination invites denial." (Loftus, 1993, p. 524)

Loftus' research, and her testimony in such famous trials as those of serial killer Ted Bundy and the McMartin preschool molestation case thrust her firmly into the limelight. Opinions concerning her research seem to be divided between angered disbelief and admiration. Although controversial and frequently critiqued, she retains the highest respect of many of her colleagues and is acknowledged as an important figure in research on memory and eyewitness testimony. Her list of publications shows her long-standing and continued interest in this area of research including: *Human Memory* (1976), *Cognitive Processes* (1979), *Eyewitness Testimony* (1979), *The Myth of Repressed Memory* (1994), and "Remembering Dangerously" (1995). In all, Loftus has published eighteen books and over 250 journal articles! She has been the recipient of a number of awards, grants, and fellowships. Most recently she received the Distinguished Contribution Award from the American Academy of Forensic Psychology (1995).

Women like Loftus and Gilligan and many of the other women psychologists presented in this chapter have made discoveries that have helped change the course of psychology, opened new areas of research, or caused psychology to question old assumptions.

The women in our history of psychology also exist as a living and vital record of the changing conditions in psychology and society, and thus, these women and their accomplishments will not soon be forgotten.

Summary

We examined the work of some prominent women in psychology as well as some of the sociocultural factors affecting the ability of women to work in psychology. Women have often been confined to the margins of the historical page as a consequence of their lack of access to education and early exclusion from functioning in leadership roles.

We discussed the contributions of women in psychology who were able to overcome these barriers to education and to leadership roles including Hildegard von Bingen, Dorothea Lynde Dix, Mary Whiton Calkins, Margaret Floy Washburn, Maria Montessori, Anne Anastasi, amd Florence Denmark. We also considered factors that influenced where women worked (whether they chose the academic or the applied setting) as well as what women chose to study, such as the many contributions of women who questioned established beliefs about gender difference and the work of women in developmental psychology. This chapter shows not only how far women have come, but also how much distance remains to be traveled in achieving gender parity in psychology.

Chapter 14—Women in the History of Psychology

Discussion Questions

- What are some of the functions of history and what implications do these functions have for the history of women in psychology?
- Should contributions of women to psychology be discussed separately from the general history of psychology or should female contributors be incorporated into discussion of the work of their male contemporaries and peers?
- What are some of the educational barriers that women have historically faced and how have these barriers changed over time?
- Is the shifting of women in psychology from the academic to the applied setting primarily the result of sociocultural factors, innate gender differences, or both?
- Current demographic trends in psychology indicate that women will potentially become the majority practitioners in the discipline. If this trend continues, what, if any, future impact will this have on the experience of male psychologists?

Racial Diversity in American Psychology

CHAPTER OVERVIEW

In this chapter we discuss the issue of racial diversity in psychology. Embracing diversity has been a long-standing problem in psychology just as it has been for the larger cultural context. To describe fully all of the social and cultural forces contributing to the problem of racial intolerance as well as the issues that arise from a failure to embrace diversity is a task far beyond the scope of this chapter. Although our experience of racism is very real, in the simplest sense, the concept of race is a product of what sociologists call the "social construction" of reality (Johnson, 2001). The experience of race, since it is a cultural construct, differs from one cultural context to another. For the sake of simplicity, we have further limited the scope of this chapter to American psychology. Our discussion includes a brief examination of the experiences and contributions of some key minority figures in American psychology.

We begin by presenting an overview of the unique challenges faced by African Americans in psychology and highlighting the contributions of four prominent African-American psychologists: Kenneth B. Clark (1914–2005), Francis Cecil Sumner (1895–1954), Dalmas A. Taylor (1933–1998), and Norman Anderson. We then discuss briefly the contributions of Asian-American, Hispanic American, and Native American individuals within psychology, highlighting challenges and barriers that are unique to each respective group. Some of the individuals whose contributions are discussed include: Stanley Sue (1944–   ), Richard Suinn; Martha Bernal (1931–2001), and Carolyn Attneave (1920–1992).

We conclude with a discussion of the present state of American psychology as it relates to diversity. While significant strides have been made over the last two decades, psychology will need to continue addressing the issue of low representation of ethnic minority groups within its professional ranks. Given the increasingly diverse population in the United States, undergraduate- and graduate-level programs will need to take an active role in recruiting more individuals from minority groups and to enhance our awareness of the need to be culturally sensitive in all areas of psychological practice, in both clinical and research settings.

LEARNING OBJECTIVES

When you finish studying this chapter, you will be prepared to:

- Identify at least three barriers encountered by African Americans in psychology in the United States
- Discuss briefly the factors contributing to the formation of the Association of Black Psychologists
- Discuss Kenneth B. Clark's role in *Brown v. Board of Education*
- Discuss the contributions of Francis Cecil Sumner, Dalmas A. Taylor, and Norman Anderson to psychology
- Describe the goals and contributions of the Asian American Psychological Association
- Discuss the contributions of Stanley Sue and Richard Suinn
- Discuss barriers encountered by Hispanic Americans and Native Americans in psychology

- Discuss the contributions of Martha Bernal, particularly to the treatment of children with behavior problems and the advancement of a multicultural psychology
- Discuss the contributions of Carolyn Attneave, particularly to the development of a family networks approach to family therapy
- Describe the current status of minority group representation within American psychology and the implications for professional practice as well as academic training

INTRODUCTION

Throughout this text we have discussed the innumerable accomplishments of psychologists around the globe. But a complete history of psychology must include its failings as well as its successes; its challenges as well as its accomplishments. A particular challenge that psychology has faced throughout its history is the development of unified theories while at the same time remaining open to diversity. As a science focused on understanding human behavior, it would be easy to assume that psychology should stand as a shining example of inclusiveness and tolerance. But an honest examination of the history of psychology reveals the restrictiveness and intolerance that has often been perpetuated in the field. As Graham Richards (1997) so aptly states, "Psychology is never separate from its host culture, the psychological concerns of which it shares, articulates, and reflects" (p. 153).

Sociologist Allan Johnson (2001, p. 19) has stated that the trouble around diversity "is produced by a world organized in ways that encourage people to use difference to include or exclude, reward or punish, credit or discredit, elevate or oppress, value or devalue, leave alone or harass." Whether an individual differs from the majority on the characteristic of race, gender, ethnicity, physical ability, age, or even sexual orientation, cultural systems often function in ways that inhibit the full realization of an individual's potential. Unfortunately, the infrastructure of psychology has historically been organized in ways that selectively reward or oppress individuals as a function of difference from the majority.

In writing this chapter, we can only begin to address a few of the barriers within psychology limiting the full participation of minority practitioners. A deeper understanding of the myriad ways in which the "-isms," such as racism, genderism, and even ethnocentrism, have impacted the history of psychology is beyond the scope of a single chapter. In chapter 14, Women in Psychology, we examined the role genderism has played in the history of psychology. In this chapter, we attempt a limited examination of the role played within American psychology by yet another "-ism," racism, by highlighting the experiences and accomplishments of a few key African-American, Asian-American, Hispanic American, and Native American psychologists.

SOME FACTORS IN THE EXPERIENCE OF AFRICAN AMERICANS IN PSYCHOLOGY

African-American psychologists have faced a twofold burden of discrimination in trying to combat racially biased theories proposed and promoted by psychology that have led to discriminatory practices in society as a whole, and numerous academic and employment barriers within the profession. Some outstanding African-American psychologists have played a pivotal role in revealing the fallacy and harmfulness of such theories and practices, thereby enhancing the profession as well as society.

In the early days of African-American involvement in psychology during the late 19th and early 20th centuries, African Americans were only beginning to gain access to higher education and frequently found their opportunities limited to the black colleges and universities located predominantly in the southern states. But even within such institutions, opportunities in psychology were limited; as of 1940, only four black colleges in the United States offered undergraduate programs in psychology. Compared with all-white colleges, such institutions were smaller and tended to have limited facilities, staffing, and funds. The majority of these colleges and universities provided only undergraduate-level programs. Fortunately, a few northern universities such as Clark University in Massachusetts accepted and even encouraged enrollment of black students seeking graduate degrees. However, policies at even such liberal institutions frequently required graduates from black colleges to complete an extra year of undergraduate training, to earn a second degree at the white university, before accepting their enrollment to graduate studies (Guthrie, 1996). As a further barrier, in the 1930s and 1940s many predominantly white schools did not allow black students to live on campus.

Black applicants frequently faced more severe financial barriers than their white peers and had fewer resources for financial support. This often led to a significant delay in graduate training while potential black graduate students worked to acquire sufficient funds. As late as the 1950s, the median age of black graduate students was ten to fifteen years higher than their white counterparts (Guthrie, 1996). Ultimately, this contributed to a significant decrease in career length for blacks with graduate-level degrees, thus hampering overall career advancement potential. Despite such barriers, between 1920 and 1950, thirty-two African Americans earned doctoral degrees in psychology. Although this represented a significant achievement, a sobering sense of perspective is gained from contrasting this low number with the fact that between 1920 and 1966 more than 3,700 doctoral degrees were granted in psychology in the United States (Guthrie, 1996; Russo & Denmark, 1987).

After surmounting barriers to graduate-level education, black psychologists then found themselves facing significant professional and employment challenges. Options were limited for those individuals seeking a career in academia since few universities hired African Americans as faculty members. Black colleges and universities were often the only option for employment; however, the limited resources and heavy teaching loads within these institutions limited the chances of achieving professional recognition. A. P. Davis, a professor at one black college, described the atmosphere at these institutions in 1936:

> (The black college professor) is criminally underpaid . . . if he is fortunate enough to get a position, he can look forward to an average salary of less than two thousand dollars a year. . . . He teaches from eighteen to twenty-one hours a week. . . . Lack of money, over-work and other unpleasant factors make it practically impossible for him to do anything outstanding in the field of pure scholarship. He cannot buy books on a large scale himself, and he cannot get them at his school libraries, because there are no really adequate libraries in the Negro schools. Probably the worst handicap of all is the lack of a scholarly atmosphere about him. There is no incentive, and, of course, no money for research in most schools. (Davis, 1936, pp. 103–104)

According to Benjamin and Crouse (2002), many Americans, including psychologists, began to reexamine their views on race as a result of their experiences of World War II and revelations concerning the horrific consequences of Adolf Hitler's vision of a master race. The American Psychological Association (APA) also began to engage in a deeper examination of its own policies and practices. For example, upon becoming aware that African-American members of APA were being discriminated against in convention hotels, APA's Council of Representatives adopted a policy in 1950 of not meeting at hotels or venues where minority members would face discrimination (Benjamin & Crouse, 2002).

The Association of Black Psychologists

The year 1968 was a tumultuous one for race relations in the United States and this was true also for relations within the APA. Martin Luther King Jr., was assassinated on April 4, 1968, and one month later the Poor People's March on Washington, DC, which had been organized by King prior to his death, took place. On August 26–29 of that same year, protestors and other crowd members were brutally beaten by police at the Democratic National Convention in Chicago. At the APA's annual convention in San Francisco, held only a day later, the APA's Council of Representatives voted not to hold their 1969 convention in Chicago as a sign of their outrage over the events in Chicago (Pickren & Tomes, 2002).

A number of African-American psychologists present at this same 1968 convention voiced their protest of APA's failure to adequately address black issues. Their frustration led to the formation of the Association of Black Psychologists (ABPsi) on September 1, 1968, with approximately 200 original members. On September 2, representatives of ABPsi presented the APA Board of Directors with an agenda for change (Pickren & Tomes, 2002). A petition submitted a month later by the ABPsi to APA's Council of Representatives included the following demands: (1) APA should endorse the *Report of the National Advisory Commission on Civil Disorders*, which cited white racism as the major cause of social and racial unrest in the United States; (2) APA should investigate the use and misuse of psychological tests with minority populations; (3) Black psychologists should be included in the development of all APA policies of relevance to the black community; (4) APA should refuse to do business with vendors who engaged in racially discriminatory employment practices; (5) APA should create a Central Office staff position to deal with social problems; and (6) psychology graduate programs should begin to aggressively recruit African-American faculty and students (Pickren & Tomes, 2002).

APA's gradual movement to address the concerns raised by the ABPsi marked a change in the APA's stance regarding its role in social issues. Previously, APA leaders had endorsed a very limited role for psychology in social concerns, indeed, arguing that psychology and psychologists should not be concerned with social problems. As a sign of APA's increasing recognition of the need for more active involvement in social problems, it created the Board of Social and Ethical Responsibility for Psychology (BSERP), which later evolved into the current Board for the Advancement of Psychology in the Public Interest.

One African-American psychologist who played a key role in APA's changing attitude regarding its social and ethical responsibilities was Kenneth B. Clark. Together with his wife Mamie Phipps Clark (1917–1983), whose accomplishments are described in chapter 14, Kenneth Clark had a significant impact on the world of American psychology and on the face of American education.

Kenneth B. Clark

Kenneth B. Clark (1914–2005) was born in the Panama Canal Zone, the son of Arthur and Miriam Clark. He first came to the United States at the age of 7 and was educated in the public school system in New York City. A student of Francis Cecil Sumner, Clark enrolled at Howard

University in 1929 where he received his B.S. degree in psychology in 1935 and his M.S. degree just one year later. It was during his years at Howard that Clark first met Mamie Phipps, who later became his wife as well as his colleague and frequent collaborator. Together in 1946, the pair established the Northside Center for Child Development in New York City.

For his graduate studies, Clark enrolled at Columbia University where he was awarded the PhD in psychology in 1940. He subsequently found employment teaching in New York at Queens College and as professor of psychology at City College. As an educator, Clark was able to exert widespread influence on a generation of students through his activities as a visiting professor at Columbia University, the University of California at Berkeley, and Harvard University, as well as through his membership on the New York State Board of Regents and as a member of the Board of Trustees of the University of Chicago.

Clark is perhaps best known for his role in unmasking the harmful effects of segregation. The U.S. Supreme Court cited Clark's work in its 1954 decision, *Brown v. Board of Education of Topeka*, which struck down the "separate but equal" doctrine of the *Plessy v. Ferguson* decision of 1896 that was the foundation of school segregation in seventeen states and the District of Columbia. The Supreme Court cited a summary, written by Clark, of psychological theories concerning the effect of prejudice and discrimination on personality development. *Brown v. Board of Education* has been described as arguably the most important Supreme Court decision of the 20th century in terms of its influence on American history (Benjamin & Crouse, 2002).

In addition to influencing the American system of education, the *Brown* decision represented a milestone in the relationship between psychology and the legal system, since this was the first time that psychological research played a significant role in a Supreme Court decision (Benjamin & Crouse, 2002). As argued by Richards (1997) "while, in point of fact, the Supreme Court . . . stressed that its decision was taken on purely legal and moral grounds, not scientific ones, the prominence given to the involvement in the case of psychologists and sociologists overshadowed this" (p. 245).

Following the Supreme Court's decision, Clark sought to reach a broader audience than his peers in academia through his book *Prejudice and Your Child* (1955), in which he presented a summary of psychological research on the relationship between prejudice and personality development (Keppel, 2002). The message Clark conveyed in this book was that "children learn prejudice in the course of observing and being influenced by the existence of patterns in the culture in which they live" (Clark, 1989, p. 17). The evidence Clark used to support his conclusion included the results of the now famous "Doll Studies" conducted by Clark and his wife.

During the Doll Studies a group of more than 200 early school age black children were presented with four dolls, two black in appearance and the other two white, but otherwise identical. The children were then asked first to identify which doll they liked best or would prefer to play with and then to select which doll resembled the child most. Kenneth and Mamie Clark discovered that the majority of the children indicated a preference for the white doll. As Clark poignantly described the reaction of one participant: "one little girl . . . had shown a clear preference for the white doll and . . . described the brown doll as ugly and dirty" (Clark, 1989, p. 45). When the investigator responded by pointing out to the child that she herself was brown, she "broke into a torrent of tears" (Clark, 1989, p. 45). Clark concluded that such responses indicated that rigid racial segregation caused these children to accept "as normal the fact of [their] inferior social status. . . . Such an acceptance is not symptomatic of a healthy personality" (Clark, 1989, p. 45).

Prejudice and Your Child presented an overall optimistic view that significant social change could be accomplished if individuals in the general public were made sufficiently aware of the information already well known to social scientists concerning the facts of prejudice as a learned, not innate, behavior. In his later works, including the books *Dark Ghetto* (1965) and *Pathos of Power* (1974), Clark evidenced an increasingly pessimistic tone in his assessment of the willingness and ability of the American public to confront its own racism (Keppel, 2002).

Clark achieved prominence within the community of his peers and from 1970 to 1971 served as the first African American to hold the office of president of the American Psychological Association. The APA also honored Clark with the association's Gold Medal Award. He served as president of the Society for the Psychological Study of Social Issues, the same organization that awarded him the Kurt Lewin Memorial Award in 1966. He was also recognized by the National Association for the Advancement of Colored People (NAACP) for his work on behalf of civil rights when they awarded him the Spingarn Medal in 1961.

Francis Cecil Sumner

Francis Sumner (1895–1954) is often acknowledged as one of the leading African-American figures in the history of psychology. In fact, R. V. Guthrie, in his groundbreaking book, *Even the Rat Was White* (1976), referred to Sumner as the "Father of Black American Psychologists."

Born in Pine Bluff, Arkansas, Francis Sumner received his early education in Norfolk, Virginia, and later in Plainfield, New Jersey. He did not receive a formal high school education since secondary education for blacks was a rarity in the early 1900s. Sumner's father was also apparently dissatisfied with the quality of secondary education then available to black youth and Sumner's application form for employment at Howard simply states, "Private instruction in secondary subjects by father" (Bayton, 1975).

After passing a written examination, Sumner was accepted at the age of 15 as a freshman at Lincoln University in Pennsylvania, an all-black institution founded in 1854. Although his parents worked hard to contribute financially to their son's education, Sumner himself had to work at a variety of part-time jobs to help pay for his tuition.

Despite his financial struggles, Sumner graduated as valedictorian from Lincoln in 1915 and expressed an interest in becoming a writer. If his dream of being a writer was to become a reality, Sumner knew that in the meantime he would have to support himself financially through some other endeavor such as teaching or government employment. Since employment opportunities were limited for black college graduates, even at the doctoral level, financial issues remained a constant concern and barrier to participation in the academic setting, even after graduation. Many gifted black psychologists found their careers hampered by the practical need to work at part-time jobs outside of psychology to maintain financial solvency.

In 1915, Sumner enrolled at Clark University where he took a number of courses in English as well as electives in foreign languages and psychology (Guthrie, 1998). He graduated from Clark in 1916 with a B.A. in English. While a student at Clark, Sumner came under the supportive wing of one of psychology's leading figures, G. Stanley Hall. Sumner's admiration of Hall was instrumental in Sumner's consideration of graduate studies in psychology. Hall stands out in the early history of psychology for his racial liberalism and his support and encouragement of Sumner as well as many other black students.

Sumner returned to Lincoln University in 1916 as a graduate student and instructor of psychology and German. Recognizing the need to further his own studies, he began exploring his options. He initially leaned toward graduate studies in German since that seemed to offer more chances of financial assistance than would graduate studies in psychology. He first applied to American University and the University of Illinois but was not accepted at either institution. With the encouragement of his mentor Hall as well as James Porter, the dean of Clark University, Sumner began graduate studies in psychology at Clark University in 1917.

At the time he was beginning his graduate studies at Clark, the United States had just entered World War I. Knowing that the potential existed for him to be drafted into military service at any moment, Sumner dove headlong into his studies. But his own experience of racism within the United States led him to have a different perspective on American involvement in the war in Europe and he wrote several letters to the local newspaper. His opinions proved very unpopular with many of the leading citizens of Worcester, Massachusetts.

In one of these letters, Sumner wrote at length criticizing claims that the United States was "a self-appointed paragon of virtue" and making an interesting psychoanalytic analysis of racism in the United States (Guthrie, 1998). This letter prompted an intense negative reaction from local citizens, who felt Sumner's words were traitorous and an attack on American ideals. Sumner formally apologized in a letter to the newspaper.

By the end of the semester, the controversy had died down considerably, allowing Sumner to focus his attention on his studies. At this point he completed a study titled "Psychoanalysis of Freud and Adler," which he was attempting to publish. He also wrote Hall, asking him to consider the piece as a potential doctoral dissertation. Before Hall could respond, Sumner was drafted into military service.

Sumner served in the military until the fall of 1919, and upon his discharge he returned to Clark University. On June 14, 1920, Francis Cecil Sumner successfully completed his studies, thereby becoming the first African American to earn a PhD in psychology. Over the next two years, he went on to teach philosophy and psychology, first at Wilberforce University and later at Southern University in Louisiana. In the fall of 1921, Sumner accepted a position at West Virginia Collegiate Institute (WVCI) where he remained for seven years. During this time, he wrote a number of controversial articles criticizing colleges and universities for their treatment of African Americans and endorsing the views of W.E.B. Dubois and Booker T. Washington.

Sumner resigned from WVCI in 1928 to become acting chairman of the Department of Psychology at Howard University where he remained for the rest of his career. While at Howard, Sumner breathed new life into the psychology department, turning it into the premier African-American institute for the study of psychology. His students included Kenneth B. Clark. Throughout his career, Sumner's primary areas of interest were in psychological topics dealing with race and religion. His career came to an untimely end when he died of a heart attack while shoveling snow outside of his home in Washington, DC, on January 12, 1954.

Dalmas A. Taylor

At the time of Taylor's death in 1998, his longtime friend James M. Jones described Taylor as someone "who was always trying to get people involved in things, to make a difference" (Jones, 1998, p. 1). One of the many ways in which Taylor made a difference for psychology was by founding the Minority Fellowship Program at APA in 1965.

Originally from Detroit, Michigan, Dalmas Taylor (1933–1998) served in the United States Army before going on to complete a B.S. degree in chemistry at Western Reserve University in Cleveland, Ohio, in 1959. He then attended Howard University where he earned his master's degree in psychology in 1961 before completing doctoral training in psychology at the University of Delaware. It was while he was at Howard University that Taylor first began his research activities in the area of race and social justice (Jones, 2000).

Over the course of his career Taylor worked in a variety of settings including the Naval Medical Research Institute, the University of the District of Columbia, the University of Maryland, Wayne State University, the University of Vermont, the University of Texas at Arlington, and Lincoln University in Pennsylvania, but no matter where he traveled, his interest in racism and social justice remained constant.

As founding director of the Minority Fellowship Program at APA, Taylor was instrumental in assuring that departments of psychology should respond to the problem of under representation of ethnic minorities within the discipline (Jones, 2000). He also opened the APA to the inclusion of ethnic minority psychologists in a number of ways. With the help of colleagues including James M. Jones, Taylor created a Summit of Ethnic Minority Psychologists in 1978. This summit, which became known as the Dulles conference, paved the way for the later establishment of APA's office of Ethnic Minority Affairs, Board of Ethnic Minority Affairs, and Society for the Psychological Study of Ethnic Minority Issues-Division 45 (Jones, 2000).

Before his untimely death following a brief illness, Taylor published six books along with a number of journal articles and book chapters, including his early work on the subject of self-disclosure (Altman & Taylor, *Social Penetration: The Development of Interpersonal Relationships*, 1973). With collaborator Phyllis Katz, Taylor edited *Eliminating Racism: Profiles in Controversy* (1988); this text has been described by Jones (2000, p. 341) as including "the best scientific and social policy perspectives on race relations in recent times." When he became ill, Taylor was working on a book about affirmative action, which he asked his daughter, Monique Taylor, an assistant professor of sociology at Occidental College in California, to complete after his death.

While African Americans have made significant strides in overcoming academic and professional barriers within psychology (thanks in part to the work of individuals like Clark, Sumner, and Taylor), an examination of current demographics within the profession in the United States reveals the remaining presence of barriers. For example, looking at the demographics within APA in the year 2000, data indicate that the number of minority participants as a whole remains far below being representative of the minority population in the United States. APA members identifying their ethnicity as black represent only 1.7% of the total membership of APA (APA Research Office, 2000). In addition, African Americans, as well as other ethnic minority psychologists, have found it difficult to breach the upper leadership levels within the profession. In the current generation of American psychologists, Norman B. Anderson is another African-American psychologist who has succeeded despite remaining barriers within the profession and society at large.

Norman B. Anderson

Norman Anderson once described himself as having come from a family of psychologists and ministers (Anderson, 2002). In an interview for the *APA Monitor* given in 2002 when Anderson assumed the post as APA's Chief Executive Officer, he discussed the similarities he perceived between psychology and the ministry:

When you lead in a very large church like my parents did, there are a lot of relationship issues that you are constantly dealing with. Ministers are often addressing people's emotional needs and their psychological well-being. So, in fact, there are a lot of similarities between being a psychologist and being a minister, and perhaps on some level, growing up as a preacher's kid may have piqued my interest in psychology. . . . There's also lots of similarities between pastoring a large church and being CEO of an organization like APA, where you have many different constituencies with sometimes overlapping and sometimes competing interests. It's the job of the minister, and partly the job of the APA CEO, to bring such disparate groups together to find common ground. (Anderson, 2002, p. 5)

Over the course of his career, Anderson has served in a number of leadership roles in addition to working as a professor of health and social behavior at Harvard University's School of Public Health. He was the founding director of the Office of Behavioral and Social Sciences Research as well as associate director of the National Institutes of Health (NIH).

A graduate of North Carolina Central University in Durham, Anderson completed his master's and doctoral studies in clinical psychology at the University of North Carolina at Greensboro as well as additional clinical and research training at the Schools of Medicine at Brown and Duke Universities (Souter, 2002).

Anderson's research interests have long dwelled upon the intersection of health and behavior and of health and race (APA, 2002). While an associate professor of psychology and psychiatry at Duke University (1985–1995), Anderson conducted research studies on the role of stress in the development of hypertension in African Americans. He also directed the Exploratory Center for Research on Health Promotion in Older Minorities funded by the NIH (APA, 2002).

Anderson has identified four points of emphasis he wishes to address during his tenure as Chief Executive Officer (CEO) of APA, including: (1) increasing the financial solvency of the APA, (2) facilitating the use of psychological knowledge by society, (3) changing the demographic makeup of American psychology to assure that a diverse population of psychologists is prepared to address the needs of America's increasingly diverse society, and (4) improving the working environment within the APA (Souter, 2002).

ASIAN-AMERICAN CONTRIBUTIONS TO PSYCHOLOGY

Asian-American psychologists, like their African-American peers, have faced a variety of barriers to their full participation in the discipline; however, the exact nature of the barriers experienced has been quite different. In examining the barriers faced by Asian-American psychologists one of the first hurdles to overcome is the use of the term *Asian-American*.

Applying a term like Asian-American implies a common shared experience, but this would be far removed from reality since the label "Asian-American" is applied to a widely diverse and growing population containing as many as thirty-two distinct cultural groups. Just who is an Asian-American psychologist? Is this person a third-generation American of Chinese descent? Or the child of Japanese Americans subjected to forcible internment in relocation camps during World War II? Or perhaps a Vietnamese refugee? As emphasized by previous authors (Dana, 1993; Kitano & Daniels, 1988), Asian-Americans of different national origins have different histories of immigration and acculturation.

The Asian American Psychological Association (AAPA)

The Asian American Psychological Association (AAPA) was founded in December of 1972 by a group of Asian-American psychologists and mental health professionals in the San Francisco Bay Area. At the time of its founding, the few Asian-Americans working in the field of psychology had very few mentors available to help them navigate within the profession. By 2002, AAPA included nearly 500 members (APA, 2002b).

The primary goals of the AAPA have always been to advance understanding and knowledge within the profession of psychology concerning Asian-American psychology and mental health issues, to increase training and education opportunities for Asian-American mental health professionals, and to function as a resource for peer collaboration and networking. As part of its effort to advocate on behalf of Asian-Americans, the AAPA was instrumental in convincing the U.S. Bureau of the Census of the need to include Asian-American subgroups in its census data (AAPA, 2003). Throughout the course of its existence, the AAPA has been at the forefront of advancing understanding of the need for cultural competence within all arenas of psychology, including research, training, and service. Two of AAPA's earliest members, Stanley Sue and Richard Suinn, have succeeded in achieving high levels of influence within American psychology.

Stanley Sue

Stanley Sue was born in 1944 in Portland, Oregon, where he was also raised. His father was a Chinese immigrant and his mother was an American-born person of Chinese descent. As Sue amusingly recalled in an autobiographical account, his early childhood goal was to become a television repairman (Sue, 1994). Fortunately for the discipline, when he was in high school Sue decided to explore the field of psychology instead. He was joined in this pursuit by three of his brothers.

In his autobiography, Sue discussed one interesting barrier to the participation of Asian-Americans in psychology, and that is the relative invisibility of the profession to many Asian-Americans. When Sue first told his parents of his intention to become a clinical psychologist his father, who was born in China, had no concept of what the profession of psychology entailed (Sue, 1994). Sue (1994) attributed this reaction to the general lack of familiarity with psychology of many Chinese and other Asian-Americans that was due in part to the under-utilization of psychological services by this population.

Stanley Sue completed his undergraduate degree at the University of Oregon and then attended the University of California, Los Angeles (UCLA) where he earned his master's in 1967 and his PhD in 1971. Although Sue initially prepared himself primarily for a career as a clinical therapist, his interests changed after gaining exposure to research and teaching (American Psychological Association, 1997). For his dissertation research, he investigated processes involved in the reduction of cognitive dissonance.

During the 1960s, Sue developed an interest in ethnic research as a consequence of his exposure to the turmoil present across many university campuses related to the issues of civil rights and American involvement in the Vietnam War. He began to realize the general absence of knowledge within psychology concerning ethnic research on such relevant topics as socialization, culture, cultural bias, and effective intervention and prevention efforts with respect to ethnically diverse populations (American Psychological Association, 1997).

After earning his PhD, Sue joined the faculty of the psychology department at the University of Washington where he spent ten years before returning to his alma mater, UCLA, as a professor of psychology. He remained at UCLA until 1996, at which time he assumed a position as professor of psychology and psychiatry at the University of California, Davis, where he also still serves as director of the Asian American Studies Program.

Included among his many accomplishments are his establishments of both the Asian American Psychological Association in 1972, in association with his brother Derald, and the National Research Center on Asian American Mental Health in 1988. Through these and other endeavors, Sue has been at the cutting edge of research on ethnicity and mental health. In recognition of his accomplishments, he has received numerous awards, including the 1986 Award for Distinguished Contributions to Psychology in the Public Interest from APA, the 1990 Distinguished Contributions Award for Research on Ethnic Minorities from APA-Division 45, and the 1990 Distinguished Contributions Award from the Asian American Psychological Association.

Richard M. Suinn

In the early days of the AAPA, Stanley Sue was joined by fellow Asian-American psychologist Richard Suinn. In 1999, Suinn became the first Asian-American to be elected president of the American Psychological Association (APA). At the time, Suinn was only the third ethnic minority individual to hold this position in the history of APA.

Suinn was born in Hawaii and received his bachelor's degree in psychology from Ohio State University. He completed both his master's and PhD degrees in clinical psychology at Stanford University. Suinn's primary area of interest within psychology is the field of sports psychology and he has authored eight books and numerous articles on such topics as sports psychology, peak performance, and anxiety management.

Suinn has had a number of unusual and varied experiences during the course of his career as a psychologist, including serving as team psychologist for four Olympic teams and as mayor of Fort Collins, Colorado, in the 1970s. He was the first sports psychologist to be included in the Olympic sports medicine team. His research activities include a case study Suinn conducted concerning the use of mental imagery to enhance performance. Suinn pioneered the use of visualization techniques.

Included among his more traditional accomplishments within psychology, Suinn is an emeritus professor and former chair of the Department of Psychology at Colorado State University. Prior to assuming the role of APA president, Suinn was appointed, in 1995, to lead the APA Commission on Ethnic Minority Recruitment, Retention, and Training. In 1994, he received the APA's Career Contribution to Education Award.

HISPANIC AMERICAN CONTRIBUTIONS

Like the Asian-American population, there is no single Hispanic or Latino population, but rather a collection of distinct groups whose culture, language, and/or geography have Latin roots (Padilla & Salgado de Snyder, 1985). At the present time, the Latino population is the fastest-growing group in the United States; the number of Latinos in the United States more than doubled between 1980 and 2000, accounting for 40 percent of the growth in the country's population during that period, and in 2003 the U.S. Census Bureau designated Latinos as the nation's largest minority group (Saenz, 2004). Despite the rapid growth in size of the Hispanic American population, their representation within psychology remains limited. For example, demographic data for APA membership in 2000 indicated only 2.1% of APA members identified their race as Hispanic (APA, 2000).

Martha Bernal

Martha Bernal (1931–2001) was born in San Antonio, Texas, the daughter of Alicia and Enrique de Bernal, who both emigrated from Mexico as young adults. Raised primarily in El Paso, Texas, Bernal earned her doctoral degree in clinical psychology from Indiana University, Bloomington, in 1962. Bernal was the first Latina to receive a PhD in psychology in the United States.

In addition to overcoming the barriers often encountered by fellow ethnic minority psychologists within professional or academic arenas, Bernal also encountered obstacles at home. The more successful she became in her academic endeavors, the more Bernal realized that her father did not support her goals because he believed that women were to be married and that college education for women was a waste (Vasquez & Lopez, 2002). Her father eventually relented and grew to support her efforts under the influence of Bernal's own persistence and the unwavering support of her mother and older sister.

Bernal is most remembered for her contributions to two important areas in the field of psychology: (1) the treatment of children with behavior problems, and (2) the advancement of a multicultural psychology (Vasquez & Lopez, 2002). Bernal was instrumental in bringing the use of learning theory and methods to the treatment and assessment of children with behavior problems, resulting in an increase in use of empirically validated interventions in the treatment of children (Vasquez, 2003). Active in professional as well as scholarly activities, Bernal helped to advance psychology toward a more multicultural perspective that recognizes the importance of diversity in training, recruitment, and research (Vasquez, 2003).

In the early 1970s, Bernal's research activities focused attention on the fact that psychology was significantly lacking in adequate representation of ethnic minority practitioners within the discipline. In articles published in journals that included *American Psychologist* (e.g., Bernal & Castro, 1994) as well as *The Counseling Psychologist* (Quintana & Bernal, 1995), she called attention to the low numbers of minority graduate students and faculty members in psychology departments across the United States (Vasquez, 2003).

While at the University of Denver and Arizona State University, Bernal implemented a number of strategies designed to increase the presence of minority students (Vasquez, 2003). She also received a number of financial awards from various foundations, including the National Institute for Mental Health (NIMH) to study training of clinical psychologists to work with ethnic minority populations.

Bernal was also an active leader in the profession of psychology, including serving on the task force responsible for establishing what is now called the National Latina/o Psychological Association (NLPA) in 1986. She served as NLPA's second president and as a treasurer. Bernal also was actively involved in a variety of public interest initiatives including APA's Commission on Ethnic Minority Recruitment, Retention, and Training (CEMRRAT); the Board for the Advancement of Psychology in the Public Interest; and the Committee on Lesbian, Gay, and Bisexual Concerns.

In recognition of the importance of her efforts on behalf of the profession of psychology, Dr. Bernal received a number of awards, including the Distinguished Life Achievement Award from Division 45 of APA (Society for the Psychological Study of Ethnic Minority Issues), the Hispanic Research Center Lifetime Award from Arizona State University, and the Carolyn Attneave Award for contributions to ethnic minority psychology. Sadly, Bernal received this latter award only a few weeks prior to her death from cancer on September 28, 2001, in Black Canyon City, Arizona.

NATIVE AMERICANS AND AMERICAN PSYCHOLOGY

As Dana (1993) emphasizes, Native Americans do not constitute a homogeneous group, and their various subcultures are neither intact nor fully functional. However, Native Americans appear to share a common core of worldview characteristics that have persisted. According to Dana (1993), this sense of Native American identity has not only minimized the degree of assimilation into the larger Anglo-American culture, but has also sustained the Native American population despite conditions of poverty, lack of educational opportunities, isolation, and discrimination.

Despite constituting a numerically small group, the Native American population represents 517 different native entities recognized by the federal government, and state governments recognize 36 tribes with unique customs, social organization, and ecology (Dana, 1993; LaFramboise & Low, 1989). According to data from the U.S. Bureau of the Census (2000a), approximately 2.5 million people, or 0.9% of the total population, identified themselves as American Indian or Alaska Native, and an additional 1.6 million people reported mixed ethnicity, including American Indian and Alaska Native and at least one other race.

Research indicates significant underutilization of mental health services by the Native American population. A variety of causes for this underutilization have been theorized including the basic reality that mental health services are often not available, especially in reservation communities (LaFramboise, 1988). In addition, the few professional mental health service providers present on reservations, many of whom are Anglo-American, are often disadvantaged by their tendency to approach their clients from a typical medical model that is at odds with the more informal, equalitarian relationships typical of Native American culture (Dana, 1993).

As of 1983, only 180 Native Americans were identified as holding master's or doctoral degrees in psychology (Stapp, Tucker, & VandenBos, 1985), and most were involved in research or education and not in the direct provision of clinical services. APA membership data from 2000 included 208 individuals identifying themselves as American Indian.

Access to education remains a significant barrier for the Native American population. According to data from the U.S. Bureau of the Census (2000b), 70.9% of American Indian and Alaska Natives report completing at least a high school education, 11.5% have completed a bachelor's degree, and only 3.9% have completed advanced degrees (please note that these data reflect responses from individuals identifying themselves as American Indian or Alaska Native only and do not include respondents of mixed racial identity).

Carolyn Attneave

Like Martha Bernal, Carolyn Attneave (1920–1992) was a native Texan. Born in El Paso, Attneave was the daughter of a Swedish-American father and a Delaware Indian mother. In an autobiographical account, Attneave (1990) described herself as a "maverick" and reviewing accounts of her life path certainly confirms the aptness of this description. Following the path of her father, who fought in World War I, Attneave served as a naval officer during World War II. She was the youngest commissioned officer in the United States Coast Guard and a member of the Coast Guard's first class of women (Attneave, 1990). After leaving military service, her interests turned to the profession of psychology. Her primary area of interest was in family therapy and she emerged as one of the field's leading figures.

After completing her graduate degree in psychology at Stanford University in the early 1950s, Attneave continued to develop her interest in **General Systems Theory** (GST) that stimulated her during her graduate years. As described by Attneave (1990), just as "Unified Field Theory" was the goal of so-called hard sciences in the 1980s, the goal of general systems theorists was to unify explanations and descriptions of social, biological, and mechanical actions and reactions that were developed from multidisciplinary perspectives. Attneave had experienced Stanford's approach to the concept of GST through participation in a series of seminars in which invited students joined in discussions with faculty from such diverse departments as Psychology, Engineering, Medicine, Physics, and Anthropology (Attneave, 1990).

GST interested Attneave in part because it provided a theoretical foundation for her Native American understanding of the interrelationships present among all phenomena of the world (Kliman & Trimble, 1993). Attneave is best remembered for her groundbreaking work in network intervention. During the mid-1960s in Oklahoma, she began to utilize the social networks of underserved populations, including Native Americans, African Americans, and poor whites, to compensate for the inadequate services provided by the mental health and social service systems (Kliman & Trimble, 1993).

In 1970, at Philadelphia Child Guidance, Attneave began collaboration with Ross Speck. Together, she and Speck introduced the network approach to family therapy with their book *Family Networks: A Way toward Retribalization and Healing in Family Crises* (Speck & Attneave, 1973). In this book, Speck and Attneave presented the radical concept that just as an individual's difficulties and strengths are embedded and can be treated within the context of his or her family, so too are the family's difficulties and strengths embedded and can be treated within the context of its social networks (Kliman & Trimble, 1993; Speck & Attneave, 1973).

Attneave then moved to Boston where she lived from 1969 to 1974. During her years there she taught at the Boston Family Institute and worked at the Harvard School of Public Health where she evaluated mental health services provided nationally by Indian Health Services. Attneave also helped found Boston City Hospital's Minority Training Program, a psychology internship and service program serving Boston's inner-city population. She led numerous training seminars in family and network therapy through the auspices of the Massachusetts Psychological Association's Professional School for Psychologists.

Attneave moved across the continent to Seattle in 1975 to take a joint position as Director of American Indian Studies and professor of psychology at the University of Washington. She remained there until her retirement in 1987. Attneave once asked her colleagues where they would place her within the variety of subclassifications within the field of family therapy. As befits a maverick, the best description her colleagues could devise was "eclectic." She agreed with this description but felt the need to describe the "meta-structure" underlying her overall approach to family therapy. In summary, Attneave (1990, p. 42) felt that the wide variety of human behaviors could be divided into four classifications:

1. **The physical systems.** This would include chemical interactions and basic biophysiological systems that are the primary fields of medicine.
2. **The emotional/cognitive systems.** These represent the mental life of people as they perceive and contemplate their environment.
3. **The social systems.** These are based on people's interactions in dyads, triads, and larger groups.
4. **Systems of values.** Included within this less often defined category are religious practices and principles, moral and ethical assumptions, value orientations, and ethnic and cultural traditions.

In addition to her many contributions to the field of family therapy, Attneave cofounded the American Indian Psychologists Association and served as its president from 1978 to 1980 and was an active member of the Association for Indian Affairs. In recognition of her efforts to enhance APA's level of multicultural awareness, Attneave was posthumously awarded APA's 1992 Psychologist of the Year award. She died on June 20, 1992, after a year-long battle with lung cancer. She left behind a network of colleagues spanning both sides of the continent who were deeply influenced by her approach to family therapy.

CURRENT DEMOGRAPHICS IN AMERICAN PSYCHOLOGY: THE CHALLENGE FOR THE FUTURE

Despite significant gains, minority groups continue to be underrepresented in psychology. Ponterotto et al. (1995) stated that demographic projections indicate that within three to four decades minority persons as a collective group will constitute the numerical majority within the United States, representing over 50% of the population. This means that professional psychologists will have to meet the needs of an increasingly diverse population. Clearly, the current ethnic makeup within American psychology is far from representative of minority presence within the United States population.

In an effort to improve the profession's ability to adequately meet this future challenge, professional psychology programs have begun to devote increasing attention to multicultural training issues as well as intensified recruitment of minority students and faculty to graduate psychology programs (Hammond & Yung, 1993; Ponterotto et al., 1995). To truly embrace diversity, the profession of psychology needs to engage in deep self-reflection. This is a process that still remains in its infancy, and it includes gaining a richer understanding of the history of minority participation in psychology.

■ Summary

In this chapter we discussed briefly the issue of racial diversity in psychology, focusing primarily on psychology within the United States. Embracing diversity has been a long-standing problem in psychology as well as the larger cultural context, and recent historical events around the globe have only served to heighten global racial tensions, thus increasing the need to address intolerance in all forms. One initial step toward embracing diversity in American psychology is to enhance our understanding of the history of minority-group participation within psychology.

We began by presenting an overview of the unique challenges faced by African Americans in psychology and highlighting the contributions of four prominent African-American psychologists: Kenneth B. Clark, Francis Cecil Sumner, Dalmas A. Taylor, and Norman Anderson. We then discussed briefly the contributions of Asian-American, Hispanic American, and Native American individuals within psychology, highlighting challenges and barriers that are unique to each respective group. Some of the individuals whose contributions were discussed include: Stanley Sue, Richard Suinn, Martha Bernal, and Carolyn Attneave. Many of these individuals have contributed significantly to the profession's understanding of ethnic minority issues in addition to their contributions to general psychological theory.

While significant strides have been made over the last two decades, psychology will need to continue addressing the issue of low representation of ethnic minority groups within its professional ranks. Given the increasingly diverse population in the United States, undergraduate- and graduate-level programs will need to take an active role in recruiting more individuals from minority groups and enhancing our awareness of the need to be culturally sensitive in all areas of psychological practice, in both clinical and research settings. Progress toward fully embracing diversity will require each of us, as individuals, to examine our own role in perpetuating intolerance. Psychology as a profession also needs to be open to a similar degree of self-examination if significant progress is to be made in building a psychology that can adequately meet the needs of our changing and increasingly diverse world.

■ Chapter 15—Racial Diversity in American Psychology

Discussion Questions

- How are the barriers encountered by African Americans in psychology similar to the barriers encountered by women practitioners? How are they different?

- What were some of the educational barriers faced by African Americans in psychology? What were some of the professional and employment barriers?

- What was the impact of *Brown v. Board of Education* on the American education system? What was its impact on the relationship between psychology and the legal system?

- If the famous Doll Study conducted by Kenneth B. and Mamie Phipps Clark were replicated today, would you expect the results to be the same or different? Why?

- Why does use of the labels "Asian-American" and "Hispanic American" present a problem when discussing issues of race and diversity?

- What barriers have been encountered by Hispanic Americans and Native Americans in psychology?

- What is the current status of minority-group representation within American psychology and what are the consequent implications for professional practice? What are the implications for academic training?

Psychology in Russia

CHAPTER OVERVIEW

In this chapter, we present an overview of the development of psychology as an independent scientific discipline in Russia. Particular emphasis is placed on ways in which Russian psychology is similar to and differs from psychology as it exists in Western Europe and the United States. For example, three key features that distinguish Russian psychology from Western psychology include: (1) the close relationship that continues to exist between psychology and philosophy in Russia compared with the division that exists between these two disciplines in the West, (2) the stronger and more overt influence of political and social changes on the practice of psychology in Russia, and (3) a strong thematic undercurrent existing in Russian psychology that emphasizes environmental influences over heredity.

Given the strong influence of political and social events on the practice of Russian psychology, this chapter begins with an overview of the history of Russia, beginning prior to the reign of Czar Peter the Great in the 18th century and Russia's emergence as a world power and as an active member of the European community. Our coverage of the history of Russia continues through the 19th century with the expansion of Russian territories, the rising discontent of Russia's citizens with the existing imperial monarchy of the czars, the abolition of Russia's practice of serfdom, and increasing social trends of intellectualism, liberalism, and political radicalism. By 1917, events occurred that led to the rise of the Bolshevik Party, a group of political revolutionaries led by Vladimir Ilyich Lenin and dedicated to the social and economic principles of philosopher Karl Marx. Following the October Revolution of 1917, the Bolsheviks assumed political control of Russia and the country evolved into a new political entity as the Union of Soviet Socialist Republics (USSR).

Our discussion continues, thereafter, with a history of communist Russia beginning with the political repression and isolationism that existed from the 1920s to the early 1950s under the leadership of Vladimir Lenin and his successor Joseph Stalin. Our coverage of the Soviet period concludes with Mikhail Gorbachev's attempt in the 1980s to restructure Soviet socialism through his twin policies of Glasnost or "openness" and Perestroika or "restructuring"; these ultimately led to the dismantling of the Soviet Union and a period of social and political turbulence.

This general overview of the history of Russia is presented as a backdrop for the history of Russian psychology and emphasis is placed on the many ways in which unfolding political events in Russia shaped the practice of psychology as a scientific discipline. The history of Russian psychology prior to 1917 emphasizes the strong ties and close similarities between Russian psychology and psychology in Western Europe. Russian psychology, prior to 1917, was also strongly influenced by practitioners from the medical-scientific field of physiology. Two physiologists who profoundly impacted Russian and world psychology were Ivan Michailovich Sechenov (1829–1905), who proposed that all psychical phenomena could be explained through the concept of the reflex arc, and Ivan Petrovich Pavlov (1849–1936), whose research on digestive processes in dogs led to his concept of the conditioned reflex. The work of both of these individuals brought into Russian psychology a strong materialist focus that continues to the present.

Another prominent figure in Russian psychology was Vladimir Bekhterev (1857–1927) who, in addition to founding the Psychoneurological Institute of St. Petersburg and the Institute for Brain Research, developed a school of Russian psychology called "reflexology," which focused on the method of associative reflexes and was similar to behaviorism in the United States.

The Soviet government's increasing emphasis on Marxism as the only acceptable ideological basis for any scientific activity, including psychology, began to impact seriously the development of Russian psychology in the 1920s. As a consequence of this increasing focus on mechanistic materialism and the elimination of idealism, Russian psychology began to discredit any notions of consciousness and was in jeopardy of losing legitimate standing as a scientific discipline separate from medical physiology. Two prominent Russian psychologists who struggled to defend the psychology of consciousness were Georgy Chelpanov (1862–1936) and Konstantin Kornilov (1879–1957).

Beginning in the 1930s, pressure from the Soviet government for Russian psychological theory and practice to conform to Marxist ideology became increasingly rigid to the degree that no works in psychology could be published unless they directly cited and referenced the writings of Marx and Lenin, both of whom were philosophers and political ideologues but not psychologists. Dialectical Materialism, a Marxian interpretation of reality that viewed matter as the subject of change and all change as the product of conflict between opposites arising from inherent internal contradictions, arose as the only acceptable organizing principle around which Russian psychology could be developed.

Two subfields of psychology that were particularly subject to active repression under communism were pedology, which focused primarily on child development, and psychotechnics, which was similar to American industrial-organizational psychology. Pedology and psychotechnics were of particular concern to Soviet ideologists due to the frequent use of aptitude tests and interest inventories, which the government criticized as tending to perpetuate artificial class differences.

Despite active governmental repression, Russian psychologists in the fields of pedology and psychotechnics were able to make significant contributions to Russian psychology. Included in this chapter is the work of Lev Vygotsky (1896–1934), who developed a stage theory of child development centered on the child's exposure to her or his environment and its gradual assimilation into the child's own mental activity. Vygotsky's students Alexander Luria (1902–1977) and Aleksei Leontiev (1903–1979) expanded upon his work.

In 1950, a joint session of the Academy of Sciences and the Academy of Medicine was organized under direct order of Joseph Stalin. The session celebrated and idealized the contributions of Ivan Pavlov to Russian psychology and what followed was a period of "Pavlovian psychology." Nikolai Bernstein (1896–1966) is discussed briefly in this chapter as one of the few Russian psychologists to challenge the Pavlovianization of Russian psychology. Bernstein proposed the study of feedback mechanisms in the physiology of body movements, an early precursor of cybernetics, as an alternative to Pavlovian doctrine.

The political and social destabilization of the USSR as a consequence of Perestroika and Glasnost led to its collapse, and to significant changes in Russian psychology. We conclude this chapter with a discussion of the impact of these changes on Russian psychology, such as the severe impairment of funding for research, a lack of stable infrastructure, a reopening to the influence of Western psychology, and an increasing focus on applied activities to address social-psychological problems arising from current conditions in Russian society, including alcoholism and depression, the adoption of a capitalist economy, and ethnic conflict.

LEARNING OBJECTIVES

When you finish studying this chapter, you will be prepared to:

- Describe two ways in which Russian psychology differs from Western psychology
- Describe the changes that occurred in Russian psychology following the October Revolution of 1917 and the emergence of the Union of Soviet Socialist Republics (USSR)
- Present an overview of the relationship between Western and Russian psychology and how this relationship changed over the course of the pre-Soviet, Soviet, and post-Soviet eras of Russian history
- Describe the significance of Sechenov's publication of *Reflexes of the Brain*
- Describe the significance of Pavlov's research on the conditioned reflex
- Define mechanistic Marxism and dialectical Marxism and describe the influence of both on the development of Russian psychology
- Describe the key principles of Vladimir Bekhterev's reflexology
- Define Dialectical Materialism
- Describe the impact of Russian sociopolitical changes on the work of Georgy Chelpanov and Konstantin Kornilov
- Describe the work of Alexander Luria, Lev Vygotsky, and Aleksei Leontiev
- Define psychotechnics and pedology and describe why both of these fields were particularly victimized by communist repression
- Describe current trends in Russian psychology following the collapse of the USSR

INTRODUCTION

In preceding chapters, our primary focus has been the historical development of a predominantly Western psychology. The pursuit of a scientific psychology, however, has never been restricted to the West and to limit the history of psychology to its development in America and Western Europe results in an incomplete portrait of the discipline. A richer understanding of the history and scope of psychology results from expanding our discussion to psychology in the East, beginning with one of the first Eastern countries to pursue systematic development of a scientific psychology, namely, Russia.

A particularly striking contrast between Western and Russian psychology lies in the deeper and more overt influence of politics on academic life and, indeed, on life in general, that is evident in the former Union of Soviet Socialist Republics or the USSR (1917–1991). Likewise, politics has certainly influenced Western psychology in many ways as, for example, through immigration of German psychologists to the United States as a consequence of political developments during the Second World War, through bureaucratic or social policies restricting the pursuit of psychology by minority practitioners, and most directly through government funding of research. In Western psychology, however, the influence of politics can be described as simply that, an influence, while in Russian psychology politics played a much more pervasive role in shaping the discipline.

AN OVERVIEW OF RUSSIAN HISTORY (1860–PRESENT)

Due to the close relationship between Russian psychology and Russian politics, we begin this chapter on the history of Russian psychology with a general overview of the history of Russia. The era of Russian history relevant to psychology begins in the 1860s in what we call the Pre-Revolutionary Period (1860–1917), is followed by the Soviet Period (1917–1991), and concludes with the Post-Soviet Period (1991–present).

The Pre-Revolutionary Period (1860–1917)

Prior to 1917, the Russian empire was an autocratic imperial monarchy ruled for over 300 years by the czars of the Romanov dynasty, a "part" of Europe and yet, at the same time, "apart from European culture," exotic and remote. The segregation of Russia from Europe was partly rooted in religious differences. As recently as the early 18th century, "Europe" was a term largely used as a geographic expression while its inhabitants thought of and referred to themselves by yet another term, "Christendom."

Although the citizens of Russia, too, were Christian, they were never included in the Christian fraternity of the West with its center in Rome, and instead practiced a faith they termed "orthodoxy," rooted in eighth-century Byzantium and the struggle over Christian doctrine that led to the separation of the Greek East from the Latin West. The Greek empire steadily declined in area and strength while the Latin West grew increasingly powerful and prosperous. The Greeks eventually reunited with Rome at the Council of Florence in 1439, leaving Russia, the primary remnant of a once proud Byzantine Empire, in the role of supplicant and subordinate to a European Christendom bent on the religious conversion of its neighbors (Malia, 1999). Russia found itself increasingly landlocked and isolated from industrial and economic development in Europe. Over the next three centuries, from the 1400s to the 1700s, Europe developed a negative image of Russia as a backward and poor "country-cousin" of little or no significance.

This image changed dramatically as a result of Peter the Great's military triumph in the Great Northern War between Russia and Sweden between 1700 and 1721. Russia emerged as a world power under Peter's rule and was suddenly opened to European influence, standing on almost equal footing with France, England, and Austria, and politically superior to a declining Spain and Holland.

Russia's entry into the cliquish European community engendered different attitudes among Europe's constituent countries, attitudes varying from the welcoming embrace of England and Prussia, to the cautious interest of Austria, to the blatant antagonism of France. But while enjoying its position as a newly fledged member of Europe, Russia's unique strength lay in its presence as a "flank power" due to its location on the geographic periphery of Europe and the resulting freedom from the close vigilance of European neighbors (Malia, 1999).

While Russia, under Peter's rule, began to "Europeanize," it retained social and political features that distinguished Russia from its newly adopted European brethren. Most striking of these differences was its universal service system, which obligated members of the nobility to military duty to the czar while in turn placing the peasantry, or serfs, at the base of the system in what was essentially a state of slavery to the nobility. While serfdom had been similarly practiced in most of Western Europe, it had disappeared by the end of the thirteenth century, but in Russia, serfdom not only remained, it was strengthened.

The fortunes of Russia as a member of Europe waxed and waned in the centuries following the twenty-five years of Peter's rule, but the overall trend was one of gradual expansion of Russia's borders through military conquest, and particularly under the rule of Catherine the Great, the adoption of European art and culture. Following the French Revolution, however, Europe's evolving value system was increasingly liberal and Russia's status as an autocratic monarchy that openly practiced serfdom led to Russia's appearance as something alien and somewhat anachronistic in the eyes of Europe (Malia, 1999). Along with an increase in liberalism in the 1800s, Europe experienced a growth both in intellectualism and in the size of its middle class. These trends brought with them an increase in political radicalism that filtered into Russia as well, particularly within Russian academia.

The atmosphere of Russian academic life during the 1860s was oddly similar to the atmosphere in college campuses across the United States a century later in the 1960s. In America of the 1960s, protests led primarily by students across many U.S. college campuses focused against the military draft, the war in Vietnam, and dominant social prescriptions concerning appropriate dress, behavior, and ideologies. The mid-1800s in Russia were similarly turbulent times; the serfs won their freedom in 1861; liberalism was sweeping through political, cultural, and scientific arenas of thought; and revolutionary thinkers were communicating to students a thirst for learning. Science played a particularly prominent role with intellectuals who embraced the belief that science was to lead humankind out of the darkness (Wells, 1956).

The Soviet Period (1917–1991)

By 1905, discontent abounded throughout all classes within Russia including the peasant and worker class, the military and educated professionals, ethnic and religious minorities, and segments of the bourgeoisie and the aristocracy. The Russo-Japanese War (1904–1905) in particular revealed both the corruption and the incompetence of the regime of Czar Nicholas II. What came to be known as the Revolution of 1905 began in January when military troops opened fire on peaceful demonstrators marching to the winter palace in St. Petersburg (which was then the Russian capital) to petition the czar for democratic and social reforms. The massacre, which was called "bloody Sunday," triggered months of political unrest throughout Russia, ending in October when the czar granted basic civil liberties and established a parliament or Duma. In the following years, a second and third Duma were both quickly dissolved and the government ruthlessly suppressed any revolutionary activities.

Russian involvement in World War I, which began in 1914, brought the political situation in Russia quickly to a head as a result of Russian military defeats, famine, and inept government. Rioting and workers' strikes occurred in both Petrograd (formerly called St. Petersburg) and Moscow and a discontented military was increasingly reluctant to put down these strikes. In mid-March of 1917, the czar tried unsuccessfully to dissolve the fourth Duma; insurgents seized Petrograd and the Duma appointed a provisional government under Prince Lvov, forcing Czar Nicholas to forfeit his throne.

The provisional government had limited support and was in conflict with the Petrograd **Soviet** or **Workers' and Soldiers' Council**, which controlled all troops, communications, and transportation. The provisional government also suffered increasing unpopularity due to its failure to address public demands to end Russian involvement in World War I, or to address demands for land redistribution from wealthy and aristocratic land owners to the property-less lower classes. In April 1917, Vladimir Ilyich Lenin, leader of a small group of revolutionaries known as the Bolsheviks and dedicated to the principles of Karl Marx, returned to Russia from exile abroad.

In July, Kerensky replaced Prince Lvov as head of the provisional government but by September (October in the old-style Julian calendar), those who wanted to limit the power of the Soviet rallied under General Z. G. Kornilov, who attempted to seize the capital in a military coup. Kornilov's attempt to seize power was stopped primarily through the efforts of the Bolsheviks and other socialists, and the Bolshevik leader, Lenin, urged the Bolsheviks to take power away from the provisional government. On October 24 (old-style calendar), the Bolsheviks seized control and set up Lenin as their party chairman. The "October Revolution" of 1917 marked the birth of Soviet Russia as the Union of Soviet Socialist Republics (USSR).

The Petrograd Soviet approved the Bolshevik coup, immediately called for an end to Russian involvement in World War I, and began addressing issues of land redistribution. The Bolsheviks soon gained control of Moscow and other major Russian cities. What followed was a period of civil war between Bolshevik (Red) and anti-Bolshevik (White) forces that lasted until the early 1920s. A final Bolshevik victory was won at great cost to the Russian people in terms of the loss of countless lives as well as the negative impact on industry and agriculture.

Lenin took the helm of the new Bolshevik regime and remained in power until his death in 1924, at which time leadership was assumed by Lenin's right-hand man, Joseph Stalin. The years between 1917 and 1921 were marred by civil war, famine, and the general destruction of industry. Social and political chaos characterized the time period and the country struggled to find some ideology or social program that would reestablish some sense of order. From its early inception, interpreters of Marx's economic model believed that if a socialist economic system could be established, then natural forces within the system would lead to the elimination of class distinctions between such groups as educated professionals and "blue-collar" workers, thereby creating a utopian society. This view of socioeconomics was described as mechanistic Marxism, according to which positive change would arise spontaneously. Others, particularly Lenin and Stalin, were convinced that the Communist Party must serve as the "vanguard of the proletariat (working class)" and that Soviet citizens must play an active role in the creation of a socialist society (Gilgen & Gilgen, 1996). This active view of the process of social change advocated by Lenin and Stalin is known as dialectical Marxism. As power and control shifted within the Communist Party, the reformative approaches of mechanistic Marxism gave way to the revolutionary approaches of dialectical Marxism. In the words of historian Beryl Williams (2000, p. 143), "If the working class could not build socialism, then they had to be taught to do so." As a consequence of Stalin's belief in furthering the movement toward a socialist society through the active process of dialectical Marxism, the Soviet Union under Stalin's regime became increasingly repressive and closed to outside political influence. Travel and communication with Western Europe, the United States and other noncommunist countries were restricted severely; the so-called "Iron Curtain" had lowered, enclosing the Soviet Union.

The Post-Soviet Period (1991–Present)

Following Stalin's death in 1953, Nikita Khrushchev came into power and set about criticizing Stalinist policies. In 1964, Leonid Brezhnev in turn replaced Khrushchev and led the Soviet Union until his death in 1983. The Brezhnev era was characterized by a regression to a more static and repressive state that continued under his successor Yuri Andropov and later Konstantin Chernenko. A reopening of the Soviet Union to world influence did not arise until Mikhail Gorbachev assumed leadership of the Soviet Union in 1985 and began to radically restructure Soviet socialism through his united policies of **Glasnost** or "openness," and **Perestroika** or "restructuring."

Gorbachev, however, underestimated the impact of Perestroika and instead of the revolution within Soviet socialism that he envisioned, his policies put in place the seeds ultimately leading to the dismantling of the Soviet Union. Beginning in 1991, when Boris Yeltsin assumed power, Russia suffered from economic, political, and social strife. By December of 1991 the Communist Party was officially banned and the Soviet Union dissolved as a unified political entity.

In summary, the major principles that emerge from this brief account of Russian history include the following:

- Turmoil balanced by control
- Mutual interdependence of economic and social systems
- Persistence of hierarchical relationships despite the utopian goal of equality of persons

PRE-REVOLUTIONARY PSYCHOLOGY (1860–1917)

Prior to the dramatic events surrounding the Bolshevik Revolution in October 1917, Russian scholars had long been at work developing a Russian scientific psychology. Indeed, prior to the revolution it would have been difficult to separate Russian from Western psychology. Essentially, the first Russian universities in Moscow and St. Petersburg would have been almost indistinguishable from their counterparts in such places as Vienna and Berlin, where psychology was also beginning to develop as a field of study separate from philosophy.

Pre-revolutionary Russian psychologists generally came from two different academic backgrounds: philosophy and medicine. The work produced by Russian psychologists during this period exhibited several important features including a tendency toward methodological pluralism, ideological tolerance, and strong interest in and ties to the work of their European counterparts (Kozulin, 1984). A great deal of effort was expended by Russian scholars in translating the work of leading Western psychologists into Russian and by October of 1917, Russian psychologists had at their disposal a library of psychological texts very similar to what would have been available to Western psychologists. In addition, prior to the 1917 Revolution there was even an active interplay between Russian and Western scholars, with many Russian scholars traveling to Europe to complete at least part of their academic studies.

The year 1879 is considered to be the date of birth of psychology around the globe as an independent science, due to Wilhelm Wundt's (1832–1920) introduction of the experimental method into psychology. The laboratory founded by Wundt became the nerve center of the world's first professional community of this new breed of scientist-psychologist. Psychologists from different countries came to Leipzig to learn Wundt's experimental method of research and then returned to their own countries and opened similar psychological laboratories. Historians have recorded 136 German, 14 American, 10 British, 6 Polish, 3 Russian, and 2 French scientists who studied under Wundt (Petrovsky & Yaroshevsky, 1994, p. 93). The establishment of new standards in psychological research along with active development of different forms of communication began within this growing global scientific community. Magazines on psychology were published, international psychological assemblies began to meet, and psychological societies began to form in Russia as well as in the West.

The Moscow Psychological Society was founded in 1885 and functioned as an interdisciplinary forum for philosophers and physicians with an interest in psychological problems (Kozulin, 1984). Soon thereafter, in 1889, the first Russian psychological journal, called *Problems of Philosophy and Psychology*, made its debut. Two of the most significant events in the early history of Russian psychology were the establishment of the Psychoneurological Institute in St. Petersburg in 1907 and the Moscow Institute of Psychology in 1912, both of which became active training institutions for almost all Russian psychologists in the years that followed. Initially, Russian psychology was centered primarily in Moscow and St. Petersburg; however, it was not long before psychological laboratories were also established in Kazan (by Vladimir Bekhterev), Kiev (by Georgy Chelpanov), and Odessa (by Nikolai Lange).

A difference that began to emerge between Western and Russian psychology during the late 19th and early 20th centuries was in the relationship between philosophy and psychology. In Europe and the United States, while a few scholars such as William James and John Dewey pursued interests in both empirical philosophy and psychology, the overall trend was toward a widening division between the two disciplines. However, in Russian academic circles philosophy and psychology remained tightly linked to each other.

Another difference between Western and Russian psychology developed as Western (particularly American) psychology began to expand its scope beyond the academic setting into more applied fields. Pre-revolutionary Russian psychology and early Soviet psychology remained almost exclusively an academic discipline with only a few psychologist-practitioners who emerged mainly from the medical field (Kozulin, 1984). Although they could not be considered psychologist-practitioners, two of the earliest and most respected names in Russian psychology emerged from this same medical background, namely, the renowned physiologists Ivan M. Sechenov and Ivan P. Pavlov.

Ivan Michailovich Sechenov

Ivan Sechenov (1829–1905) was born on August 1, 1829. After early training in the Military Engineering School in St. Petersburg and a year and a half in the army, Sechenov developed an interest in medicine and decided to attend the medical school of Moscow University where he completed his M.D. degree in June 1856. Sechenov then studied abroad where he came under the influence of European scientists, including DuBois Raymond and Claude Bernard in France and Johannes Müller and Herman von Helmholtz in Germany (Wells, 1956). After returning to Russia in 1860, Sechenov was appointed assistant professor of physiology in the Medico-Surgical Academy and began a series of lectures in physiology that strongly impacted the Russian academic world due to his emphasis on inhibitory features of the nervous system which, prior to his work, was considered exclusively as an excitatory system.

Sechenov returned briefly to Claude Bernard's laboratory in Paris in 1862 where he carried out experiments investigating the neural centers inhibiting reflex movements (Wells, 1956). He wrote of his Parisian work when he returned to Moscow and after a brief struggle with tsarist censors over the content, Sechenov was able to publish his article titled "Reflexes of the Brain" (1862). The work caused an immediate sensation within the Russian scientific community due to the strong challenge Sechenov presented to then accepted beliefs concerning the fundamental operations of the nervous system.

Sechenov's aim in "Reflexes of the Brain" was to demonstrate that the soul, or psyche, was far from being an entity independent of the body and was in fact a function of the central nervous system, particularly of the brain. His work was the earliest instance of the materialist perspective that later dominated much of Russian psychology. Sechenov developed his argument around the concept of the **reflex arc**. The reflex arc, which was a concept already known and studied by physiologists, was the basic mode of sensory-motor activity. This reflex arc was thought to have a three-part structure: first was stimulation from the external environment via sensory receptors; second, the transmission of neural impulses to the spinal cord or to the brain; and third, the transmission of neural signals outward again to muscles leading to activity (Wells, 1956).

Earlier research on the reflex arc, however, had been confined mostly to research on simple neuro-motor responses in lower animals. Sechenov's radical thesis was that all forms of psychical phenomena, even complex and diverse human behaviors, could be explained through the concept of the reflex arc. Sechenov did not confine his thesis to psychical phenomena involving only motor activity but included thought as well. Although he had no means of demonstrating this experimentally, Sechenov postulated the existence of centers within the human brain that served to augment or inhibit the third or muscle-activity phase of the reflex arc. He further proposed that emotion was the result of an augmented muscular response while thought involved an inhibited muscular response. Another key element of Sechenov's argument was the strong focus on external causation, his primary concern being to show that "the real cause of every human activity lies outside man" (Wells, 1956).

"Reflexes of the Brain" was such a novel and daring work that it rapidly became known all over Russia, although the article met with a less than favorable response from official governmental circles. Even prior to the Revolution of 1917, academic activities in Russia were subject to intense governmental scrutiny and control. In Sechenov's case, intense criticism of his work began even prior to its publication and climaxed when the work was published in book form in 1866. The sale of the book was forbidden by the Petersburg Censorial Committee and this same committee asked the attorney general to bring criminal charges against Sechenov on the grounds that this extreme materialist book "undermines the moral foundations of society and thereby destroys the religious doctrine of eternal life" (Wells, 1956). Sechenov ultimately was saved by the overwhelming popularity of the book, which deterred the attorney general from prosecuting him.

Sechenov lived for forty-two years following the publication of *Reflexes of the Brain* and spent much of that time as professor of physiology at Moscow University. Sechenov also taught without pay at the Women's Pedagogical Society and at a school for factory workers as part of his lifelong struggle against the dominant social, economic, and political ideology that prohibited the education of women and the working class in czarist Russia.

Another eminent figure in Russian psychology, Ivan P. Pavlov, was dramatically influenced by the work of Sechenov and, in a telegram to a session of the Moscow Scientific Institute commemorating the 10th anniversary of Sechenov's death, Pavlov wrote: "Sechenov's teaching on the reflexes of the brain is, in my opinion, a sublime achievement of Russian science" (Wells, 1956).

Ivan Petrovich Pavlov

Ivan Petrovich Pavlov (1849–1936) was born in the Russian city of Ryazan, the son of a parish priest whose intellectualism and love of books instilled in Ivan Pavlov a love of learning and a deep respect for scholarship. After completing his early education at the Ryazan church school, Pavlov entered the local theological seminary.

Pavlov began his studies during the previously described vibrant period of Russian intellectual history in the 1860s. It was then that his interest turned to the natural sciences. While still at the seminary he encountered and was profoundly influenced by two books in particular: Ivan Sechenov's *Reflexes of the Brain* (1866) and Charles Darwin's *On the Origin of Species* (1859).

Rejecting his earlier plans for a career in the priesthood, Pavlov left the seminary to enroll at the University of St. Petersburg where he completed his course of study with an outstanding record and received the degree of Candidate of Natural Sciences in 1875. The title of "Kandidat" in Russian academia was roughly equivalent to the American doctoral degree (Gindis, 1992). The next several years were difficult for Pavlov, mainly because universities at that time were tightly controlled by political appointees of the czarist regime and obtaining academic appointments was often more a matter of achieving political favor than doing solid science. A rigorous scientist, but not a politician, Pavlov spent four years drifting from laboratory to laboratory before attending the Military Medical Academy in St. Petersburg and graduating with a gold medal award for research in 1879.

Pavlov then spent the next ten years in charge of the physiological laboratory attached to the medical clinic run by S. P. Botkin, a professor of internal medicine at St. Petersburg. While these years were rich in terms of the opportunity for Pavlov to develop his reputation and skill as a scientific researcher, they were not so rich in financial terms. At one point, he and his wife Serafima were so poor that he had to live at the laboratory while his wife lived with relatives. Pavlov finally achieved some measure of financial and academic security when he was appointed professor of pharmacology at the Military Medical Academy in 1890, and in 1891 when he was invited to organize and direct the department of physiology in the newly established Institute of Experimental Medicine. He remained head of this department for the next forty-five years and it was there that he did the bulk of the experimental work for which he achieved world fame.

In 1904, Pavlov won the Nobel Prize for his research on digestive processes conducted at the Institute. Other tangible evidence of Pavlov's growing success as an academician included his appointment as professor of physiology at the University of St. Petersburg in 1895 and his election to the Russian Academy of Sciences in 1907, the latter representing the pinnacle of Russian academic achievement.

The area of Pavlov's research with the most immediate relevance to psychology was his introduction and systematic study of the concept of **the conditioned reflex**, which, interestingly, emerged as an accidental discovery during Pavlov's work on digestive processes in dogs (see chapter 10 for further treatment of basic and applied Pavlovian Conditioning). Utilizing skilled surgical techniques, Pavlov devised a method by which the dogs' production of saliva could be observed, measured, and recorded. Although Pavlov's initial focus was on the dog's production of saliva as a direct response to the physiological stimulus of food placed in the dog's mouth, an incidental and important finding in the course of his experiments was that occasionally saliva would flow before the food came in contact with the dog's mouth, such as when the dog saw the food, or in the presence of the man who regularly fed the dogs. Pavlov reasoned that the dogs had somehow developed a connection between the unlearned response of salivation and previously neutral stimuli (e.g., the sight of food or of the caretaker) that the dogs had been conditioned to associate with the presence of food. Pavlov differentiated salivation in response to the physiological stimulation of direct contact of the dog's mouth with food in contrast with salivation in response to a stimulus associated with the presence of food. He regarded the former to be an unlearned, innate, or unconditioned reflex and referred to the latter, learned response as a conditional reflex. In translating Pavlov's work from Russian into English, W. H. Gantt used the term *conditioned* rather than conditional and thus **conditioned reflex** became the commonly accepted term.

Initially, when writing about the conditioned reflex, Pavlov focused on the mentalistic experience of the dog and wrote of the animal's judgment, will, and desire in subjective and human terms, although he gradually dropped these references in favor of a more objective and descriptive approach (Wells, 1956). Thus, in effect, Pavlov had demonstrated that higher mental processes could be studied and discussed in purely physiological terms and without any reference to consciousness. The foundational idea emerging from this demonstration was that complex human and infrahuman behavior could be reduced and submitted to experimentation under laboratory conditions. This was a profound scientific development for experimental psychology in both Russia and the West.

Ironically, despite his indelible impact on the field of psychology, it was only late in his life that Pavlov referred to himself as an experimental psychologist. Indeed, his early opinion of psychology seemed to reflect that of his inspirational source, I. M. Sechenov, who stated that:

> The new psychology will have as its basis, in place of the philosophizing whispered by the deceitful voice of consciousness, positive facts or points of departure that can be verified at any time by experiment. And it is only physiology that will be able to do this, for it alone holds the key to the truly scientific analysis of psychical phenomena. (Sechenov, 1866, in Frolov, 1938, p. 6)

As complex as Pavlov's relationship was to psychology, it was matched equally by his relationship with the Soviet government. His early struggles with tight governmental control under the czarist regime have already been discussed. Under the Soviet regime following the 1917 Revolution, Pavlov was no less conflicted. He was openly critical of the 1917 Revolution and the entire Soviet system, writing letters of protest to Soviet leader Joseph Stalin, as well as boycotting Russian scientific meetings as a demonstration of his disapproval of the Soviet government. Despite his strong and public criticism of the Soviet government, Pavlov and his work were embraced by the political establishment; he received generous financial support and was allowed to conduct his research relatively free of government interference. While the Soviet regime may not have suited Pavlov, his work did suit the aims of the Soviet regime in controlling the development of psychology.

REVOLUTION: THE DEVELOPMENT OF SOVIET PSYCHOLOGY (1917–1991)

The social and political events sparked by the Bolshevik Revolution in 1917 led to dramatic changes in the practice of psychology in the newly created Soviet Union. Russian or now Soviet psychology had reached a metaphoric fork in the road and the developing path of Soviet psychology separated it further and further from the practice of psychology in the West.

The impact of the change in Bolshevik political strategy from mechanistic Marxism to one of dialectical Marxism had a profound impact upon higher education. Initially, universities were thrown open to all students over age 16, and entrance exams and degrees were abolished in 1918 with both maneuvers reflecting the new regime's intense desire for control and its dislike of what it perceived as bourgeois elitism or the controlling influence of the minority educated middle class (Williams, 2000). Tenure of academic staff was ended and anyone who had held an academic post for more than ten years was forced to undergo reelection by his or her students and junior colleagues. A new constitution regulating universities was passed in September of 1921 and ended university autonomy by putting the government in control of appointing rectors (i.e., presidents) to governing boards. Soviet leader Vladimir Ilyich Lenin settled faculty strikes that followed such actions by expelling the strike leaders and promising better working conditions. Lenin and his fellow Soviet leaders were deeply suspicious of pre-revolutionary intellectuals, and any academics who did not demonstrate skills that could prove useful to the state could find themselves branded as enemies of the new regime.

Two separate branches of Russian science began to develop during the period of rebuilding that followed the end of the Civil War (1917–1922). One branch was formed by the Academy of Science and the universities that had managed to survive the events between 1917 and 1922. The pre-revolutionary scholars and academics employed by these institutions were still guided by primarily academic principles as opposed to political ideology. The new regime, however, was eager to raise a new generation of intellectuals committed to communist ideology to replace those "unreliable" scholars who did not share the Bolshevik ideal, and established new institutions to achieve this goal including the Communist Academy, the Institute of Red Professors, and the Academy of Communist Education, all of which functioned under the direct supervision of the Communist Party (Kozulin, 1984).

For a while, these two branches of Russian science seemed to coexist peacefully and pre-revolutionary Russian psychologists operating within this system remained free from political interference regardless of any reservations they may have expressed regarding the Bolshevik dictatorship.

Vladimir Bekhterev

Vladimir Bekhterev (1857–1927) was one of the pre-revolutionary Russian psychologists who managed to survive, at least initially, the transition to life under the new Bolshevik regime. It is interesting to explore the life and works of Vladimir Bekhterev, particularly in contrast with Ivan P. Pavlov. Strong parallels existed in the early lives of these two individuals, even though they went on to develop their professional careers along divergent, and at times adversarial, paths.

Both Pavlov and Bekhterev were born in small towns to lower-middle-class families; Pavlov's father was a priest while Bekhterev's was a police inspector. Both men studied in St. Petersburg and both pursued medical degrees. Bekhterev, like Pavlov, also traveled and studied in Europe, first in Flechsig's laboratory in Leipzig, Germany, where he also attended Wundt's seminars on psychology, and later in Paris where he did clinical work at the mental hospital, Sâlpetrière, while studying the treatment of hysteria and the use of hypnosis under

Jean Martin Charcot (1825–1893). It was at this point that Bekhterev's and Pavlov's professional paths began to diverge from each other.

In 1881, at the age of 24, Bekhterev earned his doctorate and began to pursue actively his medical career, in contrast to Pavlov who never actually practiced medicine and who was 34 years old before earning his medical degree in 1879. Bekhterev also progressed more rapidly than Pavlov in the initial phase of his career in that it was only four years later, in 1885, that Bekhterev was invited to become chair of psychiatry at Kazan University.

While Pavlov was a specialist who began with an interest in the physiology of digestive processes and only later progressed to brain research, Bekhterev was interested in neurological problems from the beginning of his career. While working in Kazan, from 1885 to 1893, Bekhterev founded one of the first psychophysiological laboratories in Russia, established a hospital for nervous diseases, organized the Society of Neuropathologists and Psychiatrists, and established the journal *Herald of Neurology* (Kozulin, 1984). In 1888, his years of work analyzing the anatomy and physiology of the nervous system led to his publication of *Conductive Paths of the Brain and Spinal Cord*.

In 1893, Bekhterev left Kazan to work in St. Petersburg where he was appointed professor of mental and nervous diseases at the Military Medical Academy. In St. Petersburg, he organized a neurological hospital and launched the Russian Society of Normal and Pathological Psychology and a new journal, *Review of Psychiatry, Neurology, and Experimental Psychology*. Between 1903 and 1907 he published a seven-volume series titled **Bases for Teaching about the Functioning of the Brain**, which became an internationally respected encyclopedia of neuroscience (Kozulin, 1984). Bekhterev was well on the way to establishing himself as a major figure in Russian psychology.

As early as the 1880s, Bekhterev thought he had found an objective method for the study of human behavior through his investigation of reflexes. In his early research, he studied the localization of functions in the cortex via the observation of animal subjects following extirpation (i.e., removal) or electrical stimulation of various regions of the cortex. Later, Bekhterev progressed to the study of artificial associative reflexes. For example, electrical stimulation of the sole of a human's foot was presented in association with other visual and auditory stimuli. After several paired trials, the reflex of the sole could then be evoked without the need of electrical stimulation exclusively through presentation of the previously neutral yet associated stimuli. While similar to Pavlov's experiments with dogs in that the goal was induction of a physiologic response to associative stimuli, Bekhterev's method had advantages over Pavlov's in that no surgery was required and experiments could be done directly on human subjects. Conflict between Bekhterev and Pavlov quickly developed. Bekhterev questioned the validity of public recognition of Pavlov as the "founder" of the method of reflexes. Pavlov in turn questioned Bekhterev's experimental methodology.

Despite the intense and heated conflict with Pavlov, Bekhterev remained committed to his belief that the method of associative reflexes would be a major tool for the behavioral sciences. Accordingly, he developed a general physiological-psychological theory which he termed "reflexology." In 1907, Bekhterev opened the Psychoneurological Institute in St. Petersburg, which was the first major center for the comprehensive study of complex human psychological phenomena in the world. His humanistic aim was to integrate knowledge in anatomy and physiology with an understanding of human individual and social behavior. This idea became one of the main lines along which the rest of the development of Russian psychology progressed from then until the present day. Bekhterev's interpretation of psychology's role in the comprehensive study of humans was very close to that of behaviorism in the United States. The initial popularity of Bekhterev's reflexology was such that in some places the very term *psychology* was replaced in Russian college curricula by "reflexology" (Kozulin, 1984).

The Psychoneurological Institute was administered as a private university and was unprecedented in Russia for its democratic structure. In contrast to the majority of Russian universities, which were state-controlled, no political loyalty certificates were required at the institute and no nationality quotas (i.e., limits to numbers of students from certain ethnic groups such as the Jewish population) were observed (Kozulin, 1984). An interesting side effect of the vibrant atmosphere that developed in Russian academic life in the 1860s was the state's recognition of the danger represented by the thriving atmosphere of political activism in academic circles. In the interest of reducing the number of students in metropolitan centers such as Moscow, and thus to diminish the danger of political unrest, nationality quotas were observed and students were often encouraged to take scholarships and study abroad. As a private institution, Bekhterev's institute was free from enforcing such restrictions upon the student body.

The freedom experienced at the institute attracted hundreds of students and an eclectic selection of many of the most open-minded and gifted professors, and included historian Eugene Tarle, sociologist Maxim Kovalevsky, and psychologist Alexander Lazursky (Kozulin, 1984). The institute was widely popular as well as very productive. Applications of the method of associative reflexes proved useful in such diverse areas as the detection of functional versus simulated blindness and deafness, and the development of a behavioral therapy for alcoholism.

In the early 1900s, however, with increasing levels of political unrest, the police and the government were becoming more suspicious and repressive of activities on Russian college campuses. Bekhterev's institute was a prime target for such fears, for example, in the following lines from a police dossier of "academician Bekhterev":

> Institute Assembly, more than 150 professors and lecturers, has obvious antigovernmental attitudes. . . . In the tearoom of the institute a library of illegal literature was seized. . . . All political parties without exceptions have their members in the institute. . . . Huge crowd of students organized a meeting and were being dispersed by Cossacks when academician Bekhterev appeared in his general of medical corps uniform and ordered withdrawal of the forces. (Kozulin, 1984, p. 55)

Bekhterev actively stood his ground against what he perceived as nationalistic oppression and openly published essays deploring the policy that confined Jews to ghettos and argued against nationalism quotas in universities. These and similar activities angered Bekhterev's superiors and worsened his relations with the government, and he was discharged from the Military Medical Academy under the pretext that he had exceeded the term required for retirement. At the same time the Minister of Education refused to approve Bekhterev's nomination for the next term as director of the Psychoneurological Institute. However, by then it was 1917 and the eve of revolution. When the Bolsheviks seized power, Bekhterev, having experienced hardship under the old regime, initially welcomed the new regime with its promise of sweeping democratic reforms.

At first, his optimism seemed warranted as Bekhterev was allowed by the new regime to organize an Institute for Brain Research in which he could continue the studies he had begun at the Psychoneurological Institute, and he continued to publish, establish new journals, and lecture publicly. While the primary aim of the Institute for Brain Research was the further development of reflexological studies, Bekhterev wisely did not try to reduce all human behavior to a product of motor reflexes. The result, however, was that the Institute for Brain Research incorporated an eclectic range of methodologies and subject matter almost all of which were confusingly organized under the terminology of reflexology.

All of this came to an abrupt end, however, with Bekhterev's death in 1927 under somewhat mysterious circumstances. Official statements varied; one stated he had died after consuming spoiled canned meat, while one obituary claimed a heart attack as the cause of death. Rumor made note of the fact that Bekhterev, still a practicing physician, had been a neurologist-consultant for Kremlin rulers and could potentially reveal to the general public negative information concerning the mental status of key Kremlin officials (Kozulin, 1984). With the growing trend toward ideological compliance with Marxist-Leninist principles in all academic pursuits that began at the end of the 1920s, Bekhterev's eclectic theories were again a political target and his disciples were unable to remain committed to the central principles of his original theories.

Despite the ultimate demise of reflexology, Bekhterev left a rich legacy to Russian psychology including a half dozen research institutes and a generation of former students and colleagues influenced by his theories.

SOVIET REPRESSION AND REACTOLOGY

The effects of the October Revolution of 1917 did not immediately reach psychology, primarily because the efforts of the new political regime were concentrated initially on establishing mastery by military means. It was only following the Civil War in the early 1920s that the Bolshevik regime began to actively impact the practice of science, including psychology. The ideological basis for this activity came, in part, from Lenin's publication of an article in 1922, "On the Significance of Militant Materialism," in which Lenin proclaimed that Marxism was the only correct philosophy and ideology, and deviations from Marxism were seen by the ruling Communist Party as hostile acts against the state.

"Clean-ups" of those professors who chose not to follow strict Marxist principles began in the universities, and in 1922, by direct order of Lenin, a program of forced deportation of outstanding scientists and philosophers was begun. While forced emigration from Soviet Russia ended up saving their lives, these scientists were forever taken away from their motherland.

Georgy Ivanovich Chelpanov

Georgy Chelpanov (1862–1936) was a tragic victim of the Soviet initiative to construct a purely Marxist psychology. Chelpanov's role in Russian psychology closely parallels Wundt's role in psychology outside of Russia in that they both came to be the organizers of the first and biggest scientific schools in their respective countries and provided the initial impetus for the development of psychology as an independent science.

Chelpanov studied philosophy at Novorossijsk University in Odessa and psychology in Germany under both Wilhelm Wundt and Carl Stumpf. In 1907, Chelpanov accepted a chair of philosophy and psychology at Moscow University where he began to champion actively the concept of psychology as an independent discipline connected with but not absorbed by philosophy or physiology (Kozulin, 1984). The successes of Sechenov, Bekhtherev, and

Pavlov, unfortunately, endangered the future of Russian psychology as their focus on the physiology of involuntary and voluntary behaviors raised questions concerning the legitimacy of psychology as a separate scientific discipline.

While both Bekhterev and Pavlov accepted psychology's right to exist as an independent scientific discipline, they both considered Wundt's methodology of introspection as incompatible with objective methods of research. In contrast, Chelpanov, profoundly influenced by Wundt, claimed that the development of "common," "theoretical" or "philosophical" psychology was necessary in addition to empirical psychology. At that time Russian psychology still remained tightly bound to philosophy and Chelpanov believed that an integrated understanding of multifaceted psychic phenomena could only come from combining philosophy with empirical psychology. Chelpanov's plan to create a scientific-educational institution reflected his interests not only in research, but also in the preparation of future generations of professional psychologists. To further this plan, Chelpanov founded the Moscow Institute of Psychology in 1912.

The Moscow Institute produced a small but impressive group of young researchers, among them two future directors of the institute, Konstantin Kornilov (1879–1957) and Anatoli Smirnov. The Moscow Institute of Psychology was equipped with the best psychological research equipment of its time and was the first building in Europe designed exclusively for such purposes. In the spirit of professional competition, when Wundt learned of the founding of the Moscow Institute, he arranged to have another floor added to his Leibnitz Institute (Umrikhin, 1994). In 1917, Chelpanov started to publish a new psychological journal titled *Psychological Survey*.

Chelpanov's paper, "On Experimental Method in Psychology" (1913), openly criticized followers of both Pavlov and Bekhterev by stating that those who tried to discredit the notion of consciousness in an attempt to establish a purely objective psychology only deceived themselves. They could avoid mentalistic terminology and references to consciousness by replacing it with references to reflexes, but to be consistent, Chelpanov argued they should then abandon the very idea of psychological research and confine themselves to the framework of pure physiology (Kozulin, 1984). Despite the fact that he was criticizing two different major research programs led by increasingly influential scientists, Chelpanov was initially able to maintain his standing and reputation, and in 1921 was reappointed as head of the Moscow Institute of Psychology.

After the Soviet regime came into power and Marxist psychology became the only acceptable psychology, Chelpanov's deviation from Marxist materialism began to negatively impact his career. The final confrontation between the evolving science of psychology and political communist doctrine came in 1923 when Georgy Chelpanov was not only fired as director of the Moscow Institute of Psychology, but his works were also "purged" from the institute he had founded and led for a decade. Chelpanov's former students and colleagues did nothing to prevent or protest his dismissal. Interestingly, Chelpanov's student, Konstantin Kornilov, had endeared himself to the Soviet regime by making an active public bid to reconcile the principles of empiricism with those of Marxist ideology, and was soon appointed the new director of the Moscow Institute of Psychology (Kozulin, 1984).

Konstantin Kornilov

Kornilov (1879–1957) tried to integrate the contents of introspective psychology and behaviorism intending to overcome the one-sidedness of each of these approaches. Actively promoting the concept of dialectic synthesis, borrowed from Marxist ideology, Kornilov described the psychology of consciousness as the thesis and behaviorism as its anti-thesis. In Marxist ideology, **dialectic synthesis** represented the principle that the new appears and develops as the negation of the old. For Kornilov the task of achieving a dialectic synthesis in psychology could be solved by "**reactology**," the term Kornilov coined to describe the psychological theory he developed based on the study of human responses. The subject matter of reactology was the reaction of a human as a biosocial entity, which included both objective (external stimulus and response) as well as subjective (consciousness) components. External stimulus and response mechanisms were studied through objective methods while consciousness remained available solely through self-observation.

In 1923, Kornilov led the fight for the reconstruction of psychology on the basis of Marxism. After Kornilov's active participation in the events leading to the firing of Chelpanov as director of the Institute of Psychology, Kornilov took over as the new director and changed the direction of the institute's research activities toward the study of different types of reactions. Several scientists were displeased with the reforms implemented by Kornilov and left the institute in protest.

DIALECTICAL MATERIALISM, PEDOLOGY, AND PSYCHOTECHNICS

Payne (1968) has labeled the years from 1917 to 1930 the "Mechanistic Period" in Soviet psychology and during this time, in his view, Soviet psychologists were primarily focused on eliminating idealism with the result that a mechanistic materialism had emerged by the late 1920s. Dialectical materialism did not formally appear in psychology until the 1930s. In its most idealized form, **dialectical materialism** is defined as the following: a Marxian interpretation of reality that views matter as the sole subject of change and all change as the product of a constant conflict between opposites, arising from the internal contradictions inherent in all events, ideas, and movements.

In the time period between the 1920s and 1960s, Soviet psychology became an increasingly repressed science. Psychologists were deprived of work, arrested, and physically humiliated. Psychology also suffered as natural developmental trends in the discipline were altered radically under the powerful pressure of communism. Increasing pressure was placed on researchers to develop a psychological theory and practice that conformed to Marxist ideology and from the 1920s until the collapse of the USSR in 1991, no works in psychology could be published unless they cited and referenced the writings of Marx and Lenin!

One of the first victims of direct government repression was none other than the leader of Marxist psychology of the 1920s, Kornilov himself. Criticism of Kornilov's reactology was raised based on the theory's eclecticism and was started by Kornilov's young co-workers. Dreadful consequences were not long in coming; Kornilov was fired from his position as director of the institute and as editor-in-chief of the journal *Psychology* (Umrikhin, 1991). His scientific teachings were purged and, in the beginning of the 1930s, the few psychological journals still in existence in Russia—*Psychology, Pedology,* and *Soviet Psychotechnics*—began to close one by one. The Communist Party assumed the role of determining the criteria for scientific truth in psychology as well as in other disciplines.

The next repressive action toward psychology was the decision of the Communist Party to abolish **pedology**—a special subdiscipline of scientific psychology in Russia, which focused on a wide variety of psychological phenomena related to child development. Pedology was a vibrant field in Russian psychology in the early 20th century and encompassed such concepts as the diagnosis and correction of mental development, individual and age-related features of psychic phenomena, the psychology of learning, and the impact of family upbringing upon human development. The Communist Party's decision to abolish pedology particularly impacted those researchers who were considered to be the most active leaders within this subfield of psychology, including Blonsky, Vygotsky, and Zalkind, as well as many others. The name Vygotsky, in particular, became an unvoiced taboo for many years.

Lev Vygotsky

Lev Vygotsky (1896–1934) graduated from Moscow University in 1917 and joined the Moscow Institute of Psychology in 1924. He continued to work at the institute and at other research institutions, such as the Academy of Communist Education, until his untimely death in 1934.

Vygotsky was relatively unknown in the circles of Russian psychology until his appearance as a participant in the Second Russian Psychoneurological Congress in 1924. At the Congress, Vygotsky attracted attention by choosing to speak on a challenging and controversial subject, namely, the relationship between reflexes and consciousness.

Targeting the theories of the leaders of reflexology, Vygotsky argued that while reflexes provide the foundation for behavior, they provide no insight concerning the "building" that is constructed on this foundation (Kozulin, 1984). He pointed out that in searching for universal building blocks of human and infrahuman behavior, proponents of reflex theory overlooked the very phenomenon that makes humans unique, namely, consciousness. Vygotsky concluded that this was a mistake and that scientific psychology cannot ignore the existence of consciousness. This stance challenged the positions of almost all leading Soviet behavioral psychologists including followers of Pavlov, and Bekhterev who rejected consciousness as an "idealist superstition" (Kozulin, 1984).

Vygotsky further developed his theory in his 1925 article, "Consciousness as a Problem in the Psychology of Behavior." He started with the claim that consciousness must be examined as a structure of cognitive functions such as thinking, feeling, and volition. The conscious mind thus functions as a regulatory and structuring mechanism of human experiences and behaviors.

Another key element of Vygotsky's theory was his thesis that establishing a scientific psychology required resolution of the problem of interaction between the "lower" mental functions, such as elementary perception, memory, and attention, and those "higher" mental functions, such as thought, that are uniquely human. Most of Vygotsky's contemporaries sought to resolve the gap between lower and higher mental functions by presenting them as differing quantitatively. Vygotsky disagreed, and he argued forcefully that the difference between lower and higher mental functions was qualitative and not quantitative in nature.

According to Vygotsky, a newborn child exhibits only lower or so-called "natural" psychic functions such as perception, memory, and attention; however, unlike animals, humans then absorb the world of culture. Vygotsky proposed a special experimental method for the study of higher mental processes, which he called the "method of dual stimulation," and which he used to carry out a series of experiments on mental processes such as active attention and voluntary recall. His findings showed that the meaning of a word changes during the course of a child's development and plays a different role both in how the word appears to reflect reality and in how the word mediates mental activity at various stages of development (Luria, 1969). Vygotsky used this approach to study objectively the formation of higher mental functions and their disintegration in pathological brain states, such as in mental illnesses like schizophrenia (Luria, 1969).

Through the activities of Vygotsky, and later his students, Luria and Leontiev, processes that formerly had at best only been described were now explainable as the products of complex development, during which a child's exposure to the world around her or him is gradually assimilated to constitute the child's own mental activity. Their work dramatically impacted the Russian field of educational psychology.

Alexander Luria

A student and later a colleague of Vygotsky, Alexander Luria (1902–1977) was acutely interested in psychoanalysis and advocated its acceptance in Soviet psychology on an equal footing with psychological theories based on the politically correct teachings of Marxism-Leninism. Despite his failure to achieve this goal, Luria was able to conduct research that brought him world acclaim.

Luria's research concerned affective complexes (i.e., feelings and associated physiological and behavioral indices of an emotional state) that an individual would be unaware of or would intentionally strive to hide. Such affective complexes had been previously studied by Carl Jung utilizing word association methodology. Luria added the recording of muscle-motor activity to the use of the method of word association, thus greatly increasing the sensitivity of the associative method. Luria's methodology, which involved electrophysiological recordings of such measures as heart rate, respiratory rate, and the galvanic skin response as indices of hidden affective complexes, was widely used later in the criminal justice system, especially in the United States, as the "lie detector" test (Homskaya, 2001; Luria, 1982).

Luria and Vygotsky worked closely together on the study of cultural-historical concepts. One of their studies was conducted in Middle Asia—Uzbekistan and Kirgizia—and was a cross-cultural study of various subcategories of the population, including people who lived in remote settlements and people who were educated and had been exposed to European culture. The results showed significant differences in the majority of learning processes, including perception, memory, and thinking, depending on the cultural conditions under which the various subjects developed (Luria, 1974; Vygotsky & Luria, 1930/1992). In general, Luria and Vygotsky found that enriched environments enhanced the above psychological processes while barren and monotonous environments degraded such processes.

Due to the political situation at the time, Luria's and Vygotsky's research on cultural differences between population groups was abruptly stopped and the results of their studies remained unpublished for more than four decades. Luria, under the direction of Vygotsky, began to research the problem of brain organization of higher psychic functions. This research was stimulated by Russia's participation in the events of World War II, when Luria and Vygotsky saw hundreds of wounded soldiers with a variety of injuries to the central nervous system.

Another famous student of Vygotsky was Blyuma Zeigarnik (1900–1988), whose achievements have already been described in chapter 11, Gestalt Psychology. In addition to her discovery of the Zeigarnik effect, Zeigarnik studied psychopathology under the direction of

Vygotsky and the breadth of her research on the subject of psychopathology is a testimony to her role as one of the founders of this area of research in Russian psychology (Zeigarnik, 1986). While Vygotsky taught and inspired a number of famous Russian psychologists, perhaps one of his most famous and influential students was Aleksei Leontiev.

Aleksei Nikolayevich Leontiev

After working with Vygotsky and Luria to develop further the central ideas of their culturo-historical theory of human development, Aleksei Nikolayevich Leontiev (1902–1979) moved to Harkov, Ukraine, and began to develop his own separate school within Russian psychology. Adhering to the general principles taken from Vygotsky, Leontiev began to take the sociohistorical explanation of human psychic activity in a new direction by introducing the concept of **activity** as the primary explanatory principle of psychology. This principle described the mode of relationship between the subject and the environment. Activity was proposed as a universal process exhibited not only by human psychic phenomena but also those of infra-humans.

Leontiev's doctoral dissertation (1940) was devoted to the problem of unity of different types of psychic phenomena, their stages of development, and the biological mechanisms of the evolution of psychic phenomena. His major conclusion concerned the relationship of external and internal activity through the latter's existence as the result of the "interiorization" of the former, that is, we become in large measure our environments. Leontiev's activity theory became one of the main theoretical foundations for research in almost all branches of Russian psychology.

Later, Petr Yakovlevich Galperin (1902–1988) described in detail the mechanism of interiorization of external actions into internal actions. Aside from its theoretical significance, Galperin's approach became one of the most operational and "technological" approaches in Russian psychology for the effective application of pedology.

Soon after pedology became a victim of communist repression another applied branch of Russian psychology was also destroyed, namely, **psychotechnics**. The applied fields of pedology and psychotechnics were of particular concern to Soviet ideologists due to their frequent use of aptitude tests and interest inventories, many of which were taken or borrowed from American and English psychologists focused in the area of mental testing. The primary criticism of mental testing was that it "tended artificially to perpetuate class differences by stamping certain children as incapable of benefiting equally with others from the opportunities available in the Soviet Union" (Viteles, 1938, p. 90). In 1936, the field of pedology and the use of mental testing were both banned, and the Soviet government shut down the research centers of leading psychotechnicians.

Similar to American industrial-organizational psychology, psychotechnics studied a wide range of psychological factors affecting human labor, ranging from professional selection and human adaptation to machinery to social problems of industrial organizations. As part of the persecution of this branch of psychology, the leader of Soviet psychotechnics, Isaac Shpilrein (1891–late 1930s) was arrested and executed (Gilgen & Gilgen, 1996).

Further political repression of psychology began in the late 1940s following Russian and Allied victory in World War II. This time government repression developed in response to the fact that millions of Soviet soldiers returning from the West had seen with their own eyes that what the Soviet government had described as a "rotting" Western bourgeois society was in actuality providing Western Europeans with a much higher standard of living than was experienced in Soviet society. The "Iron Curtain" was created to protect Soviet culture and citizens from exposure to such outside influences and a campaign began promoting the advantages and achievements of the Soviet system, including those within science. Soviet scientists were deterred from expressing interest in the activities of science outside of the Soviet Union and particularly aggressive repression was placed on the work of Jewish scientists.

At the same time Ivan Pavlov, already long deceased, was labeled an "outstanding Soviet scientist." In 1950, a pivotal joint session of the Academy of Sciences and the Academy of Medicine was organized under the direct order of Joseph Stalin and was dedicated to the issues of Pavlov's physiological studies. The purpose of the "Pavlov Session" was to develop propagandist ideology within psychology as well as to serve as a forum for the accusation of "deviant" psychologists. Russian psychology barely survived this period of Pavlovianization and it took immense efforts by Russian psychologists to protect the right of psychology to exist as a science separate from physiology.

Nikolai Bernstein (1896–1966) emerged as one of the few Russian psychologists who tried to challenge the Pavlovianization of Russian psychology. In place of Pavlovian doctrine, Bernstein proposed the study of feedback mechanisms in the physiology of body movements, an early precursor of the movement later known as cybernetics (Gilgen & Gilgen, 1996). Bernstein's proposed alternative to Pavlovian theory did not survive the Pavlov Session of 1950, partly because Bernstein himself was a Jew and therefore a target of the rising anti-Semitism evident in the Soviet Union following World War II.

THE SOVIET UNION IN THE 1960s

As a result of Nikita Khrushchev's campaign against Stalinist policies following Stalin's death in 1953, psychology and Russian science in general were to some extent liberated. The years under the leadership of Brezhnev, and later Andropov and Chernenko (1964–1985), were characterized by a sociopolitical regression to a more static and repressive state. A reopening of Soviet psychology to the influence of the world did not arise until Mikhail Gorbachev assumed leadership of the Soviet Union in 1985 and began to restructure radically Soviet socialism through his united policies of **Glasnost** (openness) and **Perestroika** (restructuring). Of particular relevance to psychology was the fact that in 1990, Gorbachev declared the Soviet Academy of Sciences to be a self-governing organization, freeing it from the stranglehold of government control. In general, both Glasnost and Perestroika inspired Soviet psychologists to open up the process of professional exchange between themselves and Western psychologists. Increasingly, however, their efforts were hampered by a lack of funding and insufficient infrastructure to support active scientific exchange, such as inadequate computer access and networking capabilities as well as inefficient and unsafe transportation systems.

As Gilgen & Gilgen (1996) point out, articles published in the United States in 1992 summarized the intense difficulties facing Russian scientists. For example, the journals *Nature* and *Science* featured articles titled "Russian Science Faces Economic Crisis," "Cut Off from Mainstream, Ukrainian Science Drifts," "Problems Delay Emergence of Moscow Research Centre," "Internal Politics Block Proposal by Russians to Create Foundation for Basic Research," "A European Plan [to help] Gathers Support," "Small Quick Grants Proposed as Lifeline."

A further blow to psychology came in 1995 when Boris Yeltsin's government created the Ministry of Science and Technology Policy to oversee the Russian Academy of Science as well as other branches of academia. Of particular importance were legal deliberations taking place in the Duma (the lower chamber of the Russian parliament, similar to the U. S. House of Representatives) concerning the relative hierarchy of Russia's various scientific organizations. In these deliberations, the definition of what constituted a science was vague and failed to include any of the social sciences or humanities.

POST-SOVIET PSYCHOLOGY: PICKING UP THE PIECES AFTER PERESTROIKA

The most immediate impact of the above changes in governmental policy to Russian psychology includes the severe impairment of funding for the discipline, the relative destabilization of the institutional infrastructure required to support the work of the discipline, increased openness to Western psychology, increasing need for and reliance on communication technologies such as e-mail and the Internet, and an increasing focus on applied fields within psychology. This latter focus on applied activities has developed in direct response to social-psychological problems arising from conditions in Russian society. Particular areas of interest include the treatment of alcoholism and depression, facilitating adaptation from a socialist to a capitalist economy, and ethnic conflict.

A scientist in Russia has always been more than a scientist in the strictest sense of the word; he or she has always been a benchmark of morality, a carrier of culture, and a source of enlightenment. Science throughout Russian, Soviet, and again Russian history has always been ideological. Therefore, the transition from one ideology to another has been essentially reflected in science, especially social sciences like psychology. For example, during the Soviet era the scientific achievements of Ivan Petrovich Pavlov were overly exaggerated while now he is much more popular abroad than he is in his native land of Russia.

Russian scientists have avidly consumed the wealth of information from the West that became accessible upon the 1991 collapse of the totalitarian Soviet system along with the USSR's policy of isolationism. In recent times, foreign literature on psychology has again become available in Russia both in original and translated forms. Russian psychologists once again have the opportunity to meet with their colleagues from abroad and participate in collaborative research. There is no doubt that this new stream of psychological thought strongly affects the state of psychology in Russia; however, Russian psychology that has been opened to the world also influences the global development of psychology as well.

■ Summary

In this chapter, we presented an overview of the development of Russian psychology with particular emphasis on differences and similarities between Russian psychology and the psychology of Western Europe and the United States. Three key features explored distinguishing Russian psychology from Western psychology include: (1) the close relationship that continues to exist between Russian psychology and philosophy compared with the division that exists between these two disciplines in the West, (2) the stronger and more overt influence of political and social changes on the practice of psychology in Russia, and (3) Russian psychology's strong emphasis on environmental influences over heredity.

We opened this chapter with an overview of the history of Russia beginning prior to the reign of Czar Peter the Great in the 18th century, and continued through the 19th century with the expansion of Russian territories; the rising discontent of Russia's citizens with the existing imperial monarchy of the czars; the abolition of Russia's practice of serfdom; and increasing social trends of intellectualism, liberalism, and political radicalism. We then briefly explored events that led to the rise of the Bolshevik Party and the October Revolution of 1917, which heralded Russia's evolution into a new political entity as the Union of Soviet Socialist Republics (USSR).

We continued our discussion with a history of communist Russia, beginning with the political repression and isolationism that existed from the 1920s to the early 1950s under the leadership of Vladimir Lenin and his successor Joseph Stalin. Our coverage of the Soviet period concluded with Mikhail Gorbachev's political policies of Glasnost and Perestroika which, in the 1980s, ultimately led to the dismantling of the Soviet Union and a period of social and political unrest that continues to the present time.

Throughout this general overview of the history of Russia we emphasized the many ways in which unfolding political events in Russia shaped the practice of psychology as a scientific discipline. The history of Russian psychology prior to 1917 was closely tied to and not very different from psychology as it existed in Western Europe. Russian psychology prior to 1917 was also strongly influenced by practitioners from the medical-scientific field of physiology. The work of two physiologists, Ivan Michailovich Sechenov and Ivan Petrovich Pavlov, brought into Russian psychology a strong materialist focus that continues to the present.

Vladimir Bekhterev and his development of "reflexology" were then described. Bekhterev's career was impacted heavily by the repressive influence of the Soviet government following the Bolshevik Revolution.

Beginning in the 1920s, as the Soviet government increased its emphasis on Marxism as the only acceptable ideological basis for any scientific activity, Russian psychology increasingly focused on mechanistic materialism and the elimination of idealism and began to discredit any notions of consciousness. Russian psychology was in jeopardy of losing legitimate standing as a scientific discipline separate from medical physiology. Dialectical Materialism arose as an acceptable organizing principle around which Russian psychology could be developed. Two prominent Russian psychologists who struggled to defend the psychology of consciousness were Georgy Chelpanov and Konstantin Kornilov.

Two subfields of psychology, pedology and psychotechnics, were particularly subject to Soviet repression due to their frequent use of aptitude tests and interest inventories, which the government criticized as tending to perpetuate artificial class differences. Despite active government repression, Russian psychologists in the fields of pedology and psychotechnics were able to make significant contributions to Russian psychology, some of which were described herein including the work of Lev Vygotsky and his students Alexander Luria and Aleksei Leontiev.

In 1950, a joint session of the Academy of Sciences and the Academy of Medicine celebrated and idealized the contributions of Ivan Pavlov to Russian psychology and ushered in an era of "Pavlovian Psychology." Nikolai Bernstein was one of the few Russian psychologists to challenge the Pavlovianization of Russian psychology.

We concluded this chapter with a discussion of Perestroika and Glasnost and the resultant collapse of the USSR, which has impacted Russian psychology in ways that present both challenges as well as opportunities in the continued development of Russian psychology.

Chapter 16—Psychology in Russia

Discussion Questions

- What are three key features which distinguish Russian psychology from Western psychology?
- How did the relationship between Western and Russian psychology change over the course of the pre-Soviet, Soviet, and post-Soviet eras of Russian history?
- What is the significance of Pavlov's research on the conditioned reflex?
- What is the difference between mechanistic Marxism and dialectical Marxism, and how have both influenced the development of Russian psychology?
- What are some of the key principles of Vladimir Bekhterev's reflexology?
- What was the impact of Russian sociopolitical changes on the work of Georgy Chelpanov and Konstantin Kornilov?
- What are psychotechnics and pedology and why were both of these fields particularly victimized by communist repression?
- What effects have Glasnost and Perestroika had upon Russian psychology?
- How have sociopolitical changes in the United States potentially affected the development of American psychology?

Psychology in China

CHAPTER OVERVIEW

In this chapter, we present an overview of the history and development of Chinese psychology. When compared with the so-called Western psychology that has dominated global practice of the discipline, Chinese psychology exhibits subtle differences attributable to factors unique to China's cultural context. Examination of the similarities as well as the differences between Western and Chinese psychology provides useful insight and furthers the development of a more universal, global psychology.

Chinese psychology has been influenced at a fundamental level by China's philosophical heritage, which differs dramatically from the Judeo-Christian-Islamic roots of Western psychology. The deepest philosophical influences on Chinese psychology come from the three "isms": Confucianism, Taoism, and communism. We begin this chapter with a discussion of the first two "isms," providing an overview of the basic underlying principles of Confucianism and Taoism as well as their relevance to Chinese psychology. Both Confucianism and Taoism took inspiration from the *I Ching*, which is one of the world's oldest and most important philosophical texts. We include a brief discussion of the *I Ching* in the section on the philosophical roots of Chinese psychology including psychologist C. G. Jung's proposal of interesting differences between Western and Chinese views of the concept of causality evident in the *I Ching*.

Chinese psychology has also been influenced by encounters with the West. Some of the earliest Western influence on Chinese psychology came from Jesuit missionaries who traveled to China in the 16th and 17th centuries. We continue this chapter with a brief overview of some of these Jesuit scholars who have particular relevance for Chinese psychology, including Matteo Ricci (1552–1610), Julius Alenis (1582–1649), and Franciscus Sambiasi (1582–1649).

The Chinese medical model has also affected the development of Chinese psychology, particularly in the areas of abnormal and counseling psychology. We briefly describe some of the concepts from Traditional Chinese Medicine of relevance to psychology including Chi as well as Yin and Yang.

Western scientific psychology was first introduced to China in the late 19th and early 20th centuries, at which time it blended with China's philosophical belief systems and the Chinese medical model yielding a unique indigenous psychology. We briefly discuss important events during the early era of Chinese scientific psychology (between 1900 and 1949), including the contributions of Cai Yuanpei (1868–1940), landmark developments in the infrastructure supporting scientific practice, and the growing influence of American psychology.

In 1949, China became a communist nation known as the People's Republic of China (PRC). This pivotal event in Chinese social and political history had a profound effect on Chinese psychology. We provide an overview of the impact of this third "ism," communism, both philosophically through the influence of dialectical materialism and Marxist principles as well as structurally through dramatic upheavals within Chinese academic circles.

In the years between 1966 and 1976, China experienced a period known as the Cultural Revolution. Chinese psychology suffered severe setbacks during the Cultural Revolution as a consequence of Communist Party leader Mao Zedong's (1893–1976) radically repressive policies and attitudes toward educated academic scientists and intellectuals.

Since the death of Mao Zedong in 1976, China has adopted a policy of economic reform embracing a market economy and opening China to cultural, economic, and technological exchanges with the West. Economic reform has been a two-edged sword in that it has led to rapid growth and improvements in quality of life while at the same time creating inflation, high levels of unemployment, and increased levels of stress. We conclude this chapter with an overview of current challenges and opportunities in Chinese psychology.

LEARNING OBJECTIVES

When you finish reading this chapter, you will be prepared to:

- Identify the three "isms" that have influenced Chinese culture and hence Chinese psychology
- Discuss the individual philosophical contributions of Kung Fu-Zi, Meng Tzu, and Xun Zi that are of relevance to Chinese psychology
- Describe the basic underlying principles of Taoism and discuss Taoism's effect on the development of Chinese psychology
- Discuss C. G. Jung's theory regarding Chinese and Western differences in their relative conceptualizations of "change" and the implications for the practice of psychology
- Discuss the contributions of Jesuit missionaries to Chinese psychology
- Discuss China's system of civil service examinations and its relevance to psychology
- Discuss the influence of the Chinese Medical Model on the development of Chinese psychology, particularly on the areas of abnormal and counseling psychology
- Describe the contributions of Cai Yuanpei to Chinese psychology
- Discuss the impact of the formation of the People's Republic of China on Chinese psychology
- Discuss the impact of China's Cultural Revolution on Chinese psychology
- Describe the general effects of Chinese economic reform upon Chinese psychology
- Compare and contrast so-called Western versus Chinese psychology

INTRODUCTION

While humanity's search for greater self-knowledge has been a universal endeavor, the approach undertaken and the answers obtained have been greatly shaped by individual cultural contexts. Psychology, as a global science, has played a pivotal role in this universal endeavor by helping to pick apart the relative importance of cultural and environmental influences versus genetic or innate physiological characteristics: What role in human behavior is played by nature versus nurture? Ironically, psychology is itself subject to two forms of influence: the "nature" of scientific psychological practice and the "nurture" of the individual cultural context within which such scientific practice is undertaken.

Some of this cultural influence has already been explored in previous chapters. Cultural influence is evident in the unique flavor of American psychology as compared with the European psychology from which it sprung. Cultural influence is also evident in the development of psychology in Russia. Western psychology has dominated the discipline globally, providing a theoretical basis and an infrastructure design; however, psychology does not have a single, unified global character but can instead be described as a collection of indigenous psychologies. Yet while psychology as practiced in America, Great Britain, Germany, or Russia might exhibit some variations, there is at the base a common philosophical and scientific heritage that is loosely classified as Western.

In this chapter, we examine the development of psychological science in China, which, while at times readily accepting of ideas imported from the West, is built upon a philosophical and scientific base that is very different from the "Socratic," Judeo-Christian-Islamic roots of Western psychology. China is one of the oldest civilizations on the planet and Chinese psychology has, in one sense or another, been practiced throughout China's history. According to Bond (1996, p. xviii), there is great value to be found in understanding the differences as well as the similarities between Western psychology and Chinese psychology, in that:

> Chinese culture has the necessary age, coherence, and difference from Western traditions to provide a litmus test to the presumptions of universality that tend to characterize psychology done in the mainstream. If a construct or process is universal, then Chinese human beings should give evidence of its validity.

A blending of Western and Eastern (Chinese) psychology also may ultimately yield a richer, more robust and useful meta-psychology, more capable of providing answers in our ongoing search for self-knowledge.

PHILOSOPHICAL ROOTS OF CHINESE PSYCHOLOGY

As we have described in earlier chapters, the history of Western psychology has grown from the early philosophical seeds planted by Greek philosophers such as Pythagoras, Socrates, Plato, and Aristotle, and influenced by Islamic and Judeo-Christian religious systems. The influence of the Renaissance on the development of scientific methodology and practice further shaped the emergence of scientific psychology in 19th-century Europe, and in earlier chapters we discussed the contributions of individuals such as Galileo, Newton, Bacon, and Descartes. The result of these various influences is a Western psychology that is crafted on a natural science model and characteristically experimental, reductionistic, physiologically rooted, and idiographic in its orientation.

Chinese psychology has arisen from an equally old but radically different philosophical lineage, the influence of which remains to this day. In contrast to Western psychology and as a result of its culturo-philosophical inheritance, Chinese psychology is crafted more along the lines of a human science model and is characteristically more philosophical, humanistic, and nomothetic (i.e., focused on identifying principles that apply to all members of the collective or culture). The strongest forces in Chinese culture leading to these differences between Chinese and Western psychology are the three "isms": Confucianism, Taoism, and more recently, communism.

Confucianism

As discussed in chapter 4, Philosophical Foundations of Psychology, Confucianism is not a religion in the classic or Western sense of an organized belief system, centered upon the existence of a deity, and structured around institutions such as the church. Confucianism can instead be described as a system of social and/or ethical philosophy that is built on an even more ancient foundation of Chinese polytheistic and animistic religious beliefs. Sociologist Robert Bellah referred to Confucianism as a "civil religion," meaning a religious identity and common moral understanding at the foundation of a society's central institutions (Berling, 1982). Confucianism has also been called a "diffused religion," the institutions of which are not a separate church but those of society and family and whose specialists are not priests, but rather the respected figures present in everyday life such as parents, teachers, and government officials (Berling, 1982).

Confucianism was founded in the Zhou dynasty by K'ung Fu-zi, or Master K'ung, whose name was later latinized as Confucius (551−479 B.C.). Confucius lived during a time of social and political unrest in which Chinese citizens were questioning their ancient belief systems and seeking answers as to what forms the base of a stable, unified, and enduring social order. Two dominant and competing Chinese philosophical factions of the time, the Realists and the Legalists, believed that strict law and statecraft were the answer (Berling, 1982). Confucius, however, believed the answer lay in Zhou religion and its rituals, or *li*. He radically reinterpreted the *li* of Zhou religion as embodying cultural patterns of civilized behavior developed through generations of human wisdom, and forming the ethical basis of Chinese society (Berling, 1982). This ethical basis for moral and civilized behavior was centered on human relationships and structured around defined roles and patterns of mutual obligation. To behave in a civilized and morally/ethically sound manner required each individual to understand and conform to his/her proper defined role and to fulfill one's pre-defined obligations. The cultivation of individual moral maturity, and hence societal perfection, required deep self-knowledge as well as broad education and reflection on one's actions. Confucius referred to the state of individual moral perfection as **Jun-zi** or nobility, which any person can achieve through personal reflection, discipline, and education.

Confucius shared his philosophical vision through his disciples who compiled the *Confucian Analects* after his death. The *Analects* became one of the four great books taught and memorized by generations of Chinese people for more than a millennium. Some key principles of Confucian philosophy relevant to Chinese psychology are Confucius' belief in a common human nature, and his conviction that personal development and mental change can be achieved through education. This process was poetically described by Confucius in the *Classic of Rituals* (cited in Berling, 1982, p. 1):

> Only when things are investigated is knowledge extended; only when knowledge is extended are thoughts sincere; only when thoughts are sincere are minds rectified; only when minds are rectified are the characters of persons cultivated; only when character is cultivated are our families regulated; only when families are regulated are states well governed; only when states are well governed is there peace in the world.

A key difference between the Western Judeo-Christian and Islamic moral and ethical belief systems and Confucianism is the latter's lack of emphasis on an afterlife. Unlike the Western religious emphasis on moral and ethical rectitude as a means of earning a heavenly afterlife, Confucianism views the goal of moral and ethical behavior in everyday life as the creation of a utopian existence on earth.

While Confucius had many disciples, his vision did not gain broad acceptance in Chinese culture until the Han dynasty when Emperor Wu (ruled 140−87 B.C.) accepted Confucianism as state ideology and promoted Confucian values as a means of maintaining law and order.

Influential philosophers who built upon Confucianism included Meng Tzu, latinized as Mencius (370–290 B.C.) and Xun Zi, latinized as Xuncius (298–238 B.C.). Meng Tzu, who studied with the grandson of Confucius, was called "The Second Sage" in acknowledgment of his importance as secondary to that of only Confucius himself. His system of thought was based on the concepts of **jen**, or "humaneness," "humanity," "benevolence," and **i,** or "righteousness." Meng Tzu believed that the level of "humaneness" or "benevolence" owed to a person was influenced by the relationship shared with that person. This relationship was defined both by your relative positions as well as the obligations owed. Meng Tzu believed that all humans were innately good or benevolent but that most people fail to act in a benevolent manner due to environmental factors and a failure to cultivate one's virtue.

Ironically, while Meng Tzu advocated a doctrine of human benevolence, he was himself viewed at different times in Chinese history as a dangerous philosopher and his books have often been banned. The danger in Meng Tzu's philosophy was his early development of a form of social contract known as the doctrine of the Mandate of Heaven, which potentially placed rulers in a tenuous position. Meng Tzu, like Confucius, believed rulers were divinely appointed to guarantee peace and order; however, unlike Confucius, Meng Tzu also believed that if a ruler failed to bring peace and order then the people had a divine right to revolt.

Xun Zi (298–238 B.C.) argued a generation later that human nature was not innately benevolent but was instead negative. Xun Zi claimed that it is human nature to strive for wealth and to exhibit a hedonistic need for sensual satisfaction (Jing & Fu, 2001). Human nature, if allowed to flourish uncontrolled, will cultivate conflict and violence. Contradicting Meng Tzu while remaining in alignment with Confucian ideas, Xun Zi stressed the need for education and strict adherence to social norms as the prerequisites for social harmony and order (Jing & Fu, 2001).

Confucianism remained at the very heart of Chinese culture until as recently as the late 1890s. Confucianism suffered brief public disfavor during the Communist Revolution and the formation of the People's Republic of China (PRC) in the late 1940s. Despite changes in public espousal, Confucianism is so central to Chinese cultural identity that its teachings remain and retain their influence on all aspects of Chinese daily life. Confucianism's impact on the development of Chinese psychology, however, was more implicit than explicit until as recently as the 1970s. In other words, while the influence of Confucianism on the larger Chinese culture had an impact upon the nature and character of Chinese psychology throughout its history, Confucianism was not explicitly explored in terms of its direct implications for and relevance to psychology until the late 1970s and early 1980s.

Taoism

Another pillar of Chinese philosophy is Taoism. Taoism is radically different from Confucianism but the two philosophical branches are not contradictory and it is therefore not impossible for something to be both Confucianist and Taoist simultaneously (see chapter 4 for further discussion of Taoism). Confucianism, while it is a philosophical belief system, is concerned with mundane day-to-day existence; Taoism takes a more mystical and transcendent vision and is inherently naturalistic in focus. The central concept of Taoism is that behind all material things and behind all change or action in the world lies one fundamental and universal principle: the **Tao** or **the Way**. Existence, as we normally perceive it, exhibits a bewildering kaleidoscope of multiplicity and contradiction whereas the Tao exhibits unity.

To live life according to the Tao permits one to transcend contradiction and multiplicity and return to a state of unity with the universe. Regarding human activity, to live according to the Tao requires living passively, calmly, and by means of nonaction (**wu wei)**. The two accredited authors of the earliest known writings on the concept of Tao are Lao Tzu (298–212 B.C.) and Chuang Tzu (369–286 B.C.).

The *I Ching*

The *I Ching*, or *Book of Changes*, is one of the most important books in the world. Its origin dates back to antiquity, and its early history is somewhat shrouded in mystery. Both Confucianism and Taoism have common roots in the teachings of the *I Ching*. The *I Ching* is predominantly known as a Book of Oracle, meaning it was used as a tool for making predictions about future events and to guide decision making; however, in addition to its use as an oracle, the book's greater significance lies in its use as a Book of Wisdom imparting philosophical as well as moral/ethical guidance. Lao Tzu's writings take obvious inspiration from the *I Ching* and the version of the *I Ching* that has come down to us today was edited and annotated by Confucius himself.

The underlying concept of the *I Ching* is the idea of change. The story goes that Confucius, standing by a river, once said, "Everything flows on and on like this river, without pause, day and night" (Wilhelm & Baynes, 1950, p. lv). This poetically expresses the idea of change as conceptualized in the *I Ching*. Once the meaning of change is understood, our attention is no longer distracted by transitory individual material things, and we can perceive instead the immutable, eternal law at work in all change; this law is the Tao. C. G. Jung (1950), in the preface to a modern translation of the *I Ching*, proposed that at the heart of the *I Ching* lies the fundamental difference between Chinese and Western thinking, namely, their differing understanding of the nature of causality.

As described by Jung (1950), Western philosophy and science is fundamentally based upon the principle of causality. This basic understanding of causality has been shaken by recent developments in postmodernist thinking and dynamic systems or chaos theory, which have revealed that the cause-and-effect relationships previously deemed to be natural laws may merely be statistical truths and therefore subject to exceptions. Western science was built in and for the laboratory with its ability to control and restrict chance. In reality, every process is partially or totally subject to randomness to the degree that a course of events that absolutely conforms to a "natural law" is almost an exception.

According to Jung (1950), the Chinese mind is at work in the *I Ching* and appears to be almost exclusively occupied with the chance aspects of events. The *I Ching* presents a radically different view of cause and effect. Instead of a linear chain of causal processes, what is important is the configuration formed by chance events at the moment of observation. In seeking to understand an event, the Western mind looks for the proximate causal Event A which led to the occurrence of Event B. The Chinese mind looks at the complete context of Event B and examines the interrelationships between all the components existing within that context. As a result, Chinese logical processes are focused upon the importance of relationships and placement or role within a context. Jung's hypothesis, although it has not been subjected to experimental validation, does represent an interesting and thought-provoking content analysis of one of China's oldest existing philosophical texts.

Certain characteristics present in modern Chinese psychology are directly attributable to the influence of ancient Chinese philosophers such as Confucius, Meng Tzu, and Lao Tzu, and those characteristics include: the Chinese understanding of human nature, of the nature of the mind; the relationship and relative importance of nature and nurture; and particularly the role of education in shaping the human mind (Jing & Fu, 2001).

East Meets West: Early European Influence

In 1275, China experienced its first historically recorded encounter with Westerners when Marco Polo (1254–1324) arrived in Beijing with his father and uncle. Upon his return to Venice seventeen years later, Polo authored his *Description of the World* (published in 1477), capturing the imagination of Europeans and arousing interest in China. Actual direct interchange between the two cultures, however, remained virtually nonexistent for almost 250 years until Jesuit missionaries traveled to China in the 16th and 17th centuries exposing the Chinese to Western science and technology. One such missionary, Matteo Ricci (1552–1610), was responsible for translating the *Four Books*, including the *Analects of Confucius*, and introducing these works to the West. Other Jesuit scholars who traveled to China during this period included the German astronomer Adam Schall von Bell (1591–1666) and Belgian scholar Ferdinand Verbiest, who became a close friend and advisor of the Chinese emperor Kangxi. The Jesuits introduced the Chinese to Euclidean geometry, the world map, the telescope, the clock, and the gun. This last contribution was particularly ironic given that it was the Chinese who were responsible for first introducing gunpowder to the West.

The Jesuits also brought to China some of its earliest exposure to psychology, including a 1596 treatise Matteo Ricci wrote on memory in which he introduced the idea that memory is a function localized to the brain, including specifying different parts of the brain as the location for certain kinds of memory (Jing & Fu, 2001). Chinese physician Li Shizhen, in an earlier work titled *Encyclopedia of Chinese Herbal Medicine* (1590), first introduced to China the idea that the brain is also related to one's temperament (Jing & Fu, 2001). Another work by Matteo Ricci, *Mnemonic Arts*, is of particular importance to psychology and had a significant impact on China's early utilization of psychological testing.

PSYCHOLOGICAL TESTING

As mentioned previously, one of the hallmarks of Confucianism is its emphasis on education, leading to the later development of China's system of civil service examinations, which were a requirement to hold any political office in the years between A.D. 606 and 1908. One requirement of these examinations was the ability to memorize a vast number of Chinese classical texts including the *Four Books*. Ricci had a phenomenal memory and had developed a mnemonic system for memorization borrowing from various mnemonic methods known in the West since Greek times. Ricci published his treatise on mnemonic arts with the hope of impressing the Chinese nobles with his ability to contribute to Chinese culture (Jing & Fu, 2001).

In the early 1600s, another Jesuit, Julius Alenis (1582–1649), introduced the Chinese to the ideas of Aristotle and Thomas Aquinas. In his works, *A General Account of Western Studies* and *Introduction to Human Nature*, Alenis shared the Christian concepts of soul and body, and Western ideas concerning the five senses, human faculties, memory and dreams, awareness, ageing, and death (Jing & Fu, 2001). A contemporary of Alenis, Franciscus Sambiasi

(1582–1649) wrote a two-volume work in 1624 titled *Study of the Soul*, in which he discussed the works of Aristotle and Saint Augustine. These two Jesuit scholars in particular were responsible for bringing to China knowledge of psychology as it was understood in the West at that time.

After the death of Emperor Kangxi and the dissolution of the Jesuit order in China in 1773, open cultural exchanges between China and the West effectively came to an end. China suffered a period of internal political, economic, and social decay; the nation stagnated and its social structure was torn apart by internal rebellions and civil unrest. Meanwhile, Europe was reaping the benefits of the Industrial Revolution and had developed unprecedented power along with an irresistible urge toward expansion and colonialization. The combined result of these forces was China's increasing suspicion of and hostility toward outsiders.

THE CHINESE MEDICAL MODEL

In addition to its roots in Chinese philosophy, Chinese psychology was also influenced by the Chinese medical model, particularly in its understanding of psychopathology. Traditional Chinese Medicine has at its foundation the concepts of **yin and yang** and of **chi**, both of which were first explicated by Han philosophers in the *I Ching*.

The concepts of yin and yang are related to Taoist philosophy and they represent dualistic and complementary elements or forces in nature. Together, yin and yang constitute chi. Early Chinese philosophers theorized a great primal beginning for all that exists, **t'ai chi**, and later philosophers speculated upon its nature. T'ai chi was represented by a circle divided into complementary components of light and dark, representing yin and yang:

In Traditional Chinese Medicine (TCM), physical and psychological well-being was dependent upon maintaining a balance between yin and yang elements of chi. Consequently, the focus of TCM and of Chinese psychological practice was upon restoring and maintaining equilibrium of forces. Practices such as acupuncture, which dates back over 3,000 years, and organ therapy are intended to aid in this balancing of chi. Another concept of TCM of relevance to psychology is its view of the mind–body relationship. In TCM and Chinese philosophy the mind dominates; however, mental processes are nurtured by the body.

The first reference to mental illness in classical Chinese medicine appeared in the *Huang-ti Nei-ching* (*Yellow Emperor's Classic of Internal Medicine*, written from the third to the fifth centuries B.C.). In this text the term *tien k'uang* was used to describe symptoms of disturbed affect and behavior (Cheung, 1986). The etiology of mental illness followed the same principles as physical illness in the Chinese medical system and was rooted in the body. The lack of direct reference to psychodynamic causes of mental health and illness may have led to later allegations that the Chinese somatize emotional problems (Kleinman, 1977; Tseng, 1975).

The lack of differentiation between physical and mental illness contributed to Chinese psychology's lack of development of the areas of counseling and abnormal psychology. Instead, psychopathology is treated within the general Chinese medical system.

PSYCHOLOGY IN CHINA AS AN EXPERIMENTAL SCIENCE

Although writings exist in China describing an interest in human psychology that dates back over 2,000 years, the first introduction of modern scientific psychology came not from within China but from beyond the Great Wall. Following the contributions of the Jesuits in bringing the work of Western philosophers to the attention of Chinese scholars, the first acknowledged introduction of Western scientific psychology to China occurred in 1899, the year in which Joseph Haven's *Mental Philosophy* was translated by Yan Yongjin into Chinese. Yan subsequently taught the subject of psychology in church schools in China as part of a general moral education program (Blowers, 1996). One problem encountered by Yan in the translation of Haven's book was the difficulty involved in finding appropriate equivalent Chinese terms that would not distort the original meaning of the English text. Interestingly, the term *psychology* had no existing Chinese equivalent so Yan chose three Chinese characters not previously conjoined, **xinlingxue**, which in combination translates back into English literally as "pneumatology," or the study of spirit (Blowers, 1996). Later, the Chinese term **xinlixue**, literally "knowledge of the heart," was adopted as the accepted term for the discipline (Blowers, 1996).

Foreign Imports

Early in the 20th century, a group of Chinese scholars left their home country to study in the West and upon their return to China, they brought with them Western scientific psychology. Cai Yuanpei (1868–1940) was one of these foreign-educated Chinese scholars and he later became one of the most influential figures in Chinese psychology. Born in Shaoxing, in Zhejiang Province, Cai's family led a comfortable life supported by his father's income as manager of a local bank. Cai received a traditional Chinese education and, after successfully completing civil service examinations, went on to earn the Chinese equivalent of a doctorate at the age of 22. Soon thereafter, he took a position at the Hanlin Academy where most of his time was spent compiling, translating, and interpreting classic Chinese texts.

Following the Sino-Japanese War of 1894–1895, in which China was abruptly faced with its vulnerability to the threat of Western science and technology, Cai turned his focus toward translating European texts, seeking to understand the reasons behind Western successes and their technological supremacy. He then taught at various government and private schools, attempting to disseminate some of the Western knowledge gleaned from his studies. By 1901, Chinese educators were acknowledging the value in Cai's efforts, and when the Chinese Educational Association was established that year, Cai Yuanpei was elected president.

In 1907, Cai traveled to Germany, enrolling at Leipzig University where he studied experimental psychology. He briefly returned to China to serve as Minister of Education in 1911 but resigned the post in 1912 in protest against the autocratic rule of Yuan Shikai. After a few years, during which Cai continued his studies in Germany and in France, he returned to China in 1916 where he went on to become one of the leading liberal educators of early 20th-century China. Cai was the first Minister of Education as well as Chancellor of Beijing University, where he founded the first Chinese psychology laboratory in 1917, and the founder and first president of the Academia Sinica, China's most renowned national research institute.

Cai severely criticized the existing Chinese system of education, advocating radical educational reforms. His call for action spurred an educational renaissance in China. The reforms advocated and implemented by Cai Yuanpei led to a period of increased openness to the West and decreased dogmatic adherence to rigid traditional ways of thinking. In many ways, Cai was ahead of his time in presaging the current trend toward globalization:

> We must follow the general rule of freedom of thought and freedom of expression, and not allow any one branch of philosophy or any one tenet of religion to confine our minds, but always aim at a lofty universal point of view which is valid without regard to space or time. For such an education I can think of no other name than education for a world view. (Cai, cited in Zhang, 2000, p. 2)

Cai's establishment of China's first psychology laboratory was one of three important events occurring around the 1920s that were of significance to Chinese psychology. Cai also was responsible for establishing the Institute of Psychology in 1929.

Another significant event in the history of Chinese psychology was the establishment of China's first department of psychology at Nanjing Higher Normal College in 1920. This was soon followed in 1921 by the establishment of the Chinese Psychological Society (CPS), which began publishing the Chinese academic journal *Psychology* (*Xinl i*), one year later.

Several influential figures in Chinese psychology emerged during this period including: Chen D. Q., who in 1918 published the first Chinese psychology text, *Principles of Psychology*; Kuo Zing Yang (1898–1970), a strict behaviorist who conducted research on instinct and heredity in animals; Ai Wei (1890–1970), who specialized in educational and experimental psychology; Lu Zhiwei (1894–1970), a memory researcher; and Chen Li (1902–   ), a key researcher in industrial psychology.

By the late 1920s, ten psychology departments had been established at Chinese colleges and universities; however, disrupting events during the Sino-Japanese War of 1937–1945 and the Second World War forced China to close several psychology departments and institutes, leading to the dissolution of the CPS. Despite these setbacks, a few Chinese psychologists continued to teach and conduct research, keeping the embers of a Chinese psychology flickering.

In the beginning, Chinese psychology was heavily influenced by Western—most particularly American—psychology. The needs of the Chinese people were very practical and applied in nature and American psychology's pragmatic and applied elements were particularly suited to meet those needs. Confucianism's strong focus on the power and value of education as a force for behavioral and social change, coupled with the guiding influence and educational interests of Cai Yuanpei and other early leaders in Chinese psychology, led to a heavy emphasis in the areas of educational and developmental psychology. John Dewey's work was highly regarded in China and Dewey himself lectured in Beijing in 1919 and 1920. In the 1930s, John Watson's work in behaviorism became very influential. By the late 1940s, psychology in China was almost entirely "American" in nature and was heavily focused on structuralism, functionalism, and behaviorism.

The Impact of Communism

In 1949, China emerged as a communist nation with the founding of the People's Republic of China (PRC). With a stable system of government in place, an infrastructure supporting academic and scientific endeavors was developed and by 1950 the Chinese Psychological Society resumed operation after a thirteen-year hiatus.

In general, the 1950s represented a growth spurt in Chinese psychology. In 1956, Chinese psychology benefited from the Chinese Academy of Sciences' establishment of the Institute of Psychology, which became one of the largest psychological research institutes in China. Three influential psychology journals started publication: *Acta Psychologica Sinica*, *Psychological Information*, and *Psychological Translations*. China also held its First National Psychology Conference in 1955. Coupled with the stability that allowed for growth and institutional development, the Chinese communist government also brought with it strong political and ideological ties to the Soviet Union. For Chinese psychology, this meant an increasing interest in Soviet psychology and the work of Russian psychologists such as Pavlov, Bekhterev, and Kornilov. For a time, Pavlov's theory of conditioned reflexes was the main theoretical focus in Chinese psychology. Western schools of psychology lost favor in China during this era.

The period between 1950 and the 1970s was characterized by a trend in Chinese psychology that was in many ways similar to the development of Russian psychology of that same era. Political ideology co-opted the developmental path of most scientific endeavors, including psychology, and the main goal of Chinese psychology became that of developing theory guided by Marxist dialectical materialism that was ideologically compatible with socialism. One particular theme emerging in Chinese psychology as a consequence of this Marxist influence was the idea that mental activity is a reflection of social reality. In other words, social and cultural factors shape the mind of an individual instead of the combined minds of individuals shaping society and culture; for example, if collectivism governs social interactions then the individual will think collectively and thus give priority to the needs of the group over those of the individual.

Chinese psychology retained its applied focus and a great deal of research during the period between the mid-1950s and mid-1960s responded to national needs related to China's social, economic, and cultural development. Administratively speaking, there were no independent psychology departments in universities and, instead, psychology departments were subsumed under either philosophy or education departments or teachers' colleges.

During the 1960s, the influence of Soviet psychology fostered a shift in focus toward physiological psychology with much of the research focused in the areas of perception, memory, and the cognitive development of children. Some applied research conducted during this period included a study on a comprehensive therapy for neurasthenia, research on color light signals for the railway system, and the development of lighting standards for the school system. In addition, three important Chinese psychology texts were published in the 1960s: Zhu Zi-Xian's *Child Psychology* (1962); Cao's *General Psychology* (1963); and Pan's *Educational Psychology* (1964). Toward the end of the 1960s, a growing number of Chinese students were majoring in psychology and programs in psychology were opening in several colleges and universities. Unfortunately, social and political forces led to an abrupt halt in the further development of Chinese psychology.

The Cultural Revolution

The period between 1966 and 1976 in Chinese history is referred to as the Cultural Revolution. During the Cultural Revolution, the Chinese communist government under the leadership of Mao Zedong (1893–1976) enforced radically repressive policies in an attempt to eradicate social stratification based on class or economic standing, thereby creating a communist utopia in which everyone shared everything equally and no one owned anything. Anything that was viewed as potentially contributing to the development of social strata or hierarchies was discouraged, including family emotional ties, economic forces, and even education. Psychology was condemned as elitist "bourgeois science" and psychologists along with other scholars and professionals were banished to the countryside for "re-education." The goal of such re-education efforts was to induce conformity to Maoist thought and the psychological and social elimination of individualistic thought and action. Psychological research was replaced by speculative philosophy and authoritative politically based decrees.

The Cultural Revolution ended in 1976 with the death of Mao Zedong and by 1978 China, under the leadership of Deng Xiaoping, had adopted more of an open-door policy of cultural, economic, and technological exchanges with the West, thus breaching the ideological wall that had separated China from many parts of the world since 1949.

Chinese Economic Reform

In the latter third of the 20th century, Chinese leader Deng Xiaoping abandoned communist economic principles in favor of a market economy when he proclaimed, "To get rich is glorious." China's move toward a market economy has brought prosperity and economic freedom to many Chinese; however, it has also resulted in periods of inflation, unemployment, and increased levels of stress. Prior to economic reform many Chinese citizens depended upon the so-called "Iron Rice Bowl" of noncompetitive, state-owned enterprises that had guaranteed lifelong employment.

Beginning in 1976, Chinese psychology entered another period of rapid growth. Psychology departments and research laboratories were once again opened in institutes of higher learning across the country. Thousands of undergraduates enrolled in psychology programs. In 1978, the Chinese Academy of Sciences (CAS) worked with colleges and universities in China to establish thirty master's and twelve doctoral programs in psychology. By 1999, more than fifty psychology departments had been created in China.

In 1980, Chinese psychology formally joined the international psychological community when the Chinese Psychological Society (CPS) joined the International Union of Psychological Science (IUPS), ushering in a new era of free and open intercultural exchange. The former president of CPS, Jing Qicheng, served on the executive committee of IUPS (1984–1992) and later as that organization's vice president (1992–1996).

CHINESE PSYCHOLOGY FACES FORWARD: CURRENT CHALLENGES AND OPPORTUNITIES

Chinese psychology is attempting to respond to both the opportunities and pressures of adopting an open and global market economy. In return, China's cultural attitude toward psychology has changed dramatically; in fact, a recent Chinese government report listed psychology as one of half a dozen disciplines deserving priority government funding over the next few decades (Clay, 2002a).

At the 1998 International Congress symposium "Psychology as a Profession in China," Zhang Houcan, a professor of psychology at Beijing Normal University, gave an overview of recent developments in Chinese psychology (Martin, 1998). Although independent psychology practices are still rare, a rising number of medical centers are offering psychotherapy services and schools and universities are setting up counseling centers for students. In the field of industrial psychology, a long-standing area of interest in Chinese psychology, Chinese companies are relying on the expertise of psychologists in testing employee competence and in setting human-resource policies. Psychologists are also well-respected for their work in helping people adapt to new jobs—essential when economic reform has resulted in tremendous numbers of people leaving government-sponsored posts for work in the private sector. In addition, China's booming interest in information technology has sparked a growing interest in psychological research on the human use of information technology. In China's overcrowded urban settings, Chinese psychologists are also contributing in the areas of traffic management, crime control, and market research.

The growing number of school counseling centers is in response to China's identification in the 1980s of the extreme pressure put on children to succeed academically (Martin, 1998). As mentioned earlier in this chapter, Confucian ideology placed a high level of importance on education, encouraging parents to push their children to excel in school. This drive to excel academically was further enhanced by the generation of parents born during the Cultural Revolution who saw firsthand the opportunities lost when education was suppressed and devalued. At the same time, China has a limited but growing number of colleges and universities and competition for placement in secondary education institutions is intense (Martin, 1998). Responding to the psychological problems resulting from this intense pressure to achieve academically has opened up a variety of new roles and opportunities for psychologists. Their expertise is being utilized to improve teaching methods, to revise and streamline curricula, to improve understanding of individual personality development and moral development, and to prevent mental health problems.

Another growing problem in China that requires the attention of psychology is the extremely high rates of depression and suicide. China has one of the highest suicide rates in the world, particularly among women; the current Chinese suicide rate is an estimated 30.3 per 100,000 compared with 10.7 per 100,000 in the rest of the world (Clay, 2002a). In a study released in the British medical journal *Lancet* in November 2002, researchers in China partially blame the high number of deaths in these suicide attempts to the ready availability of lethal pesticides and rodent poisons in rural areas and the absence of mental health services in much of the country (Rosenthal, 2002). In previous papers, one of the study's co-authors, Dr. Michael Phillips, a psychiatrist at the Huilongguan Hospital in Beijing, estimated that 287,000 Chinese commit suicide each year, making it the fifth-largest cause of death in the country (Rosenthal, 2002). In November of 2002, Phillips and his colleagues officially opened the Beijing Suicide Research and Prevention Center, financed by the Beijing city government, to respond to this crisis. This national health care crisis is partially attributable to the stress associated with the displacement and change encountered in China's rapidly developing society. As a sign of the growing interest in and acceptance of psychology, Western pop psychology books like *Who Moved My Cheese?* which deals with coping with change, are on the Chinese best-seller list (Rosenthal, 2002).

China is also culturally becoming more accepting of individual counseling, particularly in urban and commercial areas. Young women appear most likely to seek out services; in one study of 1,400 people receiving counseling by telephone in the city of Shenzhen in southern China, 63% of callers were women and 88% were under the age of 30 (Martin, 1998). In this same study, the counseling requested could be roughly divided into six categories: 47% had mental health problems including neuropathy, personality problems and relationship problems; 32% had medical problems; 10% had gynecological and obstetrical questions; 8% had questions about sexuality; and 3.2% had questions concerning child rearing. Telephone hotlines and counseling centers are growing in popularity but many are established independently and most of the counselors are medical doctors, educators, and teachers; thus the quality of service provided by these centers is questionable and they do not adhere to any set standards. The Chinese Psychological Society and the Chinese Association of Mental Health have called for these workers to be certified in psychological counseling.

Health psychology is another critical area requiring further development within Chinese psychology, particularly in response to China's rising HIV/AIDS epidemic. In 2002, the Joint United Nations Programme on HIV/AIDS estimated that a million Chinese are already infected (Clay, 2002a). They further estimated that by 2010, ten million Chinese would be infected (Bodeen, 2002). "Stopping the epidemic of AIDS in China has mainly been a governmental issue," says Yongming Chen, president of the Chinese Psychological Society. "However, Chinese psychologists have started to pay attention to this problem" (Chen, cited in Clay, 2002a). One of the key roles played by psychologists in addressing this problem will be in devising effective education campaigns to hopefully limit the spread of the disease. Psychological expertise will also be invaluable in helping individuals already infected to cope with the stresses and issues related to the disease.

Addressing the aggressive agenda of Chinese psychology will require a far greater number of well-trained psychologists than are currently available in China. At present, China has only approximately 10,000 psychologists working in a variety of arenas including research institutes, education, medicine, and other fields. This relatively small number of practitioners services a country with more than a billion inhabitants!

In addition, China has lost a number of potential practitioners to the West. Since the beginning of the open-door policy in 1978, 210,000 Chinese scholars have gone overseas to complete their education; however, approximately 80% of these students are not returning to China and those that do return face many challenges in working openly within a still relatively closed society (Greenberger & Johnson, 1997). At the same time, the Chinese economy, which has an extremely high rate of inflation, is pushing many of those scholars who choose to remain in China out of the universities and into the private and commercial sector (Blowers, 1996).

Another key goal of the Chinese psychological community is to define educational standards in psychology. This lack of standards is partly a consequence of academia's rising and falling status within China's political and social system throughout the 20th century, particularly during the Sino-Japanese War and the Second World War, and later as a consequence of the Cultural Revolution. Even the most well-respected members of China's psychological community often lack advanced degrees (Clay, 2002a). The Chinese Psychological Society has set a priority of strengthening training of psychologists in order to develop a labor pool in psychology that is adequate to meet China's needs (Clay, 2002a).

To accomplish this goal, almost every university now offers at least a few psychology classes and eighteen Chinese educational institutions now have psychology departments and/or research laboratories. Many of the students trained in these programs will be exposed to a blend of both Western and Chinese traditions. Explains Jin Pang Leung, PhD, an associate professor of psychology at the University of Hong Kong:

> There are two camps of people here. . . . One camp just treats psychology as the study of universal human phenomena and doesn't worry about whether the subjects of study are Westerners or Chinese. The other camp believes that psychology is only meaningful as far as the cultural context is known to us. (Leung, cited in Clay, 2002a)

■ Summary

In this chapter, we presented an overview of the history and development of Chinese psychology. Chinese psychology exhibits some differences from Western psychology attributable to factors unique to China's cultural context, and examining these differences can provide useful insight into psychology as a global enterprise and not just as a collection of indigenous psychologies.

We discussed the role of the three "isms," Confucianism, Taoism, and communism, in the development of Chinese psychology. We presented an overview of the basic underlying principles of Confucianism and Taoism as well as their relevance to Chinese psychology and their relationship to one of the world's oldest and most important philosophical texts, the *I Ching*. We presented a brief discussion of the *I Ching*, including C. G. Jung's proposal of differences between Western and Chinese views of the concept of causality evident in this influential Chinese text.

We also explored early Western influences on Chinese psychology stemming from Jesuit missionaries who traveled to China in the 16th and 17th centuries, including Matteo Ricci, Julius Alenis, and Franciscus Sambiasi. In addition to external influences from the West, Chinese psychology also reflects the internal influence of Traditional Chinese Medicine (TCM) and we presented an overview of some of the key principles of TCM including chi as well as yin and yang.

Western scientific psychology was first introduced to China in the late 19th and early 20th centuries. At that time the Western academic infrastructural model and Western psychological theories combined with China's philosophical belief systems and the Chinese medical model, yielding a unique indigenous psychology. We briefly discussed important events in Chinese psychology occurring during this introductory phase of Chinese scientific psychology, including the contributions of Cai Yuanpei, landmark developments in the infrastructure supporting the practice of psychology, as well as the growing influence of American psychology.

We then provided an overview of the philosophical and structural impact on Chinese psychology of China's third "ism," communism, between the years 1949 and 1966. During this period, Chinese psychology was increasingly influenced by Marxist principles and dialectical materialism impacted theory and practice. The work of Soviet psychologists also rose in prominence in China while American psychology waned.

We then briefly discussed the impact of China's Cultural Revolution during which Chinese psychology suffered the fallout of radically repressive policies and attitudes toward educated academic scientists and intellectuals. Following the death of Mao Zedong in 1976, Chinese economic reform has reopened China to exchanges with the West. We presented an overview of the impact of economic reform and concluded this chapter with a brief discussion of current challenges and opportunities in Chinese psychology, including a growing interest in psychotherapy and counseling services, developments in industrial psychology responding to China's changing economy, and the need to address China's HIV/AIDS crisis and its extremely high national suicide rate.

China currently has a population of more than a billion inhabitants presently served by a workforce of approximately 10,000 psychologists. The need to develop new undergraduate and graduate programs in psychology, to define educational standards, and to develop a certification process for counseling psychologists is critical if Chinese psychology is to serve adequately the needs of China's growing population.

■ Chapter 17—Psychology in China

Discussion Questions

- How is the relationship between the Chinese medical model and Chinese clinical psychology different from or similar to the relationship between the Western medical model and Western clinical psychology?

- In what ways could the practice of Western clinical psychology benefit from incorporation of the Chinese medical model? In what ways could Chinese clinical psychology benefit from incorporation of approaches from the Western medical model?

- What role did Jesuit missionaries play in the history of psychology in China?

- What role did Cai Yuanpei have in the Chinese education system? What effect did he have on the development of Chinese psychology?

- Why was American psychology, and the work of such individuals as John Dewey and John Watson, particularly suited to the needs of Chinese psychology prior to the 1940s?

- How is the history of psychology in China different from the history of psychology in Russia? How are they similar?

- What were the effects of the rise of Chinese communism and the Cultural Revolution upon the development of psychology in China?

- What effect has economic reform had on the development of psychology in China?

Indigenous Psychologies: Latin America, South Africa, and India-Asia

---

CHAPTER OVERVIEW

Globalization has become and will continue to be a guiding force in all aspects of life, including psychology. As people around the world become increasingly interdependent and attempt to establish common goals, the unique needs and goals of individual nations and cultures also develop and sometimes clash with the forces of globalization. Nations around the world are influenced greatly on an international level and also have to address the challenges they face at home, which arise in most part as a result of past political, economic, and social pressures.

As human beings we are all similar in our fundamental structure and physiological functions. We are comprised of a skeleton, organs and tissues, and functional systems such as the nervous or circulatory systems to achieve the primary goal of survival and subsequent procreation. Although each of us embarks on our own unique journey in fulfilling these goals, there exists a clear and distinct common thread connecting us all together. Similarly, all nations are comprised of a similar infrastructure and have political, economic, educational, religious, and social systems by which a nation achieves survival. Each nation, like a person, has past challenges that influenced its current and future states as a nation, as a people, and as an indigenous psychology.

Indigenous psychologies have developed throughout the world to address the political, economic, religious, and social needs of individuals as well as the cultures to which they belong. Although indigenous psychologies are influenced by international psychology, it is essential to understand the role they play in addressing the specific needs of a particular country and/or culture.

The major focus of this chapter is on the nature of indigenous psychologies throughout selected nations and regions that represent the population engines of the world and are continuing to emerge as dominant forces on the global stage. Special attention is given to the historical and current state of formal governmental and educational institutions as well as to the impact of social needs of the nation and culture(s) upon the field of psychology. Although the specific institutional and social influences differ between Latin American, South African, Indian, and Asian psychologies, common themes exist. In particular, there are three common themes present in each nation or region, including a shortage of resources, professional versus scientific priority for psychology, and the challenge of integrating psychology with the culture for a more complete understanding of the human **affective, behavioral**, and **cognitive** systems.

LEARNING OBJECTIVES

When you finish studying this chapter, you will be prepared to:

- Define indigenous psychologies and their components
- Describe the relationship between international and indigenous psychologies
- Discuss the key factors in the future success of indigenous psychologies
- Identify both distinctive and similar features of psychology in Latin America, South Africa, India, and Asia
- Appreciate the impact of unique political, economic, academic, and social factors on each indigenous psychology

INTRODUCTION

Indigenous psychologies have been in existence for a very long time, although not until recently have such psychologies been examined in the context of developing a global psychology. The development of indigenous psychologies is rooted in the systematic influences of formal political and educational institutions as well as social factors that have and will continue to drastically change the state of psychology.

Indigenous psychologies grow out of the basic political, economic, religious, and social components of each culture. Heelas and Lock (1981) have defined indigenous psychology as consisting of the cultural views, theories, classifications, and assumptions coupled with overarching social institutions that influence psychological topics in each respective culture. Consequently, each indigenous psychology is unique, although similar to other indigenous psychologies in its aspiration to address the forces that shape affective, behavioral, and cognitive human systems that in turn underlie the attitudes, behaviors, beliefs, expectations, and values of the members of each unique culture. Paranjpe realized in 1981 that an increasing number of Eastern and Western psychologists had recognized the importance of indigenous psychologies, and had turned to Eastern psychologies for inspiration and insight. Accordingly, global psychology embraces and is comprised of indigenous psychologies with the aspiration of a continuous unity of dissimilarities.

Indigenous psychologies are similar in that they usually include two distinct categories of psychological knowledge, namely, scientific and applied knowledge reflected in scientific and professional psychology. Each indigenous psychology prioritizes the two in a unique manner; however, trends exist between more industrialized nations such as the United States and some of the countries that we will examine in more detail throughout this chapter, including Latin American countries, South Africa, and Indian-Asian countries. These latter countries tend to focus primarily on the application of psychological knowledge to overcome the challenges facing their culture, such as strengthening education, employment, health, population control, ethnic and religious conflict, rather than allocating limited resources to expand the scientific research infrastructure of psychology in their country. Two main challenges lie along the road to achieving a successful applied psychology in each culture. The first challenge is finding adequate resources in what has historically been a predominantly understaffed and poorly funded field of study. Second, indigenous psychologies face the challenge of integrating with or molding the practice of psychology into each culture.

As we move into the future and psychology becomes more specialized, it is important to distinguish between indigenous psychologies and specialty psychologies. Specialty psychologies, for example, consist of developmental, health, organizational, and social psychology, whereas indigenous psychologies are culturally specific, pragmatic, and aspire to integrate culture with science. The hope is that the global psychological community will consider various indigenous psychologies as resources that contribute to the formation of psychologies tailored to fit each culture around the world yet linked to an evolving global psychology.

LATIN AMERICAN PSYCHOLOGY

Psychology in Latin America, which is made up of twenty-one independent nations, has progressed much more rapidly as a profession than as a science. There are many pressing social problems requiring timely solutions, and psychologists as problem solvers rather than knowledge creators are rewarded, although there is growing realization that both applied interventions and research are necessary for indigenous psychologies in Latin America in the 21st century (Salazar, 1995). Latin America is one in a long list of examples of indigenous psychologies that have been influenced by the formal institutions of government and academia as well as the social pressures evident in their respective nations. Latin America continues to feel the repercussions of the political and economic instability that began decades ago. In particular, economic instability has greatly hindered the development of psychology as a science while at the same time stimulating its development as a profession. The social pressures resulting from the strife associated with economic and political instability have restricted the resources available to psychologists while creating an immediate demand for the applied intervention of the profession. This example illustrates a phenomenon present across the majority of non-northwestern indigenous psychologies: the prioritization of professionally applied intervention to address pressing social and economic problems instead of basic research in academic or other institutional settings.

Formal Institutions

The lack of political and economic stability in Latin America over the past forty-plus years has hindered the development of psychology as a profession and a science while concurrently creating an unstable society. Although psychological practice laws had been established in countries such as Brazil (1962) and Venezuela (1978), dictatorships and persecutions lined the political horizon in the 1970s until the rise of democracies in the 1980s (Ardila, 1992). Democratic systems were a relief to these nations and specifically to the psychological community and professional organizations that witnessed not only developmental challenges under dictatorships but also the persecution of its leaders. The disappearance of the president of the Association of Psychologists of Buenos Aires; the closure of psychology courses in Uruguay; and the assassination of Ignacio Martin-Baro, a leader in developing psychology in El Salvador and throughout other Latin American countries, were just the beginning. Although the rise of democracy brought initial hope to psychologists and all citizens alike, such systems were not enough to rectify the large amounts of external national debt of multiple Latin American countries leading to further economic instability and unrest (Salazar, 1995).

Economic instability throughout Latin America served to both hinder and facilitate the professional and scientific fields of psychology. Economic instability translated into a lack of funding for bibliographic materials, research, and research training programs (Salazar, 1995). Without funding for these key resources, research psychologists faced a challenge in developing a literature infrastructure from which professional psychology could build. Thus, the deteriorating in-country working conditions and resources restricted the growth of psychology in its applied or professional and academic or research domains, creating a lack of properly trained professionals or what is commonly known as a "brain drain" (Diaz-Loving et al., 1995). The deteriorating conditions hindered the development of psychology, particularly the scientific side, due to a lack of economic resources, yet simultaneously generated a need for the professional field due to social and economic instabilities. Although some of Wilhelm Wundt's students established the first laboratories in Latin America around the late 19th century, the education and training of students did not begin until the late 1940s. Interestingly, the Interamerican Society of Psychology (ISP) was established in the early 1950s, yet it was not until the late 1950s that the majority of Latin American psychology programs were established. Since that time, the focus has been on applied professional psychology to address a variety of social problems arising from inadequate educational, employment, and medical opportunities and facilities. Latin America has seen the professional side of psychology thrive as a result of its citizens' social unrest (Salazar, 1995). Such indigenous psychologies are typical of countries in political and economic distress in that the scientific field is driven by the professional field's need for a larger body of applied research.

Social Problem Solvers

Latin American psychology has developed as a profession faster than it has as a science. In fact, the social demand for professional psychologists has in turn catalyzed and directed the need for psychology. Many Latin American psychologists have been rewarded for their efforts to meet the social demands and apply psychology to the problems on their doorstep; however, applied research is necessary to keep pace with the changing social and economic conditions of many Latin American countries.

Although Latin American psychologists are interested in a variety of general theoretical issues, as a result of limited resources and cultural demands the majority of them have focused primarily on applied studies (Salazar, 2002). Fortunately, recent developments in areas of research have been established to address some of the pressing Latin American social issues such as population control, economic development, community psychology (Freire, 1970), national psychology (Diaz-Guerrero, 1984) and child development (Recagno, 1982). Applied interventions will ultimately be enhanced from these and other lines of research, providing a more systematic method for addressing the affective, behavioral, and cognitive psychological systems of members of a particular culture.

Martin-Baro's **liberation psychology** was developed in the 19th century as an initial attempt to create a research program focused on applied issues such as urban overcrowding, land reform, and violence. Martin-Baro defined **liberation psychology** as a paradigm in which theories don't define the problems of the situation; rather, the problems demand or select their own theorization (Martin-Baro, 1989). Many nations in political, economic, religious, and otherwise cultural discord have adopted this theory, and thereby created unique indigenous psychologies.

According to Salazar (1995, 2002), although there are many challenges to overcome, the outlook for psychology in Latin America is bright, especially if psychology is grounded in the concrete realities of each of the major cultures of this region. As financial resources and human capital continue to increase, the key to a prosperous Latin American psychology is a spirit of optimism and steadfast dedication to maintaining a field focused on developing a scientific literature base from which direct applications to society's concrete reality can be derived. This approach will ultimately facilitate psychologists, both scientific and professional alike.

SOUTH AFRICAN PSYCHOLOGY

Psychology in South Africa has been strongly influenced by the nation's political turmoil, particularly over the past sixty years. Colonial, apartheid, capitalist, and patriarchal forces all influenced South African psychology, resulting in the formation of a psychology faced with many challenges. The apartheid period intentionally neglected and isolated the field of psychology so that when South Africa held its first democratic elections in 1994, the problems facing psychology as a science and profession were just beginning to be exposed (Murray, 2002).

Formal Institutions

Apartheid was the dominant social and political policy in South Africa throughout the latter half of the 20th century (1948–1994), which has influenced dramatically the country's current state. Whites began to settle in South Africa around 1652 and in the early 1900s the Boer War was sparked between two groups of whites, the British and the Dutch, when diamonds were discovered. Although the two groups shared power for a period, in 1948 the Afrikaner National Party gained power and created the system of apartheid to maintain control over the country's social, economic, and political systems. The apartheid system based upon segregation laws grew in severity over the years. Initially, prohibitions and regulations were placed on a variety of fundamental social activities and institutions such as marriages between whites and nonwhites and "white-jobs." In the later stages of apartheid, segregated citizens were required to carry pass-cards that identified them as being in one of three categories: "white," "black," and "colored." The government then required that all blacks live in African homelands, thus losing their South African citizenships and exiled from their own country! Throughout this period there were multiple uprisings, brutal murders, imprisonments, and banishments of those black South Africans fighting for equality.

As anti-apartheid pressure mounted in the early 1990s within South Africa, in addition to external pressures from the United States and Great Britain imposed by selective economic sanctions, South African president F. W. de Klerk began reluctantly to dismantle the apartheid system. Formerly banned black congressmen were legalized and imprisoned black leaders were released in 1990, and in 1994 the South African Constitution was rewritten and the first general elections were held. When Nelson Mandela was elected as South Africa's first black president in 1994, the last vestiges of the apartheid system were finally outlawed.

South African psychology during the apartheid period was dominated by these political influences, resulting in a grossly underdeveloped field at the time of the fall of apartheid. For example, today South Africa has over forty-three million people, 13.6% of whom are white, with only approximately 5,000 psychologists, 90% of whom are white (Murray, 2002). Furthermore, practicing clinical psychologists greatly outnumber research psychologists, leaving few South African psychologists capable of crafting broad-scale psychological interventions. The new post-repression democratic system has and will continue to facilitate the improvement of the psychological education system. Recruiting efforts have already begun to pull everyone, but especially blacks, into South African psychology and improve basic and applied psychological research. Efforts to extend South African psychology beyond its borders are now well underway because apartheid no longer isolates the field from international scholarship.

Shifts in Research

The first steps for South African psychology in the aftermath of apartheid were to take a more collectivist orientation, indigenous focus, rigorous scholarship, and international exchange. South African psychologists face the challenge of balancing the need to incorporate an international influence and an indigenous psychology based on South African perspectives. The changing political front influenced psychology in more ways than freeing human and financial capital resources; it also changed the subject matter of psychology. The period of apartheid focused psychology on the social construction of the black body, the early historical and legal origins of psychology, racially skewed research practices, sociocultural context of psychological testing, and the marginalization of the mentally disturbed (Seedat, 1998). Before the fall of apartheid there was limited collaboration between academic authors, the majority of whom were white (75%) males (65.5%) from British or Afrikaanas universities; this culminated in an inefficient and disjointed literature base at best (Seedat, 1998).

South Africa desperately needs psychologists to assist in overcoming the aftermath of apartheid, especially social issues such as violence, poverty, racism, and HIV/AIDS. According to Saths Cooper, past president of the Psychology Society of South Africa and the country's Professional Board for Psychology, the goal of this balanced perspective is an insight into the apartheid-wrought psychological trauma that underlies many of the country's problems (Murray, 2002). This goal calls for a move away from the exclusionary character of apartheid that supported a colonial and patriarchical psychology toward an inclusionary psychology (Seedat, 1998). The inclusionary characterization of psychology meant efforts to solve the frequently dismissed public concerns such as how to help the 30% of pregnant women in rural areas infected with HIV/AIDS, and how to shift the wealth so that 10% of people, mostly whites, do not control 80% of the riches.

The resources available to South African psychologists are limited as a result of the past apartheid constraints; however, measures are being taken to expand the number of psychologists trained to be basic researchers and field clinical psychologists. Psychologists in South Africa race to respond to the social pressures and constraints placed on the field in the apartheid aftermath. There are now multiple efforts underway to develop South African psychology as both a profession and a science.

INDIAN-ASIAN PSYCHOLOGY

Continuing our examination of indigenous psychologies around the globe, we now travel east of Africa into India and Asia. As demonstrated by both Latin American and South African psychologies, Indian-Asian psychologies suffer from a lack of resources stemming from the political and economic instability of both regions (Sinha, 1995). Both Indian and Asian, specifically Chinese, psychologies felt initial influences of European and American psychology before being shaped by their local social, religious, and philosophical pressures and beliefs. Since the British rule has receded in India and the Chinese have begun their open-door policy, the shift toward applied professional psychology versus scientific research psychology has gained momentum.

Formal Institutions

Indian-Asian psychologies have been greatly influenced by the formal institutions in which they were both cultivated and oppressed. The political landscape throughout much of India and Asia was turbulent at best. Indian-Asian psychologies were affected further by factors similar to Latin American psychologies. Some areas were affected by the lack of intellectual infrastructure as a result of scarce financial resources. The resulting impoverished sociocultural context and centralized governmental control of resources presented both challenges and opportunities to the field. At the same time that psychology was being negatively impacted by the socioeconomic repercussions of an impoverished collectivist government, the political restrictions on academic advancements were further limiting the development of the field.

Despite the government's direct impact on the development of psychology and the challenge of communicating through the region's twenty-four native languages, each with various dialects, persistence has prevailed throughout India, Pakistan, and Bangladesh (Clay, 2002). Psychology has been established in the formal academic setting since Western psychology entered through Calcutta in the early 20th century. The first Indian university psychology department was established in 1916 along with multiple psychological departments, associations, and journals (Paranjpe, 1981). Although this may appear as a fair amount of resources at first, the shortage of resources across this region was and still is very real. As recently as two years ago, India reported having seventy universities teaching psychology in a country whose population tops one billion (Clay, 2002; Dalal, 1990). Similar to India, Bangladesh suffers from a lack of resources with only two universities offering psychology programs (Begum, 1990). Furthermore, the region has neither an accreditation nor licensing system for psychology programs and practicing psychologists, respectively (Clay, 2002). Countries such as China were prevented by the government from reaping the benefits of their well-established formal educational institutions. Even when the government restored access to the universities in 1978 through the open-door policy, 210,000 Chinese scholars had already gone overseas and approximately 80% of the students have not returned to China. The 20% that do return face many challenges in working openly in what is still considered a relatively closed society (Greenberger & Johnson, 1997).

Shifts in Research

As a result of political and other social changes many Indian psychologists have cultivated an indigenous psychology born from or rooted in Indian thought and ethos while at the same time reflecting the behavioral perspective and Indian's psychologically relevant existential problems (Rao, 1988). Those with formal Western training have molded their instruction to better fit their culture, thereby integrating cultural and traditional components into their practices. For example, native psychologists have learned to place emphasis on the extended family and feeling of community as opposed to the concentration on individualism in Western cultures. Various other Indian ideas and values such as a holistic worldview, the importance of self-discipline, the transitory nature of human experience, the comprehensive human experience (analysis of all states including waking, dreaming, and sleeping), lucid consciousness, yoga, meditation, self-discovery, and belief in both spiritual and material worlds have been incorporated along with Western psychology, yielding the current indigenous Indian psychology (Auluck, 2002; Clay, 2002; Peters, 1998).

In the process of integrating immediate social needs and tradition into imported Western psychology, three central strands of psychology have developed. The strands are unique to the Asian and South Asian region and are defined by Rao (1988) to be general psychology, country- and region-specific psychology, and native-based weltanschauung psychology. General psychology is psychology that has universal relevance and application while country- and region-specific psychology develop out of the study of geographically bound persons. Finally, the native-based weltanschauung psychology is the most unique component of an indigenous psychology. This psychology is driven by the understanding of geographically bound persons yet differs from country- and region-specific psychology in its highly theoretical or philosophical component.

These three strands of psychology, in addition to the specific social topics addressed by more recent Indian-Asian psychology, demonstrate the efforts of indigenous psychology to integrate culture into an applied focus despite a lack of resources. The main requirement for psychology to survive in this region is a dedication to continued development of the applied field and a concentration on the development of a scientific literature base from which systematic interventions can be designed.

■ Summary

As we learned, cultural views, theories, and assumptions within social institutions have influenced psychological topics in each culture for centuries, yielding a variety of indigenous psychologies. An analysis of indigenous psychologies proceeded with a closer look at the historical influences, current state, and future of indigenous psychologies as influenced by the pressures of formal institutions and society at large. For example, Latin American psychology was demonstrated to be greatly influenced by its political and economic instability. These historical instabilities were then examined in terms of their long-term effects on the field of psychology as both a profession and a science. The shortage of resources and an increasing demand for applied psychology to address numerous social problems were outcomes of the instability. Subsequently, we examined the benefits and drawbacks of the rapid development of an applied psychological field without the required scientific psychology base.

This chapter continued with a similar analysis of South African psychology. The shortage of resources and the necessity for an applied focus to deal with the post-apartheid problems were identified. Indian-Asian psychologies were examined last with a particular concentration on the unique social demands and traditional culture. More so than in other countries reviewed in this chapter, the success of Indian-Asian psychologies was identified as requiring the integration of traditional cultural methodologies with international psychology. Methods such as self-discipline and meditation in conjunction with social pressures were shown to have created a unique indigenous psychology. The current and future states of Indian-Asian psychologies, as well as all other indigenous psychologies, require the sustained growth of their scientific research base at the same pace as their applied professional interventions.

■ Chapter 18—Indigenous Psychologies: Latin America, South Africa, and India-Asia

Discussion Questions

- What are some of the key characteristics of indigenous psychologies?
- How will indigenous psychologies play a key role in psychology's future?
- How has the political and economic instability in Latin America affected the professional and academic fields of psychology?

- How did the persecution of Latin American psychological leaders affect the development of the discipline?
- How was psychological research influenced by apartheid in South Africa?
- How have Indian and Asian psychologies been particularly influenced by cultural traditions?

Epilogue

In this book, we have approached the history of psychology from the perspectives of globalization, culture, and the individual. The history of psychological inquiry before the establishment of psychology as a unique and separate science and professional practice covers centuries of ideas and actions revolving around foundational questions. Some of these questions are still being addressed and expanded—revised answers are part of the present and future of psychology. Some of these questions, which we have addressed in our treatment of the history of psychology, include: What is the relationship between the mind or psychological processes and the brain? How do we learn most efficiently and effectively? What is the best way(s) to live out our individual and collective lives? How can we best address ignorance, poverty, disease, aggression, and war, the extinction of other species, and the wasteful consumption of our natural resources?

Psychology, as both a science and a profession, has evolved from philosophical and biological foundations. We identified and discussed some of the foundational ideas, events, and persons that have contributed to each of these two foundations. Each of the schools of psychology focused upon issues of subject matter, method(s) of acquiring knowledge, research findings, and applications to address some or most of the above foundational questions. Likewise, we examined how different cultures and groups of individuals constructed psychology and the barriers that they have faced, and in some cases continue to face, in the further development of psychology.

We know a lot about the affective, behavioral, and cognitive systems and their interaction in a variety of human and nonhuman species in a variety of contexts. Psychology is a noble enterprise, and fortunately, many issues remain to be addressed, meaning that history is in the hands of our readers and still has a future. Some of the issues humanity faces can benefit from a solid knowledge of the history of psychology and need to be addressed in collaboration with other sciences, professions, the arts and humanities, scholars, economists, and politicians. Such issues include the following:

■ We need to better understand the dynamics, benefits, interactions, and barriers to effective adaptation to a continuously changing world. Such an understanding should incorporate the contexts of personal, cultural, religious, spiritual, ethnic, intellectual, and scientific values and practices.

■ We need to better understand the brain, especially diseases such as Alzheimer's, Parkinson's, and Lou Gehrig's (Amyotrophic Lateral Sclerosis, ALS) diseases, as they strike more and more of the world population.

■ We need to better understand how to construct and deploy behavioral prevention and intervention strategies to deal with HIV/AIDS and similar epidemics, and other affectively, behaviorally, and cognitively based challenges to health and well-being.

■ We need to better understand the conditions that lead to aggression, war, and terrorism to find more humane and productive ways to resolve conflict at the individual and collective levels.

443

- We need to better modulate the greed of the few and the misery of the many in developed and emerging sectors of the world.
- We need to better understand and regulate population growth and consumption to promote the well-being of people, other creatures, and the natural resources that we all seem to take for granted.
- We need to better understand human strengths and virtues to promote the further development of healthy and effective individuals and communities.

The above list is intended only to be suggestive; there are many other challenges before all of us. We hope this book assists in some manner those individuals who address these and other issues now and in the future. Please feel free to contact us regarding any question or comment you have about our book at **robert.lawson@uvm.edu.**

References

Abir-Am, P. G., & Outram, D. (1987). *Uneasy careers and intimate lives: Women in science (1789–1979).* New Brunswick, NJ: Rutgers University Press.

Achterberg, J. (1991). *Woman as healer.* Boston, MA: Shambhala.

Adair, J. G. (1995). The research environment in developing countries. Contributions to national development of the discipline. *International Journal of Psychology, 30,* 643–662.

Adair, J. G., Pandley, J., Begum, H. A., Puhan, B. N., & Vohra, N. (1995). Indigenization and development of the discipline: Perceptions and emotions of Indian and Bangladesh psychologists. *Journal of Cross-Cultural Psychology, 26,* 392–407.

Aiton, E. J. (1985). *Leibniz: A biography.* Boston: Adam Hilger.

Albee, G. W. (1959). *Mental health manpower trends.* New York: Basic Books.

Albee, G. W. (1970). The uncertain future of clinical psychology. *American Psychologist, 25,* 1071–1080.

Albee, G. W. (1990). The futility of psychotherapy. *The Journal of Mind and Behavior, 11,* 369–384.

Albee, G. W. (1998). Fifty years of clinical psychology: Selling our soul to the devil. *Applied and Preventive Psychology, 7,* 189–194.

Albee, G. W. (2000). The Boulder model's fatal flaw. *American Psychologist, 55,* 247–248.

Alexander, F. G., & Selesnick, S. T. (1966). *The history of psychiatry: An evaluation of psychiatric thought and practice from prehistoric times to the present.* New York: Harper & Row.

Allport, G. (1967). Autobiography. In E. G. Boring & G. Lindzey (Eds.), *A history of psychology in autobiography* (Vol. 5, pp. 1–25). New York: Appleton-Century-Crofts.

Allport, G. (1968). The genius of Kurt Lewin. In G. Allport (Ed.), *The person in psychology: Selected essays* (pp. 360–370). Boston: Beacon Press.

Altman, I., & Taylor, D. A. (1973). *Social penetration: The development of interpersonal relationships.* New York: Holt, Rinehart and Winston.

American Psychological Association. (1992). Evelyn Hooker. *American Psychologist, 47*(4), 501–503.

American Psychological Association. (1995). APA–accredited doctoral programs in professional psychology: 1995. *American Psychologist, 50,* 1069–1080.

American Psychological Association. (1997). Award for distinguished contribution to research in public policy: Stanley Sue. *American Psychologist, 52*(4), 351–353.

American Psychological Association. (2002). Norman B. Anderson named next CEO of the American Psychological Association. *APA Press Release, September 10, 2002.* Retrieved August 25, 2003, from http://www.apa.org/releases/anderson.html.

American Psychological Association. (2002b). AAPA marks 30 years. [Electronic version]. *Monitor on Psychology, 33*(7).

American Psychological Association. (2004). *APA membership statistics: 2004.* Retrieved June 7, 2004, from http//www5.apa.org/membership/memstat.cfm.

American Psychological Association. (2004a). Gold Medal Award for Life Achievement in the Science of Psychology: Janet Taylor Spence. *American Psychologist, 59,* 361–363.

American Psychological Association. (2004b). Gold Medal Award for Life Achievement in Psychology in the Public Interest: Florence L. Denmark. *American Psychologist, 59,* 358–360.

American Psychological Association Research Office. (2000). *Profiles of APA membership.* Retrieved August 26, 2003, from http://research.apa.org/2000profiles.pdf.

Anastasi, A. (1937). *Differential psychology.* New York: Macmillan.

Anastasi, A. (1954). *Psychological testing.* New York: Macmillan.

Anastasi, A. (1964). *Fields of applied psychology.* New York: McGraw-Hill.

Anastasi, A. (1965). *Individual differences.* New York: Wiley.

Anastasi, A. (1972). Reminiscences of a differential psychologist. In T.S. Krawiec (Ed.), *The Psychologists: Volume 1* (pp. 3–39). New York: Oxford University Press.

Anderson, N. (2002). A conversation with Norman Anderson. [Electronic version]. *Monitor on Psychology, 33*(9).

Anderson, W. (Ed.). (1996). *The Fontana postmodernism reader*. London: Fontana Press.

Angell, J. R. (1907). The province of functional psychology. *Psychological Review, 14*, 61–71.

Antonuccio, D., Danton, W. G., & DeNelsky, G. Y. (1995). Psychotherapy vs. medication for depression: Challenging the conventional wisdom. *Professional Psychology: Research and Practice, 26*, 574–585.

Appadurai, A. (1990). Disjuncture and difference in the global cultural economy. *Public Culture, 2*, 1–24.

Ardila, R. (1992). Columbia. In V. Staudt-Sexton & J. D. Hogan (Eds.), *International psychology: Views from around the world*. Lincoln: University of Nebraska Press.

Arnett, J. J. (2002). The psychology of globalization. *American Psychologist, 57*, 774–783.

Arnheim, R. (1969). *Visual thinking*. Berkeley: University of California Press.

Arnheim, R. (1974). *Art and visual perception*. Berkeley: University of California Press.

Arnheim, R. (1986). The trouble with wholes and parts. *New Ideas in Psychology, 4*, 281–284.

Ash, M. G. (1998). *Gestalt psychology in German culture, 1890–1967: Holism and the quest for objectivity*. Cambridge, UK: Cambridge University Press.

Asher, L. M., Barber, T. X., & Spanos, N. P. (1972). Two attempts to replicate the Parrish-Lundy-Leibowitz experiment on hypnotic age regression. *American Journal of Clinical Hypnosis, 14*, 178–183.

Asian American Psychological Association. (2003). *A brief history of AAPA*. Retrieved August 2, 2003, from http://www.west.asu.edu/aapa/HISTORY.HTM.

Attneave, C. (1990). A maverick finds an identity. In F. Kaslow (Ed.), *Voices in family psychology* (Vol. I). Newbury Park, CA: Sage Publications.

Auluck, S. (2002). Psychology in Indian philosophical thought. *Journal of Indian Psychology, 20*, 13–22.

Baddeley, A. (1990). *Human memory: Theory and practice*. Boston: Allyn & Bacon.

Bakan, D. (1966). The influence of phrenology on American psychology. *Journal of the History of the Behavioral Sciences, 2*, 200–220.

Bakan, D. (1969). *On method: Toward a reconstruction of psychological investigation*. San Francisco: Jossey-Bass.

Baker, D. B., & Benjamin, L.T. Jr. (2000). The affirmation of the scientist-practitioner: A look back at Boulder. *American Psychologist, 55*, 241–247.

Baldwin, J. W. (1971). *The scholastic culture of the middle ages: 1000–1300*. Lexington, MA: D. C. Heath & Company.

Bandura, A. (1973). *Aggression: A social learning analysis*. Englewood Cliffs, NJ: Prentice-Hall.

Bandura, A. (1982). Self-efficacy mechanisms in human agency. *American Psychologist, 37*, 122–147.

Bandura, A. (1986). *Social foundations of thought and action*. Englewood Cliffs, NJ: Prentice-Hall.

Bandura, A. (1997). *Self-efficacy: The exercise of control*. New York: W. H. Freeman.

Barber, T. X. (1969). *Hypnosis: A scientific approach*. New York: Van Nostrand Reinhold.

Bass, E., & Davis, L. (1988). *The courage to heal*. New York: Harper & Row.

Bass, E., & Thornton, L. (1991). *I never told anyone: Writings by women survivors of child sexual abuse*. New York: Harper Perennial.

Baudrillard, J. (1983). *Simulations*. New York: Semiotext (e).

Baumeister, R. F. (1987). How the self became a problem: A psychological review of historical research. *Journal of Personality and Social Psychology, 52*, 163–176.

Bayton, J. A. (1975). Francis Sumner, Max Meenes, and the training of Black psychologists. *American Psychologist, 30*, 185–186.

Beatty, J. (1994). Language and communication. In L. L. Adler & U. P. Gielen (Eds.), *Handbook of cross-cultural psychology: Vol. 2. Methodology* (pp. 41–51). Westport: Praeger.

Begum, H. A. (1990). Bangladesh. In G. Shouksmith & E. A. Shouksmith (Eds.), *Special report in teaching in eleven countries* (pp. 43–85). Bangkok: UNESCO.

Bell, C. (1965). Bell on the specificity of sensory nerves. 1811. In R. J. Herrnstein & E. G. Boring (Eds.), *A sourcebook in the history of psychology* (pp. 23–26). Cambridge, MA: Harvard University Press. (Original work published 1811).

Bem, S. L. (1993). *Lenses of gender: Transforming the debate on sexual inequality*. New Haven, Conn.: Yale University Press.

Bem, S. L. (1999). *Transforming the debate on sexual inequality: From biological difference to institutionalized androcentrism*. [Online]. Available at: http://www.spsp.clarion.edu/topss/tptn7052.htm.

Benjamin, L. T., Jr. (1993). *A history of psychology in letters*. Dubuque, IA: Brown & Benchmark.

Benjamin, L. T., Jr. (1996). Introduction: Lightner Witmer's legacy to American psychology. *American Psychologist, 51*, 235–236.

Benjamin, L. T., Jr. (1997). The origin of psychological species: History of the beginnings of American Psychological Association Divisions. *American Psychologist, 52*, 725–732.

Benjamin, L. T., Jr., & Baker, D. B. (2000). Boulder at 50: Introduction to the Section. *American Psychologist, 55*, 233–236.

Benjamin, L. T., & Crouse, E. M. (2002). The American Psychological Association's response to *Brown v. Board of Education. American Psychologist, 57*(1), 38–50.

Benjamin, L. T., Jr., Durkin, M., Link, M., Vestal, M., & Accord, J. (1992). Wundt's American doctoral students. *American Psychologist, 47*, 123–131.

Berling, J. A. (1982). Asian religions. [Electronic version]. *Focus on Asian Studies, 2*(1), 5–7.

Bernal, G. (1985). A history of psychology in Cuba. *Journal of Community Psychology, 13*, 222–234.

Bernal, M., & Castro, F. (1994). Are clinical psychologists prepared for service and research with ethnic minorities? *American Psychologist, 49*, 797–805.

Bernard, W. (1972). Spinoza's influence on the rise of scientific psychology: A neglected chapter in the history of psychology. *Journal of the History of the Behavioral Sciences, 8*, 208–215.

Berry, J. W. (1980). Introduction to methodology. In H. C. Triandis & J. W. Berry (Eds.), *Handbook of cross-cultural psychology: Vol. 2. Methodology* (pp. 1–28). Boston: Allyn & Bacon.

Berry, J. W., Poortinga, Y. H., Segall, M. H., & Dasen, P. R. (1992). *Cross-cultural psychology: Research and applications.* Cambridge, England: Cambridge University Press.

Beutler, L. E., Williams, R. E., Wakefield, P. J., & Entwistle, S. R. (1995). Bridging scientists and practitioner perspectives in clinical psychology. *American Psychologist, 50*, 984–994.

Birch, H. G. (1945). The relation of previous experience to insightful problem-solving. *Journal of Comparative Psychology, 38*, 367–383.

Bjork, R. A., & Bjork, E. L. (1988). On adaptive aspects of retrieval failure in autobiographical memory. In M. M. Gruneberg, P. E. Morris, & R. N. Sykes (Eds.), *Practical aspects of memory: Current research and issues* (Vol. 1, pp. 283–288). Chichester, England: Wiley.

Blatz, W. E. (1966). *Human security: Some reflections.* Toronto, Canada: University of Toronto Press.

Blowers, G. H. (1996). The prospects for a Chinese psychology. In M. H. Bond, (Ed.), *The handbook of Chinese psychology* (pp. 1–14). Hong Kong: Oxford University Press.

Blume, E. S. (1990). *Secret survivors: Uncovering incest and its after effects in women.* New York: Ballantine.

Blumenthal, A. L. (1975). A reappraisal of Wilhelm Wundt. *American Psychologist, 30*, 1081–1086.

Bodeen, C. (2002, December 1). Dire warning on AIDS gains credence in China. *The Burlington Free Press*, p. 11A.

Boeree, C. G. (1997a). *Erich Fromm: 1900–1980.* [Online]. Available at: http://www.ship.edu/~cgboeree/fromm.html.

Boeree, C. G. (1997b). *Abraham Maslow: 1908–1970.* [Online]. Available at: http://www.ship.edu/~cgboeree/maslow.html.

Boeree, C. G. (1998). *Rollo May: 1909–1994.* [Online]. Available at: http://www.ship.edu/~cgboeree/may.html.

Boeree, C. G. (2002). *Carl Rogers: 1902–1987.* [Online]. Available at: http://www.ship.edu/~cgboeree/rogers.html.

Bond, M. H. (Ed.). (1996). *The handbook of Chinese psychology.* Hong Kong: Oxford University Press.

Boorstin, D. J. (1998). *The seekers.* New York: Random House.

Boring, E. G. (1934). Seven psychologies. *American Journal of Psychology, 46*, 157–159.

Boring, E. G. (1942). *Sensation and perception in the history of experimental psychology.* New York: Appleton-Century-Crofts.

Boring, E. G. (1957). *A history of experimental psychology.* New York: Appleton-Century-Crofts.

Bouton, M. E. (2002). Context, ambiguity, and unlearning: Sources of relapse after behavioral extinction. *Biological Psychiatry, 51*, 976–986.

Bouton, M. E., Mineka, S., & Barlow, D. H. (2001). A modern learning theory perspective on the etiology of panic disorder. *Psychological Review, 108*, 4–32.

Bower, G. H., & Spence, J. T. (Eds.). (1969). *The psychology of learning and motivation* (Vol. 3). New York: Academic Press.

Bower, G. H. (1993). The fragmentation of psychology? *American Psychologist, 48*, 905–907.

Bowers, K. S. (1966). Hypnotic behavior: The differentiation of trance and demand characteristic variables. *Journal of Abnormal Psychology, 71*, 42–51.

Bowers, K. S. (1992). Imagination and disassociation in hypnotic responding. *International Journal of Clinical and Experimental Hypnosis, 40*, 253–275.

Bowers, K. S., & Davidson, T. M. (1991). A neodissociative critique of Spanos's social-psychological model of hypnosis. In S. J. Lynn I. & J. W. Rhue (Eds.), *Theories of hypnosis: Current models and perspectives* (pp. 105–143). New York: Guilford Press.

Bowie, F., & Davies, O. (1990). *Hildegard of Bingen: An anthology.* London, UK: SPCK.

Breasted, J. H. (1930). *The Edwin Smith surgical papyrus.* Chicago: University of Chicago Press.

Breger, L. (2000). *Freud: Darkness in the midst of vision.* New York: John Wiley & Sons.

Brentano, F. (1874). *Psychology from an empirical standpoint.* Leipzig, Germany: Duncker & Humbolt.

Bretherton, I. (1992). The origins of attachment theory: John Bowlby and Mary Ainsworth. *Developmental Psychology, 28*(5), 759–775.

Brett, G. S. (1965). *A history of psychology* (2nd rev. ed.). (Edited and abridged by R. S. Peters). Cambridge, MA: MIT Press.

Bringmann, W. G., Balance, W. D. G., & Evans, R. B. (1975). Wilhelm Wundt 1832–1910: A brief biographical sketch. *Journal of the History of the Behavioral Sciences, 11,* 287–297.

Bringmann, W. G., Bringmann, M. W., & Early, C. E. (1992). G. Stanley Hall and the history of psychology. *American Psychologist, 47,* 281–289.

Bringmann, W. G., & Tweney, R. D. (Eds.). (1980). *Wundt studies: A centennial collection.* Toronto: C. J. Hogrefe.

Broca, P. (1965). Paul Broca (1824–1880) on the speech center, 1861. In R. J. Herrnstein & E. G. Boring (Eds.), *A sourcebook in the history of psychology* (pp. 223–229). Cambridge, MA: Harvard University Press. (Original work published 1861).

Brogden, W. J. (1939). Sensory pre-conditioning. *Journal of Experimental Psychology, 25,* 323–332.

Brogden, W. J. (1947). Sensory pre-conditioning with human subjects. *Journal of Experimental Psychology, 37,* 527–540.

Bronstein, P. (1988). Personality from a sociocultural perspective. In P. Bronstein & K. Quina (Eds.), *Teaching a psychology of people: Resources for gender and sociocultural awareness* (pp. 60–68). Washington, DC: American Psychological Association.

Brooks, D. (2001, April). The organization kid. *The Atlantic Monthly, 287,* 40–54.

Brown, J. F. (1929). The methods of Kurt Lewin in the psychology of action and affection. *Psychological Review, 36,* 200–221.

Bruhn, A. R. (1990). *Earliest childhood memories: Vol. 1. Theory and application to clinical practice.* New York: Praeger.

Brush, S. G. (1974). Should the history of science be rated X? *Science, 183,* 1164–1172.

Bryson, R. B., Bryson, J. B., Licht, M. H., & Licht, B. G. (1976). The professional pair: Husband and wife psychologists. *American Psychologist, 31,* 10–16.

Buckley, K. W. (1989). *Mechanical man: John Broadus Watson and the beginnings of behaviorism.* New York: John Wiley.

Buhle, M. J. (1998). *Feminism and its discontents: A century of struggle with psychoanalysis.* Cambridge, Mass.: Harvard University Press.

Burbles, N. C., & Rice, S. (1991). Dialogue across differences: Continuing the conversation. *Harvard Educational Review, 61,* 393–416.

Burnham, J. C. (1968). *Psychoanalysis and American Medicine, 1894–1918: Medicine, science, and culture.* New York: International Universities Press.

Calkins, M. W. (1892). A suggested classification of cases of association. *Philosophical Review, I* (4s), 411–412.

Calkins, M. W. (1909). *A first book in psychology.* New York: Macmillan.

Calkins, M. W. (1916/1901). *An introduction to psychology.* New York: Macmillan Company.

Calkins, M. W. (1930). In C. Murchison (Ed.), *History of psychology in autobiography* (Vol. 1). Worcester, MA: Clark University Press.

Caporael, L. R. (1976). Ergotism. *Science, 192,* 21–26.

Carr, H. A. (1925). *Psychology: A study of mental activity.* New York: Longmans, Green.

Carveth, D. (2002). *Winnicott's theories.* [Online]. Available at: http://www.yorku.ca/dcarveth/Fairbairn.htm.

Cassius Felix. (1879/447). *De medicina: Ex graecis logicae sectae autoribus liber, translatus sub Artabure et Calepio consulibus.* Lipsiae, in aedibus B. G. Teubneri.

Cattell, J. M. (1890). Mental tests and measurements. *Mind, 15,* 373–381.

Cha, J. H. (1987). Psychology in Korea. In G. H. Blowers & A. M. Turtle (Eds.), *Psychology moving East: Status of Western psychology in Asia and Oceania.* Boulder, CO: Westview Press.

Chan, W. (1967). *Confucius.* In P. Edwards (Ed.), *Encyclopedia of philosophy* (Vol. 2). New York: Macmillan and Free Press.

Chaplin, J. P., & Krawiec, T. S. (1960). *Systems and theories of psychology.* New York: Holt, Rineheart and Winston.

Charcot, J. M. (1889). *Clinical lectures on the diseases of the nervous system* (T. Savill, Trans.). London: New Sydenham Society (Original work published 1887).

Chaves, J. F. (1994). Hypnosis: The struggle for a definition. *Contemporary Hypnosis, 11,* 145–146.

Chelpanov, G. I. (1901). On the relation of psychology to philosophy. *The Issues of Philosophy and Psychology, 89,* 309–323.

Chernikoff, R., & Brogden, W. J. (1949). The effect of instructions upon sensory pre-conditioning of human subjects. *Journal of Experimental Psychology, 39,* 200–207.

Cheung, F. M. C. (1986). Psychopathology among Chinese people. In M. H. Bond (Ed.), *The psychology of the Chinese people.* Hong Kong: Oxford University Press.

Clark, E. (1972). Eduard Hitzig. In C. C. Gillispie (Ed.), *Dictionary of scientific biography* (Vol. 6, pp. 440–441). New York: Scribner.

Clark, K. B. (1989). *Prejudice and your child* (3rd ed.). Middletown, CT: Wesleyan University Press.

Clay, R. A. (2002a). Psychology around the world: "Seizing an opportunity" for development Chinese psychology moves from "pseudoscience" to an increasingly accepted field. *APA Monitor, 33*(3), [Online]. Available at: http://www.apa.org/monitor/mar02/seizing.html

Clay, R. A. (2002b). Psychologists in India blend Indian traditions and Western psychology. *APA Monitor, 33*(5), [Online]. Available at: http://www.apa.org/monitor/may02/india.html

Cohen, I. B. (1985). *Revolution in science.* Cambridge, MA: Belknap Press.

Cohen, S., Doyle, W. J., Skoner, D. P., Fireman, P., Gwaltney, J. M., & Newsom, J. T. (1995). State and trait negative affect as predictors of objective and subjective symptoms of respiratory viral infections. *Journal of Personality and Social Psychology, 68,* 159–169.

Cohen, S., & Rodriguez, M. S. (1995). Pathways linking affective disturbances and physical disorders. *Health Psychology, 14,* 374–380.

Colby, A., & Damon, W. (1983). Listening to a different voice: A review of Gilligan's *In a Different Voice. Merrill-Palmer Quarterly, 29,* 473–481.

Cole, M., & Maltzman, I. (1969). *A handbook of contemporary soviet psychology.* New York: Basic Books.

Condon, R. G. (1988). *Inuit youth: Growth and change in the Canadian Arctic.* New Brunswick, NJ: Rutgers University Press.

Confucius. (1979). *The Analects* (D. C. Lau, Trans.). New York: Penguin Books.

Consumer Reports (1995, November). Mental health: Does therapy help? pp. 734–739.

Coon, D. J. (1992). Testing the limits of sense and science. American experimental psychologists combat spiritualism, 1880–1920. *American Psychologist, 47,* 143–151.

Coplestone, F. (1962). *A history of philosophy. Vol. 2: Medieval philosophy,* part II. New York: Image Books.

Cornford, F. M. (1957). *From religion to philosophy: A study of the origins of Western speculation.* New York: Oxford University Press.

Craig, A. M., Graham, W. A., Kagan, D., Ozment, S., & Turner, F. M. (1994). *The heritage of world civilizations* (3rd ed.). New York: Macmillan.

Craik, F. I. M., & Lockhart, R. S. (1972). Levels of processing: A framework for memory research. *Journal of Cerebral Learning and Verbal Behavior, 11,* 671–684.

Crewsdon, J. (1988). *By silence betrayed: Sexual abuse of children in America.* Boston: Little, Brown.

Crooks, R., & Baur, K. (1990). *Our sexuality.* Redwood City, CA: Benjamin/Cummings.

Crutchfield, R. S. (1961). Edward Chace Tolman: 1886–1959. *American Journal of Psychology, 74,* 135–141.

Cunningham, S. (1985). Humanists celebrate gains, goals. *APA Monitor,* May, pp. 16, 18.

Cushman, P. (1992). Psychotherapy to 1992: A historically situated interpretation. In D. K. Freedheim (Ed.), *History of psychotherapy: A century of change* (pp. 21–64). Washington, DC: American Psychological Association.

Dalal, A. K. (1990). India: Psychology in Asia and Pacific. In G. Schouksmith & E. A. Schouksmith (Eds.), *Special report on teaching in eleven countries.* Bangkok: UNESCO.

Dallenbach, K. M. (1955). Phrenology versus psychoanalysis. *American Journal of Psychology, 48,* 511–525.

Damasio, A. R. (1999). *The feeling of what happens.* New York: Harcourt.

Damasio, A. R., & Grosset, P. D. (1995). *Descartes error: Emotion, reason, and the human brain.* New York: William Morrow and Company.

Dana, R. H. (1993). *Multicultural assessment perspectives for professional psychology.* Boston: Allyn & Bacon.

Danziger, K. (1985). The origins of the psychological experiment as a social institution. *American Psychologist, 40,* 133–140.

Darwin, C. (1874). *The descent of man.* London: Penguin Books.

Darwin, C. (1899). *On the origin of species* (6th ed.). New York: Anchor. (Original work published 1859).

Darwin, C. (1962a). *On the origin of species by means of natural selection, or the preservation of favoured races in the struggle for life.* New York: Collier Books. (Original work published 1859).

Darwin, C. (1962b). *The voyage of the* Beagle (L. Engel, Ed.). New York: Anchor. (Original work published 1939).

Davies, J. (1955). *Phrenology, fad, and science; a 19th century American crusade.* New Haven, CT: Yale University Press.

Davis, A. P. (1936). The Negro professor. *The Crisis* (April), 103–104.

De Beer, G. (1971). Darwin. In C. C. Gillispie (Ed.), *Dictionary of scientific biography.* New York: Charles Scribner's Sons.

De Bernieres, L. (1994). *Captain Corelli's mandolin.* New York: Pantheon Books.

Decker, H. S. (1971). The medical reception of psycho-analysis in Germany, 1894–1907: Three brief studies. *Bulletin of History of Medicine, 45,* 461–481.

DeFord, M. A. (1948). *Psychologist unretired: The life pattern of Lillien J. Martin.* California: Stanford University Press.

DeLeon, P. H., Sammons, M. T., & Sexton, J. L. (1995). Focusing on society's real needs: Responsibility and prescription privileges? *American Psychologist, 50,* 1022–1032.

DeLeon, P. H., & Wiggins, J. G., Jr. (1996). Prescription privileges for psychologists. *American Psychologist, 51,* 225–229.

Delprato, D. J., & Midgley, B. D. (1992). Some fundamentals of B. F. Skinner's behaviorism. *American Psychologist, 47,* 1507–1520.

DeNelsky, G. Y. (1991). Prescription privileges for psychologists: The case against. *Professional Psychology: Research and Practice, 22,* 188–193.

DeNelsky, G. Y. (1996). The case against prescription privileges for psychologists. *American Psychologist, 51,* 207–212.

Denmark, F. L. & Unger, R. K. (Eds.). (1975). *Woman, dependent or independent variable?* New York: Psychological Dimensions.

Denmark, F. L. & Paludi, M. A. (Eds.). (1993). *Psychology of women: A handbook of issues and theories.* Westport, Conn.: Greenwood Press.

Denmark, F. L. (1995). Feminist and activist. *Women & Therapy, 17* (1/2), 163–169.

Dennis, P. M. (1991). Psychology's first publicist: H. Addington Bruce and the popularization of the subconscious and the power of suggestion before World War I. *Psychological Reports, 68,* 755–765.

Derrida, J. (1976). *Of grammathology.* Baltimore, MD: Johns Hopkins University Press.

Descartes, R. (1985). *Treatise on man* (John Cottingham, Robert Stoothoff, & Dugald Murdoch, Trans.) *The philosophical writings of Descartes* (Vol. 1). Cambridge, England: Cambridge University Press. (Original work published 1664).

Desmond, A., & Moore, J. (1991). *Darwin: The life of a tortured evolutionist.* New York: W. W. Norton.

Dewey, J. (1886). *Psychology.* New York: Harper & Brothers.

Dewey, J. (1896). The reflex arc concept in psychology. *Psychological Review, 3,* 357–370.

Dewey, J. (1899). *The school and society.* Chicago: The University of Chicago Press.

Dewsbury, D. A. (1997). On the evolution of divisions. *American Psychologist, 52,* 733–741.

Dey, E. L., Astin, A. W., & Korn, W. S. (1991). *The American freshman: Twenty-five year trends, 1966–1990.* Los Angeles: Higher Education Research Institute, University of California, Los Angeles.

Diamond, S. (1977). Francis Galton and American psychology. *Annals of the New York Academy of Sciences, 291,* 47–55.

Diaz-Guerrero, R. (1984). *Psicologia del Mexicano* (4th Edn.). Mexico: Trillas.

Diaz-Loving, R., Reyes-Lagunes, I., & Diaz-Guerrero, R. (1995). Some cultural facilitators and deterrents for the development of psychology: The role of graduate research training. *International Journal of Psychology, 30,* 681–692.

Diehl, L. A. (1986). The paradox of G. Stanley Hall: Foe of coeducation and educator of women. *American Psychologist, 41,* 868–878.

Dix, D. (1824). *Conversations on common things.* New York: Munroe & Frances Inc.

Dixon, M., & Laurence, J. (1992). Two hundred years of hypnosis research: Questions resolved? Questions unanswered! In E. Framm & M. Nash (Eds.), *Contem-porary hypnosis research* (pp. 34–66). New York: Guilford Press.

Duijker, H. C. J., & van Rijswijk, M. J. (1975). *Trilingual psychological dictionary.* Bern, Switzerland: Hans Huber.

Duncan, J., Seitz, R. J., Kolodny, J., Bor, D., Herzog, H., Ahmed, A., Newell, F. N., & Emslie, H. A. (2000). Neural basis for general intelligence. *Science, 289,* 457–460.

Eagle, M. N., & Wolitzky, D. L. (1992). Psychoanalytic theories of psychotherapy. In D. K. Freedheim (Ed.), *History of psychotherapy: A century of change* (pp. 21–64). Washington, DC: American Psychological Association.

Ebbinghaus, H. (1908). *Abriss des psychologie [A summary of psychology].* Leipzig, Germany: Veit.

Eden, D. (1984). Self-fulfilling prophecy as a management tool: Harnessing Pygmalion. *Academy of Management Review, 9,* 64–73.

Edwards, D. L. (1991). A meta-analysis of the effects of meditation and hypnosis on measures of anxiety (Doctoral dissertation, Texas A & M University, 1990). *Dissertation Abstracts International, 52,* 1039B.

Ellenberger, H. F. (1970). *The discovery of the unconscious: The history and evolution of dynamic psychiatry.* New York: Basic Books.

Ellenberger, H. F. (1972). The story of Anna O.: A critical review with new data. *Journal of the History of the Behavioral Sciences, 8,* 267–279.

Elliott, M. H. (1928). The effect of change of reward on the maze performance of rats. *University of California Publications in Psychology, 4,* 19–30.

Ellis, H. (1934). Man and woman, a study of secondary and tertiary sexual characteristics (8th rev. ed.). London: Heinemann.

Erikson, E. (1942). Hitler's imagery and German youth. *Psychiatry, 5,* 475–493.

Erikson, E. (1969). *Gandhi's truth: On the origins of militant nonviolence.* New York: Norton.

Erikson, E. (1986). *Vital involvement in old age.* New York/London: W. W. Norton.

Estes, R. E., Coston, M. L., & Fournet, G. P. (1990). *Rankings of the most notable psychologists by department chairpersons.* Unpublished manuscript.

Evans, J., Hsieh, P. P., & Robinson, D. H. (2005, September). Women's involvement in education psychology journals from 1976 to 2004. *Educational Psychology Review, 17* (3), 263–271.

Evans, R. B., Sexton, U. S., & Cadwallader, T. C. (1992). *The American Psychological Association: A historical perspective.* Washington, DC: American Psychological Association.

Fagan, T. K. (1996). Witmer's contributions to school psychological services. *American Psychologist, 51,* 241–243.

Fairbairn, W. R. D. (1953). *Psychoanalytic studies of the personality.* London: Tavistock Publications Ltd.

Fancher, R. E. (1996). *Pioneers of psychology* (3rd ed.). New York: W.W. Norton & Company.

Farazmand, A. (1999). Globalization and public administration. *Public Administration Review, 59,* 509–522.

Fearing, F. (1930). *Reflex action: A study in the history of physiological psychology.* New York: Hafner.

Featherstone, M. (1990). *Global culture: Nationalism, globalization, and modernity.* London: Sage Publications.

Fechner, G. (1966). *Elements of psychophysics* (Helmut E. Adler, Trans., Davis H. Howes & Edwin G. Boring, Eds.). New York: Holt, Rinehart and Winston. (Original work published 1860).

Fechner, G. T. (1906). *Zend Avesta* (3rd ed.). Leipzig, Germany: Voss. (Original work published 1851).

Ferguson, G. O. (1916). *The psychology of the Negro: An experimental study.* New York: Science Press.

Ferris, P. (1997). *Dr. Freud: A life.* Washington, DC: Counterpoint.

Fish, S. (1996, May 21). Professor Sokal's bad joke. *New York Times,* p. A23.

Flanagan, S. (1998). Hildegard of Bingen: A visionary life. (2nd ed.). London: Routledge.

Flynn, J. R. (1999). Searching for justice: The discovery of IQ gains over time. *American Psychologist, 54,* 5–20.

Foucault, M. (1979). *Discipline and punish: The birth of the prison.* New York: Random House.

Foucault, M. (1980). *The history of sexuality: Vol. 1. An Introduction.* New York: Random House.

Franks, C. M. (Ed.). (1969). *Behavior therapy: Appraisal and status.* New York: McGraw-Hill.

Fredrickson, B. L. (1998). What good are positive emotions? *Review of General Psychology, 2,* 300–319.

Fredrickson, B. L. (2001). The role of positive emotions in positive psychology: The broaden-and-build theory of positive emotions. *American Psychologist, 56,* 218–226.

Freedheim, D. K. (Ed.). (1992). *History of psychotherapy.* Washington, DC: American Psychological Association.

Freeman, F. S. (1977). The beginnings of Gestalt psychology in the United States. *Journal of the History of the Behavioral Sciences, 13,* 352–353.

Freire, P. (1970). *Pedagogy of the oppressed.* New York: Seabury.

Freud, A. (1922). Beating fantasies and daydreams. In *The writings of Anna Freud,* Vol. 1, pp. 137–157. New York: International Universities Press.

Freud, A. (1928). *Introduction to the technique of child analysis* (L. P. Clark, Trans.). New York: The Nervous and Mental Disease Publishing Company.

Freud, S. (1895). Studies on hysteria. [with J. Breuer]. In J. Strachey (Ed. and Trans.), *The standard edition of the complete psychological works of Sigmund Freud,* Vol. 2. London: Hogarth Press.

Freud, S. (1900). The interpretation of dreams. In J. Strachey (Ed. and Trans.), *The standard edition of the complete psychological works of Sigmund Freud,* Vols. 4–5. London: Hogarth Press.

Freud, S. (1904). The psychopathology of everyday life. In J. Strachey (Ed. and Trans.), *The standard edition of the complete psychological works of Sigmund Freud,* Vol. 6. London: Hogarth Press.

Freud, S. (1908). "Civilized" sexual morality and modern nervous illness. In J. Strachey (Ed. and Trans.), *The standard edition of the complete psychological works of Sigmund Freud,* Vol. 9, pp. 179–204. London: Hogarth Press.

Freud, S. (1914). On the history of the psychoanalytic movement. In R. M. Lowenstein (Ed.), *The standard edition of the complete psychological works of Sigmund Freud,* Vol. 14, pp. 1–66.

Freud, S. (1919). A child is being beaten: the origin of sexual perversions. In J. Strachey (Ed. and Trans.), *The standard edition of the complete psychological works of Sigmund Freud,* Vol. 17, pp. 179–204. London: Hogarth Press.

Freud, S. (1925). Some psychical consequences of the anatomical distinction between the sexes. In J.Strachey (Ed. and Trans.), *The standard edition of the complete psychological works of Sigmund Freud*, Vol. 19, pp. 243–258. London: Hogarth Press.

Freud, S. (1926). The question of lay analysis. (From *The standard edition of the complete psychological works of Sigmund Freud*, James Strachey, Ed. and Trans.). London: Hogarth Press.

Freud, S. (1931). Female sexuality. In J.Strachey (Ed. and Trans.), *The standard edition of the complete psychological works of Sigmund Freud*, Vol. 21, pp. 225–243. London: Hogarth Press.

Freud, S. (1954). *The origins of psychoanalysis: Letters to Wilhelm Fliess, drafts and notes: 1887–1902*. New York: Basic Books.

Freud, S., & Breuer, J. (2000). *Studies on hysteria* (reprint, originally published in 1895). New York: Basic Books.

Frolov, Y. P. (1938). *Pavlov and his school*. London: Kegan, Paul, Trench, Trubner.

Fromm, E. (1941). *Escape from freedom*. New York: Avon.

Fromm, E. (1955). *The sane society*. Greenwich, CT: Fawcett.

Fromm, E. (1962). *Beyond the chains of illusion: My encounter with Freud and Marx*. New York: Simon and Schuster.

Fromm, E. (1970). *The crisis of psychoanalysis*. Greenwich, CT: Fawcett.

Fromm, E., Hilgard, E. R., & Kihlstrom, J. F. (1994). APA definition of hypnosis: Endorsements. *Contemporary Hypnosis, 11*, 144.

Furumoto, L. (1979). Mary Whiton Calkins (1863–1930): Fourteenth president of the American Psychological Association. *Journal of the History of the Behavioral Sciences, 15*, 346–356.

Furumoto, L. (1980a). Edna Heidbreder: Systematic and cognitive psychologist. *Psychology of Women Quarterly, 5*, 94–102.

Furumoto, L. (1980b). Mary Whiton Calkins (1863–1930). *Psychology of Women Quarterly, 5*(1), 55–68.

Furumoto, L. (1981, June). *First generation of U.S. women in psychology*. Paper presented at the Fifth Berkshire Conference on the History of Women, Vassar College, Poughkeepsie, NY.

Furumoto. L. (1985). Placing women in the history of psychology. *Teaching of Psychology, 12*, 203–206.

Furumoto, L. (1987). On the margins: Women and the professionalization of psychology in the United States, 1890–1940. In M. G. Ash & W. R. Woodward (Eds.), *Psychology in twentieth century thought and society* (pp. 93–113). Cambridge: Cambridge University Press.

Furumoto, L. (1988). *The new history of psychology*. Paper presented at the meeting of the American Psychological Association, Atlanta, GA.

Furumoto, L. (1992). Joining separate spheres—Christine Ladd-Franklin, woman-scientist (1847–1930). *American Psychologist, 47*(2), 175–182.

Furumoto, L., & Scarborough, E. (1986). Placing women in the history of psychology: The first American women psychologists. *American Psychologist, 41*, 35–42.

Gallistel, C. R. (1981). Bell, Magendie, and the proposals to restrict the use of animals in neurobehavioral research. *American Psychologist, 36*, 357–360.

Gallup, G. G., Jr. (1970). Chimpanzees: Self-recognition. *Science, 167*, 86–87.

Gallup, G. G., Jr. (1982). Self-awareness and the emergence of mind in primates. *American Journal of Primatology, 2*, 237–248.

Galton, F. (1855). *Art of travel*. London: John Murray.

Galton, F. (1891). *Hereditary genius*. New York: D. Appleton. (Original work published 1869).

Galton, F. (1907). *Inquiries into the human faculty and its development*. London: Dent.

Gamble, E. (1927). A study of three variables in memorizing. *American Journal of Psychology, 39*, 223–234.

Gardiner, H. W. (1994). Child Development. In L. L. Adler & U. P. Gielen (Eds.), *Cross-cultural topics in psychology* (pp. 61–72). Westport: Praeger.

Garraty, J. A., & Gay, P. (Eds.). (1981). *The Columbia history of the world*. New York: Harper & Row.

Garrison, D. (1981). Karen Horney and feminism. *Signs, 6* (4), 672–691.

Gawronski, D. V. (1975). *History, meaning and method* (3rd ed.). Glenview, IL: Scott Foresman.

Gay, P. (1988). *Freud: A life for our time*. New York: Norton.

Gay, P. (1989). *The Freud reader*. New York: Norton.

Gazzaniga, M. S. (1967, August). The split brain in man. *Scientific American, 217*, 24–29.

Gazzaniga, M. S. (1970). *The bisected brain*. New York: Appleton-Century-Crofts.

Gazzaniga, M. S. (1995). Principles of human brain organization derived from split brain studies. *Neuron, 14*, 217–228.

Gazzaniga, M. S. (1998, July). Groundbreaking work that began more than a quarter of a century ago has led to ongoing insights about brain organization and consciousness. *Scientific American, 278*, 51–55.

Gazzaniga, M. S., Ivry, R. B., & Mangun, G. R. (1998). *Cognitive neuroscience: The biology of the mind*. New York: W.W. Norton & Company.

Gazzaniga, M. S., & Sperry, R. W. (1967). Language after section of the cerebral commissure. *Brain, 90*, 131–148.

Geddes, P., & Thompson, J. A. (1901). *The evolution of sex* (rev. ed.). London: W. Scott.

Gendlin, E. T. (1988). Carl Rogers (1902–1987). *American Psychologist, 43*, 127–128.

Gerard, E. O. (1966). Medieval psychology: Dogmatic Aristotelianism or observational empiricism? *Journal of the History of the Behavioral Sciences, 2*, 315–329.

Gergen, K., Gulerce, A., Lock, A., & Misra, G. (1996). Psychological science in cultural context. *American Psychologist, 51*, 496–503.

Giddens, A. (1994). *Beyond left and right: The future of radical politics*. Stanford, CA: Stanford University Press.

Gies, F., & Gies, J. (1978). Women in the Middle Ages: The lives of real women in a vibrant age of transition. New York: HarperPerennial.

Gifford, G. E., Jr. (Ed.). (1978). *Psychoanalysis, psychotherapy, and the New England medical scene, 1894–1944*. New York: Science /History.

Gilbert, F. (1967). Niccoló Machiavelli. In Paul Edwards (Ed.), *The encyclopedia of philosophy* (Vol. 5). New York: Macmillan and Free Press.

Gilbreth, F. B. & Carey, E. G. (1948). *Cheaper by the dozen*. New York: T. Y. Crowell Co.

Gilbreth, L. M. (1914). *The psychology of management*. New York: Macmillan.

Gilbreth, L. M. (1927). *The homemaker and her job*. New York & London: D. Appleton & Co.

Gilgen, A. R., & Gilgen, C. K. (1996). Historical background, analytical overview and glossary. In Vera Koltsova et al. (Eds.), *Post-Soviet Perspectives on Russian Psychology*. Westport, CT: Greenwood Press.

Gilligan, C. (1982). *In a different voice: Psychological theory and women's development*. Cambridge, MA: Harvard University Press.

Gindis, B. (1992). Soviet psychology on the path of Perestroika. *Professional Psychology: Research and Practice, 23* (2), 114–118.

Glass, G. V. (1976). Primary, secondary, and meta-analysis of research. *Educational Researcher, 5*, 3–8.

Goldberg, A. (1982). Obituary: Heinz Kohut. *International Journal of Psychoanalysis, 63*, 257–258.

Goodman, E. S. (1980). Margaret Floy Washburn (1871–1939), first woman Ph.D. in Psychology. *Psychology of Women Quarterly, 5*, 69–80.

Goodwin, C. J. (1983). On the origins of Titchener's experimentalists. *Journal of the History of the Behavioral Sciences, 21*, 383–389.

Goodwin, C. J. (1999). *A history of modern psychology*. New York: John Wiley & Sons.

Gordon, B. L. (1959). *Medieval and Renaissance Medicine*. New York: Philosophical Library.

Grane, L. (1970). *Peter Abelard: Philosophy and Christianity in the Middle Ages* (F. Crowley & C. Crowley, Trans.). New York: McGraw-Hill.

Greenacre, P. (1957). The childhood of the artist: Libidinal phase development and giftedness. *Psychoanalytical Study of the Child, 12*, 27–72.

Greenberg, J. R., & Mitchell, S. A. (1983). *Object relations in psychoanalytic theory*. Cambridge, MA: Harvard University Press.

Greenberger, R. S., & Johnson, I. (1997, November 3). Chinese who studied in U.S. undercut dogmas at home. *Wall Street Journal*, p. A24.

Griffin, E. (1991). *A different voice of Carol Gilligan*. [Online]. Available at: http://www.afirstlook.com/docs/gilligan.html.

Grmek, M. D. (1974). Francois Magendie. In Charles Coulston Gillispie (Ed.), *Dictionary of scientific biography* (Vol. 9, pp. 7–11). New York: Charles Scribner's Sons.

Gross, D. (Ed.). (1997). *Forbes greatest business stories of all times*. New York: John Wiley & Sons.

Grosskurth, P. (1986). *Melanie Klein: Her world and her work*. Cambridge, MA: Harvard University Press.

Gulick, W. L., & Lawson, R. B. (1976). *Human stereopsis: A psychophysical approach*. New York: Oxford University Press.

Guthrie, R. V. (1976). *Even the rat was white: A historical view of psychology*. New York: Harper & Row.

Guthrie, R. V. (1996). *Even the rat was white: A historical view of psychology* (2nd ed.). Boston: Allyn and Bacon.

Guthrie, W. K. C. (1960). *The Greek philosophers from Thales to Aristotle*. New York: Harper & Row.

Hall, C. C. I. (1997). Cultural malpractice: The growing obsolescence of psychology with the changing U.S. population. *American Psychologist, 52*, 642–651.

Hall, G. S. (1904). *Adolescence*. New York: Appleton.

Hammond, W. R., & Yung, B. (1993). Minority student recruitment and retention practices among schools of professional psychology: A national survey and analysis. *Professional Psychology: Research and Practice, 24*, 3–12.

Harlow, J. M. (1869). Recovery from the passage of an iron bar through the head. Boston: Clapp.

Hartmann, H. (1951). Technical implications of ego psychology. In *Essays on ego psychology*. New York: International Universities Press, Inc., 1964.

Hartmann, H. (1958/1939). *Ego psychology and the problem of adaption*. (D. Rappaport, Trans.). New York: International Universities Press, Inc.

Havel, V. (1987). *Living in truth*. London: Faber & Faber.

Hayes, S. C., & Heiby, E. (1996). Psychology's drug problem: Do we need a fix or should we just say no? *American Psychologist, 51*, 198–206.

Hayman, R. (1999). *A life of Jung*. New York: W.W. Norton & Company.

Heelas, P., & Lock, A. (1981). *Indigenous psychologies: The anthropology of the self*. London: Academic Press.

Heidbreder, E. (1933). *Seven psychologies*. New York: Appleton-Century-Crofts.

Hein, A., & Held, R. (1967). Disassociation of the visual placing response into elicited and guided components. *Science, 158*, 390–392.

Held, R., & Bauer, J. A. (1967). Visually guided reaching in infant monkeys after restricted rearing. *Science, 155*, 718–720.

Held, R., & Hein, A. (1963). Movement produced stimulation in the development of visually guided behaviors. *Journal of Comparative Physiological Psychology, 56*, 872–876.

Helmholtz, H. (1850). *On the rate of transmission of the nerve impulse*. Berlin: Preussiche Akademie der Wissenschaften.

Henle, M. (1978). Gestalt psychology and gestalt therapy. *Journal of the History of the Behavioral Sciences, 14*, 23–32.

Henle, M. (1987). Koffka's principles after fifty years. *Journal of the History of the Behavioral Sciences, 23*, 14–21.

Henle, M., Jaynes, J., & Sullivan, J. J. (Eds.). (1973). *Historical conceptions of psychology*. New York: Springer.

Henley, T. B. (1988). Beyond Husserl. *American Psychologist, 43*, 402–403.

Herbert, T. B., & Cohen, S. (1993). Depression and immunity: A meta-analytic review. *Psychological Bulletin, 113*, 472–486.

Herrnstein, R. J., & Boring, E. G. (Eds.) (1966). *A sourcebook in the history of psychology*. Cambridge, MA: Harvard University Press.

Herrnstein, R. J., & Murray, C. (1994). *The bell curve: Intelligence and class structure in American life*. New York: Free Press.

Hertz, N. (2001). *The silent takeover: Global capitalism and the death of democracy*. New York: Free Press.

Hilgard, E. R. (1965). *Hypnotic susceptibility*. New York: Harcourt, Brace & World.

Hilgard, E. R. (1975). Hypnosis. *Annual Review of Psychology, 26*, 19–44.

Hilgard, E. R. (1986). Divided consciousness. *Multiple controls in human thought and action* (expanded edition). New York: Wiley.

Hilgard, E. R. (1987). *Psychology in America: A historical survey*. San Diego, CA: Harcourt Brace Jovanovich.

Hilgard, E. R. (1991). Harvey Carr and Chicago Functionalism: A simulated interview. In G. A. Kimble, M. Wertheimer, & C. L. White (Eds.), *Portraits of pioneers in psychology* (pp. 121–136). Washington, DC: American Psychological Association.

Hilgard, E. R. (1994). Neodissociation theory. In S. J. Lynn & J. W. Rhue (Eds.), *Dissociation: Clinical, theoretical and research perspectives* (pp. 32–51). New York: Guilford.

Hilgard, E. R., & Bower, G. (1966). *Theories of learning* (3rd ed.). New York: Appleton-Century-Crofts.

Himmelfarb, G. (1987). *The new history and the old*. Cambridge, MA: Harvard University Press.

Hirsch, J. (1981). To unfrock the charlatans. *Sage Race Relations Abstract, 6* (2), 1–62.

Ho, D. Y. F. (1994). Introduction to cross-cultural psychology. In L. L. Adler & U. P. Gielen (Eds.), *Cross-cultural topics in psychology* (pp. 3–13). Westport, CT: Praeger.

Hobbes, T. (1962). *Leviathan*. In Sir William Malesworth (Ed.), *The English works of Thomas Hobbes* (Vol. 3, pp. 1–714). London: Scientia Aalen. (Original work published 1651).

Hoffman, E. (1988). *The right to be human: A biography of Abraham Maslow*. Los Angeles: Tarcher.

Hogan, J. D., & Tartaglini, A. (1994). A brief history of cross-cultural psychology. In L. L. Adler & U. P. Gielen (Eds.), *Cross-cultural topics in psychology* (pp. 15–23). Westport, CT: Praeger.

Hogan, R., Hogan, J., & Roberts, B. W. (1996). Personality measurement and employment decisions: Questions and answers. *American Psychologist, 51*, 469–477.

Holland, J. G. (1992). B. F. Skinner (1904–1990). *American Psychologist, 47*, 665–667.

Hollingworth, H. (1990). *Leta Stetter Hollingworth: A biography*. Bolton, MA: Anker Publishing Company.

Hollingworth, L. S. (1914). Variability as related to sex differences in achievement. *American Journal of Sociology, 19*, 510–530.

Hollingworth, L. S. (1920). *The psychology of subnormal children*. New York: Macmillan.

Hollingworth, L. S. (1926). *Gifted children*. New York: Macmillan.

Hollingworth, L. S. (1934). *The problem of mental disorder*. New York: Macmillan.

Hollingworth, L. S. (1942). *Children above 180 IQ.* Yonkers-on-Hudson, NY: World Book Company.

Holloway, J. D. (2004). Louisiana grants psychologists prescriptive authority. *APA Monitor on Psychology, 35,* 20–21.

Holman, B. (1995). *The evacuation: A very British revolution.* Oxford: Lion.

Homskaya, E. D. (2001). *Alexander Romanovich Luria: A scientific biography* (D. Krotova, Trans.; D. E. Tupper, Ed.). New York: Kluwer Academic/Plenum Publ.

Horney, K. (1935). The problem of feminine masochism. *Psychoanalytic Review, 22,* 241.

Horney, K. (1937). *The neurotic personality of our time.* New York: W. W. Norton & Company.

Hothersall, D. (1995a). *History of psychology* (3rd ed.). New York: McGraw-Hill.

Hourani, G.F. (1961). *Averroës on the Harmony of Religion and Philosophy.* London: Oxford University Press.

Hughes, J. M. (1989). *Reshaping the psychoanalytic domain: The work of Melanie Klein, W. R. D. Fairbairn, & D. W. Winnicott.* Berkeley: University of California Press.

Hui, C. H., & Triandis, H. C. (1986). Individualism and collectivism: A study of cross-cultural researchers. *Journal of Cross-Cultural Psychology, 17,* 225–248.

Huizinga, J. (1970). The task of cultural history. *Men and ideas: Essays on history, the Middle Ages, the Renaissance* (J. S. Holmes & H. van Merle, Trans.). New York: Harper Torchbooks.

Hulin, W. S. (1934). *A short history of psychology.* New York: Holt.

Hull, C. L. (1933). *Hypnosis and suggestibility: An experimental approach.* New York: Appleton-Century-Crofts.

Hull, C. L. (1943). *Principles of behavior.* New York: Appleton-Century-Crofts.

Hull, C. L. (1951). *A behavior system.* New Haven, CT: Yale University Press.

Hunt, M. (1993). *The story of psychology.* New York: Anchor Books.

Huntington, S. (1996). *The clash of civilizations.* Cambridge, MA: Harvard University Press.

Hurtz, G. M., & Donovan, J. J. (2000). Personality and job performance: The big five revisited. *Journal of Applied Psychology, 85,* 869–879.

Huxley, A. (1927). *A note on dogma: Varieties of human type.* Proper Studies. London: Chatto & Windus.

Hyman, I. E., & Pentland, J. (1996). The role of mental imagery in the creation of false childhood memories. *Journal of Memory and Language, 35,* 101–117.

Jackson, S. W. (1969). Galen—On mental disorders. *Journal of the History of the Behavioral Sciences, 5,* 365–384.

Jacobs, M. (1995). *D. W. Winnicott.* Thousand Oaks, CA: Sage.

Jahoda, G. (1980). *Has social psychology a distinctive contribution to make?* Paper presented at the Conference on Social Psychology and the Developing Countries, University of Lancaster, UK.

James, W. (1890). *The principles of psychology* (2 vols.). New York: Henry Holt.

James, W. (1956). *The will to believe and other essays in popular philosophy.* New York: Dover. (Original work published 1897).

James, W. (1961). *Psychology: The briefer course* (G. Allport, Ed.). New York: Harper & Row. (Original work published 1892).

James, W. (1975a). *Pragmatism: A new name for some old ways of thinking.* Cambridge, MA: Harvard University Press. (Original work published 1907).

James, W. (1975b). *The meaning of truth: A sequel to "Pragmatism."* Cambridge, MA: Harvard University Press. (Original work published 1909).

Janet, P. (1889). *L'automatisme psychologique [The psychological automatism].* Paris, France: Felix Alcan.

Jaynes, J. (1973). The problem of animate motion in the seventeenth century. In M. Henle, J. Jaynes, & J. J. Sullivan (Eds.), *Historical conceptions of psychology* (pp. 166–179). New York: Springer Publishing.

Jing, Q., & Fu, X. (1995). Factors influencing the development of psychology in China. *International Journal of Psychology, 30,* 717–728.

Jing, Q., & Fu, X. (2001). Modern Chinese psychology: Its indigenous roots and international influences [Electronic version]. *International Journal of Psychology, 36*(6), 408–418.

Jing, Q. C. (1991). *Concise encyclopedia of psychology.* Beijing, China: Academy of Sciences.

Johnson, A. G. (2001). *Privilege, power, and difference.* Boston: McGraw-Hill Higher Education.

Johnson, R. C., McClearn, G. E., Yuen, S., Nagoshi, C. T., Ahern, F., & Cole, R. E. (1985). Galton's data a century later. *American Psychologist, 40,* 875–892.

Jonçich, G. (1968). *The sane positivist: A biography of Edward Lee Thorndike.* Middletown, CT: Wesleyan University Press.

Jones, E. (1953). *The life and work of Sigmund Freud, Vol. 1.* New York: Basic Books.

Jones, E. (1955). *The life and work of Sigmund Freud, Vol. 2.* New York: Basic Books.

Jones, E. (1957). *The life and work of Sigmund Freud, Vol. 3*. New York: Basic Books.

Jones, J. M. (1998). Dalmas A. Taylor, Ph.D., 1993–1998. *Variability* (Spring).

Jones, J. M. (2000). Dalmas A. Taylor (1933–1998). *American Psychologist, 55*(3), 341.

Jones, M. C., (1974). Albert, Peter and John B. Watson. *American Psychologist, 29*, 581–583.

Jones, M. C., & Bayley, N. (1950). Physical maturing among boys as related to behavior. *Journal of Educational Psychology, 41*, 129–148.

Jones, M. C., & Mussen, P. H. (1958). Self-conceptions, motivations and interpersonal attitudes of early and late maturing girls. *Child Development, 29*, 491–501.

Jung, C. G. (1902). On the psychology and pathology of so-called occult phenomena. In G. Adler, et al. (Eds.) and R. F. C. Hull (Trans.), *The collected works of C. G. Jung*, Vol. 1. London: Routledge and Kegan Paul, and Princeton, N.J.: Bollingen.

Jung, C. G. (1907). The psychology of dementia praecox. In H. Read, et al. (Eds.) and R. F. C. Hull (Trans.), *The collected works of C. G. Jung*, Vol. 3. London: Routledge and Kegan Paul, and Princeton, N.J.: Bollingen.

Jung, C. G. (1933). *Modern man in search of a soul*. New York: Harcourt.

Jung, C. G. (1939). *The integration of the personality*. New York: Farrar & Rinehart.

Jung, C. G. (1950). Foreword. In R. Wilhelm & C. Baynes (Trans.) *The I Ching, or Book of Changes*. New York: Princeton University Press.

Jung, C. G. (1961). *Memories, dreams, reflections*. New York: Pantheon Books.

Jung, C. G. (1968). *Analytical psychology: Its theory and practice*. New York: Pantheon Books.

Jung, C. G., & Baynes, H. G. (1921). *Psychological types, or, The psychology of individuation*. London: K. Paul Trench Trubner.

Jung, C. G., & Hinkle, B. M. (1912). *Psychology of the unconscious*. London: K. Paul Trench Trubner.

Kamin, L. J. (1969). Predictability, surprise, attention, and conditioning. In B. A. Campbell & R. M. Church (Eds.), *Punishment and aversive behavior*. New York: Appleton-Century-Crofts.

Kanter, J. (2000). The untold story of Donald and Clare Winnicott: How social work influenced modern psychoanalysis. *Clinical Social Work Journal, 28*(3), 245–261.

Karn, H. W. (1947). Sensory pre-conditioning and incidental learning in human subjects. *Journal of Experimental Psychology, 37*, 540–545.

Katz, P. A., & Taylor, D. A. (1988). *Eliminating racism: Profiles in controversy*. New York: Plenum Press.

Keefe, F. J., Wilkins, R. H., Cook, W. A., Crisson, J. E., & Muhlbaier, J. H. (1986). Depression, pain, and pain behavior. *Journal of Consulting and Clinical Psychology, 54*, 665–669.

Kelman, H. C. (1968). Social psychology and national development: Background of Ibadan conference. *Journal of Social Issues, 24*, 9–20.

Kemp, S. (1990). *Medieval psychology*. New York: Greenwood Press.

Kendler, H. H., & Spence, J. T. (Eds.) (1971). *Essays in neobehaviorism: A memorial volume to Kenneth W. Spence*. New York: Appleton-Century-Crofts.

Keppel, B. (2002). Kenneth B. Clark in the patterns of American culture. *American Psychologist, 57*(1), 29–37.

Kihlstrom, J. F. (1985). Hypnosis. *Annual Review of Psychology, 36*, 385–418.

Kintsch, W. (1985). Reflections on Ebbinghaus. *Journal of Experimental Psychology: Learning, Memory, and Cognition, 11*, 461–463.

Kirk, G. S., & Raven, J. E. (1957). *The presocratic philosophers*. Cambridge: Cambridge University Press.

Kirsch, I., & Lynn, S. J. (1995). The altered state of hypnosis: Changes in the theoretical landscape. *American Psychologist, 50*, 846–858.

Kirsch, I., & Lynn, S. J. (1998). Dissociation theories of hypnosis. *Psychological Bulletin, 123*, 100–115.

Kirsch, I., Montgomery, G., & Sapirstein, G. (1995). Hypnosis as an adjunct to cognitive behavioral psychotherapy: A meta-analysis. *Journal of Consulting and Clinical Psychology, 63*, 214–220.

Kitano, H. H. L., & Daniels, R. (1988). *Asian Americans: Emerging Minorities*. Englewood Cliffs, NJ: Prentice-Hall.

Kleinman, A. M. (1977). Depression, somatization, and the new cross-cultural psychiatry. *Social Science and Medicine, 11*, 3–10.

Kliman, J., & Trimble, D. (1993). In memoriam: Carolyn Attneave. *Netletter, 6*(2). Retrieved February 2, 2003, from http://www.netletter.org/archives/net793.html.

Koch, S. (1969, March). Psychology cannot be a coherent science. *Psychology Today*, pp. 14, 64, 66–68.

Koch, S. (1993). "Psychology" or "the psychological studies"? *American Psychologist, 48*, 902–904.

Koch, S. (Ed.). (1959). *Psychology: A study of science* (Vol. 3). New York: McGraw-Hill.

Koffka, K. (1924/1921). *The growth of the mind*. (R. M. Ogden, Trans.). London: Routledge & Kegan Paul.

Koffka, K. (1935). *Principles of Gestalt psychology*. New York: Harcourt Brace and Company.

Kohlberg, L., & Kramer, R. (1969). Continuities and discontinuities in childhood and adult moral development. *Human Development, 12,* 93–120.

Köhler, W. (1920). *Static and stationary physical gestalts (Die physischen gestalten in ruhe und im stationaren zustand).* Braunschweig: Friedr. Vieweg and Sohn.

Köhler, W. (1947). *Gestalt psychology, an introduction to new concepts in modern psychology.* New York: Liveright Publishing Corp.

Köhler, W. (1959). Gestalt psychology today. *American Psychologist, 14,* 727–734.

Köhler, W. (1976). *The mentality of apes.* New York: Liveright. (Original work published 1925).

Kohlstedt, S. G. (1987). Maria Mitchell and the advancement of women in science. In P. G. Abir-Am & D. Outram (Eds.), *Uneasy careers and intimate lives: Women in science (1789–1979).* New Brunswick, NJ: Rutgers University Press.

Kohut, H. (1977). *The restoration of the self.* New York: International Universities Press.

Koltsova, V. A., Oleinik, Y. N., Gilgen, A. R., & Gilgen, C. K. (Eds.). (1996). *Post-soviet perspectives on russian psychology.* Westport, CT: Greenwood Press. Retrieved April 30, 2006, from Questia database: http://www.questia.com/PM.qst?a=o&d=27300697.

Korn, J. H., Davis, R., & Davis, S. F. (1991). Historians' and chairpersons' judgements of eminence among psychologists. *American Psychologist, 46,* 789–792.

Kozulin, A. (1984). Psychology in Utopia: Toward a social history of Soviet psychology. Cambridge, MA: The MIT Press.

Kraft, W. A., & Rudolfa, E. R. (1982). The use of hypnosis among psychologists. *American Journal of Clinical Hypnosis, 24,* 249–257.

Kramer, R. (1976). *Maria Montessori: A biography.* New York: G. P. Putnam & Sons.

Krippner, S., & Winkler, M. (1996). Studying consciousness in the postmodern age. In W. Anderson (Ed.), *The fontana postmodernism reader* (pp. 157–165). London: Fontana Press.

Kristeller, P. O. (1967). Petrarch. In P. Edwards (Ed.), *The encyclopedia of philosophy* (Vol. 5). New York: Macmillan.

Kroeber, A. L., & Kluckhohn, C. (1952). *Culture: A critical review of concepts and definitions.* Cambridge, MA: Peabody Museum, Vol. 47, No. 1.

Krüll, M. (1986). *Freud and his father.* New York: Norton.

Kuhn, T. S. (1970). *The structure of scientific revolutions* (Rev. ed.). Chicago: University of Chicago Press. (Original work published 1962).

Lachman, B. (1993). *The journal of Hildegard of Bingen.* New York: Bell Tower.

LaFramboise, T. D. (1988). American Indian mental health policy. *American Psychologist, 43,* 388–397.

LaFramboise, T. D., & Low, K. G. (1989). American Indian children and adolescents. In J. G. Gibbs & L. Hwang (Eds.), *Children of color.* San Francisco: Jossey-Bass.

Landy, F. J. (1992). Hugo Münsterberg: Victim or visionary? *American Psychologist, 47,* 787–802.

Lapan, R. T., Kaidash, C. M., & Turner, S. (2002). Empowering students to become self-regulated learners. *Professional School Counseling, 5,* 257–265.

Lashley, K. S. (1929). *Brain mechanisms and intelligence.* Chicago: University of Chicago Press.

Lasley, T. (1994). *Teaching peace: Toward cultural selflessness.* Westport, CT: Bergin & Garvey.

Lattal, K. A. (Ed.). (1992). Special issue: Reflections on B. F. Skinner and psychology [Monograph]. *American Psychologist, 47,* 1265–1560.

Lau, D. C. (1979). *Confucius,* The Analects. Harmondsworth; New York: Penguin Books.

Leahy, T. H. (1987). *A history of psychology: Main currents in psychological thought* (2nd ed.). Englewood Cliffs, NJ: Prentice-Hall.

Leahy, T. H. (1992). The mythical revolutions of American Psychology. *American Psychologist, 47,* 308–318.

LeDoux, J. E. (1996). *The emotional brain: The mysterious underpinnings of emotional life.* New York: Simon & Schuster.

Leland, J. (1995, July 17). Not gay, not straight: A new sexuality emerges. *Newsweek, 126* (3), 44–50.

Lemonick, M. D., & Park, A. (2001, May 14). The nun study. *Time,* pp. 53–64.

Leonard, R. (1978). *Computers in South Africa: A survey of U.S. companies.* New York: The Africa Fund.

Leontiev, A. N. (1979). The problem of activity in psychology. In J. V. Wertsch (Ed.), *The concept of activity in Soviet psychology* (pp. 37–71). Armonk, NY: Sharpe.

Lerner, G. (1997). *Why history matters.* New York: Oxford University Press.

Lester, T. (1999, January). What is the Koran? *The Atlantic Monthly,* 43–56.

Lever, J. (1976). Sex differences in the games of children. *Social Problems, 23,* 478–487.

Levin, D. T., & Simons, D. J. (1997). Failure to detect changes to attended objects in motion pictures. *Psychonomic Bulletin & Review, 4,* 501–506.

Ley, R. (1990). A whisper of espionage: Wolfgang Köhler and the apes of Tenerife. Garden City Park, NY: Avery Publishing Group.

Lindenfeld, D. (1978). Oswald Külpe and the Würzburg School. *Journal of the History of the Behavioral Sciences, 14,* 132–141.

Lippitt, R. (1939). An experimental study of authoritarian and democratic group atmospheres. *University of Iowa Studies in Child Welfare, 16*(3), 43–195.

Lipsey, M. W., & Wilson, D. B. (1993). The efficacy of psychological, educational, and behavioral treatment. Confirmation from meta-analysis. *American Psychologist, 48*, 1181–1209.

Locke, J. (1974). *An essay concerning human understanding* (A. D. Woozley, Ed.). New York: New American Library (Original work published 1706)

Loftus, E. F. (1979). *Eyewitness testimony*. Cambridge, MA: Harvard University Press.

Loftus, E. F. (1992). When a lie becomes a memory's truth. Memory distortion after exposure to misinformation. *Current Directions in Psychological Science, 1*, 121–123.

Loftus, E. F. (1993). The reality of repressed memories. *American Psychologist, 48*, 518–537.

Loftus, E. F. (1995, March). Remembering dangerously. *Skeptical Inquirer*, 1–14.

Loftus, E. F. (2003). Make-believe memories. *American Psychologist, 58*, 864–873.

Loftus, E. F. (2004). Memories of things unseen. *Current Directions in Psychological Science, 13*, 145–147.

Loftus, E. F., Bourne, L. E., & Dominowski, R. L. (1979). *Cognitive processes*. Englewood Cliffs, NJ: Prentice-Hall.

Loftus, E. F., & Ketcham, K. (1994). *The myth of repressed memory*. New York: St. Martin's Press.

Loftus, E. F., & Pickrell, J. E. (1995). The formation of false memories. *Psychiatric Annals, 25*, 720–725.

Loftus, G. R., & Loftus, E. F. (1976). *Human memory*. Hillsdale, NJ: Lawrence Erlbaum Associates.

Logan, D. D. (1980). Mary Cover Jones: Feminine as asset. *Psychology of Women Quarterly, 5* (1), 103–115.

Lunt, I., & Poortinga, Y. H. (1996). Internationalizing psychology: The case of Europe. *American Psychologist, 51*, 504–508.

Luria, A. R. (1969). The neuropsychological study of brain lesions and restoration of damaged brain functions. In Michael Cole & Irving Maltzman (Eds.), *A Handbook of Contemporary Soviet Psychology*. New York: Basic Books.

Luria, A. R. (1974). *Ob istoricheskom razvitii poznavatel'nykh protessov* (*Cognitive Development: Its Social and Cultural Foundations*). Moscow: Nauka

Luria, A. R. (1982). *Etapy Proidennogo Puti* (*The Stages of the Traversed Path*). Moscow: MGU Press

Lynn, S. J., & Rhue, J. W. (Eds.). (1991). *Theories of hypnosis: Current models and perspectives*. New York: Guilford Press.

MacLeod, C. (1991). Half a century of research on the Stroop effect: An integrative review. *Psychological Bulletin, 109*, 163–203.

MacLeod, R. B. (1975). *The persistent problems of psychology*. Pittsburgh: Duquesne University Press.

MacMillan, M. B. (1986). A wonderful journey through skull and brain: The travels of Mr. Gage's tamping iron. *Brain and Cognition, 5*, 67–107.

Magendie, F. (1965). Francois Magendie (1783–1855) on spinal nerve roots, 1822. In R. J. Herrnstein & E. G. Boring (Eds.), *A sourcebook on the history of psychology* (pp. 19–22). Cambridge, MA: Harvard University Press. (Original work published 1822).

Maher, W. B., & Maher, B. A. (1985). Psychopathology: I. From ancient times to the eighteenth century. In G. A. Kimble & K. Schlesinger (Eds.), *Topics in the history of psychology* (Vol. 2). Hillsdale, NJ: Erlbaum.

Malia, M. (1999). Russia under Western eyes: From the bronze horseman to the Lenin mausoleum. Cambridge, MA: The Belknap Press.

Maquet, P., Laureys, S., Peigneux, P., Fuchs, S., Petiau, C., Phillips, C., Aerts, J., Del Fiore, G., Degueldre, C., Meulemans, T., Luxen, A., Franck, G., Van Der Linden, M., Smith, C., & Cleeremans, A. (2000). Experience-dependent changes in cerebral activation during human REM sleep. *Nature Neuroscience, 3*, 831–836.

The Margaret S. Mahler Psychiatric Research Foundation. (2002). *Margaret S. Mahler's biography*. [Online] Available at: http://www.margaretmahler.org/foundation/mahler/bio.html.

Marrow, A. J. (1969). The practical theorist: The life and work of Kurt Lewin. New York: Basic Books.

Marsella, A. (1998). Toward a "global-community psychology": Meeting the needs of a changing world. *American Psychologist, 53*, 1282–1291.

Martin, L. J. (1917). Mental hygiene and the importance of investigating it. *Journal of Applied Psychology, 1*, 67–70.

Martin, S. (1995, September). APA to pursue prescription privileges. *APA Monitor*, p. 6.

Martin, S. (1998). China increasingly accepts psychology [Online]. Available at: http://www.apa.org/monitor/oct98/china.html.

Martin-Baro, I. (1989). La opinion publica salvadorena (1987–1988). San Salvador: UCA Editores.

Marx, M. H., & Cronan-Hillix, W. A. (1987). *Systems and theories in psychology* (4th ed.). New York: McGraw-Hill.

Masson, J. M. (1985). *The assault on truth: Freud's abandonment of the seduction theory*. New York: Farrar Strauss.

Matossian, M. (1982). Ergot and the Salem witchcraft affair. *American Scientist, 70*, 355–357.

May, R., Angel, E., & Ellenberger, H. F. (Eds.). (1958). *Existence: A new dimension in psychiatry and psychology*. New York: Basic Books.

Mays, V. M., Rubin, J., Sabourin, M., & Walker, L. (1996). Moving toward a global psychology. *American Psychologist, 51*, 485–487.

Mazzoni, G., & Loftus, E. F. (1998). Dream interpretation can change beliefs about the past. *Psychotherapy, 35*, 177–187.

McClearn, G. E. (1991). A trans-time visit with Francis Galton. In G. A. Kimble, M. Wertheimer, & C. L. White (Eds.), *Portraits of pioneers in psychology* (pp. 1–11). Washington, DC: American Psychological Association.

McCrae, R. R., & Costa, P. T., Jr. (1997). Personality trait structure as a human universal. *American Psychologist, 52*, 509–516.

McDonald's. Retrieved August 23, 2001, from Web site: http://www.mcdonalds.com.

McDougall, W. (1908). *An introduction to social psychology*. Kennebunkport, ME: Milford House.

McGaugh, J. L. (1990). The "Decade of the Brain." *APS Observer, 3*, 2–5.

McGovern, T. V., Furumoto, L., Halpern, D. F., Kimble, G. A., & McKeachie, W. J. (1991). Liberal education, study in depth, and the arts and sciences major—psychology. *American Psychologist, 46*, 598–605.

McHenry, L. C. (1969). *Garrison's history of neurobiology*. Springfield, IL: Charles C. Thomas. National Institute of Neurological Disorders and Stroke. Retrieved August 4, 2001, from Web site: http://www.ninds.nih.gov.

McKenna, W., & Kessler, S. J. (1977). Experimental design as a source of sex bias in social psychology. *Sex Roles: A Journal of Research, 3*, 117–128.

McLuhan, M., & Powers, P. S. (1989). *The global village: Transformations in work life and media in the 21st century*. New York: Oxford University Press.

McReynolds, P. (1996). Lightner Witmer: A centennial tribute. *American Psychologist, 51*, 237–240.

Meissner, W. W. (2000). *Freud and psychoanalysis*. Notre Dame, IN: University of Notre Dame Press.

Merton, R. K. (1948). The self-fulfilling prophecy. *Antioch Review, 8*, 193–210.

Miles, W. (1949, July 1). James Rowland Angell, 1869–1949, psychologist-educator. *Science, 110*, 1–4.

Miller, J. G. (1997). Theoretical issues in cultural psychology. In J. W. Berry, Y. H. Poortinga, & J. Pandley (Eds.), *Handbook of cross-cultural psychology: Theory and method* (Vol. 1, pp. 85–128). Boston: Allyn & Bacon.

Mills, W. (1899). The nature of animal intelligence and the methods of investigating it. *Psychological Review, 6*, 262–274.

Misiak, H. K., & Sexton, V. S. (1966). *History of psychology: An overview*. New York: Grune & Stratton.

Moghaddam, F. M. (1987). Psychology in the three worlds: As reflected in the crisis in social psychology and the move toward indigenous third-world psychology. *American Psychologist, 42*, 912–920.

Moghaddam, F. M., & Taylor, D. M. (1985). Psychology in the developing world: An evaluation through the concepts of "dual perception" and "parallel growth." *American Psychologist, 40*, 1144–1146.

Montague, H., & Hollingworth, L. S. (1914). The comparative variability of the sexes at birth. *American Journal of Sociology, 20*, 335–370.

Monte, C. F. (1980). *Beneath the mask (2nd ed.)*. New York: Holt, Rinehart and Winston.

Moskowitz, M. J. (1977). Hugo Münsterberg: A study in the history of applied psychology. *American Psychologist, 32*, 824–842.

Mount, M. K., Barrick, M. R., and Strauss, J. P. (1994). Validity of observer ratings of the big five personality factors. *Journal of Applied Psychology, 79*, 272–280.

Mowrer, O. H. (1947). On the dual nature of learning—A re-interpretation of "conditioning" and "problem-solving." *Harvard Educational Review, 17*, 102–148.

Mowrer, O. H. (1960). *Learning theory and behavior*. New York: Wiley.

Münsterberg, H. (1892). *Proceedings of the American Psychological Association*. New York: Macmillan & Co., p. 11.

Münsterberg, H. (1901). *American traits*. Boston: Houghton Mifflin.

Münsterberg, H. (1908). *On the witness stand*. New York: Doubleday, Page.

Münsterberg, H. (1909). *Psychotherapy*. New York: Moffat, Yard.

Münsterberg, H. (1910). *Subconscious phenomena*. Boston: R. G. Badger.

Münsterberg, H. (1913a). *Psychology and industrial efficiency*. Boston: Houghton Mifflin.

Münsterberg, H. (1913b). The case of Beulah Miller: An investigation of the new psychical mystery. *The Metropolitan*, 16–18, 61–62.

Murchinson, C. A. (Ed.) (1952). *History of psychology in autobiography*. Worcester, MA: Clark University Press.

Murray, B. (2002). Psychology tackles apartheid's aftermath: In South Africa, psychology faces the huge task of tailoring aid to a once-oppressed majority population. *APA Monitor on Psychology, 33*.

Murray, H.A. (1938). *Explorations in personality*. New York: Oxford University Press.

Mussen, P., & Eichorn, D. (1988). Mary Cover Jones (1896–1987). *American Psychologist, 43* (10), 818.

Mussen, P. H., & Jones, M. C. (1957). Self-conceptions, motivations and interpersonal attitudes of late- and early-maturing boys. *Child Development, 28*, 242–256.

Myers, G. E. (1986). *William James: His life and thought.* New Haven, CT: Yale University Press.

Nash, M. (1987). What, if anything, is regressed about hypnotic age regression. A review of the empirical literature. *Psychological Bulletin, 102*, 42–52.

National Science Foundation. (1994). *Women, minorities, and persons with disabilities in science and engineering: 1994* (NSF 94-333). Arlington, VA: Author.

Neale, J. M., Davison, G. C., & Haaga, D. A. F. (1996). *Exploring abnormal behavior.* New York: John Wiley & Sons.

Neimark, J. (1996). The diva of disclosure, memory researcher Elizabeth Loftus. *Psychology Today, 29* (1), 48.

Neisser, U. (1982). *Memory observed: Remembering in material contexts.* New York: Frecman.

Neisser, U., Boodoo, G., Bouchard, T. J., Jr. Boykin, A. W., Brady, N., Ceci, S. J., Halpern, D. F., Loehlin, J. C., Perloff, R., Sternberg, R. J., and Urbina, S. (1996). Intelligence: Knowns and unknowns. *American Psychologist, 51*, 77–101.

Neugebauer, R. (1978). Treatment of the mentally ill in medieval and early modern England: A reappraisal. *Journal of the History of the Behavioral Sciences, 14*, 158–169.

Newman, B. (1987). *Sister of wisdom: St. Hildegard's theology of the feminine.* Berkeley: University of California Press.

Newton, I. S. (1999). The principia: Mathematical principles of natural philosophy/Isaac Newton; a new translation by I. Bernard Cohen and Anne Whitman assisted by Julia Budenz; preceded by a guide to Newton's principia by I. Bernard Cohen. Berkeley: University of California Press. (Original work published 1687.)

O'Connell, A. (1980). Karen Horney: Theorist in psychoanalysis and feminine psychology. *Psychology of Women Quarterly, 5*(1), 81–93.

O'Connell, A. N., & Russo, N. F. (1990). *Women in psychology: A biographic sourcebook.* New York: Greenwood Press.

O'Donnell, J. M. (1979). The crisis of experimentalism in the 1920s: E. G. Boring and his uses of history. *American Psychologist, 34*, 289–295.

O'Leary, A. (1994). Stress, emotion and immune function. *Psychological Bulletin, 108*, 363–382.

O'Neil, W. M., & Landauer, A. A. (1966). The phi-phenomenon: Turning point or rallying point. *Journal of the History of the Behavioral Sciences, 2*, 335–340.

Ohman, A., Flykt, A., & Lundqvist, D. (2000). Unconscious emotion: Evolutionary perspectives, psychophysiological data, and neurophysiological measures. In R. Lane & L. Nadel (Eds.), *The cognitive neuroscience of emotion* (pp. 296–327). New York: Oxford University Press.

Orlov, A. (1998). In M. Cote (Ed.), *Russian psychology in transition: Interviews with Moscow psychologists.* Commack, NY: Nova Science Publishers.

Outler, A. C. (Ed. and Trans.) (1995). *Augustine: Confessions and enchiridion.* Philadelphia: Westminster Press.

Padilla, A. M., & Salgado de Snyder, N. (1985). Counseling Hispanics: Strategies for effective intervention. In P. Pederson (Ed.) (1987), *Handbook of cross-cultural counseling and therapy* (pp. 157–164). New York: Praeger.

Paranjpe, A. (1981). Indian psychology in the cross-cultural setting. *Journal of Indian Psychology, 3*, 10–22.

Parrish, M., Lundy, R. M., & Leibowitz, H. (1968). Hypnotic age-regression and magnitudes of the Ponzo and Poggendorff illusions. *Science, 159*, 1375–1376.

Parrish, M., Lundy, R. M., & Leibowitz, H.W. (1969). Effect of hypnotic age regression on the magnitudes of the Ponzo and Poggendorff illusions. *Journal of Abnormal Psychology, 74*, 693–698.

Passons, W. R. (1975). Gestalt approaches in counseling. New York: Holt, Rinehart and Winston.

Pawlik, K. (1992). Psychologie international: Aufgaben und Chancen [International psychology: Tasks and chances]. *Psychologie in Osterreich, 12*, 84–87.

Pawlik, K. (Ed.). (1985). *International directory of psychologists* (4th ed.). Amsterdam: North-Holland.

Pawlik, K., & Rosenzweig, M. R. (Eds.). (1994). The origins and development of psychology: Some national and regional perspectives [Special issue]. *International Journal of Psychology, 29*.

Pawlik, K., & d'Ydewalle, G. (1996). Psychology and the global commons: Perspectives of international psychology. *American Psychologist, 51*, 488–495.

Pavlov, I. P. (1902). *Lectures on the work of the digestive glands* (W. H. Thompson, Trans.). London: Charles Griffin. (Original work published 1897.)

Pavlov, I. P. (1955). *I. P. Pavlov: Selected works* (J. Gibbons, Ed., S. Belsky, Trans.). Moscow: Foreign Languages Publishing House.

Payne, T. R. (1968). *S. L. Rubinstein and the philosophical foundations of Soviet psychology.* Dordrecht: D. Reidel.

Pearson, K. (1896). Mathematical contributions to the theory of evolution, regression, heredity, and panmixia. *Philosophical Transactions, 187A,* 253–318.

Pearson, K. (1924). *The life, letters, and labours of Francis Galton.* Cambridge, England: Cambridge University Press.

Pelletier, K. (1999). Psychoneuroimmunology: Toward a mind–body model. Advances, *Institute for the Advancement of Health, 15,* 27–56.

Perlman, D. (1986). SPSSI's publication history: Some facts and reflections. *Journal of Social Issues, 42,* 89–113.

Perls, F. S. (1969). *In and out of the garbage pail.* New York: Bantam.

Perls, F. S., et al. (1951). *Gestalt therapy.* New York: Dell Publishing Co.

Perry, C. W., & Chisholm, W. (1973). Hypnotic age regression and the Ponzo and Poggendorf illusions. *International Journal of Clinical and Experimental Hypnosis, 21,* 192–204.

Peters, F. (1998). Lucid consciousness in traditional Indian psychology and contemporary neuro-psychology. *Journal of Indian Psychology, 16,* 1–25.

Peterson, D. R. (2000). Scientist-practitioner or scientific practitioner? *American Psychologist, 55,* 251–252.

Petrovsky, A. V. (1967). *Istoria sovietskoi psikhologii* [*The history of psychology*]. Moscow.

Petrovsky, A. V., & Yaroshevsky, M. G. (1987). *A concise psychological dictionary.* New York: International Publishers.

Pezdek, K., Finger, K., & Hodge, D. (1997). Planting false childhood memories: The role of event plausibility. *Psychological Science, 8,* 437–441.

Phantom Limb & Causalgia: The tragic enigmas. (1998). [Online]. Available at: http://www.library.ucla.edu/libraries/biomed/his/PainExhibit/panel4.htm.

Pickard, M. E., & Bailey, R. C. (1945). *The Midwest pioneer: His ills, cures, and doctors.* Crawfordsville, IN: R. E. Banta.

Pickren, W. E., & Tomes, H. (2002). The legacy of Kenneth B. Clark to the APA. *American Psychologist, 57*(1), 51–59.

Pion, G. M. (1991). Psychologists wanted: Employment trends over the past decade. In R. R. Kilburg (Ed.), *How to manage your career in psychology* (pp. 229–246). Washington, DC: American Psychological Association.

Pion, G. M., Mednick, M. T., Astin, H. S., Sijima Hall, C. C., Kenkel, M. B., Puryear Keita, G., Kohant, J. L., & Kelleher, J. C. (1996). The shifting gender composition of psychology: Trends and implications for the discipline. *American Psychologist, 50*(5), 509–528.

Ponterotto, J. G., Casas, J. M., Suzuki, L. A., & Alexander, C. M. (Eds.). (1995). *Handbook of multicultural counseling.* Thousand Oaks, CA: Sage.

Porter, R. (1986). The scientific revolution, a spoke in the wheel? In R. Porter & M. Teich (Eds.), *Revolutions in history* (pp. 290–316). Cambridge, England: Cambridge University Press.

Posner, M. I., Petersen, S. E., Fox, P. T., & Raichle, M. E. (1988). Localization of cognitive operations in the human brain. *Science, 240,* 1627–1631.

Povinelli, D. J. (1993). Reconstructing the evolution of mind. *American Psychologist, 48,* 493–509.

Premack, D., & Woodruff, G. (1978). Does the chimpanzee have a theory of mind? *Behavioral Brain Science, 1,* 515–526.

Prilleltensky, I. (1997). Values, assumptions, and practices. Assessing the moral implications of psychological discourse and action. *American Psychologist, 52,* 517–535.

Quinn, S. (1987). A mind of her own: The life of Karen Horney. Reading, MA: Addison-Wesley Publishing Company, p. 143.

Quintana, S. M., & Bernal, M. E. (1995). Ethnic minority training in counseling psychology: Comparisons with clinical psychology and proposed standards. *The Counseling Psychologist, 23,* 102–121.

Rahula, W. (1974). *What the Buddha taught.* New York: Grove Press.

Raimy, V. C. (Ed.). (1950). *Training in clinical psychology.* Engelwood Cliffs, NJ: Prentice-Hall.

Ramachandran, V. S., & Blakeslee, S. (1998). *Phantoms in the brain.* New York: William Morrow and Company.

Rao, K. R. (1988). What is Indian psychology? *Journal of Indian Psychology, 7,* 37–57.

Read, J. D., & Lindsay, D. S. (Eds.). (1997). *Recollections of trauma: Scientific research and clinical practice.* New York: Plenum Press.

Recagno, I. (1982). *Habitos de crianza y marginalidad.* Caracas: Universidad Central de Venezuela.

Reisenzein, R., Meyer, W.-U., & Schützwohl, A. (1995). James and the physical basis of emotion. *Psychological Review, 102,* 757–761.

Rescorla, R. A. (1988). Pavlovian conditioning: It's not what you think it is. *American Psychologist, 42,* 151–160.

Rice, C. E. (1997). Scenarios: The scientist-practitioner split and the future of psychology. *American Psychologist, 52,* 1173–1181.

Richards, G. (1997). *Race, racism, and psychology: Towards a reflexive history.* New York: Routledge.

Richards, R. J. (1983). Why Darwin delayed, or interesting problems and models in the history of science. *Journal of the History of the Behavioral Sciences, 19,* 45–53.

Richet, C. (1884). *L'Homme et l'intelligence. Fragments de philosophie.* Paris: Alean.

Ridley, M. (1999, November 8). Will we still need to have sex? *Time, 154,* 67–69.

Roazen, P. (1975). *Freud and his followers.* New York: Knopf.

Roback, A. A., & Kiernan, T. (1969). *Pictorial history of psychology and psychiatry.* New York: Philosophical Library.

Roberts, J. M. (1995). *A concise history of the world.* New York: Oxford University Press.

Robertson, R. (1990). Mapping the global condition: Globalization as the central concept. In M. Featherstone (Ed.), *Global culture: Nationalism, globalization, and modernity* (pp. 15–30). London: Sage Publications.

Robinson, D. N. (1986). *An intellectual history of psychology* (3rd ed.). Madison: University of Wisconsin Press.

Robinson, J. H. (1912). *The new history.* New York: Macmillan.

Rodin, G., & Voshart, K. (1986). Depression in the medically ill: An overview. *American Journal of Psychiatry, 143,* 696–705.

Rogers, C. (1942). *Counseling and psychotherapy: Newer concepts in practice.* Boston: Houghton Mifflin.

Rogers, C. (1951). *Client-centered therapy: Its current practice, implications and theory.* Boston: Houghton Mifflin.

Rorty, R. (1989). *Contingency, irony, and solidarity.* New York: Cambridge University Press.

Rosenau, P. M. (1992). *Postmodernism and the social sciences: Insights, inroads, and intrusions.* Princeton, NJ: Princeton University Press.

Rosenthal, E. (2002, November). China begins to address massive suicide problem. *The Burlington Free Press,* p. 11A.

Rosenzweig, M. R. (1992). Psychological science around the world. *American Psychologist, 43,* 15–22.

Rosenzweig, M. R. (1999). Continuity and change in the development of psychology around the world. *American Psychologist, 54,* 252–259.

Ross, B. (1991). William James: Spoiled child of American psychology. In G. A. Kimble, M. Wertheimer, & C. L. White (Eds.), *Portraits of pioneers in psychology* (pp. 13–25). Washington, DC: American Psychological Association.

Ross, D. (1972). *G. Stanley Hall: The psychologist as prophet.* Chicago: University of Chicago Press.

Ross, W. D. (Ed.). (1931). *The works of Aristotle.* Oxford: Clarendon Press.

Rosser, S. V. (1988). *Feminism within the science and health care professions: Overcoming resistance.* Tarrytown, NY: Pergamon Press.

Rosser, S. V. (1990). *Female-friendly science.* New York: Pergamon Press.

Rosser, S. V. (1992). *Biology and feminism: A dynamic interaction.* New York: Twayne Publishers.

Rosser, S. V. (1995). *Teaching the majority: Breaking the gender barrier in science, mathematics, and engineering.* New York: Teacher's College Press.

Rosser, S. V. (1997). *Re-engineering female friendly science.* New York: Teacher's College Press.

Rossi, P. H., & Wright, J. D. (1984). Evaluation research: An assessment. *Annual Review of Sociology, 10,* 331–352.

Routh, D. K. (1994). *Clinical psychology since 1917: Science, practice, and organization.* New York: Plenum Press.

Routh, D. K. (1996). Lightner Witmer and the first 100 years of clinical psychology. *American Psychologist, 51,* 244–247.

Russell, B. (1945). *A history of Western philosophy.* New York: Simon & Schuster.

Russo, N. F., & Denmark, F. L. (1987). Contributions of women to psychology. *Annual Review of Psychology, 38,* 279–298.

Saenz, R. (2004). *Latinos and the changing face of America.* Retrieved February 2, 2006, from http://www.prb.org/Template.cfm?Section=PRB&template=/ContentManagement/ContentDisplay.cfm&ContentID=11337

Sahoo, F. M. (1993). Indigenization of psychological measurement: Parameters and operationalisation. *Psychology and Developing Societies, 5,* 1–10.

Salazar, J. M. (1995). Factors influencing the development of psychology in Latin America. *International Journal of Psychology, 30,* 707–716.

Salazar, M. (2002). Latin American Psychology *Interamerican Journal of Psychology, 31,* 295–316.

Salgado, J. F. (1997). The five factor model of personality and job performance in the European Community. *Journal of Applied Psychology, 82,* 30–43.

Salovey, P., Rothman, A. J., Detweiler, J. B., & Steward, W. T. (2000). Emotional states and physical health. *American Psychologist, 55,* 110–121.

Sampson, E. E. (1988). The debate on individualism: Indigenous psychologies of the individual and their role in personal and societal functioning. *American Psychologist, 43*, 15–22.

Sanford, N. (1968). Personality and patterns of alcohol consumption. *Journal of Consulting and Clinical Psychology, 32* (1), 13–17.

Scarborough, E., & Furumoto, L. (1987). *Untold lives: The first generation of American women psychologists.* New York: Columbia University Press.

Schacter, D. L. (1996). *Searching for memory: The brain, the mind, and the past.* New York: Basic Books.

Schacter, D. L. (1999). The seven sins of memory: Insight from psychology and cognitive neuroscience. *American Psychologist, 54*, 182–203.

Schooler, L., & Anderson, J. R. (1997). The role in the rational analysis of memory. *Cognitive Psychology, 32*, 219–250.

Schultz, D. P., & Schultz, S. E. (1996). *A history of modern psychology* (6th ed.). Fort Worth, TX: Harcourt-Brace College Publishers.

Schwartz, S. (1986). *Classic studies in psychology.* Mountain View, CA: Mayfield Publishing.

Seaman, J. D. (1984). On phi-phenomena. *Journal of the History of the Behavioral Sciences, 20*, 3–8.

Sechenov, I. (1965). *Reflexes of the brain [by] I. Sechenov. Russian text edited by K. Koshtoyants. Translated from the Russian by S. Belsky. Edited by G. Gibbons. Notes by S. Gellerstein.* Cambridge, MA: MIT Press. (Original work published 1866.)

Seedat, M. (1998). A characterization of South African psychology (1948–1988): The impact of exclusionary ideology. *South African Journal of Psychology, 28*, 74–84.

Segall, M. H., Lonner, W. J., & Berry, J. W. (1998). Cross-cultural psychology as a scholarly discipline: On the flowering of culture in behavioral research. *American Psychologist, 53*, 1101–1110.

Seligman, M. E. P. (1970). On the generality of the laws of learning. *Psychological Review, 77*, 406–418.

Seligman, M. E. P. (1975). *Helplessness: On depression, development, and death.* San Francisco: Freeman.

Seligman, M. E. P. (1991). *Learned optimism.* New York: Knopf.

Seligman, M. E. P. (1995). The effectiveness of psychotherapy: *The* Consumer Reports *study. American Psychologist, 50*, 965–974.

Seligman, M. E. P. (1998, January). Building human strength: Psychology's forgotten mission. *APA Monitor*, p. 2.

Seligman, M. E. P. (1998, April). Positive social science (President's column). *APA Monitor*, p. 2.

Seligman, M. E. P., & Csikzentmihalyi, M. (Eds.). (2000). Special issue: Positive psychology. [Monograph]. *American Psychologist, 55*, 1–200.

Sexton, V. S. (1965). Clinical psychology: An historical survey. *Genetic Psychology Mongraphs, 72*, 401–434.

Sexton, V. S., & Hogan, J. D. (Ed.). (1992). *International Psychology: Views around the world.* Lincoln: University of Nebraska Press.

Shapiro, A. E., & Wiggins, J. G. (1994). A PsyD for every practitioner: Truth in labelling. *American Psychologist, 49*, 207–210.

Shaw, J. S., III. (1996). Increases in eyewitness confidence resulting from postevent questioning. *Journal of Experimental Psychology: Applied, 2*, 126–146.

Sheldon, K. M., & King, L. (2001). Why positive psychology is necessary. *American Psychologist, 56*, 216–217.

Shields, S. A. (1975). Functionalism, Darwinism, and the psychology of women: A study in social myth. *American Psychologist, 30*, 739–754.

Shields, S. A. (1975a). Ms. Pilgrim's progress: The contributions of Leta Stetter Hollingworth to the psychology of women. *American Psychologist* (August), 852–857.

Shneidman, E. S. (1998). Evelyn Hooker (1907–1996). *American Psychologist, 53* (4), 480–481.

Shweder, R., & LeVine, R. A. (1984). *Culture theory: Essays on mind, self, and emotion.* Cambridge, England: Cambridge University Press.

Siegel, S. (1989). Pharmacological conditioning and drug effects. In A. J. Goudie & M. E. Emmett-Oglesby (Eds.), *Psychoactive drugs: Tolerance and sensitization* (pp. 115–180). Clifton, NJ: Humana Press.

Simons, D. J., & Levin, D. T. (1998). Failure to detect changes to people during a real-world interaction. *Psychonomic Bulletin & Review, 4*, 644–649.

Simonton, D. K. (1994). *Greatness: Who makes history and why.* New York: Guilford Press.

Sinha, D. (1994a). Indigenous psychology: Need and potentiality. *Journal of Indian Psychology, 12*, 1–7.

Sinha, D. (1994b). Origins and development of psychology in India: Outgrowing the alien framework. *International Journal of Psychology, 29*, 695–705.

Sinha, D., & Holtzman, W. (1984). The impact of psychology on third world development. *International Journal of Psychology, 19*, 3–192.

Sinha, J. B. P. (1995). Factors facilitating and impeding growth of psychology in South Asia with special reference to India. *International Journal of Psychology, 30*, 741–753.

Sizer, N., & Drayton, H. S. (1892). *Heads and faces and how to study them.* New York: Fowler & Wells.

Skinner, B. F. (1938). *The behavior of organisms: An experimental analysis.* New York: Appleton-Century-Crofts.

Skinner, B. F. (1948). *Walden two.* New York: Macmillan.

Skinner, B. F. (1956). A case history in scientific method. *American Psychologist, 12,* 221–223.

Skinner, B. F. (1960). Pigeons and a pelican. *American Psychologist, 15,* 28–37.

Skinner, B. F. (1971). *Beyond freedom and dignity.* New York: Macmillan.

Skinner, B. F. (1990). Can psychology be a science of the mind? *American Psychologist, 42,* 780–786.

Slamecka, N. J. (1985). Ebbinghaus: Some associations. *Journal of Experimental Psychology: Learning, Memory, and Cognition, 11,* 414–435.

Slife, B. D., & Williams, R. N. (1997). Toward a theoretical psychology. *American Psychology, 52,* 117–129.

Sloan, T. (1996). Psychological research methods in developing countries. In S. Carr & J. Schumaker (Eds.), *Psychology and the developing world.* New York: Praeger.

Smith, N. W. (1974). The ancient background to Greek psychology and some implications for today. *Psychological Record, 24,* 309–324.

Snowdon, D. (2001). *Aging with grace: What the nun study teaches us about leading longer, healthier, and more meaningful lives.* New York: Bantam Books.

Sokal, M. M. (1971). The unpublished autobiography of James McKeen Cattell. *American Psychologist, 26,* 626–635.

Sokal, M. M. (1992). Origins and early years of the American Psychological Association, 1890–1906. *American Psychologist, 47,* 111–122.

Soros, G. (1997, February). The capitalist threat. *The Atlantic Monthly, 279,* 45–58.

Souter, C. R. (2002). New chief executive officer wants to move APA forward. *Massachusetts Psychologist, 11*(7). Retrieved August 25, 2003, from http://www.masspsy.com/leading/0212_qa.html.

Spanos, N. P. (1982). A social psychological approach to hypnotic behavior. In G. Weary & H. L. Mirels (Eds.), *Integrations of clinical and social psychology* (pp. 231–271). New York: Oxford University Press.

Spanos, N. P., & Barber, T. X. (1974). Toward a convergence in hypnosis research. *American Psychologist, 29,* 500–511.

Spanos, N. P, & Gottlieb, J. (1976). Ergotism and the Salem witch trials. *Science, 194,* 1392.

Speck, R. B, & Attneave, C. (1973). *Family networks: A way toward retribalization and healing in family crises.* New York: Pantheon Books.

Spence, J. T., et al.(1976). *Elementary statistics.* Englewood Cliffs, NJ: Prentice-Hall.

Spence, J. T., & Helmreich R. L. (1978). *Masculinity and femininity: Their psychological dimensions, correlates and antecedents.* Austin: University of Texas Press.

Spence, K. W. (1952). Clark Leonard Hull: 1884–1952. *American Journal of Psychology, 65,* 639–646.

Spence, K. W., & Spence, J. T. (Eds.) (1967). *The psychology of learning and motivation: Volume I.* New York: Academic Press.

Spence, K. W., & Spence, J. T. (Eds.) (1968). *Advances in the psychology of learning and motivation research and theory.* Vol. II. New York: Academic Press.

Sperry, R. W. (1961). Cerebral organization and behavior. *Science, 133,* 1749–1757.

Sperry, R. W. (1964, January). The great cerebral commissure. *Scientific American, 50,* 703–710.

Spinoza, B. (1955). *On the improvement of the understanding, the ethics, and correspondence* (R. H. M. Elwes, Trans.). New York: Dover. (Original work published 1677).

Squire, L. R., & Zola-Morgan, S. (1991). The medial temporal lobe memory system. *Science, 253,* 1380–1386.

Stapp, J., Tucker, A. M., & VandenBos, G. R. (1985). Census of psychological personnel: 1983. *American Psychologist, 40,* 1317–1351.

Steele, R. S. (1985). Paradigm lost: Psychoanalysis after Freud. In C. E. Buxton (Ed.), *Points of view in the modern history of psychology* (pp. 221–57). Orlando, FL: Academic Press.

Sternberg, R. J. (1986). A triangular theory of love. *Psychological Review, 93,* 119–135.

Sternberg, R. J. (2000). The holy grail of general intelligence. *Science, 289,* 399–401.

Steudel, J. (1974). Johannes Peter Müller. In Charles Coulston Gillispie (Ed.), *Dictionary of scientific biography* (Vol. 9), 567–584.

Stevens, G., & Gardner, S. (1982). Women pioneers in psychology: Mary Whiton Calkins. *The Women of Psychology: Vol. 1. Pioneers and Innovators.* Cambridge, MA: Shenkman Publishing Company.

Stevens, S. S. (1935). The operational basis of psychology. *American Journal of Psychology, 43,* 232–330.

Stevens, S. S. (1961). To honor Fechner and repeal his law. *Science, 133,* 80–86.

Stocking, G. W. (1965). On the limits of "presentism" and "historicism" in the historiography of the behavioral sciences [editorial]. *Journal of the History of the Behavioral Sciences, 1,* 211–218.

Stone, A. A., Marco, C. A., Cruise, C. E., Cox, D. S., & Neale, J. M. (1996). Are stress-induced immunological changes mediated by mood? A closer look at how both desirable and undesirable daily events influence slgA antibody. *International Journal of Behavioral Medicine, 3*, 1–13.

Storr, A. (1983). *The essential Jung*. New York: MJF Books.

Storr, A. (2001). *Freud: A very short introduction*. Oxford, England: Oxford University Press.

Stroop, J. (1935). Studies of interference in serial verbal reaction. *Journal of Experimental Psychology, 18*, 643–662.

Strozier, C. B. (1985). Glimpses of a life: Heinz Kohut (1913–81). In A. Goldberg (Ed.), *Progress in self psychology* (vol. 1) (pp. 3–12). New York: The Guilford Press.

Strunk, O. (1972). The self-psychology of Mary Whiton Calkins. *Journal of the History of the Behavioral Sciences, 8*(2), 196–203.

Strupp, H. H. (1996). The tripartite model and the *Consumer Reports* study. *American Psychologist, 51*(10), 1017–1024.

Strupp, H. H., & Howard, K. I. (1992). A brief history of psychotherapy research. In D. K. Freedheim (Ed.), *History of psychotherapy: A century of change* (pp. 309–334). Washington, DC: American Psychological Association.

Sue, D., Bingham, R., Burke, L., & Vasquez, M. (1999). The diversification of psychology: A multicultural revolution. *American Psychologist, 54*, 1061–1069.

Sue, S. (1994). Change, persistence, and enthusiasm for ethnic research. In P. Keller (Ed.), *Academic paths: Career decisions and experiences of psychologists* (pp. 149–158). Hillsdale, NJ: Erlbaum.

Sur, C. W. (1993). The feminine images of God in the visions of Saint Hildegard of Bingen's Scivias. Lampeter, Dyfed, Wales: Edwin Mellen Press, Ltd.

Taylor, E. (2000). Psychotherapeutics and the problematic origins of clinical psychology in America. *American Psychologist, 55*, 1029–1033.

Tehranian, M., & Reed, L. (1997). *Human security and global governance: The state of the art: Working paper #1*. Honolulu, HI: Toda Institute for Peace and Policy Research.

Temkin, O. (1947). Gall and the phrenological movement. *Bulletin of the History of Medicine, 21*, 275–321.

Terman, L. (1944). Leta Stetter Hollingworth: A biography by Harry Levi Hollingworth. A review. *Journal of Applied Psychology, 28*, 357–359.

Terman, L. M. (1939). The gifted student and his academic environment. *School and Society, 49*, 65–73.

Terman, L. M., Buttenwieser, P., Fergeson, L. W., Johnson, W. B., & Wilson, D. P. (1938). *Psychological factors in marital happiness*. New York: McGraw-Hill.

Thibault, J. W., Spence, J. T., & Carson, R. C. (Eds.)(1976). *Contemporary topics in social psychology*. Morristown, NJ: General Learning Press.

Thompson, A. S. (1998). Morris S. Viteles (1898–1996). *American Psychologist, 53*, 1153–1154.

Thompson, R. F. (1993). *The brain: A neuroscience primer*. New York: W. H. Freeman and Company.

Thorndike, E. L. (1898). Some experiments in animal testing. *Science, 8*, 818–824.

Thorndike, E. L. (1899). A reply to "The nature of animal intelligence and the methods of investigating it." *Psychological Review, 6*, 412–420.

Thorndike, E. L. (1913). *Educational psychology* (3 vols.). New York: Teachers College, Columbia University.

Thorndike, E. L. (1991). Edward L. Thorndike: A professional and personal appreciation. In G. A. Kimble, M. Wertheimer, & C. L. White (Eds.), *Portraits of pioneers in psychology* (pp. 139–151). Washington, DC: American Psychological Association.

Thorndike, E. L. (1998). Animal intelligence: An experimental study of the associate processes in animals. *American Psychologist, 53*, 1125–1127. (Original work published 1898.)

Thorndike, E. L., & Woodworth, R. S. (1901). The influence of improvement in one mental function upon the efficiency of other functions, I. *Psychological Review, 8*, 247–261.

Thorne, B. M., & Henley, T. B. (1997). *Connections in the history and systems of psychology*. Boston: Houghton Mifflin Company.

Titchener, E. B. (1896). *An outline of psychology*. London: The Macmillan Co.

Titchener, E. B. (1905). *Experimental psychology: A manual of laboratory practice*. (First. ed.) (2 vols.). Vol. Two. New York and London: The Macmillan Co.

Tolman, E. C. (1932). *Purposive behavior in animals and men*. New York: Century.

Tolman, E. C. (1948). Cognitive maps in rats and men. *Psychological Review, 55*, 189–208.

Tolman, E. C., & Honzik, C. H. (1930). Introduction and removal of reward and maze performance in rats. *University of California Publications in Psychology, 4*, 257–273.

Tolman, E. C., Ritchie, B. F., & Kalish, D. (1946a). Studies in spatial learning. I. Orientation and the shortcut. *Journal of Experimental Psychology, 36*, 13–24.

Tolman, E. C., Ritchie, B. F., & Kalish, D. (1946b). Studies in spatial learning. II. Place learning versus response learning. *Journal of Experimental Psychology, 36*, 221–229.

Top Biography. (2002). *Eric Homberger Erikson (1902–1994).* [Online]. Available at: http://www.top-biography.com/9043.Erikson/works.htm.

Toulmin, S. (1985). *The return to cosmology: Postmodern science and the theology of nature.* Berkeley: University of California Press.

Triandis, H. C. (1971). Some psychological dimensions of modernization. *Proceedings of the 17th International Congress of Applied Psychology* (Vol. II). Brussels: Editest, pp. 1257–1265.

Triandis, H. C. (1980). Introduction. In H. C. Triandis & W. W. Lambert (Eds.), *Handbook of cross-cultural psychology* (pp. 1–14). Boston: Allyn & Bacon.

Triandis, H. C. (1996). The psychological measurement of cultural syndromes. *American Psychologist, 51,* 407–415.

Triandis, H. C., Malpass, R. S., & Davidson, A. (1972). A cross-cultural psychology. *Biennial Review of Anthropology, 1,* 1–84.

Triandis, H. C., & Vassiliou, V. (1972). A comparative analysis of subjective culture. In Triandis, Vassiliou, Vassiliou, Tanaka, and Shanmugam (Eds.), *The analysis of subjective culture* (pp. 299–338). New York: Wiley.

Tsanoff, R. A. (1964). *The great philosophers* (2nd ed.). New York: Harper & Row.

Tseng, W. S. (1975). The nature of somatic complaints among psychiatric patients: The Chinese case. *Comprehensive Psychiatry, 16,* 237–245.

Turk, D. C., Rudy, T. E., & Stieg, R. L. (1987). Pain and Depression. 1. "Facts." *Pain Management, 1,* 17–26.

Umrikhin, V. V. (1991), "The beginning of the end" of behavioral psychology in USSR. *Repressed Science,* Leningrad.

Umrikhin, V. V. (1994), "The temple of psychological science" in the dramas of Russian history. *Psikhologichesky Zhurnal [Psychological Journal], 15*(6).

Urmson, J. O. (Ed.). (1960). *The concise encyclopedia of Western philosophy and philosophers.* New York: Hawthorn Books.

Urmson, J. O. (Ed). (1967). *The concise encyclopedia of Western philosophy and philosophers* (3rd ed.). New York: Hawthorn Books.

U.S. Bureau of the Census. (2000). *The American Indian and Alaska Native population.* Retrieved August 25, 2003, from http://www.census.gov/prod/2002pubs/c2kbr01-15.pdf.

U.S. Bureau of the Census. (2000b). *Educational Attainment: 2000.* Retrieved August 25, 2003, from http://www.census.gov/prod/2003pubs/c2kbr-24.pdf.

Vasquez, M. J. T. (2003). The life and death of a multicultural feminist pioneer: Martha E. Bernal (1931–2001). [Electronic version]. *The Feminist Psychologist, 30*(1). [Online]. http://www.psych.yorku.ca/femhop/Martha%20Bernal.htm

Vasquez, M. J. T., & Lopez, S. (2002). Martha Bernal (1931–2001). *American Psychologist, 57*(5), 362–363.

Verma, S., & Saraswathi, T. S. (2002). Adolescents in India: Street urchins or Silicon Valley millionaires? In B. B. Brown, R. Larson, & T. S. Saraswathi (Eds.), *The world's youth: Adolescence in eight regions of the globe* (pp. 276–306). New York: Cambridge University Press.

Viteles, M. S. (1938). Industrial psychology in Russia. *Journal of Occupational Psychology, 12,* 85–103.

von Bingen, H. (1998). *Physica.* (P. Throop, Trans.) Rochester, VT: Healing Arts Press. (Original work published ca. 1150).

von Bingen, H. (1999). *On natural philosophy and medicine: selections from Cause et cure* (M. Berger, Trans.) Rochester, N.Y.: D.S. Brewer. (Original work published ca. 1158).

Vygotsky, L. (1925). Soznanie kak problema psikhologii povedenija. English translation reprinted in *Soviet Psychology, 17*(1979), 5–35.

Vygotsky, L. S., & Luria, A. R. (1992). *Ape, primitive man, and child: Essays in the history of behaviour* (Evelyn Rossiter, Trans.). Sydney: Harvester Wheatsheaf. (Original work published 1930 in Russian.)

Wakefield, H., & Underwager, R. (1992). Recovered memories of alleged sexual abuse: Lawsuits against parents. *Behavioral Sciences and the Law, 10,* 483–507.

Wang, Z. M. (1993). Psychology in China: A review dedicated to Li Chen. *Annual Review of Psychology, 44,* 87–116.

Washburn, M. F. (1908). *The animal mind: A textbook of comparative psychology.* New York: Macmillan.

Washburn, M. F. (1916). *Movement and mental imagery: Outlines of a motor theory of the complex mental process.* Boston: Houghton Miffin.

Watson, D. (2000). *Mood and temperament.* New York: Guilford Press.

Watson, J. B. (1912). Instinctive activity in animals. *Harper's Magazine, 124,* 376–382.

Watson, J. B. (1913). Psychology as a behaviorist views it. *Psychological Review, 20,* 158–177.

Watson, J. B. (1919). *Psychology from the standpoint of a behaviorist.* Philadelphia: Lippincott.

Watson, J. B. (1924). *Behaviorism.* New York: Norton.

Watson, J. B., & McDougall, W. (1929). *The battle of behaviorism.* New York: Norton.

Watson, J. B., & Morgan, J. J. B. (1917). Emotional reactions and psychological experimentation. *American Journal of Psychology, 28,* 163–174.

Webb, M. E. (1988). A new history of Hartley's observations on man. *Journal of the History of the Behavioral Sciences, 7,* 202–211.

Weber, E. H. (1978). *The sense of touch* (H. E. Ross, Trans.) New York: Academic Press. (Original work published 1834).

Wells, H. K. (1956). *Ivan P. Pavlov: Toward a scientific psychology and psychiatry.* New York: International Publishers.

Wertheimer, M. (1982). *Productive thinking* (Michael Wertheimer, Ed.). Chicago: University of Chicago Press. (Original work published 1945).

Wessels, M. G. (1982). *Cognitive psychology.* New York: Harper & Row.

Westen, D. (1998). The scientific legacy of Sigmund Freud: Toward a psychodynamically informed psychological science. *Psychological Bulletin, 124,* 333–373.

White, A. D. (1978). *A history of the warfare of science with theology in Christendom* (2 vols.). Gloucester, MA: Peter Smith. (Original work published 1896).

White, R. W., & Shevach, B. J. (1942). Hypnosis and the concept of dissociation. *Journal of Abnormal and Social Psychology, 37,* 309–328.

Wilhelm, R., & Baynes, C. (Trans.) (1950). *The I Ching, or Book of Changes.* New York: Princeton University Press.

Williams, B. (2000). *Lenin: Profiles in power.* Harlow, England: Pearson Education.

Wilson, K. M. (1984). *Medieval women writers.* Athens: University of Georgia Press.

Winnicott, D. W. (1953). Transitional objects and transitional phenomena. *International Journal of Psychoanalysis, 34,* 89–97.

Winnicott, D. W. (1964). *The child, the family and the outside world.* Reading, MA: Addison-Wesley.

Winnicott, D. W. (1971). *Playing and reality.* London: Tavistock Publications.

Winnicott, D. W., & Britton, C. (1947). Residential management as treatment for difficult children. *Human Relations, 1* (1), 2–12.

Wissler, C. (1901). The correlation of mental and physical tests. *Psychological Review Monograph Supplements, 3,* no. 6., 1–63.

Witmer, L. (1896). Practical work in psychology. *Pediatrics, 2,* 462–471.

Witmer, L. (1897). The organization of practical work in psychology. *Psychological Review, 4,* 116–117.

Witmer, L. (1909). William James. *Psychological Clinic, 2,* 288–289.

Wolf, T. H. (1973). *Alfred Binet.* Chicago: University of Chicago Press.

Wolfe, D. (1997). The reorganized American Psychological Association. *American Psychologist, 52,* 721–724

Wolpe, J. (1958). *Psychotherapy by reciprocal inhibition.* Palo Alto, CA: Stanford University Press.

Wood, N. (1968). Niccoló Machiavelli. In David Sills (Ed.), *International encyclopedia of the social sciences* (Vol. 9, pp. 505–511). New York: Macmillan and Free Press.

Woodworth, R. S. (1910). Racial differences in mental traits. *Science, 31,* 171–186.

Woodworth, R. S. (1918). *Dynamic psychology.* New York: Columbia University Press.

Woodworth, R. S. (1931). *Contemporary schools of psychology.* New York: The Ronald Press Co.

Woodworth, R. S. (1938). *Experimental psychology.* New York: Henry Holt and Company.

Woodworth, R. S. (1958). *Dynamics of behavior.* New York: Holt.

Woody, E. Z., & Bowers, K. S. (1994). A frontal assault on dissociated control. In S. J. Lynn & J. W. Rhue (Eds.), *Dissociation: Clinical, theoretical and research perspectives* (pp. 52–79). New York: Guilford Press.

Woolley, H. T. (1910). Psychological literature: A review of the recent literature on the psychology of sex. *Psychological Bulletin, 7,* 335–342.

Wundt, W. (1904). *Principles of physiological psychology* (5th ed.) (E. Titchener, Ed.). New York: Macmillan. (Original work published 1874).

Wundt, W. (1916). *Elements of folk psychology* (Edward Leroy Schaub, Trans.). New York: Macmillan.

Wundt, W. (1969). *Principles of physiological psychology* (E. B. Titchener, Trans., 5th ed.). New York: Kraus Reprint Co. (Original work published 1873; 5th edition published in 1910).

www.clas.ufl.edu/users/gthursby/taoism/ttcstan3.html#1.

Zeigarnik, B. V. (1986). *Abnormal psychology.* Moscow: MGU Press.

Zhang, L. (2000). Cai Yuanpei [Electronic Version]. *Prospects: The Quarterly Review of Comparative Education*, vol. XXIII (1/2), 147–157. [Online]. Available at: http://www.ibe.unesco.org/publications/Thinkerspdf/caie.pdf

Zusne, L. (1984). *Biographical dictionary of psychology.* Westport, CT: Greenwood Press, p. 243.

Name Index

Page numbers with *f* indicate figures; page numbers with *t* indicate tables.

469

Subject Index

Page numbers with *f* indicate figures; page numbers with *t* indicate tables.